THE

IRANIAN
NUCLEAR CRISIS

A MEMOIR

THE
IRANIAN
NUCLEAR CRISIS

A MEMOIR

SEYED HOSSEIN MOUSAVIAN

CARNEGIE ENDOWMENT

FOR INTERNATIONAL PEACE

WASHINGTON DC ▪ MOSCOW ▪ BEIJING ▪ BEIRUT ▪ BRUSSELS

Carnegie Endowment for International Peace
1779 Massachusetts Avenue, N.W.
Washington, D.C. 20036
202-483-7600, Fax 202-483-1840
www.ceip.org

The Carnegie Endowment does not take institutional positions on public policy issues; the views represented here are the author's own and do not necessarily reflect the views of the Endowment, its staff, or its trustees.

To order, contact:
Hopkins Fulfillment Service
P.O. Box 50370, Baltimore, MD 21211-4370
1-800-537-5487 or 1-410-516-6956
Fax 1-410-516-6998

Cover design by Jocelyn Soly
Composition by Oakland Street Publishing
Printed by United Book Press

Library of Congress Cataloging-in-Publication Data
Mousavian, Seyyed Hossein, 1967-
   The Iranian nuclear crisis : a memoir / Seyed Hossein Mousavian.
      p. cm.
   Includes bibliographical references and index.
   ISBN 978-0-87003-268-4 (pbk. : alk. paper) -- ISBN 978-0-87003-267-7 (cloth : alk. paper) 1. Nuclear nonproliferation--Iran. 2. Nuclear weapons--Iran. 3. Iran--Politics and government--1997- 4. Iran--Foreign relations--1997- 5. Mousavian, Seyyed Hossein, 1967- I. Title.

JZ5665.M68 2012
623.4'51190955--dc23

                    2012012698

CONTENTS

ACKNOWLEDGMENTS   vii

FOREWORD   ix

INTRODUCTION   I

CHAPTER ONE   39
THE ORIGIN AND DEVELOPMENT OF IRAN'S NUCLEAR PROGRAM

CHAPTER TWO   57
THE FIRST CRISIS

CHAPTER THREE   97
FROM TEHRAN TO PARIS

CHAPTER FOUR   157
FROM THE PARIS AGREEMENT TO THE 2005 PRESIDENTIAL ELECTIONS

CHAPTER FIVE   185
THE LARIJANI PERIOD

CHAPTER SIX   225
TO THE SECURITY COUNCIL

CHAPTER SEVEN   259
BACK TO THE SECURITY COUNCIL AND A
NEW DOMESTIC SITUATION

CHAPTER EIGHT   289
IRAN ALONE: THE JALILI PERIOD

CHAPTER NINE   321
U.S. ENGAGEMENT

CHAPTER TEN   371
THE CRISIS WORSENS

CONCLUSION   431

NOTES   471

INDEX   553

ABOUT THE AUTHOR   597

CARNEGIE ENDOWMENT FOR
INTERNATIONAL PEACE   598

ACKNOWLEDGMENTS

I would like to offer my sincere thanks to a number of individuals and institutions for their help in making this book possible. Professors Frank von Hippel of the Program on Science and Global Security at Princeton University's Woodrow Wilson School of Public and International Affairs, and Zia Mian, a researcher in the program, were the principal investigators who read the manuscript, made valuable comments, and raised funding for the project. George Perkovich, vice president for studies and director of the Nuclear Policy Program at the Carnegie Endowment for International Peace and a top global expert on weapons of mass destruction, made valuable comments on multiple drafts of the manuscript. The Program on Science and Global Security and its director, Christopher Chyba, steadfastly supported my work and provided me with a base of operations. I thank also the Liechtenstein Institute on Self-Determination, the Institute for the Transregional Study of the Contemporary Middle East, North Africa, and Central Asia, and Daniel Kurtzer, Abraham Chair in Middle East Policy of the Woodrow Wilson School of Public and International Affairs at Princeton University. The Ploughshares Fund, the Rockefeller Brothers Fund, and the Carnegie Endowment for International Peace all contributed generously with grants to Princeton University for this research. I am grateful to the reviewers, Mark Fitzpatrick, director of the International Institute for Strategic Studies program on nonproliferation and disarmament, and Pierre Goldschmidt, a nonresident senior associate at Carnegie Endowment and former deputy director general of the IAEA, for the useful comments they made on the manuscript, and to M. Mahdavi Emad Kiyaei, who helped on finding and translating some Persian sources. Lastly, I offer my thanks to my research assistant, Noah Arjomand.

I dedicate this book to my beloved family, who endured great difficultly as a result of my unjust and illegal arrest in April 2007 because of the responsibilities tasked to me on Iran's nuclear file. During this period, our negotiating team did the utmost to resolve the crisis through diplomacy while preserving the nation's rights for peaceful nuclear technology and preventing referral to the UN Security Council that would pave the way for sanctions. My family and I paid a high price for such efforts and I am forever grateful for their unrelenting support, dedication, and belief in me.

FOREWORD

Dr. Seyed Hossein Mousavian has written a unique book, a hybrid of four genres.

As a contemporary history, *The Iranian Nuclear Crisis: A Memoir* is the first detailed Iranian account of the diplomatic struggle between Iran and its interlocutors during the nuclear crisis that began in 2002 when news emerged that Tehran was secretly constructing facilities to enrich uranium and produce plutonium. Drawing on extensive research and firsthand knowledge, Mousavian's narrative adds much-needed Iranian material to the historical record. It is a treasure trove for scholars, journalists, and policy analysts.

The Iranian Nuclear Crisis is also a memoir. From 1997 to 2005, Mousavian was the head of the Foreign Relations Committee of Iran's Supreme National Security Council. In 2003 he was named the spokesman of Iran's nuclear negotiating team led by the secretary of Iran's National Security Council, Hassan Rouhani. In this position, he gained an intimate knowledge of Iran's dealings with the International Atomic Energy Agency, France, the United Kingdom, Germany, Russia, China, and, indirectly, the United States. Mousavian provides firsthand accounts of many of these interactions. Rarer still, he takes the reader into Iran's internal deliberations, where Khamenei, Khatami, Ahmadinejad, and other leaders wrestle with their internal and external adversaries.

The most vivid memoir sections of this volume recount his arrest and interrogations, beginning in 2007, on charges of committing espionage by allegedly providing classified information to the United Kingdom. Public-ly accused by President Mahmoud Ahmadinejad, Mousavian was tried two times on these charges and found not guilty, and then later was charged with criticizing the government of Iran, which he admitted. He was put on probation with the proviso that he not speak or write publicly against government policies. These dramatic episodes, and other insider accounts of diplomatic missions in the 1980s and 1990s, tell much about the author and the swirling dynamics of Iranian politics and diplomacy.

This is also an analytical volume. Mousavian at times steps back to con-ceptualize the challenges Iran faced and the options it weighed in dealing with them. He analyzes the policies and diplomatic moves of the United States, the United Kingdom, France, Germany, Russia, China, and other players in this drama. This analysis extends into the future, as Mousavian compares the potential costs and benefits of the options available to Iran and its counterparts to resolve the nuclear crisis and mend the broader re-lationship between Iran and the international community. He weighs the likely effects of American and/or Israeli military strikes, of covert action, sanctions, and containment, and of diplomatic engagement, concluding that there is still an opportunity for diplomacy to prevent Iran from decid-ing to produce nuclear weapons.

The final genre is that of the polemic. In comparing and contrasting the approaches that Iran has taken under the Khatami and the Ahmadinejad administrations, Mousavian does not hide his fundamental and specific disagreements with the latter. Upon first taking office in 2005, Ahmadine-jad interviewed Mousavian for the position of foreign minister, only to be told, as the book recounts, that Mousavian could not support the new president's view of the world and the policies he was inclined to pursue. It would be unnatural for the author, after having been arrested and inter-rogated multiple times, not to have a certain animus toward Ahmadinejad and his administration. Nevertheless, the critiques in this volume are suf-ficiently analytical to be judged on their merits.

Anything having to do with Iran since 1979 can be the subject of in-tense controversy in the United States. The current atmosphere of bellicos-ity—replete with assassinations of nuclear scientists in Iran and an alleged Iranian assassination plot against the Saudi ambassador in Washington—

make it all the more difficult for Iranians and Americans to express the value of understanding the interests and perspectives of "the other side."

Thus, the question arises of why a Washington-based think tank would want to publish a book by an Iranian protagonist. The answer is that the Carnegie Endowment for International Peace is a global think tank. We believe that the most serious international conflicts cannot be resolved—or mitigated—if the antagonists do not understand each other's perceptions, interests, and strategic cultures. Understanding does not necessarily lead to reconciliation; often, understanding clarifies differences. This is likely to be the case with the present volume. Nevertheless, we are convinced that serious, earnest studies such as Hossein Mousavian's can be invaluable to historical knowledge and contemporary policymaking.

The pedagogical value of this book extends to its "style." Readers will notice that analytical points and presentations of costs and benefits of particular policy options are often conveyed in lists of "bulleted" text. If Western writers included such lists we would edit them into narrative paragraphs. However, Ambassador Mousavian has explained that Iranian rhetoric often relies on lists of arguments for and against particular propositions, with as much (or more) weight given to the quantity of points on each side as to quality. In order, then, to convey Iranian points of view and styles of thinking, we have chosen not to make the entire text conform to Western editorial style.

A final editorial point: this is largely a book of contemporary history, and as such it strives for factual accuracy. Yet, even distant history is factually disputed. The causes of World War I are still debated, for example. Contemporary history is more uncertain or contested. And when the history involves subjects and relationships as fraught with conflict as those surrounding the Iranian nuclear crisis, agreement on facts is especially problematic. Therefore, Ambassador Mousavian graciously agreed that when his narrative treats as fact something that the editor thinks is in dispute, or in need of qualification, the editor can note that on the page. This does not mean that the author agrees with these notes, or that the editor agrees with passages that do not contain notes. Rather, the notes appear where the editor thinks a given statement is factually problematic enough to need to be qualified.

Obviously, this procedure is severely limited by the editor's knowledge or lack thereof. Some readers will no doubt find passages that they would dispute and wonder why they went unnoted. Other readers will disagree with the editor's notes. Beyond acknowledging imperfection, we can only say that one of the values of *The Iranian Nuclear Crisis: A Memoir* is to encourage further study and dialogue by and among its readers.

—GEORGE PERKOVICH
Vice President for Studies
Carnegie Endowment for International Peace

In the name of God, the compassionate, the merciful

INTRODUCTION

I ran's nuclear crisis began in earnest in the summer of 2003, when a report from the director general of the International Atomic Energy Agency (IAEA) triggered a resolution from the agency's Board of Governors that laid out major points of dispute over Iran's nuclear activities, some of which remain unresolved to this day. The case has had many ups and downs in the past few years and has intertwined with many domestic and international developments. The case has already engaged two presidents and three secretaries of Iran's Supreme National Security Council and has posed a challenge to world powers and international organizations, including the European Union (EU), NATO, the Non-Aligned Movement,[1] and the Gulf Cooperation Council. Despite the significance of recent developments in the Middle East and North Africa, with political upheaval in Tunisia, Egypt, Yemen, Bahrain, Libya, and Syria, the Iran nuclear issue continues to occupy President Barack Obama's agenda as a top foreign policy priority.

The nuclear crisis has been the most important challenge facing the Islamic Republic's foreign policy apparatus since the 1980–1988 war between Iran and Iraq. The issue's serious political and economic consequences, such as the referral of Iran's nuclear case to the UN Security Council and the imposition of harsh economic sanctions against Iran, are undeniable and have partly affected the political, economic, and even social and cultural realities of Iran.

1

Hostilities between Iran and the United States date back more than three decades following the Islamic Revolution in 1979. The recent nuclear crisis is part of a broader set of issues—among them terrorism, human rights, the Middle East peace process, energy, and Persian Gulf security—that complicate the relationship between Iran and the West. From a U.S. perspective, the nuclear issue arguably is an opportunity to unite the international community against Iran, with the ultimate goal being regime change. From the Iranian perspective, the nuclear issue is an opportunity to resist U.S. hegemony and its regime change policy. The nuclear issue is a matter of national consensus and pride that enables the Iranian government to unite the nation around the flag and resist the West.[2]

A well-informed retired U.S. politician listed the *U.S. security objectives* in the region as follows:

- Iran without nuclear, chemical, and biological weapons.
- To avoid a proliferation domino effect in the region.
- Iraq stability as U.S. troops withdraw and beyond.
- Afghanistan more self-sustaining and stable over the next two years.
- Israel achieving peace with neighbors and an agreement on the Palestinian issue.
- No military conflict with Iran.
- No accidental war in the region in which the United States might be drawn in.
- Iran to cease its military support of Hizbollah, Hamas, the Palestinian Islamic Jihad, and the Popular Front for the Liberation of Palestine–General Command.

The fact is that any U.S. policy or set of policies that seeks to achieve these objectives will have to take into account Iran's objectives, intentions, and interests. Iran's approach to each of these seven U.S. security objectives varies in intensity. Some of the U.S. objectives are more amenable to Iran's cooperation with the United States than others. But none of these U.S. objectives will be achieved without dealing with Iran's interests. *Iran's security objectives* are in conflict with U.S. objectives, though not in every case. Having been involved in Iran's security and foreign policy issues for two decades, I believe some of the major Iranian security objectives in the region are as follows:

- Iran with self-sufficiency on nuclear, chemical, biological, and missile technology consistent with the Non-Proliferation Treaty (NPT), the Chemical Weapons Convention, and the Biological Weapons Convention.
- U.S. troops out of Iraq and Afghanistan.
- An end to the U.S. military presence in the region. The United States has significantly expanded its military presence in the region since Iran's 1979 Islamic Revolution and today has military bases in countries surrounding Iran, including Saudi Arabia, Bahrain, the United Arab Emirates, Qatar, Pakistan, and Afghanistan. The fact is that Iran is virtually surrounded by U.S. military forces.
- Iran as the key regional ally of Iraq and Afghanistan.
- A stable political–economic system in Iran.
- A regional cooperation system for security, stability, and peace in the Persian Gulf.
- Israel weakened by increased pressure from the Islamic nations and the international community.
- No military conflict with Israel or the United States, no accidental war, and an end to threats from the United States and Israel that "all options are on the table."
- Preventing the militarization of the region. Since the Islamic Revolution, Western countries, especially the United States, have exported hundreds of billions of dollars' worth of sophisticated armaments to upgrade the military capabilities of regional countries against Iran, while working by all means to prevent Iran from obtaining weapons to build up its own military capabilities. This is viewed by Iranian security and political officials as a clear and serious threat and has stimulated Iran to upgrade its own military capabilities to the extent possible.
- The end of U.S. policies to achieve "regime change" in Tehran. Iran believes that U.S. efforts to promote democracy and human rights in Iran mask covert efforts to foster a "velvet revolution" against

the system. Iran seeks an end to U.S. support for violent anti-regime groups (for example, the Mujahideen-e Khalq, or MEK, also known as the PMOI, Jundallah, People's Free Life Party of Kurdistan, and others).

- Iran relieved of the UN Security Council sanctions, with normalized relations with the IAEA, with access to foreign investment and trade, and developing a relationship of mutual respect with other countries in the region and beyond.

By taking into account security objectives and identifying those areas in which some overlap might be found, Tehran and Washington should formulate a revised set of policies that would be more apt to achieve at least some of their security objectives. Neither country can expect full satisfaction in achieving all of its objectives. The challenge for both parties is to identify which objectives are most important and whether they will give some ground on other objectives in order to achieve their primary ones. A zero-sum approach will not work for either side.

If Iran's leader could be convinced that his country could achieve some of its objectives through dealing directly with the United States on the range of security issues that threaten its security in the region, the United States would have a better opportunity to address with Iran the major concerns it has with Iran's nuclear program. Tehran will not seriously consider having a dialogue with the United States on Weapons of Mass Destruction (WMD) questions unless and until the United States agrees to discuss Iran's security objectives in addition to America's security objectives. The obstacles to Washington and Tehran opening such a dialogue are serious but not insurmountable as each nation becomes more cognizant of the mounting threats to its security.

The two negotiating counterparts—Iran and the five permanent members of the UN Security Council (the United States, Great Britain, France, China, and Russia) plus Germany (P5+1)—reiterate that diplomacy is the best avenue for resolving the dispute over Iran's nuclear program. Diplomacy has failed thus far because the West has tried to force Iran to compromise on its policies by utilizing sanctions, pressure, sabotage, and threats. Some observers in the West argue that Iran's actions, policies, and internal dysfunction during President Mahmoud Ahmadinejad's term in office provoked the West to resort to these international pressures. Nevertheless, Iran has based its policy on resistance to threats, defending its independence, and perseverance in the face of tyranny. This is the main reason that the Iranians have responded to the P5+1 threats by accelerating their uranium enrichment program to reach a point of no return; it's a way of forcing the West to negotiate with them on an equal basis.

Five options generally have been discussed by international politicians and commentators as means to resolve the Iranian nuclear crisis:

1. A preemptive strike
2. Behavior change through sanctions, paired with containment and deterrence
3. Espionage and covert action to sabotage the program
4. Learning to live with an Iranian bomb and relying on containment and deterrence to prevent threats from Iran to regional peace and security
5. A diplomatic solution.

The first is seen by many as a last resort. The second and third have been the focus of efforts thus far. The fourth would cause damage to the nonproliferation regime. And the fifth has not worked despite eight years of attempts.

One of the main purposes of this book is to explain first why engagement has failed thus far and then, with that background, how it might succeed. We start here with a review of the other options.

1. A PREEMPTIVE STRIKE

WikiLeaks has provided a level of insight into U.S. foreign policy and positions taken by various actors that is deeper than any to date. Of 3,373 State Department cables released by the whistle-blowing website as of February 1, 2011, 323 are tagged as directly relating to Iran. The cables reflect a stereotypical U.S. fear-based view of Iran and contain very few, if any, positive statements toward normalizing relations or concrete mechanisms to reduce tension and misunderstanding. This perspective reflects more than thirty-two years of strained relations between the United States and Iran that is very much shaped by the regional actors' views on Iran and how they relay this information to U.S. officials.

In 2009, Egyptian President Hosni Mubarak called Iranians "liars," informing George Mitchell, the U.S. envoy to the Middle East, that he did not oppose the United States talking with Iran—as long as "you don't believe a word they say."[3] In the same meeting, Mubarak expressed the belief that Iran seeks to destabilize Egypt and the region. Similarly, the King of Qatar, in discussions with U.S. Senator John Kerry, chairman of the Senate Foreign Relations Committee, advised him in 2010 that "based on 30 years of experience with the Iranians, they will give you 100 words. Trust only one of the 100."[4]

The king of Saudi Arabia was quoted in a 2008 cable as urging the United States to "cut off the head of the snake,"[5] implicitly encouraging the United States to attack Iran. According to the cable, the king was adamant on the point of attacking Iran to put an end to the Iranian nuclear program, a request that he apparently made frequently. This view appears to have been understood well by the United States, with Secretary of Defense Robert Gates informing the French foreign minister in 2010 that the Saudis want to "fight the Iranians to the last American."[6]

And there is more. The president of the Jordanian Senate, Zeid Rifai, warned a visiting U.S. official in a 2009 cable, "Bomb Iran, or live with an Iranian bomb. Sanctions, carrots, incentives won't matter."[7] This was communicated despite his belief that a military strike would have a "catastrophic impact on the region."[8] In the same cable, the Jordanians are quoted as describing Iran as "an octopus whose tentacles reach out insidiously to manipulate, foment and undermine the best-laid plans of the west and regional moderates."[9]

King Hamad bin Isa al-Khalifa of Bahrain appeared to have expressed similar views in 2009 to U.S. General David Petraeus, who had command of U.S. military operations in the region. The king pointed to Iran as a source of "trouble" in the region and discussed the rationale for strikes against Iran, with the U.S. diplomat who authored the cable noting that "he argued forcefully for taking action to terminate their nuclear program, by whatever means necessary. 'The danger of letting it go on is greater than the danger of stopping.'"[10]

A number of cables have also made clear the position taken by the United Arab Emirates. In a meeting in 2009 between U.S. Treasury Secretary Timothy Geithner, Abu Dhabi Crown Prince Sheikh Muhammad bin Zayed al Nahyan, and Foreign Minister Sheikh Abdullah bin Zayed al Nahyan were noted to have expressed their fear of the Iranian government and to have advocated military strikes. The crown prince is said to have viewed "a near term conventional war with Iran as clearly preferable to the long-term consequence of a nuclear armed Iran."[11]

The crown prince also speculated that, within six months, Iran would be attacked by Israel and that an Israeli strike, by itself, would not be able to halt Iran's nuclear program.[12] The 2009 statement by the crown prince endorsing military action is consistent with his message in 2007 to General Michael Moseley, the U.S. Air Force chief of staff, when he recommended, "Delay their program—by all means available,"[13] as well as his comments in 2005 to U.S. Air Force Lieutenant General Michael Dunn. When Dunn voiced doubt regarding the chances of success in destroying "locations of concern" via aerial attack only,[14] the crown prince exclaimed, "Then it will take ground forces!"[15]

The Israeli government has expressed its position clearly on many occasions. Ministry of Defense Director General Pinchas Buchris was quoted in a 2009 cable as stating that there should be a finite period of time for U.S.-Iran engagement and that "all options must remain on the table."[16] In a 2007 cable, the Mossad director, Meir Dagan, is quoted as informing Frances Fragos Townsend, assistant to the U.S. president for homeland security and counterterrorism, that "Jordan, Saudi Arabia, and the Gulf States all fear Iran, but want someone else to do the job for them."[17]

The fear and resultant hostility shown toward Iran appear to have grown more intense in recent years. The cables show, for example, that the arrest of foreign citizens, as in the case of the British Embassy employees after the 2009 presidential election in Iran and the three U.S. hikers who crossed the border later in 2009, has added to the concerns of London and Washington and has exacerbated dealings with Iran.[18]

In a 2010 cable, Muhammad Omar Daudzai, Afghanistan's former ambassador to Iran, was noted to have stated that the Afghan president, Hamid Karzai, "had maintained excellent relations with Iran and Khatami [Muhammad Khatami, the former president of Iran] personally. . . . Relations had become more complicated with Ahmadinejad's election."[19] Another indication of mistrust was provided in a 2009 cable documenting the exchange between U.S. Senator Joseph Lieberman, chairman of the Senate

Committee on Homeland Security and Governmental Affairs, and Gamal Mubarak, a high-ranking member of his father's ruling party. When asked if the United States should reengage with Iran, Mubarak noted, "As long as Ahmadinejad is there, I am skeptical."[20]

The cables indicate that there are conflicting assessments of Iran's nuclear program and capability even among Israeli officials. A cable from 2005 notes that Defense Minister Shaul Mofaz "cautioned that Iran is 'less than one year away,' while the head of research in military intelligence estimated that Iran would reach this point by early 2007," while the head of the strategic affairs division of the Ministry of Foreign Affairs "recalled that [Israeli government] assessments from 1993 predicted that Iran would possess an atomic bomb by 1998."[21]

A cable from 2009 further illustrates the apparent lack of reliable intelligence on Iran's nuclear program, with Prime Minister Benjamin Netanyahu stating that he did not know "for certain how close Iran was to developing a nuclear weapons capability, but that 'our experts' say Iran was probably only one or two years away."[22] Interestingly, another 2009 cable notes, "It is unclear if the Israelis firmly believe this or are using worst-case estimates to raise greater urgency from the United States."[23] This comment was made in reference to Brigadier General Yossi Baidatz, the head of the Defense Ministry's Intelligence Analysis Production, who stated that "it would take Iran one year to obtain a nuclear weapon and two and a half years to build an arsenal of three weapons. By 2012 Iran would be able to build one weapon within weeks and an arsenal within six months."[24]

An analysis of the cables makes it reasonable to conclude that regional actors as well as the U.S. administration have deep concerns and fears in regard to Iran's true nuclear intentions. The cables have also made it clear that, while the U.S. administration and regional actors publicly support engagement with Iran, in reality they are increasingly suspicious and concerned about Iran's role in the region. In fact, they have opted to pursue a policy of increased pressure on Iran rather than options for dialogue and restoration of normal relations between Iran, its neighbors, and the United States.

Although the Iranian media paid a good deal of attention to WikiLeaks, President Ahmadinejad publicly dismissed the leaks as a staged and "worthless" psychological warfare campaign meant to bring down further pressure on Iran and said that they would not affect Iran's foreign relations.[25]

I am confident that in reality, Iran's strategists have analyzed the WikiLeaks cables closely as a means of better understanding U.S. foreign policy.

According to a survey conducted between April 7 and May 8, 2010, the publics in 22 countries, 16 Western and some Arab, indicated their approval of military action against Iran. In this poll, 66 percent of Americans, 59 percent of French, 51 percent of Germans, 55 percent of Egyptians, and 53 percent of Jordanians favored military action against Iran.[26] However, state media in Iran claim that according to another poll, 95 percent of people in Arab countries were in favor of Iran's nuclear program and 70 percent even believed that Iran should acquire nuclear weapons.[27]

Some politicians and academics, both in the Middle East and the West,[28] believe that, after eight years of negotiations without results, military strikes by the United States or Israel are the only remaining viable option to stop, or at least delay, Iran's nuclear bomb program. They reiterate that any air strikes should be precision attacks, aimed only at nuclear facilities, to minimize the costs and risks. Air strikes would also serve to remind Iran of the reach of U.S. military strength, they point out, and that many other valuable sites could be bombed if Iran were foolish enough to retaliate.[29]

Some believe a nuclear Iran would transfer nuclear materials and technologies to terrorist groups and countries such as Syria, Sudan, or Lebanon and argue that such a threat can be contained only if Washington is prepared to use force against Iran's enrichment facilities.[30]

Just days before the November 2010 congressional elections yielded major Republican gains, Senator Lieberman stated, "It is time to retire our ambiguous mantra about all options remaining on the table. Our message to our friends and enemies in the region needs to become clearer: namely, that we will prevent Iran from acquiring a nuclear weapons capability—by peaceful means if we possibly can, but with military force if we absolutely must."[31] After the election, Lieberman said that Congress would focus on pressing the administration on sanctions, but he also invited Congress to pass an "Iran War Resolution," suggesting that Congress might decide to formally endorse the options of military action against Iran.[32] He encouraged President Obama to forge a "bipartisan foreign policy" by cooperating with the new Republican leadership in the House of Representatives to thwart "anti-war Democrats and isolationist Republicans."[33]

After the election, Lindsey Graham, a leading Republican senator on defense issues, said that any military strike on Iran to stop its nuclear program must also strive to take out Iran's military capability. According to Graham, the United States should consider sinking the Iranian navy, destroying its air force, and delivering a decisive blow to the Revolutionary Guard to "neuter" the regime, precluding any ability to fight back, and hope that Iranians would use the opportunity to rise up against the government.[34]

Senator Graham outlined his plan for confronting Iran during a speech at the Johns Hopkins School of Advanced International Studies. He said: "If sanctions fail, and the President believes they're going to fail, then you have to put on the table military force." Graham urged U.S. action, because "the worst possible thing that could happen in the Mid-East is an Israeli strike against Iran because that changes the whole equation. The Iranians would be able on the 'Arab street' to have traction they wouldn't have otherwise."[35] This of course ignored the reality that a U.S. attack would have the same effect on regional public opinion.

Stephen Hadley, President George W. Bush's former national security adviser, and Israeli Brigadier General Michael Herzog wrote in a paper published by the Washington Institute for Near East Policy in July 2009,

> By the first quarter of 2011, we will know whether sanctions are proving effective . . . the administration should begin to plan now for a course of action should sanctions be deemed ineffective by the first or second quarter of next year. The military option must be kept on the table both as a means of strengthening diplomacy and as a worst-case scenario. . . . [36]

Bush's former ambassador to the United Nations, John Bolton, has insisted that neither diplomacy nor sanctions, no matter how tough, will be sufficient to dissuade Tehran from acquiring nuclear weapons and that military action—preferably by the United States, but if not, by Israel—will be necessary, sooner rather than later.[37]

The Israeli Right is constantly encouraging the United States to attack Iran. Prime Minister Netanyahu said in a March 2011 interview, "The current United Nations sanctions on Iran for its failure to come clean about its nuclear program were not enough. The only thing that will work is if Iran knows that if it fails to cooperate, military action will be taken. Such actions would be aimed at knocking out Iran's nuclear facilities, be 'preferably' led by the United States, and is not that complicated. Could be done. It's not easy, but it's not impossible."[38] Netanyahu has frequently called upon the United States to take military action rather than expect sanctions to be effective.[39]

Although it is widely believed in Washington that Obama is trying to avoid a war with Iran and to restrain Israel, Vice President Joseph Biden, Secretary of State Hillary Clinton, and Admiral Mike Mullen, until recently the chairman of the Joint Chiefs of Staff, have all reiterated that, in dealing with Iran's nuclear program, "all options" remain on the table, including that of a military strike.[40] For his part, Obama sought to reassure Israel in an interview with the Israeli TV Network 2, stating, "Iran acquiring a nuclear weapon is unacceptable, and we will use all the means [at] our disposal to prevent such an event from happening."[41]

It seems that White House decisionmakers believe in a military strike as a possible last resort. First, they will wait and hope that the severe pressure Iran faces today will compel a change in its behavior. They have kept open the door for diplomacy only to check whether this approach is succeeding. If Iran continues its defiance, despite all pressures and sanctions, they may consider the military option more seriously. Washington is determined to ensure the security of Israel and reassure Arab governments, and it believes—and this belief crosses party lines—that preventing Iran from acquiring nuclear weapons must ultimately trump other concerns.[42]

Nevertheless, differences exist on the question of who should launch the air strikes: Israel or the United States or both? Israeli officials regard Iran's nuclear capability as an "existential" threat and hence are willing to engage in military action if necessary to destroy the enrichment facilities.[43] Some in Washington favor letting Israel do the dirty work to avoid exacerbating anti-American sentiment in the Islamic world. Others, however, argue that the United States should carry out the strike because its sophisticated weaponry would be more effective. They claim that because of its great capacity and global reach, only the U.S. military could prevent Iranian retaliation.[44] In November 2011, Moshe Ya'alon, Israel's strategic affairs minister, said he preferred an American military attack on Iran to one by Israel.[45]

A preemptive strike, however, is basically unrealistic and unfeasible. Contrary to the past assertions of Israel's current prime minister, Iran does not pose an existential threat to Israel.

Iran's defense spending is a small fraction of Israel's and an even far tinier fraction of America's. Apart from the Iran-Iraq war, which Saddam Hussein clearly started, Iran has not launched an attack across another country's borders in more than a hundred years. Despite some aggressive rhetoric on Iran's part, an examination of the history of its actions shows that Iran's ultimate goals are no different than other countries' goals: survival and influence. In fact, the best and probably only way to make Iran an existential threat to Israel would be for Israel to attack Iran.[46] At the same time, there should be no doubt that any Israeli attack would have immediate ramifications on U.S. interests both regionally and internationally.

Should there be an Israeli strike, the United States would be considered complicit and would become embroiled militarily in any Iranian retaliation, whether it's aimed directly at Israel or more generally at the region. Iran could and would, for instance, make the already tenuous situations in Iraq and Afghanistan much more troublesome for the United States while Washington is trying to scale down its presence in both countries.[47] Difficult as those conflicts have been, the U.S. wars in Iraq and Afghanistan were like a picnic compared to a war with Iran.

Iran is allied with movements throughout the Middle East. In the case of any military strikes, Iran's military would use both its own resources and those movements to quickly spread the conflict throughout the Middle East and even the entire Islamic world. Iran also would hit Tel Aviv with long-range missiles and attack Americans and U.S. infrastructure in Iraq, Afghanistan, and the broader Middle East, engulfing the region in an open-ended war. As Mohamed ElBaradei, the former head of the IAEA, has written, an attack on Iran would be an "an act of madness" that would trigger "Armageddon in the Middle East."[48]

An Israeli or U.S. strike could produce a diplomatic split between the United States and Russia, China, Non-Aligned Movement countries, and even European and regional U.S. allies, reminiscent of the tensions over the Iraq war.

The safe passage of oil and gas through the strategic Strait of Hormuz, which the Iranian military has considerable capacity to attack or block, would be in danger. Iran's sophisticated missile batteries arrayed in the mountains overlooking the strait could strike any fleet deployed below. Iran also has in its speedboat fleet a very powerful naval weapon with speed and advanced abilities to avoid radar detection, capable of inflicting terrible damage on any ships. Iran would attempt to block the strait by mining, cruise missile strikes, or small boat attacks. The price of oil might rise dramatically, and European dependence on Russian oil and gas would increase.

The economies of Japan, China, and even South Korea are very much dependent on imported oil and gas from Iran and the rest of the Persian Gulf countries. China has signed contracts with Iran for $70 billion worth of oil and natural gas. China is developing the Yadavaran oil field in Iran to purchase 150,000 barrels of oil per day and 250 million tons of liquefied natural gas over the next three decades. Obviously these countries would have to defend their national interests.*

President Obama's efforts to improve relations with the Muslim world are very important for U.S. strategic interests. In a June 4, 2009, speech in Cairo, Obama called for a "new beginning" between the United States and Muslims, one "based upon mutual interest and mutual respect."[49] Anti-American sentiment is on the decline in the Muslim world. If Israel were to conduct a military strike, however, the United States would be viewed as strategic partner of Israel in war against a Muslim country. One consequence of such a perception would be the deterioration of U.S. relations with the Muslim world. Despite President Obama's efforts to improve America's image in the Muslim world and also increase U.S. defense cooperation with Arab allies, American credibility is in decline, and global opinion of the United States is generally negative in countries such as Jordan and Egypt, which are key U.S. partners.[50] In a war between the United States and Iran, Arab leaders who may even now be encouraging attacks on Iran would likely not only condemn the military strikes but also distance themselves from military and political cooperation with Washington.

The atmosphere created by a military attack on Iran would create golden opportunities for al-Qaeda and other terrorist groups to gain sympathy and recruits from among Muslims for terrorist activities against America all over the world.

An Israeli or U.S. strike on Iran would kill any chance for rapprochement between Tehran and Washington after Obama's engagement policy,

---

* Editor's note: At the same time, Russia and other states have said that Iran's acquisition of nuclear weapons would be unacceptable, leaving open the possibility that their perspectives on costs could change.

the official exchange of letters between President Obama and Iran's leader and president, the high-level meeting between officials on October 1, 2009, in Geneva, and many other developments have created hopes for détente after thirty years of hostilities.

The popular anger aroused domestically by a military strike would help radicals and undermine moderates in Iran. Hard-line radicals would face fewer constraints in consolidating their power. There is no doubt that Iranians of all stripes would rally around the flag to defend their country. Any military strike also would unify Iranians around the necessity of having nuclear weapons to deter attacks and threats to their land, integrity, identity, and rights.

Peaceful enrichment technology is extremely important for Iran, not only for industrial development but also as a "virtual deterrent." A military attack might change Iran's objective from a virtual to a real nuclear deterrent. It would certainly strengthen the influence of Iran's military establishment in government policy and cause Iran to accelerate its drive to modernize its military.

An Israeli strike would dash any hopes for progress in Israeli-Palestinian peace negotiations. Washington and Tel Aviv would be preoccupied managing the huge consequences of the attack against Iran. Hamas or Hizbollah or both would retaliate against Israel. In such a situation, a further setback of any revival of the peace process is predictable. In the view of Muslim and Arabs, the Israel-Palestinian peace process is by far the central concern in the region. An Israeli attack could also weaken unity among Democrats and Republicans in support of Israel and bring severe consequences for the alliance between Jerusalem and Washington.[51]

Iran would withdraw from the NPT, suspend nuclear talks with the P5+1, kick out inspectors from all nuclear sites, and henceforth hide the progress of its nuclear program.*

A former U.S. Marine commander who served in Beirut offered a historical perspective as well as a warning of the consequences an attack could unleash. Timothy J. Geraghty wrote in 2010,

> Since the 2006 Israeli-Hezbollah war, Iran has rearmed Hezbollah with 40,000 rockets and missiles that will likely rain on Israeli cities—and

---

* Editor's note: Iran has in the past, as recently as 2009 at Fordow, hidden the progress of its nuclear program.

even European cities and U.S. military bases in the Middle East—if Iran is attacked. Our 200,000 troops in 33 bases are vulnerable. . . . Iran is capable of disrupting Persian Gulf shipping lanes, which could cause the price of oil to surge above $300 a barrel. Iran could also create mayhem in oil markets by attacking Saudi oil refineries. . . . Iran could unleash suicide bombers in Iraq and Afghanistan or, more ominously, activate Hezbollah sleeper cells in the United States to carry out coordinated attacks nationwide. . . . On Nov. 28, 2009, reacting to increased pressure from the International Atomic Energy Agency, Iran warned it may pull out of the Nuclear Non-Proliferation Treaty. . . . Two days later, Iran announced plans to build 10 new nuclear plants within six years. . . . I have seen this play before. In 1983, I was the Marine commander of the U.S. Multinational Peacekeeping Force in Beirut, Lebanon. Iran's Islamic Revolutionary Guard Corps' (IRGC) Lebanon contingent trained and equipped Hezbollah to execute attacks that killed 241 of my men and 58 French Peacekeepers on Oct. 23, 1983.[52]

Finally, and needless to say, the U.S. budget is already under tremendous pressure and cannot afford another war. And given the consequences of the invasions of Iraq and Afghanistan, I believe that the United States is not interested in another war in the Middle East and neither is Israel. The crises in Libya, Egypt, and Yemen are more than enough to occupy America's security establishment. Keeping the military option on the table is mainly a ploy to increase pressure on Iran for a possible deal. Given the realities of U.S. challenges and limitations domestically and internationally, many Iranian politicians do not view the U.S. military threat as credible. They claim that the military option is no longer being seriously examined.[53] Nevertheless, we should keep three realities in mind:

1. Military threats are counterproductive because Iran will refuse to compromise under the threat of military strike and will view any U.S. offer for rapprochement under such conditions as suspect. The war talk makes confidence-building measures ineffectual.
2. Issuing military threats over and over again will create expectations for action[54] and put pressure on the U.S. government to repeat on a more catastrophic scale the mistake of invading Iraq.

3. Using the language of war is therefore simply counterproductive, and it is best set aside. This is especially the case in that military strikes against Iran would not set back Iran's program for very long and would greatly increase Iran's incentive to withdraw from the NPT and go straight to building a nuclear bomb at secret locations, just as Iraq did after Israel destroyed its Osirak reactor in 1981.[55]

2. BEHAVIOR CHANGE THROUGH SANCTIONS, PAIRED WITH CONTAINMENT AND DETERRENCE

John Limbert, who served as U.S. deputy assistant secretary of state for Iran in 2009–2010 and who as a foreign service officer newly posted to Tehran was one of the 52 Americans taken hostage in the U.S. Embassy in 1979, summed up the imposition of sanctions as a fallback position that ultimately is ineffective:

> Actually since 1979, we've used sanctions against Iran. They're something we know. We know how to apply them, how to negotiate them, how to negotiate with the Russians or with the Chinese or with the P5+1, how to get them through the UN. [But we do not know how to change] the unproductive relationship that we've had with Iran for the last 30 years. That's hard. That is very hard. That is very hard.[56]

Indeed, the majority of Westerners commentators and policymakers believe that efforts to negotiate with Iran should be abandoned but that military strikes on Iran's nuclear sites should not be considered as an alternative. They suggest a policy of compelling Iran to comply with IAEA and UN Security Council resolutions through unilateral and multilateral sanctions and political pressure. They stress that sanctions serve as an important tax on Iran's economy and help disrupt Iran's ability to purchase equipment vital to its nuclear and missile programs. In parallel with efforts to press Iran to change its behavior, advocates of this policy urge the United States and Iran's neighboring states to take steps to contain and deter its capacity and inclination to conduct asymmetric coercion outside its borders. Overall, they argue that this combination of policies has better chances of success than either military attack or the current path of extended inconclusive negotiations.[57]

Some of these commentators and policymakers also believe that promoting regime change in Tehran through comprehensive and global sanctions is the best approach to support nonproliferation, by leaving Iran's present leadership with the choice of giving up its nuclear program or losing power. Their position is predicated on the belief that, after the June 2009 presidential election in Iran, the situation completely changed and that the Iranian people are ready to rise up and demand change. They encourage the U.S. president to realize that this is his "tear down this wall" moment. They believe that Iran's leaders are rushing to obtain a nuclear weapon to strengthen their hands domestically as well as internationally. Moreover, they warn the White House that Israel's patience will not be infinite.[58]

Richard Haass, the president of the Council on Foreign Relations, was among those who believed that after the 2009 election Iran was closer to profound political change than at any time since the revolution that ousted the Shah thirty years ago. He argued that the government overreached in its manipulation of the election and then made matters worse by repressing those who protested. He wrote in 2010 that Ahmadinejad and the supreme leader of Iraq, Ayatollah Ali Khamenei, had both lost much of their legitimacy and that the opposition Green Movement had grown larger and stronger than many predicted. Accordingly, he advised the United States, European governments, and others to shift their Iran policy toward increasing prospects for political change because "now is the first good chance in decades to bring about a regime change in Iran."[59] He changed his mind in 2011. He said: "You've got to hope for regime change in Iran, which unfortunately doesn't look like it's happening. Can you ratchet up sanctions? Can you go after the Iranian export of oil? Now, that's really going to the edge of economic warfare. But might that not be preferable to going to the edge of warfare warfare."[60]

Some hawks in Washington advocate regime change in Iran through supporting terrorist groups. In November 2010, the neoconservative group Freedom Watch held a symposium entitled "National Security, Freedom, and Iran: Is It Time for U.S. and Western Intervention?" The gathering was aimed at convincing the new Congress, now that the House of Representatives was going to be in Republican hands, to push harder for U.S. and Western intervention for regime change in Iran through direct U.S. support for the MEK. The following month, a group of prominent Republicans, including former New York mayor Rudy Giuliani, former homeland security secretary Tom Ridge, former attorney general Michael Mukasey, and Townsend, the former homeland security official, flew to Paris to speak in support of the MEK. A resolution urging the Obama administration to drop the MEK from the State Department's list of terrorist organizations had surfaced in the House earlier in 2010; it had 112 sponsors, but it died in committee. Britain and the European Union, meanwhile, had already dropped terrorist designations for the group.[61]

On August 2011, the *Christian Science Monitor* revealed that "many former high-ranking U.S. officials ... have been paid tens of thousands of dollars to speak in support of the MEK."[62]

There's a reason the MEK is on the list of terrorist organizations: It *is* a terrorist organization. It was formed in the 1960s as an urban guerrilla movement against the Shah of Iran. It was responsible for the assassination of six Americans before the 1979 revolution and hundreds of Iranian civilians and officials afterward. In addition to murder, it is known to have engaged in arson and acts of general sabotage in Iran.[63] In the Iran-Iraq war in 1980s, the MEK fought alongside Saddam Hussein, against Iran. Saddam later deployed the group to crush the Kurdish rebellion that came immediately after Iraq's defeat in the Persian Gulf War. Since Saddam's ouster, the Iraqi government has been working to try to expel the group from the country.[64]

The MEK remains on the State Department's list, but it is not for lack of trying to get off. The *Financial Times* reported that the group has spent millions of dollars in a lobbying effort to be removed from the list. The newspaper reported that the group has paid tens of thousands of dollars to more than 40 former U.S. officials across the political spectrum—from conservative John Bolton to liberal Howard Dean to retired general James L. Jones—to speak at events organized by MEK supporters.[65]

The policy of increasing pressure, whether through imposing sanctions or calling for regime change, has thus far failed to make a change in Iran's nuclear program. After the October 2009 impasse in Geneva talks over a "confidence-building" deal in which Iran would have traded most of its stockpile of low-enriched uranium for fuel for the Tehran nuclear research reactor, Denis McDonough, chief of staff at the U.S. National Security Council, said that the United States was reaching out to its international partners in an effort to gain support for a fresh round of sanctions against the Islamic Republic.[66] Shortly thereafter, Hillary Clinton stated that the aim was not incremental sanctions, but sanctions that would "bite."[67] In June 2010, following this strategy, the United States, supported by Europe, Russia, and China, was successful in passing UN Security Council Resolution 1929, which did indeed produce harsh new sanctions.

Since the adoption of Resolution 1929 and additional unilateral sanctions by the United States[68] and other countries including EU member states, Japan, South Korea, and Australia,[69] more and more international companies and foreign subsidiaries of American companies have stopped doing business in Iran.[70] Investors in Iran's energy sector are pulling out of projects, making it more difficult for Iran to modernize its infrastructure or develop new oil and gas fields. In the first seventeen months after Resolution 1929 was adopted, Iran's currency (the rial) experienced a drop in value by 20 percent as of September 2011.[71] On December 31, 2011, U.S. President Barack Obama signed a bill calling for new sanctions against financial institutions doing business with Iran's state banking institutions. The bill, approved by Congress earlier in December, aimed at reducing Tehran's oil revenues. After this announcement, the Iranian currency lost over 60 percent of its value against major foreign currencies.[72] Merchants in several cities, including Tehran and Shiraz, went on strike to protest government plans to impose value-added taxes on certain goods.[73] The prices of some goods have increased by 10 to 40 percent since Resolution 1929 took effect. This was due in part to a decision by Iran's government to drastically cut domestic subsidies, which raised the prices of gasoline and other necessities. The deterioration of Iran's economy, then, was not just because of sanctions but also because of mismanagement. Increasing oil prices have provided enormous revenue to the Iranian government and thus greater latitude in economic policy. Iran's foreign exchange reserves are quite high, and its foreign debt is low. Iran's trade has shifted from the West to neighboring countries and Asia, where financial sanctions are less effective.

Iranian hard-liners consider the sanctions "a joke." In fact, they welcome the sanctions and call them a "gift of God to the Iranian nation." Ahmadinejad himself believes that they strengthen the autarky of the Iranian economy, serve the national interest, and have had no impact on people's livelihoods.[74] In November 2010, General Muhammad Reza Naqdi, the head of the Basij militia, declared, "I thank the Lord that our country is under sanction and I pray that the sanctions increase every day, and if the universities of our country attain greater scientific progress these sanctions will be to our benefit."[75]

Even so, the reality is that the sanctions have hurt Iran's economy, which is why Ali Akbar Hashemi Rafsanjani, the former president who is now the head of the Expediency Council, said publicly that Iran had never been faced with so many sanctions and that all the country's officials should take the sanctions seriously and not treat them as a joke.[76] His remarks stand in contrast to those of Ahmadinejad. The president has continually insisted that the sanctions have had no effect on Iran's economy, calling them "pathetic" and likening Resolution 1929 to "a used handkerchief that should be thrown in the dustbin."[77]

But will the sanctions achieve their goal of forcing Iran to change its nuclear policy? The answer, in a word, is "no." Those who support pressuring Iran through sanctions understand that further international sanctions will not compel a change in Iran's nuclear policies, but they think there are five good reasons to pursue additional sanctions anyway: to influence Iranian policy, to promote positive change in the nature of the Iranian regime, to degrade Iranian military and power projection capabilities, to set a deterrent example for other aspirant proliferators, and to provide an alternative to two unattractive options: either doing nothing to respond to the Iranian nuclear program or going to war to prevent it.[78] But there are clear reasons that sanctions will not change Iran's nuclear policy:

The Islamic Republic has experienced a number of episodes of severe economic pressure, and not one of them has generated the kind of foreign policy changes that the West seeks.[79] Pressure through sanctions is a policy that has been applied against Iran for thirty years and yet in spite of it, the Islamic Republic today is regionally and internationally more powerful than ever. Even though there is no evidence of diversion of nuclear, chemical, and biological activities for military purposes, Iran has been able, despite sanctions, to acquire the capability for long-range missiles, ura-

nium enrichment, and advanced chemical and biological technologies.*
This suggests that Iran's lack of weapons of mass destruction is a matter of
Iran's policy choice and that it cannot be coerced through sanctions.

As former U.S. ambassador James Dobbins[80] put it:

> Historically, sanctions have seldom forced improved behavior on the
> part of targeted regimes. Sanctions did not compel the Soviet Union to
> withdraw from Afghanistan, Pakistan to halt its nuclear weapons pro-
> gram, Saddam Hussein to evacuate Kuwait, the Haitian military regime
> to step aside, [Slobodan] Milosevic to halt ethnic cleansing in Bosnia
> and Kosovo, or the Taliban to expel Osama bin Laden. Stiff sanctions
> were applied in all of these cases, but it took either a foreign military
> intervention, violent domestic resistance, or both to bring about the
> desired changes.[81]

Virtually all Iranians support Iran's efforts to master the nuclear fuel
cycle, and sanctions that are applied to coerce Iran into giving up its enrichment program could well increase support for the system against foreign meddling rather than the reverse. As Mohamed ElBaradei reflects in
the 2011 memoir of his time as the IAEA's director general, "From what
we repeatedly observed, a policy of isolation and sanctions only served to
stimulate a country's sense of national pride; in the worst case, it could
make the targeted country's nuclear project a matter of national priority."[82]

The use of sanctions as a prelude to invasion is another matter. Sanctions can reduce economic activity and military power, as was certainly
true in Saddam's Iraq, Haiti, Serbia, and Afghanistan, and in each case,
comprehensive and widely enforced sanctions led to an eventual American
military intervention. But a sanction policy as a prelude to invasion and
occupation is totally unrealistic in the case of Iran.[83]

Some politicians believe that the United States should seek to impose
more sanctions as a way to postpone an Israeli military strike against Iran.
This may be a stopgap measure, but it is not a solution to the problem, and
in fact it complicates the situation in the long term.

---

* Editor's note: As noted below and throughout, the IAEA and UN Security Council recognize that beyond the issue of diversion, the overriding requirement under the NPT is that
all of a state's nuclear activities must be exclusively for peaceful purposes and that none be
hidden and outside of safeguards.

Unfortunately, existing U.S. legislation does not include broad authority for the president to waive or terminate sanctions in response to changing conditions. In the immediate aftermath of the U.S. interventions in Afghanistan and Iraq, the Islamic Republic made far-reaching overtures for cooperation with Washington. But Washington was either unable to respond to the opportunities for rapprochement or ignored them. That was a great strategic mistake. When another such opportunity arises, the U.S. president should be in a position to respond rapidly.

Finally, America's use of the UN Security Council sanctions as a tool to serve a broader political agenda on Iran has damaged the body's credibility. According to ElBaradei, in addition to being counterproductive, Resolution 1929 was "a misuse of the council's authority under Chapter VII of the UN Charter."[84,*] Such misuse of international institutions delegitimizes them in the eyes of not only Iran but also other developing countries.

At the same time that sanctions were being pursued in Iran's case, the IAEA found that South Korea and Egypt had failed to disclose past nuclear activities, but they were not charged with noncompliance because of their close relations with the United States. According to ElBaradei: "In Egypt, the IAEA encountered a similar [to South Korea] case of undeclared nuclear experiment . . . uranium extraction and conversion and reprocessing had in fact occurred. Egypt failed to report to [the] IAEA both activities."[85] An even worse inconsistency has been American policy toward Israel, India, and Pakistan; when they went nuclear, their reward was strategic relations with the United States.

As I wrote after taking up residence at Princeton University in September 2009, "Regime change is not part of Iran's outlook in the near future, and Iran is not in a pre-revolutionary state." I continued to press for the United States to engage Tehran in a bid to reduce regional tensions, and in an interview with the *Wall Street Journal*, I made it very clear that "the target of the recent [UN sanctions] resolution was to soften Iran's position in regard to its nuclear program, but in reality it will only serve to radicalize its position . . . the United States should still shape a compre-

---

* Editor's note: The fact that the Security Council has voted for sanctions on this basis four times indicates that the leading states of the international community do think such action is within the council's responsibilities to protect international peace and security and to enforce the NPT.

hensive dialogue with Iran based on shared interests in stabilizing Iraq and Afghanistan."[86]

3. ESPIONAGE AND COVERT ACTION TO SABOTAGE THE PROGRAM

Proponents of clandestine action against Iran's nuclear facilities believe it would be more effective and less risky politically than an Israeli or American military operation that might not stop Iranian enrichment but could make Tehran retaliate across the region and become even more determined to obtain a nuclear weapon as a deterrent.[87]

U.S. covert action in Iran has a long history, beginning in 1953 when the United States toppled the popularly elected Prime Minister Muhammad Mossadegh, and continuing after the 1979 revolution.[88] In 1995, the Central Intelligence Agency (CIA) allocated $18 million for covert efforts to destabilize Iran.[89] In 2005, the U.S. Congress authorized a $3 million fund to support democracy and human rights in Iran.[90] Three years later, President George W. Bush signed a "non-lethal presidential finding" that initiated a CIA plan involving "a coordinated campaign of propaganda, disinformation and manipulation of Iran's currency and international financial transactions."[91]

The 1981 Algiers Accords between Iran and the United States very clearly state that "it is and from now on will be the policy of the United States not to intervene, directly or indirectly, politically or militarily, in Iran's internal affairs."[92] The U.S. sabotage activities are a serious violation of the Algiers Accords.

In early 2009, the *New York Times* reported that the Bush administration had organized covert action intended to sabotage Iran's nuclear program in 2008 after sanctions failed to curb Iran's nuclear ambitions.[93] According to the article, the administration briefed Israel on the covert program after Washington rejected an Israeli request for a new generation of bunker-busting bombs required for a possible attack on Iran. Mark Fitzpatrick, former deputy assistant secretary of state for nonproliferation and now a senior fellow at the International Institute for Strategic Studies, said: "Industrial sabotage is a way to stop the program, without military action, without fingerprints on the operation, and really, it is ideal, if it works.

One way to sabotage a program is to make minor modifications in some of the components Iran obtains on the black market, and because it's a black market . . . you don't know exactly who you are dealing with."[94]

Many published reports have confirmed that a malicious computer worm known as Stuxnet was developed to target the computer systems that control Iran's huge enrichment plant at Natanz.[95] The then-vice president and head of the Atomic Energy Organization, Ali Akbar Salehi, provided a clear government confirmation that Iran has been fighting espionage at its nuclear facilities. Iran announced the arrest of several nuclear spies and battled a computer worm that it says is part of a covert Western plot to derail its nuclear program. An industrial control security researcher in Germany who has analyzed Stuxnet said it had been created to sabotage a nuclear plant in Iran.[96]

In January 2011, the *New York Times* published a report revealing that Stuxnet was designed as an American-Israeli project to sabotage the Iranian nuclear program. The report confirmed that the worm was tested at the Israeli nuclear site of Dimona before being directed toward Iranian nuclear facilities.[97]

Quoting the head of the Mossad, Hillary Clinton also confirmed damage to Iran's nuclear program by a combination of "sabotage and sanctions."[98] This is the first time that state-sponsored cyber warfare has become entirely public worldwide. According to the *New York Times*, the cyber attack was largely managed by the Obama administration. It said that the Bush administration's covert computer sabotage program "has been accelerated since President Obama took office."[99]

David Albright, president of the Institute for Science and International Security (ISIS) in Washington, has confirmed that foreign intelligence agencies now appear to be targeting Iran's nuclear activities with a variety of methods. These include cyber attacks, the sabotaging of key equipment Iran seeks abroad, infiltration and disruption of Iran's purchasing networks, and the assassination of nuclear experts.[100] He believes that, given the delays caused both by these secret projects and actual technical difficulties, the world has some number of years to work on this impasse before Iran is in a position where it could make a political decision whether to build nuclear weapons.[101]

IAEA reports on Iran show a drop in the number of operating centrifuges in the Natanz plant. After reaching a peak of 4,920 machines in May 2009, the number of centrifuges declined to 3,772 in August 2010.[102] Nevertheless, based on IAEA findings in September 2011, 53 cascades were installed in Natanz as of August 2011, 35 of which were being fed with uranium hexafluoride, or UF_6, a chemical compound used during the uranium enrichment process. Initially each installed cascade comprised 164 centrifuges; Iran has subsequently modified twelve of the cascades to contain 174 centrifuges each. Therefore, Iran reached about 8,800 centrifuges as of August 2011.[103]

Iranian authorities have said that all industrial computers in Iran have been cleansed of the Stuxnet worm. An official in the Ministry of Industries and Mines reported that Iranian engineers were successful in eradicating Stuxnet from all computers in use at industrial facilities.[104] Intelligence Minister Heydar Moslehi also officially revealed that five spies had been arrested.[105] The most direct confirmation that sabotage has paid off came from Ahmadinejad, who said in November 2010 that the Stuxnet computer worm had damaged the Natanz operation. "They [spies] succeeded in creating problems for a limited number of our centrifuges with the software they had installed in electronic parts," he said.[106]

On April 25, 2011, Brigadier General Gholamreza Jalali, a senior Iranian military official who heads the country's anti-sabotage Passive Defense military unit, announced that Iranian computer systems had been hit with additional computer malware. Though he did not specify the facilities that were targeted, Jalali suggested that the Stars virus was part of a foreign campaign to sabotage Iran's nuclear program.[107]

Meanwhile, international media reported that Israel planned to target Iranian nuclear scientists with letter bombs and poisoned packages, possibly as part of a campaign of psychological warfare.

When Iranian nuclear scientist Ardeshir Hosseinpour was killed in 2008, sources told the *New York Times* that the Israeli intelligence service had assassinated him.[108] Later, Iran announced the arrest of several people who it said were linked to Israel and involved in a bomb attack that killed Masoud Alimohammadi, a nuclear scientist, in January 2010.[109] Two other nuclear scientists were attacked in Tehran on November 29,

2010. One of them, Majid Shahriari, died when a bomb was stuck to the door of his car and detonated. The other, Fereydoon Abbasi Davani, who was under a UN travel ban because of his work, was badly injured.[110] Iran said the attacks were part of a covert campaign by the United States, the United Kingdom, and Israel to sabotage its nuclear program.[111] Some days later, Iran's intelligence minister announced the arrests of suspects in the most recent attacks.[112] A week after that, the Iranian interior minister announced that those arrested had confessed that they were trained and charged by the U.S., UK, and Israeli intelligence agencies to assassinate the two Iranian scientists.[113]

Following these incidents, Ahmadinejad publicly stated that "I swear to God, if this act of assassination is once more repeated, I will bring every member of the UN Security Council to trial."[114]

A few months later in July 2011, a thirty-five-year old postgraduate student, Daryoush Rezayeenejad, was shot dead near his home in south Tehran by two gunmen firing from motorcycles. An official from a member nation of the IAEA said Rezayeenejad participated in developing high-voltage switches, a key component in setting off the explosions needed to trigger a nuclear warhead.[115] Iranian Parliament Speaker Ali Larijani strongly condemned the killing, which he said indicates the U.S. and Israeli animosity toward Iran. *Der Spiegel* reported that Israel was responsible for the assassination. An unnamed Israeli source told the German newspaper that it was the first "serious action" taken by the new Mossad chief, Tamir Pardo.[116] Iran's intelligence minister said, however, that no signs had been found so far to suggest that foreign intelligence services were behind the incident.[117]

And then on January 11, 2012, Mostafa Ahmadi Roshan, a thirty-two-year-old director at the Natanz uranium enrichment plant, was assassinated after a metallic explosive device attached to his car by a motorcyclist detonated during the morning rush hour in Tehran.[118] Iranian leader Ayatollah Khamenei blamed the CIA and the Mossad, Israel's intelligence agency, for killing the Iranian nuclear scientist.[119] Ahmadinejad has not fulfilled his promise of placing on trial any members of the UN Security Council. But at the Geneva talks in December 2010, the Iranian delegation had displayed a photograph of Majid Shahriari, the scientist killed in November, and persuaded Catherine Ashton, the EU foreign affairs chief, to condemn such "terrorist" attacks.[120]

Meanwhile, eighteen people were killed in an explosion that occurred at one of Iran's missile bases in the province of Lorestan in October 2010. The European and Iranian media reported that the explosion was one phase of a greater master scheme of sabotage planned by the United States, United Kingdom, and Israeli intelligence services against Iranian military and nuclear infrastructure.

All of the nefarious activities may have had an impact in buying time. Outgoing Mossad chief Meir Dagan said in January 2010 that Iran couldn't build a bomb before 2015 at the earliest because of "measures that have been deployed against them."[121] U.S. and Israeli officials concluded that, as a result of covert sabotage, Iran's nuclear program had been slowed, and due to the delay caused by a combination of sabotage, sanctions, and Iran's own technical problems, a military showdown with Iran could be postponed.[122] Hillary Clinton said that any delay in Iran's nuclear program should not undercut international determination to keep the pressure on Iran, through sanctions and other means, to come clean about its atomic work.[123] In addition, there has been a deluge of irresponsible statements from some in the United States. Former Republican presidential candidate Rick Santorum ranted[124] that the murders of Iranian nuclear scientists are "a wonderful thing." Iranians and others hear this as nothing less than support of terrorism by a U.S. presidential candidate.[125]

In what can be interpreted as an official confession of covert activity, spying, sabotage, and interference in the internal affairs of Iran, John Sawers, former British nuclear negotiator and now the chief of MI6, the UK's intelligence service, stated in October 2010 that spying is crucial to stop Iran's nuclear drive. "Diplomacy is not enough to stop Iran developing nuclear weapons," he said, urging an "intelligence-led approach to stopping Iran's nuclear proliferation."[126] Immediately following the assassination of Ahmadi Roshan, Iran's foreign ministry blasted the U.S. and UK governments for the assassination in an official note to the UK Ministry of Foreign Affairs. The note pointed out that the assassination of Iranian nuclear scientists immediately followed the remarks of Sawers, who had discussed the launch of intelligence operations against Iran. The note also argued that Iran's Foreign Ministry "voices its strong protest to the outcome of the mentioned British approach and underscores that the UK is responsible for such acts of terror."[127] "We have reliable documents and evidence that this terrorist act was planned, guided and supported by the CIA," the Iranian foreign ministry said in a separate official note handed to the Swiss ambassador in Tehran.[128] (The Swiss embassy represents U.S. interests in a country where Washington has no diplomatic ties.)

The strategy pursued by the United States, United Kingdom, and Israel as described above constitutes a declaration of war on Iran, and a first strike. Stuxnet actually did attack Iran's nuclear program; it can be called the first unattributed act of war against Iran. By pursuing the sabotage option, the United States is taking the preliminary steps toward war and sacrificing its long-term interests for short-term achievements. Such policies certainly thicken the wall of mistrust and ultimately could disrupt engagement policy and confidence-building measures between Tehran and Washington. In response, Iran may look toward retaliatory measures by launching a cyber counterattack against Israeli and U.S. facilities. After the Stuxnet attack, and under the directive of Iran's supreme leader, Iran's army established new structures for cyber warfare (that is, offense as well as defense).[129] Thousands of mourners chanted "Death to Israel" and "Death to America" during the funeral of slain nuclear expert Ahmadi Roshan. An unnamed Iranian intelligence official said, "Iran's intelligence community is in a very good position to design tit-for-tat operations to retaliate for assassinations carried out by Western intelligence services. Iran's response will be extraterritorial and extra-regional. It follows the strategy that none of those who ordered or carried out (the attacks) should feel secure in any part of the world."[130]

Proponents of clandestine action against Iranian nuclear facilities may believe that strategy to be more effective and less risky than an Israeli or American military operation. However, it makes Tehran all the more determined, even pushing Iran to redouble its nuclear efforts. This mentality can be seen in the appointment of Abassi Davani to head the Atomic Energy Organization of Iran after he had been targeted by assassins.

Iran also might conclude that information gathered by IAEA inspectors has been used to create computer viruses and facilitate sabotage against its nuclear program and the assassinations of nuclear scientists. Such conclusions would push Iran to limit technical-legal cooperation with the IAEA on remaining questions. Strategies to undermine Iran's nuclear program may also encourage Iranian hard-liners to push in favor of developing a bomb instead of a peaceful enrichment program. Some Iranian officials claimed that the International Atomic Energy Agency (IAEA) has publicized the identities of Iranian nuclear officials and exposed them to the risk of terrorist acts. Foreign Minister Salehi accused the IAEA of disclosing confidential information about Iran's nuclear activities, saying that "the IAEA has no right to make public any sensitive information about [the] nuclear activities of its member states . . . Unfortunately, the agency has failed to carry out its duties accordingly. Even the IAEA chief (Yukiya Amano) has apologized for such mistakes in the past, but for Iran, it is just too late," he said.[131]

Although the United States and Israel insist that Iran has actively promoted and enabled attacks on their personnel in Lebanon, Israel, Saudi Arabia, and Iraq, Iran has not made a single attack against the United States or Israel since the 1979 revolution.[132] It is an undeniable fact that American intelligence and logistical support played a crucial role in arming Iraq in its invasion of Iran (1980–1988). During the war in 1988, the United States launched the largest American naval combat operation since World War II, striking Iranian oil platforms in the Persian Gulf. On July 3, 1988, the U.S. Navy guided missile cruiser *USS Vincennes* shot down an Iranian Airbus A300B2 that was on a scheduled commercial flight in Iranian airspace over the Strait of Hormuz, apparently mistaking it for an F-14. The attack killed 290 civilians from six nations, including 66 children; the U.S. refused to apologize for the loss of innocent life.[133]

Actions like the Stuxnet computer worm leveled against Iran only assist those radical political figures who are used to pointing fingers at the United States and Israel. This sympathetic attention serves to hide their dysfunctional management. While it is true that covert actions and espionage have damaged Iran's nuclear program, they can only delay Iranian progress on uranium enrichment, not stop it. Iran has sophisticated computer technologists and has recovered from the major damage caused by Stuxnet. To give up on the nuclear program because of such actions is out of the question.

According to the IAEA report, between October 18, 2010, and November 1, 2011, Iran produced 1,787 kilograms of low-enriched UF_6, which would result in a total production of 4,922 kg of low-enriched UF_6 since production began in February 2007. As of November 2, 2011, about 9,000 centrifuges were installed, and as of September 13, 2011, 720.8 kg of low-enriched UF_6 had been fed into the cascade(s) in the production area since the process began on February 9, 2010, and a total of 73.7 kg of UF_6 enriched up to 20 percent U-235 had been produced.[134] This is enough low-enriched uranium to produce perhaps two nuclear weapons, if Iran decided to enrich the low-enriched uranium up to weapon grade (90 percent). Contrary to statements by U.S. officials and many experts, Iran clearly does not appear to be slowing down its nuclear drive. On the contrary, it has a greater enrichment capacity and seems to be more efficient at enrichment.[135]

The IAEA confirmed that Iran has mastered and tested advanced centrifuges, called the IR–2m and the IR–4, at its pilot enrichment plant at Natanz. Former IAEA safeguards chief Olli Heinonen indicated that the IR-2m has about three times the potential capacity of the P-1, named for being Pakistan's first-generation centrifuge.[136]

These facts all show that Iran has been successful in continuing on the path of nuclear enrichment and that the maximum impact of the sabotage scenario would only slow Iran's nuclear progress—a short-term achievement with negative long-term consequences. It is also possible that rather than slowing Iran's nuclear progress, covert operations could accelerate Iran's march toward the ultimate deterrent. Worsening Iranians' siege mentality by covert actions and violations of the country's territorial sovereignty could compel the leaders in Tehran to double down on acquiring nuclear weapons. Iran could be pondering now the reality that the United States is not waging a covert war on North Korea (because it possesses a nuclear bomb), Muammar Qaddafi lost his grip on power in Libya after ceding his nuclear program, and Iraq and Afghanistan were invaded (because they had no nuclear weapon).

4. LEARNING TO LIVE WITH AN IRANIAN BOMB, AND RELYING ON CONTAINMENT AND DETERRENCE TO PREVENT THREATS FROM IRAN TO REGIONAL PEACE AND SECURITY

Many officials and observers in the U.S., Israel, and Arab states argue that all possible steps including military strikes should be taken to try to prevent Iran from acquiring nuclear weapons. However, others believe that

Iran cannot be dissuaded or compelled to forego acquiring nuclear weapons, or a latent nuclear weapon capability, but that Iran can nevertheless be contained and deterred from precipitating war and potentially using nuclear weapons.

For example, former U.S. ambassador James Dobbins believes that it is "perfectly logical for Iran to be pursuing nuclear weapons."[137] He points out that three major nuclear powers—Pakistan, India, and Israel—are in Iran's region and that all three are at a level of sophistication and proficiency that allows them to achieve nuclear capability. "If Barack Obama or George W. Bush were elected president of Iran, they would be pursuing nuclear capability; any leader in that geopolitical context would be."[138] He also raises the points that Iran is not threatening its neighbors and that creating incentives and disincentives to stop Iranians from pursuing their legitimate rights on nuclear technology is not realistic. "Iran crossing the nuclear threshold," he testified at a congressional hearing, "is not necessarily the end of the world."[139]

The debate over whether a nuclear-armed Iran could be contained and deterred from threatening regional peace and security is worthwhile, but I believe it is unnecessary and indeed may distract the world and Iran from a more positive outcome that is still achievable. There is no credible evidence that Iran has made the final decision to acquire nuclear weapons—as distinct from acquiring a nuclear weapon option. "During my time at the agency," Mohamed ElBaradei recounted to journalist Seymour Hersh, "we haven't seen a shred of evidence that Iran has been weaponizing, in terms of building nuclear weapons facilities and using enriched materials."[140] To adjust the IAEA's position in accordance with the judgment of Western intelligence, ElBaradei's successor, Yukiya Amano, has emphasized evidence that Iran, at least in the past, has conducted activities that raise serious questions over whether all of its nuclear activities have been and are only for peaceful purposes. Amano therefore has called on Iran to provide the transparency necessary to answer questions related to this evidence.[141] Yet, Amano, like U.S. intelligence officials, does not cite evidence to conclude that Iran is determined to make nuclear weapons.

Rather than focus international policy on deterring and containing a presumed nuclear-armed Iran, I believe greater attention should be paid to reinvigorating diplomatic creativity and energy to resolve the crisis peacefully.

5. DIPLOMATIC SOLUTION

My belief that Iran is not attempting to acquire a nuclear bomb is based on the following facts:

- Iran's supreme leader issued a religious order (*fatwa*) against all weapons of mass destruction in 1995, eight years before Iran's enrichment program became known to the West.[142] All Shi'i grand ayatollahs have the same religious *fatwa*. Evidence for the seriousness of the ayatollahs' revulsion toward WMD is provided by the fact that chemical weapons were used against Iran during the 1980–1988 war with Iraq, and thousands of Iranian soldiers and civilians were killed or injured. But Iran did not retaliate because Imam Ruhollah Khomeini issued a *fatwa* against the use of weapons of mass destruction.

- Iran acknowledges that possession of nuclear weapons would provide only a short-term regional advantage that would turn into a longer-term vulnerability, because sooner or later Egypt, Turkey, and Saudi Arabia would follow suit and a regional nuclear arms race would be inescapable.

- The technical choices Iran has made in the configuration of its nuclear program demonstrate a preference for a robust enrichment capability rather than for a rapid nuclear weapons breakout capability. Iran's development program is focused on next-generation technology (IR-2m), rather than mass production or maximum installation of IR-1s and IR-2s, a more advantageous configuration if Iran were determined to acquire weapons in the near term, however efficient.

- Iran's nuclear dual-use work does not indicate a sense of urgency. Not only are the activities detailed in the November 2011 IAEA report not directed at one specific warhead design, but also the weapons program "halt" in 2003 (as theorized by the 2007 U.S. National Intelligence Estimate) still seems plausible, even more so with the recent evidence provided by the IAEA.

- Iran recognizes the fact that even Russia and China would not tolerate an Iranian nuclear bomb and that they would join the

United States in instituting sanctions that would paralyze Iran's economy and more if Iran diverted its program toward nuclear weapon production.

- Iran also understands that Israel will perceive a nuclear-armed Iran as an existential threat, increasing the possibility of a preemptive military attack.

- Iran's ultimate strategy is to be a modern nation, fully capable of competing with the West in terms of advanced technology. This strategy could not be fulfilled if Iran were to divert its nuclear activities to military uses. Despite some rhetoric from radicals, the majority of Iran's prominent politicians and the vast majority of Iranian diplomats believe that a nuclear bomb would in the long term be a threat to the national interests of Iran regionally and internationally. They would hate for Iran to be in a situation of extreme isolation like North Korea.

- It is frequently said that Iran is interested in the "Japan model," meaning that it would like to be capable of building the bomb in short order if its security or existence were threatened. This is both true and false. Iran wants to be treated like other NPT member states without discrimination. Iran would be ready to accept the commitments on transparency measures required by the international community if its legitimate rights were respected. That's why Iran wants to be treated like other NPT members like Japan, Germany, or Brazil.

That is why we should concentrate on diplomacy to resolve the dispute.

China and Russia were the only countries noted in the WikiLeaks cables on Iran to be urging the United States to talk with Iran. A 2009 cable noted that the Chinese West Asia deputy director for the Ministry of Foreign Affairs, Ni Ruchi, urged the U.S. side to make a clear statement abandoning the notion of regime change. He suggested seeking a "cooperative partnership" with Iran on shared concerns such as security in Iraq and Afghanistan, and in doing so, recognizing Iran as a major regional power. He recommended offering concrete and immediate benefits, especially economic incentives and a relaxation of existing sanctions, in response to positive overtures on the Iranian side. These efforts could start small, he added, but should be focused on sending a clear signal of sincere intentions to Tehran.[143]

Another 2009 cable, from the U.S. Embassy in Moscow, noted that the Russian foreign minister informed his Israeli counterpart that "nothing new would happen with Iran until after the U.S. began its dialogue with Tehran."[144]

Clearly, the WikiLeaks cables indicate the distrust between the Persian Gulf states and Iran during President Ahmadinejad's tenure. During the Rafsanjani presidency, great efforts were made to bring about closer relations with Iran's neighbors, especially Saudi Arabia. I was personally involved in this effort, and it is worth recounting briefly here because it shows another face of the system in Tehran—a face that, if it could be engaged again, could lead to a diplomatic solution of the impasse over Iran's nuclear program.

The animosity between Iran and its Persian Gulf neighbors reached its peak during the Iran-Iraq war in the 1980s, when Persian Gulf countries gave full support to Saddam Hussein to wage war on Iran and to a great extent bankrolled his war effort. Tensions also boiled over when more than 400 Iranian pilgrims were killed by Saudi security forces in Mecca in 1988.

In this tense climate, during the Organization of the Islamic Conference meeting in Senegal in the early 1990s, Crown Prince Abdullah bin Abdul-Aziz of Saudi Arabia and President Rafsanjani met and agreed to take measures to improve relations.[145] The first step in this endeavor was to send Rafsanjani's special envoy to discuss the revival of the relations between the two capitals.

Some time after that meeting, the Iranian president's office called me in Bonn, where I was the Iranian ambassador to Germany, requesting that I return to Tehran immediately to meet with the president. President Rafsanjani explained the situation and the task ahead to mend relations with the Saudis.[146] It became clear very quickly that he had selected me to negotiate with the crown prince of Saudi Arabia. I insisted that my expertise was with Western countries and that there were many individuals with expertise in the region who would be better suited for the assignment. However, he insisted that I go and said that his son Mehdi would accompany me on the trip.

The first meeting with Amir Abdullah was scheduled to take place in his summer villa in Casablanca. I was given assurances from the Saudis that there would be no need for visas or any other arrangements; everything would be taken care of. The Saudis kept their promise, and upon landing I was escorted to the private villa of Amir Abdullah.

My first meeting with Amir Abdullah, which lasted three hours, touched on regional and bilateral issues. At the end of the meeting, Prince Abdullah said, "This was not a negotiation, this was an evaluation," adding, "My aim in this meeting was to evaluate you and see whom Rafsanjani has chosen to negotiate with me and if I can make a deal with him or not." Finally, he said, "You are the right man, and I congratulate Rafsanjani for his selection."

After our meeting, he extended an invitation to my wife and me, as well as Rafsanjani's son and his wife, to go to Jeddah. Once we arrived there a month later, the negotiations took place at Amir Abdullah's private home over three nights, from midnight until four or five in the morning. The negotiations were extremely tough, and the only people present were Amir Abdullah, his assistant, Rafsanjani's son, Muhammad ali Azarshab, as the interpreter, and myself. There was a wide range of topics and issues to discuss ranging from security in the region and bilateral relations to Saudi government relations with the Sunni population of Iran and the Iranian influence on the Shi'i population within Saudi Arabia. The discussions also included expansion of economic, social, and political relations. All the major issues and policies were discussed. At dawn on the final day, we shook hands and agreed on a comprehensive package to revive Saudi-Iranian relations.

We needed to obtain final approval of the package from the leadership in Tehran and Riyadh. For this purpose, Amir Abdullah asked me to meet with the Saudi interior minister, Amir Nayef bin Abdul-Aziz, to discuss the security issues surrounding the comprehensive package. He agreed to the security framework that Amir Abdullah and I had negotiated. We presented the package to King Fahd bin Abdul-Aziz. I believe the meeting was mainly for protocol purposes. After half an hour of discussion, he approved it with no alterations. The king said to me, "Ambassador, the security of the region relies on three regional powers, Iran, Iraq, and Saudi Arabia. We are very disappointed with the Iraqi situation, as we cannot have a trilateral relationship, but we are happy to build a bilateral relation between Riyadh and Tehran and keep praying for a time when Iraq can join us."

I returned to Tehran to brief President Rafsanjani and Foreign Minister Ali Akbar Velayati on the negotiations. They were both happy with the result. The only other approval required was from the supreme leader of Iran, Ayatollah Khamenei, who had the final say. Within days, he reviewed the package and agreed with no reservations to all the items.

A new dawn began in Tehran-Riyadh relations, and the implementation of the negotiated package greatly improved it. Within a few months, the countries exchanged diplomatic visits, with Amir Abdullah making an official trip to Tehran, the first since the revolution. Relations had warmed to such a level that joint security institutions were established to cooperate on regional matters. Economic activities increased immensely, leading even to business visas for Iranians to establish companies in Saudi Arabia. On the political front, foreign ministers from both countries met on a regular basis and discussed mutual concerns. The warm relations continued under President Khatami, leading to a new era in Iran's relations with other Persian Gulf countries.

This background is essential to explain the dismay I feel now in witnessing relations between the Persian Gulf and Iran having hit such a low point during President Ahmadinejad's tenure that the same man I negotiated with, Amir Abdullah, demanded that the United States "cut off the head of the snake."[147]

Since 2003, the nuclear issue has played an important role in domestic political rivalries. I witnessed this firsthand as a member and spokesman for Iran's nuclear negotiating team during the first two years of the crisis. Iran's two dominant political currents have traded recriminations over one another's conduct of nuclear diplomacy; the degree of factionalism was so great that, after the inauguration of Iran's ninth government under President Mahmoud Ahmadinejad in 2005, the new administration accused the previous nuclear team of betraying the country. In April 2007, the Ahmadinejad government arrested me and generated a huge propaganda campaign trumpeting President Ahmadinejad's nuclear policies and charging the former nuclear negotiating team with "passivity" and even "treason." Ahmadinejad claimed that former nuclear negotiation team members—myself included—had transferred classified information to other countries and were lackeys for Western countries. After a year of baseless accusations and huge media propaganda supported by the government, the judiciary formally acquitted me on April 2008 of charges of "espionage" and "treachery in the nuclear case." Despite my acquittal, Ahmadinejad's administration continued to hurl accusations,[148] going as far as to posit that I should have been hanged.

Although all Iranian governments are divisive, they all have pushed for Iran's right to peaceful nuclear technology—whether under Mir-Hossein Mousavi, Akbar Hashemi Rafsanjani, Mohammad Khatami, or Mahmoud Ahmadinejad. Nevertheless, their approaches to nuclear diplomacy and the international circumstances under which they operated have been very different. As my arrest and the wrangling over the nuclear issue in Iran's domestic political arena attest, these differences in approaches have been extreme and are of central importance to anyone analyzing Iran's foreign policy or seeking a resolution to the international controversy around its nuclear program. With this book, then, I hope to shed light on the Iranian nuclear strategy, its connection to both domestic issues and Iran's relations with global powers, and its evolution over the past eight years.

In the ten chapters of this book, I will review the history of Iran's nuclear activities, Iran's nuclear policy, and interactions with the international community during Khatami's and Ahmadinejad's tenures, President Obama's engagement policy, and a comparison of the nuclear policies taken during the Khatami and Ahmadinejad presidencies, and I will assess the advantages and disadvantages of the two presidents for Iran's national interest. These chapters will explore some of the mistakes and missed opportunities of the West in dealing with Iran, the failures and shortcomings of attempts at diplomatic engagement since the Islamic Revolution, and the reasons for the emergence and continuation of the nuclear crisis in terms of Western policies toward Iran. And finally I will discuss a mutually acceptable and comprehensive package to resolve the issue peacefully and provide for the beginning of a thaw in U.S.-Iran relations.

Despite the failure so far to reach a negotiated resolution to the crisis, I will argue that a comprehensive deal is not only possible, but also essential to addressing the interests and concerns of Iran and the international community, and indeed essential to the credibility of multilateral diplomacy as a means of ensuring the nonproliferation of nuclear weapons while protecting the rights and sovereignty of nations under international law.

My hope is that this book will facilitate such a resolution by providing a better understanding of the Iranian perspective and decisionmaking process. It is, after all, of the utmost importance that Iran's negotiating partners understand the thinking and goals of their Iranian counterparts if they are to strike a deal that leaves both sides victorious and the world safer.

_____

CHAPTER ONE

THE ORIGIN AND DEVELOPMENT OF
IRAN'S NUCLEAR PROGRAM

Iran's nuclear activities far predate the current crisis and even Iran's Islamic Republic. Understanding the history of Iran's atomic program and the role of the West in its founding is important for any analysis of both the political and technical disputes of the current crisis. Indeed, Iran's accusations in recent years of double standards and discrimination by the United States and international community are rooted in the support that the West lent to the Iranian monarchy but then withdrew after the Islamic Revolution,[1] helping to spur Iran's drive for nuclear self-sufficiency that continues to this day.

THE SHAH AND THE COLD WAR

With Iran's strategic location and vast oil reserves, its international standing has long been a function of its relationships with the great powers. Mohammad Reza Shah Pahlavi succeeded his father to the throne of Iran during World War II, and during the Cold War became a key ally of the United States, which in 1953 collaborated with the British in instigating a coup against democratically elected Prime Minister Mohammad Mossadegh in the Shah's favor.

Until the Shah's overthrow in 1979, the United States propped up his sultanistic regime, providing considerable military and economic aid including assistance for the development of Iran's infrastructure and energy sector. From the early 1950s until 1979, tens of thousands of students—myself included—were sent to the United States each year to receive education at American schools and universities in all fields, including medicine, nuclear physics, networks for communications, and all aspects of engineering and dam building, as well as all forms of business, banking, and commerce. This large group of American-educated Iranians still plays a constructive role in Iran.

Such was American influence over Iran that the country's foreign policies were largely dictated by its membership in the anticommunist bloc. The United States brought Iran tightly into the fold of its Cold War alliance system, including through the Central Treaty Organization (CENTO) that Iran signed with American-allied Iraq, Turkey, Pakistan, and the United Kingdom. President Richard Nixon and his secretary of state, Henry Kissinger, referred to Iran as "the linchpin of stability in the Middle East."[2]

What the U.S. government did not do was urge the Shah to allow a democratic political process or enact a just system under the rule of law. Doing so could have prevented the 1979 revolution in Iran and could have had huge positive consequences for the long-term partnership between Iran and the West and specifically the United States. Instead, the Shah's regime became increasingly unpopular and was perceived as brutal and deeply corrupt. Efforts made by the U.S. government in the late 1970s to persuade the Shah to open up the political system to democratic governance were too late to be effective. To the end, the Pahlavi regime remained an autocracy. Although he relied on the counsel of a coterie of trusted advisers, the Shah was the ultimate decisionmaker for all of the state's policies, foreign and domestic.

IRAN-WEST NUCLEAR COOPERATION
BEFORE THE ISLAMIC REVOLUTION

The United States Laid the Foundation for a Nuclear Iran

The year 1956 is considered the starting point of Iran's interest in nuclear energy. It was then that the Iranian government's negotiations with the White House resulted in the first agreement for the nonmilitary use of nuclear energy, which was concluded in 1957,[3] the year I was born. The agreement, which laid a framework for nuclear collaboration between Iran and the United States, consisted of a preamble and eleven articles that were ratified by the National Consultative Assembly on February 1, 1959. Made possible by the general alignment between Tehran's and Washington's economic and political interests, and the spirit of the American Atoms for Peace initiative, the agreement laid the foundation for a nuclear Iran.

Existing evidence shows that despite relative sensitivity of the White House toward the possibility of diversion of Iran's nuclear program to military use, that concern was not expressed as seriously with Iran as with some other countries. The United States was supportive of enrichment facilities in Iran but skeptical about plutonium reprocessing, though the Shah firmly pushed for the development of both technologies in Iran. The United States had also set rules for nuclear cooperation with other countries that were enforced through bilateral agreements. Those rules, which put special emphasis on disposal of spent nuclear fuel, constituted a model for organized cooperation to address concerns about possible diversion.

As nuclear cooperation between Tehran and Washington developed, the Nuclear Science Institute of CENTO was relocated from Baghdad to Tehran in 1957 and based at the University of Tehran. The institute admitted students from Iran and other countries, including Turkey and Pakistan, and was a forerunner to the Tehran Nuclear Research Center, which was formally established by Mohammad Reza Pahlavi in 1959. Later on, U.S. President John F. Kennedy, in accordance with the Atoms for Peace agenda, endorsed the construction of a five-megawatt (MW) research reactor in Tehran. Known as the Tehran Research Reactor (TRR), it used highly enriched uranium to produce radioactive isotopes for medical uses and plutonium production.

Iran signed the Nuclear Non-Proliferation Treaty in 1968, on the very day the NPT opened for signature. The Tehran Research Reactor finally came into operation in November 1967 after six years of construction. The United States delivered 5.54 kg of highly enriched uranium and 112 grams of plutonium to the University of Tehran in September 1967,[4] signaling a turning point in the Iranian government's ten years of nuclear activities. Using the Tehran Research Reactor and banking on hot cell facilities,[5] which had been given to Iran by the United States to separate plutonium, Tehran eventually came up with a long-term plan for the all-out development of nuclear technology. The plan included the manufacture of accelerators and establishment of a nuclear medicine center at the University of Tehran.[6] The Shah also signed nuclear cooperation agreements with other countries. For example, Iran signed a scientific cooperation agreement with Canada ensuring support for the development of Iran's nuclear activities, especially "nuclear equipment, materials, and facilities." The agreement was signed on January 7, 1972, and underlined the need for "free access to equipment and facilities" by both countries' scientists as well as bilateral "scientific visits."

Meanwhile, the prospect of greater export revenue from elevated global oil prices in 1973 and 1974, in addition to considerations of Iran's political weight in the Persian Gulf and the Middle East, prompted Iran's government to take serious measures to use nuclear technology for domestic power generation.[7] With U.S. encouragement, the Shah in March 1974 announced plans to generate 23,000 MW of nuclear energy within twenty years, beginning with two reactors at Bushehr, and to acquire a full nuclear fuel cycle—including facilities to enrich uranium, fabricate fuel, and reprocess spent fuel.[8] The Nixon administration was eager to take part in this plan. Dixy Lee Ray, the chairman of the U.S. Atomic Energy Commission, was sent to Tehran in May 1974 and offered to provide a "clearinghouse" for Iranian investments. According to a recently declassified State Department memo, she "urged Iran to embark on the job as soon as possible."[9]

The Shah's government reached an agreement in 1974 with the Massachusetts Institute of Technology for the education of a large number of Iranian students in the field of nuclear technology. Iran provided MIT with millions of dollars in funding, and MIT admitted dozens of Iranian students for a three-year master's program. Ali Akbar Salehi, Iran's foreign minister and the former president of Iran's Atomic Energy Organization (from 2009 to 2010), earned his Ph.D. from MIT in the late 1970s, though not as part of this special program.[10]

This push for progress in nuclear technology and expertise was viewed as essential for the achievement of Iran's development goals and was even recommended by some American politicians. The Stanford Research Institute, which Iran's Plan and Budget Organization commissioned in 1974 to formulate the country's "Twenty-Year Vision Plan," recommended that the government diligently follow plans for power generation from a variety of sources. The institute's report, which in twenty volumes addressed Iran's economic, social, and cultural development plans, advised the Iranian government to take all necessary measures to generate 20,000 MW of nuclear power in twenty years (from 1974 to 1994).

The decision to commit to "nuclear power generation" was a watershed moment, entailing other significant steps, including the establishment of the Iran Atomic Energy Organization (IAEO). The IAEO was charged with developing civilian nuclear science and technology, building the country's nuclear infrastructure, and managing international nuclear cooperation and representation, including through the International Atomic Energy Agency.

Considerable resources were poured into the organization as nuclear energy emerged as a symbol of national pride and modernization. On the Shah's order, its employees were the most highly paid in the government. By 1976, the IAEO's budget was $1.3 billion, the largest of any public economic institution except Iran's state oil company.[11]

Nuclear power generation was one of the most important goals of the IAEO. The available evidence indicates that the Iranian government pursued short- and long-term plans to supply nuclear fuel to power plants. Purchasing fuel was the most important short-term strategy, while mastering the nuclear fuel cycle and fuel production was the country's long-term goal. Thus, extensive negotiations were undertaken with foreign partners for the purchase of enrichment technology and equipment in parallel to Iran's signing of nuclear fuel purchase contracts with the United States, West Germany, and France in the mid-1970s. Iran dispatched specialists to Western countries, and the IAEO hired scientists from the United States, United Kingdom, India, and Argentina to help build local nuclear fuel-cycle capability. These foreign scientists, hired by the IAEO as advisers, played a significant role in technology transfer and the buildup of domestic nuclear capability.[12]

Before the Islamic Revolution, Western countries, including the United States, France, Germany, the United Kingdom, and Canada, by and large supported Iran's nuclear activities; indeed, they competed for lucrative nuclear projects to nuclearize Iran. Iran followed short- and long-term strategies to develop nuclear power generation and build a nuclear fuel-cycle capability. Following the logic of Atoms for Peace and widespread expectations that nuclear energy would fuel global development and bring profits to exporters, Western countries encouraged the Iranian government's nuclear ambitions. The economic attraction to industrialized countries of selling Iran nuclear power plants initially was powerful enough to brush aside any concern about possible deviation toward a military nuclear program.[13] Some believe that the Carter administration strengthened U.S. nonproliferation policy as it applied to Iran,[14] but from a geopolitical perspective, the dependence of the Pahlavi dynasty on the United States, as well as Iran's situation in the Middle East as envisaged by the White House, added strategic importance to nuclear collaboration between Iran and the United States. It also meant that Mohammad Reza Shah's late efforts to build nuclear weapons would be largely ignored until his downfall.[15]

The U.S. offer, details of which appear in declassified documents reviewed by the *Washington Post*, proves that the United States tried to accommodate Iranian demands for plutonium reprocessing, which produces the key ingredient of a bomb. According to the newspaper, after balking initially, President Gerald R. Ford signed a directive in 1976 offering Tehran the chance to buy and operate a U.S.-built reprocessing facility for extracting plutonium from nuclear reactor fuel. The deal was for a complete "nuclear fuel cycle"—reactors powered by and regenerating fissile materials on a self-sustaining basis. That is precisely the ability the current administration is trying to prevent Iran from acquiring today.[16]

The United States laid the foundation for a nuclear Iran. The first nuclear test by India in 1974, however, created an international crisis about nuclear proliferation that prompted a pullback and eventually led to the ratification of relevant regulations by the U.S. Congress in 1978. Although that pullback was also extended to Tehran, Iran was in practice usually treated with more lenience.[17] While Secretary of State Henry Kissinger initially pursued a policy of restricting fuel-cycle technology to a few centers internationally, he never protested Mohammad Reza Shah's obvious efforts to enrich uranium (revealed by, among other things, Iran's role in prospecting for uranium at mines in Namibia).

U.S. National Security Council documents declassified in the second half of the 1990s clearly prove that the United States pursued two goals in its negotiations with Iran during the 1970s. The first was to allow the establishment of fuel reprocessing facilities in Iran that would be used by other regional states. The second was to prevent Pakistan from building independent nuclear facilities by securing Islamabad's agreement to commission plutonium reprocessing facilities in Iran.[18]

Washington did its best to advance U.S. economic interests through its nuclear cooperation with Iran. This was done by imposing regulations to guarantee the United States exclusive rights and through the imposition of special contracts. Akbar Etemad, the former head of the IAEO, said in a 1997 interview that Iran was obliged to accede to U.S. regulations, which were designed to guarantee Washington's economic interests and its control over Iran's lucrative nuclear activities.

During that period, the United States had indicated its readiness to sell eight light-water reactors to Tehran and also to provide Iran with complete facilities to build several additional nuclear power plants. This deal, whose economic value has been estimated at $6.4 billion,[19] was signed after a number of prominent congressmen visited Iran in the mid-1970s with a letter from President Ford addressed to the Shah calling for the speedy implementation of the agreement.

A 1976 Ford strategy paper noted that the "introduction of nuclear power will both provide for the growing needs of Iran's economy and free remaining oil reserves for export or conversion to petrochemicals." Etemad recounted this cooperation from the Iranian perspective:

> Iran and the U.S. established a joint economic cooperation commission, of which I was a member. . . . Iran was obliged to purchase eight nuclear power plants according to that contract, although this was not our initial mission. . . . This issue was never put up for discussion in commission meetings. This shows that the pressure was high. Could Iran purchase eight nuclear power plants from the United States at once? This was to be recorded in official cooperation documents of the two countries. Political pressure was high. Senators later came to meet with the Shah. He was also regularly visited by the U.S. President's special envoys. They insisted that a bilateral agreement be prepared [for the power plant purchase].[20]

The U.S. Department of Energy granted Jeffrey Eerkens, a nuclear physicist and expert in uranium enrichment, a license to sell four lasers to Iran, and the lasers were shipped in October 1978. The lasers could be physically modified to enrich uranium.[21]

Developments in the 1970s introduced unresolved tensions. The United States and other nuclear technology exporters promoted nuclear power in major developing countries such as Iran. The United States was especially keen on nuclear cooperation with Iran for economic reasons and due to its strategic partnership with the Shah. And yet, after the Indian nuclear test of 1974, international concern over nuclear proliferation was growing. Much of this concern focused on plutonium reprocessing that could yield weapons-grade material; at that time, it was assumed that uranium enrichment was technologically beyond most developing countries. These interests and considerations pointed in different, potentially conflicting directions, which would become more apparent when revolution came to Iran and events in India and Pakistan highlighted the potential of nuclear proliferation.

Iran-France Nuclear Cooperation

The election of Valéry Giscard d'Estaing in the French presidential elections and subsequent visit to Paris by the Shah in June 1974 set the stage for nuclear cooperation between the two countries. In the wake of the first global oil shock starting in October 1973, Giscard was a proponent of turning to nuclear power as a major source of energy for France, and he oversaw a rapid expansion of the country's nuclear activities.

Negotiations during Mohammad Reza Shah's stay in Paris laid the foundations for the first nuclear agreement between Tehran and Paris on June 27, 1974. The agreement ensured bilateral cooperation for fifteen years and was later known as the "Mother Agreement" as it gave birth to many more protocols and agreements between Iranian and French nuclear companies and institutes. All of those agreements followed three major goals: first, Iran's contribution to the uranium enrichment industry in France and, in fact, Iran's contribution to the international fuel-cycle industry; second, the construction of a nuclear research and development center in Isfahan; and third, generation of 5,000 MW of nuclear power in Iran.

A letter of intent was signed between the IAEO and the French company Framatom on November 2, 1974, for the construction of two pressurized water reactors at the Darkhoein oil field near Ahvaz, in southwestern Iran, each capable of generating 950 MW of electricity. On September 19, 1977, an agreement worth eight billion francs, or 31.8 trillion rials, was signed by the IAEO and a consortium of French companies led by Framatom and Alstom Atlantic. The agreement was implemented without problem through summer 1978. In October of that year, however, progress halted because of the escalation of popular demonstrations against the Shah, and in June 1979 the French consortium canceled the agreement.

Another instance of Iran-France nuclear cooperation was between the IAEO and the Tricastin-based firm Eurodif. Eurodif runs one of the world's biggest uranium enrichment facilities, which has been producing enriched uranium for France and other countries, including Japan, since 1980. Eurodif signed a contract with the IAEO in the mid-1970s for around $1.2 billion in joint investments, as well as the loan, purchase, and provision of enrichment services. Its goal was to facilitate the supply of fuel to Iran's nuclear power plants and ultimately support the completion of the nuclear fuel cycle in Iran.

Eurodif is, according to its charter, a completely European entity (its main stockholders were Spanish, Belgian, Italian, and French) and could not assimilate non-European partners. As a way around this impediment, Iran and France established a joint venture company called Sofidif (with 60 percent French and 40 percent Iranian ownership) to represent it in the Eurodif consortium. The French Atomic Energy Commission agreed to sell 25 percent of Eurodif's stocks to Sofidif, allowing the IAEO to own 10 percent of Eurodif's stocks and enabling Iran to buy the firm's products.[22]

Establishment of the Iran Nuclear Research and Development Center was another issue on the agenda between Tehran and Paris. The IAEO and French Atomic Energy Commission signed a protocol on November 18, 1974, requiring Paris to provide Iran with the necessary technical assistance and facilities to launch the center in Isfahan. This protocol eventually led to the signing of a memorandum of understanding between representatives of the two sides on March 12, 1977, which set out conditions and a construction schedule for the Isfahan Nuclear Technology Center.

Iran-Germany Nuclear Cooperation

Nuclear cooperation between Iran and (West) Germany dates to 1975. The first cooperation agreement between Tehran and Bonn was signed on June 30, 1975, and was succeeded by another contract promulgated on July 4, 1976. The latter agreement, signed by the IAEO and the West German government, ensured extensive bilateral cooperation in nuclear technology research and development, in addition to the peaceful use of nuclear energy. The agreement covered various areas related to nuclear fuel, the safety of nuclear facilities, staff training, and nuclear power technology. The two sides also agreed to collaborate in creating nuclear power plants and research institutes, generating nuclear power, and producing radioisotopes.

Two more contracts were signed on July 1, 1976, one for the design, construction, and commissioning of two 1,150-MW light-water nuclear power plants 18 kilometers from Bushehr, and the other for the supply of nuclear fuel to those power plants. Kraftwerk Union, the main contractor, agreed both to commission the Bushehr power plants and to supply them with fuel for thirty years. Kraftwerk Union set out to implement the contract immediately. Based on existing reports, about 80 percent of construction and 65 percent of electromechanical operations were complete before the Islamic Revolution.

Until this point, the IAEO had paid a total of 5.7 billion deutsche marks to the Kraftwerk Union, but, because of the escalation of unrest leading to the Islamic Revolution, the contractor suspended the project and the Iranian government did not pay the thirteenth installment of the payment schedule (464 million deutsche marks). The German contractor then informed the Iranian government of the annulment of both contracts on July 30, 1979. Agreements for the construction of two other nuclear power plants in Isfahan, each capable of producing 1,290 MW of electricity, and two more plants in Saveh also were canceled by the Germans.

In the meantime, Iran had signed a cooperation agreement with a nuclear research center in the German city of Karlsruhe in April 1977 concurrent with a nuclear technology conference in Shiraz and dispatched 21 nuclear experts to Germany. A draft agreement for educational cooperation between the IAEO and the Physikalisch-Technische Bundesanstalt Institute of Germany, an agreement signed in June 1976 with Kraftwerk Union of Siemens for the delivery of fuel rods, partnership with Urangesellschaft to prospect for uranium, and a contract with Prakia Company in 1976 were other instances of nuclear cooperation between the two countries that ceased entirely after the Islamic Revolution.

Other International Cooperation on Iran's Nuclear Program

As has been demonstrated, Iran's nuclear activities under Mohammad Reza Shah Pahlavi were directed toward nuclear power generation. The production of nuclear fuel and development of a domestic nuclear fuel cycle were major goals pursued in tandem with the development of Iran-West economic relations. In addition to infrastructural cooperation with the United States, the Iranian government launched various joint ventures, with France and Germany as its main partners and some other countries as temporary ones.

Of Iran's nuclear partners, the United Kingdom enjoyed a special status, and the IAEO had signed a contract with British companies in the United Kingdom and South Africa. The contract, signed on July 16, 1975, guaranteed sales of 2,400 tons of uranium to Iran by the United Kingdom. It was also a forerunner to a contract signed by Iran with British companies in 1977 to convert uranium to UF_6. The first contract obligated Tehran to grant 3.4 million South African rand to its British partners as a gratuitous loan to develop Iran's uranium mines. The loan was to be amortized through uranium delivery to Iran. The second contract, signed on April 7, 1977, provided for the conversion of 775 tons of triuranium octoxide, or U_3O_8, a uranium compound whose milled version is commonly known as yellowcake, to UF_6 in several stages.[23] This latter contract was, however, never completely fulfilled due to nonpayment of the cost of the third consignment (125 tons of uranium).

Iran also purchased shares of the British-Australian Rio Tinto-Zinc Corporation, which was active in Namibia. The measure was part of the Iranian government's efforts to procure uranium and made way for the IAEO to prospect in one of the world's biggest uranium mines in Namibia.

EVIDENCE OF THE FORMER REGIME'S EFFORTS TO BUILD NUCLEAR WEAPONS

Although it has not been definitively proved that the Shah intended to develop nuclear weapons, there is considerable evidence to that effect. The Shah signed the NPT, but he was also an ardent nationalist who dreamed of regional hegemony and built up Iran's military with American backing.

When the Shah was asked by a French journalist in 1974 whether Iran would pursue a nuclear weapon, he replied, "Certainly, and sooner than one would think." After India tested a nuclear device that same year, he said, "If other nations in the region acquire nuclear weapons, then perhaps the national interests of any [other] country will demand the same."[24]

Etemad, the head of the IAEO and a confidant of the Shah, described the monarch's strategic thinking in a 2008 interview: "I think that if the shah had remained in power he would have developed nuclear weapons because now Pakistan, India and Israel all have them."[25]

It is important to note that the Shah's interest in nuclear weapons was closely related to Iran's competition with those other regional powers, as well as with Iraq, the only one that had not developed nuclear weapons by the 1980s. Therefore, he had ample motivation to build the "weapon of the century." As a recently declassified 1974 Central Intelligence Agency report stated, "If [the Shah] is alive in the mid-1980s and if other countries [particularly India] have proceeded with weapons development, we have no doubt that Iran will follow suit."[26]

There is other evidence of the Pahlavi regime's aspiration to obtain nuclear weapons. The Atomic Energy Organization of Iran engaged in negotiations with the famous American scientist Jeffrey Eerkens in 1976 and 1977. Eerkens, who designed a process of uranium enrichment using laser technology, delivered four laser parts to Iran in a deal endorsed by the U.S. Department of Energy. Eerkens seems to have camouflaged Tehran's main goal of using his enrichment method by emphasizing that those parts were to be used in plasma research. The parts were transferred to Iran in October 1978, just a few months before the downfall of Mohammad Reza Shah.

The Pahlavi regime launched extensive and clandestine negotiations with South Africa on a $700 million contract to buy uranium concentrate (yellowcake). Confidential documents dating to 1976, which were recently declassified by the U.S. Department of State, show that U.S. officials were kept abreast of those negotiations.

The Tehran Atomic Research Center carried out extensive studies on "reprocessing technology" to replace highly enriched uranium with plutonium from spent nuclear fuel. Plutonium reprocessing is a technically highly complex process that yields material suitable for use in nuclear weapons. This was in fact one of the few areas of Iran's nuclear programs that raised red flags for the U.S. government. In the mid-1970s, a debate over controls involving plutonium reprocessing resulted in a brief impasse in Iran-U.S. nuclear cooperation that subsided only when, on the suggestion of Pentagon officials who argued that the plutonium issue was "poisoning other aspects of U.S.-Iran relations," the Ford administration backed down and agreed to a policy of accommodating the Shah's plans.[27] President Ford signed a directive in 1976 offering Tehran the chance to buy and operate a U.S.-built reprocessing facility for extracting plutonium from nuclear reactor fuel.[28] This came just two years after India used plutonium separated under the Atoms for Peace program for a "peaceful nuclear explosion."

Shortly before the Islamic Revolution, the Shah assigned a group of Iranian scientists to study nuclear weapons. Since Mohammad Reza Shah was intent on keeping information from and about the research highly classified, it is quite possible that the researchers were not aware of the results of each other's studies.[29]

Akbar Etemad relates,

It is true that the government instructed me only to generate nuclear power, that the Shah was not thinking about nuclear weapons at that time, and that nobody told me anything about them, but the life of a nation cannot be summarized in a single snapshot. . . . It was quite possible that military and political conditions in the region would change suddenly, in which case Iran would need to have nuclear weapons. If so, the country's need would have to be met on short notice. . . . The interesting point was proposals related to nuclear research and entities which offered them. I didn't tell them anything, but I allowed them to do their work. . . . I always put those research plans together in my mind as pieces of a puzzle in order to get the whole picture. . . . It showed that the IAEO was pursuing a long-term goal, but was trying to hide its true intent from the public, especially the press and domestic and foreign spies. . . . I never saw myself as obliged to either hinder certain research for political reasons or to deprive Iran of having the option of building nuclear weapons in the future.[30]

IRAN'S ISLAMIC REVOLUTION AND U.S.-IRAN RELATIONS

Iran's 1979 revolution had a clear anti-American and anti-British aspect stemming from the 1953 CIA coup d'état and subsequent American support for the Shah. U.S.-Iran relations reached a new low when Iranian students seized the U.S. Embassy in Tehran and took 52 Americans hostage in symbolic retribution for the 1953 covert action, sparking a lengthy international crisis.

The antagonism continued when the United States supported Iraq's leader, Saddam Hussein, during the Iran-Iraq war in the 1980s. Iran perceived the U.S. silence during Iraq's use of chemical weapons against Iran[31] and Iraq's missile attacks on Iranian cities during the "War of the Cities" in 1985 as implying tacit support for Iraq's actions. When in 1988, the *USS Vincennes*, a U.S. warship engaged in a battle with Iranian high-speed gunboats in the Persian Gulf, mistook an Iranian civilian jetliner for an attacking Iranian F-14 fighter plane and shot it down with a missile, Iran decried the incident, which resulted in the deaths of 290 passengers, as a "barbaric massacre."[32]

The United States had its own list of grievances against Iran that would grow in the years after the revolution. In addition to the sharp and painful memories impressed on the American public by the hostage crisis of 1979, the United States suspected Iran of involvement in the bombing of its Beirut embassy in 1983, the bombing of the Asociación Mutual Israelita Argentina in Buenos Aires in 1994, and the attack on the Khobar Towers in Saudi Arabia in 1996, for which Iran denied any involvement.

INTERNATIONAL NUCLEAR COOPERATION
AFTER THE ISLAMIC REVOLUTION

Imam Khomeini, the Islamic Republic's founding religious leader, opposed weapons of mass destruction on ideological and moral grounds. The supreme leader also opposed the Shah's ambitious nuclear plan.[33] Even during the Iraq-Iran war, as Saddam Hussein's (Western-backed) military made widespread use of chemical weapons, Iran neither reciprocated with WMD attacks nor sought to fast-track the Shah's agenda to develop nuclear weapons. In fact, Saddam's use of weapons of mass destruction made Iran rethink its national nuclear program.

In 1979, after the Islamic Revolution, the IAEO requested that the French join them in talks to negotiate resumption of bilateral agreements. The French, however, rejected the idea and froze Iranian assets including two loans worth more than $1 billion. In October 1991, France and Iran initialed an agreement to settle their twelve-year-old loan dispute; France agreed to pay $1 billion to cover the balance of repayment plus interest.[34] In December 1991, France lost a case that it had brought against Iran for breach of a 1973 contract under which France was to construct two pressurized water reactors at Karun.[35]

In the end, the standoff led to the total suspension of Iran-France nuclear cooperation and the dissolution of Coredif Company despite opposition from Iran's government.[36] The United States stopped all of its agreements with Iran, including supply of highly enriched uranium for the Tehran Research Reactor. Germany, the United Kingdom, and other Western countries followed the lead of the United States and terminated their nuclear agreements with Iran.[37]

Iran's nuclear program did, however, make some quiet progress during the war years. According to IAEA reports, Iran's gas centrifuge program started in 1985 and in 1987 Iran was able to acquire key components from the A. Q. Khan network, a nuclear supply complex operating from within Pakistan's uranium enrichment establishment.[38] The components included technical drawings for a P-1 centrifuge and a design for a gas centrifuge enrichment plant.[39] Iran discovered "high-quality uranium" in the Saghand region of Yazd province after several years of exploration work. Pakistan and Iran signed an agreement for Iranian engineers to be trained in Pakistan.[40]

Iraq bombed the Bushehr plant in 1987. With the nation's resources overwhelmingly devoted to fighting Iraq, Iran's civilian nuclear program was largely put on hold until the end of the war and the 1989 election of a moderate, technocratic government under Ayatollah Ali Akbar Hashemi Rafsanjani. Together with his Servants of Construction Party, Rafsanjani made the reconstruction of Iran's war-shattered economy a top priority and accordingly moved to secure international cooperation to complete nuclear projects inherited from the Shah and develop new ones.[41]

Iran started activities in uranium mining infrastructure, uranium conversion, heavy-water reactor, and uranium enrichment programs. South Africa supplied Iran with uranium concentrate. India also signed an agreement to supply Iran with a 10 MW research reactor, as part of a memorandum of understanding on scientific and technical cooperation.[42]

At Rafsanjani's initiative, China and Iran signed a ten-year nuclear cooperation agreement in early 1990. China agreed to build a 27 MW research reactor and to supply additional calutrons and other uranium enrichment technology.[43] In mid-1991, Prime Minister Li Peng, during talks with Rafsanjani, agreed to provide expertise and technology on nuclear reactors.[44] According to an IAEA report published in 2003, Iran conducted tests on centrifuges installed at Kalaye Electric Company, an IAEO subsidiary, using the Chinese-supplied UF_6.[45] China was supposed to build a uranium hexafluoride complex known as the Isfahan uranium conversion facility (UCF). In 1991, Iran imported from China one metric ton of UF_6 to feed gas for centrifuges, which would later become part of the "case" against Iran because it was not reported to the IAEA, as required under Iran's Comprehensive Safeguards Agreement.[46] In December 1991, China withdrew its offer to sell Iran a nuclear reactor. Part of the planned facility in Isfahan was delivered by China, but when China joined the Nuclear Suppliers Group in 1992, it ceased nuclear cooperation with Iran under American pressure.

According to a 2006 report by the Argentine judiciary, Iran signed three agreements with Argentina's National Atomic Energy Commission in 1987–1988. The first Iranian-Argentine agreement involved help in converting the U.S.-supplied Tehran Nuclear Research Center reactor from highly enriched uranium fuel to 19.75 percent low-enriched uranium, and to supply the low-enriched uranium to Iran.[47] The required uranium was delivered in 1993.[48] The second and third agreements were for technical assistance, including the provision of components for the building of pilot plants for conversion of UF_6 into uranium dioxide and fuel fabrication. Under U.S. pressure, Argentina also ceased nuclear cooperation with Iran.[49]

The Bushehr reactor was badly damaged by Iraqi air strikes during the Iran-Iraq war. Iran's president, Rafsanjani, signed a comprehensive bilateral nuclear agreement with the USSR in 1989. In 1993, Iran signed a contract with Russia for the restoration and completion of the power plant in

Bushehr. The United States pressed Moscow to stop work on the Bushehr plant, but Moscow rejected these demands. Nevertheless, American pressure succeeded in persuading Russia to delay completion of the program for more than a decade. Finally, in May 2010, the Bushehr reactor partly came into service at a low level under IAEA safeguards.[50] Russia also committed to deliver nuclear fuel to be used by the Bushehr plant and to take back spent fuel after its use in the reactor. In addition to the Bushehr project, Iran and Russia negotiated secretly for cooperation on an enrichment facility in Natanz and heavy-water reactors in Arak, but Russia halted this cooperation under pressure from the United States in the late 1990s. Iran also began constructing the underground enrichment facility of its Natanz plant in early 1990.

While the Iranian government continued with mixed effect to seek international cooperation in developing its nuclear program from the late 1980s and into the 1990s, it also pursued diplomacy to promote regional WMD disarmament. In May 1998, President Khatami paid a visit to Saudi Arabia, where Iran and Saudi Arabia issued a joint statement expressing support for the elimination of weapons of mass destruction from the Middle East. They said Israel's production and stockpiling of nuclear weapons, along with its noncompliance with international laws and treaties, posed a serious threat to peace and security in the region.[51]

The United States remained suspicious of Iran's nuclear aspirations throughout the 1990s and early 2000s. Intelligence reports surfaced that North Korea assisted Iran in uranium exploration and mining in the early 1990s.[52] In March 2000, President Bill Clinton signed the Iran Non-Proliferation Act, which allowed the United States to sanction individuals and organizations providing material aid to Iran's nuclear chemical, biological, and ballistic missile weapons programs.[53]

On December 31, 2001, the U.S. Department of Defense listed Iran in its Nuclear Posture Review "among the countries that could be involved in immediate, potential, or unexpected contingencies" that could require a U.S. nuclear response. This review represented a significant shift in U.S. policy, expanding the potential uses of nuclear weapons and including the possibility for the use of nuclear weapons against non–nuclear-weapon states not attacking the United States or its allies or forces in concert with another nuclear-weapon state.[54]

CHAPTER TWO

THE FIRST CRISIS

DEVELOPMENTS PRECEDING THE IAEA'S
FIRST RESOLUTION IN SEPTEMBER 2003

President Rafsanjani and his successor, Muhammad Khatami, followed a policy of international engagement to reduce tensions with the West, and particularly the United States, that had erupted after the Islamic Revolution. Hand in hand with Rafsanjani's postwar reconstruction agenda, his government sought to improve economic ties with the West, as well as neighbors such as Turkey, Afghanistan, Pakistan, and the Arab states. What Rafsanjani established in 1990 as a policy of "dialogue" was promoted in Khatami's reformist administration to "dialogue of civilizations" to reach a lasting understanding with the West.[1]

The Iranian government condemned the terrorist attacks of September 11, 2001, and assisted the United States and its allies in toppling the Taliban regime and setting up a new government in Afghanistan. This newfound collaboration was unexpectedly cut short when, in January 2002, President George W. Bush shocked the world by labeling Iran a member of an "axis of evil" together with Iraq and North Korea, a move that heralded a new era of Iran-U.S. hostility.[2]

The tension heightened when, on August 14, 2002, a spokesman for the Iranian dissident MEK[3] claimed during a news conference in Washington that the Islamic Republic of Iran engaged in covert nuclear activities at nuclear sites in Isfahan, Natanz, and Arak. About four months later, on December 13, 2002, CNN aired a documentary about the Institute for Science and International Security's report that included satellite images of the three nuclear sites. Both the MEK spokesman and the CNN report alleged that Iran was pursuing secret nuclear activities aimed at developing nuclear weaponry.

In 2002, three huge nuclear complexes were indeed under construction in Isfahan, Natanz, and Arak. Isfahan's Uranium Conversion Facility was under direct supervision of the International Atomic Energy Agency from the very beginning, and no covert activities were conducted there. At Natanz, the IAEA was not informed of the construction of the facilities, which raised strong suspicions that equipment and material related to them had been imported by Iran also without being reported, as was required under Iran's Comprehensive Safeguards Agreement with the IAEA.[4] Iran's failure to report imported nuclear material from China was mentioned in the IAEA June 2003 report. Arak, meanwhile, was a heavy water production plant that was not required to be under Iran's Safeguards Agreement with the IAEA.

The Nuclear Non-Proliferation Treaty was built on three pillars: nonproliferation, disarmament, and the peaceful use of nuclear energy. Accordingly, the treaty recognizes the peaceful use of energy as an inalienable right of all signatory states, provided that they meet nonproliferation obligations. In signing the treaty, non–nuclear-weapon states agree to accept Safeguards Agreements with the IAEA to verify that their nuclear programs are not being diverted for military purposes and that all of their nuclear activities are exclusively for peaceful purposes.

At the time, Tehran was not a signatory to the IAEA's 93+2 Additional Protocol,[5] which provides the agency's inspectors with greater authority to monitor nuclear activities within a state.[6] Nor had Iran committed to recommended "subsidiary arrangements" specifying details for the IAEA and the state's implementation of the Safeguards Agreement.[7] Subsidiary arrangements to Comprehensive Safeguards Agreements include the requirement that countries under their purview report plans for construction activities related to atomic facilities to the IAEA six months in advance of introducing nuclear material into the facility. In their revised form (Code 3.1), subsidiary arrangements require a state to declare any nuclear facility as soon as a decision has been made to construct it.

The international community has required Iran to implement the modified version of the subsidiary arrangements (Code 3.1). Iran signed the modified version in December 2003 but later withdrew after the nuclear file was reported to the UN Security Council. In that Iran was not a signatory to either the revised Subsidiary Arrangements or the Additional Protocol prior to December 2003, the country's commitments to the NPT did not oblige it to inform the IAEA about the construction of the Natanz and Arak facilities in advance of the introduction of uranium into them. Despite these facts, claims made by the MEK and the ensuing wave of media attention contributed to heightened suspicions about Iran's nuclear activities.

Between September 2002 and February 2003, the IAEA requested inspections of Iran's nuclear facilities at Natanz but because of administrative problems on the part of Iran in arranging high-level meetings for IAEA Director General Mohamed ElBaradei, his visit to Iran was delayed, raising suspicions in the international community that Iran was stalling to cover up evidence.

On February 22, 2003, ElBaradei visited Tehran to continue his negotiations with officials of the Islamic Republic of Iran. During that trip, he toured nuclear installations at Natanz and within a few weeks presented a report to the IAEA Board of Governors confirming Iran's uranium enrichment capability. The report indicated the seriousness of the crisis and noted that Iran's nuclear dossier would be brought to the Board of Governors' agenda for the first time since 1979. ElBaradei welcomed Tehran's cooperation with the IAEA and reiterated that Iran should sign the Additional Protocol strengthening and extending the safeguards system.

Against this backdrop, the White House had turned its attention in the region to attacking Iraq and toppling Saddam Hussein. The apparent quick victory of the U.S. military in Iraq and prevalence of military and security-based discourse among American neoconservatives, however, set the stage for a full-blown crisis with the Islamic Republic of Iran, despite its recent conciliatory developments with the IAEA. Starting in April 2003, the Bush administration decided to increase pressure on Iran.

A meeting of the American Israel Public Affairs Committee held in early April 2003 offered an indication of what was to come. During that meeting, Secretary of State Colin Powell, National Security Adviser Condoleezza Rice, and John Bolton, at the time undersecretary of state for arms control and international security, made harsh remarks about Iran's nuclear activities. Their comments reflected the trend of Western politicians emphasizing the necessity for Iran to implement the Additional Protocol. At both this meeting and the first session of the Preparatory Commission for the 2005 NPT Review Conference, Iran was faced with requests for the implementation of the Additional Protocol. High-level Western diplomats reiterated that request in most negotiations with their Iranian counterparts. On April 24, 2003, for example, French Foreign Minister Dominique de Villepin used a meeting with his Iranian counterpart, Kamal Kharrazi, to urge Iran's acceptance of the Additional Protocol. Similar requests were repeated at various news conferences and in the course of political negotiations with Iran up to early May of that year.

At the second session of the Preparatory Commission for the NPT Review Conference, a consensus was reached against Iran. The meeting, which was held from April 28 to May 9, turned into a venue for strongly worded remarks about Iran's nuclear program, with delegates from the United States, France, Australia, United Kingdom, New Zealand, Canada, and the European Union adopting tough stances. In his address to the session, John Wolfe, at the time the U.S. assistant secretary of state for nonproliferation, clearly announced that Iran was treading the same path of deceiving the international community that incapacitated IAEA inspectors in North Korea and Iraq.[8] Andrew Semmel, Wolfe's deputy, referred to the necessity for Iran to accede to the Additional Protocol, saying that Iran's nuclear activities constituted an unacceptable threat to global security. The Australian envoy, John Dauth, read a statement describing Iran's ambitious policy for obtaining sensitive nuclear technology allowing uranium enrichment and a complete fuel cycle as a source of concern. Delegates from New Zealand and Canada made similar remarks and called for Iran's "rapid" and "unconditional" signing of the 93+2 Additional Protocol.

Iran's representatives—Ambassador to the UN Javad Zarif,[9] Deputy Minister for International Affairs Gholamali Khoshrou,[10] and Director General for International Affairs Amir Zamaninia[11]—tried to give Iran's response to the charges of the April 29 statement but remained silent about Iran's final decision on whether to implement the protocol. In response, the British envoy delivered a speech asking why Iran was so reluctant to implement the protocol if, as it claimed, the country had no secret nuclear weapons program. The EU delegation, in its statement, criticized the position taken by Iran's envoy, and it, too, called on Iran to sign the Additional Protocol.

The EU statement, which expanded on a similar argument introduced at the Preparatory Commission's first session, highlighted another important point providing a legal backing for further altercations between Iran and the West.[12] The statement included an interpretation of the NPT's articles that directly linked the basic rights of state parties to their obligations. According to this argument, the development of nuclear energy for peaceful purposes is considered the "right" of a state party only as long as there is no diversion toward a weapons program. The West's interpretation is that the rights under Article IV of the NPT are linked with fulfillment of Article III, which is the safeguards provision. Iran and other members of the Non-Aligned Movement contend that even countries suspected of diversion to a weapons program are obliged to fully cooperate with the IAEA only until all such concerns are removed and the nature of their peaceful programs is verified.

In the Western point of view, it was entirely possible for a country to violate its treaty obligations even without any diversion of civilian nuclear activities to military applications. A state could have secret, parallel facilities to develop the components of nuclear weapons without diverting materials or resources from civilian facilities. So, according to this viewpoint, which draws on the NPT's and the IAEA Statute's repeated emphasis that legitimate nuclear activities in non–nuclear-weapon states must be exclusively for peaceful purposes, the issue of compliance and legality was broader than the matter of diversion alone. This would be demonstrated in the IAEA Board of Governors' Resolution in September 2005, which cited Article XII, Paragraph C of the IAEA Statute in defining noncompliance as diversion or any other use of nuclear energy for military purposes.

From the Iranian point of view, however, the IAEA could at most claim that Iran had failed to report some of its nuclear activities in a timely fashion. Condemnation that secrecy was evidence of military nuclear activities was unjustified because Iran, due to sanctions and pressure from the West, had no option other than to obtain materials and technology for its civilian nuclear program secretly and on the black market. For Iran to declare to the IAEA far in advance its intention to build a new enrichment facility would only make it easier for Western countries to prevent Iran from obtaining the necessary materials and technology. Thus, in Iran's view, it was the West that had violated the NPT on a grand scale by cutting off all nuclear cooperation with Iran—as mandated by the treaty—after the 1979 Islamic Revolution and violating its existing contractual obligations. By comparison, Iranians believe that the country's failures to report activities to the IAEA were minor when viewed against the West's violations and to the diversion of nuclear activities for military purposes.[13,*]

On May 21, 2003, three days after the second session of the Preparatory Commission, the International Conference on Drug Abuse and Illicit Trafficking convened, with Iranian Foreign Minister Kamal Kharrazi among its participants. Kharrazi's French, British, Italian, German, Russian, Canadian, and Greek counterparts used meetings on the sidelines of the conference to express their viewpoints on Tehran's nuclear activities, with special emphasis on the necessity for Iran to sign the Additional Protocol.

At the end of a summit meeting of major industrialized economies in June 2003 in Evian, France, G8 leaders issued a statement expressing concern over Iran's nuclear program. In that statement, the G8 called on Iran to fully comply with its obligations under the NPT and to try to build confidence with the world.[14] According to reports produced by Iran's Foreign Ministry for high Iranian officials, the nuclear issue was a major focus of further discussions between European diplomats and their Iranian counterparts.

Despite the fact that Bush "rewarded" Iran for its cooperation with the United States in Afghanistan after the 9/11 attacks by labeling Iran as part of an "axis of evil" in January 2002, in a non-paper, Iran offered the

---

* Editor's note: The issue of reporting is vital to the determination whether a state's nuclear activities are exclusively peaceful.

U.S. government a comprehensive plan for negotiations and cooperation, which addressed all mutual concerns. The memorandum, sent to the U.S. government via Tim Guldimann, the Swiss ambassador in Tehran, was intended for a broad-based negotiation on major bilateral, regional, and international issues to remove thirty years of hostilities with the United States. The major outline of the proposal is as follows:[15]

Iranian Aims

The United States accepts a dialogue "in mutual respect" and agrees that Iran put the following aims on the agenda:

- Halt hostile U.S. behavior and rectify status of Iran in the United States (interference in internal or external relations, "axis of evil," terrorism list).
- Abolishment of all sanctions: commercial sanctions, frozen assets, judgments (Foreign Sovereign Immunities Act), impediments in international trade and financial institutions.
- Iraq: democratic and fully representative government in Iraq, support of Iranian claims for Iraqi reparations, respect for Iranian national interests in Iraq and religious links to Najaf/Karbal.
- Full access to peaceful nuclear technology, biotechnology, and chemical technology.
- Recognition of Iran's legitimate security interests in the region with corresponding defense capacity.
- Terrorism: pursuit of anti-Iranian terrorists, above all the MKO and support for repatriation of their members in Iraq, decisive actions against anti-Iranian terrorists, above all MKO and affiliated organizations in the United States.

U.S. Aims

Iran accepts a dialogue "in mutual respect" and agrees that the United States put the following aims on the agenda:

- WMD: full transparency for security that there are no Iranian endeavors to develop or possess WMD, full cooperation with IAEA based on Iranian adoption of all relevant instruments (93+2 and all further IAEA protocols).

- Terrorism: decisive action against any terrorists (above all, al-Qaeda) on Iranian territory, full cooperation and exchange of all relevant information.
- Iraq: coordination of Iranian influence for activity supporting political stabilization and the establishment of democratic institutions and a nonreligious government.
- Middle East:

    1) cease any material support to Palestinian opposition groups (Hamas, Jihad, and others) from Iranian territory, put pressure on these organizations to stop violent actions against civilians within borders of 1967.

    2) action on Hizbollah to become a mere political organization within Lebanon.

    3) acceptance of the Arab League Beirut declaration (Saudi initiative, two-states approach).

- Steps:

    Communication of mutual agreement on the following procedure.

    I. Mutual simultaneous statements: "We have always been ready for direct and authoritative talks with the U.S./with Iran in good faith and with the aim of discussing—in mutual respect—our common interests and our mutual concerns based on merits and objective realities, but we have always made it clear that such talks can be held only if genuine progress for a solution of our own concerns can be achieved."

    II. A first direct meeting on the appropriate level (for instance, in Paris) will be held with the previously agreed aims:

    a. of a decision on the first mutual steps

- Iraq: establishment of a common group, active Iranian support for Iraqi stabilization. U.S.: commitment to actively support Iranian reparation claims within the discussions on Iraq foreign debts.
- Terrorism: U.S.: commitment to disarm and remove MKO from Iraq and take action in accordance with UN Security Council Resolution 1373[16] against its leadership. Iran: commitment for

enhanced action against al-Qaeda members in Iran, agreement on cooperation and information exchange.

- Iranian general statement "to support a peaceful solution in the Middle East involving the parties concerned."
- U.S. general statement that "Iran did not belong to the 'axis of evil.'"

U.S. agrees to halt its impediments against Iran in international financial and trade institutions.

    b. of the establishment of three parallel working groups on disarmament, regional security, and economic cooperation. Their aim is an agreement on three parallel road maps; for the discussions of these working groups, each side accepts that the other side's aims (listed above) are put on the agenda:

        1) Disarmament: road map, which combines the mutual aims of, on the one side, full transparency by international commitments and guarantees to abstain from WMD with, on the other side, full access to Western technology (in the three areas).

        2) Terrorism and regional security: road map for aims mentioned above on the Middle East and terrorism.

        3) Economic cooperation: road map for the abolishment of the sanctions, rescinding of judgments, and unfreezing of assets.

    c. of agreement on a timetable for implementation.

    d. and of a public statement after this first meeting on the achieved agreements[17]

The offer made by Iran was an incredible opportunity which the United States dismissed. Unfortunately, the United States responded by protesting to the Swiss foreign ministry and criticizing Tim Guldimann for having even deemed Tehran's proposal worthy of consideration. The absence of a response to Iran in 2003 convinced Tehran that Washington was not sincere in its stated desire for rapprochement. My graduate students at Princeton and I met with Tim Guldimann in early November 2011 in Berlin and found him very pessimistic about a possible rapprochement between Iran and the United States in the near future.[18]

THE FIRST IAEA BOARD STATEMENT, JUNE 2003

On June 6, 2003, Mohamed ElBaradei presented his report on the implementation of the Safeguards Agreement in Iran, the main topic of discussion at the IAEA's session that month, to members of the agency's Board of Governors. From legal and technical perspectives, despite some positive points, the general findings presented in the report were fairly damning for Iran.

The eight-page report cited without ambiguity failures and breaches of safeguards by Iran and called for more inspections. In the report, the IAEA announced that Iran had failed to observe the provisions of the Comprehensive Safeguards Agreement and the Non-Proliferation Treaty, at least with regard to the following five issues:

- Failure to declare the importation of natural uranium in 1991, or its subsequent transfer for further processing.
- Failure to declare the activities involving the subsequent processing and use of the imported natural uranium, including the production and loss of nuclear material, and the production and transfer of waste from such activities.
- Failure to declare the facilities where such material (including nuclear waste) was received, stored, and processed.
- Failure to provide in a timely manner updated design information on the MIX Facility[19] and for the Tehran Research Reactor.
- Failure to provide information on waste storage at Isfahan or Arak in a timely fashion.

The report implied that Iran had provided information only under duress, after being presented with incriminating information obtained by the IAEA, and that it had done its best to disclose as little information as possible. The director general also revealed the IAEA's concerns about the nature of Iran's nuclear program. Reference to a heavy water program and emphasis on the necessity of taking samples at Kalaye Electric Company were other important points. More importantly, sampling at Kalaye was deemed necessary for "further follow-up on information regarding allegations about undeclared enrichment of nuclear material."

In summary, the June 2003 report stressed such themes as Iran's failures under the Comprehensive Safeguards Agreement and its breaches of the agreement. As for the IAEA, it stressed such themes as the agency's lack of trust in corrective measures and its concern about the possibility of diversion, possible military use of nuclear facilities, and the existence of many technical ambiguities. The director general also emphasized in the report to the Board of Governors that Iran's acceptance of the 93+2 Additional Protocol was a necessary step to restore Iran's credibility.

The IAEA Board of Governors convened several days after the report's presentation. In that meeting, Cuba was the only country that called for Iran's nuclear program to be removed from the agenda because of the lack of any evidence showing a breach of the Safeguards Agreement by Tehran. The Non-Aligned Movement, meanwhile, issued a statement professing support for Iran while "appreciating transparency" and the "cooperation of Iran with [the] IAEA." China took a relatively mild stance on Tehran, also calling on Iran to be more transparent and build confidence with the international community. Those countries were in agreement in recognizing Iran's right to have peaceful nuclear technology and opposing referral to the UN Security Council, and they thus formed a bloc whose activities strengthened Iran's position.

The Europeans constituted the second bloc in that meeting. Aside from some differences in the tone of statements and extent of criticism of Tehran, the bloc was united on two points: first, the need for Iran to immediately and unconditionally accept the Additional Protocol, and second, concern about Iran's failures mentioned in the director general's report.

A third bloc, led by the United States, was the most outspoken against Iran. The United States focused its statement on the prospect of an Iranian nuclear bomb, arguing that Iran's reluctance to sign on to the Additional Protocol was evidence of military and non-peaceful activities on the part of Tehran.

As ElBaradei remembers in his 2011 memoir, the American bloc took the fact that Iran had engaged in clandestine nuclear activities as "proof positive that Tehran intended to produce nuclear weapons . . . U.S. statements of certainty regarding Iran's nuclear weapon intentions soon began to be echoed by others in the West. Many representatives of developing countries were, by contrast, more sympathetic to Iran's need to go underground to evade the sanctions."[20]

The American bloc turned into a powerful minority at the meeting after supportive, though less confrontational, statements by Canada, Australia, and the United Kingdom. In addition to deploring Iran's failures and asking Iran to unconditionally accept the Additional Protocol, the four countries agreed on a demand that Iran suspend the initiation of uranium enrichment at the Natanz facility. This request was the first official international request that Iran suspend part of its nuclear activities.[21]

The meeting of the Board of Governors concluded on June 19, 2003, with the issuance of a statement containing conciliatory terms[22] but also very important demands. The statement[23] called on Tehran to rectify its declared shortcomings and accept the 93+2 Additional Protocol without any conditions. The statement also encouraged Tehran to suspend the introduction of nuclear material into centrifuges and cooperate with IAEA inspectors in environmental sampling.

It should be noted that the predominant international disposition at that time was to accept virtually any measures to prevent the development of weapons of mass destruction. The U.S. government had indicated that it would spare no effort in establishing a security-based international atmosphere aimed at protecting the security interests of the United States. Moreover, as would later be revealed through WikiLeaks, Washington's Arab allies were pressing it to act decisively to prevent Iran from acquiring nuclear-weapons capabilities. Therefore, agreement among G8 leaders and a unified stance against Iran taken on both sides of the Atlantic could have had dire consequences for Tehran.[24]

On July 3, 2003, less than a month after the IAEA Board of Directors meeting, Mohamed ElBaradei visited Tehran again, this time armed with the demands of the international community and IAEA. ElBaradei met with Kamal Kharrazi and President Khatami. Apparently, the director general left Iran without receiving any firm assurances from Iran on the two main requests of the IAEA: transparency and full cooperation, and acceptance of the Additional Protocol. However, ElBaradei said in an interview with *Al-Hayat* several months later that Iran's president had provided assurances that his country would cooperate completely with the IAEA.[25] I was surprised about ElBaradei's claims of Khatami's assurances because we hadn't had any discussion or decision on the Additional Protocol issues in the Supreme National Security Council. Some days after ElBaradei's visit, I had a private meeting with Dr. Velayati, the supreme leader's adviser on foreign affairs and Iran's foreign minister from 1981 to 1997.[26] As the head of the Foreign Relation Committee of the Supreme National Security Council, I was trying to understand the different viewpoints on the Additional Protocol. Dr. Velayati told me that Iran would not accept the Additional Protocol. He equated the Additional Protocol with the 1828 Treaty of Turkmenchai. Viewed by Iranians today as a betrayal and a black mark in their history, the treaty surrendered much of present-day central Armenia, Nakhchivan, and Azerbaijan to Russia following the Russo-Persian War.

In this meeting, which Mehdi Akhondzadeh, my deputy in international affairs in the Supreme National Security Council (and current deputy foreign minister for international affairs) also attended, I failed to persuade Dr. Velayati to adopt the protocol.

Meanwhile, international pressures on Iran were mounting. The foreign ministers of France, the United Kingdom, and Germany sent a joint letter to their Iranian counterpart on August 6, 2003, explaining the EU's viewpoint, followed by a similar letter from Russian Foreign Minister Igor Ivanov outlining Moscow's viewpoint. In this way, two transregional powers—the EU and Russia—showed that despite cooperation with the United States in June, they would pursue their own interests and their own courses of action to resolve the crisis in a relatively independent manner. The most pressing demand from the Europeans and the Russians was for Iran's signing and implementation of the 93+2 Additional Protocol.

The letters included another important point, which was described by some experts as a short-term solution to circumvent the more aggressive U.S. strategy. Both Russia and the European Union asked Iran in clear terms to cease its nuclear enrichment activities. The letter from France, the United Kingdom, and Germany stated that the three countries did not question the right of any country that complied fully with international obligations to generate electricity using nuclear power. They did, however, request that Iran halt the development of facilities—including those for enrichment or reprocessing—that would give it the capability to produce fissile material.

Igor Ivanov, in his letter to Iran's foreign minister, wrote that as long as the Additional Protocol had not been implemented by the Islamic Republic, it would be to Iran's own benefit to avoid producing fissile material. The Russian foreign minister argued that international experience has proved that any economically feasible model for nuclear energy use would have to rely on international cooperation for purchasing nuclear fuel, rather than a country's own capacities for fissile material production, enrichment, and conversion.

The viewpoints of Europe and Russia regarding Iran's interaction with the International Atomic Energy Agency were clear. France, the United Kingdom, and Germany wrote in their letter to Iran's foreign minister that they expected the Iranian government "to sign and ratify an Additional Protocol without delay or precondition. This will promote international confidence of the peaceful nature of Iran's nuclear program." They called on Iran to immediately implement the Additional Protocol even as formalities related to its final ratification proceeded. The letter from Moscow noted that Russian officials had frequently and clearly told Tehran that the commitment to transparency demonstrated through signing and implementing the Additional Protocol and the Safeguards Agreement would protect Iran's interests. The letter argued that the measure would help Iran build confidence with the international community about the peaceful nature of its nuclear program, particularly if Iran took measures to implement the Additional Protocol even before its formal ratification.

Both blocs thus called on Iran to cease nuclear activities related to fuel-cycle development and pushed for the speedy signing and ratification of the 93+2 Additional Protocol as a confidence-building measure and implementation of its contents. In this period, I discussed the importance of the nuclear case for the country's national security with Hassan Rouhani,[27] the secretary of the Supreme National Security Council, and we decided to become more active on the issue. From this point on, the Supreme National Security Council began holding regular meetings with high-level officials from pertinent ministries and organizations, such as the Foreign Ministry, Atomic Energy Organization, and Defense Ministry, to discuss the issue and to hear their analyses. My colleagues at the Foreign Ministry, including Ambassadors Javad Zarif, Amir Zamaninia, and Gholamali Khoshrou, were very glad to see the Supreme National Security Council engaging with the nuclear issue. They had been worried that officials at the Atomic Energy Organization, which had previously taken the lead in handling the issue, had been overly optimistic and failed to predict the emergence of the nuclear crisis because of their focus on straightforward technical matters rather than the quite significant political dimensions of the problem.

THE FIRST IAEA BOARD RESOLUTION, SEPTEMBER 2003

The next meeting of the IAEA Board of Governors was scheduled in September. The White House considered the meeting an opportunity to reach a definite decision on Iran.[28] Iran had still not declared its official and final position on the requests of the IAEA and other international parties; however, Iran's international standing and the IAEA's requests were being discussed at the highest decisionmaking level of the Islamic Republic of Iran. Tehran decided to send positive signals on the 93+2 Additional Protocol, in what was considered a pragmatic gesture in view of the upcoming Board of Governors meeting. Immediately after this decision was made by senior officials of the Islamic Republic, major diplomatic activities were put on Iran's agenda. On August 25, Ali Akbar Salehi, Iran's representative to the IAEA in Vienna, communicated to the IAEA director general Iran's declaration of readiness to negotiate with the IAEA on the Additional Protocol. Dr. Salehi met separately with Mohamed ElBaradei, officials of the agency's secretariat including Tariq Rauf, the head of verification and security policies of the secretariat, IAEA Deputy Director General Pierre Goldschmidt, and the Malaysian envoy to the IAEA (who was serving as the head of the Non-Aligned Movement). Foreign Minister Kharrazi, meanwhile, negotiated with the president and foreign minister of China on August 25, 2003, and the prime minister and foreign minister of India, as well as the prime minister and foreign minister of Japan. In the diplomatic scramble, Iranian officials also engaged in extensive negotiations with officials of Turkey, Germany, Bulgaria, Italy, the Czech Republic, Spain, Panama, Colombia, and Morocco. In all those meetings, the foreign parties called on Iran to take measures to speedily implement the Additional Protocol and to cooperate transparently with the IAEA.

On August 26, 2003, one day after Tehran's letter was submitted to the IAEA, the director general's report on Iran's nuclear activities was forwarded to members of the Board of Governors. ElBaradei's report acknowledged that between the June and September meetings, Tehran had cooperated with the IAEA's inspectors in various ways, including allowing them to do environmental sampling (which was not required by the Safeguards Agreement), submitting statements, and indicating its willingness to implement the Additional Protocol. Despite that cooperation, the report included enough criticism to turn the September meeting of the Board of Governors into a venue for intense international censure of Iran.

The resolution adopted by the Board of Governors at the meeting's conclusion included stringent requirements for Tehran. The requirements were so onerous that the head of the Iran Atomic Energy Organization described them as being totally impractical: "It seems that the resolution has been engineered in such a manner as to guarantee noncompliance."[29] In the Iranian point of view, it was impractical because the resolution required open-ended suspension and unlimited access for inspectors, meaning access beyond the requirements of the NPT.

The initial reaction from Tehran was one of surprise and anger, rejecting out of hand compliance with the resolution. Ali Akbar Salehi, Iran's representative to the IAEA, announced soon after the ratification of the resolution that Iran would possibly reduce its cooperation with the IAEA or even cut it off entirely.[30] Likewise, Iranian Foreign Ministry spokesman Hamid Reza Asefi announced on September 14, 2003, that concerned authorities in Iran were considering reviewing Iran's cooperation with the IAEA and that Iran's decision would be announced in the near future.[31] Dr. Salehi further told the BBC that the Iranian government did not consider itself committed or accountable to a resolution which had been ratified in an unusual manner of voting, and which was against the letter and spirit of international law.[32] Such statements and Dr. Salehi's walkout from the Board of Governors' meeting—a protest that was construed by Western media as an unprecedented measure—showed in unambiguous terms Iran's anger with the Board of Governors.

These harsh positions by Salehi and the Foreign Ministry were not discussed or decided upon beforehand by the Supreme National Security Council. I talked to Dr. Salehi before the IAEA's Board of Governors' meeting, and I found him optimistic about the meeting, believing that the board would take a soft stance on Iran.

Ambassador Salehi had a close and friendly relationship with Mohamed ElBaradei. They could communicate in Arabic very well, as Salehi was born in Karbala, Iraq. Salehi was also chancellor of Sharif University of Technology, the best university in Iran, from 1982 to 1985,[33] when ElBaradei was an adjunct professor of international law at New York University's School of Law.[34] Their amicable personal relationship may in part explain Dr. Salehi's perhaps unwarranted optimism about Iran's relationship with the agency. After the IAEA's resolution, I asked Salehi about his impression. He told me that it was completely unexpected and that he was shocked about the resolution.

The Iran nuclear question was of critical importance at the IAEA's September 2003 meeting, and the resolution issued by the Board of Governors brought the issue even more to the fore. The resolution expressed concern about low and highly enriched uranium contamination in Iran's centrifuges, significant and material changes in Iran's statements, increased ambiguities, the introduction of nuclear material into centrifuges, and Tehran's failure to declare all of its activities. The Board of Governors asked Iran "to promptly and unconditionally sign, ratify and fully implement the Additional Protocol" and "suspend all further uranium enrichment-related activities." The board also gave Iran a window of fifty days to take "essential and urgent" steps toward confidence building and to take "corrective measures." These measures included "providing a full declaration of all imported material and components relevant to the enrichment program" and "granting unrestricted access, including environmental sampling, for the Agency to whatever locations the Agency deems necessary for the purposes of verification of the correctness and completeness of Iran's declarations." The September resolution also noted that Iran had breached its previous commitments, providing legal grounds for reporting Iran's nuclear dossier to the UN Security Council if the country ignored the resolution.

A great crisis engulfed the country. The IAEA's October 31 deadline gave Iran a short time to respond to the international demands. Suspension of a considerable portion of Iran's nuclear activities was the most important demand of the resolution, which was supported by the West as well as powers such as Russia and China. The Board of Governors called on Iran "to suspend all further uranium enrichment-related activities, including the further introduction of nuclear material into Natanz, and, as a confidence-building measure, any reprocessing activities, pending provision by the Director General of the assurances required by member states, and pending satisfactory application of the provisions of the Additional Protocol." Iran was faced with a dilemma: conform to the demands of the Board of Governors and shut down a large part of its nuclear activities without gaining any clear concession or any prospect for a compromise; or reject the resolution, leading to accusations that Iran had breached its international obligations and lending credence to U.S. claims of an Iranian nuclear threat.

Some Western analysts have questioned the very idea of granting Iran concessions in exchange for its adherence to its international obligations and Board of Governors' requests. But in the Iranian view, no international treaties could bind member countries to cooperate with the IAEA beyond the Comprehensive Safeguards Agreement of the Non-Proliferation Treaty or its Additional Protocol. Therefore, the request of the IAEA for cooperation beyond the Comprehensive Safeguards Agreement and Additional Protocol had no legal base and would be accepted not as an international obligation but as a gesture of goodwill and a confidence-building measure. Furthermore, the IAEA and international community could demand only that Iran cooperate in terms of transparency and verification; suspension, in Iran's view, had nothing to do with transparency, and the international community could not legally force an NPT member state to suspend its legitimate nuclear activities. More generally, it was up to sovereign states to decide whether to join international treaties, and the international community had no authority to force any country to accept a treaty, as the IAEA Board of Governors and EU3 (the United Kingdom, France, and Germany) demand that Iran implement the Additional Protocol seemed to suggest. Iran expected concessions in return for such acceptance because it was purely voluntary and part of a policy of building confidence with the international community. From the European point of view, not referring Iran to the UN Security Council was a concession, as Article XII of the IAEA Statute calls for such a referral.

As previously noted, another requirement of the resolution was that Iran immediately ratify and implement the Additional Protocol.[35] In view of Iran's earlier declaration of readiness, this left no room for negotiations about the Additional Protocol as part of talks with international parties and the IAEA. Between the IAEA's meetings in June and September, some diplomats had warned Iran that delaying acceptance of the Additional Protocol would reduce its leverage in further political bargaining, and the September resolution seemed to confirm that.

The wording of the resolution suggested that adopting the Additional Protocol was not just a diplomatic "initiative," but an international "obligation." The September resolution pointed to such issues as:

- The existence of two levels of highly enriched uranium in Iran.[36]
- Considerable modifications to the facilities of the Kalaye Electric Company had been made prior to inspections, which could have affected the accuracy of environmental sampling.[37]
- The fact "that some of Iran's statements to the IAEA have undergone significant and material changes, and that the number of outstanding issues has increased since the report."
- The necessity of "resolving questions regarding the conclusion of Agency experts that process testing on gas centrifuges must have been conducted in order for Iran to develop its enrichment technology to its current extent," and for Iran to accept the Additional Protocol and grant "unrestricted access" to inspectors.

The resolution called on Iran to take all necessary actions. This included providing a full declaration of all imported material and components relevant to the enrichment program, especially imported equipment and components stated to have been contaminated with highly enriched uranium particles, and collaborating with the IAEA in identifying the source and date of receipt of such imports and the locations where they have been stored and used in Iran. The resolution also called for Iran to provide complete information regarding the conducting of uranium conversion experiments.

IRAN'S DOMESTIC AND FOREIGN SITUATION AT THE TIME OF THE CRISIS

Iran's official assessments earlier in 2003 did not anticipate the emergent crisis or the broad-based international consensus evident in the September resolution.[38] Most Iranian politicians knew little about the technical aspects of disputes between Iran's Atomic Energy Organization and the IAEA. The IAEO, for its part, was confident that there were no major problems that could lead to a serious international crisis, even as some Foreign Ministry diplomats, who knew little about the technicalities of

Iran's nuclear program, sensed that trouble was brewing in the international community over the issue.

The Islamic Republic of Iran found itself suddenly on the verge of referral to the UN Security Council under Article XII, Paragraph C of the IAEA Statute if it did not comply with the Board of Governors' resolution.

Iran was in no way prepared to handle the consequences of such a referral, which would threaten the country with isolation and transform the dispute into a matter of international security. America's neoconservatives, fresh from their victories in Afghanistan and Iraq, were at the time mulling over whether to attack Iran or Syria. Far from a political bluff, threatening to report Iran's nuclear dossier to the Security Council would lend credence to their warnings about the dangers of Iran and help drum up support for political confrontation or even war. Also, once the case had been brought to New York, the United States could have used the nuclear issue to bring attention to other areas of mutual difference such as terrorism, the peace process in the Middle East, Iran's missile activities, and even human rights.

Aside from Israel, all countries referred to the UN Security Council during its sixty years of existence had been forced to accept maximum requirements of the Security Council. In all such instances, the Security Council—with the United States exercising great influence—came out victorious.

The general consensus among Western countries in the lead-up to the September resolution had become an international consensus against Iran. Suspicion of Iran had spread not only to Russia and China, but also was rife in the capitals of Muslim countries, especially Iran's neighbors. That developing consensus was not solely the result of American political pressure. Some of the IAEA's findings, as well as failures on the part of Tehran, lent credence to the international media's allegations about Iran's nuclear activities.

Iran's technical and legal interactions with the International Atomic Energy Agency were reaching a breaking point. Reports presented by the director general as well as the resolution issued by the Board of Governors clearly cited Iran's failures to meet safeguards commitments, and Tehran had not provided a convincing response. Tehran's complex relationship with the IAEA was fraught to the point of providing the United States with an excuse to confront Iran unilaterally. Tehran hence faced enormous pressure to cooperate with the IAEA while formulating a long-term plan to resolve all technical and legal problems it had with the agency.

However, dawdling on the part of Iran, bred by incorrect assessments of the extent and severity of the crisis and bureaucratic passivity, exacerbated the diplomatic shift away from Iran and the development of near-unanimous international support for the demand that Tehran implement the Additional Protocol. Further delay by Iran carried the risk of encouraging a broad-based front against Iran's nuclear activities as a whole.

Domestic political disputes were so virulent at the time of the crisis that they provided another major obstacle to a rational solution to the issue. Political squabbling over Iran's nuclear activities had much more destructive consequences than other factors. Responding to the September resolution, as an issue closely related to national security and even to the territorial integrity of the country, demanded collective wisdom and consensus. Therefore, the contradictory signals sent by Tehran constituted a full-blown catastrophe for Iran's policymaking system.

There were two main factions in the country's political scene: hardliners who argued against showing any signs of flexibility to the West, and reformers and pragmatists who had been working to improve relations with the international community. Each side accused the other of treason, or at least of misinformation and ignorance, when the nuclear crisis broke. The first faction comprised those who believed that signing the Additional Protocol would be treasonous. They called on Iran to reject the Board of Governors' resolution and even to withdraw from the Non-Proliferation Treaty. Any form of cooperation with the international community, they maintained, would be futile.

Hossein Shariatmadari, a leading figure among Iran's hard-liners and the editor-in-chief of *Kayhan* newspaper, which consistently reflected the radicals' school of thought, has been particularly influential on the issue. He is a confidant of Iran's supreme leader, who appointed him directly as editor, and has strongly supported President Mahmoud Ahmadinejad since 2005. He has an insider's access to Principlist[39] political circles and valuable links to Iran's security apparatus.[40]

The second faction in Iran's domestic debate on the nuclear issue was composed of those who believed that resistance to the resolution would be detrimental to national security. This group advocated an urgent response and implementation of the Additional Protocol. The main political grouping representing this school of thought was the reformist Mosharekat Party (officially called the Islamic Iran Participation Front), which was loyal to President Khatami and held a majority in Parliament until 2004.

In this way, the country's foreign policy became the scene of an exhausting struggle, with the result that Tehran sent two contradictory messages to the world. That struggle, with both groups using official outlets as their mouthpieces, depleted a large part of Iran's capacity to form a coherent response to the September resolution.

In this atmosphere of IAEA and U.S. condemnation and Iranian inaction, international public opinion was stacked against Iran. Under the influence of calculated, professional, and far-reaching propaganda by the international media, global public opinion had been mobilized against Iran. The "Clash of Civilizations" discourse following 9/11 and the security atmosphere that had been established as a result of the U.S. invasions of Afghanistan and Iraq had greatly affected the perceptions of citizens of the global village. The image of Iran in Western public opinion was violent, despotic, abusive of human rights, and, most importantly, seeking to build an atomic bomb. A transnational Gallup poll conducted at that time in Western countries and the Middle East illustrates the attitude of the global public opinion toward Iran. According to the poll, a majority of Americans and other Westerners believed that Iran was trying to produce an atomic bomb and viewed Iran's nuclear activities as dangerous.[41]

Public opinion had become an issue inside Iran as well. Lack of a coherent public platform by state media and criticism from official news outlets led to wavering public support for the government's nuclear policies. The public was not convinced that Iran's nuclear activities were a source of "national pride." Despite support from elites and some domestic groups, negative attitudes toward nuclear activities and their consequences for the country were commonplace.

The "September shock" from the IAEA resolution gave rise to grave concerns among Iranians of various social strata. The trend of emigration increased as the future appeared less and less predictable, and as rumors of war with the United States abounded. Iraq's occupation and the aggressive rhetoric used by the Israeli and U.S. governments against Iran did little to allay such concerns.

The crisis in September 2003 similarly contributed to economic pessimism and uncertainty that spurred the flight of capital from the country. The *Economist* claimed in mid-October 2003 that about $1 billion of capital had been transferred from Iran to the United Arab Emirates during the last forty-five days of the summer. Both Iran's domestic production and capital market stagnated.

Previous Iranian plans to attract international investments were also stymied. During this period, Japan suspended investments in one of the biggest upstream oil projects in Iran. Iran's economic risk rating by European financial institutions deteriorated to grade E, and international insurance firms reduced their dealings in Iran's economy to a minimum. A spokesman for Italy's SACE Insurance Company went so far as to announce that as long as the nuclear confrontation between Iran and the West continued, the company would not cooperate with Iran. Despite efforts made by officials of the Islamic Republic to assure the capital market and production sectors, the domestic economy was experiencing real stagnation. Naturally, continuation of that trend would have had grave implications for employment and the labor market in Iran.

The combination of international pressure and domestic paralysis brought about by the September crisis made Iranian opposition groups, hoping for instability leading to regime change, quite ecstatic.

Tehran's quick rejection of the resolution was considered a turning point in the opposition's activities, and Europe- and U.S.-based groups opposed to the regime started the countdown to the collapse of the Islamic Republic.[42] Therefore, various efforts were made to create a temporary union among various opposition groups. The mood was such that some opposition figures even went so far as to propose a conference similar to the 2001 Bonn Conference, a meeting of anti-Taliban groups that determined the future government of Afghanistan shortly before the country was invaded by the United States.

In the same vein, Republican Senator Sam Brownback of Kansas presented a plan to the U.S. Senate in the spring of 2004 calling on the White House to financially support the Iranian opposition.[43] These developments point to the fact that at the time of the crisis, the Iranian opposition was drawing serious attention from some hard-line politicians in Washington.

DOMESTIC PLAYERS AND TEHRAN'S STRATEGIES IN RESPONSE TO THE CRISIS

Iranian leaders tried to present the country as unified to improve perceptions of the nation's capacity for countering threats and to ensure that the eventual decision of the Islamic Republic of Iran on the nuclear issue was viewed as final and definitive.[44] However, continued domestic political differences resulted in contradictory signals sent to the West. These policy differences were closely watched; powerful factions in the United States viewed Iran's nuclear dossier as a major source of debate between reformists and conservatives in Iran.[45]

Iranian decision makers and political factions represented and debated six alternative approaches. Each of these approaches was based on different assumptions and prescribed different treatment of three major issues, that is, how to interact with the IAEA, how to respond to the September resolution of the Board of Governors, and whether to accept the 93+2 Additional Protocol.

The Confrontational Approach

The first approach called for the discontinuation of cooperation with the International Atomic Energy Agency and rejection of the Board of Governors' resolution. Advocates of this approach led Tehran's angry response to the resolution.

Proponents of this approach believed that the September resolution was merely the result of American pressure on the international community and viewed it as a prelude to a military assault on Iran. Signing the Additional Protocol was considered to be "humiliating." Members of this group maintained that in addition to rejecting the resolution, Tehran ought to leave the NPT and immediately suspend its cooperation with the IAEA.[46]

Instead of bargaining with the IAEA or great powers, the confrontationalist group argued that Iran should make use of its assets and influence in Iraq, the greater Middle East, and other areas. The main assumption in this approach was that reporting Iran's case to the UN Security Council was an ineffective political bluff and posed no real threat to Tehran. The group also asserted that both sides of the Atlantic were following similar approaches toward Iran and that there was no substantive difference between the American "stick" and the European "carrot." Hence, they believed that all-out resistance by Iran in the face of the resolution would eventually lead both Washington and Brussels to back down.

Hossein Shariatmadari, the *Kayhan* editor, was not the only hard-liner to encourage Iran's withdrawal from the NPT. Abu Muhammad Asgarkhani, professor of law and political science at the University of Tehran, had raised the idea of withdrawing from the NPT during the Iran-Iraq war in the mid-1980s and has advocated this stance in hundreds of interviews with the Iranian media, state radio, and television over the past twenty-five years.[47] Akbar Alami, a prominent figure in Parliament, wrote an official letter to Kofi Annan, the secretary general of the United Nations, in September 2003 rejecting demands for the implementation of the Additional Protocol.[48]

The Nuclear Rights Approach

The second approach emphasized the technical and legal aspects of Iran's nuclear dossier. From this viewpoint, any negotiation with global powers or international organizations on the nuclear issue was considered incorrect. Proponents of this approach believed that Tehran ought to continue to cooperate with the IAEA while rejecting the Board of Governors' resolution as politically motivated.

They maintained that Tehran needed to take action to answer questions posed by the International Atomic Energy Agency but only on the basis of the Safeguards Agreement and without crumbling to global pressure. They were against temporary suspension of uranium enrichment and provisional implementation of the Additional Protocol as confidence-building measures. This approach ignored all international pressure, the September resolution, and political and security threats posed by the United States, while abiding by existing commitments to the IAEA. Proponents of this view also underestimated the problem that Iran's declarations to the IAEA depended on information supplied by the nuclear technologists and that IAEA investigators frequently discovered contradictions or incompleteness in those declarations. This led the IAEA to conclude that Iran would have to take extraordinary steps to redress its breaches and build confidence that all of its nuclear activities were peaceful.

Just days after Mahmoud Ahmadinejad came to office in August 2005, the newly appointed nuclear spokesman, Javad Va'idi, and Ali Asghar

Soltanieh, the current Iranian ambassador to the IAEA, participated in a roundtable at the Center for Strategic Research. They advocated the nuclear rights approach and criticized the policies of the Khatami negotiation team between 2003 and 2005. In my view, like many Iranian politicians, they underestimated the political dimension of the issue, believing it was a simple legal case and thus capable of a straightforward technical resolution.

The Grand Bargain Approach

This approach put much emphasis on the political context of the September crisis. Its proponents believed that the standoff was merely a manifestation of a broader confrontation with the Western bloc and viewed it as a component of U.S. strategy for the region. They believed that the nuclear issue is a subsidiary component of Iran-West relations, specifically U.S. hostilities toward Iran. Therefore, the proponents maintained that the crisis would continue until a resolution was found for problems between Tehran and Washington.

The advocates of this approach considered that a critical juncture had been reached that provided a very good opportunity to start direct talks with the United States. They believed that Iran's influence in Afghanistan and Iraq would provide the country with considerable leverage to push for concessions during any possible negotiations. The situation in the Middle East and the existing gap between Europe and the United States caused by the U.S. invasion of Iraq were other factors that bolstered Tehran's standing in any possible talks with Washington.

This approach prescribed extensive cooperation with the IAEA in tandem with negotiations with the United States and Europe. I was among the proponents of such an approach. I tried at every opportunity to suggest the terms of a Grand Bargain and comprehensive package for rapprochement between Iran and the United States since joining the Foreign Ministry in 1986. When I raised the idea in an annual seminar of ambassadors in Mashhad in 1993, I was severely criticized by diplomats such as Hossein Sheikholeslam, then–deputy foreign minister for African and Arab affairs, and Hojatoleslam Morsali, then–deputy foreign minister for consular and parliamentarian affairs. Other prominent diplomats such as Hossein Kazempour Ardebili, then-ambassador to Japan, and Muhammad Ali Najafabadi, then-ambassador to the United Arab Emirates, supported my proposal. This issue became the most challenging one of the seminar. Dr. Velayati, then the foreign minister, intervened to stop the discussion by criticizing me and reiterating that the issue was a redline for the Islamic Republic that must not be crossed. Two days later, the ambassadors met with Hashemi Rafsanjani, who criticized the seminar for omitting discussion of major foreign policy issues. The ambassadors interpreted Rafsanjani's criticism as support for my position.

Rapprochement between Tehran and Washington was the most important foreign relations issue under dispute by Iranian politicians after the passing of Imam Ruhollah Khomeini in 1989. Hashemi Rafsanjani, who was the president at the time, was the leading political figure endorsing rapprochement, though the supreme leader, Ayatollah Khamenei, blocked any such attempts.[49] In an interview in July 2011, Rafsanjani said that he had tried during his time in office to initiate a dialogue with Washington but that effort had been vetoed by Ayatollah Khamenei.[50] Rafsanjani, who was president from 1989 to 1997, during the U.S. presidencies of George H. W. Bush and Bill Clinton, said: "In my time, the Americans showed signs of wanting to soften their stance, but we responded coldly because we followed the policy of the leader [Khamenei], who did not favor normalization with the U.S. . . . They [the Americans] moved forward as much as I showed openness. Maybe if we had treated the Americans in the same way that we treated the Europeans, we would have faced fewer problems."[51]

However, the supreme leader continued to strenuously oppose the establishment of diplomatic relations with the United States or even any direct negotiations up to Ahmadinejad's rise to the presidency in 2005. Former president Rafsanjani said Ahmadinejad had already "broken the taboo of negotiations with the U.S." by "sending letters to American officials that remain unanswered," referring to letters Ahmadinejad wrote to Presidents George W. Bush and Barack Obama.[52]

The Eastern Bloc Approach

This approach stressed the political nature of the crisis and the necessity to cooperate with the IAEA. However, its proponents believed that the only way to control the crisis was to create a powerful bloc supporting Iran against the West. They considered the apparent disparity between Europe and the United States on the Iran nuclear issue as different sides of the same old "carrot and stick" approach. They asserted that the United States and European Union pursued the same goals with regard to Iran's nuclear dossier. The group hence recommended that instead of relying on Europe or the United States, the Islamic Republic of Iran should try to work toward consensus with developing countries, the Islamic world, and such powers as China, Russia, and India.

The "Eastern Bloc Approach" was based on the assumptions that the Non-Aligned Movement and countries such as China and Russia would be able to reach a consensus on supporting Tehran's nuclear activities and that the Eastern bloc, specifically Russia and China, would be willing to resist heavy U.S. pressure in siding with Iran.

With this in mind, the proponents of this approach recommended that Tehran focus on the East to balance out the Western bloc and as a supplement to cooperation with the IAEA. Ali Larijani was the head of Iranian state radio and TV and also one of two representatives of the supreme leader to the Supreme National Security Council during President Khatami's tenure. He was a close friend of mine, and we would discuss foreign relations issues privately about twice a month in my office when I was the head of the Security Council's Foreign Relations Committee (1997–2005). He was an advocate of Iran's focusing on the Eastern bloc in resolving the nuclear crisis, and this was always a disputed issue in our private chats on foreign policy. It was no surprise, then, when he launched a "Look to the East" policy immediately after Ahmadinejad named him as Iran's top nuclear negotiator in August 2005.

The Conciliatory Approach

Proponents of this fifth approach believed that Iran ought to give up enrichment activities, following the Libyan model, which had become known only in December 2003. They believed that crippling sanctions by the international community and/or a military strike by the United States or Israel would be disastrous for the country's industrial and economic infrastructure. Supporters of this approach were very much in the minority.

The Pragmatic Approach

Beyond the above approaches, there was a sixth approach based on the balance of world power at the time and realpolitik assessments. This approach maintained that the nuclear crisis was purely political, though it also paid attention to the technical aspect of Tehran's activities as well as some failures on the part of Iran. Proponents of this approach maintained that in addition to heavy pressure from the United States, there were serious concerns among regional and transregional powers regarding the nature of Iran's nuclear programs. Therefore, interaction with the global community was deemed necessary to build confidence and to quiet concerns.

Advocates of this approach believed that expelling IAEA inspectors and withdrawing from the Non-Proliferation Treaty in protest of the September resolution would just cause a repeat of Iraq's experience. They argued that such confrontational behavior had been predicted by the United States and that American plans had been made accordingly. Therefore, withdrawing from the NPT would have transformed the budding international isolation of Iran into a new phase of outright hostility to all of Tehran's plans. The White House would be given a pretext to refer Iran's case to the UN Security Council and even to militarily attack Iran's nuclear installations. Proponents of the pragmatic approach construed Tehran's angry reaction to the September resolution as a sign of U.S. success.

Reporting Iran's case to the Security Council was considered by the hard-liners to be a bluff—an empty and ineffective threat—while those of us who subscribed to the Grand Bargain approach believed it was a credible threat, a clear goal of Washington and Tel Aviv, and one that would have had seriously deleterious consequences if achieved. This issue was one of the main items of dispute between us and the hard-liners. The pragmatic approach also included cooperation with the IAEA. Two points are important in this regard. First, full cooperation with the IAEA was impossible without acceptance of the September resolution; the proposal to cooperate with the IAEA while rejecting the resolution was a non sequitur. Second, even acceptance and implementation of the resolution could not guarantee that Tehran's case would not be reported to the UN Security Council. Hence, proponents of the pragmatic approach stressed the need for political interaction with the international community to break the consensus against Iran's nuclear program.

Advocates of the pragmatic approach maintained that Iran had only three options to choose from with regard to diplomatic interactions: direct talks with the United States; bargaining with the European Union; or relying on an alternative bloc, comprising Non-Aligned Movement countries, China, and Russia.

Since Iran's supreme leader at the time rejected any calls for direct negotiations with the United States, what was deemed the best possible approach was the combination of engagement with the European Union as the main negotiating party, continued talks with the Non-Aligned Movement and East Asian powers, and full cooperation with the IAEA in order to resolve outstanding disputes and eliminate technical and legal ambiguities. Rafsanjani supported this approach, as did Khatami, Rouhani, Kharrazi, and the majority of Iranian diplomats, including Khatami's nuclear negotiation team.

WHY NEGOTIATE WITH THE EUROPEAN BLOC? WHY NOT WITH THE EASTERN BLOC?

In the situation in which Tehran found itself, it was infeasible not to pursue diplomacy in all directions—with Europe, with the Eastern bloc, with the Non-Aligned Movement, and others. Nor were these diplomatic approaches mutually exclusive. Still, there was not enough time and leadership attention available to do everything at once and with equal priority. There were several important reasons for focusing diplomacy more on the European bloc than the Eastern bloc.

Advocates of concentrating on Europe proposed that outreach to the East and South should be a supplementary strategy to achieve Iran's goals, particularly to bolster leverage for bargaining in Brussels. After all, although Russia, China, and the Non-Aligned Movement exercised considerable clout in international diplomacy, they could not be relied on as a dynamic coalition leading the way toward a resolution of Iran's nuclear issue. This stemmed in part from the fact that the Eastern bloc is a concept left over from Cold War diplomacy. The designation does not provide an accurate assessment of the international balance of power and alliances since the implosion of the Soviet Union, particularly in the face of international developments after the September 11 terror attacks. Interactions among member countries of this "bloc" and the United States have shifted frequently since the 1990s.

Importantly, a combination of the Non-Aligned Movement, Russia, and China could never realistically form a unified bloc, as it would include countries lacking strong strategic bonds or sufficiently overlapping national interests. The Eastern bloc is an amalgam of profiteer powers without strong strategic bonds. As a result, the United States faces little difficulty in creating rifts among those countries. In many instances, cohesion among Non-Aligned Movement countries suffers from paltry differences and conflicts. This problem has been on full display in the diplomatic wrangling surrounding Iran's atomic activities. Countries such as India, Russia, China, and Malaysia have taken significantly different approaches to Iran's nuclear case, and U.S. pressure has predictably exacerbated this disunity. In sum, the Eastern bloc did not have enough power to withstand the pressure from a cohesive alliance of the United States and the European Union.

At the same time, it seemed that interaction with the European Union could potentially deepen the transatlantic divide. This theory was the basis of an approach stressing the prioritization of negotiations with the European countries without ignoring the Non-Aligned Movement or the rest of the Eastern bloc. The proponents of the sixth approach maintained that, by widening the rift between Washington and Brussels, diplomatic activism with Europe could also increase the relative power of the Eastern bloc and lower the political cost of its support for Iran.

We firmly believed that the Eastern bloc would not be able to prevent referral of Iran's case to the UN Security Council and that UN sanctions would be detrimental to the interests of the Islamic Republic's national security and interests. Iran would also have to make heavy concessions to world powers to mitigate the pressure from the sanctions. We were always reiterating to hard-liners that if the United States and the West succeeded in portraying Iran as a nuclear threat to the international community and coordinated world public opinion for a confrontation with Iran, the dossier on other issues of contention, such as human rights violations, missile capability, terrorism, and weapons of mass destruction would be on the U.S. agenda.

APPROACHES TAKEN BY MAJOR POWERS TO IRAN'S NUCLEAR DOSSIER

It is obvious that when one formulates a strategy to control a nuclear crisis, simplistic divisions such as "the West" and "the Islamic Republic of Iran" fall short of accurately describing the complexities of the international system. Situating the issue within an implacable conflict between East and West serves little purpose in understanding Iran's position or resolving the crisis. Such divisions as the "Islamic world" versus the "Western world" or "developing countries" versus "colonialist powers" are useful only for reducing the complex calculations of the twenty-first century into a simplistic polemic.

Understanding Iran's situation and perspective depends not only on an accurate and realistic recognition of goals, approaches, convergences, and divergences among such powers as the United States, Europe, Russia, and China in the light of developments following the September 11 attacks, but also on Iran's security concerns and the significance of the Israeli-Palestinian conflict. In this context, interests and rivalries are so intertwined that any delineation of definite and permanent "sides" supporting and opposing Iran is deeply flawed. Hence, the approaches adopted by three European powers, Russia, and China need to be analyzed with reference to interactions among those powers and the United States and Israel. My understanding of approaches taken by major powers to Iran's nuclear dossier is as follows:

1. The United States

The events of September 11, 2001, provided the United States with an opportunity to promote its political-military dominance and push international diplomatic discourse to focus on security issues on the pretext of fighting terror. Neoconservatives used every means in their power to remove obstacles to their hard-line political strategy. The militarization of the international environment after September 11, 2001, was among the most significant outcomes of the terror attacks, making the Middle East once again a focus of the United States. From the U.S. point of view, the emergence of Iran as a hostile regional power had long been considered one of the most important threats to the vital interests of the United States in the Persian Gulf and the Middle East.

An analysis of U.S. policies in the face of Iran's nuclear aspirations suggests the formulation of a trilateral strategy in the White House for containing Iran at domestic, regional, and international levels by any means possible. The United States tried to present Iran, perhaps most notably in President Bush's "axis of evil" speech, as the most significant threat to international peace and security.

The U.S. strategy was thus based on proving to the world that Iran was trying to build nuclear weaponry in violation of the Non-Proliferation Treaty. This agenda was pursued at technical, political, propaganda, and security levels, via the IAEA secretariat and Board of Governors, and the UN Security Council. The U.S. goals were the dismantling of Iran's enrichment and reprocessing facilities, bringing Iran's nuclear program to complete and permanent cessation, and even barring the country from building its nuclear power plant. Although the U.S. position on Bushehr and a peaceful nuclear program shifted at the end of the Khatami period, Washington opposed offering any incentives to encourage Iran to respond with confidence-building measures or objective guarantees that the nuclear fuel would not be diverted for military purposes. If this strategy succeeded, Iran would end up totally isolated in political and economic terms. Thus, marginalizing Iran in the region and the world would greatly reduce the cost of confronting Tehran.

From the American point of view, Iran sponsors terrorism, threatens Israel, seeks to thwart the Middle East peace process, disrupts democracy in Iraq, and denies the aspirations of its people for freedom. With this in mind, the nuclear issue and other concerns can ultimately be resolved only through regime change. In Tehran, the U.S. strategy was seen as a multipronged approach to bring about regime change in Iran.[53]

2. The European Union

Approaches taken on the other side of the Atlantic to Iran's nuclear case must be evaluated with a more nuanced view than the standard "good cop (Europe)/bad cop (United States)" portrayal. After the U.S. invasion of Iraq, Europe was torn between two contradictory inclinations. One was to reduce the polarization of the international political arena and promote joint security interests; the other was to push for the reemergence of Europe as a major diplomatic player and through multilateralism counterbalance an aggressive and hegemonic United States.

It seems that these competing interests translated into a policy of political circumspectness aimed at keeping Europe's options open, particularly with regard to the Iranian nuclear issue. A European victory in resolving Iran's nuclear issue could reestablish the old continent as the main champion of diplomatic and nonmilitary approaches to solving international crises. Whether or not European leaders had this in mind, in Tehran it was recognized by the Khatami team that successful European diplomacy on the nuclear issue could weaken U.S. hegemony in arbitrating future crises in the Middle East, with the United States forced to pay renewed attention to transatlantic cooperation, which had been largely dismissed since the buildup to the military invasion of Iraq. At the same time, Europe's failure to deal with the nuclear crisis would be a nail in the coffin of transatlantic cooperation and the EU foreign policy apparatus, with the European Union playing only a marginal role in future international crises.[54]

To present an accurate picture of the interactions between Europe and Iran, another point should be taken into account. Relations inside the European Union in 2003 could perhaps best be understood as dominated by two separate axes: London-Washington and Paris-Berlin. These two axes acted differently and in some ways complemented each other. The Paris-Berlin axis was responsible for the main push to strengthen the union and strove for international convergence within the framework of the European Union. The London-Washington axis was the guarantor of external links between the European Union and the United States, given traditional and strategic ties between Britain and the United States. Because of this link, negotiations of the EU3—the United Kingdom, France, and Germany—with Tehran were in practice understood as talks between a European/American side and an Iranian side.

It could be predicted that interactions within the European Union would directly affect quadrilateral negotiations on Iran's nuclear dossier. Internal rivalries within the EU3 would create conditions that would make negotiations more complicated and achieving a final agreement more difficult. Tehran, however, could find more room for maneuver as a result of the differences among the three countries, which would increase its chances of achieving temporary agreements. The competition between the German and the French focus on finding a solution to the crisis within the framework of the European Union and the British aim to address the crisis through the London-Washington axis would make U.S. efforts to report Iran's case to the Security Council more difficult. The major implications of this situation were increased bargaining capability for Tehran in negotiations with the three European countries on uranium enrichment, yet greater difficulty in achieving a final resolution, because any resolution would still have to involve the United States.

There was undeniable convergence between the European Union and the United States on Iran's nuclear activities, particularly on a shared opposition to Iranian uranium enrichment. Nevertheless, there were fundamental disagreements on how to interact with Tehran, Iran's peaceful use of nuclear energy, as well as nuclear and even strategic cooperation with Tehran. Iran could seek to exploit and intensify these gaps between the United States and Europe in negotiations. But even taking advantage of this opportunity, forging a final agreement between Tehran and the EU3, though not impossible, would likely require a relatively long period of confidence-building measures and diplomatic interaction.

3. Russia

Russia's approach to Iran's atomic program was inconsistent and mixed, which has made it difficult to accurately predict Moscow's behavior at critical junctures. In reality, nuclear cooperation between Iran and Russia has always been closely related to Russia's relations with the Western world (especially the United States). Russia and China were the two great powers supportive of Iran. However, Russian authorities have clearly noted that they take seriously U.S. concerns about Iran's atomic programs and draw up policies accordingly.[55]

Moscow believes that its nuclear cooperation with Tehran is important to its economic interests and geopolitical considerations, as well as its security concerns. From an economic viewpoint, nuclear cooperation with Iran is very lucrative for Russia, particularly as long as Iran remains dependent on Russia for nuclear fuel. The economic interests plus the general nonproliferation strategy of Russia prompted the Kremlin to pursue preventing Iran's access to complete the fuel cycle as its main policy. Moscow is in this regard totally attuned to the United States and the European Union. Of course, considerable differences in opinion exist on how to pressure Tehran. Russian Foreign Minister Igor Ivanov's letter to Iran's foreign minister,

Kamal Kharrazi, in the summer of 2003 called explicitly for the suspension of enrichment activities. In that letter, the Russian foreign minister questioned the "economic feasibility" of enrichment and called on Iran to purchase fuel from other countries. In addition to trying to allay proliferation concerns posed by Iran's enrichment-related activities, the policy was clearly aimed at advancing Moscow's economic interests and the country's exclusive rights to providing Iran with nuclear fuel.

A general outline of the Russian view of relations with Iran is as follows:

- From a geopolitical viewpoint, Tehran is considered a very valuable conduit for the expansion of Russia's influence in the Middle East and warm waters of the Persian Gulf.

- Good relations between Tehran and Moscow are considered an important factor in bolstering Russia's position in Central Asia, especially after Iran proved during conflicts in Chechnya and Tajikistan that it is a committed and responsible partner for Russia.

- Despite these factors, Russia has pursued an unwavering policy of opposing Iran's development of nuclear capability. The Soviet Union had cooperated with the United States in drafting and negotiating the NPT, and Russia has continued to believe that nonproliferation is strategically important. Russia's conflicting economic and geopolitical interests, along with its complicated relationship with the United States, have made Moscow's policy multifaceted and often unpredictable.

- Continued nuclear cooperation with countries like Iran is one of the main means of preventing a complete collapse of the nuclear industry inherited from the Soviet Union. Moscow's representatives have presented this argument in talks with Washington, saying that they were economically compelled to seek out markets like Iran for their nuclear industry.

- By transferring nuclear technology to Tehran despite international pressures, Russia looked to become the sole player in Iran's nuclear industry. This would provide Russia with leverage to pressure Iran on such key issues as legal rights to the Caspian Sea and détente with the West.

- Command over some aspects of Iran's nuclear program provides a good bargaining chip for negotiations with the United States. Such bargaining may even be based on disclosing secret information about Iran's nuclear activities.

Analyzing the interplay of these Russian interests, Iranian experts have offered three competing views of nuclear cooperation between Iran and Moscow. One holds that the pro-American part of the Kremlin will do its best to control the transfer of nuclear technology and material to Iran but in the end will fail. A second view posits that Russia considers continued nuclear cooperation with Iran to be in its interest to the degree that it will buck U.S. pressure for a full-scale freeze of Iran's nuclear program. The third interpretation is that Russia is intentionally stalling in dealing with Iran to wring concessions from the United States. That is, while offering Iran some support, it also has an eye on bargaining with the United States on important points.

It seems that Russia is in practice following a combination of these three approaches. That said, Russia's diplomatic record on the issue suggests that sudden convergence between Moscow and the American and European blocs has always been a possibility if pressures and incentives line up correctly. This reflects, in part, Russia's strong and consistent view that additional states should not acquire nuclear weapons.

4. China

The Supreme National Security Council's political assessment suggested that the interest of Chinese officials in expanding their relations with the United States would ultimately trump the various ties between Tehran and Beijing. This was based on the following judgments:

- Relations between Tehran and Beijing lack lasting strategic bonds. Although economic cooperation between the two countries has risen dramatically over the past few years, especially in the field of energy, bilateral relations are still at an incipient stage.
- China enjoys fewer bargaining chips than Russia when dealing with the United States on the Iran issue. We believed that if pressured

by escalating tension into a definite choice between Iran and the United States, Beijing would do what it can to maintain "impartiality" but would ultimately be more likely to side with Washington.

- Strategic cooperation between Iran and China could be in China's economic interests while catering to Iran's immediate needs.
- To maintain bargaining power when dealing with Washington over the Taiwan issue, China has expanded arms sales and cooperation with some adversaries of the United States, including Iran. However, this cooperation has always been limited, conditional, and under China's full control.

IRAN'S OBJECTIVES IN THE FINAL STRATEGY TO MANAGE THE CRISIS

The nuclear standoff involved a great number of domestic and international factors. The number of those factors and the domestic and foreign consequences of the September 2003 resolution were such that it had reached a crisis pitch. The international context of the crisis in the wake of the September 11 terror attacks and American invasion of Iraq lent it special urgency.

Until Iran's Supreme National Security Council[56] became directly involved in the case and appointed a team of nuclear negotiators on October 6, 2003, Tehran did not provide a clear-cut response to the international community's demands or the IAEA Board of Governors' resolution. The most important official comment up until that time came from the Expediency Council chairman and former president, Hashemi Rafsanjani,[57] who indicated that the Islamic Republic of Iran had decided to negotiate on accepting the Additional Protocol with reservations, as the United States had done. Rafsanjani gave little indication as to Iran's position on such issues as the suspension of uranium enrichment or further cooperation with IAEA inspectors.

I had regular meetings with Rafsanjani to discuss foreign and domestic developments during my time at the Supreme National Security Council because I found him an extremely clever political strategist. We discussed Iran's nuclear status in the summer of 2003, even before the IAEA's September resolution. He was supportive of the pragmatic approach, while he was skeptical about adopting the Additional Protocol or suspending enrichment. During these discussions he told me that the pragmatic approach was the best option, but that one should keep in mind that without America on board, the Europeans would not be willing or able to make a final deal with Iran on the nuclear issue and therefore could use negotiations only to buy time and provide stopgap measures rather than resolving the issue. Finally, he said that implementation of the Additional Protocol with reservations would be possible along with very short-term suspension as confidence-building measures, but that if this did not suffice, negotiations would fail because Iran would not accept long-term suspension.

As soon as the nuclear case was referred to the Supreme National Security Council, a pyramidal structure was created for decisionmaking. In that period I was the head of the Security Council's Foreign Relations Committee. We decided to study and discuss the developments at three different levels before reaching final decisions at a meeting of the highest level. At the lower level of the pyramid, we established a committee, headed by one of the Foreign Ministry's directors and comprising experienced scholars from relevant organizations. In that committee, all developments related to the nuclear issue were studied from various angles.

The second level of the pyramid comprised another expert committee. Its participants were at the level of deputy ministers of relevant organizations and headed by the secretary of the Supreme National Security Council. This committee supplemented activities of the lower committee.

The pyramid's third level was a high committee, which was also headed by the secretary of the Supreme National Security Council and whose membership consisted of various ministers and heads of relevant organizations, five members of the Supreme National Security Council (the foreign minister, the defense minister, the intelligence minister, and the two representatives of the supreme leader at the Security Council), plus Gholam Reza Aghazadeh, the head of the Iran Atomic Energy Organization and adviser to the supreme leader. This high committee was to be the main decisionmaker, though its decisions could be implemented only after obtaining the supreme leader's approval.[58] The supreme leader attended important meetings of this high committee, as did all eleven members of the Supreme National Security Council plus Rafsanjani, Dr. Velayati, Mir Hossein Mousavi,[59] and Mohsen Rezaee,[60] and other prominent politicians whom the supreme leader wished to include in the decisionmaking process to create greater domestic consensus on nuclear policies.

Early assessments of the September resolution suggested that Tehran faced something of a Catch-22. Iran's policymakers were suspicious and concerned that even if Iran cooperated with the IAEA in accordance with the resolution, the United States might use Iranian disclosures about past activities to justify proceeding with reporting Iran's case to the UN Security Council.[61] Tehran could choose between two paths, but both seemed to lead to New York. In the first path, the Board of Governors of the IAEA had asked Iran in its September resolution to provide the agency with full disclosure of its nuclear activities. In view of Iran's past failures, if the full scope of Iran's nuclear activities were exposed, it would have provided grounds for the referral of Iran's case to the UN Security Council.* But in the second path, rejecting the request of the Board of Governors would have been construed as evidence of noncooperation and an affront to the international community, which would also provide an opportunity for the United States to implement its strategy of taking Iran's case beyond the IAEA.

Studies at that time determined that neither the "confrontation" nor "surrender" option was in line with the large-scale interests of the Islamic Republic of Iran. Hence, experts scrambled to formulate an alternative, multifaceted strategy in an attempt to control the crisis.

---

* Editor's note: The Libyan case suggests the possibility of an alternative. After Libya decided to provide full transparency and reveal all its past nuclear activities, its case was reported to the UN Security Council in a favorable way, with no further sanctions or penalties.

CHAPTER THREE

FROM TEHRAN TO PARIS

FRAMEWORK OF IRAN'S NEW NUCLEAR DIPLOMACY (2003–2005)

H assan Rouhani was appointed to the newly created post of Iran's chief nuclear negotiator by general consensus in a meeting of high-ranking officials on October 1, 2003. Rouhani told me, "I declined to take on this responsibility but then changed my mind following a private meeting with the Leader on October 5, where he told me, 'This is a responsibility on my shoulders, relieve me of it and take on the responsibility.'" Rouhani and his team then set out to design a framework for a new strategy in dealing with the nuclear issue.[1] The members of this team had been suggested by Ali Akbar Velayati, the supreme leader's adviser on international affairs and a former foreign minister, and approved by the ministerial level committee.

Tehran's new approach was based on several basic premises:

- If Iran's case were reported to the UN Security Council, it would have dire consequences for Iran in view of domestic conditions and a lack of contingency plans.

- If Iran's case were taken out of the IAEA's purview in Vienna and to the UN Security Council in New York, it would be a triumph for the United States and Israel.
- Pressure from the United States, damaging anti-Iran propaganda, and some failures on the part of Iran had led to a widespread global consensus against Iran.
- Iran needed to consider the nuclear case to be far more serious than ordinary diplomatic disputes and as closely related to the long-term grand strategy of the United States for the Middle East.
- Emotional and angry reactions to the September resolution would merely make the case more complicated and intensify existing disputes.
- The final goal should be engagement with the West.

In formulating a crisis resolution strategy, Iran sought to achieve the following goals at minimum cost and in the shortest possible time:

1. Do away with the threat of the IAEA Board of Governors' reporting Iran's nuclear case to the United Nations Security Council.
2. Diminish the opposition by the international community to an Iranian nuclear program in principle.
3. Address the serious concerns of various countries about the nature of Iran's nuclear activities.
4. Greatly increase the cost of a possible U.S. or Israeli military attack aimed at destroying Iran's nuclear facilities.[2]
5. Transform tense relations between Iran and the International Atomic Energy Agency into more amicable interactions.
6. Present a plan for the resolution of all technical and legal ambiguities that were enumerated by the IAEA.
7. Lay the groundwork for the transfer of nuclear technology to Iran and for nuclear cooperation with diverse partners other than Russia.
8. Manage existing political and other pressure on Iran.
9. Reduce hostility to Iran in world public opinion and correct misunderstandings about the country's nuclear activities.
10. Eliminate negative social and economic effects of the crisis domestically.
11. Secure greater understanding and support for the government's position among the Iranian public.

12. Reduce to a minimum domestic political rifts and confrontations over Iran's interaction with the IAEA and the international community.

13. Pursue a long-term strategy of "turning threats into opportunities" and, in this way, resolve some long-standing problems facing the Islamic Republic of Iran, especially with regard to economic, technological, security, political, and nuclear cooperation with the West, including the United States.

In line with these goals, a logical approach to and treatment of the crisis depended on Iran's formulation of a comprehensive strategy with legal, technical, political, and public relations aspects. This strategy had to be pursued through diplomatic negotiations, not through either confrontation or surrender. Hence, many discussions in various scholarly and decisionmaking meetings focused on the prospect of negotiations. As far as partners for negotiations, Iran had three major options to choose from: the United States, Europe, and a third bloc comprising the Non-Aligned Movement and such countries as Russia and China. High-ranking authorities in the country did not give the go-ahead for negotiations with the United States, as the supreme leader considered the establishment of diplomatic relations or even conducting direct negotiations with the United States to be redlines.[3] From the two remaining options and in view of the nature, bargaining power, and behavior of the Non-Aligned Movement plus Russia and China, Iran opted to negotiate with Germany, France, the United Kingdom, and Russia (dubbed the 3+1 group) as the main focus of its diplomatic policy. Thus, Tehran chose to follow the "sixth approach" explained in the previous chapter.

Europe and Russia, frustrated with Washington's unilateralism, had their own reasons for getting involved in the escalating crisis. Brussels was striving to restore the status of the European Union within the hierarchy of international power. A new rhetorical emphasis on "European strategy" as an effective alternative to "American militarism" was evidence of that effort. The European Union and Russia were trying to prevent a repetition of the Iraq war and to remove sources of tension that threatened to deepen the transatlantic rift. Europe and Russia were trying through "soft power" approaches to counter the domination of the United States over the Middle East and to establish themselves as relevant to the region's future. The leaders in Paris and Berlin wanted to bolster their strategic cooperation, and the European Union also wanted to mend the "Germany-France-Britain" triangle. Russia considered Iran an important neighbor and was willing to play a key role in diplomacy and the management of Iran's nuclear crisis.

DEVELOPMENTS LEADING TO THE SA'DABAD NEGOTIATIONS— OCTOBER 2003

After Iran's main strategy to face the nuclear crisis was approved and a framework for bargaining was determined, plans were made to initiate talks with Brussels and invite the foreign ministers of the EU3. The maneuvering space available to Iran's diplomats and even subsequent measures to be taken in the face of the September resolution were laid out in detail in the meeting.[4] The most important objective of Iran's negotiators was to obtain maximum concessions from their foreign counterparts in return for cooperation.

Iran's invitation to the foreign ministers of the three European countries was immediately welcomed. The EU3, however, insisted that a simultaneous visit to Iran by French, British, and German diplomats was a necessary prerequisite for high-level negotiations. The request was granted by Iran, and preparations were made for the reception of the EU3 ministries.

EU3 diplomats weren't Tehran's only visitors. IAEA chief Mohamed ElBaradei arrived in Tehran on October 16, 2003. At the time of his visit, Tehran had not yet revealed its final stance on the September resolution. Aside from the Additional Protocol, the most important issues discussed with ElBaradei included the import of centrifuges to Iran and aspects of Tehran's peaceful nuclear program. The International Atomic Energy Agency had announced long before that Iran's remarkable progress in developing the nuclear fuel cycle could not have been possible without testing centrifuges or the introduction of UF_6.

That claim had led to an important technical dispute between Iran's Atomic Energy Organization and the IAEA. Tehran's denial and the agency's insistence that UF_6 must have been introduced into centrifuges in Iran was important because introducing gas into centrifuges without informing the IAEA could have been construed as noncompliance on the part of Iran with its obligations, and thus provide legal grounds for the referral of Iran's nuclear case to the UN Security Council. Therefore, the United States insisted that the director general include Iran's "noncompliance" with the Non-Proliferation Treaty in his next report to the Board of Governors.

During talks with Rouhani and Gholam Reza Aghazadeh, the head of the Atomic Energy Organization of Iran, ElBaradei called for the suspension of Iran's fuel-cycle activities. The main topic discussed by Rouhani and ElBaradei was the definition of "suspension." A one-on-one meeting between Rouhani and ElBaradei was held in Sa'dabad Palace on October 17, 2003. Immediately after the meeting, I asked Dr. Rouhani about El-Baradei's view on the definition of suspension, the key issue for a possible agreement. Rouhani told me that ElBaradei had made it clear that if Iran avoided the introduction of gas into the centrifuges, it would be considered to have suspended fuel-cycle activities.* ElBaradei also explains in his 2011 memoir that, technically, suspension required only halting the introduction of gas into centrifuges.[5]

Rouhani also told the negotiation team that he raised this question three times with ElBaradei and that the director general repeatedly confirmed that by suspending the introduction of gas into the centrifuges, Iran would meet the IAEA suspension requirements. This definition could enable the negotiation team to persuade the leaders of the Islamic Republic of Iran to accept suspension of the fuel cycle because such suspension would be much more limited than what the September IAEA resolution had called for and could be construed as a triumph for Iran in its bargaining with the IAEA. Officials in Tehran assured the director general that they would accept provisional implementation of the Additional Protocol and pursue a policy of full transparency as a confidence-building measure.[6]

Just as ElBaradei was leaving Iran, directors general of the EU3 foreign ministries arrived in Tehran on October 19, 2003. This crossing of paths allowed a brief talk between the European diplomats and Dr. ElBaradei at the VIP pavilion of Tehran's Mehrabad International Airport. In three rounds of negotiation between EU3 directors general and Iranian diplomats, we expected to finalize the main elements of the draft agreement between the EU3 foreign ministers and Rouhani. I led Iran's negotiation

---

* Editor's note: ElBaradei in his memoir does not mention that he defined suspension in his October 2003 meeting with Rouhani, or that his definition was different from the September IAEA board resolution requiring Iran to suspend "all enrichment-related activities." The differences between ElBaradei's privately communicated definition and that of the IAEA board proved durably problematic.

team. The EU3 directors general welcomed my offer to include in our agreement cooperation on political, security, and economic issues and on combating terrorism and weapons of mass destruction. We concluded the draft agreement with only the suspension issue left for a ministerial-level meeting with Rouhani. The four-hour discussion between Rouhani and the EU3 ministers on October 21 was one of the most difficult and complicated diplomatic negotiations I had witnessed in my career.

The sticking point was the suspension issue. EU3 ministers were reiterating suspension, while Iran's top negotiator, Dr. Rouhani, was rejecting it. Reaching the conclusion that they would not be able to agree, the EU3 ministers decided to end the negotiation, cancel their planned meeting with President Khatami, and leave directly for the airport. I proposed a recess and privately told Rouhani that we ought to avoid a breakdown of negotiations, suggesting that he talk with the president and the office of the supreme leader to get permission to compromise on the definition of the suspension agreed to by the IAEA. We had been assured by ElBaradei that the suspension of the introduction of gas would be sufficient, but now the EU3 were insisting on more. Rouhani called the president and the office of the leader and explained the status of the negotiations. After a twenty-minute telephone conversation, both the president and the office of the leader finally consented to the idea, and intense quadripartite talks resumed. They agreed that Iran would temporarily and voluntarily suspend enrichment, based on ElBaradei's definition and nothing further.

Though Italy was at the time rotational head of the European Union, the diplomatic delegation of the EU3 was led by the director general of the French Foreign Ministry. This showed that the EU3 was determined to settle the crisis. The Paris-Berlin axis, as the driving force behind the European Union and for European convergence in the face of American hegemony, was not willing to include Italy directly in negotiations. The willingness of France and Germany to engage in multilateral interaction with Iran as an alternative to Washington's unilateralism indicated increased resistance within Europe to pro-U.S. tendencies of such EU members as Britain and Italy. Nevertheless, I believe Italy wanted to participate in negotiations for prestige and to protect trade with Iran.

The situation created both threats and opportunities for Iran. The rift inside the European Union made bargaining between Iran and the world powers easier in some aspects and more difficult in others. Britain's delegation to negotiations aimed to ensure U.S. interests. However, the simultaneous presence of France and Germany stood to widen the transatlantic gap and weaken the U.S. position. And despite the United Kingdom's close relationship with the United States, British Foreign Secretary Jack Straw shared with his German and French counterparts the goal of using negotiations to remove any pretext for another American preemptive war. During the October negotiations, Straw and German Foreign Minister Joschka Fischer told me that the objective of EU3 engagement with Iran was to serve as a "human shield" to prevent an American or Israeli military strike. ElBaradei recounts in his memoir that Straw and Fischer told him the same thing.[7]

It should be noted that during those talks, the EU directors general urged Iran to "cease" its nuclear activities, not to "suspend" them. We categorically rejected their request and were firm that no talks would be held on that matter. Finally, the European side accepted the idea of conducting negotiations with Iran on the basis of short-term "suspension" and not "complete cessation" of Iran's peaceful nuclear activities. During those talks, the negotiating parties accepted a framework of "mutual commitments of both sides," that is, Iran and the European Union, to replace the unilateral requests contained in the IAEA resolution. This principle, which was accepted by the EU3 after heavy pressure and bargaining from Iran's diplomats, changed considerably, in Tehran's favor, the political calculus created by the September resolution.

The possibility of a ministerial meeting between Tehran and the EU3 elicited surprisingly strong reactions from various circles. At that time, Israel considered any agreement between Iran and the international community a success for Iran and a failure for Washington. Israel basically believes that bolstering Tehran's international standing would weaken its own position. This approach has compelled Israel to use the most provocative rhetoric and make the worst accusations against the Islamic Republic. From a Western point of view, Israel was concerned about direct threats via Iranian activities in Lebanon and Syria and support for Palestinian groups, while historically, Israel welcomed Iran as a counter to the Arabs.

Weeks before the meetings, on September 28, 2003, Israeli military intelligence officials stressed the necessity of attacking Iran's atomic installations. Also, the head of the Foreign Intelligence Department of the Mossad presented a report to the Knesset claiming that Iran's nuclear activities were a major threat to the very existence of Israel and declared his country's readiness to launch a military offensive on Iran's atomic facilities.[8] Israeli Defense Minister Shaul Mofaz announced on December 7, 2003, that Iran would reach the point of no return within a year. He called on the international community to prepare for "confronting Tehran's nuclear ambitions." Just two days before that, Israel had announced that it had purchased twenty advanced fighter-bomber aircraft from the United States that were capable of attacking Iran's nuclear installations.[9] Those positions, which were revealed in September through December 2003, clearly showed that Israel was working seriously to increase tensions between Iran and the international community.

Inside Iran, the possibility of a simultaneous visit to Tehran by foreign ministers of the EU3 was powerful enough to provoke sensitivities and cause resistance in some quarters. Several groups opposed the negotiations.

The first group comprised those who believed, on the basis of revolutionary ideology rather than expert analyses, that negotiations with the Europeans were categorically against the national interests of the country.

The second group included those who viewed the crisis through the lens of its effects on upcoming parliamentary and presidential elections and had little desire to see their opponents achieve high-profile success. Factional tendencies unfortunately led this issue of national interest to be seen as a political football for short-term disputes.

The third group included those who maintained that more tension and serious confrontation between Iran and the West serve their interests best. That tendency was observed both in expatriate opposition groups that sought to topple the Islamic system and among some political activists inside the country.

The last group consisted of those who, due to personal problems with negotiating diplomats, hoped to see them fail to contain the crisis. Dr. Rouhani was one of the potential candidates for the 2005 presidential elections. Rouhani's competitors were well aware that success in the nuclear negotiation would be a boon to his electoral prospects.

Of course, some political developments in Tehran in October 2003 reduced the Islamic Republic of Iran's bargaining power during negotiations with the Europeans. The decision by some reformist members of the Parliament (Majles) to pass a "triple urgency plan" to force the government into accepting the Additional Protocol was one such development. The bill, which was never passed, would have taken away a valuable bargaining chip and greatly reduced Iran's ability for diplomatic maneuvering in negotiations with the West.

The premature announcement of Iran's willingness to implement the 93+2 Additional Protocol and to "suspend part of its enrichment activities" was another step that reduced the leverage held by Iran's diplomats in political dealings. Before the beginning of the Sa'dabad negotiations, some Iranian authorities had implied that Iran was willing to implement the Additional Protocol. President Mohammad Khatami's remarks during a news conference after meeting with the Pakistani prime minister[10] and Foreign Minister Kamal Kharrazi's statements in press interviews were examples of positions taken by Iran's officials that made it clear to the EU3 that Iran would ultimately accept the Additional Protocol.

Before the Sa'dabad meeting between the EU3 ministers and Dr. Rouhani, high-ranking Iranian officials, including the president, indicated Tehran's readiness to accept short-term and limited suspension of enrichment activities to build confidence with the world and reduce political pressure. That decision was the result of requests by Iran's strategic partners and the International Atomic Energy Agency, along with the general air of crisis at the time. Iran sought to include partial suspension of enrichment in the political negotiation process with the international community.

However, when the ministers had arrived in Tehran and begun negotiating, two major sources of friction between Iran and the EU3 became evident. The EU3 considered suspension of Iran's enrichment program a legal obligation based on the September resolution of the IAEA Board of Governors. Relying on the September resolution, the EU ministers insisted that all activities related to enrichment in Iran be suspended immediately.

After four rounds of negotiations in two days (on October 21–22) at the expert and ministerial levels, Rouhani accepted suspension only because Mohamed ElBaradei had assured him a week earlier that requirements of suspension would be fulfilled if Iran abstained from introducing gas into centrifuges, which was a less demanding requirement than the suspension of all enrichment-related activities called for in the September IAEA resolution. On the basis of this understanding, the supreme leader confirmed the temporary suspension. The "Tehran statement" was agreed upon and made public at 2 p.m. on October 21, 2003.

I do not know whether ElBaradei informed the EU3 or the United States about his negotiations and agreement with Rouhani on the definition of suspension, but there are six important points to note on this matter. First, the IAEA Board of Governors' June statement requested only that Iran suspend the introduction of gas into centrifuges. Second, Rouhani clearly mentioned to the EU3 ministers in a meeting held in Tehran on October 21 that he was accepting the suspension based on ElBaradei's definition and nothing more. Third, in a meeting on November 8, 2003, where I was present, Rouhani complained about the changes made to the scope of suspension and ElBaradei responded, "Yes! This is still my view but it changed due to the decision of others." Fourth, as ElBaradei explains in his 2011 memoir, there is a distinction between purely technical definitions and political demands: technically, suspension required only halting the introduction of gas into the centrifuges; the Europeans' broader definition was based more than anything on their political agenda.[11] Fifth, in a meeting held in Brussels on November 17, 2003, in which I participated, Rouhani told the EU3 ministers: "In Tehran, we agreed on suspension based on the IAEA's definition as ElBaradei defined it for us and we accepted. Yet, you put him under pressure and wrote him a letter asking to widen the scope of the suspension. We were supposed to be sincere to each other. You violated your commitments...." In response, the EU3 ministers said that in their view and also of the technicians of the IAEA, suspension should include all enrichment-related activities, adding that ElBaradei was *not* the IAEA. Sixth, I privately discussed the negotiations with ElBaradei with my EU3 counterparts, stressing that Iran had accepted suspension only because of the definition agreed to with ElBaradei in his private meeting with Rouhani, and I found that they already knew about ElBaradei's interpretation of suspension. This suggested to me that ElBaradei had already discussed this technical definition with them but that they had rejected it in favor of their own politically determined definition.

THE "TEHRAN STATEMENT" AND ACHIEVEMENTS OF SA'DABAD NEGOTIATIONS

The Tehran agreement seemed to be a mutual victory for Iran and the EU3. The results of the Sa'dabad meeting took the wind out of the sails of the American push for international convergence against Tehran's interests, which could have ended in a repetition of Iraq's experience. This reality was clearly noted by the supreme leader, who said in an address to government officials that,

> The international community is afraid of atomic weapons and a staunch foe of Islam—of which the nation of Iran is aware—and has raised sensitivities in the world's public opinion and among many states by falsely claiming that Iran is trying to build nuclear weapons so as to attain its goal of forging an international consensus against the Islamic Republic of Iran. For this reason, the Islamic Republic of Iran has chosen a wise alternative to both preserve its nuclear technology and expose its nuclear activities to the world to refute false propaganda launched by the Americans and Zionists.[12]

The Tehran negotiations constituted a comprehensive step forward, and were a far cry from what some domestic media called "giving in to the pressures of the West."[13] The achievements of those negotiations were so significant for Iran that some Israeli media outlets, as well as others close to White House neoconservatives, described them as an Iranian success in cheating Europe. The talks signified undeniable importance because they marked a balancing point between two contradictory policies, that is, submission to the demands of the IAEA Board of Governors and maintaining Iran's basic position to meet the country's long-term interests through the implementation of a broad-based strategy.

The Sa'dabad negotiations had been planned not as an endgame but as a step toward a final goal (achieving an internationally accepted peaceful nuclear program) and aimed at controlling the existing crisis. Fundamentally, the Tehran statement opened a middle road between submission and confrontation, extricating Iran to a degree from the demands of the September resolution.

That Tehran secured the agreement of the EU3 to oppose the referral of Iran's case to the UN Security Council was one of the most important achievements of the Sa'dabad conference. The assurances of the European foreign ministers at Sa'dabad that they would use their Security Council vetoes if the United States managed to bring Iran's case to New York was construed as a major international breakthrough for Iran. The meeting's concluding statement, which emphasized the necessity of solving all problems within the framework of the International Atomic Energy Agency, was the legal rendition of the Sa'dabad agreement.

The agreement that the "full implementation of Iran's decisions after being upheld by [the] director general of the IAEA should resolve the current situation within the Board of Governors" also increased Iran's power to pressure the international community to close the case as soon as possible and reduced the ability of the United States to escalate the crisis. It promised to effectively transform a "political and security dispute" into a "technical and legal dispute."

The agreement also lowered tensions over points of technical and legal dispute with the IAEA. The Board of Governors' request that Iran provide a complete picture of its past nuclear activities was one of the most challenging technical and legal issues of the case. Whichever course Iran followed—either offering a comprehensive report about past nuclear activities (which would have reflected Iran's failures to inform the IAEA) or refraining from preparing it (which would have been construed as noncompliance with the requests of the international community)—could potentially lead to Iran's referral to the UN Security Council.

The Tehran negotiations provided an opportunity to break the deadlock and get the EU's support for Iran's taking corrective measures with the IAEA on mutually acceptable terms. The wording of the agreement, which expressed that "Iran . . . should clarify and compensate any possible failure within the framework of the IAEA," was along these lines. It showed that even if the Islamic Republic of Iran's failures were proven, the EU3 would prevent referring its case to New York.

All this was a considerable departure from the Board of Governors' September meeting, when the European Union aligned closely with the U.S. position and refrained from upholding Iran's right to pursue its nuclear program peacefully. At that time, under pressure from the Non-Aligned

Movement and South Africa, European countries had finally accepted the inclusion of a general phrase about nuclear rights in the resolution, but it did not contain any direct reference to Iran. In reality, despite some lip service, before the Sa'dabad meeting the EU was not willing to accept Iran's right to peaceful nuclear technology. This was quite evident in diplomatic negotiations as well as the political signals sent by Brussels. With this in mind, the Tehran statement was a very important turning point. The EU3 had not only accepted Iran's basic right to nuclear energy in the final statement of the meeting, but had also suggested peaceful nuclear cooperation with Iran to develop nuclear technology.

This recognition of Iran's basic rights was linked to a revised view of the suspension issue. The September 2003 resolution had called on Iran "to suspend all further uranium enrichment-related activities, including the further introduction of nuclear material into Natanz, and, as a confidence-building measure, any reprocessing activities, pending provision by the Director General of the assurances required by Member States."

The suspension requested in the September resolution seemed to represent an international consensus and was arguably obligatory. With the Sa'dabad (Tehran) statement, however, Iran's suspension of nuclear and all related activities was downgraded to a *voluntary* act, and just for confidence building.[14] Moreover, the Iranian leadership had obtained ElBaradei's judgment that suspension need only apply to the introduction of nuclear material into centrifuges, and not all enrichment-related activities. All of this was a considerable victory, and the more limited definition of suspension was more palatable to Iran's leadership.

The European approach to the issue of the Additional Protocol was similarly toned down, opening up the possibility for a more amicable resolution. The European foreign ministers stressed that adopting the Additional Protocol would by no means compromise the "sovereignty, credibility, dignity, or national security" of Iran. That approach contrasted sharply with the imperative tone of the September resolution. The statement made it clear that Iran's Parliament was the ultimate authority on implementation of the Additional Protocol and that the Khatami administration had committed itself only to provisionally implementing the Additional Protocol as a confidence-building measure.

Negotiations in October were considered the first step in a long process for solving problems between Iran and the European Union. The promise of "easier access to modern technology and other items in various fields" indicated a positive outlook for bilateral strategic cooperation and undermined U.S. sanctions. The agreement also laid out a new and positive prospect for future security cooperation between Iran and the European Union in the region. In doing so, the agreement precluded possible military measures against Iran's nuclear installations by the United States or Israel and paved the way for the protection and development of Iran's infrastructure.

Furthermore, the statement emphasized the importance of creating a region free from weapons of mass destruction in a veiled reference to Israel, which possessed such weapons and was considered Iran's staunchest enemy.

The simultaneous visit to Tehran by three European foreign ministers was a unique event. The meetings showed that Iran was a major power in the region and an important country in the developing order of the Middle East, as well as a credible negotiating partner.

The negotiations also provided an opportunity to prepare plans to bargain with other powers and respond to domestic and foreign public opinion, as well as cope with economic aspects of the crisis and reduce its social impact. Iran also managed to forge considerable accord among political factions inside the country through the agreement. The foreign policy consensus reached its climax after the supreme leader declared his resolute support for the agreement on November 3, 2003.

When one analyzes the consequences of the Sa'dabad negotiations, it is necessary to pay attention to an important point. In reality, all stipulations included in the October 21 statement had been approved by high-ranking Iranian officials a few days earlier. Iran was determined to accept the Additional Protocol (and had in August 2003 declared its readiness to implement it) and to boost cooperation with the IAEA. Negotiations by Dr. ElBaradei in Tehran and his definition of enrichment suspension also made palatable Iran's agreement to short-term suspension of part of the fuel cycle. Various debates were carried out at different levels of Iran's government about how to proclaim those decisions: whether unilaterally or through negotiations with other powers. Iran managed to gain more concessions through the Sa'dabad negotiations on October 21 with the

EU3 than it would have had it pledged to accept the Additional Protocol and to suspend enrichment unilaterally.

Nevertheless, a political protest organized in front of Sa'dabad Palace during negotiations on October 21 was a clear sign of plans among some in Iran to oppose engagement with the West to resolve the nuclear impasse. The demonstrators decried the outcome of the talks even while we were still negotiating and nobody knew what the result would be.

RESOLUTION OF TEHRAN-IAEA DISPUTE THROUGH POLITICAL NEGOTIATIONS

The agreement signed between Iran and the EU3 in October 2003 provided the guarantees Tehran had sought to prevent the referral of its nuclear dossier to the UN Security Council. This facilitated cooperation between Iran and the IAEA and marked the beginning of a confidence-building process. In the wake of the September 2003 resolution, Iran had, as previously discussed, seemingly faced two options, both of which led to the UN Security Council. After getting out of this quandary, Iran decided to respond immediately to one of the main requests of the IAEA Board of Governors by presenting a complete report on its nuclear programs.

The Iran Atomic Energy Organization drew up the report, which was delivered to the IAEA on October 22, a move applauded in diplomatic circles as Iran's first practical step to address the September resolution. The report was in a way a formal confession of its major past failures to inform the IAEA of some nuclear activities in a timely fashion.

I believe that the IAEA was already aware of major aspects of Iran's nuclear activities. Information submitted to the agency by Iran's nuclear partners, intelligence gathered from espionage activities, and the accidental leak of secret information in scientific publications had left no major gaps in the IAEA's knowledge.[15,*] In view of that reality, Iranian officials knew that denying past failures would merely intensify international suspicions and threaten the interests of the country.[16] Thus, the decisionmaking apparatus in Iran considered the official release of information about all aspects of the country's nuclear activities and its cooperation with the

---

* Editor's note: Subsequent investigations by the IAEA raised additional issues, about which the IAEA has sought more information and greater transparency.

IAEA to be a tactical measure. The centrifuge testing with uranium hexafluoride, uranium conversion, and the issue of plutonium were included as major themes in the report because denying Iran's activities in those fields was no longer possible. The Tehran agreement thus paved the way for open discussion of several issues:

1. Centrifuge Testing with Uranium Hexafluoride

The issue of introducing gas to centrifuges at Kalaye Electric Company and testing gas centrifuges was one of the most important technical issues of the nuclear case. The IAEA clearly asserted that Iran's progress in developing technology would have been impossible without enrichment tests involving the introduction of uranium hexafluoride gas into centrifuges. That conclusion was taken to be so certain by the agency that it had even been cited in the September 2003 resolution.[17]

That resolution had in so many words called on Tehran to confirm the introduction of gas to centrifuges in cooperation with the IAEA's inspectors. As the IAEA was pressing its point despite Tehran's denial, samples taken at Kalaye Electric Company showed that traces of enriched uranium existed in those installations. Samplings at other places, including the Natanz facility, also revealed evidence of highly enriched uranium.[18] That discovery, combined with Iran's denial of any nuclear testing, contributed to major international suspicion about the goals and nature of Tehran's nuclear programs. Suspicion was one of the most important factors that bolstered the hard line of the United States and led to the adoption of the strongly worded Board of Governors' resolution in September 2003.

The discovery of highly enriched uranium particles at Iran's installations was first reported by the IAEA to a representative of Iran's Atomic Energy Organization in Vienna on June 10, 2003. The news caused grave concern in Tehran. We called for an urgent meeting of the National Security Council to discuss the case. At the meeting the conclusion was reached that, because Iran had not undertaken non-peaceful nuclear activities, the discovery of the highly enriched uranium particles could be a plot by the Israeli or U.S. intelligence services. In further meetings, the Atomic Energy Organization suggested a new hypothesis: that the traces of highly enriched uranium could have been from secondhand imported centrifuges that had been contaminated before they were transferred to Iran from Pakistan. With these two possibilities in mind, experts decided that continued secrecy would only intensify suspicions on the part of the IAEA and the international community and would preclude the possibility of a practical solution to the crisis.

In the comprehensive report submitted to the IAEA in October 2003, Iran finally admitted that it had carried out undeclared tests on centrifuges using UF_6 at Kalaye Electric Company[19] and had enriched uranium-235 up to 1.2 percent. Tehran also announced that higher levels of enrichment were due to contamination of imported centrifuge parts that had been probably used as part of a nuclear weapons program by another country before transfer to Iran.[20] The IAEA concluded that the tests of the environmental samples in question showed that Iran's explanation about the foreign origin of the highly enriched uranium contamination was likely true.[21] The diplomats on the nuclear negotiation team were not informed about the technical aspects, including the above-mentioned cases.

2. Conversion Process

Until the October 22 report and most notably in a February 2003 statement, Iran denied having done any testing or having experience in complex processes such as converting uranium dioxide, or UO_2, to UF_4 (uranium tetrafluoride), or UF_4 to UF_6. After further inspections by the IAEA revealed contradictions in Iran's statement, Tehran admitted in August 2003 that it had carried out tests and experiments in a radiochemistry laboratory of Tehran Nuclear Research Center to convert UO_2 to UF_4 using depleted UO_2, which had already been declared to the IAEA by Iran.

When Iran offered its full report to the IAEA in October 2003, the country expanded on its previous statements and admitted that major tests and experiments had been carried out on the scale of grams and kilograms, including on the conversion of U_3O_8 to UO_2, in research at Tehran Nuclear Research Center that dated back to the 1980s. From 1991 to 1993, Iran had begun converting UF_4 to UF_6 in a series of tests and experiments at the research center. After the release of the October report, the IAEA insisted that these disclosures had been offered only after the agency discovered the tests.[22]

It should be noted that even before the October report, Iran had announced that a trivial amount of UF_4 had been lost in the process of conversion to metal. However, Tehran admitted in October 2003 that the "lost" UF_4 was in fact used in experiments in converting UF_4 to UF_6 in the early 1990s. According to Tehran, most of the equipment used in conversion and reduction experiments in 1999 was no longer active and had been sent to a waste storage facility.

3. Tests on Plutonium

The issue of plutonium reprocessing is one of the most thought-provoking points in Iran's October 2003 report. Limited plutonium testing was carried out as one of the most secret parts of Tehran's nuclear activities. However, during Mohamed ElBaradei's visit to Iran the week before the report's issuance and during subsequent negotiations with IAEA's inspectors, the IAEA made clear that it had been informed of those limited laboratory activities.

Iran admitted in its October 2003 report that it had carried out tests and experiments on reprocessing at Tehran Nuclear Research Center between 1988 and 1992. According to Iran's announcement, a few kilograms of depleted UO_2 pellets had been produced at Isfahan Nuclear Technology Center and irradiated for about two weeks at the Tehran Research Reactor. About half of the irradiated pellets were reprocessed using three shielded boxes that were put in a hot cell inside the nuclear security building of Tehran Nuclear Research Center, and the separated plutonium—in the form of a plutonium nitrate solution—had been stored at the laboratory of the pharmaceutical firm Jaber Ebne Hayyan. The other half of the irradiated UO_2 pellets had been kept in highly shielded boxes before being buried at the Tehran Nuclear Research Center.[23]

NUCLEAR DEVELOPMENTS LEADING TO THE NOVEMBER 2003 RESOLUTION

After this presentation of what the Iran Atomic Energy Organization told us was a complete picture of past nuclear activities to the IAEA, the crisis management process commenced in political, legal, and technical areas. Tehran dispatched a top diplomat—Deputy Foreign Minister for International Affairs Gholamali Khoshrou—to Moscow and Beijing during the EU3 negotiations to garner further support for the imminent November meeting of the IAEA Board of Governors. Tehran's main goal was to launch broad-based negotiations with the Eastern bloc parallel to diplomacy with the West. However, because of opposition from the Russian Foreign Ministry to Tehran's call for negotiations on the very day that the Sa'dabad meeting was launched (October 21), the meetings were postponed. Dr. Khoshrou flew to Beijing on October 22 and visited Moscow on October 24 to inform officials in both countries of Tehran's new nuclear policy.

The November meeting of the IAEA's Board of Governors was fast approaching. The White House was going to make its demand for the referral of Iran's case to the UN Security Council, and this was the main topic that Tehran and Washington were discussing separately with other global powers. The European media confirmed that there was considerable support for involving the Security Council in the case.[24]

Reports of U.S. diplomatic activities and the possibility that the U.S. government would succeed in reporting Iran's case to the UN Security Council prompted Iran's nuclear team to step up its political and legal efforts. Between November 1 and November 6, 2003, intense negotiations were held between Iran's diplomats and the director general of the IAEA and representatives of the European countries, as well as ambassadors from Russia, China, and the Non-Aligned Movement countries. However, these frenetic efforts did not succeed in securing for Tehran the guarantees it had hoped for, especially with regard to ElBaradei's report.

To continue the country's diplomatic push, Dr. Rouhani, Iran's nuclear negotiation chief, and the negotiation team planned their first visits to Vienna and Moscow on November 8. At this juncture, two basic goals were of the utmost importance to Iran.

The first was to prevent the UN Security Council's involvement in the case. The possibility of referral to the Security Council and imposing sanctions on Iran was imminent. That is why from the early days of the crisis, we decided to mobilize the country to resist possible sanctions. In this pursuit, we established a special committee in the National Security Council to identify and prepare strategies in the event that sanctions were placed on Iran. Such measures included the stockpiling of goods, policies to diversify Iranian assets held outside of the country, and conversion of foreign currency reserves from the U.S. dollar to the euro. A directive on national mobilization and preparedness for possible sanctions was issued, instructing all related ministries to begin implementation.

The second goal was to persuade the IAEA to support Iran's corrective measures and prevent the characterization of Iran's past activities as noncompliance. Iranian diplomats finally convinced the director general that the nuclear case ought to be handled by the IAEA, explaining the reasons for Iran's strong opposition to the involvement of the Security Council. The director general was also persuaded during the course of these negotiations that the term "noncompliance" should not be applied to Tehran's past failures or breaches. ElBaradei also said in his report that there was no evidence that Iran's nuclear program had been diverted to military activities.

Iran's nuclear negotiating team, headed by Hassan Rouhani, arrived in Russia on November 9.[25] The visit to Moscow by Iran's chief negotiator after the Sa'dabad agreement showed that negotiation with the EU3 was essential but only a piece of the larger puzzle. Negotiations with high-ranking Russian officials, including President Vladimir Putin and Foreign Minister Igor Ivanov, clearly indicated that in its negotiation strategy Iran was paying attention not only to the European countries, but also to all world powers.

Negotiations between Iran's foreign minister, Kamal Kharrazi, and the Japanese prime minister on November 13, as well as Dr. Kharrazi's talks with Chinese officials around the same time provided further evidence of Iran's broad strategy, as did the official announcement of uranium enrichment suspension by Iran's chief negotiator while in Russia on November 10.

Concurrently with negotiations in Moscow and Tokyo, ElBaradei submitted to the Board of Governors his report on the implementation of the Safeguards Agreement in Iran and Tehran's nuclear activities. The official announcement of the start of enrichment suspension by Iran in Moscow and the presentation of a letter to the secretariat of the IAEA denoting Iran's acceptance of the Additional Protocol were two major steps taken by Iran on that same day. ElBaradei's report referred to some past breaches of the Safeguards Agreement by Iran. However, the director general also pointed to Iran's corrective measures. His noting that no evidence had been found that Iran was involved in military nuclear activities drew a harsh response from Washington.

John Bolton, at the time the U.S. undersecretary of state for arms control and international security, criticized ElBaradei's report on November 13, 2003, and noted that the White House was angry with the sentence about the lack of evidence of military diversion.[26] Within hours, IAEA spokeswoman Melissa Fleming responded to Bolton's criticism by defending the IAEA position.[27]

The director general's report prompted the United States to increase pressure to report Iran's nuclear dossier to the UN Security Council. American efforts were strongly supported by Israel in a media and diplomatic campaign. In response, Iran scrambled to escalate its own diplomatic activities. Following the Sa'dabad negotiations with the EU3, Iran had received the guarantee it had sought that its nuclear dossier would not be sent to the Security Council.

Despite these assurances, some media and diplomatic reports suggested that Washington had prevailed upon some European countries to agree to the referral of Iran's case to the UN Security Council. Some European (especially British) diplomats argued that guarantees given during the October negotiations were solely related to "reporting" the case and had nothing to do with "notifying" the Security Council.[28] The expression of this interpretation immediately met with a strong response from Iran.

BOARD OF GOVERNORS' NOVEMBER 2003 RESOLUTION: A SUCCESS FOR IRAN

The next meeting of the IAEA's Board of Governors started on November 20, 2003. Iran, which had already received assurances from the EU3 countries that they would object to the use of the word "noncompliance" in the resolution, or to reporting the case to the UN Security Council, started negotiations with member countries of the Board of Governors on the phrasing of the imminent resolution. The United States, accompanied by Canada, Australia, Japan, New Zealand, the Netherlands, South Korea, Italy, and even Spain, pressured the board to report the case to New York. The U.S.-led bloc also insisted that the word "noncompliance" be used in the resolution. On the other side of the table, the EU3, helped by Russia, China, and the Non-Aligned Movement, launched intensive efforts to placate Washington while reducing U.S. demands.

Another problem for Iran in that meeting stemmed from the public relations situation of the EU3 and some countries sympathetic to Iran. The foreign ministers of France, Germany, and Britain were under heavy pressure from propaganda and criticism by the U.S. media. A large part of the American and Israeli media claimed that the Sa'dabad agreement had been a move by Iran to deceive Europe.[29] They alleged that Tehran was going ahead with its clandestine activities, the true dimensions of which would be revealed in the future. The pressure prompted the European diplomats to emphasize during negotiations that the support the EU3 offered to Iran was based on the condition of full transparency and honesty and that if further clandestine activities were revealed in the future their support would be immediately withdrawn. Britain, France, and Germany were unanimous in their implied threat to punish Iran if more secret activities were revealed down the road.

As a result of strenuous efforts by Tehran and measures taken by the EU3, the resolution that was finally passed by the IAEA Board of Governors on November 26, 2003, largely conformed to Iran's aims. Tehran had succeeded in changing the meeting's atmosphere in its own favor. Negotiations among Iranian diplomats and the ambassadors of the EU3, Non-Aligned Movement, and other countries, along with intensive lobbying over every word and phrase used in the initial draft, led to many changes in the resolution. The unfriendly atmosphere of the meeting created by the U.S. bloc led to some sharp arguments between Iran's delegation and representatives of some countries. However, the final output of the Board of Governors' November meeting was far different from the September resolution and quite distant from what the U.S. bloc had hoped for: the announcement of Iran's "noncompliance" and that its nuclear dossier would be reported to the UN Security Council.

The November resolution adopted by the Board of Governors "welcomed" Iran's decision for "active cooperation and honesty" with the international community. It also noted with satisfaction "the decision of Iran to conclude an Additional Protocol to its Safeguards Agreement" and spoke favorably of Iran's decision to suspend enrichment and reprocessing activities. The Board of Governors, however, called on Iran "to undertake and complete the taking of all necessary corrective measures on an urgent basis." The resolution strongly deplored "Iran's past failures and breaches of its obligation to comply with the provisions of its Safeguards Agreement" and urged Iran "to adhere strictly to its obligations under its Safeguards Agreement in both letter and spirit." The Board of Governors also reiterated that "the urgent, full and close co-operation with the Agency of all third countries" was essential for the resolution of outstanding questions concerning Iran's nuclear program. The IAEA required the close cooperation of third countries such as Russia and China to clarify remaining questions about Iran's nuclear program.

The resolution included two additional noteworthy points. First, it officially announced that suspension of uranium enrichment by Tehran had been a "voluntary" measure. This announcement, which was the result of extensive negotiations between Iran and all member countries of the Board of Governors and of the Sa'dabad meeting, was considered a major breakthrough because the Board of Governors officially, legally, and in opposition to conventional interpretations of the September resolution, reiterated that the suspension was voluntary.[30]

The other important point in that resolution was Paragraph 8, which called for what the international media labeled a "trigger mechanism." The United States tried to insert a sentence in Paragraph 8 to secure direct referral to the UN Security Council in the instance that further Iranian failure to disclose its nuclear activities and comply with IAEA requests came to light. Although efforts made by Iranian diplomats led to major changes in the early draft of the resolution, including Paragraph 8, pressure exerted by the United States and decisions made by European countries resulted in its final inclusion. According to the paragraph, "should any further serious Iranian failures come to light, the Board of Governors would meet immediately to consider, in the light of the circumstances and of advice from the Director General, all options at its disposal, in accordance with the IAEA Statute and Iran's Safeguards Agreement."

On the whole, the resolution adopted by the Board of Governors in November 2003 was much more satisfactory to Iran than the one just two months earlier had been. Positive developments for Tehran included:

- The decision by the IAEA not to report Iran's case to the Security Council, contrary to Washington's pressure.
- Exclusion of the word "noncompliance" from the resolution.
- Emphasis included on the voluntary nature of enrichment suspension by Iran.
- The watering down of Paragraph 8 of the resolution.

P-2 CENTRIFUGES AND THE ESCALATION OF EUROPE'S SUSPICIONS OF IRAN

In the aftermath of the November resolution, Iran took the required steps to resolve technical problems and bolster the outlook for strategic cooperation with the European Union. Ali Akbar Salehi, Iran's representative to the IAEA at the time, signed the 93+2 Additional Protocol on December 18, 2003. The measure, which had been approved by high-ranking Iranian officials, was another step toward confidence building and settlement of the crisis. The situation prompted the United States to propose direct talks with Iran to avoid being further sidelined as diplomacy moved forward. U.S. Secretary of State Colin Powell announced on December 30, 2003, that the United States was ready to engage in direct talks with Iran about its nuclear program.[31]

Even as the wall of distrust between Tehran and Brussels began to break down, new technical problems, as well as new developments related to existing technical problems, popped up one after another.[32] Some of these problems were significant enough to even temporarily create tension in Tehran's relations with the IAEA. The most important of these issues faced by Tehran from the November 2003 meeting up until March 2004 were as follows:

1. The Centrifuge Crisis

Iran had announced in its declaration in October that it had informed the IAEA of all aspects of its past activities. The Board of Governors indicated its concern about this issue in Paragraph 8 of the November resolution. The Paragraph meant that if any further serious Iranian failures came to light, it would open the door to greater pressure from the United States through the IAEA Board of Governors. It was in this state of affairs that the IAEA, scrutinizing Iran's October claims about P-1 centrifuges, learned from documentation provided by Libya that Tehran may have also gotten its hands on drawings for more advanced P-2 centrifuges.

Iran's announcement, which took place after the IAEA asked questions about purchasing drawings of P-2 centrifuges, caused many problems, in part because once again Iran was acknowledging facts after they had been discovered by others rather than before. The IAEA and the EU3 construed Iran's failure to mention the drawings in its October declaration as deliberate concealment. The issue was once again blown up by the American media as evidence of the non-peaceful nature of Iran's nuclear activities and the continuation of its past secrecy. Media and diplomatic circles scoffed at Iran's defense: that information about the P-2 centrifuges would have been in accordance with the implementation of the Additional Protocol but the disclosure of that information had not been required under its previous commitment to only the Safeguards Agreement.[33]

Another new challenge was that Tehran was informed in early 2004 that Libya had relayed all information about its own nuclear programs to the United States and the IAEA. A portion of that information was related to purchasing equipment and technical drawings from a dealer who had already sold P-1 drawings and centrifuges to Iran. Security forces in Malaysia arrested the dealer, who was identified as a Sri Lankan named Buhary Syed abu Tahir. The information from Libya revealed that the dealer had provided Tripoli with both P-1 and P-2 centrifuges and drawings, as well as drawings related to some kind of atomic bomb.[34] Buhary Tahir, for his part, told the Malaysian authorities that he had transferred two consignments of used centrifuge parts from Pakistan to Iran by freighter in 1994 and 1995 in return for $3 million in cash.[35]

These disclosures exposed Iran to suspicion that, in addition to P-1 centrifuges and their drawings, it might have received the same package of P-2 centrifuge materials that Tahir had sold to Libya.[36] Iran emphatically rejected this claim but admitted in January 2004 that it had purchased general information in 1995 for designing P-2 centrifuges. At the same time, Iran stressed that no practical steps had been taken to develop those centrifuges until many years later because the P-1 program had been a higher priority.[37]

2. The Polonium Crisis

In January 2004, Rouhani and a group of senior Iranian diplomats set off for Vienna. During the trip, detailed negotiations were carried out between Iran's delegation and the director general of the IAEA, as well as his deputies. Dr. ElBaradei told Iran's chief negotiator that the IAEA had obtained information about Iran's experiments with polonium.[38] The director general demanded an explanation from Iran, since polonium had not been mentioned in Iran's October statement.

Polonium is a highly radioactive neutron source with some applications in military and nonmilitary industries. The potential use of polonium in manufacturing the explosive charges of nuclear weapons made the IAEA quite sensitive about the issue. The Iran Atomic Energy Organization announced that experiments with polonium were intended for developing the use of the substance in batteries and related research. The document released by Iran in response to ElBaradei's report in March 2004 noted that the irradiation of a sample of bismuth metal for the production of polonium-210 had been carefully examined by IAEA inspectors and that a 41-page document had been presented to the agency.[39] Several points made in this document are noteworthy:

- Under the Safeguards Agreement, there was no need to declare bismuth irradiation.
- The bismuth irradiation project had been abandoned and mothballed thirteen years earlier.
- Complete information about bismuth irradiation had been provided in reports about the Tehran Research Reactor, which had been under the IAEA's supervision for approximately thirty years.
- In the bismuth irradiation research project, only two samples of bismuth (0.5 g and 1.5 g) were irradiated, and efforts to produce and extract polonium from the first sample were unsuccessful.
- According to technical and scientific texts presented to the IAEA, polonium-210 has many applications for peaceful purposes. Even if polonium-210 were to be used as a neutron source, it has peaceful applications in reactors, and for oil and gas extraction.

3. The Contamination Crisis

Samplings by the IAEA in the spring of 2003 revealed traces of enriched uranium contamination in some nuclear installations of Iran. After the Tehran statement was issued in October, the results of analysis of IAEA's samples proved the existence of 36 percent enriched uranium. The properties of the uranium isotope found and its similarities to Russian uranium convinced the IAEA that this contamination was different from other instances[40] and came from reprocessing imported Russian power plant fuel.[41]

4. The Gas Test Crisis

As already stated, the International Atomic Energy Agency firmly believed in the summer of 2003 that Iran's progress in developing a complete nuclear fuel cycle would not have been possible without introducing uranium hexafluoride gas into centrifuges. Iran persistently rejected the IAEA's claims before the issuance of the Tehran statement. However, the IAEA noted during an inspection of UF_6 gas reserves that their quantity had been slightly reduced. In response to the IAEA question about the loss, Iran's Atomic Energy Organization announced that the loss was caused by leakage from a UF_6 cylinder.[42] The lost gas had, in fact, been used to test centrifuges, and the IAEA's rejection of the Iranian claims soured its relations with Iran.

5. The Plutonium Crisis

Tehran disclosed the existence of plutonium experiments in the statement issued in October 2003, although questions remained about the amount of plutonium produced.[43] Samples taken by the IAEA from plutonium solution and vessels containing irradiated UO_2 in shielded boxes showed a discrepancy with the Tehran statement: Iran's estimated amount of produced plutonium was less than the actual amount. The IAEA also declared that the lifetime of the dissolved plutonium samples was less than the twelve to sixteen years claimed by Iran. Although later statements by Tehran cleared up the controversy, the revelation of this discrepancy at the time exacerbated feelings of distrust.

BRUSSELS AGREEMENT IN FEBRUARY 2004 AND EXTENSION OF SUSPENSIONS

Neither Dr. Rouhani, the head of Iran's nuclear negotiation team, nor the members of the team were informed about these technical problems by relevant officials of the Iranian nuclear program, and specifically the Iran Atomic Energy Organization. Thus the problems that emerged after the November meeting of the Board of Governors came as a surprise to us and increased European and IAEA skepticism toward Iran, providing grounds for a renewed American diplomatic and public relations push against Iran.

In the plane on our way back from our January 2004 meeting with ElBaradei, I told Dr. Rouhani that our nuclear strategy risked a serious impasse, as we had been pressed to respond to questions about new issues such as P-2 centrifuges and experiments with polonium-210 that we were hearing about for the first time. I told Rouhani that it is unimaginable that he was also not informed of the issue. He replied, "Hossein! I would not be surprised if you and other members of the negotiating team think like this, but believe it or not they told me that they had found some information about P-2 centrifuges on the Internet and are studying it! I did not know that they have got the drawings through the broker. I also was not informed about the plutonium issue...."[44] Being blindsided by these new revelations was dismaying for Iran's nuclear negotiation team.

The next Board of Governors meeting was to be held in March 2004. The American and European media referred to Paragraph 8 of the November resolution to suggest that, in light of the technical crises that had arisen, Iran's dossier should be referred to the UN Security Council.

During this period (November 2003 to January 2004), the IAEA asked Tehran to extend the range of nuclear suspensions. With the definition of suspension provided by ElBaradei in the lead-up to the October 21 agreement in mind, we asked the IAEA to clarify its request, confident that its definition would consist of only the suspension of the introduction of gas. But surprisingly, the IAEA delivered a non-paper[45] in November 2003 that introduced a different, very broad definition that included suspension of production and assembly of centrifuge parts, and even of nuclear facility construction. This was inconsistent with the definition of suspension that ElBaradei had given to Dr. Rouhani the previous month. We were totally shocked. Later we were told by reliable sources in the IAEA that ElBaradei had been under heavy pressure from the United States and EU to present this new definition. ElBaradei corroborated our views of the highly politicized nature of the redefinition of suspension in his 2011 memoir:

> Once again we found ourselves at an intersection of technology and politics. A purely technical definition would only require suspending the introduction of nuclear material into a centrifuge enrichment cascade . . . [but] the Europeans wanted a broader definition.[46]

This development became a major source of Iran's distrust toward the IAEA and also the core issue of the disputes and failures of EU3-Iran nuclear negotiations in 2003–2005.*

Despite this issue, in early February 2004, Tehran stepped up its efforts to bring the issue of the IAEA's nuclear dossier on Iran back under control. Confident that the country had shown its commitment to the peacefulness of its nuclear activities through confidence-building measures such as implementing the Additional Protocol, suspending enrichment, providing a long report on the history of its nuclear activities, Iran took a bold step toward a grand bargain with the United States. ElBaradei confirms in his memoirs that he delivered the message directly to President Bush in March 2004 in a meeting at the White House:

> Many members of Iran's political establishment wanted above all else to reestablish ties to the United States, preferably as part of a "grand bargain" that would address security, trade, Israel's perception of an Iranian military threat, and other issues relevant to full normalization of relations. This was the gist of Rouhani's note. But neither Bush nor Rice [Condoleezza Rice, Bush's national security adviser and future secretary of state] seemed, at that time, open to such a prospect.

Unfortunately, ElBaradei's impression from his visit to Washington was that "the only U.S. strategy . . . was to put pressure on Iran, through the IAEA and the press, in hopes that damning evidence would come to light or that an informant would come forward with a 'smoking gun.'" This was to be America's continued policy despite the fact that George Tenet told ElBaradei a full year later, after leaving the directorship of the CIA, that the United States had no concrete proof and no "actionable information" that Iran intended to develop nuclear weapons.[47]

In the face of continued American implacability, getting Iran's dossier on the right track depended on two different processes. First, it was necessary to find solutions to technical problems involved in the case and to reassure the IAEA that there was no diversion of nuclear materials or activities

---

* Editor's note: ElBaradei in his memoirs does not mention that he alone had told Rouhani in October 2003 that suspension could be defined as restraint from introducing UF_6 into centrifuges. The differences between ElBaradei's privately conveyed definition of suspension and that of the EU3 became a major source of confusion in Iran and tension between it and its international counterparts.

for military purposes and that the Safeguards Agreement would be fully implemented. Second, negotiations would need to succeed with members of the Board of Governors to undermine support for the American stance and persuade the Board of Governors to close Iran's nuclear case.

ElBaradei believed that if Iran extended suspension and cooperated fully with IAEA inspectors, the technical and legal grounds would be satisfied for returning Iran's nuclear case to normal in June 2004. From a political viewpoint, Tehran decided that if Europe provided assurances to close the nuclear case at the June 2004 meeting of the Board of Governors, Iran would extend nuclear suspensions as requested by the IAEA within the framework of the Board of Governors' resolutions for a maximum one-year period while Iran-EU3 nuclear negotiations finalized a permanent solution.

The September 2003 resolution requested that Iran suspend all uranium enrichment-related activities. Tehran managed through the Sa'dabad negotiations, and by changing the legal framework into voluntary measures rather than requirements, to limit the IAEA's (or ElBaradei's) suspension demands to the introduction of gas into centrifuges. After considerable internal debate, Iranian officials reached the conclusion that a short-term extension of suspension in return for an agreement by the EU3 to push for the closure of Iran's case in the June 2004 meeting of the IAEA would be a win-win solution, in keeping with the pragmatic approach described in the last chapter for breaking the international consensus against Iran's nuclear program through diplomatic interaction.

After this decision was reached, Iran made plans for complicated and difficult negotiations with the EU3 to clarify the terms of suspension and of further negotiations to resolve the nuclear case. This time, Iran's diplomatic delegation was headed by our ambassador to the United Nations, Javad Zarif, who joined other members of the nuclear negotiation team in Brussels. I did not attend this meeting. The negotiations ultimately led to the conclusion of the second agreement, called the Brussels Agreement, between Tehran and the EU3 on February 23, 2004. According to that agreement:

- Iran agreed to suspend the manufacture of parts and assembly of centrifuges.

- The EU3 promised to do its best to normalize Iran-IAEA relations and close Iran's nuclear dossier in the June meeting of the Board of Governors.
- The reasons for the deficiencies found in Iran's October statement of disclosure about its nuclear activities were explained.
- No direct relationship was established between the director general's conclusions and reports and the three countries' commitment to close the nuclear case in June.
- A time schedule was partially agreed upon for quadrilateral negotiations on solutions that would guarantee the continuation of Iran's peaceful nuclear program.

The content of the Brussels Agreement and the terms the EU3 agreed to were quite significant, but unfortunately the deal immediately drew strong opposition from the United States. After assessing the agreement, U.S. officials argued that, once the case was closed, Iran would be able to simply give up "voluntary" suspensions and go back to the situation that existed before September. Meanwhile, the six-month calm would have allowed Iran time to bring its nuclear technology and capacities to a higher level than they had been in September. The real reason the Brussels Agreement came under heavy fire from the White House as well as conservative American and European media is that it threatened to deprive the United States of its main leverage to pressure Iran through the IAEA.[48]

THE IAEA'S THIRD RESOLUTION IN MARCH, ACCEPTING THE BRUSSELS AGREEMENT

After the IAEA director general's highly critical report on the implementation of the NPT Safeguards Agreement in Iran was issued on February 24, 2004, the international community prepared for the March meeting of the IAEA Board of Governors. It was anticipated that the issues of the P-2 centrifuges, plutonium, and uranium contamination would be the major points raised in the meeting.

Tehran braced itself for the March meeting, as controversy over technical problems and a heavy propaganda campaign by the international media about Iran's deceitful behavior and the November resolution of the Board of Governors had created an environment ripe for the referral of Iran's nuclear dossier to the UN Security Council. Even in this state of affairs, the Brussels Agreement and explicit promise by the EU3 to normalize the case in June 2004 gave Iran more bargaining power in dealing with the meeting and its possible resolution.

The EU3, which respected its obligations according to the Brussels Agreement, believed that the results of the March meeting would not affect efforts to normalize Iran's case in June 2004.

However, the United States dominated the IAEA Board of Governors meeting from its start on March 8, presenting a surprising and harsh draft resolution. Citing some problems in Iran's October statement, as well as the IAEA's findings after the November meeting, and playing up such issues as P-2 centrifuges, polonium, and laser enrichment, Washington's draft, if approved, would have been the harshest resolution ever on Iran's case. The European Union rejected the draft resolution, characterizing it as rash, nontechnical, and nonlegal. The EU said it should be revised.[49]

It appeared that the draft was prepared by the United States solely to create a deadlock and stymie the implementation of the Brussels Agreement. Iran believed that certain parts of the director general's report, especially those drawing an analogy between the nuclear programs of Iran and Libya and exaggerating the significance of a heavy-water project at Arak and a polonium project, were incorrect yet served to legitimize the U.S. draft proposal.

Tehran also maintained that the main goal of Washington was to bring work on the Brussels Agreement to a standstill and put more pressure on the EU3 to comply with the U.S. agenda. Therefore, we decided to launch extensive negotiations with the European bloc, Non-Aligned Movement, China, Russia, and even Japan, New Zealand, South Korea, and the Netherlands (as members of the U.S. bloc). In addition to urging Moscow and Non-Aligned Movement countries to stand up to U.S. pressure, we had to treat the EU3 harshly during negotiations in Vienna and in four European capitals. The result of Tehran's pressure and bargaining and its resistance to every word and paragraph of the draft resolution was the unprecedented prolongation of the Board of Governors' meeting. This experience demonstrated to the United States the difficulty of diplomatically outmaneuvering Iran.

Iran's multifaceted activities, efforts made by the EU3, a statement issued by a bloc sympathetic to Iran, including the Non-Aligned Movement,[50] and the insistence of the Non-Aligned Movement that Iran's continued co-operation with the IAEA be supported led to many changes in the early draft. The final resolution was still by no means satisfactory to Iran, and we harshly criticized the Board of Governors and the EU3 in particular.

At the end of the meeting, the EU3 announced its continued determination to bring the case back to normalcy in the next meeting, scheduled for June. Britain and France cited three conditions as necessary for normalization: that Iran immediately ratify the Additional Protocol; that the director general declare in the next meeting that Iran's cooperation had been complete and that good progress had been achieved on various issues; and that no more failures to meet international obligations be found on Iran's side.

Despite Iran's efforts, the Board of Governors issued its resolution on March 13, 2004. It was the direct result of the technical crises that followed the November meeting of the board and U.S. efforts to sink the Brussels Agreement. The resolution expressed satisfaction over the implementation of the yet-to-be-ratified Additional Protocol and described Iran's decision to suspend processing and enrichment activities as a "positive step." The Board of Governors also "recognized" Iran's "active cooperation with the Agency in providing access to locations requested by the Agency." The resolution, however, put forth a diverse range of "concerns," "emphases," and "requests" to Iran, the most important of which were as follows.*

The IAEA Board of Governors:

1. Notes with serious concern that the declarations made by Iran in October 2003 did not amount to the complete and final picture of Iran's past and present nuclear program considered essential by the Board's November 2003 resolution, in that the Agency has since uncovered a number of omissions—for example, a more advanced centrifuge design than previously declared, including associated research, manufacturing and testing activities; two mass spectrom-

---

* Editor's note: These IAEA concerns reflect the fact that issues beyond the diversion of declared nuclear materials are germane to the ultimate need to demonstrate compliance with IAEA and NPT obligations that all of a non–nuclear-weapon states' nuclear activities must be exclusively for peaceful purposes.

eters used in the laser enrichment program; and designs for the construction of hot cells at the Arak heavy-water research reactor—which require further investigation, not least as they may point to nuclear activities not so far acknowledged by Iran.

2. Noting with equal concern that Iran has not resolved all questions regarding the development of its enrichment technology to its current extent, and that a number of other questions remain unresolved, including the sources of all [highly enriched uranium] contamination in Iran; the location, extent, and nature of work undertaken on the basis of the advanced centrifuge design; the nature, extent and purpose of activities involving the planned heavy water reactor; and evidence to support claims regarding the purpose of polonium-210 experiments.

3. Noting with concern that, although the timelines are different, Iran's and Libya's conversion and centrifuge programs share several common elements, including technology largely obtained from the same foreign sources.

4. As Iran's cooperation so far has fallen short of what is required, calls on Iran to continue and intensify its cooperation, in particular through the prompt and proactive provision of detailed and accurate information on every aspect of Iran's past and present nuclear activities.

5. Calls on Iran to extend the application of this commitment (voluntary suspension) to all such activities throughout Iran, and requests the Director General to verify the full implementation of these steps.

6. Deplores that Iran, as detailed in the report by the Director General, omitted any reference, in its letter of 21 October 2003, which was to have provided the "full scope of Iranian nuclear activities" and a "complete centrifuge R&D chronology," to its possession of P-2 centrifuge design drawings and to associated research, manufacturing, and mechanical testing activities—which the Director General describes as "a matter of serious concern, particularly in view of the importance and sensitivity of those activities."

7. Echoes the concern expressed by the Director General over the issue of the purpose of Iran's activities related to experiments on the

production and intended use of polonium-210, in the absence of information to support Iran's statements in this regard.

8. Calls on Iran to be pro-active in taking all necessary steps on an urgent basis to resolve all outstanding issues, including the issue of [uranium] contamination at the Kalaye Electric Company workshop and Natanz; the issue of the nature and scope of Iran's laser isotope enrichment research; and the issue of the experiments on the production of polonium-210.

9. [Therefore, the Board of Governors] decides to defer until its June meeting, and after receipt of the report of the Director General referred to above, consideration of progress in verifying Iran's declarations, and of how to respond to the above-mentioned omissions.

Some diplomats considered this ninth paragraph of the March resolution to be its most important. Deferring any consideration of progress by Iran until the June meeting was a purely political decision that was directly dictated by the United States. All issues mentioned in the resolution, as well as conflicts between Iran's October statement and findings of the IAEA, could now be raised again in the next meeting, giving the United States another chance to argue for reporting Iran's case to the UN Security Council. The ratification of this paragraph in the final resolution, even with some changes made as a result of Tehran's lobbying efforts, earned the EU3 harsh criticism from Iran.

EU FAILURE AND CANCELLATION OF THE BRUSSELS AGREEMENT

Despite the results of the Board of Governors' meeting in March 2004, which focused heavily on the problems of Iran's experiments with polonium, P-2 centrifuges, and mass spectrometers, the Brussels Agreement had greatly increased Iran's leverage in confronting the diplomatic ramifications of those problems. The agreement not only raised a realistic prospect for the normalization of the nuclear case, but also widened the transatlantic divide. In our opinion, voluntary and short-term suspension of the assembly and manufacture of centrifuges was not a high price to pay for normalization of the case with the IAEA. Iran's acceptance of the agreement faced different types of resistance inside and outside the country.

Inside Iran, some groups that did not fully understand the situation or the implications of the February agreement accused us of giving in to the West's demands. Beyond Iran's borders, American neoconservatives and anti-Iranian U.S. and Israeli media outlets claimed that Europe had granted a major concession to Iran through the Brussels Agreement without getting anything in return. They maintained that the normalization of Iran's nuclear case would deprive the West of its most important leverage over Tehran. They also maintained that Iran should have agreed to suspend centrifuge manufacture much earlier in accordance with the September resolution.

Following the ratification of the Board of Governors' resolution on March 13, 2004, Tehran heightened its diplomatic efforts to get the nuclear case back on a normalized track at the next meeting, as promised by the Brussels Agreement. Examples of those efforts included Dr. Rouhani's visit to Japan (March 13), phone conversations between President Khatami and his Russian counterpart Vladimir Putin, a meeting between foreign ministers of Iran and Russia on the sidelines of the Caspian Sea conference, and meetings between Foreign Minister Kharrazi and high-ranking French officials (April 22), the British prime minister and foreign secretary (April 23), the prime minister and minister of foreign affairs of the Czech Republic (April 29), the Belgian prime minister (May 4), the chancellor of Germany (May 6), Russia's Putin (May 7), and high-ranking officials of Poland (May 25) and Spain (May 27). In addition to these meetings, many rounds of negotiations were carried out, as Iran's senior diplomats and experts met with high-ranking diplomats and officials of the European Union, Pakistan, Malaysia, Non-Aligned Movement countries, and other member countries of the IAEA's Board of Governors. A number of meetings were also held with the director general of the IAEA and his deputies in Vienna.

Despite Tehran's efforts, conditions were not being met that would motivate Brussels to honor the February agreement. There were a host of reasons for Europe's unwillingness to close Iran's nuclear case in the June Board of Governors meeting:

1. The main reason for the failure of the EU3 to abide by the Brussels Agreement was enormous pressure from the United States.[51]

The United States, which considered the February 23 agreement an obstacle to its goals and strategies, took extensive measures to force the three countries to renege on their obligations.

2. The psychological warfare launched by the Western media against Iran and the atmosphere it created were other factors that reduced Europe's motivation to implement the Brussels Agreement. At that time, rumors were flying about Iran's "clandestine programs." The issue of Shiyan[52] constituted a major propaganda campaign against Tehran in June 2004 and led Europe to adopt a more conservative approach. There were reports that enrichment activities had taken place in Shiyan, east of Tehran. Some Western countries believed that the Iranian government had removed soil from the site and destroyed all buildings and converted it into a park in order to cover up evidence before inspectors had access to the site. The IAEA sent a team to investigate the rumors; it found no evidence of contamination.

3. Libya's unconditional surrender on the nuclear issue under U.S. pressure was another factor that undermined Europe's strategy vis-à-vis the United States. The U.S. success in subduing Tripoli through "threat and pressure" tactics made Brussels hesitant to go out on a limb in negotiations with Iran for fear that failure would discredit its softer approach.

4. Statements made by the IAEA on the conflict between Iran's statements and its investigators' findings, along with its presentation of evidence of Tehran's continued secrecy after the Sa'dabad negotiations, increased the skepticism of European officials toward Iran's objectives and honesty.

5. Furthermore, many technical problems were still in dispute between Iran and the IAEA.

6. In the midst of diplomatic efforts to prepare for the June meeting, the inauguration of the uranium conversion facility in Isfahan brought a new wave of negative international attention to Iran's nuclear activities. The facility, whose inauguration was announced during this period by the head of the Iran Atomic Energy Organization in a news conference after a meeting with ElBaradei, elicited immediate condemnation from the EU, United States, and some other countries.

7. Iran's round-the-clock activity in centrifuge assembly just before suspension began in April 2004 gave Europe another reason to be doubtful about Iran's intentions. European countries maintained that such activities discredited the Brussels Agreement. Iran had, according to the agreement, agreed to suspend the manufacture of parts and the assembly of centrifuges in return for a commitment from the EU3 to push for the normalization of the nuclear case in the next meeting of the Board of Governors. The EU3 assumed that Iran would begin the suspension right after the Brussels Agreement, while Tehran believed that it was committed to suspending the manufacturing and assembly of centrifuges before the June meeting of the IAEA Board of Governors. This allowed Iran to compensate for delays resulting from suspension in advance by working around the clock between when it accepted the Brussels Agreement (February 23) and the official start of suspension in early April 2004, which was to last for no more than forty days.

Revelations of such activities in the European media were met with consternation in Brussels and fueled propaganda by the American media against Iran. With the two April events—that is, the launch of the Isfahan facility and round-the-clock efforts before the scheduled date of suspending centrifuge assembly—as evidence, European and American observers reached the conclusion that Tehran was insincere and using its agreement with Europe simply as a stopgap measure.[53] With this interpretation of events in mind, American media outlets and Bush administration officials spearheaded anti-Iranian propaganda and labeled the European Union the main loser in negotiations with Tehran. Less publicly, some Western countries and, surprisingly, some of Iran's regional Arab neighbors, were pushing the United States to take a hard line on Iran.

The above mentioned seven factors provided ample incentive for the EU to breach the obligations of the Brussels Agreement. A resolution adopted by the U.S. House of Representatives against Iran's nuclear activities on May 8, as well as direct calls on the EU by the United States to support sanctions against Tehran and end trade talks with Iran, clearly showed that further resistance to Washington's agenda would cost Brussels dearly.[54] The press statement released at the end of a G8 meeting in the United States in June likewise reflected American determination on the issue.[55]

The IAEA director general's next report on the implementation of the NPT Safeguards Agreement in Iran, issued on June 1, triggered another marathon session of the agency's Board of Governors. In this report, the director general emphasized progress in Tehran-IAEA relations and commended Iran's cooperation. Yet, he wrote, the inauguration of the Isfahan facilities conflicted with the IAEA's interpretation of "the range of Iran's decision on suspension." Dr. ElBaradei mentioned issues related to the origins of contamination of low-enriched uranium and highly enriched uranium and to Iran's efforts at importing, manufacturing, and operating P-1 and P-2 centrifuges as two key problems that had yet to be solved. Iran was also charged with giving "contradictory information" on some issues.

The report, factored in with pressure from the United States and the prevailing political atmosphere, led to a European draft resolution that went against the Brussels Agreement and Tehran's expectations. This turnabout contributed considerably to the loss of confidence in EU3 nuclear diplomacy on the part of the supreme leader and other Iranian policymakers. One of the chief challenges faced by Khatami's nuclear negotiation team was the impatient expectation of many within the country that the level of cooperation with the IAEA and confidence-building measures already taken were enough for the resolution of the issue and for Iran's nuclear dossier to be taken off the agenda of the Board of Governors.

Most of Iran's policymakers felt that Iran had already done more than enough for the EU3 to go through with its end of the bargain reached in the Sa'dabad statement in fall 2003 and that further compromise by the nuclear team would be unnecessary and a sign of weakness. We on the negotiating team, however, recognized that the confidence-building process and resolution of all technical issues would take longer than our domestic critics assumed. We were essentially trapped between the unrealistic demands, on the one hand, of the Western countries, which expected that the status quo of suspension and access for inspections beyond the NPT's requirement should continue for years, and, on the other hand, of the Iranian politicians who wanted these measures to be concluded in the space of a few months.

The June meeting of the Board of Governors started on June 14, 2004, amid sharp criticism from Iran's Foreign Ministry over the draft resolution prepared by Brussels two days earlier. President Khatami wrote a letter to leaders of the EU3 on June 13 implying that Iran might end talks with the European countries if they failed to comply with their obligations under the Sa'dabad and Brussels Agreements. In a news conference on June 16, the president stipulated that Iran would end enrichment suspension if the European side ignored its commitments.[56]

The Board of Governors released its final resolution on June 18, 2004. In it, the board reiterated "its appreciation that Iran has continued to act as if its Additional Protocol were in force" and commended "Iran's voluntary decisions to suspend all enrichment-related and reprocessing activities and to permit the Agency to verify that suspension" while "noting with concern that, as the verification was delayed in some cases," the suspension was not comprehensive. The board, however, acknowledged that "there has been good progress on the actions agreed during the Director General's visit to Tehran in early April 2004."

The resolution went on to call on Iran "to take all necessary steps on an urgent basis to help resolve all outstanding questions," especially that of low-enriched uranium and highly enriched uranium contamination found at various locations in Iran, "including by providing additional relevant information about the origin of the components in question and explanations about the presence of a cluster of 36 percent [highly enriched uranium] particles; and also the question of the nature and scope of Iran's P-2 centrifuge program." While welcoming "Iran's submission of the declarations under Articles 2 and 3 of its Additional Protocol," the board emphasized "the importance of Iran continuing to act in accordance with the provisions of the Additional Protocol to provide reassurance to the international community about the nature of its nuclear program."

Through intense diplomatic negotiations with various power blocs, notably the Non-Aligned Movement and the EU3, Iran was able to tone down the resolution somewhat. However, Tehran firmly believed that the EU3's political obligations and Iran's cooperation with the IAEA merited the normalization of the nuclear case. Tehran hence reacted angrily when Britain, France, and Germany breached their obligations under the Brussels Agreement to normalize the course of Iran's nuclear dossier in the June meeting of the Board of Governors. In its protestation, Tehran highlighted two major points: first, the inability of Europe to get the dossier back on the normal track as promised in the Brussels Agreement because the United States was not on board and the Europeans were incapable of finalizing an agreement in America's absence; second, the content of the Board of Governors' June resolution did not bode well for the prospect of future cooperation between Iran and the IAEA.

Most of Iran's politicians played down the importance of newly arisen technical problems and their political ramifications and expected a final resolution of the issue regardless of these new technical and political realities.

With regard to the first issue, Tehran's reaction was firm and decisive, reneging on its own end of the bargain struck in Brussels: the expansion of enrichment suspension.[57] As for the contents of the June resolution, remarks made by Iranian officials showed that Tehran had no intention of giving in to the demands of the resolution. The most important requests were detailed in Paragraphs 7 and 8 of the resolution: the extension of suspension to the Isfahan project and a review of Iran's decision on the Arak heavy water project. Negotiations between Iranian diplomats and various member countries during the Board of Governors' meeting led to the modification of Paragraphs 7 and 8. And, even after the resolution's ratification, member countries of the Non-Aligned Movement issued a statement criticizing the two paragraphs.[58]

Less than a week after the resolution's passage, Iran wrote a letter to the director general of the IAEA and to foreign ministers of the EU3 officially announcing that Tehran would no longer respect the Brussels Agreement. The renewed manufacture of parts and assembly of centrifuges by Iran conveyed two clear political and legal messages to the world: Iran would not accept any unilateral obligation; and Iran's suspension needed to be acknowledged as a voluntary measure taken as part of a political bargain. This acknowledgement needed to be expressed not only in word but also in deed.

Iran's decision to resume assembling centrifuges immediately met with condemnation from various countries. Unusually bellicose remarks were made by U.S. National Security Adviser Condoleezza Rice and Defense Secretary Donald Rumsfeld about "testing all possible ways" to prevent Tehran from obtaining nuclear weapons. Tensions with Israel heightened considerably as media reports pointed to the possibility of an Israeli attack on Iran's nuclear installations similar to the air raid on Iraq's Osirak reactor in 1981. The *Washington Times* carried a report on July 4, 2004, that outlined a plan that the paper claimed was formulated by the Israeli army to launch "limited surprise attacks" on Iran's nuclear installations. Details of the plan were republished in various languages by the mass media in Europe and the Persian Gulf states.

However, a warning issued by British Prime Minister Tony Blair to Israeli Prime Minister Ariel Sharon on August 21 about the consequences of any Israeli attack on Iran's nuclear installations, remarks to similar effect made by the German chancellor, and Jacques Chirac's opposition to any "undiplomatic treatment" of Tehran indicated that any such action would come at a huge political cost to Israel. Finally, on September 15, 2004, Sharon denied that Israel had intended to attack Iran.

THE SECOND CRISIS IN TEHRAN-BRUSSELS RELATIONS

The cessation of suspension, heightened pressure by the EU3 on Tehran, and the dismay of Iranian authorities and political activists led to a new low in Iran's relations with the EU3. The quarrel was exacerbated by domestic and international developments both in Tehran and in the European capitals.

In response to Iran's termination of the suspension of centrifuge assembly and European opposition politicians criticizing the EU3's turnaround on the Iran nuclear issue, the European Union put forth the request that Iran return to the understanding that existed before the June meeting. This was stated as something of a diplomatic ultimatum by the foreign ministers of Britain and France, who said that negotiations would be halted until Iran reinstituted enrichment suspension. The imminent presidential elections in the United States and increased political and electoral debate in Washington about how to handle Iran and Iraq were other factors for Brussels to consider.

Iran's moderates were disappointed with the EU3 and under heavy pressure from domestic political groups and media. Inside Iran, hard-liners argued that the failure of the Brussels Agreement showed that the Khatami administration's engagement policy was futile at best. Some political factions even talked of leaving the Non-Proliferation Treaty and expelling the IAEA's inspectors. The Majles insisted on a plan that required the government to pursue peaceful nuclear technology—by means of uranium enrichment, among other things—to show its dissatisfaction with the EU3.

In this climate, official channels for negotiations were practically cut off between Tehran and the EU3. In July 2004, limited meetings were held between the two sides' diplomats in Europe without any notable accomplishment. The talks were mostly private and unofficial meetings meant for the exchange of viewpoints. And even as these talks went on, a propaganda war, stoked by the U.S. and Israeli media, raged between the two sides, continuing until late July.

Meanwhile, Tehran decided to convert 37 tons of yellowcake to uranium hexafluoride gas, which led to a further escalation of political and propaganda pressure on Iran. Earlier, the inauguration of Isfahan's uranium conversion facility on March 28, 2004, had been mentioned by the Europeans as a reason for their turn away from normalizing the nuclear case in the June meeting of the Board of Governors. The new decision by Tehran to convert yellowcake to UF_6—a decision that later evidence showed was premature from a technical standpoint and politically motivated[59]—threatened to push the EU3 even further from reconciliation.

The controversy once again triggered a media countdown for the referral of Iran's nuclear dossier to New York at the upcoming September meeting of the IAEA Board of Governors. The main goal behind this decision to convert yellowcake to UF_6 was to convince Europe that Iran's right to enrichment would not be forgotten by extending suspension, and that long-term suspension would ultimately be counterproductive. At the same time, the reality was that Iran's intention to demonstrate its firmness on the issue of enrichment rights threatened to create more distrust toward Iran in the international community, further complicating Iran's nuclear dossier.

To salvage diplomacy with the Europeans without drawing further accusations of weakness from Iran's hard-liners, the nuclear team drew up a new plan that was mutually agreed upon by the country's leadership. On July 24, 2004, Tehran proposed this plan for a "framework of mutual guarantees," which included a large-scale strategy for crisis management. Such an Iranian initiative could have led to a major breakthrough. The plan was conveyed to the EU3 during a quadripartite meeting in Paris on July 29, 2004.[60]

Iran's plan, which had been drawn up in four different sections—"mutual guarantees," "advanced technology," "energy," and "security"—sought a way to promote bilateral strategic cooperation through confidence building and mutual guarantees. According to the plan, Tehran promised the EU3 that it would:

1. Under no conditions divert its peaceful nuclear activities for military purposes, nor would it leave the NPT.
2. Guarantee cooperation with the IAEA's inspectors according to the 93+2 Additional Protocol.
3. Provide assurances about the responsible application of advanced technology, especially regarding materials with both peaceful and military applications.
4. In return for these commitments, Iran sought assurances from the EU3 on the following points:
   • Recognition of Iran's basic rights as per the Non-Proliferation Treaty and its right to develop the fuel cycle. Europe's commitment to accepting and enforcing Iran's nuclear right and providing the country with honest support was Iran's most urgent and important demand.
   • The promotion of relations with Tehran to the level of strategic relations and cooperating with Iran on regional security and counterterrorism. Iran sought assurances on defense cooperation with a commitment to the idea of a Middle East free from weapons of mass destruction.
   • The transfer of advanced technology, including technologies with both peaceful and military applications, expansion of economic cooperation, and collaboration in building nuclear power plants in Iran and supplying needed equipment.

Despite some positive signals on the Tehran plan, the international tension and political climate in the wake of the cancellation of suspension, coupled with continued operations at Isfahan's uranium conversion facility, made practically impossible a return to the situation that had existed before the IAEA Board of Governors' meeting in September 2003. The United States insisted that Iran's case be reported to the UN Security

Council in September 2004. The atmosphere created by the international media, along with rhetoric by Israel and claims already raised by the terrorist opposition group MEK, made such a referral seem quite plausible.

Tehran once again intensified its diplomatic efforts ahead of the Board of Governors' meeting. Given the poor standing of its relations with the EU3, Iran focused on negotiations with other blocs, especially the Non-Aligned Movement and the Eastern bloc, as an alternative approach, even as it continued to bargain with the EU3. Considerable importance was attached to negotiations with Malaysia, India, South Africa, Cuba, China, and Russia. More than 35 meetings were held at various diplomatic levels on the issue throughout late August and early September 2004. Those negotiations, pursued in the face of European countries' request that Iran suspend its enrichment activities, the U.S. push to report Iran's case to the UN Security Council, and the IAEA's urging for more cooperation and transparency from Iran, were aimed at softening the expected blow of the next Board of Governors' resolution, hindering Washington's agenda, and blocking the imposition of more demands on Iran.

The Board of Governors' meeting on September 13, 2004, was held in a politically charged atmosphere. The meeting turned into a tug of war between the American-led bloc and other countries on reporting Iran's case to the UN Security Council. The disputes forced the American bloc to eventually agree to a compromise that set a deadline for the next meeting in November, which would undertake an exhaustive review of Iran's case. In his statement to the board, Mohamed ElBaradei emphasized that although the IAEA was making progress, more time was needed to assess the nature of the Iranian program. On several occasions, he also strongly opposed setting an artificial deadline for concluding the IAEA's investigations in Iran.[61]

In the Iranian view, the threat in the Board of Governors resolution to refer Iran to the UN Security Council unless its demands for the adoption of the Additional Protocol, indefinite enrichment suspension, and unlimited access for inspection for an indefinite period were met contravened the Non-Proliferation Treaty.[62]

The September 2004 resolution, which was a direct consequence of Iran's abandonment of centrifuge assembly suspension and the inauguration of Isfahan's uranium conversion facility, brought Tehran's nuclear dossier another step closer to being referred to the UN Security Council.

In the resolution passed by the Board of Governors in September 2004:

- The general positive trend of Iran's cooperation with the IAEA was confirmed. However, serious concern was expressed over Iran's inattention to suspending all enrichment and reprocessing activities.[63]
- The Board of Governors stressed the need for cooperation with the IAEA on P-2 centrifuges and plutonium separation tests and expressed concern over Tehran's decision to introduce 37 tons of yellowcake into the Isfahan uranium conversion facility.[64]
- Iran was urged to respond positively to the director general's requests for access and information at any time and was specifically urged to provide further explanation for the sources and reasons of enriched uranium contamination and about the import, manufacture, and use of centrifuges.
- The board expressed deep concern over Iran's reversal of the suspension agreement and called on Tehran to suspend activities related to enrichment in all sectors immediately and in a verifiable manner.
- It was requested that Iran voluntarily reconsider its decision to start construction of a heavy-water research reactor in Arak as a further confidence-building measure.
- The Board of Governors also urged Iran once again to ratify the Additional Protocol without delay.
- It was requested that the director general submit a report on the implementation of the September 2004 resolution and a recapitulation of the agency's findings on Iran's nuclear program since September 2002, as well as a full account of past and present Iranian cooperation with the agency, before the November board session.[65]

It was announced that the Board of Governors would decide in its subsequent session whether further steps were appropriate with regard to Iran's obligations under its NPT Safeguards Agreement and the requests made of Iran by the board in that resolution and previous ones. All in all, the resolution was a boon to the American camp.

DEVELOPMENTS LEADING TO THE PARIS AGREEMENT: ACHIEVEMENTS AND FAILURES

The September 2004 resolution once again brought Tehran's case closer to the UN Security Council. The director general, following a thorough review of the resolution, referred to the requests of the Board of Governors as the "November 25 deadline" in his first official statement.

The situation was an outcome of different measures and developments that greatly worsened the existing crisis:

- In the aftermath of the June resolution, Tehran ended its voluntary suspension of the manufacture and assembly of centrifuges.
- The introduction of 37 tons of yellowcake into Isfahan's uranium conversion facility and the facility's operations was a confrontational move by Iran to the requests put forth by the Board of Governors.
- Revelations concerning contamination, P-2 centrifuges, polonium, and plutonium increased the agency's suspicions.
- Tremendous political pressure exerted by the United States on Europe, which was intensified as a consequence of the Brussels Agreement and the introduction of yellowcake at the Isfahan facility, greatly limited the room for political maneuvering by Europe, and even by Russia and China. Part of that pressure resulted from polls conducted during the U.S. presidential campaign.
- Because of Iran's consternation at Europe's inability to normalize the case in June (as per the Brussels Agreement), the country virtually closed normal channels of negotiation with Europe in July 2004. European negotiators told me that Tehran's decision to inaugurate the Isfahan facility in March 2004 was a clear provocation and, contrary to previous board resolutions, caused the EU-3 inability to normalize the case in June.
- Extensive propaganda including daily claims about Iran's secrecy by media in the United States, Israel, and the EU, and by MEK and other political circles further worsened the situation.
- Some signals that were sent out by certain political circles in Tehran were exploited by neoconservative politicians at the White House.

For example, news about a triple urgency plan proposed by some Majles deputies to force the Iranian government to withdraw from the NPT[66] prompted the U.S. media to draw an analogy between Iran and North Korea.

- Israel's public statements about a possible limited military attack on Iran had caused the political discourse governing global interactions to take a more violent turn. Out of concern over the worsening situation in the Middle East, Europe was trying to take control of the situation by supporting harsher treatment of Iran.

The September resolution, which was a result of the conditions stated above, reduced to a minimum the level of diplomatic negotiations between Iran and the EU3. For various reasons, Tehran decided to temporarily halt all talks with the EU3, which sent clear signals to the European side that Iran was very angry but determined. Parallel to the obstruction of political channels between Tehran and Brussels, various negotiations were carried out with other countries, which confirmed Iran's decision to continue interacting with the international community. Kharrazi, then Iran's foreign minister, went to New York on September 21, 2004, and conferred with other power blocs on the sidelines of the UN General Assembly session. Similarly, Rouhani negotiated with officials in South Africa and Kazakhstan on October 11, while other Iranian diplomats continued talks with Russia and representatives of important member states of the Non-Aligned Movement. In an interview with the *Asia Times*, I—as the spokesman of Iran's nuclear negotiating team—once more called on all countries to take part in Iran's nuclear activities. The report read,

> Speaking to *Asia Times Online* in Vienna on the sidelines of the latest meeting of the IAEA's board of directors on the question of Iranian nuclear programs, Mousavian said that besides inviting the West's main exporters of nuclear plants to take a "substantial part" in Iran's nuclear projects, Tehran is also ready to offer them a "golden package" that would include full cooperation in fighting international terrorism and restoring peace and security in the region, as well as in trade and investment.[67]

The report went on to suggest that if the West did not respond to Iran's offer, Russia would likely gain a monopoly on the country's nuclear activities even beyond the $1 billion deal it already had at the Bushehr plant. My intention in the interview was to invite the West to agree on a grand bargain that would include all the above-mentioned areas of mutual interest.

Under these circumstances, Europe decided to change the situation and initiate a new trend in order to gain more control of the crisis. News circulating in the European and American media in October 2004 attested to Europe's decision to reach a compromise on Iran's nuclear dossier with the United States and other powers. Jack Straw, then the British foreign secretary, went to Washington in early October to discuss the latest developments in the situation. Negotiations were also carried out between Javier Solana, the European chief negotiator,[68] and the U.S. secretary of state as well as Democratic leaders of congressional committees involved in U.S. foreign policy. It was announced in late October that negotiations between Europe and the United States on Iran's nuclear activities had failed.[69] At any rate, evidence showed that Europe was seeking a way to pursue nuclear negotiations, through the support of bigger powers, on the basis of a broad agenda.

The meeting of the G8 on October 15, 2004, was a turning point in Europe's international efforts. Sporadic media reports contained ambiguous indications of G8 agreement on how to interact with Tehran. However, there was no official public statement on the subject. The reports were confirmed a few days later, when the United Kingdom, France, and Germany made public their first comprehensive plan. The plan, which was offered to Iran as a "way out," delineated a wide range of mutual cooperation aimed at achieving a long-term strategic agreement. The first comprehensive plan to be offered by the EU3 was an official response to Tehran's past diplomatic initiative.[70]

The EU3 plan outlined the two sides' commitments, as well as approaches for the short term (for dealing with the upcoming November session of the IAEA Board of Governors) and the long term. The following points are noteworthy about the plan:

- It started by recognizing Iran's right to research, produce, and use nuclear energy for peaceful purposes.
- Tehran was requested to totally suspend all enrichment and reprocessing activities in a way that could be verified by international observers. Tehran was to implement the suspension without delay.

- The European Union stipulated that if Iran accepted the suspension, negotiations would begin immediately to achieve a long-term agreement. From this viewpoint, the EU3 emphasized that it would continue efforts to normalize the situation in the next meeting.
- It was clearly stated that Iran's opposition to full suspension of the fuel cycle would cause the EU to support referral of the nuclear case to the UN Security Council. This paragraph was construed by the international media as a threat on the part of the European Union and a sign of some convergence of the viewpoints on the two sides of the Atlantic.
- Iran would be obliged to work toward preventing the proliferation of weapons of mass destruction and to settle remaining problems with the IAEA.
- Tehran was required to commit that it would take the necessary measures to ratify the Additional Protocol by the end of 2005 and open all of its nuclear installations to IAEA inspections.
- Europe also requested Iran to replace the "heavy-water" research reactor that it was constructing with a "light-water" reactor and provide objective guarantees to assure lack of diversion of the program to nuclear weapons. Finally, Iran was supposed to implement long-term suspension of its enrichment and reprocessing activities.
- As a party to the NPT, the EU3 was obligated to recognize and support without discrimination Iran's rights to development, research, production, and utilization of nuclear energy for peaceful purposes.
- Other commitments to be undertaken by the European countries included providing Iran with needed guarantees for access to the nuclear fuel market, cooperating with Iran on nuclear safety and protection, and supporting Iran's drive to obtain a light-water reactor.
- The three European countries announced that as soon as suspension of Iran's nuclear activities was confirmed, they would resume trade talks with Tehran and support Iran's accession to the World Trade Organization.
- Other offers made by the EU3 were cooperation with Iran to boost its influence in regional security arrangements; prosecuting MEK elements; facilitating the establishment of a WMD-free zone in the

Middle East; fighting illicit drugs; and supporting Iran's participation in the greater Middle East initiative.

"The way out" was promptly rejected by Iran. Tehran was satisfied with certain political outcomes of its negotiations, particularly the support lent by the United States and other industrial countries to interact with Tehran. The plan was an indication of the West's acceptance, for the first time since the Islamic Revolution, of the necessity of Iran's effective participation in international interactions. However, the contradiction between some paragraphs of the plan and Iran's viewpoints and long-term interests led us—after many hours of intensive internal discussion—to the decision to reject the EU3 proposal. The main reasons for rejection can be enumerated as follows:

1. The European Union threatened Iran that in case of opposition to suspension, it would support the reporting of Iran's case to the UN Security Council.
2. The requested period of suspension was unlimited.
3. The plan contained a wide definition of global nonproliferation policies and also referred to UN Security Council Resolution 1540, which paved the way for putting more pressure on Tehran with regard to missile activities.
4. Iran was obliged to ratify the Additional Protocol by the end of 2005.
5. Iran was requested to take necessary measures to ratify the Comprehensive Test Ban Treaty.
6. Full transparency of Iran's program was demanded. This could have amounted to more requests that could have transcended the limits of 93+2 Additional Protocol.
7. Finally, the "objective guarantees" requested by Europe to assure that Iran would not divert materials toward nuclear weapons were taken to mean "stopping" the nuclear program, which was our redline.

Realizing that the achievements of an entire year of negotiations were in jeopardy as a result of the September 2004 developments, Europe increased diplomatic contacts with Tehran immediately after "the way out" package was rejected.[71] On October 21, high-ranking expert talks started in Vienna between diplomats from the EU3 and Iran. Less than a week later, on October 27, a new round of talks was held in the same city, though the spokesman for Iran's delegation described those talks as fruitless.

In the course of these negotiations, the ambassadors from France, Germany, and Britain offered Iran a "draft agreement" at 9 a.m. on Tuesday, November 2. Tehran rejected the plan and offered an alternative proposal at 8 p.m. the following day. Although this latest European plan was less defective than "the way out," it still diverged considerably from the viewpoints of the Islamic Republic of Iran.

The necessity of reaching an agreement ahead of the November meeting of the IAEA Board of Governors and thus easing the crisis prompted the four countries to meet again on November 5, 2004, in Paris. Prior to the Paris meeting, the nuclear negotiation team received instruction from high-level authorities to include the following seven points in the agreement with the EU3:

- Recognition of Iran's rights to the peaceful use of nuclear technology;
- Suspension only for the period of negotiations;
- Suspension should not prevent the AEOI from continuing its work on other elements of the program;
- Negotiation period not to exceed six months;
- Removal of Iran's file from IAEA Board of Governors' agenda;
- Positive resolution in November's IAEA session; and
- Iran's attendance at the Multilateral Approach to Nuclear Fuel Cycle.

We entered Paris talks with such a mandate. These talks evolved into one of the most complicated and lengthy rounds of quadrilateral negotiations since October 2003, taking about 23 hours. The negotiations in Paris commenced on a weekend, early on Saturday, allowing for only a short break for the Iranians to pray and rest a bit late at night, and went on until late Sunday.

At the negotiating table, the European delegations were more than three times the size of the Iranian delegation. The Europeans were under tremendous pressure from the Americans; this became apparent as the British delegation would confirm each step of the negotiations with Washington. The Iranian delegates, meanwhile, were also under enormous pressure; politicians and the Iranian public had lost patience with the whole process and would not tolerate further suspension of uranium enrichment.

The goal of the negotiations was to compare the proposals from Tehran and Brussels paragraph by paragraph and bargain over the demands of each side. Diplomats from the four countries finally reached an agreement on a single text that covered to the greatest extent possible the minimal interests of both Iran and the European countries. The text became known as the "Paris Agreement."

THE PARIS AGREEMENT

The negotiations leading to the Paris Agreement were among the most grinding of my career, and I had been involved in a number of highly sensitive international issues: negotiations for the release of German hostages in Lebanon in the early 1990s and European and American hostages in 1988–1989; the Salman Rushdie affair; arranging the largest humanitarian exchange between Hizbollah and Israel with Germany's mediation in the mid-1990s; Iran-U.S. cooperation to fight the Taliban and al-Qaeda in Afghanistan in 2001–2002; and more. After the Paris Agreement, Iran's nuclear negotiation team returned to Iran to report back to the high-level authorities. After submitting our report, we left for the next IAEA Board of Governors' session in Vienna.

On the second day of the IAEA session, we were informed that the supreme leader had rejected the Paris Agreement because of its provision for suspension. He had told Dr. Rouhani that Iran would continue talks if the EU3's concern is about "non-diversion" but must be halted if the EU3 are seeking "cessation." The main reason for the leader's rejection was that the EU3 would not even accept 20 centrifuges to function for lab experiments. Furthermore, he was suspicious that the EU3 intended to prolong the negotiations and the suspension. My experience in almost two decades of diplomacy aimed at improving relations between Iran and the West told me that Ayatollah Khamenei was extremely suspicious of the policies of the West toward Iran, the Persian Gulf, the Middle East, and the Islamic world. My understanding was that he was supportive of the Saʾdabad statement between Iran and the EU3 but began to lose faith in the diplomatic process when the ElBaradei-limited definition of suspension expressed in

October 2003 (before the Tehran statement) was broadened dramatically by the IAEA's non-paper that was issued the following month.

This event caused the revival of the supreme leader's suspicion of the West, as he was principally against any type of long-term suspension and stressed repeatedly to the nuclear negotiation team that there was a substantial difference between "transparency" and "suspension." His argument was: We have no problem with transparency, but why should we suspend our legitimate rights under the NPT if the IAEA has no evidence of any diversion in our nuclear program?* His reasoning was logical and legitimate, but the problem remained of how to face the reality of international suspicions.

The supreme leader's rejection of the Paris Agreement came as a particular surprise to President Khatami and Dr. Rouhani. We found ourselves shocked, stranded, and stumped. We tried repeatedly to call Dr. Rouhani to inform him about the critical situation in Vienna.

At the urging of Ayatollah Hashemi Rafsanjani, who met with Ayatollah Khamenei along with President Khatami and Dr. Rouhani to explain that Iran was not committing to open-ended suspension, the supreme leader acquiesced to the Paris Agreement, but only conditionally. He accepted the extension of the suspension for only the three-month period during which working groups would, according to the Paris Agreement, meet to discuss and define mutual commitments to "firm guarantees" for Iran-EU cooperation and "objective guarantees" of non-diversion. This was a breakthrough and, as Rouhani told me later, the last chance to save Iran-EU nuclear diplomacy.

The Paris Agreement called, on the one hand, for temporary suspension of Iran's nuclear fuel-cycle activities, and on the other, for EU support for the resumption of those activities after the period of suspension. Europe would meanwhile undertake to grant other concessions to Tehran and lay the grounds for long-term strategic cooperation with Iran.[72] Both parties were committed to hammering out a precise definition for this main task during three months of working group meetings on political, economic, and nuclear issues. In the Paris Agreement, it was clear that suspension would continue only if and when the working groups, after

---

* Editor's note: Here again appears the key issue of the broader need to demonstrate that, beyond the question of diversion, all of a state's nuclear activities are exclusively peaceful.

150

three months of negotiations, came closer to determining mutually agreeable long-term arrangements. This was obviously not unconditional or unlimited suspension.

The Paris Agreement showed that achieving an agreement that would support Iran's enrichment program was possible. Its main goal was to promote talks aimed at achieving a solution that would be acceptable to both sides. This was a good opportunity for the European Union and the international community, as the past year of negotiations and positions taken by Iran's officials showed that Tehran would accept an agreement only if it defended Iran's rights to nuclear technology, including enrichment technology. The EU3's agreement to enforce Iran's basic nuclear rights showed that such a basis for a lasting solution was achievable and that they had recognized that they would ultimately have to accept Iran's enrichment activities. The agreement's call for Iran to provide "objective guarantees" on the peaceful nature of its nuclear program was further demonstration that the EU3 was prepared to give up calling for Iran to stop all of its nuclear activities, and it was understood that such a guarantee would be provided in the context of ongoing enrichment activity.

The Paris Agreement emphasized the enrichment suspension as a voluntary and temporary confidence-building measure.[73] Prior to the agreement, the United States and even Europe had in various sessions of the Board of Governors' meetings pushed for the suspension of Iran's nuclear activities with the ultimate aim of forcing Iran to give up its nuclear program. The Paris Agreement contained the most explicit acknowledgment in any official agreement that the IAEA resolutions calling for suspension were not legally binding.

Even more important than recognizing Iran's basic nuclear rights under the Non-Proliferation Treaty, the Paris Agreement called for the enforcement of those rights without discrimination by the European Union. This came as the United States was, on the basis of Iran's past failures and alleged aspiration to develop nuclear weapons, questioning Iran's right to have nuclear energy according to the NPT. The Paris Agreement squarely opposed the argument that an exception had to be made in Iran's case.[74]

Furthermore, the Paris Agreement reaffirmed Europe's commitment to prevent the referral of Iran's nuclear case to the UN Security Council. The events following the June session of the Board of Governors—Iran's resumption of centrifuge assembly and launch of Isfahan's uranium conversion facility—had shaken the fundaments of the Sa'dabad negotiations. The Paris Agreement reminded Europe of its commitments in a firm and undeniable manner.

This reaffirmation of European opposition to reporting Iran to the UN Security Council was quite significant, as intervention by the Security Council had up to that point been considered in some circles the sole remaining option for dealing with the Iran nuclear issue. With the Paris Agreement, Tehran managed to channel the nuclear case in a direction much more in accordance with its national interests. Until the very last moments before the conclusion of the agreement, Brussels had pushed for the inclusion of a trigger mechanism in the draft agreement, by which Iranian rejection of uranium suspension would have led to the case's referral to the Security Council.

Europe had also insisted that normalization of the case be made conditional on a conclusive confirmation by the IAEA director general that there was no sign of diversion of nuclear materials for military purposes. Tehran succeeded in softening the conditions for normalization considerably. The last paragraph of the September resolution had insisted that the Board of Governors remain seized of the matter; the Paris Agreement contravened that paragraph.

Europe's emphasis in the Paris Agreement on noninvolvement by the UN Security Council and the normalization of the case within the IAEA, as well as its agreement that Iran deserved a seat at the Committee on Multilateral Approaches to the Nuclear Fuel Cycle, further opened the possibility that Iran's nuclear program could be regarded as peaceful by the international community. Thus, in Iran's view, the Paris Agreement amounted to a refutation of claims raised by the American bloc that Iran posed a threat to world peace, and it undermined the arguments of American and Israeli (war) hawks.

The Paris Agreement and Europe's readiness to develop broad-based relations was a first for the Islamic Republic of Iran. Over the preceding twenty-five years, the West had sought to isolate Iran politically and in terms of security. The Paris Agreement could have been a true turning point. The new strategic cooperation that it promised between Tehran and Brussels through the creation of political and security cooperation and technology, and nuclear working groups stood to greatly enhance Iran's position in regional and global security arrangements and entail many benefits for Tehran.

The Paris Agreement called on the European Union as a whole to engage in negotiations along with the EU3, which was a sign of promotion of negotiations compared with October 2003 and increased the strategic weight of Iran's nuclear dossier. The foreign ministers of the EU3, who had visited Tehran in October 2003, engaged in negotiations with Iran in Paris having the full support of the European Union and the G8.

In reaching the agreement, Tehran and Europe once more took the initiative and circumvented American political maneuvering. In view of the failure of diplomacy leading to the Iraq war, a diplomatic settlement of the nuclear crisis by Europe would have greatly enhanced Europe's political credibility. Brussels' failure to deal with the nuclear dispute, however, would have greatly shored up the American neoconservatives' standing in the international arena. Furthermore, the Paris Agreement deepened the transatlantic gap while pressuring the White House to follow Europe's policy terms. Continuation of the trend of improving relations with Europe could have made U.S. economic sanctions against Iran ineffective.[75]

The agreement provided for Iran-Europe cooperation even beyond the nuclear issue. Its call for cooperation in Iraq's political crisis was a clear message to the United States, which aimed to obstruct Iran's presence in Iraq. The Paris Agreement reiterated the stipulations of the October 2003 Tehran statement that Europe would cooperate with Iran for the promotion of security and stability in the region, including efforts to establish a WMD-free zone. Therefore, the Paris Agreement seemed to increase Iran's ability to play an effective role in the Middle East on issues ranging from Israel's weapons of mass destruction to the crisis in Iraq. It also stressed cooperation in fighting the MEK and al-Qaeda terrorist groups.

Another major achievement of the Paris Agreement was that it laid the foundation for coherent and purposeful negotiations on economic relations by an economic committee and the resumption of trade talks. A review of Iran-EU economic ties shows that until that point relations were mainly focused on trade and were to Europe's advantage. Iran's non-oil exports to the EU declined by 25 percent between 1996 and 2003, from about $1 billion to about $800 million. Also, the ratio of Iran's non-oil exports to the European Union to total non-oil exports of the country during the same period fell from 33 percent to 13 percent. During the same period, Iran's imports from EU member states increased by more than 80 percent, from $5.8 billion in 1996 to $10.6 billion in 2003.

The negotiations of the newly created cooperation and technology working group therefore stood to provide Iran's industries, scientific community, and economy with a major opportunity. In view of unilateral U.S. sanctions against Iran that aimed to bar the transfer of technology (especially dual-purpose technology) to the country, this was a very important breakthrough.

Furthermore, the Paris Agreement reiterated, on the basis of Europe's obligations under the Tehran statement, the need for Brussels to support Iran's accession to the World Trade Organization and integration into the global economy. The United States had persistently opposed Iran's accession to the WTO for two decades. The initiation of negotiations on Iran's membership in the WTO, which was made possible only through nuclear talks, was a major stride toward bolstering the country's economic capabilities and realizing its sustainable development. Since economics, politics, and security are closely interrelated, WTO membership would have bolstered Iran's standing in other international bodies.

The Paris Agreement reassured the international community that Iran would opt for negotiations rather than confrontation. As the crisis had escalated, a large part of Iran's international cooperation, especially in economic fields, had slowed down. Assuring private companies and governments that the country's international relations were on a smooth track promised to enhance Iran's economic exchanges with the rest of the world. For example, Germany's Hermes insurance firm signed on to cover an industrial project in Iran worth $1 billion within ten days of the Paris Agreement. The agreement likewise quieted concerns in Iran's domestic economic sphere, reassuring the market, enhancing investment, and reducing capital flight.

The perception that Iran was moving to resolve the crisis amicably was also reflected in international media coverage, in which a good deal of support for the agreement was found. This shift increased the political cost to the United States of continuing to pursue a hard line against Iran.

The most important achievement for the international community, meanwhile, was the complete suspension of enrichment and granting of time for confidence building. Iran agreed, for the first time, to suspend its nuclear program as defined by Board of Governors' resolutions. Hence, after the conclusion of the Paris Agreement, Isfahan's uranium conversion facility and the Natanz facility stopped operating, which brought tremendous domestic political pressure down upon the nuclear negotiating team. At the time, many were concerned that requiring Tehran to suspend enrichment activity was a ploy to gain enough time to introduce a new international mechanism on the fuel cycle.

Ample evidence existed to this effect. The United States and EU had proposed at the end of 2003 that the IAEA Board of Governors establish a committee within the IAEA to devise a new approach on the issue of enrichment and production of nuclear fuel, issuing a joint statement that countries that violated the NPT or were under close inspection by the IAEA (due to a breach of the Safeguards Agreement) could not be accepted as members of the committee.[76]

Dr. ElBaradei also prepared a proposal according to which countries that had not achieved the full nuclear fuel cycle should stop all their activities for at least five years. Based on his proposal, which was supported by the United States, a new multilateral nuclear approaches committee was established in 2004.

The joint goal of the IAEA and the United States was to create a new mechanism for oversight of the fuel cycle, and they would pursue that goal through three international processes: the Committee on Multilateral Approaches to the Nuclear Fuel Cycle, the 2005 conference on the revision of the Non-Proliferation Treaty, and the director general's report to the summit meeting of the UN General Assembly. The fuel-cycle committee was authorized to transmit its final report on the new multilateral nuclear approach to the Board of Governors or send it to the conference on the revision of the NPT to pave the way for the ratification of new regulations. Given the importance of the committee, Tehran was determined to become a member of it.

At first, Tehran's efforts to have one of its diplomats join the fuel-cycle committee failed because of opposition from the United States. Tehran conducted many negotiations in September 2004 (after the Paris Agreement) to get the backing of European countries for its membership in the committee. The talks finally led the European Union to declare to the director general that it was not opposed to Iran's membership in the fuel-cycle committee. Renewed opposition from the United States meant months more of diplomatic wrangling, but Iran eventually prevailed upon Europe to fully support Tehran's request. On December 6, 2004, the IAEA officially invited Iran to become a member state of the committee.

The presence of an Iranian diplomat at the fuel-cycle committee was of more benefit than had originally been imagined. It very much changed the course of meetings of the committee, which had previously threatened Iran's interests. When Iran joined, the United States was trying to get the agreement of the committee to limit the right of enrichment to countries that had already attained the complete fuel cycle and ban enrichment in countries that were just developing their nuclear energy capacity. Iran, along with the Non-Aligned Movement and countries such as Canada and Australia, played an important role in defeating this proposed rule.[77]

The Paris Agreement changed the direction of the American bloc and international media, which had sought to get Iran's nuclear dossier to the UN Security Council even sooner than was originally expected. The change in attitude in the IAEA, the European Union, Russia, China, India, and even some countries in the American bloc, such as Australia and Japan, showed that Tehran's crisis management had been successful in November. The sole overt opposition to the agreement came from Israel and opposition groups abroad.

CHAPTER FOUR

2005 PRESIDENTIAL ELECTIONS

DEVELOPMENTS OF NOVEMBER 2004 AND
OUTCOMES OF REALISTIC CRISIS MANAGEMENT

Iran faced a long and difficult process after the conclusion of the Paris Agreement. This process can be divided into short-term and long-term phases. The former included measures to guarantee EU compliance with the agreement. Tehran maintained that dropping the nuclear case from the provisional agenda of the November session, along with Iran's immediate membership in the multilateral nuclear approaches committee, would be early signs of Europe's good faith. One of the EU3 negotiators told me that it was simply impossible because the IAEA director general had been requested by the Board of Governors to report on Iran in November and that the EU did not have the authority to remove an item from the IAEA agenda. In the interval leading up to the November session of the Board of Governors, Iran focused its efforts in three areas: cooperation with the IAEA to solve the remaining technical problems and to negotiate the expansion of suspensions; bargaining with the European Union on the content of the Board of Governors' resolution; and extensive negotiations with Non-Aligned Movement countries, China, and Russia.

The EU3 agreed for the first time to include Iran's representatives in consultations to draft a resolution on Iran's nuclear activities for the November session of the IAEA board. This agreement was taken as the first sign of Europe's willingness to cooperate with Iran to normalize the nuclear situation. On November 27, 2004, quadrilateral negotiations began in Vienna on the content of the draft resolution. Some Western media at that time indicated that the draft resolution presented by Europe had already been discussed in the EU's negotiations with Washington, as well as in the course of expert sessions of the G8. Reuters reported that major differences had surfaced between European and American diplomats on the main paragraphs of the resolution. Tehran's complete opposition to some paragraphs of the draft resolution and U.S. pressures led to extensive and difficult negotiations among all sides.

There were major differences between Iran and the EU (as well as between the United States and the EU) on a number of issues: how to quote from the director general's report on Iran's past breaches and failures; suspension and its scope; legal aspects of settling the case in the IAEA; IAEA inspections and the consequences of the emphasis put on the need for Tehran's full transparency (Tehran accepted inspectors only on the basis of the Safeguards Agreement and the Additional Protocol and rejected transparency measures that went beyond this); Iran's corrective measures; normalization of the situation; and Iran's controversial request to exclude twenty centrifuges from the suspension.

Intense negotiations by Iranian diplomats, and the confidence built by the Paris Agreement, finally turned the November 2004 resolution of the IAEA's Board of Governors, adopted on November 29, into one of the board's best and most positive resolutions on Iran's nuclear program. Iran's corrective measures on some of the past breaches were confirmed,[1] as was the fact that all declared nuclear materials in Iran had been accounted for, with no diversion to prohibited activities.[2,*] The Paris Agreement was confirmed with an emphasis on the voluntary, not legally binding, nature of enrichment suspension as a confidence-building measure.

---

* Editor's note: This still left open the questions related to possibly undeclared nuclear materials and activities in Iran.

Although the resolution had mentioned continuation and extension of suspension of all activities related to enrichment and reprocessing as an "essential" measure, the emphasis put on the "voluntary and not legally binding" nature of that measure indicated that the goals of Article 18 of the Safeguards Agreement and Article XII of the IAEA Statute had not been met. According to Article 18, when an issue is considered essential and urgent by the Board of Governors, the government of that country is compelled to take the required action without delay, irrespective of whether procedures have been invoked pursuant to Article 22 of the Safeguards Agreement for the settlement of a dispute. The resolution also stipulated that the IAEA's activities in Iran would be carried out within the framework of the 93+2 Additional Protocol.[3] It should be noted that prior resolutions had called for unlimited access and inspections beyond the Additional Protocol. Finally, according to the November resolution, Iran's case was removed from the Board of Governors' provisional agenda. This was an outcome of the Paris Agreement.

Compared with the Board of Governors' past demands, the substance of the November 2004 resolution showed that Tehran had been largely successful in crisis management. The achievement, especially in view of the board's decision to remove the nuclear issue from its provisional agenda, signified that the crisis could be ended in the foreseeable future and that Europe was willing to normalize the situation. The Board of Governors' request that the director general report to the board on his findings "as appropriate" was much less demanding than the closing paragraphs of previous resolutions.

Hence, after fourteen months of negotiations and diplomatic efforts, Tehran found itself in November 2004 in a new position, one that contrasted sharply with its earlier status.

In September 2003, Iran had nearly been referred to the UN Security Council, a course that was now reversed. At that same time, Tehran had been required to suspend all nuclear activities, while now this suspension was considered to be voluntary, for the purpose of confidence building and not legally binding. At that time, too, a host of evidence had been presented by Western countries in an effort to prove diversion of Iran's civilian nuclear activities to military goals or the existence of a secret military nuclear program parallel to its declared peaceful activities. In November

2004, however, the Board of Governors showed the first credible signal that Iran's activities were peaceful and that there was no diversion to military programs. The IAEA resolution of September 2003 had focused on Iran's secrecy; in November 2004, more emphasis was put on Iran's corrective measures.

At the outset of the crisis, Tehran was facing global consensus against it. By November 2004, not only had the transatlantic gap widened, but some countries of the American bloc were also opposed to the U.S. stance. Washington, which earlier was prepared for a limited military attack on Iran, now looked toward direct talks with Iran and signaled readiness to give concessions following Tehran's interactions with the international community and developments in Iraq. And the international community, now moving away from its earlier view of Iran's nuclear activities as a threat to international peace, recognized Iran's rights and agreed to their enforcement in November 2004, postponing that enforcement for several months while outstanding issues were resolved and mutual confidence was built. Even Russia and the EU, which considered suspension of Iran's nuclear fuel cycle to be in line with their economic interests, were sending positive signals and giving their nod to a gradual start of the fuel cycle in Iran.

It should be noted that all concessions given by Iran to Europe were limited to the requirements of the September 2003 resolution. Tehran diplomatically accepted part of those requirements in November 2004. In return, the EU, IAEA, and the majority of countries, specifically the 118 members of the Non-Aligned Movement, accepted the following: suspension as voluntary (not legally binding), limited to the period of negotiation and dependent on progress; Iran's right to develop peaceful nuclear energy, including its fuel-cycle technologies, and no evidence of diversion to military activities; stipulation that inspections would be limited to the Additional Protocol; and admission that Iran had corrected its major past failures.

The conclusion to be reached by these points was that Iran's nuclear activities did not constitute a threat to international peace and security. The EU agreed to grant concessions asked by Tehran to pave the way for the expansion of strategic relations with Iran and also to engage in nuclear cooperation with Iran and fulfill obligations undertaken by nuclear-weapon states as per the NPT. Tehran was offered a good opportunity to continue development of the technical know-how of its scientists in a calm atmosphere.

BROAD-BASED NEGOTIATIONS
TO SUPPORT THE PARIS AGREEMENT

The removal of the nuclear case from the Board of Governors' provisional agenda, and consensus on the terms of the November 2004 resolution, were construed as the first signs of the EU's compliance with its commitments under the Paris Agreement. Assertions by European officials concerning "the commencement of a new chapter in Iran-EU cooperation"[4] and the IAEA's official invitation to Iran, extended on December 6, 2004, to become a member of the fuel-cycle group provided the necessary grounds for resumption of long-term talks with the EU3.

The Paris Agreement had projected that long-term negotiations between Iran and the EU would be pursued simultaneously through three working groups: political and security, economic cooperation and technology, and nuclear. On January 17, 2005, Iran proposed to the EU an unprecedented comprehensive package of 33 articles on political and security relations.[5] We worked carefully on this package in Iran's Supreme National Security Council. We offered full cooperation with the EU on major security issues including combating terrorism; the elimination of weapons of mass destruction in the Middle East and control on exports of WMD technologies and expertise; respecting all international norms and commitments; full implementation of all WMD conventions (chemical, nuclear, and biological); combating organized crime and drug trafficking; exchanging intelligence; and the general peace and stability of the Persian Gulf. To demonstrate the maximum goodwill on the nuclear issue, we reiterated in the package our readiness to commit to the non-diversion of capabilities toward the production of nuclear or other weapons of mass destruction. Unfortunately, the EU did not accept this offer on nuclear, WMD, and other security issues, even though the EU3 had put forth no initiative of its own on "objective guarantees" for non-diversion.

The most difficult aspect of the diplomacy related to the "objective guarantees" required by the EU to ensure that Iran's nuclear program would not be used for military applications. Many rounds of talks were held on the question of "objective guarantees" and "firm guarantees." According to the Paris Agreement, Tehran had agreed to give "objective guarantees" that its nuclear fuel cycle would not be used for military purposes. Europe had also pledged to provide Iran with "firm guarantees" for development of political, economic, security, technological, and nuclear cooperation with Tehran. European diplomats were seeking guarantees that would not be affected by changing political conditions.

Some Western analysts argued that Iran did not truly need to produce fuel by itself, as it could obtain what it needed for the Tehran Research Reactor and Bushehr reactor from Russia and the international market, and that because it did not need to enrich itself, the best way to reassure the international community about objective guarantees on non-diversion was for Iran not to have any enrichment facilities. However, the Iranian view, based on the experience of Western countries breaching their contracts with Iran after the 1979 Islamic Revolution, was that it could not trust promises from the international community to provide the fuel it needed in the long term. Furthermore, the rights to enrichment were inalienable under the NPT, regardless of whether depriving a country of those rights would be an expedient means of guaranteeing non-diversion.

The difference in Iran's and Europe's understanding of this issue accounted for the lion's share of negotiations. In this round of critical negotiations on "objective guarantees" that the Iranian program would be used exclusively for peaceful purposes, Tehran maintained that the NPT, the Safeguards Agreement, the Additional Protocol, transparency, and cooperation with the IAEA were the best "objective guarantees" that no diversion would occur in Iran's peaceful nuclear program. Official recognition of Iran's right was the key prerequisite for compromise on the "objective guarantees."

However, the Europeans were not able to convince the Americans on this issue, and so they had no other option than to play for time. Ambassador Sirous Nasseri,[6] the head of Iran's working group for nuclear negotiations, did everything possible to reach a solution, but the EU did not consider the guarantees Iran proposed as sufficient because the United States was not on board. In private, I told our EU negotiation partners that the issue of the fuel cycle would never be negotiable, and that this was the last opportunity to save the negotiations. The supreme leader's patience had reached an end, and if the nuclear working group could not show tangible progress, enrichment would restart soon. One of our EU negotiation partners told me that they were ready to compromise but that the United

States was the obstacle. Later, Dr. Rouhani told me that in 2006, Joschka Fischer had told him that "[the] EU3 and Iran have reached a compromise but the United States prevented it from succeeding." As time went by and negotiations slowed down, Tehran took critical positions and threatened to leave negotiations if that trend continued.

At that time, some of our opponents in Iran believed that the time-honored "good cop/bad cop" routine was being deployed and considered negotiations with Europe and threats from the United States as political and security tactics to contain Iran. There was a lot of evidence to prove otherwise, however, especially considering developments in Iraq. Sharp re-actions from the European Union to President Bush's remarks in an NBC interview were along the same lines.[7] The president, asked about potential military action against Iran, had replied, "I hope we can solve it diplo-matically, but I will never take any option off the table." Luxembourg (as rotational head of the European Union) had issued a statement critical of Bush's remarks, and similar positions were taken by the foreign policy commissioner of the European Union, the German chancellor, France's Chirac, and the French foreign minister.

High-ranking diplomatic efforts by Iran were pursued by the country's top nuclear negotiator, the foreign minister, and the head of the Atomic Energy Organization of Iran. Negotiations between Iran's foreign minister and the Australian prime minister, John Howard, on January 30, 2005, ne-gotiations between Gholam Reza Aghazadeh[8] and the foreign ministers of Portugal and Belgium on February 1, and meetings of Iran's foreign minis-ter and the Japanese prime minister and minister of foreign affairs in Tokyo on February 9 exemplify Iran's diplomatic efforts. The February 13 visit to Algeria by Rouhani, Iran's chief nuclear negotiator, and his subsequent vis-its to Russia, Tunisia, France, and Germany within a one-week period also demonstrate that Tehran had launched a major drive to achieve its goals.

Negotiations with the Russian president, Vladimir Putin, and French president, Jacques Chirac, were more important in the eyes of internation-al observers. Rouhani's second trip to Russia signaled Tehran's attempt to use Moscow as leverage in the face of Europe's dawdling. Putin's stress on Iran's basic rights and the Kremlin's support for those rights reflected that strategy. Iran's emphasis on the need to establish strategic relations between the two countries at a time when difficult talks on Iran's strategic relations with Europe were going on demonstrated Tehran's effort to draw on the traditional sensitivities of Western Europe.

During that trip, private and official negotiations with Putin lasted about three hours. In this discussion we tried to make it clear that the Paris Agreement would lead to three months of working group negotiations to conclude "firm guarantees" for establishing good relations and "objective guarantees" that Iran's nuclear program would not be diverted to non-peaceful purposes. If the working groups failed, Iran would not be able to continue broad suspension. Putin expressed very positive views toward Iran's nuclear policy and encouraged us to remain patient.

In his 2011 memoir, Mohamed ElBaradei likewise recognized Iran's commitment to resolving the nuclear issue in the ultimately squandered period of opportunity after the November 2004 Paris Agreement: "Iran's cooperation with the IAEA stayed strong; there were only a few remaining inspection issues. At the March 2005 Board meeting, Iran's nuclear program was not on the agenda for the first time in almost two years."[9]

ANOTHER CHANCE FOR A COMPROMISE

The meeting between Iranian and French authorities was another significant chance for a face-saving solution. Dr. Rouhani and President Chirac agreed in Paris in March 2005 to let the IAEA solve the sole remaining problem, "objective guarantees," by defining the necessary mechanics of such guarantees. I was very much surprised when the French foreign minister and director general of the French Foreign Ministry, who were present at the meeting, opposed Chirac. It is important to note that in some instances, the French permanent government under the country's presidents has taken a harder line on Iran than the United States.

Chirac, however, noted that the IAEA, as the sole international authority to guarantee the peaceful nature of nuclear activities of member countries, was in the best position to define such mechanisms. From Paris, we left for Berlin and a meeting with the German chancellor, Gerhard Schroeder. Schroeder said that he had been informed about the meeting with Chirac, which was also discussed between the EU3 and the United States, but that, unfortunately, even if the EU3 accepted the proposal, the Americans would not.

By March of 2005 the nuclear working group was practically stagnant. Tehran insisted that its right to produce nuclear fuel was not negotiable and asked the European side to offer its proposals on objective and firm guarantees as envisaged in Brussels. However, the inability of the Europeans to persuade the United States and to come up with an effective proposal nearly caused the negotiations to grind to a halt. In a meeting on April 12, 2005, François Nicoullaud, the French ambassador in Tehran, told me that "for the U.S., the enrichment in Iran is a redline which the EU cannot cross." Following the meeting, I sent the minutes of the meeting to the high-level authorities. Just two weeks later, on April 26, 2005, the Leader instructed Dr. Rouhani to restart the UCF activities in Isfahan. Under these circumstances, we tried to end the deadlock by offering generous new proposals to Paris and Berlin. Tehran's proposals could have led to major developments on two counts. First, the proposals offered to France mainly pertained to weaknesses in negotiations and structural problems. From that angle, it seemed that reducing bureaucracy and bargaining with more powers could promote talks. The Iranian side asked Chirac to elevate the level of negotiations on the European side to facilitate further talks. Second, Iran's negotiating team made a key initiative in focusing on how the IAEA should arbitrate differences between the two sides' positions, especially concerning the definition of mechanisms for providing "objective guarantees."

THE SECOND SESSION OF THE NUCLEAR NEGOTIATIONS STEERING COMMITTEE

Tehran took two important steps following the steering committee's[10] March 2005 session in Paris. First, it announced that it would stop negotiations with the political and economic working groups. At that time, the evidence strongly suggested that Europe was willing to grant concessions within the framework of the political and economic working groups to secure Iran's agreement on long-term suspension of the fuel cycle.

The EU3 proposed elements of a nuclear deal, under which indefinite suspension of Iran's enrichment would be met with EU promises for the following:

- Recognition of the rights of Iran to develop a power plant program.
- Support for Russian-Iranian cooperation in the fields of power plants and fuel supply.
- Political support for Iran in accessing the international nuclear fuel market, with spent fuel being returned.
- Cooperation in the field of nuclear safety.
- Support for Iranian light-water research reactors.
- Resumption of negotiations for a trade agreement with Iran.
- Support for Iran's accession to the WTO.
- Cooperation in sectors such as investment, civil aviation, the petrochemical industry, communications, railroads, and car manufacturing.
- Confirmation of security assurances for Iran.
- Cooperation in counterterrorism, including against the MEK as a terrorist organization.
- Comprehensive security and political dialogue on regional security.
- Support for a Middle East free of WMD.
- Support for Iranian participation in the G8 broader Middle East initiative.
- Cooperation in combating drug production and trafficking.[11]

These points, the products of the three working groups, were the incentives the EU put on the table. Iran was prepared to accept a deal only if the EU recognized the complete rights of Iran including enrichment. Iran offered objective guarantees for non-diversion; the EU3 proposed nothing in return about the definition of objective guarantees to secure the Paris Agreement. By withdrawing from political and economic negotiations, Tehran showed that it had not forgotten the main goal of the Paris Agreement and was still pursuing its main objective, that is, peaceful enrichment with objective guarantees to assure non-diversion and firm guarantees for good relations.

Second, Iran presented another innovative plan to build confidence with Europe and resume enrichment activities on the basis of mutual agreement with every objective guarantee the IAEA and the EU required on transparency and non-diversion. This "fourth plan" offered by Iran's negotiating team was a proposal for a phased approach. According to the plan, presented on March 23, 2005, Tehran was supposed to gradually restart fuel-cycle activities while building confidence with Europe:

A.1. Actions for Iran in Phase 1:
- Cabinet approval of the Additional Protocol
- Policy declaration not to reprocess spent fuel
- Presentation of draft legislation to Parliament banning the production or use of nuclear weaponry
- Resumption of uranium conversion at the Isfahan facility
- Storage of uranium conversion products under IAEA surveillance

A.2. Actions for the EU in Phase 1:
- Declarations guaranteeing Iran's access to EU's markets and investments
- Declaration recognizing Iran as a major source of energy supply
- Commencement of a feasibility study for building EU nuclear power plants in Iran

B.1. Actions for Iran in Phase 2:
- Policy declaration not to enrich above the level of LEU
- Policy declaration to convert all enriched uranium to fuel rods
- Presentation of the Additional Protocol to Parliament for ratification
- Parliamentary and cabinet decisions on strengthening legal export mechanisms
- Assembly, installation, and testing of 3,000 centrifuges in Natanz

B.2. Actions for the EU in Phase 2:
- Declaration of guarantees for Iran's access to advanced and nuclear technology
- Declaration of readiness to build nuclear power plants in Iran
- Signature of contracts for building nuclear power plants

C.1. Actions for Iran in Phase 3:
- Parliamentary approval of legislation on banning the production or use of nuclear weaponry
- Permission for the continuous on-site presence of IAEA/EU inspectors at Isfahan and Natanz
- Commencement of operation of a pilot centrifuge plant at Natanz
- Immediate conversion of all UF_6 produced by the pilot plant to fuel rods
- Commencement of work to complete an industrial-scale centrifuge plant at Natanz

C.2. Actions for the EU in Phase 3:
- Normalizing Iran's status under G8 export control regulations
- Issuing guarantees on nuclear fuel supply
- Presentation of the EU's initiative to establish a WMD-free zone in the Middle East

D.1. Actions for Iran in Phase 4:
- Parliamentary approval of the Additional Protocol
- Beginning of operation of an industrial centrifuge plant in Natanz
- Immediate conversion of all industrial plant products to fuel rods

D.2. Actions for the EU in Phase 4:
- Conclusion of contracts for defense sales to Iran
- Beginning of construction of a new nuclear power plant in Iran

Iran's four-stage plan was immediately sent to Paris, London, Berlin, and the EU by European diplomats in Tehran. It was a realistic proposal providing for both Iranian "objective guarantees" of non-diversion and EU "firm guarantees" for good relations with Iran, and in fact the last official proposal offered by Iran as a face-saving solution. Tehran insisted that the plan provided the basis for further negotiations. The Europeans told us that they were ready to consider Iran's proposal but not as the foundation of nuclear negotiations. The European side insisted on simultaneous assessment of both sides' plans culminating in agreement on a resultant joint plan.

At the Iran-EU3 Steering Committee meeting in late April 2005 in London, in which I did not participate, Iran's negotiation team tried its utmost to make its EU counterparts understand the domestic pressure it faced: Back in Iran, we were accused of having been "tricked" into accepting suspension and getting nothing in return. We warned our European partners that we would be forced to start activities at the conversion plant in Isfahan if they stalled the talks. This was not a bluff. The supreme leader had told Rouhani that the uranium conversion plant in Isfahan should be put into operation and that Rouhani should not wait any longer for an EU response.

Hence, Iran's negotiating team offered a revised version of its March 23 proposal, but with a greater focus on short-term, confidence-building measures. The proposal provided for Iran's adoption of the Additional Protocol, assurances against reprocessing, and continuation of enrichment suspension for six months, with the EU3 for its part agreeing to joint task forces on export controls and counterterrorism and declaring Iran a major source of energy for Europe.[12] The EU3 could not come to an agreement on the Iranian proposals due to U.S. opposition to any agreement that included Iran's right to enrichment.

PRESIDENTIAL ELECTION FEVER
AND REASONS FOR FAILURE

The remarks of negotiators and credible evidence from the media showed that Europe was on the verge of accepting Tehran's enrichment activities.[13] However, between the meeting of the steering committee in Paris on March 23, 2005, and the London meeting on April 19, a new factor, rooted in Iran's domestic political atmosphere, was introduced into Tehran's talks with the European Union. Iran's nuclear dossier was a major topic of debate among candidates in the presidential race. As will be discussed in greater detail in the next chapter, during and after the presidential election campaign, some hard-liners labeled President Khatami's nuclear negotiating team spies, traitors, and tools of the West who sold out the rights and ambitions of the country. This rhetoric was used to transform the nuclear issue into one of national pride and to sideline moderate and reformist political camps.

This domestic sparring had an impact on Iran's ability to conduct a coherent foreign policy. Conflicting signals were sent to the Europeans that mirrored a wide range of political stances. At one end of the spectrum, some political figures said that enrichment was useless to Iran and that Tehran should completely stop its fuel cycle. On the other end of the spectrum, it was argued that Iran should confront the international community, not implement the Additional Protocol, and even withdraw from the Non-Proliferation Treaty.

The London session of the steering committee showcased this discordance. Tehran—due largely to domestic pressures—offered another plan and called for the speedy inauguration of the Isfahan uranium conversion facility and continuation of negotiations. In the previous plan, the inauguration of the complex had been projected for July 2005. Europe, however, asked Iran to adjourn negotiations until after Iran's presidential elections.

The discrepancy between the two sides' viewpoints led to a rapid escalation of political disputes. The remarks by the Atomic Energy Organization of Iran and Dr. Kamal Kharrazi about Iran's decision to launch the Isfahan facility triggered a new dispute between Tehran and Brussels. The EU3 asked Iran in an official letter on May 10, 2005, to continue suspension of the nuclear fuel cycle.

Following Tehran's decision to resume operations at Isfahan and widespread reactions in the West to Iran's decision, the EU3 sent a letter to Iran's chief nuclear negotiator calling for a high-level quadrilateral meeting. Plans for the meeting were overshadowed by the escalation of tensions. In view of Iran's decision to launch the Isfahan plant and Europe's insistence on the postponement of negotiations until after Iran's presidential elections, most observers predicted that the quadrilateral meeting in Geneva would fail. Some reporters close to European diplomatic circles said that they had been unofficially invited to attend a news conference to be held by the EU3's foreign ministers at the European headquarters of the United Nations to report the failure of the negotiations. The development indicated that the European foreign ministers had met with Rouhani presuming that negotiation would fail and that the news conference was arranged at UN headquarters to announce the necessity of reporting Iran to the UN Security Council.

At the same time, three important international meetings were under way or pending: the NPT review conference in New York, a World Trade Organization meeting, and the IAEA's Board of Governors' session in June.

During the May 25, 2005, Geneva meeting, the three European foreign ministers asked that Brussels be given three months to present Europe's final plan to Iran. They also noted that Europe was willing to boost cooperation with Iran and provide guarantees on some key issues, including:

- Full support for nuclear energy for peaceful purposes in Iran, including the provision of nuclear plants by Western countries.
- Assurances for long-term fuel supplies to power plants backed by the IAEA and United Nations.
- Guarantees related to Iran's territorial integrity, independence, and national sovereignty and the prevention of aggression against the country.

- Bolstered political and security relations between Tehran and Brussels.
- Recognition of Iran as a major source of energy, including oil and gas, for the EU.
- Gradual removal of obstacles to sending dual-use equipment or advanced technology to Iran and to technological cooperation with Tehran.
- Strengthening cooperation between Iran and Europe in fighting terror and illicit drugs.
- Rapidly finalizing an Iran-Europe trade agreement and Iran's membership in the World Trade Organization.

The meeting's timing and the acceptability of Europe's proposals persuaded Tehran to agree to grant a two-month deadline to the EU to present a final proposal. I notified the EU3 ministers of Iran's official response after the return of the nuclear negotiating team to Tehran and high-level discussions there on June 1, 2005. Although Rouhani gave the green light to a maximum two-month period for the EU to present its final proposal, he made it clear and said three times during the meeting that any proposal that excluded enrichment would be rejected in advance. Therefore, the EU3's positive stance was taken as a sign of willingness to support enrichment in Iran. Reuters, meanwhile, reported that President Bush had agreed to limited enrichment in Iran.[14]

The two-month interval would allow the nuclear team to wait until electioneering in Tehran was finished before returning to the negotiating table.

Because Tehran's "fourth plan" faced some opposition in Brussels, I paid an unofficial visit to the EU3 capitals in spring 2005. Berlin was my first stop. I met my German counterpart, Michael Schaefer, for lunch in a pizza restaurant in Berlin. I told him that regardless of the results of the election, Iran would restart the uranium conversion facility at Isfahan and later the enrichment activities in Natanz because the supreme leader had already decided on the matter and issued the relevant orders. I reiterated that neither we nor any other administration would ever compromise on the legitimate rights of Iran for peaceful nuclear technology, including enrichment. I reminded him that we had shown considerable cooperation and goodwill by agreeing to suspension of the nuclear fuel cycle, implementing the Additional Protocol and Subsidiary Arrangement, and allowing IAEA inspections even beyond the Comprehensive Safeguards Agreement and Additional Protocol. I argued that the way to save the current round of negotiations would be for Europe to demonstrate its recognition of Iran's nuclear rights to enrichment in practice; otherwise, the current conciliatory nuclear policy would be scrapped and Iran would continue to develop its nuclear activities in accordance with its legitimate rights unilaterally even if Rafsanjani were to become the next president.

I unofficially proposed to Michael Schaefer the "fifth and the last" package as a contingency if the EU3 was not ready to accept Iran's fourth plan. The general outlines of the fifth package were as follows:

- In the first step, Iran would resume uranium conversion at the Isfahan plant and would export its product to an agreed-upon country in exchange for yellowcake.
- In the second step, Iran would begin enrichment at Natanz in a limited pilot plan with some 3,000 centrifuges but export all enriched uranium to an agreed-upon country.
- Negotiations would continue for a maximum of one year to reach a final compromise on "objective guarantees" of non-diversion and "firm guarantees" for comprehensive relations.
- The timetable for the industrial-level production of fuel would be agreed upon based on Iran's fuel requirements.

The reality was that the Bushehr nuclear power plant accounted for most of Iran's nuclear fuel consumption needs, and Russia had already contracted to provide the plant with fuel for ten years.

After two and a half hours of discussion, Michael Schaefer expressed a positive reaction to the package and encouraged me to discuss the same proposal with Paris and London. After the meeting I sent a report to Dr. Rouhani through our embassy. I got a positive signal from him to pursue the same discussion with the United Kingdom and France. I left for Paris and had that discussion with our French counterpart. Sadeq Kharrazi, our ambassador to Paris, was also in the meeting. Paris seemed to be on the fence: the French Foreign Ministry's political director, Stanislas Lefebvre de Laboulaye, expressed interest in the idea without either explicitly agreeing to it or rejecting it, and emphasized the importance of London's reaction. In London I discussed the proposal with John Sawers, who was at the time director general for political affairs at the Foreign Ministry. After two hours of very difficult negotiations, John told me that Washington would never tolerate the operation of even one centrifuge in Iran, but would be willing to talk about such a package after Iran's presidential election.

A note on John Sawers: over the course of two years of nuclear negotiations, I found Sawers to be something of a mystery. When we had our first meeting with the EU3 directors general in 2003, he was the one who first raised and pushed for the proposal for cessation of Iran's enrichment activities. During ministerial meetings with Dr. Rouhani in October 2003, there were times when tensions got very high over the suspension issue. I noticed at two points that, just as it seemed that the UK's foreign secretary, Jack Straw, was ready to show flexibility, John Sawers whispered something in his ear and then Straw immediately changed his position. One or twice more over the next two years I saw the same thing: when Jack Straw took a moderate stand and showed flexibility, a whisper by John Sawers was all that was needed for Straw to revert to a more rigid position.

ElBaradei recollects such tensions between the positions and styles of Straw and Sawers in his memoir, as well as the limitations that Straw faced in determining policy toward Iran. ElBaradei writes of Straw,

> In all our dealings, I found that he had an ability to grasp the big picture, a sense of fairness, a deep respect for cultural nuance, and a pragmatist's willingness to consider commonsense solutions. . . . Straw had told me [in early 2006] that it was clear that the Americans no longer trusted him. When reports had circulated alleging U.S. plans to use bunker-busting weapons in Iran, Straw had been quoted as saying the idea was "completely nuts," telling BBC News there was "no smoking gun." One month later, Blair had removed Straw as foreign secretary, replacing him with Margaret Beckett, a foreign policy neophyte.[15]

In 2007, around the time of my arrest in Iran, Sawers was posted as the UK ambassador to the UN and later was appointed chief of MI6. When I heard about his new assignment, I was totally shocked. I took it as clear evidence that Sawers was from the start a high-level intelligence operative, rather than a diplomat. This suggested to us that behind the scenes of the negotiations, intelligence services were playing a key role and even preventing European diplomats from making necessary compromises.

After my discussions with the EU3, on July 18, Rouhani sent a message to the EU3 proposing an agreement on initial limitations on uranium enrichment at Natanz; negotiations for the full-scale operation of Natanz; arrangements to import material for uranium conversion and to export UF_6; and negotiation of an "optimized" IAEA monitoring mechanism for Natanz.[16]

In general and to my understanding, the Europeans were ready to accept operations at Isfahan's uranium conversion facility, but only after Iran's June 2005 presidential election. However, when it came to the pilot plant in Natanz, Berlin and Paris could accept a limited number of centrifuges operating at the pilot level, while London was reluctant to acquiesce on any because of Washington's stance. In my opinion the postponement of discussion of the proposal was a strategic mistake by the EU3, because, as I told them, the supreme leader had already decided to start the facility at Isfahan, and the postponement of talks until after the election would kill Iran's current nuclear policy.

After I returned to Tehran, I met Rouhani and he informed me that our leadership had agreed with the package on three conditions: first, the number of pilot centrifuges should not be less than 3,000; second, negotiations should not take longer than one year; and third, agreement on the formula should be reached before the presidential election.

Later, the new Iranian foreign minister, Manouchehr Mottaki, said in an interview with Japan's NHK television that Europe had reacted positively toward Iran's proposal.

Disappointed by the latest efforts to convince the EU3 to agree to the fifth package, we decided to meet with the president of South Africa for mediation. Rouhani visited South Africa in late July before the reopening of the Isfahan uranium conversion facility. The trip's achievements could have led to major developments and even the settlement of the nuclear crisis. South African President Thabo Mbeki proposed that the products of the Isfahan facility be exported to his country in return for yellowcake. Immediately after the meeting, he wrote a letter to the leaders of the EU3 and the U.S. president about the idea. The letter was delivered in less than 24 hours, but responses were late in coming.

In the interim, the ninth presidential election was held in Iran, and Mahmoud Ahmadinejad was elected president. Almost two weeks later, Abdul Samad Minty, South Africa's nuclear negotiator, called and told me that the official response was not negative and the EU3 heads of state had written to Mbeki reiterating they were ready to discuss the idea in principle. I told my South African colleague that it was too late.

Ahmadinejad's election shocked the world—Iranian politicians included—and led to a heavy propaganda campaign against Iran. The atmosphere that was created by the Western media and the positions taken by some political activists pushed Western governments to ratchet up pressure on Tehran. As a result, the international community's tone toward Iran changed significantly. Tehran emphasized that nuclear policies were adopted at the highest level and were not affected by transient developments such as a turnover of the presidency. This argument, however, went unheeded for various reasons.

It was in this context that the EU3 ambassadors presented their comprehensive package of incentives to me on August 5, 2005. Two weeks prior to this meeting, we received credible information that the EU3 would propose indefinite suspension in its upcoming package. This prompted us to deliver an official letter to the IAEA on August 1, 2005, informing the agency that Iran had reached a decision to restart the UCF plant in Isfahan. The presidential election result, which had taken the Western world by surprise, also influenced the content of the incentives package. When submitting the package to me, European diplomats stressed that the door was still open to negotiations and that the European Union was prepared to promote fuller cooperation with Iran.

THE EUROPEAN PACKAGE

The goal of Europe's proposed package was to prevent the possibility of diversion of Iran's nuclear activities to nuclear weapon development and to foster better relations and cooperation with Iran on the basis of mutual respect while building confidence with the world regarding the peaceful nature of Iran's nuclear program.

With the package, the Europeans showed that, to create the right conditions for negotiations, they were ready to take the following steps:

- Reaffirm Iran's right to develop nuclear energy for peaceful purposes in conformity with its NPT obligations, and, in this context, reaffirm their support for the development by Iran of a civil nuclear energy program.
- Commit to actively support the building of new light-water reactors in Iran through joint international projects, in accordance with the IAEA Statute and the NPT.
- Agree to suspend discussion of referral of Iran's nuclear program to the Security Council upon resumption of negotiations.

In return, Iran was expected to:

- Commit to addressing all outstanding concerns of the IAEA through full cooperation with the agency.
- Suspend all enrichment-related and reprocessing activities under IAEA monitoring, as requested by the IAEA Board of Governors, and commit to continue suspension for the duration of negotiations. In fact, they hoped to secure an agreement for long-term suspension.
- Resume implementation of the Additional Protocol.

Areas of future cooperation to be covered in negotiations on a long-term agreement included:

- Reaffirmation of Iran's inalienable right to nuclear energy for peaceful purposes without discrimination and in conformity with Articles I and II of the NPT, and cooperation with Iran in the development of a civil nuclear power program.
- Active support for the building of new light-water power reactors in Iran through international joint projects in accordance with the IAEA Statute and the NPT and using state-of-the-art technology.
- Provision of a substantive package of research and development cooperation, including the possible provision of light-water research reactors, notably in the fields of radioisotope production, basic research, and applications of nuclear technology in medicine and agriculture.
- Legally binding assurances for the provision of nuclear fuel to Iran.
- Support for a new conference to promote dialogue and cooperation on regional security issues.

- Improvement of Iran's access to international markets and capital through practical support for full integration into international structures including the World Trade Organization, as well as the creation of a framework for increased direct investment in and trade with Iran.
- Civil aviation cooperation, including the possible removal of restrictions on U.S. and European manufacturers in exporting civil aircraft to Iran.
- Establishment of a long-term energy partnership between Iran, the EU, and other willing partners.
- Support for the modernization of Iran's telecommunications infrastructure, including the possible removal of relevant U.S. and other export restrictions.
- Support for agricultural development in Iran, including possible access to U.S. and European agricultural products, technology, and farm equipment.

The new Iranian government, however, was determined to resume activities at the Isfahan uranium conversion facility. With the Europeans initially proposing that Iran agree to total suspension of enrichment activities for an indefinite period, Tehran decided to withdraw from the November 2004 Paris Agreement. In the meeting of August 2005, the EU3 ambassadors raised with me an unrealistic idea of a ten-year suspension, but El-Baradei had already called for a five-year suspension. I believe a three-year suspension of the enrichment facility of Natanz was as far as the Europeans could go toward a compromise with Iran on restarting the uranium conversion project at Isfahan because the United States was not on board; Washington was taking a zero enrichment stance on Iran.

Nevertheless, we were ready to accept a shorter term of suspension in subsequent talks. With the EU's clear acceptance of the legitimate rights of Iran to peaceful nuclear technology, including enrichment and "firm guarantees" for comprehensive relations, we were able to persuade high-level decisionmakers to allow us to negotiate "objective grantees" that our nuclear activities were peaceful, acceptance of a period of suspension of a few months for finalizing details of the deal, and cooperation on political and security issues bilaterally, regionally, and internationally. The latter included such delicate issues as Iraq, Afghanistan, al-Qaeda, terrorism, a WMD-free zone in the Middle East, and even the Israeli-Palestinian peace process. The Iranian negotiating team felt it was a golden opportunity for world peace and security.

Unfortunately, our EU partners didn't view it that way. Speaking to the press at the Élysée Palace, Tony Blair and Jacques Chirac urged Iran to suspend enrichment. Also, Jacques Chirac subsequently joined Vladimir Putin and Gerhard Schroeder at Kaliningrad, where they reviewed Iran's nuclear case and called on Iran to suspend enrichment and continue negotiations. Following these developments, the United States, which had already shown signs of flexibility on, at least, the uranium conversion project in Isfahan, expressed opposition even to the construction of the Bushehr nuclear power plant.

At the beginning of nuclear talks in 2003, the United States had aimed for not just permanent or indefinite suspension, but for the "dismantlement" of Iran's enrichment and reprocessing activities, and it rejected the idea of any provision of nuclear power plants to Iran, even if Iran abandoned fuel-cycle activities. The United States also had opposed any incentives to Iran because it believed that there should be no incentive for compliance with NPT obligations.[17] Later, U.S. policy changed to support the EU's initiative after the February 2005 visit by George W. Bush to Europe and his meetings with the heads of the EU3. Washington realized that the talks were going to fail and decided to show support in order to ensure that Tehran, not Washington, would be blamed for the failure of the talks. This would in turn encourage the EU3 to support sanctions if and when the file was referred to the UN Security Council.[18] But we should not forget that the EU missed a great many opportunities for a face-saving solution during nuclear talks just because the United States was not prepared to play a constructive role to support an initiative other than its own ramping up of pressure during negotiations from 2003 to 2005.

As already mentioned, a few days before the reopening of the Isfahan uranium conversion facility in August 2005, Abdul Samad Minty, a representative of the South African president, called me to relay a message from Thabo Mbeki. In that message, which was later rejected by Iran's leadership, Mbeki stated that the leaders of the three European countries were ready to accept his country's plan and were willing to negotiate with

Iran. Minty also asked Iran's leaders to postpone the inauguration of the Isfahan facility for a couple of weeks to allow time for an agreement with the EU3. This initiative, however, came too late, and we were not able to take any action because we had been informed that replacing our nuclear negotiation team was the first priority of the new administration. When we received Mbeki's message, we were in the process of packing up to leave the Supreme National Security Council.

In the last days of Khatami's presidency, we had to reactivate the Isfahan uranium conversion facility, and the seals on the facility were removed in the presence of IAEA inspectors. The next day, Iran's official letter on the resumption of activities at Isfahan was submitted to the IAEA. Dr. ElBaradei reported the reopening of the Isfahan facility to the Board of Governors, which held an emergency meeting on August 7, 2005. Two days later, a resolution was issued calling on Iran to reinstate the suspension.

RECAP: IRAN'S OBJECTIVES AND ACHIEVEMENTS

A recap of these developments shows that following the Khatami team's grand strategy to handle the crisis, specific goals, and approach to negotiations with Europe, Iran was successful in achieving the following major objectives:

- The serious international crisis and its domestic consequences were checked, and the Islamic Republic managed to prevent the referral of its nuclear dossier from the IAEA's Board of Governors to the UN Security Council.
- Iran's peaceful nuclear capability was protected and enhanced through interaction with the international community and various confidence-building measures. Meanwhile, negotiations provided time for Isfahan's uranium conversion project to be finished and commissioned, the number of centrifuges at Natanz increased from 150 to 1,000, and software and hardware for Iran's nuclear infrastructure to be further developed. The heavy-water reactor project in Arak came into operation and was not suspended at all.
- Warmongering U.S. unilateralism was undermined. Progress through diplomacy showed that solving international issues through multilateral negotiations, or the European approach, could

be more fruitful and entail few adverse effects. American bullying, meanwhile, achieved little. For its part, Tehran showed that it was possible to exploit the gap between Europe and the United States to achieve Iranian objectives.

- The U.S. attempt to keep Iran out of the sessions of the IAEA's committees failed. Instead, Iran attained membership on the multilateral approaches committee, giving it a greater ability to influence committee/IAEA decisions on the nuclear fuel cycle.

- The world's understanding of "suspension" was changed from a legally binding obligation (according to the September 2003 resolution) to a voluntary and short-term undertaking aimed at confidence building. Other requirements and obligations included in the September 2003 resolution of the IAEA Board of Governors with regard to the Additional Protocol were also changed to voluntary and confidence-building measures.

- By renouncing suspension on two occasions, Tehran demonstrated the voluntary nature of suspension and showed that the timing for the resumption of enrichment activities would be determined by Tehran, not a foreign authority or power. Iran's suspension freezes, along with the wording of IAEA resolutions, underlined the fact that "safeguards requirements" were totally separate from voluntary "confidence-building measures."

- Technical questions raised by the IAEA about Iran's activities were addressed in clear, logical, and undeniable fashion, despite fears in Tehran that the great powers could determine the IAEA's decisions. As ElBaradei mentions in his 2011 book, although some ambiguities and questions about Iran's nuclear activities remained, the major legal and technical issues that the United States raised to prove Iranian noncompliance with the NPT were largely resolved.*

- To maintain friendly political relations with Iran, countries such as Pakistan were forced to cooperate with the IAEA and accept responsibility for some problems related to the nuclear dossier. This helped resolve some of the most problematic ambiguities cited by the IAEA. The issue of highly enriched contamination, for exam-

---

* Editor's note: more challenging issues were to arise through subsequent IAEA investigation.

ple, was largely diffused when it became clear to the IAEA that the source of the highly enriched uranium contamination was centrifuges imported from Pakistan.

- Iran's general stance that it had a legitimate right to and interest in developing the nuclear fuel cycle, and particularly its rejection of the monopolization on the production and sale of nuclear fuel by members of an exclusive club, gained support among developing countries and the Non-Aligned Movement.

- Efforts by the United States and its allies to convince the international community that Iran had clandestine military aims for its nuclear program made little headway. The world gradually came close to believing that Iran's nuclear activities posed no security or military threat to regional countries, as the IAEA repeatedly confirmed that Iran's nuclear activities had not been diverted for military purposes. Public opinion in the West, which was totally against Tehran's nuclear program in September 2003, softened a good deal. Although the IAEA could not announce that all Iran's nuclear activities were exclusively peaceful, the U.S. National Intelligence Estimate said that Iran halted its nuclear weapons development program in the fall of 2003, contradicting claims by the Bush administration.[19]

- Grounds were provided for the gradual elimination of economic and political pressures that the West had exerted on Iran for twenty-seven years, and a thaw had commenced in Iran's relations with the West, particularly with the EU. The removal of barriers to Iran's membership in the World Trade Organization and resumption of Iran-Europe trade talks were the most important signs of that development.

- Iran's economic recession was put to an end, and concerns among citizens about the economy gave way to new hopes. This was due in part to Iran's improved relations with Europe resulting from progress in nuclear negotiations. Positive developments were evident in indicators of Iran's economic relations with the world. Iran was high on the list of credit coverage by major European insurance firms. Germany's Hermes Company provided the highest degree of insurance coverage for Iran.

- Prospects were raised for cooperation on nuclear activities with EU member states and freedom from dependence on a single country

(Russia) for power plant construction. Likewise, it seemed that Iran would be able to attain agreements for the transfer of advanced nuclear technology to Iran for medical, agricultural, power plant, and other applications, in a departure from the nuclear sanctions of the preceding twenty-seven years.

- A new mechanism was devised for planning broad-based relations between Iran and Europe through establishment of political, security, economic, and nuclear working groups. The basis for a "Europe without the U.S." approach was thus developed. And by securing Europe's agreement to ensure investment in Iran, hopes were raised that widespread U.S. sanctions against Tehran would be dropped as futile.

- An "Iran-Europe security partnership" suggested that a new regional order could be established for stability and security of the Middle East and the management of regional crises. This could ultimately have engaged the United States and led to a new order in the Middle East.

- In agreeing to cooperation between Iran and Europe to free the Middle East of weapons of mass destruction, efforts were made to attract global attention to the need for WMD disarmament by Israel.

- Finally, tremendous pressure exerted by the United States to totally isolate Iran in the international scene and to force Tehran out of political and security equations of the region and Middle East failed, and the cost of undiplomatic treatment of Tehran considerably increased.

Although we failed to attain our ultimate goals, gaining such achievements was not easy as we were faced with an unbalanced political, diplomatic, and technical situation. America was not on board. Hawks in Washington and Tel Aviv were pushing for radical policies toward Iran. The Russians and the Chinese were on the periphery of the negotiations, although the Russians were more actively engaging with Tehran and the EU3. For the first time, the three major European powers, Germany, Britain, and France, established a triangular diplomatic forum called the EU3. This was their first experience in a joint diplomatic mission facing multiple challenges. On one hand, London was committed to communicating every detail with Washington, while the French and Germans wanted to use this occasion to show the importance of the EU on the global diplomatic scene. On the other hand, some European nations, such as Italy, were hesitant regarding the composition of the EU3.

Impediments existed on the Iranian side, too. Despite the fact that all decisions on nuclear negotiations were approved by the supreme leader, he showed reluctance and reservation. Such reluctance opened the door for Principlist (Conservative) politicians to attack the nuclear policy of the reformist government of President Khatami. Principlist members of Parliament were extremely critical of the Khatami team's nuclear policies, and on occasions they recalled Dr. Rouhani to appear at parliamentary hearings to explain the policies. This fueled the negative atmosphere surrounding the nuclear issue in the domestic media, leading to public opinion becoming negative toward our nuclear policy. As a result, the Iranian negotiating team felt intimidated, leaving me to be the only member of the negotiation team to explain and defend the policies to the public.

Thus, not only did the nuclear negotiating team have to fend off pressure from the hawks in Washington and Tel Aviv, but we had to resist domestic pressure as well. In addition, we had to resolve the IAEA's technical ambiguities on Iran's nuclear program, while we often lacked information on technical details and developments in the nuclear program that were controlled beyond the negotiating team's purview.

CHAPTER FIVE

THE LARIJANI PERIOD

DIFFERENT POLITICAL INTERESTS, APPROACHES, AND SLOGANS

The ninth government came to power at a time when there was potential for an agreement between Iran and the EU3 for launching uranium enrichment in the pilot facility at Natanz and restarting activities at the Isfahan uranium conversion facility.[1] At the beginning of the Ahmadinejad period, the difficulties faced when the crisis first began in late 2002 were less intensive. The EU3 was replaced by the P5+1, which brought Washington, Beijing, and Moscow to the negotiation table. With Ahmadinejad in power, the nuclear policy became aligned with the supreme leader's real intentions. For the first time in the history of the Islamic Republic, the parliament, judiciary, executive, military, and security establishments were in the hands of Principlists (Conservatives), in line with the supreme leader's policies. This concentration of power prompted all media outlets and public opinion to be supportive of the nuclear policies of the ninth government.

However, political changes in Iran since Ahmadinejad's election, as well as dawdling by Europe in cooperating with Khatami's government, led to dramatic changes in the negotiations. Tehran's approach to the nuclear crisis and the West's approach to Iran changed with the inauguration of the ninth government.[2]

During the last round of unofficial negotiations I held with European diplomats, my European counterpart emphasized that pursuant to indirect agreements between Tehran and Brussels, the European Union had decided to give the go-ahead to the restart of activities at the Isfahan uranium conversion facility as part of the planned August 2005 package deal. The European diplomat said that the agreement was not made public because Britain maintained that room should be left for more bargaining. Iran's new foreign minister, Manouchehr Mottaki, later confirmed that the Europeans did not oppose enrichment on a laboratory scale.[3] The same point was also mentioned in a report submitted to former president Khatami by Dr. Rouhani.[4]

The ninth government adopted an approach that was totally different than that of its predecessor. The difference was so profound that the new president was sometimes vociferous in criticizing the approach taken by Iran to the nuclear standoff over the previous two years. The Iran-EU3 Steering Committee had only one meeting with European partners after the election. This meeting was held in London about one or two weeks after the election. The office of the president-elect called and invited me to meet with Mr. Ahmadinejad just a day before the steering committee met. On July 19, 2005, at 5 p.m., I met the new president in his temporary office, located in the former parliament building. The meeting was scheduled to last twenty minutes but took more than two hours. Mojtaba Hashemi Samareh, the president's close friend, aide, and adviser, was taking notes.

Mr. Hashemi Samareh was formerly the director of the Inspection and Evaluation Department of the Foreign Ministry, where he headed a delegation that assessed my work as Iran's ambassador to Germany. He spent about a month in Germany in 1996, after which his delegation suggested to Dr. Velayati, the foreign minister at the time, that my policies and activities in the political, economic, cultural, administration, and consular sections of the embassy be used as a model for all other Iranian embassies worldwide. After reading the report, Dr. Velayati praised my work in an official letter, and Hashemi Samareh sent letters of commendation to all my deputies. I believe this background was the only reason for Ahmadinejad to invite me to meet him as his administration began.

President-elect Ahmadinejad and I discussed not only the nuclear issues but also the broader question of Iran's relations with the West. We did not have a single point of agreement in our basic views. I had the opportunity to hear directly about his foreign policy strategy, which was the most radical position I had ever heard from an Iranian politician since the revolution. He told me in clear terms that he did not care about the IAEA resolutions, nor the possible referral of the nuclear file to the UN Security Council, nor possible UN sanctions, nor the positions of the international community toward Iran, nor about relations with Western countries. He even said that he would welcome sanctions by the international community because these sanctions would be in Iran's long-term interest, forcing the country to become more independent and self-sufficient.

After almost two hours of discussion on the nuclear issue, he told me that I was one of his five candidates to lead the Foreign Ministry. He asked me to write a report for him on my foreign policy strategy and program for the ministry. After hearing his stance on nuclear and foreign policy, I told him that I had had views like his in 1980, when I was twenty-three years old and the editor-in-chief of *Tehran Times*, an English-language daily, but that I had modified them after more than two decades of diplomatic experience. I told him that we didn't share a common understanding of the realities of the world and Iran's foreign relations interests, and hence I could not be his foreign minister. After the meeting Mr. Hashemi Samareh complained about my negative reaction to the new president's offer. But I promised to send him a report on my views on foreign policy strategy, and later did so.

After this meeting I understood that Iran was bound for new confrontations regionally and internationally, and I had no doubt that President Ahmadinejad would order the start of enrichment activities without any compromise with the IAEA or international community. Nor did I doubt that Iran's nuclear dossier would be referred to the UN Security Council and that sanctions would be in place very soon. I informed Dr. Rouhani of my views immediately after the meeting and offered to resign. The next day we left Tehran for London to participate in the last steering committee meeting with the EU3, saying goodbye to sixteen years of Rafsanjani and Khatami strategies in foreign policy aimed at lowering tensions with the West.

Dr. Rouhani met Ahmadinejad on August 9, 2005. After the meeting, he briefed me about their talks. In their meeting Dr. Rouhani explained to Ahmadinejad that the nuclear file would be referred to the UNSC if Iran restarted the UCF plant in Isfahan because the West provides a major share of the IAEA budget and therefore controls the IAEA's decisions. Ahmadinejad told Rouhani, "Call ElBaradei right now and tell him Iran would pay the IAEA's full budget!" Rouhani responded, "First of all, such a decision has to go through the Majles and, second, international organizations have their own rules and structures and Iran cannot individually decide on such matters." In anger, Ahmadinejad commanded Rouhani: "I am instructing you and you should obey." In response, Rouhani stated, "You should nominate another person to follow such instructions. I resign as of now."

After this heated exchange, Rouhani resigned as secretary of the Supreme National Security Council and head of Iran's nuclear negotiating team in August 2005 for the same reasons I did. Though major decisions in Iran are always made at the top level and thus not wholly determined by a change in presidents, it was clear that nuclear negotiations would dramatically change course now that the supreme leader had a president whose mind-set on nuclear and foreign policy issues was similar to his own. Khatami's nuclear negotiation team, led by Rouhani, had a farewell meeting with the Leader on August 15, 2005. In this meeting, where I was present, the Leader praised the work of the nuclear negotiation team and stated, "During this period (2003–2005), the work was implemented rationally, precisely, and in a calculated manner. You have all done a great job and worked under immense pressure and heavy burdens. The nuclear negotiation team was our front line and must be supported. . . ."

AHMADINEJAD'S MAJOR CRITICISMS OF THE PAST APPROACH

President Ahmadinejad's low opinion of the past administration's foreign policy was clear from the time of the presidential election campaign. His often strongly worded criticism of the approach taken by Khatami and his nuclear negotiating team was along the following lines:

- The new government maintained that threats to refer Iran's case to the UN Security Council were merely "political bluffs"[5] and that the negotiating team had committed suicide for fear of death. (Today, it is crystal clear that threats of referral to the Security Council were not bluffs and that we had a realistic grasp of the state of affairs.)
- New administration officials believed that during the first two years of talks, Iran had made important concessions such as suspending enrichment and accepting the Additional Protocol in return for practically nothing. In 2004 Dr. Larijani, the head of State Radio and TV (and who became the new administration's chief nuclear negotiator in August 2005), remarked that the negotiating team had exchanged "a pearl for a lollipop."[6] Mohsen Rezaei, former commander of the Islamic Revolutionary Guard Corps and a serious critic of Khatami's nuclear policy, said in a September 2005 interview that the Khatami administration's diplomacy "was based on excessive trust in Europe and giving numerous concessions such as unconditional acceptance of the Additional Protocol, voluntary submission of information, giving in to inspections which went beyond the Additional Protocol, voluntary suspension of enrichment, suspension of centrifuge manufacture as well as suspension of activities at Isfahan, which caused unilateral obligations for Iran without getting any clear concessions in return from the European side."[7]
- The new government maintained that the former negotiating team had revealed "top secret" information. Media outlets critical of past nuclear negotiations used strong words of denunciation. Baztab, one of the most prominent conservative news websites, led criticism of Iran's previous nuclear diplomacy, going so far as to label some members of the former negotiating team as "traitors." Conservatives critical of Khatami claimed that the October 2003 Tehran statement and information provided to the IAEA were aimed at "disclosing secrets of the Islamic Order."[8]
- New officials claimed that agreeing to suspension was different from being "transparent" and that acceptance of suspension was a mistake from the very beginning.[9]
- The new government was generally opposed to cooperation and interaction and confidence building with the West and maintained

that Europe was not powerful or trustworthy enough to be a credible negotiating partner of Iran. The strategy of "looking to the East," which was introduced by Ali Larijani as the new secretary of the Supreme National Security Council, was the result of this view.

- The ninth government was basically against any compromise on Iran's nuclear rights and believed that development of the nuclear fuel cycle was the legitimate and non-negotiable right of Iran.[10] They were of the opinion that the right to enrichment should be realized not through negotiations and confidence building, but through resistance.[11]

- The new administration maintained that Tehran had turned a straightforward legal dossier with the IAEA into a political one in the first two years of negotiations.[12]

The high-water mark of the criticism came when Dr. Ahmadinejad delivered a speech before the Assembly of Experts[13] declaring that the nuclear agreements reached in Sa'dabad and Paris were worse than the Turkmenchai and Golestan treaties of the nineteenth century.[14] Iranians consider the Russian-imposed Turkmenchai and Golestan treaties, which ceded large swaths of territory in northern Iran, including seventeen large cities, over to imperial Russia, to be the most humiliating treaties in Iran's history.

LOOKING TO THE EAST: STRATEGY OR TACTIC?

The radical new president allotted most of his energy to the settlement of challenges in the arena of foreign policy. Iran's major foreign policy challenges were seen as the results of efforts by the United States to influence Iran's nuclear dossier and of insecurity in Afghanistan and Iraq. This prompted Ahmadinejad and his top diplomats to look to the East in the hope of finding new allies.

Foreign policies followed by Hashemi Rafsanjani and Khatami aimed for the expansion of relations with all countries, and especially détente in relations with regional and Western countries. The diplomacy adopted by both administrations during sixteen years of their rule was watchful of the influence of Western countries in international forums and kept an eye on the economic and political exigencies of the country, aiming to mend

fences with the West, especially the European Union, through three principles: "dignity, wisdom and expediency (interest)."

Both former presidents looked for a trusting partner in Europe to bring
an end to a quarter of a century of hostility between Tehran and the West.
This choice of Europe as the main political partner came under fire inside
the country, but interactions between Iran and Europe, specifically Britain,
France, and Germany, reached a high point during negotiations on the
nuclear dossier. The European countries turned into top economic partners during that period. Iran's foreign policy had found a new direction
after a period of turbulent foreign relations after the Islamic Revolution,
with new partners found in addition to Eastern friends.

The victory of Ahmadinejad, considered by the Europeans to be a symbol of Islamic fundamentalism, signaled the end of amicable relations between Iran and Europe. During and after his presidential campaign, Ahmadinejad put much emphasis on promoting a "regional-based" foreign
policy that focused on "a regional approach to international relations giving priority to political, economic, and cultural ties" and to the "Islamic
world, Persian Gulf, Central Asia, Africa, Latin America, and Pacific" over
the West.[15] Iran's president announced that he was committed to the "expansion of relations with independent and non-aligned states according to
national interests as well as establishment of just relations and cooperation
with Islamic countries in order to form an Islamic pole in the multi-polar
international system of [the] future."[16]

Ahmadinejad clearly indicated his diplomatic intentions by appointing
Ali Larijani as secretary of the Supreme National Security Council and
Manouchehr Mottaki[17] as his foreign minister. Larijani, who was Ahmadinejad's rival candidate in the presidential election, and then was named
chief nuclear negotiator of his government, also stressed the importance of
ties with China and Russia.

Ahmadinejad and his team preferred to use the phrase "expansion of capacities" over "looking to the East" to describe their diplomatic approach.
The new government's lack of faith in relations with Western countries led
it to examine the "expansion of capacities" approach.

Another viewpoint maintained that the "looking to the East" approach
was more a tactic to weather the nuclear crisis than a well-defined long-
term strategy. However, many, myself included, believed that "looking to

the East" or "giving priority to the East" while "marginalizing the West" was not plausible. The main reasons include:

- Economic relations between Iran and Europe were so close and well established that finding an alternative was a remote possibility.
- Eastern countries did not have great enough influence at the international level. Therefore, we could not rely on them to protect our national interests.
- Iran's neighbors, Persian Gulf littoral countries, and members of the Non-Aligned Movement enjoy good relations with the West and the United States. Therefore, even if it relied on the East, Iran would still come under indirect pressure from the West.
- Conflicting interests of Eastern countries threatened to cause many problems for Iran in its bid to balance its relations with India, Russia, and China. Member states of the Non-Aligned Movement were conflicted over Iran's nuclear program and often did not act in concert.
- Eastern countries generally lacked the capacity to meet Iran's technological needs. Those countries did not produce many of the technologies that Iran needed, and, like Iran, imported them.
- China, India, and Russia enjoyed broad-based relations with the West and even Israel. They would not have been ready to put their large-scale interests at risk on behalf of Iran. Moscow's acquiescence on the Iran nuclear issue with EU3 countries and then within the framework of the P5+1 demonstrated this fact. Further evidence to this effect is provided by a look at the slow pace of nuclear cooperation between Iran and Russia for the construction of the Bushehr atomic power plant. Russia originally committed to complete the Bushehr nuclear power plant by 1997. A fifteen-year delay in the project's completion could not be just because of technical problems, but was definitely the result of pressure on Russia from the West.
- The close relations of countries in Iran's region with the United States and other Western countries, along with various disputes between Iran and some regional states, were a major impediment to expansion of strategic relations in the region. Establishment of the (Persian) Gulf Cooperation Council and covert relations between

Arab governments and Israel were examples of divisions with Iran. The wars in Iraq and Afghanistan and the Israeli-Palestinian conflict were other divisive issues in relations with some countries in Iran's neighborhood. Changing this situation would be very difficult under existing conditions, with the United States pressuring its regional allies to restrict their relations with Tehran. Regional countries, for their part, had little desire to see a nuclear Iran, and they encouraged the United States to prevent Iran from attaining nuclear weapon capability.

- The security of Iran's neighbors hinges on the military presence of the United States. Many of the region's rulers seized power through covert and overt support from Britain or the United States and have allowed them to establish many military bases on their soil in return for continued support. They cooperated with Washington in military attacks on Afghanistan and Iraq. How could one expect them to suddenly give up their ties to the United States in return for the "establishment of strategic relations with Iran"?

In view of these points, I believed from the beginning that the "looking to the East" approach adopted by Ahmadinejad's government as its main strategy would be nothing but a temporary and ephemeral policy. Later developments upheld my view, and the "looking to the East" strategy soon went downhill.

The resumption of talks with the EU3, negotiations between Ali Larijani and EU foreign policy chief Javier Solana, numerous trips by Iranian officials to European nations, a letter written by Iran's president to his American counterpart, and emphasis by Tehran on Iran's readiness to talk to Europe and even the United States all indicate that the "looking to the East" policy was flawed from the beginning and that Iran needed to continue bargaining with the West.

COUNTING ON U.S. LIMITATIONS

Since the 1979 Islamic Revolution in Iran, the United States has adopted misguided policies toward the Islamic Republic of Iran. "Dual containment," "military invasion," "regime change," and recently "limited negotiations" are major themes of American policy toward Iran. All of them have proven useless.

The similarity in the current standoff between Tehran and Washington and the Cold War is undeniable. While Europe was practically buried under the rubble of World War II, a similar dispute was going on between the United States and the Soviet Union, with each side trying to boost its influence. Washington had adopted a policy based on the ideas of George Kennan, according to which the United States should rely on its economic might and find new allies to isolate the Soviet Union through a policy of containment, while simultaneously exerting military and diplomatic pressure on Moscow. Now, the same strategy has been adopted by the United States in the Middle East, especially toward Iran. Instead of a direct military encounter or compromise, the United States is trying to isolate Tehran through heavy pressure. At the same time, fears about a possible military strike by the United States on Iran have been soaring on the other side of the Atlantic.[18]

A note on the Iranian perspective on the prospect of an American military attack is necessary here. The view of Iranian policymakers was that America's success in Afghanistan in 2001 was made possible only by Iran's cooperation. Likewise, they viewed the 2003 American invasion of Iraq's initial success as owing a great deal to Iran. Iran rejected secret overtures from Saddam Hussein for an alliance against the United States. Tehran cooperated with the UN Security Council resolutions on Iraq, sponsored the most powerful anti-Saddam resistance groups, including the Supreme Council of the Islamic Revolution in Iraq and the Dawa Party, and continued to back them in the consolidation of post-Saddam Iraq's political system. The United States was also allowed to use Iran's airspace to launch air strikes in Iraq from warships in the Persian Gulf.

Iran's Supreme National Security Council intelligence estimates made at the time of the emergence of the nuclear crisis considered an American military attack a real possibility. However, the majority of Iranian policymakers were confident that the United States would be hesitant to go through with such a strike for numerous reasons, including the fact that it lacked the crucial regional support and cooperation with which Iran had provided it in its previous military actions in Iraq and Afghanistan.

The main reason for Iran's cooperation with the IAEA and agreement to additional confidence-building measures during the Khatami era, then, was not the fear of an American attack but, rather, the understanding of the president, foreign minister, secretary of the Supreme National Security Council, and many other high-level officials that as long as Iran did not pursue nuclear weapons, the best approach was to show goodwill to the international community to demonstrate the country's peaceful intentions. The goal was to earn international recognition of Iranian nuclear rights and to secure the resumption of cooperation with the international community, and especially the West, in the development of Iran's peaceful nuclear program, thus helping to give rise to a new era of cooperation with the West.

Iran maintains that the United States is concerned about the increasing influence of Iran in the Middle East and is trying to prevent the emergence of a new regional hegemonic power. Tehran also contends that the main reason for the current standoff is to keep Iran dependent on the industrial powers and to impede the country's economic and industrial progress. Iranian leaders have frequently noted that the "United States should recognize Iran as a regional power."[19] That strategic request, which has stood since the victory of the Islamic Revolution, is being followed by the ninth government through its aggressive foreign policy.

One may ask what the implications would be of the United States "recognizing" Iran as a regional power, and what it would allow Iran to do that it is currently unable to do. Iran plays an influential role even without U.S. endorsement, but U.S. recognition of Iran's role would be a prelude to a grand bargain and comprehensive cooperation between the top global power and the top regional power to resolve the region's political crises. Of course, the United States would have to be mindful of the concerns and interests of the Arab governments with which it has had close relations, and it would be very difficult for Iran to assure these same governments and the United States that a clearer acceptance of Iran's major role in the region would be beneficial. But the sort of confidence building pursued by the Rafsanjani and Khatami governments offered the only hope for this, and a U.S. military attack on Iran would provoke such opposition from Arab Muslim populations that the United States would be worse off.

Iranian theorists have frequently pointed to the case of China to explain their resistance to heavy pressure from the United States. The United States refrained from negotiating with China for twenty-five years after the 1949 revolution, but in time American politicians came to realize the power of China. Kissinger flew to Beijing, kissed Mao Zedong's hand, and problems were solved.[20] From this point of view, officials of the ninth government are ready to face more pressure and threats because they maintain that "the Americans have not reached that stage" with regard to Iran. Tehran really believes that the White House has no choice but to accept Iran as a major regional power.[21] Foreign policy officials of the ninth government have frequently noted that the United States should learn from its relations with China: despite adamant opposition to its domestic and some foreign policies, Washington has established complete relations with Beijing.

The case of North Korea has also encouraged some Iranian theorists about the possible repetition of the Chinese model. A lesson learned by some Iranian analysts from North Korea was that, even after sanctions and mutual threats, the two sides had no other choice but to sit at the negotiating table.

Under such conditions, some new politicians saw that the U.S. difficulties in Iraq and Afghanistan and the U.S. need for Iran's assistance presented a good opportunity to press their point. Apart from the situation in Afghanistan and Iraq, internal differences in the White House, such as the heavy pressure exerted by Democrats on President George W. Bush, as well as the empowerment of Islamist forces in the Middle East and overflowing oil revenue, were other factors that would turn the current juncture into a golden period for Iran.

Taking into account the experiences of China and North Korea, Tehran was confident that Washington would finally give in to its demands. Many European analysts have also emphasized the need for the United States to engage in direct talks with Iran. They maintained that President Bush and his foreign policy team should have learned from their policy toward North Korea and started negotiations with Iran and Syria in order to find a lasting solution to end the current catastrophic situation in Iraq, and also to find a peaceful solution to Iran's nuclear case.

Thus, a number of factors convinced Tehran's new administration that the United States would have no other choice but to get along with the reality of Iran.

A few months before Ahmadinejad's election, the then-U.S. Secretary of State Condoleezza Rice took part in an interview with the al-Arabiya network and admitted that the United States had chosen the wrong policies toward Iran over the previous twenty-seven years. Rice also noted that she had proposed a U-turn in those policies.[22] Such remarks emboldened the ninth government's foreign policy theorists in their approach to the issue.

Officials of the new Iranian government invariably noted that Iran should be resolute in the face of the United States to prove its new status and, if need be, should pay the price of its resistance. They maintained that the United States will not go further than a certain point and will have to reach a compromise with Iran. The most important arguments for this view include the following:

- Iran is the sole country in the region that can play a key role in establishing stability and peace in Iraq and Afghanistan. While the political fate of the Republicans hinged on Iraq and George W. Bush was doing his best to establish security in Afghanistan and Iraq, ignoring a big regional power like Iran would have cost the White House dearly. Proponents of resistance (at any cost) against the United States thus expected that Bush would finally have no choice but to negotiate with Tehran.

- All observers assessed that a full-blown military strike on Iran and entry of the U.S. military into Iran was well-nigh impossible, or at least too dangerous and costly. A limited attack on Iran (if successful) could cause a delay in Iran's nuclear program, but it would also greatly strengthen the radical positions inside Iran, adding to U.S. problems in the Middle East. Foreign aggression is the surest way to persuade a nation's people to rally behind those in power to resist threats to the country's integrity, which in turn limits the prospects for democratic opposition or political reform. Also, in case of such an attack, Iran might decide to walk out of the NPT and really move toward building a nuclear bomb to deter potential threats.

- It seems that despite the relative agreement of Beijing and Moscow with economic sanctions imposed by the United States on Iran, they were not likely to back a military option against Tehran. In case of unilateral action, U.S. politicians, especially the Republicans, would have suffered the heavy psychological, political, and financial costs of a third war in the Middle East without broad support among the U.S. public.

- Although the United States had been partially successful in arousing the sentiments of Arab countries against Iran, those states were not likely to support a military attack on Iran because of the great economic and security consequences it would have for the entire region.

- Apart from having to convince China, Russia, and some Arab countries of its imperative to act, the United States would have faced another problem, namely international public opinion. Lacking a network of reliable informants in Iraq, the United States based its attack of that country on speculation, and the same would be true about Iran. World public opinion would not forget what proved to be the falsity of Washington's claims about Iraq.

- Proponents of resistance to U.S. pressure also pointed to the warnings issued by militant Palestinian groups against a possible attack on Iran by the United States or Israel as another difficulty for Washington. An attack on Iran, they argued, would sink the Middle East into such turmoil that, according to Vali Reza Nasr, an Iranian member of the U.S. Council on Foreign Relations, twenty years of effort made by the West to forge a Middle East peace accord would be undone. Iran would consider the United States and Israel to be part of a united enemy in the instance of an attack on Iran by either of them, and hence would retaliate against Israel using regional assets such as Hizbollah, Hamas, and Jihad al-Islami as a first response, and then target the American presence in the region.

- Oil and the Strait of Hormuz, two powerful advantages for Iran, are the Achilles' heel of the United States. Senior Iranian officials had constantly warned that any possible invasion of Iran could lead to closure of the Strait of Hormuz and disruption of oil exports from the Persian Gulf.

- Another problem faced by the United States was Iranian public opinion. Iran had successfully won its citizens' support for its nuclear program, and all political factions, despite their other differences, were unanimous that peaceful nuclear technology is an inalienable right of Iran. When the United States attacked Iraq, 80 percent of the population consisted of Shi'a who opposed Saddam and his Baath Party. Although the Iranian people's support for the nuclear program was an achievement of past governments, the ninth government began by using it to good effect.

- Supporters of the government also emphasized that the Bush administration was under tremendous pressure domestically to pave the way for negotiations with Tehran by reducing its threats and showing more flexibility, even temporarily. This was evidenced in the Baker-Hamilton report,[23] the speech delivered by Nancy Pelosi, as well as in reports prepared by the Council on Foreign Relations.

There was also a contrary body of evidence that Bush was not willing to move in the direction set by his Democratic critics and was even ready to withstand their all-out pressure. Bush vetoed legislation by Democratic lawmakers requesting a schedule for withdrawal of U.S. troops from Iraq. What would prevent him from carrying out military operations with regard to Iran, as he did in Iraq? Despite all pressure and requests, including warnings issued by Nouri al-Maliki, the Iraqi prime minister, the White House had thus far refrained from releasing Iranian diplomats who had been arrested on the grounds of fomenting unrest in Iraq. There was little evidence that the Bush administration would budge from its position on suspension of uranium enrichment by Iran as a precondition to talks.

Senior neoconservative officials of the Bush administration, including the president himself and his vice president, did not reject the possibility of a military attack on Iran. An unprecedented letter written by Iran's president to his American counterpart[24] in February 2006 proposing "new ways" to resolve the disputes fell on deaf ears in the White House. President Ahmadinejad noted in the letter that Iran had discarded the reverse gear of the nuclear train and would not brake or go backwards. Five hours later, Secretary of State Rice said Iran did not have to go back but should push the stop button.[25]

AGGRESSIVE RHETORIC AND FORCEFUL DIPLOMACY

One of the most prominent features of the ninth government is what its theorists describe as "aggressiveness." The idea is that to seize the initiative, Iran should reject the existing political order and rules that have been imposed on international bodies by the West, while providing conditions that compel the United States to acknowledge Iran's power. This approach is different from what was pursued by the former nuclear team. The former team believed more in negotiation and mutual understanding than provocation or aggressiveness and emphasized that aggressive approaches would merely provide grounds for pessimism about the feasibility of a diplomatic solution to the confrontation over Iran's nuclear program.

The idea that Iran should adopt an aggressive diplomacy in order to have the upper hand in the international arena[26] is based on the hypothesis that interactions between the Hashemi and Khatami governments and the West were a failure. Critics of the foreign policies adopted by the two presidents claimed that in return for concessions made to the West, no concessions were given to Iran, and new questions were raised even as old ones were resolved. From this viewpoint, analysts supporting the ninth government have maintained that instead of a gradual retreat from one bunker to the other, Iran should have resisted to the last in the first bunker.

The former nuclear team maintained that although Iran's position on the nuclear issue was supported by public opinion in Iran as well as the Islamic world,[27] it could be turned into an acute security matter due to the behavior of Western media and the international atmosphere following the 9/11 terror attacks. We assumed that the United States would not be able to forge a major consensus on any other difference like the nuclear one. The nuclear case was the sole case in which Washington could bank on global sensitivities about nonproliferation in order to launch directed propaganda against Iran's peaceful goals and also take advantage of security concerns of regional countries—even such powers as Russia—to build a major consensus against Tehran. This analysis, in addition to other conditions set out in previous chapters, made Tehran conclude after the issuance of the IAEA Board of Governors' resolution in September 2003 that the least costly option was "a face-saving solution through negotiation and understanding" with the West, not "provocation and aggressiveness." Of course, we understood at the same time that the nuclear issue would also be the one issue around which the ninth government could mobilize domestic support vis-à-vis the upcoming challenges with the West.

The new government put too much emphasis on the value of propaganda. For example, it tried to claim as its own achievement the introduction of the fuel cycle, even though IAEA Director General ElBaradei, following a visit to nuclear facilities in Natanz in winter 2003 (more than two years before Ahmadinejad's presidency), had announced that Iran was among ten countries with access to fuel-cycle know-how and technology, and President Khatami, in an interview with domestic and foreign media, had officially declared the breakthrough as a major historical achievement for Iran. At any rate, the propaganda policy of the ninth government was such that Western countries were prompted to note that Iran was exaggerating its nuclear achievements.

RESTART OF THE ISFAHAN URANIUM CONVERSION FACILITY

On June 24, 2005, just one day before official announcement of the final election results, President Khatami stated that "our fundamental policies with regard to foreign issues as well as nuclear and other issues are quite clear, and regardless of poll results, I don't think that Iran's foreign policy will undergo a basic change."[28] However, the resignation of Hassan Rouhani, who was in charge of nuclear diplomacy, and changes in the nuclear negotiating team after the presidential election clearly showed that Iranian diplomacy was in for a major upheaval.[29]

On August 1, 2005, in the final days of the Khatami administration, Iran sent an official letter to the IAEA declaring its decision to restart uranium conversion at Isfahan. The announcement prompted a strong reaction from the European countries, which threatened to walk out of negotiations. The EU sent a letter to ElBaradei declaring that the decision to resume activities at the Isfahan facility would be a breach of both the Paris Agreement and the IAEA Board of Governors' resolution dated November 29, 2004. The EU also called on the Iranian government not to resume "suspended" nuclear activities. Stefan de Rynck noted that the European Commission was optimistic about finding a negotiated solution to the problem and expressed hope that no measures would be taken that could jeopardize achieving that solution.[30]

Senior American and EU3 officials also reacted angrily to Tehran's decision. Britain, which was then the rotational head of the European Union, expressed regret over Iran's decision to reject the EU3 proposals and indicated London's deep concern over the resumption of Iran's nuclear activities.[31] London described Tehran's new decision as being destructive. The French foreign minister, Philippe Douste-Blazy, asserted that resumption of Iran's nuclear activities would amount to a blatant breach of the Paris Agreement and, further, that Iran's tone was unsettling and against the spirit of negotiations that had been carried out during the preceding years.[32] Joschka Fischer, then the German foreign minister, warned Iran about the disastrous consequences of the new decision.[33] Both Fischer and German Chancellor Schroeder noted that resumption of any negotiation with Iran would depend on suspension of those activities and threatened Iran with referral of its nuclear dossier to the UN Security Council as a prelude to more strict sanctions.[34] In addition, the secretary general of the United Nations, Kofi Annan, called on Tehran to show self-restraint and continue with negotiations while complying with its obligation to suspend enrichment.[35] At the same time, ElBaradei issued a statement warning Iran about taking any unilateral action.[36]

Iran's politicians newly elected in 2005 maintained that operating the Isfahan facility would not lead to Iran's nuclear dossier being reported to the UN Security Council. They argued that by aggressively seizing the initiative and issuing warnings about the consequences of measures taken by Western countries, the United States and Europe would be scared off from sending Iran's case to the UN Security Council. It was for this reason that Iranian officials warned, even before any meeting of the Board of Governors and later, before Security Council sessions, that if the nuclear case were referred to the UN Security Council for the imposing of new sanctions on Iran, Tehran might leave the Non-Proliferation Treaty.[37]

The new statesmen took the position that they would no longer negotiate over enrichment. Their approach was "negotiation *after* the beginning of enrichment." The new government maintained that the way to enrichment passes through crisis and resistance, and that negotiations with the European countries would never bear fruit. Nor did the new government consider the United Nations Security Council as its redline. The former nuclear negotiating team had two redlines: to secure the legitimate rights of Iran on nuclear technology including enrichment, and to prevent the referral of Iran's nuclear dossier to the UN Security Council. We were certain that Iran's nuclear program would be considered a threat to international peace and security and that sanction resolutions would be prepared one after another.

I was the only ex-nuclear negotiation team member appointed by Dr. Larijani (the new secretary of the Supreme National Security Council and the new chief of the nuclear negotiation team) and was named his foreign policy adviser. I was invited to his first convening of the Secretariat of the National Security Council on nuclear issues. At the meeting I understood that the new team was willing to risk referral of Iran's nuclear dossier to the UN Security Council. After hearing the new debates, I left the meeting, sending a note to Dr. Larijani as follows:

> The discussions in this meeting have left no doubt for me that the nu-
> clear file will be referred to the UN Security Council in less than three
> months, and the economic-political sanctions resolution will be passed,
> greatly harming the national interest of Iran. This will make a black
> mark on the current policy makers in the history of Iran which I do not
> want to share. That is why I prefer not to attend your meetings anymore.
> This was my first and last participation in the new nuclear negotiation
> team meetings.

The previous nuclear negotiating team had by no means been allowed to negotiate with the United States. However, the new team was allowed to do so. The unprecedented measure taken by Ahmadinejad in writing a direct letter to U.S. President George W. Bush and, later, the official start of open talks between Iran and the United States on Iraq and the nuclear issue—following three decades of completely severed relations— proved that the ban was lifted for the new administration and that the taboo concerning direct talks with Washington was broken. This was a major development in U.S.-Iran relations, which will be further explored in later chapters.

In its last proposal to Iran on August 5, 2005, the EU3 called on Tehran for indefinite suspension and to totally desist from building a heavy-water research reactor. In return, Iran was promised political and security coop-eration, long-term support for its civil nuclear program, as well as econom-ic and technological cooperation. The proposal, however, was categorically rejected by the new government, which described it as humiliating.[38]

In return for asking Tehran to suspend the nuclear fuel cycle for an indefinite period[39] and not build a heavy-water research reactor in Arak,[40] several important concessions were proposed by the European countries in their August 2005 offer.[41] First, recognition of Iran's inalienable right according to Article IV of the NPT to develop research, production, and application of nuclear energy without discrimination according to its obligations under the NPT. Despite the fact that this article includes Iran's right to build civil nuclear power and enrichment plants, the EU announced that it aimed, by general agreement, to support Iran's plan to develop civil nuclear power that would conform to Iran's needs and be in line with the economic and scientific criteria of nonproliferation. The EU also promised to support long-term cooperation between Iran and Russia on developing civil nuclear technology. However, the EU kept silent about the rights of Iran to enrichment by asking for the continuation of suspension.

The EU also confirmed that Iran would have access to the international market of nuclear technologies, where contractors offered technologies on the basis of free and official competition. The EU had intended to provide Iran with a more concrete offer of a deal with France's government-owned nuclear technology group, but Washington scuttled the idea. As ElBaradei writes in his 2011 memoir, "The United States had refused to give the green light to Areva, so the Europeans' offer simply made a vague statement about giving Iran access to the foreign nuclear technology markets."[42]

The EU further made clear its support for the development of Iran's civil nuclear program. The support would include aid for allocation of equipment needed for the construction of more research reactors in Iran and cooperation in other fields of peaceful nuclear energy, except for activities related to the nuclear fuel cycle. Europe also promised to support the development of cooperation in such fields as production of radioisotopes, basic research, and useful application of nuclear energy in agriculture and medicine as well as cooperation among Europe, Iran, and the IAEA for the implementation of nuclear security regimes, including international safeguards. Tehran raised major objections to the August 2005 plan:[43]

- The proposal contained a set of unilateral and selfish proposals that were not legal and called on Iran to deny its sovereign and inalienable rights.
- The plan aimed to scare Iran into accepting inspections beyond the Safeguards Agreement and even the Additional Protocol to lay a foundation for Iran outside the jurisdiction of the IAEA.

- The plan called on Iran for indefinite suspension of all enrichment activities.
- It also aimed to impose arbitrary and discriminatory criteria on Iran's nuclear program.
- The plan included no firm guarantees or even specific offers for serious cooperation with Iran.
- With regard to security, the plan simply repeated articles of the UN Charter and other general obligations that had been already accepted by all member states.
- With regard to nuclear cooperation, the proposal carried no indication that EU countries were determined to reduce their violations of international rights and the NPT in preventing Iran from developing nuclear energy, let alone offering any guarantees thereof. For example, while the three European countries are bound by the NPT to facilitate Iran's access to nuclear energy for peaceful purposes, the plan consisted of only a conditional and vague proposal that European countries would not bar Iran's access to nuclear energy.[44]
- As for economic cooperation, the plan consisted of only a conditional report on arrangements and obligations that existed already.

After operations were restarted at the Isfahan uranium conversion facility, South Africa offered a proposal to break the deadlock, including a proposal for South Africa to supply needed uranium to Iran.[45] According to that plan, Iran would have converted uranium to UF_6 at the Isfahan plant before exporting the gas back to South Africa, thus minimizing stockpiles of UF_6 on Iranian soil as a confidence-building measure. While Iran welcomed the proposal, European diplomats described South Africa's proposal as unrealistic: They claimed that it would enable Iran to solve its problems of producing needed uranium gas for enrichment, amounting to a big victory for Iran and a fiasco for Europeans. South African officials withdrew the proposal.[46]

Dr. ElBaradei finally reported to the Board of Governors on August 8, 2005, that Iran had started uranium conversion activities at Isfahan and had therefore partially ended suspension. The European Union, which had already warned Tehran about such a decision, called for an extraordinary meeting of the IAEA Board of Governors. The meeting was held on

August 9, 2005, and a resolution was issued two days later, asking Iran "to re-establish full suspension of all enrichment related activities."

In the resolution, the Board of Governors noted that full compliance with suspension by Iran as a voluntary and non-legally binding measure was necessary before the outstanding issues were resolved.[47] Expressing serious concern over the new decision of Tehran,[48] the Board of Governors called on the director general "to provide a comprehensive report on the implementation of Iran's NPT Safeguards Agreement and this resolution by 3 September 2005."

Negotiations between Iran and the EU3 were called off by the European side on August 31. The Europeans realized that the incentives they had proposed to persuade Iran to indefinitely suspend uranium enrichment constituted an unrealistic offer in the face of Iran's determination to develop this dual-use nuclear technology that Tehran insisted was for peaceful purposes. Tehran sensed that Europe aimed to deprive it of its inalienable right one way or another.

Ali Larijani, the new secretary of the Supreme National Security Council, at this time took charge of Iran's nuclear dossier. Before flying to Vienna, Larijani noted that Iran held to its policy of continued negotiations and understanding to build confidence with the international community and that Iran welcomed negotiations with all member states of the Board of Governors, including the European countries and member countries of the Non-Aligned Movement within the framework of the NPT. Expressing regret over positions taken by the EU3 in calling off the talks with Iran, he underscored Iran's determination to go on with negotiations.[49]

Significantly, before meeting with ElBaradei in Vienna, Dr. Larijani visited India[50] and Pakistan,[51] two countries that occupied a central place in his theory of "looking to the East." Back from his trip, he noted that Iran was planning to increase the number of negotiating countries and, in fact, to reduce the role of the European countries. This plan led to many later problems—and eventually to the resumption of talks with the European countries after receiving no result from negotiations with Russia, China, India, and the Non-Aligned Movement.

In his report to the Board of Governors' session on September 10, ElBaradei announced that results of inspections related to highly enriched uranium found in Iran supported Tehran's remarks that the contamination came from centrifuge components that had been imported from a country that was known for producing highly enriched uranium. ElBaradei also noted that Tehran had not given full answers to requests put forth by the IAEA and that the IAEA was therefore not able to confirm that Iran's nuclear activities were totally peaceful. Some European diplomats argued that his report paved the way for sending Iran's case to the UN Security Council. A French diplomat reacting to ElBaradei's report asserted, for example, that the report was a complete indictment of Iran and provided sufficient reasons for taking the country's nuclear dossier to the UN Security Council. The report pointed to many breaches of the NPT by Iran and showed that Iran had not heeded IAEA requests to stop its nuclear activities.[52] Tehran criticized the report, saying that it violated the IAEA's obligation to remain impartial.[53] Gholam Reza Aghazadeh, head of the Atomic Energy Organization in Iran, left for Moscow on August 13 to promote Iran's policy for increasing the number of negotiating parties.

AHMADINEJAD'S PROPOSAL FOR A CONSORTIUM TO MANAGE IRAN'S ENRICHMENT PROGRAM

In his September 2005 visit to Vienna, Larijani met with ElBaradei and conveyed a message to him from the new Iranian president. The new initiative aimed to break the deadlock over the nuclear dossier and prevent Iran's case from being referred to the UN Security Council. Although Iran's newly ensconced politicians revealed no details of the proposal before Ahmadinejad's speech to the Security Council, they had explained it during negotiations with international parties behind closed doors and had organized heavy propaganda around it. Larijani said in his news conference in Vienna that the initiative was the most important thing that the new president could come up with in a reasonable period of time[54] and announced that ElBaradei had welcomed the proposal.[55]

In late September 2005, after being elected president, Mahmoud Ahmadinejad traveled to New York, his first foreign trip. Importantly, the trip provided the world with an opportunity to listen to the views of the new Iranian president. There was considerable advance publicity about an Ahmadinejad initiative to end the standoff between Iran and the West, which raised new hopes.

Iran's nuclear dossier seemed to have reached a stage where everybody expected that the new initiative offered by Ahmadinejad would break the deadlock in negotiations with Europe. The word "initiative," after all, implied that a basic solution would be presented that would seem reasonable to both sides of the negotiations. The announcement that Iran would propose a new initiative was made during Larijani's first visit to Vienna and was communicated to the IAEA director general during a meeting between Larijani and ElBaradei.[56] Encouraged by the extensive media coverage, the EU looked forward to hearing Iran's new proposal.

In his September 2005 speech at the UN General Assembly, President Ahmadinejad proposed as a confidence-building measure a consortium with other countries on Iran's enrichment activities. Although details of such a consortium were never discussed, the proposal was that transparency would be guaranteed and the concerns of regional and Western countries allayed by international participation in the fuel-cycle and enrichment activities. The global reaction to Ahmadinejad's proposal in his UN speech was cold. The United States reacted negatively,[57] and the proposal was denounced by Western media a few weeks later.

I personally was shocked to hear about the initiative because, as the spokesman of Iran's nuclear negotiating team, I had proposed just such an initiative in an interview with the Russian news agency ITAR-TASS a year earlier. I had not coordinated the proposal with anyone before the interview. My proposal received great attention—and derision—in the global media. One of the EU3 ambassadors told me that it was ridiculous and that the West would never invest in enrichment in Iran. He told me that Iran's P-1 centrifuges were 1950s technologies and obsolete for economic purposes and that for any investment in Iranian enrichment to be feasible, Western countries would have to bring the latest enrichment technology to Iran. He suggested not repeating such an initiative because the West would never agree to it.

Rouhani, meanwhile, called me immediately after the interview and asked me to deny the report because high-level authorities were surprised and angry with the proposal. I told him that I could not deny having made the proposal, as I made it on the record in an interview, but that I could resign. In the end, he managed the problem in Tehran but he reiterated that I should never repeat the proposal in the future. I therefore was shocked when the new president made the same proposal a year later. Although I had been sharply rebuked, Ahmadinejad received strong domestic support from the supreme leader and conservatives.

Iran's ambassador to the IAEA, Ali Asghar Soltanieh, told *Arms Control Today* that:

> Since our president [Iranian President Mahmoud Ahmadinejad] issued an invitation in the UN General Assembly, to all private and governmental sectors to come for a joint venture and contribute to our enrichment project, we will welcome any initiative and any country or companies that are interested to have a joint venture with us. And, therefore, we would welcome [it] if China or other countries are interested, even Europeans that are interested to jointly work together. And this is the maximum transparency that we could ever give and confidence building, that we are opening our enrichment activities and not only the IAEA inspectors will be there, all experts from different countries will be present. Therefore, this is maximum transparency and nobody will have any doubt that these activities will remain peaceful.[58]

In any case, the United States and the rest of the P5+1 did not buy into the initiative and increased pressure to send Iran's case to the UN Security Council in New York. In reaction to IAEA Board of Governors' threats to refer Iran to the Security Council and the unenthusiastic international reaction to Ahmadinejad's initiative, Larijani warned that if force were used against Iran, the country would undoubtedly begin enrichment, stop implementing the Additional Protocol, and consider withdrawing from the NPT.[59]

It should be noted that the new nuclear negotiation team believed that the West's threats to refer Iran's nuclear file to the Security Council and pass sanction resolutions were nothing more than a political bluff. They charged us as being "cowed diplomats," likening us to one who is scared into committing suicide merely by the threat of death. Mahmoud Vaezi, the deputy president of the Center for Strategic Research, invited me and the new nuclear negotiation team and some other scholars and diplomats to discuss nuclear policy in September 2005. In the meeting, my successor as the nuclear team spokesman, Javad Va'idi, and Ali Asghar Soltanieh, Iran's ambassador to the IAEA, repeated the argument that the IAEA Board of Governors would not refer the file to the UN Security Council and that the nuclear issue was just a legal one that could be resolved easily with the IAEA. I argued that the Iran nuclear issue was very important to the West as a political and security issue, that legal aspects with the IAEA were secondary issues, and that the file would most certainly be referred to the UN Security Council and Iran confronted with sanctions. This reading of the IAEA and the West was the core issue of difference between the former and new nuclear negotiation teams. Just a few days after this discussion, the IAEA Board of Governors passed a resolution declaring Iran in noncompliance, which set the stage for reporting the case to the UN Security Council in February 2006.

IAEA BOARD RESOLUTION DECLARING IRAN'S NONCOMPLIANCE (SEPTEMBER 2005)

The meeting of the Board of Governors started on September 19. Three days later, the board noted in Paragraphs 1, 2, and 3 of its resolution that Iran's failure to comply with its NPT Safeguards Agreement obligations according to Article XII, Paragraph C and Article III, Paragraph B4 of the IAEA Statute and Iran's concealment of the history of its nuclear activities "have given rise to questions that are within the competence of the Security Council." The resolution was approved even though the IAEA's inspectors had not reported anything new to show that Iran had failed to comply with its NPT safeguards obligations during their inspections. The Europeans believed that Iran was discovered to be noncompliant in 2003. The IAEA and the EU3 had made a concession to Iran between November 2003 and September 2005 by not declaring and reporting this noncompliance to the Security Council. A further concession was to negotiate to find ways to clarify past activities and build confidence that Iran's nuclear program was and is exclusively peaceful, without reporting Iran to the Security Council, as required by Article XII, Paragraph C of the IAEA Statute.

The resolution was welcomed and supported by all the powerful members of the IAEA. The September meeting of the Board of Governors was the first serious reaction by the international community to the nuclear policies of the new Iranian government. Despite claims by Iran's nuclear negotiating team that Europe had withdrawn its initial draft resolution, the final document that came out of the Board of Governors was based on the resolution that had been proposed by France, Germany, and Britain to report Iran to the Security Council.[60] This proposal was ultimately included in Paragraph 3 of the resolution, though no exact schedule was presented for this notification of the Security Council.

The resolution was ratified on September 23, 2005, with 22 ayes, 12 abstentions, and only one nay.[61] It relied on the following legal arguments, though Iran's new nuclear negotiators downplayed their importance.

First, the UN Security Council is the main body responsible for maintaining international peace and security, and it is legally charged with handling cases referred to it by the IAEA. The Non-Proliferation Treaty and the IAEA's Safeguards Agreement signed with Iran clearly state that the Security Council should be involved in cases that lie within its competence. Article III, Paragraph B4 of the IAEA Statute likewise notes that "if in connection with the activities of the Agency there should arise questions that are within the competence of the Security Council, the Agency shall notify the Security Council, as the organ bearing the main responsibility for the maintenance of international peace and security."

Second, noncompliance of a country with its NPT obligations constitutes a serious case that should be referred to the Security Council. According to Article XII, Paragraph C of the IAEA Statute, noncompliance can be defined as any diversion from peaceful use of nuclear energy or the use of nuclear energy for military purposes. Articles 18 and 19 of the Comprehensive Safeguards Agreement are also noteworthy. Article 18 pertains to those instances in which the government in question should take action without delay to allow verification of non-diversion of nuclear material covered by the Safeguards Agreement to military applications following a decision made by the Board of Governors. Article 19 applies to cases in which the Board of Governors reaches the conclusion that the IAEA is unable to verify that nuclear material has not been used for illegal purposes. In such a circumstance, the Board of Governors is authorized to notify the Security Council. The sequence of Articles 18 and 19 of the Safeguards Agreement shows that measures stipulated in Article 18 should be taken first. However, if the country in question does not take corrective measures and the IAEA, as a result, is unable to verify the true nature of its activities, then the Board of Governors may move on to notifying the Security Council.[62]

Historically, a limited number of cases—until now, North Korea, Romania, and Libya—have been reported to the UN Security Council for noncompliance with the obligations of their Safeguards Agreements. It should be noted that from a legal standpoint, there is a major difference between "reporting to the Security Council" and "notifying the Security Council." "Reporting" occurs when the IAEA cannot verify the true nature of a country's activities because the country has not cooperated with the agency. Of course, "reporting" is not the final step for the IAEA. "Notifying" the Security Council occurs when a country that has been found in violation of safeguards has cooperated with the IAEA and taken corrective measures, after which the agency "notifies" the Security Council about the violations and the measures taken to redress them so that the IAEA judges that the country's nuclear program is exclusively peaceful. For example, in 1992 IAEA inspectors went to Romania at the request of the new government that succeeded Nicolae Ceaușescu's regime and carried out special inspections to explore irregular activities that had taken place there. The agency then notified the Security Council according to its Statute, suggesting no further action was necessary. In the case of Libya in 2003, the IAEA notified the Security Council that Libya had violated its safeguards requirements and indeed had been pursuing nuclear weapons but that Libya then admitted all of this and allowed the IAEA to verify that Libya was now compliant with all of its obligations as a non–nuclear-weapon state. The Security Council did not deem further measures such as sanctions to be necessary because in each case the country in question had provided full transparency and taken corrective measures.

Iran is the only country that has been referred to the Security Council in line with Article III of the IAEA Statute since the agency's creation. In the cases of Iraq, Libya, and Romania, the Security Council had been notified in line with Article XII, Paragraph C of the Statute due to noncompliance with their obligations. However, the September 2005 resolution relied on both Articles 18 and 19 of the Comprehensive Safeguards Agreement, which are clearly related to threats against international peace and security.

In ElBaradei's view, as recorded in his memoir, this referral was based less on the facts of Iran's nuclear activities than on the search of the United States and its allies for a legal argument to force Iran to halt enrichment:

The Agency had made substantial progress in verifying Iran's nuclear program. The eventual referral, when it came, was primarily an attempt to induce the Security Council to stop Iran's enrichment program, using Chapter VII of the UN Charter to characterize Iran's enrichment—legal under the NPT—as "a threat to international peace and security."[63]

With Iran slated for referral to the Security Council, the only points left unresolved were the timing of reporting and contents of the report that was to be submitted to the Security Council,[64] which allowed for further time to build up international support for a hard line on Iran. This astute approach by the West also emboldened Russia to put forward a plan, described below, that had been categorically rejected by Iran a year earlier, and thus put further pressure on Iran. Moscow thought that Iran had been put in such a weak position by the new resolution that it would accept the old proposal.

The resolution allowed the Security Council members to examine the case regardless of whether they reached political agreement or not. The important point was that even if Iran reached a political agreement with the Europeans, the Security Council could still discuss Iran's nuclear dossier. It also put Iran's case on the agenda of all subsequent sessions of the IAEA Board of Governors.

The main point of dispute shifted from adherence to the Additional Protocol to inspection that went far beyond the Additional Protocol.[65] The September 2005 resolution called for transparency measures extending beyond the formal requirements of the Safeguards Agreement and Additional Protocol, including access to individuals, documentation relating to procurement, dual use equipment, certain military-owned workshops, and research and development locations.[66] It also called on Iran to suspend all enrichment-related activity, which was understood to include the uranium conversion at Isfahan.

The resolutions referred to the director general's report to the Board of Governors in which ElBaradei mentioned reports relating to equipment, materials, and activities that have applications in the conventional military area and in the civilian sphere as well as in the nuclear military area.

The international reaction to the resolution created new economic uncertainty for Iran and put an end to the relative calm that had resulted from previous agreements between Iran and Europe that had taken Iran's case back to a routine track during the Board of Governors' November meeting.

Iran's Foreign Ministry reacted by announcing that Iran would not comply with the resolution and officially warned that "if the resolution is not corrected or IAEA insists on it, Iran will have no choice but to revoke voluntary and temporary concessions it has given to the IAEA, including implementation of the Additional Protocol before its ratification by Iran's parliament." The statement noted that "threatening Iran with sending the case to the Security Council will not change the basic stance taken by Iran and will not help improve the situation." It also took the IAEA to task by saying, "Iran considers the IAEA and its Statute as the sole competent source for establishing technological nuclear balance and considers any irresponsible and illegal intervention by the Agency a serious threat to future prospects of international nuclear management."[67]

AHMADINEJAD ADDRESSES THE SECURITY COUNCIL

The EU3 had decided to end negotiations with Iran after the restart of activities at the Isfahan uranium conversion facility. In October 2005, however, the foreign ministers of the EU countries called on Iran to return to negotiations on its nuclear program after suspending all activities related to the nuclear fuel cycle. Iran retorted that it would consent to return to negotiations only in the absence of any preconditions.[68] It seemed that the political situation of Iran's nuclear dossier was exacerbated by the IAEA Board's September 2005 resolution.

Even before the resolution's ratification, Ahmadinejad administration officials made statements against the European Union and argued for canceling all forms of suspension and restarting activities at Isfahan. This rhetoric was matched by propaganda against the new government in the Western media. The IAEA board's September 2005 resolution and the finalization of its decision to report Iran to the UN Security Council returned the situation to crisis mode. Mid-ranking Iranian officials and the domestic media fulminated about cutting relations with the IAEA, ending negotiations with Europe, and even leaving the NPT.[69] This hard-line stance further stoked the international escalation against Tehran and provided fuel to the United States and to the Israeli media.

On October 26, Ahmadinejad delivered a speech expressing hope for the annihilation of Israel's Zionist regime.[70] This rhetoric gave the West another excuse to mount more pressure on Iran and its nuclear program. Tel Aviv linked the call for the annihilation of Israel and the potential manufacture of nuclear bombs by Iran to put pressure on Iran's friends. Although the international media misinterpreted Ahmadinejad's remarks, the remarks provoked sharp reactions from many countries, with Kofi Annan, the secretary general of the United Nations, among those voicing concern over Ahmadinejad's statements.[71]

European Union leaders condemned Ahmadinejad's remarks in a meeting near London.[72] British Prime Minister Tony Blair, who hosted the meeting, said that the sentiments were totally unacceptable and stressed that they raised new concerns over Iran's nuclear program.[73] French President Jacques Chirac told reporters that he was deeply shocked by the remarks of Iran's president. He added that Ahmadinejad was taking the risk that his country would be added to the list of rogue states.[74] CNN quoted French Foreign Minister Philippe Douste-Blazy as condemning Ahmadinejad's words and saying that the French government had summoned Iran's ambassador in Paris to explain the Iranian president's remarks. He added that the right of Israel to exist should never be questioned. Russia's foreign minister, Sergei Lavrov, also stated that he had ordered the Russian ambassador in Iran to ask for an explanation of Ahmadinejad's remarks, adding that such rhetoric was not appropriate in an unstable region like the Middle East.[75]

The Irish foreign minister said that he was shocked by Ahmadinejad's remarks about wiping Israel off the map.[76] The Italian Foreign Ministry issued a statement saying that the remarks confirmed the worst fears about Iran's nuclear program.[77] A spokesman for the German Foreign Ministry told Agence France-Presse that the Iranian chargé d'affaires had been summoned to tell him that the remarks of Iran's president were totally unacceptable and should be condemned in the strongest way.[78] Canadian Prime Minister Paul Martin also condemned Ahmadinejad's remarks, describing them as unbelievable and unacceptable. Martin added that the words amounted to intolerance and anti-Semitism.[79] Israeli Prime Minister Ariel Sharon called for expulsion of Iran from the United Nations, saying that a nation that calls for the annihilation of another nation should not be permitted to be a member of the United Nations.[80]

Sean McCormack, the spokesman for the U.S. State Department, noted that Iran was a member of the United Nations and said that the world should encourage Iran to behave as a responsible member of the international community. He added that the United States was concerned about Iran's access to technology for uranium enrichment and reprocessing.[81] Even Saeb Erekat, the chief Palestinian negotiator, noted that Palestinians had recognized the state of Israel and pursued peace talks with Tel Aviv and could not accept Ahmadinejad's statements.[82]

The Norwegian ambassador met me in late 2006 in my office in Tehran (I was Dr. Larijani's foreign policy adviser and Dr. Rouhani's deputy in international affairs) and asked me about Ahmadinejad's position on the Holocaust and wiping Israel off the map. I told him that this was not the position of Iran and that our constitution makes it clear that the supreme leader is the ultimate determiner of foreign policy. Ayatollah Khamenei has frequently and publicly proposed that the resolution to the Palestinian-Israeli issue be decided by the Muslim, Jewish, and Christian populations living there in a free election. Ahmadinejad's remarks, I told the ambassador, was intended more as propaganda and for internal consumption than as the real foreign policy of Iran.

This was one of the accusations raised against me later. I defended my stance very strongly on grounds that the leader's position was the real and official position of the country, with foreign policy developed in the Supreme National Security Council and confirmed by the leader. In reality I had defended the national interest of Iran by explaining Iran's real policy on the Israeli-Palestinian conflict.

In October 2005, in an effort to prevent the referral of its nuclear dossier to the Security Council, Iran allowed IAEA inspectors access to new locations inside the Parchin military site.[83] This was the second time that IAEA inspectors were allowed to visit the site.

On November 4, Russia seized on the aggravated international atmosphere against Iran and proposed that a joint stock company be established in Russia to provide Tehran with nuclear fuel. This plan had been proposed to me in 2004 in Moscow by Sergei Kislyak, at that time the Russian deputy foreign minister. I raised the proposal in a meeting of the Supreme National Security Council, and it was unanimously rejected. But in view of mounting pressures on Iran and following Ahmadinejad's announcement during his speech at the United Nations that other countries would be allowed to cooperate in Iran's fuel cycle, Moscow renewed its proposal. The proposal had been vetted by the United States and the EU3.

According to the plan, Iran would be able to process natural uranium yellowcake into UF_6 at the Isfahan conversion facility provided that Tehran agreed to suspend other phases of the fuel cycle. The Moscow plan aimed to suspend (permanently, as it seemed to Tehran) the activities at the Natanz complex and increase the dependence of Iran's nuclear industry on Russia.

Russia's proposal put Iran in a difficult situation because either acceptance or rejection would have had negative consequences for the country. The United States and Europe welcomed Russia's proposal for the transfer of the main part of the nuclear fuel cycle—uranium enrichment—to another country. If Iran had accepted Russia's proposal, it would have lost the most important part of its nuclear technology: enrichment. But if it rejected the plan, Iran would push Russia toward the American camp and reduce the likelihood that Russia would stand up for Iran at the UN Security Council. Hence, the ninth government adopted a strategy of expressing support for the Russian proposal at critical junctures without taking practical steps to implement it.

Javad Va'idi, the Supreme National Security Council undersecretary for international affairs, presented a letter from Ali Larijani, the head of the nuclear negotiation team, to the ambassadors of Britain, France, and Germany on November 6.[84] The letter contained a message indicating Iran's readiness to resume negotiations without any preconditions. Iran emphasized that negotiations should be carried out within a clear framework and according to a specified schedule, but the EU3 did not respond to Iran's request and no negotiations took place until the November meeting of the IAEA Board of Governors.

To reduce international pressure before that meeting, Tehran stepped up diplomatic efforts with meetings between Iranian officials and the Non-Aligned Movement troika[85] on November 11 and a day later with Igor Ivanov, the former Russian foreign minister who had become secretary of the Russian National Security Council.

ELBARADEI'S REPORT TO THE IAEA
BOARD'S NOVEMBER MEETING

The five-page report presented by IAEA Director General Mohamed ElBaradei to the Board of Governors in November 2005 differed from previous reports in that it dealt mainly with Iran's performance and activities since the September 2005 resolution and not with any preceding activities by Iran. When one assesses that report, the following points should be taken into consideration:

- In accordance with the September 2005 Board of Governors resolution, the report requested access extending beyond the formal requirements of the Safeguards Agreement and Additional Protocol (including such things as access to individuals, documentation relating to procurement, dual use equipment, certain military-owned workshops, and research and development locations). The director general also called on Iran to reestablish full and sustained suspension of all enrichment-related activity, reconsider the construction of a heavy-water research reactor, and ratify and fully implement the Additional Protocol.

- ElBaradei emphasized that Iran had not suspended activities at Isfahan as the September 2005 resolution requested, nor had it reviewed its decision about building a heavy-water reactor complex at Arak, as had been requested by IAEA resolutions beginning in the Ahmadinejad period.

- ElBaradei noted that, after he met with Larijani on November 1, access was given to IAEA inspectors to visit military sites in Parchin, with no unusual activity observed. He also acknowledged that Tehran had permitted access to individuals who were previously unreachable for the IAEA, and noted that among the documents recently made available was one related to the casting and machining of uranium metal into hemispherical forms. Iran stated that it had received this document on the initiative of the A. Q. Khan network.

- Finally, ElBaradei's report contained nothing to show that past ambiguities had been resolved or that Tehran had accepted international requests.[86]

As threats to refer Iran's case to the Security Council escalated in late November 2005, Iran's Parliament approved an urgent plan that would mandate that the government stop voluntary suspension if the case were actually reported to the Security Council. The bill was passed overwhelmingly with 183 ayes and 10 nays; three members of Parliament abstained.[87]

The meeting of the Board of Governors on November 24, 2005, ended after one day of deliberations without issuing a resolution. The statement issued at the end of the session called on Iran to take transparency measures beyond the obligations of the Additional Protocol and Safeguards Agreement.[88] The board also called on Iran once again to promptly ratify the Additional Protocol. Iran's delegates to the IAEA announced that agreement on a timetable and a clear agenda were necessary before the negotiations could continue. During the meeting, the Russian proposal that had been already rejected by Iran was brought up with support from the United States and Europe. Britain's representative to the IAEA asked Iran to pay serious attention to Russia's proposal. It was the first time that the proposal was raised at the IAEA, which was taken as a sign that the proposal was supported by the West and even the agency itself.

Then, on November 27, the foreign ministers of the EU3 countries issued a reply to the letter that had been sent to them by Ali Larijani on the resumption of negotiations between Iran and Europe. The Europeans focused on the need to reach a basis for official negotiations between the two sides. On December 5, Larijani held a news conference to announce that the continuation of negotiations hinged on the recognition of Iran's right to conduct enrichment on its own soil. He emphasized that Iran would not budge on this issue.[89] It was decided that negotiations between Iran and the EU3 should begin in Vienna on December 21. However, the negotiations, which continued on January 18, were little more than an exchange of viewpoints.[90]

Meanwhile, on December 24, Russia's proposal was officially offered to Iran. At that time, some analysts maintained that Russia had offered the proposal under pressure from the United States and the European countries. Russia did not provide the details of its plan to Iran.[91]

In January 2006, Ali Asghar Soltanieh was appointed Iran's representative to the IAEA with the endorsement of the head of the Atomic Energy Organization of Iran and the president. Ali Larijani, the new Iranian nuclear negotiator, announced that Russia's proposal could be considered if it were based on an existing contract for supplying fuel to the Bushehr power plant during the first year of its operations, with nuclear waste returned to Russia. The Iranian government also emphasized that although Moscow's proposal was based on the establishment of a joint Iranian-Russian company in Russia to enrich uranium, Iran was determined to have a domestic enrichment program. Tehran started separate negotiations with Moscow to work toward a mutually agreeable revision of the proposal. This was in line with the ninth government's "looking to the East" strategy, which continued to enjoy high-level support.

RESTART OF CENTRIFUGE ENRICHMENT AT THE NATANZ PILOT PLANT

On January 3, 2006, Tehran informed the IAEA of its decision to resume nuclear research and development activities. The following day, the secretariat of the IAEA issued a press release announcing that it had received the memo sent by Iran's permanent representative informing the agency that it would resume R&D on peaceful nuclear energy, which had been voluntarily suspended as a confidence-building measure as of January 9, 2006. The press release noted that the IAEA director general was opposed to Tehran's new decision and considered it counterproductive.[92]

The official argument of the new government for resumption of R&D activities in that tense atmosphere was that "voluntary and non-legally binding suspension" of uranium enrichment had cost the country very dearly.[93] On January 10, Iran began to remove seals installed by the IAEA on the uranium suspension sites. According to an announcement by the IAEA and Iran, the seals were to be completely removed from the Natanz enrichment site as well as two related test and storage sites, Farayand Technique and Pars Trash, by January 11. On January 13, the IAEA received a letter from Britain, Germany, and France informing the agency of an upcoming meeting in Berlin before the end of January. On January 18, the IAEA Board of Governors announced that an extraordinary meeting would be held on February 2 to discuss the issue of nuclear safeguards in Iran.

Resumption of R&D activities exposed Iran to a spate of international criticism, not only from Western countries, but also Eastern bloc countries, which had been the main object of Tehran's new diplomacy. Iran sent a letter to the EU3 on January 17, 2006, calling on them to resume negotiations.[94] Iran also indicated willingness in the letter, submitted by Javad Va'idi, to remove outstanding ambiguities about its nuclear activities through dialogue. The letter noted that, despite the failure of the London meeting, Iran was determined to go on with negotiations to achieve a solution. The letter was received coldly by the EU3.[95]

Tehran, for its part, took Europe and the United States to task for their opposition to Iran's proposal. Hossein Entezami, the new spokesman for the Supreme National Security Council, described the EU's rejection of Iran's call for negotiations as illogical. Entezami confirmed that Iran had sent a letter written by the Supreme National Security Council undersecretary for international security inviting the EU3 to talks. He emphasized that resumption of R&D activities under supervision of the IAEA could not be considered a violation.[96]

Remarks by officials of the ninth government reported in the mass media in late January 2006 allow us to draw several conclusions. Despite the IAEA resolution of September 2005, Iran's diplomats evidently still believed that sending Iran's case to the UN Security Council was a political bluff and would never take place.[97] The new nuclear officials emphasized that Iran would resume R&D activities and suspension of other activities at Natanz and that production of nuclear fuel would remain in place.[98] At the same time, these officials, following what they called "aggressive diplomacy," stressed the possibility of withdrawal from the IAEA or even the NPT. Europe would oppose the U.S. approach in order to avert the consequences of reporting Iran to the UN Security Council. At this juncture, many Iranian officials repeated the threats of severing ties with the IAEA, suspending implementation of the Additional Protocol, and even leaving the NPT.[99]

After Iran announced its decision on January 10, 2006, to resume enrichment activities, Germany, Britain, France, and the United States held a meeting with Russia and China in London and called for an emergency meeting of the IAEA Board of Governors on February 2 and 3. However, the director general rejected a request by the Western countries to submit a complete report on Iran's nuclear activities to the emergency meeting. It was announced that his report would be submitted to the Board of Governors during its regular session on March 6.

The ninth government maintained that the request for an extraordinary meeting reflected a tacit acceptance in the West of Iran's determination to go on with research and development activities. Tehran also maintained that the request aimed to politicize the Board of Governors' meeting on March 6 by increasing pressure on the director general to pay more attention to political considerations when drawing up his technical report, which would be used as a basis for a possible resolution.

The ninth government had already gone through one extraordinary meeting of the IAEA Board in August 2005, when Iran restarted activities at the Isfahan uranium conversion facility under the supervision of the IAEA. ElBaradei had been asked to present a full report on the history of Iran's nuclear activities during the regular meeting of the Board of Governors in September 2005. In Paragraphs 49 and 50 of his report (presented on September 3), ElBaradei stated that the IAEA would not be able to confirm the peaceful nature of Iran's nuclear activities unless Iran granted access to the agency beyond the Additional Protocol. These paragraphs were later echoed by the Board of Governors' resolution on September 24, 2005. This earlier experience should have alerted Tehran to the possibility that ElBaradei's opposition to report to the extraordinary meeting was a legal trap for Iran.

In the meantime, Tehran threatened Western countries on several occasions that if its nuclear dossier were referred to the UN Security Council, it would retaliate and expand its activities. The most official threat was stated by Ali Larijani, the top Iranian nuclear negotiator, who emphasized that "if Iran's nuclear case were sent to the Security Council, Tehran would resume uranium enrichment for industrial purposes and would have to give up all voluntary suspension."[100] Larijani assured the international community that Iran would not withdraw from the NPT. Hossein Entezami, the Supreme National Security Council spokesman, also warned that if the nuclear case were sent to the Security Council, Tehran would end implementation of the Additional Protocol of the NPT.[101] Further, Ali Asghar Soltanieh, Iran's representative to the IAEA, threatened that if the nuclear case were sent to the UN Security Council, Tehran would end its voluntary cooperation with IAEA inspectors.[102]

Under those conditions, Ali Larijani, who was the main proponent of the "looking to the East" approach, flew to Moscow to discuss with his

Russian counterpart the Kremlin's proposal for Iran to continue enrichment activities on Russian soil.[103] Taking part in a joint news conference with Ivanov, Larijani noted that Russia's plan was "positive" and could be made more complete in a February meeting of Iran and Russia.[104] However, his remarks the next day about the limited capacity of Russia to meet Tehran's nuclear needs prompted the United States, Europe, and even China to dismiss Iran's maneuver.

CHAPTER SIX

TO THE SECURITY COUNCIL

THE IAEA BOARD REFERS IRAN'S CASE
TO THE UN SECURITY COUNCIL

On January 30, 2006, the five permanent members of the UN Security Council and Germany agreed on a statement requiring the IAEA to report Iran's case to the Security Council. The statement, which was also endorsed by the European Union foreign policy chief and issued in London, noted that the ministers agreed that the Board of Governors should make a decision in its extraordinary meeting to compel Iran to take necessary steps.[1] In the statement, the P5+1 emphasized that the UN Security Council should wait for ElBaradei's March report before making a final decision. The statement also noted that the ministers called on Iran to fully suspend enrichment and related activities such as research and development, under the supervision of the IAEA. Ali Larijani, secretary of the Supreme National Security Council, reacted by saying that the message being conveyed to Iran was that Europe lacked the capacity to solve the nuclear problem.[2]

A day later, 212 members of Iran's Parliament released a statement warning the government that it should not allow the inalienable rights of the Iranian nation to be bargained away to any government, nor bend to foreign bullying. They also noted that, if the IAEA Board of Governors wanted to bully Iran, the government would be obliged to reverse all voluntary suspensions and restart all peaceful nuclear activities. IAEA inspectors would also be allowed to act only within the limits of the NPT, conducting only ordinary inspections of Iran's nuclear centers.[3]

On February 4, 2006, the Board of Governors began its three-day extraordinary meeting on Iran's nuclear issue, confirming the referral of Iran's case to the Security Council. March 6 was set as the date when Iran's case would be taken up by the Security Council. The resolution was ratified with 27 ayes, 3 nays (Cuba, Syria, and Venezuela), and 5 abstentions (Algeria, Belarus, Indonesia, Libya, and South Africa). Sixteen member countries of the Non-Aligned Movement were present at the voting; the result shows that not only did the NAM fail to build support for Iran, but even India, Russia, and China, which were major members of the Eastern bloc, supported the resolution and voted against Iran.

According to Article 19 of the Safeguards Agreement between Iran and the IAEA, dated May 15, 1974,[4] any referral of the issue by the IAEA to the Security Council in accordance with Article XII, Paragraph C of the IAEA Statute could be possible "if the Board, upon examination of relevant information reported to it by the Director General, finds that the Agency is not able to verify that there has been no diversion of nuclear material required to be safeguarded under this Agreement to nuclear weapons or other nuclear explosive devices."

Nevertheless, it is important to note that Iran and some legal experts have questioned the legal grounding of the entire "referral process" from the IAEA to the Security Council.[5] Nowhere in the UN Charter, the IAEA Statute, the NPT, Iran's Safeguards Agreement, or anywhere else is authority given to the UN Security Council to enforce the Safeguards Agreement between Iran and the IAEA. Legally, enforcement of the agreement falls to the IAEA, which can take measures such as terminating nuclear assistance or expelling Iran from membership in the agency if the country does not comply.

This is quite significant because, while IAEA Board of Governors requests have been readily acknowledged to be *voluntary* and *not legally binding*, Security Council resolutions have restated the same requests as *requirements and demands*.[6] These demands were not made under Chapter VII of the UN Charter but were based on Iranian noncompliance with its Safeguards Agreement, which only the IAEA has the authority to enforce.

The noncompliance of a country with its Safeguards Agreement does not automatically imply that the country is a threat to international peace. In the cases of Romania in 1992, North Korea in 1993, and Libya in 2004, for example, the IAEA notified each country's noncompliance, yet no determination was made by the UN Security Council that any of them posed a threat to the peace. No further action was recommended in the cases of Romania and Libya because Libya gave up all its nuclear weapons programs, and the political aspects of the Romanian nuclear issue were totally different than the Iranian case.

Citing this discrepancy between international legal authority and the restrictions and obligations placed on Iran by the Security Council, legal expert Eric A. Brill has suggested that Iran request an independent arbitration panel to determine the legality of the Security Council's resolutions aimed at enforcing Iran's Safeguards Agreement.[7]

Some Western analysts believed that because Iran had not complied with all of its safeguards obligations and the IAEA Statute, the referral to the Security Council was legal. They question whether any state other than Iran shares the view that the referral lacks a basis in international law, and also whether Iran would win such arbitration.

One of the European former diplomats involved in the Iranian nuclear issue for five years told me that:

> The [UN Security Council] resolutions on the Iranian nuclear issue are legal but not legitimate. There is a whiff of moral illegitimacy: neither the NPT or IAEA require abandonment of enrichment when a state is found noncompliant with its safeguards regulations—all they require is that the noncompliance be corrected. UN Chapter 7 suggests measures are justified when there is a threat to the peace. Under Article 39, the [Security Council] has not been able to determine if Iranian nuclear activities have been a threat to the peace. Why does moral legitimacy matter? How the West behaves morally actually affects perceptions of Western leadership along the global order set up in 1945. The West has tried to deny Iran its NPT right to enrich uranium. There are also many

other states that are threshold states that aren't being punished as Iran is. There is also no indication that Iran wants a nuclear weapon. We also say that Iran must comply before we are willing to talk, but the only treaty Iran is noncompliant with is that it has ceased to apply Subsidiary Arrangement code 3.1.

On June 9, 2011, six former ambassadors to Iran from European countries, Richard Dalton (United Kingdom), Steen Hohwü-Christensen (Sweden), Paul von Maltzahn (Germany), Guillaume Metten (Belgium), François Nicoullaud (France), and Roberto Toscano (Italy), questioned the legitimacy of the Security Council resolution in a joint declaration:[8]

> In terms of international law, the position of Europe and the United States is perhaps less assured than is generally believed. Basically, it is embodied in a set of resolutions adopted by the UN Security Council authorizing coercive measures in case of "threats to the peace." But what constitutes the threat? Is it the enrichment of uranium in Iranian centrifuges? . . . In principle, however, nothing in international law or in the Nuclear Non-Proliferation Treaty forbids the enrichment of uranium. Besides Iran, several other countries, parties or not to the treaty, enrich uranium without being accused of "threatening the peace." And in Iran, this activity is submitted to inspections by the International Atomic Energy Agency. These inspections, it is true, are constrained by a Safeguards Agreement dating from the 1970s. But it is also true that the IAEA has never uncovered in Iran any attempted diversion of nuclear material to military use. . . . Today, a majority of experts, even in Israel, seems to view Iran as striving to become a "threshold country," technically able to produce a nuclear weapon but abstaining from doing so for the present. Again, nothing in international law or in the Nuclear Non-Proliferation Treaty forbids such an ambition. Like Iran, several other countries are on their way to or have already reached such a threshold but have committed not to acquire nuclear weapons. Nobody seems to bother them.

Soltanieh, Iran's representative to the IAEA, mentioned the following five reasons to *Arms Control Today* to explain why he believes the referral to the UN Security Council resolution is illegal and why Iran has not implemented the UN resolution and has no intention of doing so:

- The first reason is, according to Article XII.C of the [IAEA] Statute, the noncompliance of a member state should be recognized by inspectors, because the inspector has the access to the places, the materials, confidential information, and individuals. Then if they report noncompliance to the director-general, the director-general then should refer [the matter] to the board of governors. But in the case of Iran, after years of negotiation between the EU-3 and Iran and robust inspections, then in 2006, some diplomats, European and Americans, being on the board of governors, themselves judged that there was noncompliance before 2003. Therefore, this is in 100 percent contravention of the statute, [Article] XII.C.
- In Article XII.C, it says that the country that is referred to the Security Council is the recipient country. It means that when this article was written decades ago, for the country that is receiving nuclear materials and equipment from the IAEA and misuses it for nonpeaceful purposes, that is noncompliance. That is why this article says that the recipient country should be referred to the Security Council and that the country should return the equipment or materials to the IAEA. But in the case of Iran, this is not applied because we were not the recipient country of nuclear materials or equipment for Natanz enrichment or other activities.
- Referral to the Security Council has no legal basis because an issue should only be referred to the Security Council if there is proof of diversion of nuclear material to military or prohibited purposes. In the reports of the IAEA, you see language that says that there is no evidence of diversion of nuclear materials to prohibited purposes. Therefore, this does not apply to Iran.
- If there are obstacles for inspectors to go to a country, for example North Korea, when the inspectors were not permitted to [go], then this matter should be sent to New York. But in the case of Iran, you can see in all the reports of the director general over the last eight years that the director general says that the IAEA is able to continue its verification in Iran. It means that there have been no obstacles whatsoever for inspectors to come to Iran.
- In the resolutions of the EU-3 in the Board of Governors, before this matter was sent to New York or New York was involved, the

Security Council in their own resolution, they confess, confirm that the suspension of enrichment was a non-legally binding, confidence-building, and volunteer measure. If this is non-legally binding, then how is it that, after two and a half years, when we stopped the suspension, then they turned to the Board of Governors and said that Iran has violated its obligation and this is not legal, [that] Iran should continue its suspension? They admit themselves that it is not-legally binding.[9]

It is clear that Iran would most likely not win such international arbitration because of international political attitudes toward Iran's nuclear program. However, in his recent memoir, ElBaradei himself questioned the legality of the referral of Iran's nuclear dossier to the UN Security Council and mentioned that member countries of the Non-Aligned Movement shared his concerns.

The first angry reactions from Tehran to the IAEA Board of Governors' vote were predictable. Minutes after passage of the resolution, a German news agency quoted Javad Va'idi as saying that, following Parliament's instruction, Iran would end voluntary cooperation with the IAEA. He added that Iran had merely been conducting research on uranium enrichment but that it had decided now to launch full-scale enrichment.[10]

An Iran Atomic Energy Organization official also told the student news agency ISNA that it had been instructed by the Supreme National Security Council to end voluntary implementation of the Additional Protocol and all voluntary nuclear suspensions if the nuclear case were referred to the Security Council.[11]

In Paragraph 2 of the IAEA resolution, which was championed by Germany, Britain, and France, the board requested "the Director General to report to the UN Security Council that these steps are required of Iran by the Board and to report to the UN Security Council all IAEA reports and resolutions, as adopted, relating to this issue." Also, according to Paragraph 8, the Board of Governors requested "the Director General to report on the implementation of this and previous resolutions to the next regular session of the Board, for its consideration, and immediately thereafter to convey, together with any Resolution from the March Board, that report to the Security Council."[12]

The following points must be considered in an analysis of the board's February 4, 2006, resolution on Iran:

- Paragraph C of the resolution contained an important legal point that countries could not simply rely on Article IV of the NPT to claim their right to nuclear energy and the fuel cycle. The argument was that Article IV must be interpreted in the context of Articles I and II, which require that the country's overall program be peaceful. This paragraph of the resolution was the result of efforts made by the United States and the West to impose new restrictions. In the Western point of view, Iran could not enjoy the cooperation promised by Article IV because it had not complied with its Safeguards Agreement. In Iran's view, the whole nuclear issue had from the beginning been a political initiative by the West to deprive Iran of its legitimate rights under the NPT and to prevent Iran from obtaining a nuclear capability. That is why Iranian officials considered this initiative to be a new means of restricting Iran's legitimate rights.

- Paragraph D of the resolution was added to get the support of Non-Aligned Movement member states and countries such as Brazil and Egypt. It emphasized that Iran's nuclear case was a special one that would not be extended to other Non-Aligned Movement countries.

- Paragraph H implied that Iran had not shown full transparency in its dealings with the IAEA. Also, emphasis was put on Iran's failures and issues such as the history of its secret nuclear activities, and in several paragraphs doubts were expressed about Iran's intentions and the nature of its nuclear programs.

- Paragraph K used the word "extensive" in reference to the requirement of confidence building about the peaceful nature of Iran's nuclear program. This was unprecedented. The word implied that it would take a long time before the world could trust Iran. The paragraph was a response to Iran's claims that the suspension period had been too lengthy and underlined that resolution of problems between Iran and the IAEA would not be reached in the near future.

- In the final version of the resolution, the word "nuclear" had been taken out of the draft and the phrase "Iran's nuclear issue" had been replaced with "Iran's issue." It noted that "a solution to the Iran issue would contribute to global nonproliferation efforts and to realizing the objective of a Middle East free of weapons of mass destruction, including their means of delivery."[13] Paragraph M was added through the insistence of Egypt, and a compromise was reached among the United States, Egypt, and Yemen in response to Egypt's concerns about Israel. Instead of pointing to Israel's nuclear program, the paragraph implied that Iran was the main problem in the Middle East.

- Paragraph 8 contained the most important point of the resolution: The director general was requested to report on its implementation and previous resolutions to the next regular session of the board for its consideration, and immediately thereafter to convey, together with any resolution from the board in March, that report to the UN Security Council.[14]
- The request for full suspension of all nuclear activities including suspension of the uranium conversion facilities and repetition of other requests of the Board of Governors, such as the revision of Iran's decision to build a heavy-water research reactor at Arak, were other noteworthy points of the resolution.[15]

A few days after Iran's nuclear dossier was sent to the UN Security Council, Hassan Rouhani, the former Iranian official in charge of the nuclear dossier, and former president Mohammad Khatami questioned the wisdom of the ninth government's diplomatic policy. Both emphasized that Tehran should negotiate,[16] avoid taking emotional positions, and move along the lines of a realistic and overarching strategy. The ninth government had earlier talked about a possible withdrawal from the NPT, which reinforced international concerns that Iran's nuclear program was not entirely peaceful and that Iran's goal was to follow North Korea's example. Tehran now tried to take a more conciliatory position. However, this could not prevent the failure of negotiations between European ministers and Iran's foreign minister on the nuclear issue. Javier Solana, the EU foreign policy chief, told reporters after a ninety-minute meeting with Iran's foreign minister, Mottaki, that Iran's basic positions had not changed and called on Iran to be more constructive.[17]

Concurrently, Iran was carrying out important negotiations with Russia focused on the Bushehr nuclear power plant and Russia's proposal for uranium enrichment on Russian soil. Despite heavy political pressure from the West, nuclear cooperation between Tehran and Moscow had continued since 1996, and Moscow had promised to complete the Bushehr plant. Its operation, however, was postponed on various grounds. According to the last schedule for commissioning the Bushehr plant that was announced during a meeting between Aghazadeh, head of Iran's Atomic Energy Organization, and Alexander Rumyantsev, then-head of the Russian nuclear agency, both sides had agreed that the plant should be made operational in the second half of the Iranian calendar year 1385 (winter 2006/spring 2007).[18] During the meeting, which took place on February 28, 2006, the Iranian side announced that after installation of fuel in the Bushehr nuclear power plant, the plant would go through a three-month test period and would be ready for the generation of 1,000 MW of nuclear power within six months. The same day, Iran and Russia signed agreements including the timing of the return of the Bushehr reactor's spent fuel to Russia.[19] On February 25, Sergei Kiriyenko, head of the Russian Federal Atomic Energy Agency, arrived in Tehran and held intensive talks with Aghazadeh in Tehran and Bushehr. Ali Larijani also went to Russia on March 1 to continue negotiations with Sergei Lavrov and other high-ranking Russian officials.[20]

RUSSIA'S PROPOSAL: INVEST IN ITS ENRICHMENT PLANT INSTEAD OF DOMESTIC PROGRAM

On December 24, 2006, Moscow announced that it had proposed to Iran a plan that could help solve the nuclear problem.[21] The plan included a formal proposal for the transfer of Iran's enrichment program to Russia.[22]

The new Iranian government responded with uncoordinated and frequently contradictory positions on what it called the Russian plan.[23] The Foreign Ministry spokesman, Hamid Reza Asefi, basically denied the existence of such plan. Larijani stressed that the plan was worth consideration.[24] Foreign Minister Manouchehr Mottaki announced that Tehran had conditionally agreed to the Russian plan.[25] Javad Va'idi, meanwhile, characterized the plan as totally unacceptable.[26]

A review of those remarks makes clear that the officials believed that the plan did not meet Iran's national interests and the position of the ninth government. Some pro-government groups went as far as to claim that the Russian plan was "the West's new trap"[27] and warned the government against accepting it. The issue was hotly debated. Experts and Iranian members of Parliament maintained that Iran, in order to meet the country's national interests, should accept the Russian plan only if it amounted to enrichment on Iranian soil. Moscow, for its part, made implementation conditional on suspension of enrichment by Iran.[28]

Iranian and Russian experts met in Tehran on January 8 to hold a first round of talks about Russia's proposal. Negotiations finally got under way on February 20. A final round of talks between Tehran and Moscow was held on March 1, just a few days ahead of the IAEA Board of Governors' meeting on March 6. The negotiations were held at a high level, attended by Ali Larijani and Russian Foreign Minister Igor Ivanov. After the negotiations, Larijani began talks with the foreign ministers of Germany and France as well as a high-ranking representative of the British Foreign Ministry and the European Union foreign policy chief in Vienna. Finally, he announced that Iran and Russia had agreed on five or six points that would improve conditions. He warned, however, that if the United States took Iran's nuclear dossier to the UN Security Council, the Russian plan would be considered null and void.[29] He also stated that transfer of Iran's uranium enrichment activities to another country was out of the question.[30]

On March 5, speculation concerning the Russian plan took a totally new turn. After a meeting with Condoleezza Rice, his American counterpart, Russian foreign minister Sergei Lavrov announced that his country would not accept any compromise to the plan.[31]

This reality contrasted with claims by ninth government officials that Iran had achieved a final victory in the nuclear case, or at least that many of the problems had been solved. Ahmadinejad stated, "In the nuclear case, thank God, we have emerged victorious and succeeded, and they have understood that we have succeeded." Addressing the families of journalists killed while covering wars or assassinated by terrorist groups at the Salman Farsi Mosque of the presidential office, the president stated that Western countries sought concessions from Iran, but "they should know that they cannot do anything against the nation of Iran." He further said, on February 11 (the official anniversary of the Islamic Revolution), that Iran had "finished the job," with only marginal issues related to the nuclear case remaining unresolved. Ahmadinejad attributed the "victory" to "the stead-fastness of the nation, which was not afraid of any threat."[32]

In his 2011 memoir, Mohamed ElBaradei describes how, later in 2006, he worked with the Russians on a new compromise by which Iran would be allowed a small-scale R&D program with a limited number of centrifuges. The Americans, however, rejected the proposal and held to their position of demanding that not a single centrifuge run in Iran. ElBaradei's impression was that Iran might have accepted the proposal, but it was never fully developed due to American opposition.[33] I believe that if the compromise allowed Iran to expand beyond a pilot program once remaining technical ambiguities with the IAEA had been resolved, Iran would have accepted the proposal.

FIRST SECURITY COUNCIL STATEMENT

After twenty days of negotiations, the UN Security Council met on March 28, 2006, and issued a nonbinding statement on the Iran situation.

Before the London meeting, the West (United States and Europe) and East (Russia and China) were divided on how to deal with Iran. The Western countries—especially the United States—urged that the nuclear case be reported to the Security Council, but China and Russia argued that the time was not yet ripe. At the London meeting, they tried to find a middle ground. Moscow called for enrichment to be transferred to Russian soil, a plan that Beijing supported. In the view of Iranian experts who were not involved in the decisionmaking process, flirting with the plan had the benefit of, at the very least, buying some time.

There was another delicate matter occupying Iran's diplomats. While Iran's nuclear case was being discussed at the UN Security Council, Ali Larijani announced on March 16 that the chairman of the Supreme Council of the Islamic Revolution in Iraq, Abdul Aziz Hakim, had asked Iran to negotiate directly with the United States on the Iraq issue. Larijani said that Iran had accepted the offer and was appointing negotiators. This was the first time Iran had agreed to talk directly to the United States since the Islamic Revolution, and the prospect was taken seriously in Western diplomatic circles, especially those who were opposed to the unilateral militaristic policies of the U.S. government. Some European media outlets likewise expressed optimism about possible talks between Iran and the United States and argued that they should have taken place sooner.[34]

The UN Security Council's March 28 statement expressed serious concern about Iran's decision to resume uranium enrichment and about the reduction of Iran's cooperation with the IAEA. The Security Council called on Iran to take steps requested by the IAEA Board of Governors to build confidence about the peaceful nature of its nuclear program and to resolve outstanding issues. The Security Council also stressed the importance of reestablishing suspension of activities related to enrichment and reprocessing (including research and development) in a manner that could be verified by the IAEA.

At the end of the statement, the UN Security Council called on the director general of the IAEA to present a report within thirty days on Iran's compliance with the Board of Governors' requests and forward copies to the Board of Governors and Security Council.[35] A few points in the statement softened the blow to Iran. The deadline given to Tehran was increased by thirty days due to pressure from Russia and China. A paragraph that had described Iran's nuclear program as a threat to global peace and security was taken out. Iran's nuclear program therefore was not yet made subject to Chapter VII of the UN Charter.

Foreign Minister Mottaki expressed regret over the statement and rejected it.[36] Iran's representative to the IAEA, Ali Asghar Soltanieh, said that Tehran intended to continue cooperation with the IAEA but warned that putting more pressure on Iran to give up uranium enrichment would make the situation more complicated. In an interview with CNN, Soltanieh said that the Security Council statement had been issued hurriedly and that the Security Council should not get involved in Iran's nuclear case.[37]

THE FIRST GOOD NEWS

After the foreign ministers of EU member states issued a statement on April 11, 2006, calling for a diplomatic solution and for Iran to comply with the UN request to suspend its enrichment activities,[38] President Ahmadinejad responded by launching a "good news" propaganda campaign. Attending a special ceremony in Mashhad, he proclaimed, "I announce at this historical opportunity that under the blessings of Hazrat Vali Asr [the twelfth Shi'i imam] and due to endeavors of faithful and creative Iranian scientists and due to prayers of the brave and intelligent Iranian nation, the cycle for production of nuclear fuel has been completed on a laboratory scale and our youth produced uranium with the needed richness on 20 Farvardin of the current year [April 9, 2006]."[39]

During the same ceremony, Gholam Reza Aghazadeh, the head of the Atomic Energy Organization of Iran, announced that Iran had decided to become self-sufficient with regard to nuclear fuel. "Up to the present," he said, "the uranium processing facilities of Iran have produced 110 tons of UF_6 and Iran is now the eighth country in the world to master this technology."[40] The news was announced on the basis of a tenet, central to the ninth government's foreign policy program, that maintained that the West would have to get used to an atomic Iran sooner or later. By such statements, the ninth government's intention was to convince the world that it had passed the point of no return on enrichment capabilities while it would not proceed to develop a nuclear bomb. But from the Western point of view, the statement could mean only that Iran was becoming a nuclear-weapon state, once more supporting the view of those believing that this was indeed Iran's long-term objective.

The "good news" propaganda campaign made the international community more suspicious of Iran's nuclear program. In reaction to Iran's April announcement, U.S. Secretary of State Condoleezza Rice called on the UN Security Council to pass a resolution against Iran under Article 41 of Chapter VII of the UN Charter. Rice continued to state pointedly that the Security Council, unlike the IAEA, was authorized to compel a country to comply with its orders.[41]

After the thirty-day deadline set by the UN Security Council was extended, the deputy head of the Atomic Energy Organization of Iran provided the IAEA with new information about Iran's nuclear program as a last-ditch effort to change the atmosphere. Aghazadeh, the Atomic Energy Organization's head, also met with the IAEA's director general. On April 29, 2006, Ali Larijani wrote a letter to ElBaradei indicating Iran's readiness to resolve outstanding issues enumerated in the director general's March report, provided that the nuclear case remained at the IAEA and was discussed in the context of compliance with the Safeguards Agreement. The same day, the international media covered a statement by the deputy head of Iran's Atomic Energy Organization, who stated that if the nuclear case were returned to the IAEA Board of Governors, Iran was ready to give the IAEA "complementary access"[42] to its nuclear facilities.

Pressures mounted on Iran to accept incentives that had been offered by the EU3 in August 2005. Tehran argued that the proposal of August 5, 2005, simply ignored the main problem. In Iran's view, the main goal of the EU3 was to dissuade Tehran from continuing fuel-cycle activities. The new government stuck to the previous negotiating team's line that any proposal entailing enrichment suspension would be unacceptable to Iran.[43]

Faced with this resistance, the West increased its focus on encouraging the UN Security Council to adopt a resolution against Iran under Chapter VII of the UN Charter. ElBaradei had been instructed to report on Iran's compliance with the UN's March 28 request the following month. He reported that Iran had not complied with the requests of the Board of Governors to fully suspend the enrichment program, revise the decision to build the Arak heavy-water reactor, implement and ratify the Additional Protocol, and provide transparency beyond the Additional Protocol and Safeguards Agreement.

With regard to clarification of the nature of Iran's past nuclear activities, ElBaradei reported:

- Difficulty in establishing a definitive conclusion with respect to the origin of the highly enriched uranium contamination that the IAEA had found in Iran made it essential to obtain more information on the scope and chronology of Iran's centrifuge enrichment program.
- Some discrepancies existed between the information provided by Iran and information that the agency had obtained through law enforcement actions against A. Q. Khan's enrichment equipment smuggling network.
- Several reports in the press about statements by high-level Iranian officials concerning R&D and testing of P-2 centrifuges by Iran needed to be clarified.
- Continuing concern about the instructions regarding the machining of uranium metal into hemispheres, an activity relevant only to the making of a nuclear bomb.

- The plutonium samples analyzed by the IAEA were derived from source(s) other than the ones declared by Iran.
- Iran's work on missile reentry vehicles and their military applications as well as explosive tests required explanation.
- The "role of the military" in Iran's nuclear programs raised concerns that the program was not exclusively peaceful and made it difficult to obtain information about the full scope of Iran's enrichment program.

The report officially confirmed Iran's claim that it was enriching uranium to about 3.6 percent[44] at Natanz. It also confirmed the production of 110 tons of UF_6 at the Isfahan uranium conversion facility between September 2005 and the time of the report's preparation.

Finally, the report noted that Iran's decision to cease voluntary implementation of the provisions of the Additional Protocol further limited the agency's ability to make progress in clarifying various issues and confirming the absence of undeclared nuclear material and activities. Agency access to activities not involving nuclear material (such as research into laser isotope separation and the production of sensitive components of the nuclear fuel cycle) would be restricted, which also would make it difficult to verify that Iran's nuclear program was exclusively peaceful.

In the aftermath of ElBaradei's report, a P5+1 meeting was held in Paris on May 2, 2006. During the meeting, Britain and France presented key parts of the first draft of their proposed resolution, which called on Iran to immediately halt uranium enrichment activities. The meeting, which was attended by the foreign ministers of the five permanent members of the UN Security Council plus Germany, started after Tehran's announcement that it had successfully tested uranium enrichment up to 4.8 percent.[45]

That same day, U.S. Undersecretary of State R. Nicholas Burns noted that Iran's actions required moving toward using Chapter VII of the UN Charter to enforce sanctions on Iran to increase diplomatic pressure on the country to adopt a more rational policy and halt its nuclear activities. Burns added that it was quite clear that the P5+1 could not work with Iran's government under existing conditions.[46]

The Paris meeting was the first of top representatives from the United States, Russia, China, France, Britain, and Germany (P5+1) after ElBaradei sent his report on Iran's nuclear program to the Security Council. One day after the meeting, the Security Council met in New York, with the U.S. representative warning that if the Security Council did not give the go-ahead on Iran sanctions, the United States was prepared to form a coalition of countries to impose those sanctions.[47] At the same time, German Chancellor Angela Merkel met with U.S. President George W. Bush at the White House and called on him to start direct talks with Iran. Bush rejected the idea.[48]

The ninth government undertook a number of diplomatic maneuvers. President Ahmadinejad sent a letter to President Bush on May 8, 2006, in which he gave his philosophical perspective on the international situation and root causes of the crisis and offered ways to get out of the stalemate. Iran considered the letter a very important diplomatic initiative, but American officials criticized it and noted that it was more of a philosophical treatise than a set of policy proposals.[49]

The secretary of Iran's Supreme National Security Council, Ali Larijani, announced that Tehran was willing to continue negotiations on Moscow's proposal. Larijani stated in an interview, "We believe that this proposal can continue and go ahead, but they should give us more time to reach a satisfactory result with Russia."[50] Larijani dedicated most of the interview, however, to describing Iran's "carrot and stick" policy. That policy was meant to give the West two options: take Iran's nuclear dossier back from the UN Security Council and give it to the IAEA, which would lead to increased cooperation on the part of Iran with IAEA inspectors and full implementation of the Additional Protocol;* or continue hostile measures by Western countries against Iran through the UN Security Council, which would result in a discontinuation of Iran's cooperation with the IAEA.[51] At the same time, Tehran emphasized that it would never accept suspension.[52]

NEW EU INCENTIVES

One day after Ahmadinejad's letter was sent to President Bush, Britain, France, and Germany suddenly announced that they would soon propose a new incentive package to Iran. The new plan was to include provisions

---

* Editor's note: The IAEA retained the Iranian nuclear file in any case. It had sent it to the Security Council, in accordance with the IAEA Statute, because Iran had not cooperated fully with the IAEA to resolve all outstanding issues.

for loans and technology to meet Iran's energy needs, in exchange for resumed negotiations and Iran's agreement to suspend its nuclear fuel enrichment program.[53]

Representatives of the P5+1 met in May 2006 to discuss political, economic, and security incentives for Iran.[54] Javier Solana, the EU foreign
policy chief, stressed that the European package showed that Europe was
not opposed to a peaceful nuclear program for Iran. Asked about Iran's
reluctance to accept the so-called generous incentives of Europe, he replied
that rejection of the incentives would prove that Iran was not ready to
cooperate. The UN Security Council, meanwhile, moved forward with
discussions on a resolution to force Iran to comply with the demands of
the international community.[55]

Around this time, John Sawers, director general of the UK Foreign
Ministry, wrote a letter to his colleagues in Paris, Berlin, and Washington,
arguing that in order to undermine the Iranian argument that suspension
was voluntary and non-legally binding, they could push for the referral of
Iran's dossier to the UN Security Council and make suspension mandatory
through a Security Council resolution. Sawers proposed to his counterparts that, to win over China and Russia for such a resolution, they needed
to propose an incentive package to the Iranians. Once this package was
rejected by Iran (as it predictably would be if, as Sawers desired, it included
a demand for indefinite suspension), the Chinese and Russians would be
more inclined to assent to a Security Council resolution on Iran based on
Chapter VII of the UN Charter.[56]

In late May, ElBaradei made a statement that reported that Iran's new
government had shown some flexibility in talks with the IAEA. He announced to reporters a few weeks after meeting with Larijani and immediately after a meeting with Condoleezza Rice that Iran was showing more
flexibility. He said that as far as he knew, the Iranians were ready to agree
for uranium enrichment to be part of an international consortium outside
Iran for a few years.[57]

In his 2011 memoir, ElBaradei revealed that in May 2006 he also conveyed a message from Larijani to Condoleezza Rice. As he later recounted,
"The Iranians were interested in direct talks with the United States. They
were ready to discuss not only Iran's nuclear issues, but also Iraq, Afghanistan, Hezbollah, and Hamas." ElBaradei told Rice that Larijani believed that

"Iran could assist with security in Baghdad and also help establish a national unity government in Lebanon."[58] This was, together with Khatami's gesture of cooperation on Afghanistan in 2001 and Rouhani's 2003 message transmitted to President Bush through ElBaradei, Iran's third overture to the United States for a grand bargain to resolve issues of concern to both sides.

The next month, Javad Va'idi, my successor as nuclear team spokesman and Larijani's deputy on nuclear affairs, met with ElBaradei and told him, "The issue is not just the nuclear program. It is the entire future relationship between America and Iran." As ElBaradei remembered, "The Iranians were prepared to agree to suspension, but not as a precondition of the negotiations, only as an outcome. Suspension would also need to be linked to some type of security assurance." ElBaradei relayed the message to Gregory Schulte, the U.S. ambassador to the IAEA. Unfortunately, like Iran's previous overtures, these messages were spurned by the Bush administration. As ElBaradei wrote in his memoir, the only "missing ingredient" at the time was American willingness to move forward.[59]

To return to the European plan: ABC News published a report on the proposal on May 24. According to the plan, Britain, Germany, and France would declare their readiness to help Iran build a number of light-water power plants and establish a nuclear fuel bank. The European proposal expressed support for enrichment on Russian soil. The new plan also offered trade, economic, and security incentives to Iran if Tehran accepted the request of the international community. The EU3 had also added sixteen punishments to be enforced should Iran reject the incentives.[60] Elements of the revised proposal were as follows:

- The international community would reaffirm Iran's right to develop nuclear energy for peaceful purposes in conformity with its NPT obligations, and in this context, commit to actively support the building of new light-water reactors in Iran through international joint projects. Upon resumption of negotiations, it would also agree to suspend discussion of Iran's nuclear program at the UN Security Council.
- For its part, Iran would commit to addressing all outstanding concerns of the IAEA through full cooperation with the IAEA and suspend all enrichment-related and reprocessing activities as re-

quested by the IAEA Board of Governors and the UN Security Council, and commit to continue suspension during negotiations; and would resume implementation of the Additional Protocol.

The areas to be covered in negotiations on a long-term agreement would include Iran's participation as a partner in an international facility in Russia that would provide enrichment services for a reliable supply of fuel to Iran's nuclear reactors. Subject to negotiations, such a facility could enrich all the UF_6 produced in Iran. The EU3 would also support:

- An intergovernmental forum on security issues in the Persian Gulf to establish regional security arrangements including guarantees for territorial integrity and political sovereignty.
- The facilitation of a WMD-free zone in the Middle East.
- Iran's full integration into international structures, including WTO, and the creation of a framework for increased direct investment in Iran and trade with Iran, including a trade and economic cooperation agreement with the EU.
- Civil aviation cooperation and removal of restrictions on civil aircraft manufacturers from exporting such aircraft to Iran.
- Establishment of a long-term strategic energy partnership between Iran and the EU.

The European Union also threatened that in the event that Iran did not cooperate, a long list of escalating punitive sanctions could be taken:

- A freeze of assets and a ban on financial transactions and investments involving organizations and/or individuals involved in Iran's nuclear and missile programs; a travel and visa ban on individuals involved in these programs; and a ban on Iranians from studying abroad in disciplines related to nuclear and missile development.
- Suspension of technical assistance from the IAEA.
- A visa and travel ban on selected high-ranking officials and personalities, and a freeze of assets of individuals and organizations connected to or close to the regime.
- An arms embargo against Iran.

- An embargo on exports of specific products (for example, refined oil or gas products) to Iran.
- Prohibition on foreign cooperation and investment in Iran in certain sectors.
- A general freeze of assets of Iranian financial institutions.
- Reduced government support for trade and export credit insurance to Iran.

Finally, the proposal contained a delicate point overlooked in most domestic analyses. The moratorium could be reviewed if and when all outstanding technical issues between Iran and the agency were resolved; the IAEA confirmed that there were no undeclared nuclear materials or activities in Iran; and international confidence in the exclusively peaceful nature of Iran's civil nuclear program had been restored.

Some pro-Ahmadinejad analysts argued that the proposal represented a sudden turnaround in the West's approach. While Western countries, led by the United States, had always used strong words on Iran, the new plan sought a diplomatic solution to problems and a return to negotiations. They considered this development a result of Iran's steadfastness in pursuing enrichment. The changed approach, according to this line of reasoning, showed that Iran's international standing had improved and that the case for reporting Iran's dossier to the UN Security Council as a threat to international security had weakened.[61]

On May 31, 2006, the United States issued a surprising statement announcing Washington's readiness to work with the European Union in negotiations with Iran, provided that Iran suspended enrichment and reprocessing. Secretary of State Rice read the statement on live television, noting that a copy had been sent to Tehran via the Swiss Embassy and that another copy had been given to Iran's representative to the United Nations.[62] This came to mark the transition from the EU3 to the P5+1,[63] in which the United States, Russia, and China joined Britain, France, and Germany as Iran's counterparts in nuclear negotiations.

Rice said that President Bush was committed to a diplomatic solution but that all options were still on the table. Iran, she said, was entitled to a peaceful nuclear program, but it was not to continue its enrichment program without international supervision. Rice promised major economic cooperation with Iran if the country gave up its nuclear ambitions.[64]

The unprecedented change in the U.S. position was greatly welcomed by the international media. The *Financial Times* wrote that President Bush had taken one of the biggest foreign policy risks of his second term as president in withdrawing from his previous stance and embracing cooperation with Europe in negotiations with Iran.[65] Western and regional governments also welcomed the proposal. Iranian Foreign Minister Mottaki, however, immediately rejected the offer. After a meeting with the secretary general of the Organization of the Islamic Conference, Mottaki said that the statement read by Ms. Rice contained nothing new.[66]

The P5+1 officially announced after a June 2, 2006, meeting that it had reached a final agreement on the new proposal to Iran. On June 5, Javier Solana arrived in Iran amid revelations in the media that if Iran suspended its enrichment activities, the United States was ready to lift a portion of the sanctions that it had imposed on Iran since the 1990s.[67] Solana met with Ali Larijani for two hours behind closed doors and then emerged to report that the meeting had been quite positive. Larijani also told reporters that the negotiations had been constructive and would pave the way for further cooperation.[68]

The new proposal by the P5+1 increased optimism that the Iran nuclear crisis could be resolved peacefully. The *Washington Post* even quoted American and European officials as saying that the incentive package proposed by the P5+1 would make it possible for Iran to enrich uranium on its own soil.[69] An unnamed American official was cited by the paper as saying that possible enrichment by Iran had been included so that Iran would accept the proposal.

According to the proposal,[70] P5+1 would:

- Reaffirm Iran's right to develop nuclear energy for peaceful purposes in conformity with its NPT obligations, and in this context reaffirm their support for the development by Iran of a civil nuclear energy program;
- Commit to actively support the building of new light-water reactors in Iran through international joint projects, in accordance with the IAEA Statute and the NPT;

- Agree to suspend discussion of Iran's nuclear program at the Security Council on the resumption of negotiations.

And Iran will:

- Commit to addressing all the outstanding concerns of the IAEA through full cooperation with the IAEA;
- Suspend all enrichment-related and reprocessing activities to be verified by the IAEA, as requested by the IAEA Board of Governors and the UN Security Council, and commit to continue this during these negotiations; and
- Resume implementation of the Additional Protocol.

But the key point of the proposal was about the mechanism mentioned in the "Review of Moratorium" part of the proposal on conditions for termination of the suspension, as follows:

"The long-term agreement would, with regard to common efforts to build international confidence, include a clause for review of the agreement in all its aspects, to follow:

- Confirmation by the IAEA that all outstanding issues and concerns reported by the IAEA, including those activities which could have a military nuclear dimension, have been resolved;

and

- Confirmation that there are no undeclared nuclear activities or materials in Iran and that international confidence in the exclusively peaceful nature of Iran's civil nuclear program has been restored.

Those who know the IAEA's procedures understand very well that this is the wording used for an indefinite suspension.

Reconciliation seemed to be in sight. That possibility was taken very seriously by Europe, even if the United States was relying on the new Iranian government to reject any provision for suspension, thereby helping to pursue its core policy of mobilizing the other great powers to support a harder line against Iran.[71]

Iran's government followed the script expected by the Americans. The policymakers of the ninth government became more determined about the rightfulness of their approach in the face of America's skepticism and adamantly opposed any suspension. Iranians have always believed that reconciliation with the United States should come in the form of a broad-based policy, not with a piecemeal deal on the nuclear issue, unless a nuclear deal is comprehensive and covers Iran's full rights. Iran always negotiated to explore the EU3 and P5+1 packages, but the Western partners were not ready to include the rights of Iran for enrichment. Neither the American nor European proposals accounted for such a grand bargain or even a comprehensive face-saving solution to the nuclear issue including Iran's rights to enrichment. Iran thus did not consider the P5+1 or the West's proposals genuine measures for reconciliation.

Nevertheless, Europe and Russia became disillusioned by Iran's obstinacy and joined the United States in supporting referral of Iran's case to the UN Security Council. The IAEA Board of Governors held a meeting amid heavy publicity by Western media to the effect that the West was approaching possibly its last chance to prevent confrontation with Iran.[72]

Under this media blitz, Larijani canceled a trip to Europe during which he had planned to give Iran's response to the new Western plan. This cancellation showed that Tehran had not yet reached a final conclusion, or at least was not prepared to announce it. On June 13, 2006, Larijani announced in Algiers that Iran was ready for constructive talks about its nuclear program, but only if there are no preconditions. He added that the issue of uranium enrichment belonged in the negotiations and, if it were made into a precondition, the negotiations would be to no avail.[73] However, President Ahmadinejad said in Shanghai that the incentives package was a step forward and that it would be seriously considered by Tehran. Therefore, Larijani's remarks were considered not to be Tehran's final response.[74]

As time passed without an official response from Tehran, Western countries started to criticize Iran for the delay. The criticism, which was very cautious at first, called on Iran to provide an answer to the P5+1 proposal by the end of June. However, Ahmadinejad suddenly announced that Iran would respond by late August. Tehran maintained that America's failure to bring the other four permanent members of the Security Council into line for more punitive measures against Iran, along with the increased cost of the U.S. presence in Iraq and confrontations between Iran and the United States over Palestine, Iraq, and the nuclear issue, drove the United States to change its tone.

During a visit to Spain in mid-June, Foreign Minister Mottaki announced (after a string of unofficial and inconsistent statements) that Iran would respond to the P5+1 and make its own proposal in about ten days.[75] Mottaki told reporters that it seemed that the United States and its European allies, along with Russia and China, had decided to give up their past threatening postures and show more respect to Iran.

High-ranking Iranian officials started diplomatic consultations at regional and international levels. Ali Larijani traveled to Egypt for talks with Hosni Mubarak, then set off for Algeria and planned to proceed on to Spain. The diplomatic trips were so important that when Larijani was not able to go to Spain due to illness, Foreign Minister Mottaki went in his stead. President Ahmadinejad took part in a summit meeting of the Shanghai Cooperation Organization in Beijing without his foreign minister. There he met and conferred with his Russian counterpart, Vladimir Putin, and Chinese President Hu Jintao.

In this hectic period, Saud al-Faisal, the Saudi Arabian foreign minister, paid an unexpected visit to Iran and submitted a message from King Abdullah to the supreme leader. He also met with the president and chairman of the Expediency Council. Abdul Aziz Hakim, leader of the influential Supreme Council for the Islamic Revolution in Iraq, also visited Tehran. There were rumors in Tehran that his trip was aimed at possible mediation between Iran and the United States.

At the same time, remarks by Javad Va'idi, the undersecretary of the Supreme National Security Council, that suspension of uranium enrichment would be neither a precondition for negotiations nor a result of those negotiations[76] raised concerns that Iran was delaying its response simply to buy time. The *Financial Times* reported that, because of Iran's slow response to the P5+1 package, the United States and European Union planned to push for a resolution on Iran's nuclear dossier in the UN Security Council.[77]

In an unofficial ultimatum, the foreign ministers of the G8 announced that they expected a clear response from Tehran at an upcoming meeting between Larijani and Solana. Larijani, however, canceled the scheduled July 5 meeting and in later meetings with Solana gave no official response, insisting that Iran would adhere to the late August deadline set by President Ahmadinejad.[78] Mottaki reaffirmed that deadline in a news conference during a meeting of foreign ministers of Iraq's neighbor countries. Tehran wished perhaps to show that the West could not arbitrarily set a deadline for Iran.

Criticisms raised by the ninth government about the proposed package included the following:

- Some of the benefits offered by the incentives package, such as recognition of Iran's right to peaceful use of nuclear energy including construction of light-water or research reactors, were already mandated by the NPT.
- Others, such as the transfer of advanced technology and/or equipment in such fields as aeronautics, communications, and agriculture, were offers to reverse policies that were discriminatory and should have been reversed regardless of the nuclear case.
- The P5+1 countries were not genuine about recognizing Iran's nuclear rights based on the NPT and were following double standards toward international regulations.
- Many concessions offered to Iran were described using vague language open to differing interpretations.
- Any proposal aimed to reach a political compromise on Iran's nuclear program should be based on the NPT and international law, which recognize the rights of member states to enrich uranium for peaceful purposes, subject to Articles I and II of the NPT. Asking Iran to suspend enrichment activities even for a moment was a blatant breach of Article IV of the Non-Proliferation Treaty, while the West always has believed that the right for enrichment under Article IV is subject to complying with Articles I and II of the treaty.
- From the Iranian point of view, involvement of the UN Security Council in the case was unjustified because Iran remained as a member of NPT, was observing its Comprehensive Safeguards Agreement, and had not diverted its nuclear program toward non-peaceful purposes. Also, the ninth government insisted that as long as the Security Council failed to return Iran's nuclear dossier to the purview of the IAEA, there would be no possibility for the imple-

mentation of the Additional Protocol based on ratification through Parliament. The West was reiterating that Iran had been found to be in noncompliance with its Safeguards Agreement.

- The Islamic Republic continued to consider suspension a redline and would not accept any incentive to give it up.

SECURITY COUNCIL RESOLUTION 1696

On July 12, 2006, the foreign ministers of France, Britain, Russia, the United States, China, and Germany announced that the P5+1 had agreed to pass a resolution on Iran's nuclear dossier in the UN Security Council.[79] Four days later, G8 leaders issued a joint statement calling on Iran to respond to the proposed package and threatening to support the passage of a resolution in the UN Security Council in case of a negative answer.[80]

On July 20, soon after a draft resolution drawn up by France was distributed among members of the UN Security Council, Iran's Supreme National Security Council issued a statement[81] warning against approval of an anti-Iranian resolution. It noted that Iran considered diplomacy and negotiation the best way to find a solution to the nuclear case. A spokesman for the Russian Foreign Ministry reacted by saying that the statement would not change the viewpoints of the P5+1.

Finally, on July 31, 2006, the UN Security Council issued Resolution 1696 under Chapter VII of the UN Charter and set a one-month deadline for Iran to suspend its nuclear fuel-cycle activities. The resolution was passed with fourteen ayes; Qatar cast the only nay vote. The resolution was approved even as some supporters of Iran's "looking to the East" strategy were insisting that the United States would fail in its effort to get a binding resolution passed.[82]

The UN Security Council stressed that Iran should halt all activities related to enrichment and reprocessing, including those related to research and development. It asked all countries to prevent the transfer to Iran of prohibited materials, goods, and technology that could help Iran with its nuclear and missile programs. It also requested by August 31 a report from the director general of the IAEA on whether Iran had established "full and sustained suspension of all activities mentioned in this resolution."[83]

The resolution also stated that, in the event that Iran had not complied by that date, the Security Council would adopt measures under Article 41 of Chapter VII of the UN Charter to persuade Iran to comply.[84]

As ElBaradei later opined,

[The resolution] was of dubious legality. There was still no proof that Iran's nuclear activity involved a weapons program. It was quite a stretch to say that a small laboratory-scale centrifuge cascade constituted "a threat to international peace and security" when peaceful uranium enrichment is legal for all states under the NPT.[85]

Tehran immediately rejected Resolution 1696, and some circles close to the ninth government talked about the possibility of Iran's leaving the NPT. They argued that firm resistance to the demands of the international community led by the United States and Europe would force the West to accede to the status quo.

Overall, Resolution 1696 was a diplomatic defeat for Iran:

- It designated Iran's nuclear program as a threat to international peace and security.[86]
- Suspension, which had been recognized before as a "voluntary and not legally binding measure," became "obligatory."
- The UN Security Council, according to Article 40 of Chapter VII of Resolution 1696, set a one-month grace period for Iran to pave the way for further decisions to be made according to Article 41 of Chapter VII of the UN Charter (which is related to political and economic sanctions).
- Resolution 1696 referred to possible "military aspects" of Iran's nuclear program, so as to pave the way for considering Iran's peaceful nuclear activities a threat to international peace and security.
- The resolution also called on all countries to prevent transfer of materials and technology that could help Iran's uranium enrichment and missile activities.
- It further called upon all states to prevent the transfer of items that could contribute to Iran's ballistic missiles program.
- Iran also was required to comply with the Additional Protocol, even though it had not ratified the Additional Protocol.

- The resolution emphasized that if Iran did not comply with the resolution before the deadline, needed measures would be approved according to Article 41 of Chapter VII of the UN Charter.

The passage of Resolution 1696 fully displayed the West's double standards and the politicization of Iran's nuclear file. As the resolution was discussed in the UN Security Council, Israel was in the midst of a large-scale military operation in Lebanon, killing hundreds and displacing more than 700,000 Lebanese civilians. The United States was not ready to consider the possibility that Israel's actions might constitute a threat to international peace and security, rejecting along with the UK a request from UN Secretary General Kofi Annan for even a cease-fire resolution on Lebanon. Yet they considered Iran's pilot enrichment plan comprising very few centrifuges to be a threat to international peace and security. Not only were Middle Eastern countries shocked, but so was the UN secretary general, telling ElBaradei on the telephone, "This war in Lebanon was not considered a threat to international peace and security but the laboratory-scale activity in Iran was."[87]

For his part, ElBaradei saw the resolution as misguided and revealing of American inconsistency on nuclear proliferation issues:

> In my view, Security Council Resolution 1696 was not only counterproductive from a policy perspective, but also a misuse of the council's authority under Chapter VII of the UN Charter. It was staggering to compare the difference in treatment of North Korea and Iran. North Korea had walked out of the NPT and made explicit threats about developing nuclear weapons (and would in fact test its first weapons less than three months later, in October 2006), yet the Americans were ready to join them in a direct dialogue, and Chris Hill [assistant U.S. secretary of state for East Asian and Pacific Affairs] seemed to be in Pyongyang every other day. By contrast, Iran, which remained under safeguards and party to the NPT, was penalized for possibly having future intentions to develop nuclear weapons, and the Americans refused to talk to them without preconditions.[88]

Even some of Europe's top foreign policy officials were incredulous. Ali Larijani recounted a phone call with Javier Solana immediately after the resolution's passage in which Solana said resignedly, "The spoilers have done their job."[89]

252

LARIJANI-SOLANA NEGOTIATION ON THE "FREEZE TO FREEZE" INITIATIVE

On August 22, 2006, days before the deadline set by the UN Security Council and while IAEA inspectors were preparing their report on Iran's nuclear program, Ali Larijani presented to the ambassadors of the P5+1 Iran's official response to the incentives package. The European Union, Russia, and the United States immediately announced that they would study Iran's response.

Iran's 21-page response made diverse points, including citing ambiguities surrounding the European package, and posed some 100 questions to clarify them. At the same time, Iran declared its readiness to negotiate on the ambiguous points and in fact on "all issues."

French President Jacques Chirac noted that Iran's proposal was itself ambiguous, giving rise to questions about whether Iran would discontinue enrichment. Frank-Walter Steinmeier, the German foreign minister, told reporters in Brussels that Iran had asked for a guarantee against further sanctions before any talks began and that this was by no means acceptable.

Then, on August 26, President Ahmadinejad announced that Iran's heavy-water facility at Arak had been put into operation. The ninth government felt that inauguration of the project would prove the irreversibility of Iran's decision and also that mastery of the technology to produce heavy water would boost Iran's standing in world power politics.[90]

Five days later, IAEA Director General Mohamed ElBaradei reported to the UN Security Council that Iran had not complied with Security Council Resolution 1696, and the foreign ministers of the European Union gave Iran two weeks to clarify its position on a halt to uranium enrichment.[91]

Iranian policymakers were deeply frustrated by these developments. In September, Aghazadeh wrote a letter to ElBaradei complaining that, in ElBaradei's account, "the IAEA had no intention of ever closing the Iran file. The more Iran cooperated, the more questions they received from Agency inspectors."[92]

Nonetheless, as revealed in his 2011 memoir, ElBaradei remained convinced that, in his words,

The Iranians remained open to the notion of suspension, so long as it was not a precondition of negotiations. They were willing to implement the Additional Protocol on a voluntary basis during the negotiations. And they were ready to commit to permanent membership in the NPT, to allay fears of a "breakout" scenario in the style of North Korea.[93]

On this basis, ElBaradei proposed a plan based on four principles:

- Iran would suspend enrichment during the talks;
- the Europeans and Americans would in exchange suspend new Security Council sanctions;
- the P5+1 would affirm Iran's right to peaceful nuclear energy under the NPT, making clear that suspension was temporary; and
- the P5+1 would issue a statement recognizing Iran's political independence and sovereignty.

ElBaradei strongly believed that this would be a face-saving solution for both sides. The United States, however, rejected the plan, with Rice calling ElBaradei on September 5 to say, "We will have problems with giving them any security assurances. . . . You know we also cannot sit down with Iran until the suspension is in place."[94]

At this critical juncture, important talks were held between Ali Larijani and Javier Solana in Vienna. The first reports published by the European and American media as well as those close to the ninth government in Tehran indicated that Larijani had conditionally accepted suspension of part of the fuel cycle for two months in return for guarantees and concessions from the West. At the end of the first round of negotiations, both Ali Larijani and Solana announced that some misunderstandings concerning Iran's nuclear case had been eliminated.[95] Without going into details, Solana stated that there had been some progress and that a meeting was scheduled for the next week.

Six months later, on February 23, 2007, the *Washington Post*[96] published a report on more secret aspects of the September Solana-Larijani negotiations. This included a two-page agreement according to which Iran would agree not to launch new cascades for enrichment for a period of two months as a voluntary, nonbinding, and temporary measure if UN sanctions were lifted.

ElBaradei had the new "freeze-for-freeze" initiative in mind, by which Iranians would avoid adding new centrifuges, which would have precluded Iran from embarking on industrial-scale enrichment in this period, but would retain their previous centrifuges; and in response, the P5+1 countries would suspend efforts to seek a new UN sanction resolution during the negotiation period.[97]

China, Britain, France, Russia, and Germany later agreed to give Javier Solana more time to achieve a diplomatic solution with Tehran before the UN Security Council considered new sanctions against Iran under Article 41.[98]

In late October 2006, the IAEA director general confirmed that Iran was testing a new cascade of 162 centrifuges that would double the capacity of its small pilot plant. ElBaradei said in an interview that according to the latest inspections by the IAEA, no uranium had been introduced into the new cascade, but it was possible for this to take place within a week.[99] His remarks came at a time when the Western media were picturing Iran as still facing countless technical problems.

Mohammad Saeedi, deputy president of Iran's Atomic Energy Organization, proposed on November 1 that France establish a consortium to produce enriched uranium in Iran. France's government-owned nuclear technology group, Arvena, responded that Iran's proposal was politically motivated, and a spokesman for the French Foreign Ministry announced that Iran should simply halt uranium enrichment.

A draft of a second UN Security Council sanctions resolution on Iran was distributed among the P5+1 by the EU3. Moscow and Beijing, however, insisted that Security Council sanctions resolutions should not be formulated in a way that could be used as an excuse for military action against Iran's enrichment installations. Ali Larijani also warned that if the draft resolution against Iran's nuclear program were ratified, Iran would review its cooperation with IAEA inspectors.[100]

A meeting of the IAEA's 35 member countries of the Board of Governors opened on November 2 with the IAEA's technical assistance on Iran's Arak heavy-water research reactor on its agenda. Most members rejected Iran's request for safety assistance with the reactor, but all indicated their readiness to help seven other nuclear projects under way in Iran. In the final document, which was signed by member states of the Board of

Governors through consensus after three days of discussion, all requests from Iran for technical assistance were granted except for the Arak project, which many countries regarded as a potential plutonium production reactor, and which IAEA and UN Security Council resolutions had called on Iran to suspend.[101]

Soltanieh, Iran's representative at the IAEA, issued a statement at the end of the Board of Governors meeting declaring that, "The first result of the historic mistake of reporting Iran's nuclear case to the Security Council will be an end to voluntary implementation of the Additional Protocol, which has been carried out by Iran for three years prior to being ratified by the Iranian parliament."[102] He also warned that "if the UN Security Council approves any resolution on the basis of Article 41 of the UN Charter, Iran will rethink its cooperation with the IAEA."

Heated debates took place among the P5+1 concerning a new resolution against Iran. Before each meeting, Tehran would warn that no resolution would change its nuclear program but would merely make things more complicated.

TOTAL FAILURE OF THE "LOOKING TO THE EAST" POLICY

During the 1990s, Iran adopted a policy of reconstruction inside and détente outside the country as a prelude to its new regional role. Iran's nuclear program provided the West with an additional but important reason to contain the power of Iran. However, the nuclear standoff (2002 and later) was a test of Iran's power to play in a new era, and the West's policy during President Khatami's period made Iran more determined to go on with its nuclear plan and introduce a new phase of "aggressive diplomacy."

The special role of Iran became clearer when its archenemy, the United States, nearly ran aground in Iraq and Afghanistan and needed Iran's help to cope with the complicated situations there. Russia first tried to play the role of arbiter and to maximize the value of the "Iran trump card," in addition to having an opportunity to directly bargain with the West. The Russian plan was a reflection of Russian policies in that time.

When Iran rejected the Russian plan, however, Moscow realized that Iran was willing to play an active and independent role and to fend for itself in nuclear technology by reducing dependence on Russia for nuclear fuel. This opened a new chapter in the nuclear standoff in which Russia began to move closer to the West. Russia's delays in completing the Bushehr atomic power plant provided an example of Russia's duplicity at that time.

When Iran decided to put into operation a second cascade of centrifuges and the Arak heavy-water facility, Russia significantly changed its approach. In 2006–2007, the Kremlin came to oppose Iranian membership in the Shanghai Cooperation Organization. (Ahmadinejad had used Iran's status as an observer state to deliver a fiery speech at a June 2006 summit calling for the organization to transform itself into a "strong, influential institution" that could counter "threats of domineering powers to interfere in the affairs of other states").[103] Russia began to respond more quickly and positively to requests from Western countries, especially the United States, for support of anti-Iran resolutions.[104]

During that period, Israel also mounted a tremendous effort to woo Russia. The Russian press continuously reported regular, but unofficial, trips to Moscow by different Israeli officials. In November–December 2006, when the P5+1 were preparing another anti-Iranian resolution, Russia announced that it would support the resolution proposed by the West as long as it did not harm economic relations between Iran and Russia.[105] The Iranian view was that Russia was willing to use Iran as leverage and ultimately to sell out Iran in exchange for trade concessions, technology, investments, and security deals with NATO and the United States in Commonwealth of Independent States (CIS) countries.[106]

Before February 2006, when Iran's nuclear dossier was reported to the UN Security Council, Russia did not play a major role in negotiations with Iran, aside from the presentation in 2004–2005 to me by Sergei Kislyak, then–Russian deputy minister, of what would became known as the "Russian plan" for joint uranium enrichment in Russia. Under the plan, Iran would have no access to enrichment technology in Russia and there would be no cooperation between Tehran and Moscow on enrichment. When I raised this issue, Kislyak told me that even the Americans had not been able to obtain information about Russian enrichment technology and that Russia would never share this technology with any country. Thus, the Russian proposal, for all practical purposes, was about trade, not joint enrichment cooperation. Naturally, the plan was rejected by the former nuclear negotiating team.

However, as Iran's nuclear case was sent to the Security Council and Western countries escalated pressure on Iran, Moscow once more brought up its plan. The reason for doing it now was the support lent to the plan by Europe and the United States at the peak of disputes between Tehran and the West. The main goals prompting Russia to reintroduce the plan, according to which enrichment was to be carried out in that country, were to make the most of the existing standoff between Iran and the West to realize its own national interests; to continue its lucrative nuclear cooperation with Iran in other projects; and to avail itself of political and economic benefits of the plan to boost its bargaining power with Western countries.

The plan showed that Russia, like the United States and other Western countries, was unwilling to allow Iran to pursue enrichment on its soil. This was emphasized in a letter sent to the then-Iranian foreign minister, Kamal Kharrazi, by his Russian counterpart, concurrently with a letter from the EU3. Nevertheless, Russia showed reluctance to join in any resolution that would punish Iran for its peaceful nuclear activities. Many Russian politicians maintained that the Iran case provided a good arena for Moscow to flaunt its political weight in the international system at rival countries.

Thus, Russia maintained that Iran's nuclear case should be solved through political and peaceful means, and Moscow frequently rejected any forceful treatment of Iran. Like the United States and the European Union, Russia opposed any form of uranium enrichment by Iran, especially at high levels. Despite the fact that the international standing of Moscow may have suffered due to Iran's lack of cooperation or to siding with the West against Iran, pragmatic Russian politicians demonstrated that national interests are of utmost importance to them. Recognition of this reality was a major difference between proponents of the "looking to the East" strategy and those who advocated "negotiations with Europe."

BACK TO THE SECURITY COUNCIL AND A

NEW DOMESTIC SITUATION

SECURITY COUNCIL RESOLUTION 1737

On December 23, 2006, the UN Security Council unanimously approved Resolution 1737 against Iran. The resolution urged Iran to suspend all activities related to uranium enrichment that could lead to production of fuel for a nuclear power plant or the building of an atomic bomb.

The following points are noteworthy about Resolution 1737:

- The resolution relied on Article 41 of the UN Charter, which made it binding but excluded military action.
- All countries were called upon to prevent the supply, sale, or transfer of items that could contribute to Iran's enrichment-related, reprocessing, or heavy-water-related activities, or to the development of nuclear weapon delivery systems.
- Countries could use their discretion with regard to dual-use commodities that might be utilized in Iran's nuclear program. However,

the use and location of these items should be inspected and the Security Council's sanctions committee should be informed.

- The draft resolution excluded equipment and fuel for light-water reactors. This meant that the $800 million light-water reactor being built by Russia in Bushehr would not be affected.

- Foreign travel by people associated with companies or those involved in Iran's nuclear and missile programs was banned, and the UN Security Council called on all countries to freeze their assets, excluding assets related to previous contractual commitments.

- The freeze on assets included Iran's Atomic Energy Organization and companies working on centrifuges, the Arak heavy-water reactor, and the uranium enrichment facility of Natanz. Iran's aerospace industry, which produces missiles, was excluded at Russia's insistence, though its subsidiary companies remained on the list.

- Individuals named by the resolution included the Atomic Energy Organization vice president for research and development, as well as officials involved in the Arak and Natanz nuclear sites and the rector of Malek Ashtar University of Defense Technology.

- Travel bans were taken out of the resolution, but it called on countries to inform the sanctions committee about the transit through their territories of any person or representatives of groups mentioned in the resolution.

- The resolution called for the establishment of a committee to follow up on the Iranian nuclear issue. The committee would be charged with seeking information from all countries about their economic exchanges with Iran; reviewing cooperation between Iran and the IAEA; creating a list of individuals, companies, and institutions to be inspected or subject to sanctions; and reporting at least every ninety days to the Security Council.

- The resolution also requested a report from the director general of the IAEA within sixty days on whether Iran had established "full and sustained suspension of all activities mentioned in this resolution, including a halt to uranium enrichment and construction of a heavy water reactor."

- It made the ratification of the Additional Protocol "mandatory" for Iran and called upon Iran to provide unlimited access, meaning beyond the Additional Protocol, for the IAEA's inspectors.
- Finally, the resolution stated that the sanctions would be lifted only upon Iran's compliance with all requests of the UN Security Council and International Atomic Energy Agency and threatened that, in the case of noncompliance on the part of Iran, further measures were to be taken.

I was the only Iranian official to explain the content and consequences of this resolution to the Iranian public, which I did in an interview with the Mehr News Agency.[1] The interview was widely published, awakening the nation and politicians to the dangers of UN Security Council censure. The authorities did not appreciate my comments, and this interview became one of the reasons for my arrest in April 2007.

President Ahmadinejad stated defiantly that sanctions had lost their efficacy and that "all the Western powers are concerned about is that we have made everything on our own and they cannot take it away from us, because nuclear technology is the product of our own brains."[2]

In addition, 206 members of the Iranian Parliament issued a statement that Iran would not give in and would proceed with its peaceful nuclear program. Javad Zarif, Iran's representative to the United Nations, noted that the UN Security Council was employing double standards by ignoring the admissions of Israeli Prime Minister Ehud Olmert that his country possessed nuclear weapons.[3] The Western countries argue that Israel, Pakistan, and India have not signed the NPT. Such justification indirectly encourages radicals in Iran to withdraw from the NPT and thereby eliminate all compliance problems.

Mohamed ElBaradei emphasized that the nuclear standoff could still be resolved through negotiation and in a peaceful manner.[4] After UN Security Council Resolution 1737 was approved, France called on Iran to return to the negotiating table. The French foreign minister, Philippe Douste-Blazy, noted that the resolution offered a clear option to Iran to cooperate with the international community or risk more isolation as the cost of pursuing its enrichment and reprocessing programs. High-level German, British, Japanese, and Canadian officials, among others, welcomed the resolution and urged Iran to cooperate with the international community and pursue serious negotiations. China expressed hope that the resolution would be implemented seriously, even as Beijing did not believe that sanctions could be a permanent solution to the problem.

The U.S. secretary of state called for the immediate enforcement of the sanctions. Undersecretary of State Burns also noted that the resolution was not sufficient and called for additional sanctions well beyond those enforced by the Security Council to make sure that countries would cease their usual transactions with Iran. Burns said the United States was trying to persuade international and private banks to stop granting loans to Iran.[5]

TEHRAN'S STRATEGY FOLLOWING RESOLUTION 1737

Iran was now faced with three strategic options:

1. Comply with the most important demand of the resolution by suspending enrichment activities and resuming negotiations. Proponents of this option maintained that if Iran were ever to suspend enrichment, now was the time to do so. That way, Iran would have been able to accept suspension with fewer consequences and for only two to three months, provided that it was allowed to go on with research and development.

2. Make the nuclear case the most important priority for Iran's foreign policy. It would become the focal point of a confrontation with the West. Since the overwhelming majority of Iranians supported the pursuit of nuclear capability, this would give leverage to Iran's government in confronting the West. Denounce all forms of suspension, oppose inspections of non-nuclear sites, and continue to pursue missile policies, which were considered legitimate. Tehran would go on the offensive.

3. Tehran to leave the NPT and ignore the IAEA's requests entirely. Although it would have led to mounting pressures on Iran, at the same time Iran would have been increasing pressure on the other side.

To achieve the second option as the core strategy,[6] the third option was adopted and the Majles reacted to Resolution 1737 by approving a bill calling on the government to review cooperation with the IAEA and speed up nuclear activities.[7]

Seyed Mohammad Ali Hosseini, the spokesman for Iran's Foreign Ministry, announced that Iran would put 3,000 more centrifuges into operation in reaction to the UN Security Council resolution.[8] Ali Larijani also warned that if Iran were treated unfairly, it would change its position on the Non-Proliferation Treaty.[9] Only if the West backed down would Iran provide guarantees of the peaceful nature of its nuclear program and cooperate with the West and specifically with the United States on regional issues, as it had on Afghanistan in 2001–2002. Clearly, the ninth government was adhering to an aggressive "carrot and stick" policy to deal with the West.[10]

UN Security Council Resolution 1737 was the first to be issued against the Islamic Republic of Iran under Chapter VII of the UN Charter and its 41st article. In view of the resolution's incremental mechanism, it posed future political and economic threats to Iran and could even endanger the national security of the country. It is Article 42 of Chapter VII that authorizes the use of force, though even without its explicit citation the reference to Iran as a threat to international peace and security was a serious blow. The resolution was even harsher than the resolution issued in October 2006 against North Korea, whose nuclear program included nuclear weapons.[11]

Iran had limited options in challenging the resolution, because under international law no country can take legal action against UN Security Council resolutions through such entities as the International Court of Justice.

The Slovenian representative and rotational head of the IAEA Board of Governors announced in January that, as a result of the Security Council sanctions, the agency had suspended its technical assistance on projects in Iran.[12] In retaliation to that decision and, more broadly, to Resolution 1737, Iran announced that it had barred 38 IAEA inspectors from traveling to Tehran.[13]

NEW DIPLOMATIC ACTIVISM BY THE AHMADINEJAD TEAM

On January 26, 2007, during the World Economic Forum annual meeting in Davos, Switzerland, IAEA Director General Mohamed ElBaradei proposed that Iran suspend its enrichment program and, in return, that the UN Security Council suspend new sanctions. This proposal was called "suspension for suspension" or a "time-out." Although Russia welcomed the proposal and argued that it would lead to a political solution for Iran's nuclear case, it was officially rejected by the Western countries, though it was discussed unofficially among Iran, the P5+1, and the IAEA. Iran, for its part, sought to reduce pressure through diplomatic maneuvering.

Ali Akbar Velayati went to Moscow, Ali Larijani to Munich, and Manouchehr Mottaki to Monaco, while Russia's plan was presented to the supreme leader. Vladimir Putin and Ayatollah Khamenei exchanged messages, the contents of which have not yet been publicly revealed. Hopes were raised about the possibility of achieving a multilateral deal combining ElBaradei's proposal, the Russian plan, and previous agreements between Larijani and Javier Solana.

With only a few weeks remaining before the Security Council's deadline for Iran to suspend enrichment activities, all involved parties began to emphasize the need to restart negotiations. On the sidelines of a security conference in Munich, Solana declared his readiness to resume talks with Dr. Larijani.[14] At the same time, however, it was rumored (and later denied) that some new countries, including Switzerland, were willing to get involved in Iran's security case.

With the United States and the EU3 emphasizing the need for Iran to suspend enrichment and China's role in the case greatly diminished, stepped-up diplomacy between Tehran and Moscow convinced some observers that Russia was willing to play a special role in the Iran nuclear case in the near future. Moscow's approach was indicated by President Putin's reference to "mutual and dynamic dialogue at [the] working level with Iran" during a meeting with Dr. Velayati and his statement, made in response to a message from Ahmadinejad, that "I allow myself to hope that we and other parties involved in this trend, especially our Iranian friends, will be able to find a solution to [the] difficult problems with which we are faced."[15]

From this flurry of diplomatic activity, it seemed that a twelve-point agreement could be in the works, combining an eleven-point agreement reached between Larijani and Solana and the Ivanov plan. Although the media remained silent on the details of the Ivanov plan, it seemed that it was a combination of ElBaradei's proposal and a modified version of the old Russian plan. The issue of suspension, as usual, remained a sticking point.

INTERNAL WRANGLES OVER SUSPENSION

As the West was preparing to issue a new resolution through the UN Security Council, it seemed that the enrichment suspension issue had turned into a Gordian knot that precluded any compromise between Iran and the West. Developments on the nuclear case after the election of Mahmoud Ahmadinejad had turned suspension into a matter of honor and a redline for all involved parties. When the IAEA director general offered his proposal as a face-saving solution for both sides and called for a "time-out," meaning mutual suspension of enrichment and new sanctions,[16] he initially came under fire from the United States,[17] Britain, and Germany,[18] proving that the situation was worse than initially perceived. The P5+1's position later was modified, while Tehran rejected the proposal through Ali Larijani, a Foreign Ministry spokesman,[19] and Larijani's deputy Javad Va'idi.[20]

Western countries maintained that as long as Iran had not complied, at least in part, with the UN Security Council resolution and suspended enrichment activities, there would be no return to the negotiating table. A minimum of three proposals circulated in the international media to end the deadlock over Iran's nuclear contention. All of the proposals were rejected or denied after a short time. Reuters reported on February 9 that a plan offered by Swiss diplomats to Ali Larijani on the sidelines of a Munich security conference would allow Iran to keep its uranium enrichment facilities provided that it avoided introducing UF_6 into centrifuges until the end of negotiations. The proposal was immediately denied and was slammed by both the United States and Britain.

A plan for "dry enrichment"[21] also received attention in the Associated Press in late February, but was not taken seriously. Another plan, which was likewise rejected offhandedly, was proposed by Javier Solana to change technology used in Iranian centrifuges to render them unable to enrich uranium to higher level. The dismissal of all those proposals, in addition to remarks made openly by American, British, German, and French officials, clearly showed that the Western governments would not accept anything short of suspension of uranium enrichment by Iran at that juncture.

Iran was similarly intransigent. Remarks made by President Ahmadinejad that Tehran had thrown away "the brakes and reverse gear of the nuclear train" put an end to optimism that arose from remarks by Hashemi Rafsanjani, Velayati, and Larijani. Velayati, the international affairs adviser to Supreme Leader Ayatollah Khamenei, had already indicated Iran's stance on enrichment during a visit to Moscow.[22] Before that, the Iranian foreign minister and Foreign Ministry spokesman had announced that Tehran was ready to consider all possibilities, including suspension, but only during negotiations with the European side, and not before.[23] Those official positions, along with criticism of the ninth government's nuclear approach and pressure from the United States and Europe, led to speculation that change was on the horizon.

In reality, it was impossible, or at least very difficult, for either side to compromise its redline on the nuclear standoff. The West's difficulty in giving ground on suspension was not merely due to concerns about nonproliferation, but also tied to the diplomatic prestige of the United States and the European Union. Concerns about the rise of new regional powers and the empowerment of Iran as a major regional player in the Middle East was another reason for putting more pressure on Iran. Some politicians and scholars believe that if there were progress on the outstanding issues with the IAEA, the United States and the EU would recognize Iran's right to enrichment activities. This is not correct. I will present my reasons in the next few pages.

Frequent American and British diplomatic missions to the region and positions taken by Arab states against the Islamic Republic of Iran clearly indicated that the West was relatively successful in building up regional pressure on Iran to give up uranium enrichment. Even India lent its support to sanctions enforced by Resolution 1737, and South Africa called on Iran to suspend enrichment just a day after Ali Larijani conferred with Thabo Mbeki. Warnings issued to Iran by Russian officials and the passivity of the Non-Aligned Movement were among other indications of the partial success of the U.S. bloc in its bid to press Tehran to give up enrichment.

While using the "stick," the United States and Europe did not forget the "carrot." U.S. Secretary of State Condoleezza Rice announced on three occasions that if Iran suspended uranium enrichment, she would be ready to talk face-to-face with her Iranian counterpart, Manouchehr Mottaki. Also, the French foreign minister announced that if Tehran went ahead with suspension, Tehran and Paris could enjoy revitalized and "ambitious" relations.[24]

In parallel to its political and economic confrontation with the West, the government of Mahmoud Ahmadinejad acted in such a way as to make agreement with enrichment suspension costly and even impossible. Supporters of the ninth government charged the former nuclear team with giving in to U.S. pressure and even committing espionage for Western countries.[25] They also described Washington's threats to Iran as a "war of nerves" and a "bluff" and argued that Mahmoud Ahmadinejad's aggressive policy had boosted Iran's international standing and had rid the country of the passivity that occurred during sixteen years of rule by pragmatic presidents. In this atmosphere, any move toward agreement to suspension would have run against the government's propaganda and would have been attacked by Ahmadinejad's own political base as a reversal of positive progress.

In the meantime, Tehran increased the number of operating centrifuges at the Natanz facility, moving toward the capability to produce enough nuclear fuel for more than 50,000 centrifuges. Iran produced more UF_6 at Isfahan. Launching more 164-centrifuge cascades in Natanz was meant to prove to the world that Iran had reached the point of no return in its bid to achieve an industrial-scale nuclear fuel cycle.

APPROACH OF FORMER NUCLEAR TEAM TO SUSPENSION

The diplomatic approach adopted by Khatami's government had emphasized that the indefinite suspension of enrichment was a redline for Iran. However, its nuclear negotiators avoided sloganeering or sensationalism and sought to achieve their goal through multilateral negotiations, confidence building, and engaging in broad cooperation with our negotiation partners. From this perspective, it can be claimed that the governments of both Khatami and Ahmadinejad, and during the tenures of both Rouhani and Larijani as chief nuclear negotiators, sought the same goals: achieving the nuclear fuel cycle and engaging in peaceful nuclear technology. Our diplomatic approach attached more importance to "confidence building, negotiations and initiation of complete enrichment operations parallel to or after an agreement with the international community." We had defined two essential goals in our strategy: preserving the rights of Iran to nuclear technology—including enrichment—and preventing the referral of Iran's nuclear dossier to the UN Security Council.

Our successors had only one aim in mind on the nuclear issue: protecting the rights of Iran, including enrichment. Therefore they sought the same goal through confidence building, diplomacy, and negotiations, but also through initiation of complete enrichment operations without the agreement of the international community. In fact, in the first round of its nuclear diplomacy, Tehran was managing suspension demands instead of rejecting them offhandedly and tried to cut the Gordian knot through building confidence with the world and forging international understanding. In the second round, under Ahmadinejad, suspension was simply a redline.

Iran agreed to "suspension" in September 2003 when it had secured three important qualifications. The first was realized during ElBaradei's trip to Iran on October 16, 2003, during which the nuclear negotiating team succeeded in redefining suspension from "total suspension" to "introduction of gas into centrifuges" (though the EU3 did not accept this definition, and ElBaradei never made public, even in his memoir, that he had proposed it to Iran in 2003).[26] The two other major breakthroughs were achieved during negotiations in Tehran on October 21, 2003 (the Sa'dabad negotiations). According to the Sa'dabad Agreement, the EU3 agreed to pursue negotiations with Tehran on the basis of short-term "suspension" and not permanent "cessation" of Iran's peaceful nuclear activities. Also, the EU3 accepted suspension as a voluntary and not legally binding measure.

The Khatami nuclear negotiating team, in its effort to break the deadlock over suspension, presented a plan to the Europeans on July 24, 2004. This "Framework for Mutual Guarantees" plan clearly indicated Iran's insistence on enrichment and fuel-cycle development. The same approach was quite evident in Iran's reaction to the G8 plan that been proposed to Iran just a few days after a meeting of the group on October 16, 2004. That plan had demanded that "suspension" continue indefinitely until a long-term agreement was achieved. Therefore, it was immediately rejected by Iran.

Another plan, offered by Iran on March 23, 2005, to break the suspension deadlock, was evidence of the country's approach to the suspension issue. The plan stipulated that Iran intended to start all fuel-cycle activities gradually and through a confidence-building process with the European Union. The process was to begin with the inauguration of the Isfahan uranium conversion facility and end with the commissioning of industrial-scale uranium enrichment at the Natanz installations to provide fuel for the Bushehr power plant. At that time, some media reported that Europe was ready to accept the launch of a limited number of centrifuges in Natanz, and it seemed that the European countries would finally support enrichment in Iran.[27]

But Iran's plan to commission industrial-scale (50,000–60,000) centrifuges was one reason that P5+1 officials felt that even if Iran agreed to limit centrifuges to a number commensurate with its current capabilities, Iran would then seek to break the limit and deploy more centrifuges when it had the capability to do so, even if there were no civilian need for the resultant enriched uranium. The fourth plan made clear that the industrial scale would be developed gradually and only through confidence-building measures and within some years, while ultimately industrial-scale uranium enrichment in Natanz would be sufficient for Bushehr's fuel requirement.

A similar approach had already been laid out in the Paris Agreement (with the main goal being establishment of and agreement on the fuel cycle by way of bargaining and interaction). The general outline of the Paris Agreement was "short-term suspension" of the fuel cycle, on the one hand, and EU support for Iran's fuel-cycle activities (at least for a pilot program of 3,000 centrifuges) at the end of the suspension period on the other. This was evident in a letter written to the IAEA on November 15, 2004, the morning that Iran announced its consent to the Paris Agreement. In that letter, Tehran noted that only "conversion operations" would be temporarily and voluntarily suspended. The Paris Agreement itself not only emphasized that the suspension was both "voluntary" and for "confidence building," but it also stated that suspension of nuclear activities was not legally binding for Iran. That part of the agreement was the clearest reference in an official and political agreement during the crisis that admitted to the nonbinding nature of the resolutions.

A major achievement of the Khatami government's diplomacy through temporary and limited suspension and insistence on enrichment as a redline could be seen in the days that followed ratification of the November 2004 IAEA Board of Governors' resolution. From an Iranian perspective, that was the best and the most positive resolution ratified by the IAEA and officially put Iran's nuclear dossier back on the normal track. This was a major step toward confirming the peacefulness of Iran's nuclear program.

The resolution also emphasized the voluntary nature of suspension as a confidence-building measure.

The November 2004 resolution did not dissuade Iran from pursuing its main goal of continued enrichment in the face of delaying tactics by the Europeans. The introduction of yellowcake into the Isfahan facility and production of UF_4 and UF_6 in the spring of 2004, the announcement by Iran's Atomic Energy Organization that the Isfahan facility would go into operation on April 30, 2005, followed by Kamal Kharrazi's remarks days later on the sidelines of the NPT review conference in New York that Tehran was determined to immediately reopen the Isfahan facility, all demonstrated the determination of Tehran to enrich uranium during President Khatami's tenure.

As previously discussed, the suspension that did occur between 2003 and 2005 was limited and temporary. Suspension of parts manufacturing and assembly started in May 2004 and ended in July 2004. Suspension of the Isfahan facility began, in practice, in early 2005 and ended in August 2005. In the meantime, operations aimed at completing the Isfahan facility and some activities at the Natanz facility were never suspended. Hence, during the first two years of diplomacy, activities related to enrichment were ongoing, although the Paris Agreement temporarily suspended some parts of those activities.

Of course, the ninth government also tried to deal with demands for suspension, but due to the inflexibility of the Western countries and their view of Ahmadinejad's government, those efforts proved futile. Iran announced its readiness to accept the participation of foreign private and state-run bodies in its uranium enrichment activities, as suggested first by me in spring 2005 and then by Ahmadinejad in September of the same year. This plan could have led to a great degree of transparency in the field of enrichment, but it was rejected by the West. On March 30, 2006, Iran proposed the establishment of a regional consortium for the development of fuel-cycle activities to be owned jointly by a number of shareholding countries, but the proposal again fell on deaf ears. In September and October 2006, during negotiations between Iran's nuclear negotiator and the European Union, Tehran proposed the establishment of an international consortium for uranium enrichment. Although the Europeans at first welcomed the proposal, they later rejected it and went back to urging Iran to suspend enrichment.

SECURITY COUNCIL RESOLUTION 1747

At the end of the two-month deadline given to Iran by UN Security Council Resolution 1737, ElBaradei presented his report on the latest developments in the implementation of nuclear safeguards in Iran. The report noted that since August 31, 2006, centrifuges in the single-machine test stand, as well as 10-machine, 20-machine, and the first 164-machine cascades at the Pilot Fuel Enrichment Plant at Natanz had been running, mostly in a vacuum (with no gas), with UF_6 being fed into the machines intermittently. The installation of a second 164-machine cascade had been completed, and the testing of the cascade with UF_6 gas began on October 13. Between August 13 and November 2, Iran reported feeding a total of approximately 34 kg of UF_6 into the centrifuges and enriched to levels below 5 percent U-235.[28]

The report raised two important points that contributed to Western countries' discussion of Iran's nuclear case within the framework of the UN Security Council:

1. "While the Agency is able to verify the non-diversion of declared nuclear material in Iran, the Agency will remain unable to make further progress in its efforts to verify the absence of undeclared nuclear material and activities in Iran unless Iran addresses the long outstanding verification issues, including through the implementation of the Additional Protocol, and provides the necessary transparency. Progress in this regard is a prerequisite for the Agency to be able to confirm the peaceful nature of Iran's nuclear programme.

2. "Iran has not suspended enrichment activities. Iran has continued operations at test enrichment facilities and has also continued construction of a fuel enrichment plant by installing cascades and introduction of UF_6 to the enrichment site. Iran has also continued its heavy water project including construction and commissioning of a heavy water production plant."

ElBaradei's report triggered intensive negotiations among the P5+1 countries about the need for another UN Security Council resolution. The U.S. State Department announced on March 4, 2007, that the P5+1 had failed to resolve differences over a new sanctions resolution but had agreed to continue to work on the Iranian nuclear case through their representatives at the United Nations. The next day, ElBaradei announced that Iran appeared to have stopped its uranium enrichment program, at least temporarily.[29] His remarks were immediately rejected by Tehran.

The diplomatic blitz against Iran continued. Western diplomats said that Iran had refused to respond to the IAEA request for the installation of full-view cameras at a site where Tehran was assembling centrifuges for uranium enrichment.[30] Representatives of the 35 member states of the Board of Governors also ratified suspension of 23 aid programs to Iran.[31] Stopping the programs had been recommended by ElBaradei in line with sanctions against Iran that were established by the UN Security Council on December 23.

While the West was negotiating a new resolution on Iran, the ninth government adopted two parallel approaches to reduce diplomatic pressure and prevent the ratification of another resolution. In the first approach, Foreign Ministry officials announced that suspension could be discussed through negotiations with the European countries. Foreign Minister Mottaki announced that if Iran's nuclear case were returned from the UN Security Council to the IAEA, Tehran would be ready to negotiate on enrichment. Mottaki, who traveled to Geneva to take part in an international conference on disarmament, further noted that if the five permanent members of the UN Security Council returned the case to the Board of Governors, Iran was ready to provide needed guarantees to build confidence about non-diversion and undeclared material.[32] According to the second approach, ninth government officials threatened that if another resolution were approved against Iran, the country might cut cooperation with the agency, even as they stressed that Iran was once again ready to implement the Additional Protocol if the case were returned to the IAEA.

Iran sent an official letter to the director general of the IAEA to reemphasize the peaceful nature of its nuclear activities and reject the involvement of the UN Security Council in the case, while stressing that Iran would cooperate more on the basis of the Additional Protocol.[33] The letter also noted that as Dr. Larijani told ElBaradei in his report on April 27, 2006, Iran's readiness to negotiate on outstanding issues with the IAEA would depend on assurances about UN Security Council noninvolvement in the case.

Representatives of the P5+1 reached a new agreement on Iran sanctions in New York on March 15, 2007.[34] A draft resolution was accordingly introduced to the UN Security Council. South Africa submitted amendments to the draft calling for a ninety-day time-out, for focusing sanctions only on Iran's nuclear program, and for stipulating that any decision to lift the suspension would be based on the IAEA's technical judgment rather than the Security Council's political judgment. The P5+1 dismissed these proposals with little consideration.

On March 24, 2007, the UN Security Council unanimously approved Resolution 1747. The new resolution banned arms exports to Iran, froze the assets and bank accounts of persons and companies involved in Iran's nuclear and missile programs, and called on countries and international bodies not to grant new loans to Iran. The resolution banned the export of Iranian arms and the procurement of Iranian arms by other countries and called upon all states to exercise restraint in supplying Iran with battle tanks, armored combat vehicles, large caliber artillery systems, and combat aircraft. Once again, the Security Council granted a sixty-day grace period for Tehran to comply with international demands. The new resolution obliged UN member states to present their reports on enforcement to the Security Council within sixty days.[35]

CONSEQUENCES OF RESOLUTION 1747 AND EARLY REACTIONS FROM THE NINTH GOVERNMENT

About two weeks after the adoption of Security Council Resolution 1747, with the world anticipating Iran's reaction, Mahmoud Ahmadinejad declared: "With great pride, I announce as of today our dear country is among the countries of the world that produces nuclear fuel on an industrial scale," adding that "this nuclear fuel is definitely for the development of Iran and expansion of peace in the world."[36] He made this announcement at an April 9, 2007, ceremony organized by Iran's Atomic Energy Organization to name the day (the 20th of Ordibehesht, according to the Persian calendar) the "National Day of Nuclear Technology."

Ahmadinejad sought to implicitly present himself as an heir to Prime Minister Muhammad Mossadegh as the champion of the nationalization of Iran's nuclear industry. Mossadegh was prime minister in 1951 when the Majles voted, at his request, to nationalize the Anglo-Iranian Oil Company[37] and its holdings. Despite intense British pressure, and the withdrawal of the oil company from Iran, Mossadegh was able to manage the crisis and nationalize Iran's oil industry. In the nuclear case, of course, Iran had mastered enrichment technology during President Khatami's tenure (1997–2005), and even before that Rafsanjani had played a key role in establishing the foundations for an independent Iranian nuclear industry during his presidency (1989–1997).

A few hours after Ahmadinejad announced that Iran was a member of the nuclear club,[38] Ali Larijani, Iran's chief nuclear negotiator, addressed Western countries with a statement that Iran had completed the nuclear fuel cycle and was looking forward to negotiations because the time had come for an agreement.[39] Larijani's remarks indicated his willingness to engage in further negotiations to reduce tension—a willingness that would come to clash with the aggressive stance of his president. Ahmadinejad's foreign policy advisers maintained that Iran encouraged the view that its nuclear program was a fait accompli in order to get the P5+1, especially the United States and United Kingdom, to "come to grips with reality."

Opponents of the policy argued that exaggerating Iran's nuclear achievements would just narrow the transatlantic gap and make it more difficult for Russia, China, and the Non-Aligned Movement to support Iran. Therefore, many international observers and Ahmadinejad's domestic critics held that announcing Iran's membership in the "nuclear fuel producers' club" was a "great strategic mistake" and warned that it would just consolidate opposition to Iran.[40]

Ahmadinejad's so-called good tidings elicited a mix of reactions from Iran's negotiating partners. Media outlets close to White House neoconservatives and the Israeli lobby warned that Iran was now closer to a nuclear bomb and discussed the possibility of preemptive military action.[41] Both Russian and American officials, however, doubted the accuracy of Ahmadinejad's remarks, saying that there was no evidence to prove that Iran was capable of industrial-scale uranium enrichment. Sergei Kiriyenko, the head of the Russian Nuclear Energy State Corporation (Rosatom), emphasized that his country's specialists did not believe that Iran had initiated industrial-level enrichment because it was a very complicated technological process that required much more than just a certain number of centrifuges. He added, "The question is, 'Have Iranians actually overcome technical problems to start uranium enrichment on an industrial scale?' Our answer is negative."[42]

At that time, international research suggested that Iran had just commissioned a cascade of 164 centrifuges with maximum output of about 20 percent enriched uranium.[43] Most studies indicated that Iran was facing serious technical problems with installing 164-centrifuge cascades, and suspicions continued until June 2007 when the IAEA director general released his new report, saying that during "complementary access" by the IAEA on March 13, 2007, "eight 164-machine cascades were operating simultaneously and were being fed with UF_6; two 164-machine cascades were being vacuum tested; and three more were under construction." ElBaradei's report also noted that Iran was still far from producing the high volume of uranium required to meet its consumption needs.[44]

New negotiations between Ali Larijani and EU foreign policy chief Javier Solana started in the spring of 2007. The first round of talks was held in Ankara[45] and the second round in Madrid, shortly before the deadline for Iran to meet the demands of Resolution 1747. The P5+1 announced that they were waiting for the results of negotiations before deciding about tougher sanctions.[46] Foreign ministers of the G8 member countries issued a statement in Potsdam, Germany, before the Larijani-Solana negotiations to announce that if Iran continued to ignore the Security Council's demands, they would support further sanctions as warned in Resolution 1747.[47]

In Madrid, Larijani and Solana met at La Quinta Palace and talked behind closed doors for five hours. Subsequent media reports were encouraging. It was clear from the news conference in which both negotiators participated that no agreement had been reached on the main point of dispute: the suspension of enrichment activities. Larijani emphasized that Iran and Europe were wrangling over the issue of suspension as a precondition, though Solana immediately noted that the EU insisted on the Security Council resolutions, which called for suspension.[48]

There were indications of a possible bilateral agreement between Larijani and Solana on the horizon, but profound differences between Larijani and Ahmadinejad led to Larijani's dismissal a few months later. Some Western media claimed that despite his hardheadedness in negotiations with Solana, Larijani was carrying an unofficial proposal for "limited suspension" by Iran, which was turned down by the EU.[49] The proposal that was central to Larijani's effort to end the nuclear standoff was rejected outright by Ahmadinejad.

I believe that Larijani, understanding that flexibility was required of Iran, was seeking a compromise with the P5+1 countries. He was trying to show flexibility by cooperating with the IAEA to remove remaining ambiguities, and even by being willing to consider suspension of enrichment for several weeks if the P5+1 would agree to finalize a package that included Iran's right to enrich. In an interview with the German magazine *Focus* in August 2007, Larijani spoke publicly for the first time about this possibility. Asked whether suspension was a possible outcome of negotiations, he said, "It cannot be ruled out, but nobody can impede progress of this technology" in Iran. This relatively flexible position was rejected so vehemently by Ahmadinejad and pro-state media that Larijani's office subsequently claimed that Larijani's remarks had been "distorted."[50]

Larijani embarked on another diplomatic tour in July 2007 to meet separately with Mohamed ElBaradei at the IAEA's Vienna headquarters and with Solana in Portugal. This third round of negotiations with Solana was organized after the failure of previous talks to make significant headway and amid strongly worded statements issued by the G8, the European Union, and the EU3 threatening that tougher sanctions would be imposed if Tehran rejected the call for suspension of enrichment.[51]

Tehran refused to accept the Western countries' demands or the IAEA director general's "time-out" initiative, which was another version of the "suspension for suspension" option that had previously been rejected by both Iran and the West.[52] Iran did, however, announce that it would allow IAEA inspectors to visit the nuclear facility at Arak and allow them to take samples from Arak's heavy-water reactor.[53] A number of members of the Iran Parliament stated that they would have no objection to a limited and temporary suspension if it helped to "thwart U.S. plots."[54] Then, just as some Western analysts were arguing that the signs of flexibility on the suspension issue indicated a rise in the power of pragmatists in Iran's government,[55] Ali Larijani resigned as secretary of the Supreme National Security Council.

ALI LARIJANI: RESIGNATION OR DISMISSAL?

Larijani's resignation was made public by government spokesman Gholamhossein Elham, who announced that Larijani had resigned "due to personal problems and . . . Saeed Jalili will replace him."[56] Almost all domestic and foreign media, however, conjectured that the resignation had been brought about by profound disagreements between Larijani and Mahmoud Ahmadinejad and was a sign of a new surge in the power of the radical fundamentalist camp.[57]

The rift between Larijani and Ahmadinejad over the nuclear case was quite deep. In some cases, Ahmadinejad dispatched people such as his top adviser, Mojtaba Samareh Hashemi, as his special envoys to countries like France to negotiate in parallel with Larijani, thus casting doubt on Larijani's authority. Ahmadinejad's approach was idealistic and aggressive, while Larijani's was more pragmatic and tuned to international conditions and global power equations. The differences became quite evident when Ahmadinejad made sharp remarks in response to speculation (as in the August 2007 *Focus* report) that Tehran would suspend enrichment by retorting that Tehran would not suspend uranium enrichment for even a single day. Rumors about Larijani's imminent resignation circulated on at least three occasions before he actually stepped down.

The last instance of discord between Larijani and Ahmadinejad became manifest one week before his resignation and pertained to negotiations between the Russian president and the Iranian supreme leader. While Larijani clearly announced that President Putin had conveyed a "special nuclear message" to the Iranian leader, Ahmadinejad emphasized that the negotiations had nothing to do with the nuclear issue and the message was one of "peace and friendship."[58] Also, three weeks before Larijani's resignation, Ahmadinejad bitterly criticized "clandestine negotiations" between some people and the European countries. At first it was thought that the criticism was directed at Rouhani and the former negotiating team, but later developments clearly showed Larijani to be the main target of that rebuke. Some media reports maintained that Larijani's resignation had something to do with the dismissal of the chief commander of the Islamic Revolutionary Guard Corps, General Yahya Rahim Safavi, a few days after he criticized some radical measures and talked about possible war with an "angry, powerful, and illogical" enemy. Some sources maintained that Safavi had also severely criticized Ahmadinejad and his policies, which Safavi regarded as warmongering.[59] Major General Mohammad Ali Jafari, who was considered to be more in line with Ahmadinejad's policies, replaced Safavi.

Larijani's resignation from the Supreme National Security Council and its acceptance by Ahmadinejad were described as "surprising" by BBC News because of Larijani's prominence in nuclear diplomacy.[60] Most foreign media noted Larijani's role in steering the nuclear case and suggested that his resignation was a sign that Iran would adopt more radical policies.[61] One day after the resignation, there was news about changes in Iran's foreign policy structure. The expectation was that Foreign Minister Manouchehr Mottaki,[62] who had conflicts of his own with Ahmadinejad, would follow Larijani in resigning.[63] Ahmadinejad brushed aside such rumors by calling them psychological warfare,[64] and Mottaki also denied the news. But it was clear that the differences between the president and the foreign minister were serious.

Larijani was removed from nuclear negotiations after his "looking to the East" approach proved a failure and his revised approach moved toward that of the former nuclear negotiating team, which he had previously likened to "swapping a pearl for a lollipop." A few rounds of talks with the European Union and a better understanding of realities on the ground had been enough to persuade him to rethink his past views.

Although Iran's nuclear case was referred to the UN Security Council during Larijani's term as senior negotiator, and the Security Council issued a statement and adopted three resolutions (1969, 1737, and 1747) before his resignation, he made a last-ditch effort to reach a comprehensive agreement with the P5+1. In the Supreme National Security Council of the ninth government, all prominent decisionmakers including Larijani initially chose the "looking to the East" approach but modified it after two years of negotiations with Solana in favor of inclusive talks with the EU. Larijani tried to find a face-saving solution to the situation.

Larijani's resignation created a spate of criticism across the country. Ali Akbar Velayati, the supreme leader's adviser in international affairs, opined that it would have been better if the resignation had not taken place at such a time of international tension.[65] Larijani, for his part, denied the Ahmadinejad government spokesman's remarks that his resignation was based on personal motives, and the fact that he did not address political disagreement with Ahmadinejad substantiated speculation that that was the true cause of his resignation.[66]

One month after Larijani's resignation, some political figures who were critical of Ahmadinejad weighed in on the nuclear issue. Former presidents Hashemi Rafsanjani and Muhammad Khatami, as well as Hassan Rouhani and Ali Akbar Velayati, were among them. Hashemi Rafsanjani, accompanied by politicians including Hassan Rouhani, attended a conference I chaired at the Center for Strategic Research, which is affiliated with the Expediency Council,[67] to talk about Iran's nuclear issue. A few days later, Seyed Muhammad Khatami and his foreign minister, Kamal Kharrazi, took part in a seminar on Iranian and Egyptian thinkers and, for the first time since Ahmadinejad's inauguration, talked about the nuclear issue. While advising Iranian officials to be more logical when interacting with other countries, Khatami criticized the West for its rash approach to Iran's nuclear case and called on Western countries to change their ways.[68]

This was, of course, not the first time that Rafsanjani or Khatami had commented on the nuclear case, but they demonstrated that following Larijani's resignation, pragmatic politicians were concerned about radicalism dominating Iran's nuclear policy. Most of Larijani's close aides had been dismissed from the Supreme National Security Council by then and replaced by others chosen by Ahmadinejad. It was also rumored that the locus of decisionmaking had shifted away from the council and toward the president's office. Ahmadinejad's acerbic rhetoric also raised concerns that Iran was moving irreversibly toward crisis and confrontation.

MY ARREST: SIGNIFICANCE FOR THE COUNTRY AND ITS NUCLEAR DIPLOMACY

In 1997, by order of Dr. Rouhani and President Khatami, I was put in charge of the Foreign Policy Committee of the Supreme National Security Council. I held the post until 2005. In that capacity, I was involved in handling major foreign policy issues including the American invasions of Afghanistan and Iraq and Iran's nuclear case. I was the sole former official of the Supreme National Security Council who also served as a foreign policy adviser to Ali Larijani.

My arrest on April 30, 2007,[69] on espionage charges[70] therefore caused a sensation across Iran and was widely viewed as politically motivated. Although it initially seemed to be the result of a misunderstanding, later scathing rhetoric by Mahmoud Ahmadinejad against me and the opposition of the ninth government to my eventual acquittal by the judiciary demonstrated that my arrest was a political maneuver instigated by the Ahmadinejad administration. Domestic and foreign observers maintained that the arrest was related to the nuclear case.

I was the only member of Khatami's former nuclear negotiating team who was publicly defending Khatami's record on the nuclear issue and criticizing Ahmadinejad's nuclear and foreign policy as ineffectual and overly aggressive.[71] The former nuclear team had worked under the oversight of a Supreme National Security Council committee, which in turn answered directly to the supreme leader. The committee consisted of such prominent politicians as Ali Larijani, Kamal Kharrazi, Ali Akbar Velayati, Ali Younesi, Ali Shamkhani, Gholam Reza Aghazadeh, and Hassan Rouhani. All decisions of the committee were endorsed by the supreme leader. Despite this, after 2005 the committee's decisions to suspend uranium enrichment, implement the Additional Protocol to the NPT, and continue negotiations with the EU3 came under severe fire from the newly inaugurated President Ahmadinejad, who even accused the former negotiators of "treason" and "cowardice."

After Iran's nuclear case was referred to the UN Security Council and sanctions resolutions were adopted, criticism of Ahmadinejad's nuclear policies heightened. Trying to present himself as the "savior" of Iran's nuclear program and introducing Iran's achievements as his own "miracle" through his "good news" policy, Ahmadinejad assailed Khatami's nuclear policies. In numerous public remarks in the fall and winter of 2006, he lost no opportunity to laud his own government's nuclear breakthroughs while attacking his predecessors' policies.[72]

There was, of course, a major problem with this strategy. Although Ahmadinejad did his best to pose as savior, the UN Security Council adopted consecutive sanctions resolutions against Iran, thereby increasing pressure on Tehran. While Ahmadinejad announced in early 2007 that the nuclear case had been decided with Iran as final winner, the West continued to escalate its pressure on and condemnations of Iran. Thus serious doubts were cast on the credibility of the president's claims.

Faced with mounting domestic criticism in the winter of 2007, Ahmadinejad repeatedly claimed that critics were sending the wrong signals to the world, which presented Iran as weak and thus encouraged the belief that Iran would bow to new sanctions resolutions. Radical supporters of Ahmadinejad alleged that Ahmadinejad's critics were spies and traitors. Presenting me as a "spy" who worked with the former negotiating team and also symbolized Khatami's nuclear policies was nothing more than a ploy to shift blame.[73]

My arrest was also a serious warning to Ahmadinejad's other foreign policy critics. A member of the foreign relations committee of the Parliament told me that my arrest had sent a strong message to many parliamentarians, because if a policymaker as closely affiliated as I was with politically powerful figures such as Hashemi Rafsanjani, Khatami, Rouhani, Ali Akbar Nategh-Nouri (who headed the supreme leader's inspection office and was the former speaker of Parliament), Mehdi Karroubi (the former speaker of Parliament), and Ayatollah Emami Kashani (a top conservative cleric and the Friday prayer leader of Tehran appointed by the supreme leader) could be sent to jail for criticizing Ahmadinejad's foreign policy, it could happen to virtually anyone who crossed the new president. This message was taken seriously. From the time of my arrest in May 2007 to the March 2008 parliamentary elections, criticism of Ahmadinejad's policies was muted and commentators began to express more support for the government's foreign policy.

I was not only a political aide to Ayatollah Hashemi Rafsanjani and one of his senior directors at the Center for Strategic Research but was also highly trusted by him and given sensitive assignments during my diplomatic career.[74] Rafsanjani, Khatami, Rouhani, and Larijani were Ahmadinejad's four main competitors, and I was one of the few politicians connected to all four. Depicting me as a spy of the West could be a major political blow to Ahmadinejad's rivals, who were implicated by their association to me. Some pro-Ahmadinejad media speculated that I had been orchestrating clandestine arrangements between Rafsanjani and the West against Ahmadinejad. Such accusations were totally baseless.[75]

The goal of discrediting Ahmadinejad's political opponents was apparent to me during my detention. During ten days of interrogations in Evin

Prison from April 1 to April 10, I was told that the intelligence service and the administration believed that I was in contact with Westerners with the goal of bringing the Rafsanjani and Khatami factions to power again. They told me that I had been arrested to cut off this communication.

Baseless though it was, my detention was a direct message to Ayatollah Hashemi Rafsanjani. After several disappointing setbacks in parliamentary and other elections, Rafsanjani was elected chairman of the Assembly of Experts by a huge margin four months before my arrest, with observers speculating that he was making a political comeback.

The political camp he led, which was viewed as a serious threat by Ahmadinejad's supporters, decided to reorganize its political activities and make a push to regain ground in the eighth parliamentary elections scheduled for early 2008. I was arrested in the interval between the two elections (that of the Assembly of Experts and the Majles). The first election had ended in an undisputed triumph by Rafsanjani and his allies. A further victory in the Parliament would have been a serious blow to the Ahmadinejad government. Foreign media, especially in the United States, maintained that my apprehension was meant to throw the pragmatist camp off balance after its relative reinvigoration following the Assembly of Experts election.[76]

A day after I was released from Evin Prison (on May 9, 2007), I met with Rafsanjani at his home. He told me that within twenty-four hours of my arrest, reliable sources had informed him that it was the beginning of a series of arrests of top politicians from the opposition camp that would be carried out in a huge propaganda campaign against moderates and reformists prior to the 2008 parliamentary and 2009 presidential elections. Rafsanjani told me that my refusal to "confess" under threats and pressure in prison was a setback for the government's plan but that it would wait for another opportunity to make further arrests.

I was a senior director of the Center for Strategic Research. Radicals considered the center to be a locus of "intrigues" against the president. My arrest therefore was also meant to send a message to the center and its president, Hassan Rouhani, a moderate cleric and the former secretary of the Supreme National Security Council and former chief nuclear negotiator, who was expected to run in the 2009 presidential elections and was therefore a major target for the pro-Ahmadinejad media.[77]

I was a very active diplomat traveling to many countries and was well known in European and Middle Eastern diplomatic circles.[78] I was a regular attendee of international conferences and considered an unofficial spokesman of the pragmatic political current represented by Hashemi Rafsanjani.[79] Therefore, my arrest served to send a further message to the government's opponents: *There is to be no communication with the outside world except through us.*

From the day of my arrest, a huge amount of propaganda was orchestrated in the right-wing media against me, Rafsanjani, Rouhani, and Khatami. Thirteen accusations and charges were published in a very organized manner by the pro-Ahmadinejad media; none of them existed in my case file or were even raised in my interrogations. I decided to keep silent on such baseless allegations but to file suit against the publishers in court. Some months later my old friend Ahmad Tavakkoli, a prominent parliamentarian of the right-wing Principlist faction and head of the Majles's research center, called me and complained about my lawsuit against his news site Alef. I told him that he bore responsibility for following the lead of the hard-line media and publishing false information about my case. He was a member of the Majles, I reminded him, and was able to study the files of the courts and intelligence services to find the truth.

Some months later, in a move that grabbed the country's headlines, Tavakkoli issued an official statement that revealed for the first time the realities of my case file. In the statement, he said that he had studied the complete file very carefully, spoken with responsible officials in the judiciary and intelligence services, and was confident that all thirteen accusations against me were completely baseless and did not even exist in the official case file—a file that I, as the accused, had not been permitted to see. Tavakkoli listed the accusations as follow:

1. Providing the UK's intelligence service (MI6) with secret documents about "Iran's security bases in Europe."
2. Meeting with European intelligence services during frequent visits to Europe.
3. Engaging in espionage for the EU and UK on Iran's nuclear program.
4. Being in long-term contact with an American diplomat.

5. Delivering a top-secret document on Iran's nuclear policy to the British Embassy in Tehran.

6. Handing over secret Supreme National Security Council documents to foreigners.

7. Delivering confidential documents and information to the Europeans.

8. Handing over secret documents of Iran's intelligence service to the UK.

9. Requesting help from foreigners to win the majority in the 2008 parliamentarian election.

10. Obtaining financial support for the Center for Strategic Research from UK officials.

11. Urging the West to expedite sanction resolutions against Iran.

12. Equipping my home with secret surveillance cameras.

13. Warning Sirous Nasseri, a member of the former nuclear negotiation team who was indicted on corruption charges, not to return to Iran.[80]

This rebuke of the government's handling of the case by a prominent member of Ahmadinejad's own Principlist camp was quite significant, as Ahmadinejad had personally accused me of the third, seventh, and eleventh of those charges in public on several occasions. Even two years after the dismissal of the case by the judiciary and despite overwhelming evidence of my consistent opposition to sanctions and UN resolutions against Iran, he indirectly accused me of urging the West to impose sanction resolutions.[81]

Ahmad Tavakkoli officially apologized and asked me and my family for forgiveness for his participation in publishing baseless accusations harming my reputation and credibility.[82] In his statement, Tavakkoli blamed the government for the false accusations, which Ahmadinejad's office denied in an official statement.[83] I responded to Tavakkoli by publicly forgiving him.[84]

Other pro-Ahmadinejad media such as Fars News Agency, Ansarnews,[85] Edalatkhaneh,[86] and Bultannews were found culpable in a number of court cases for publishing the thirteen accusations. Some other media outlet chiefs also officially apologized, and I forgave them.[87]

My case was investigated for about a year by three different judges. All the judges found me innocent of espionage.[88] However, the second judge who cleared me of espionage charges believed that I was guilty on other grounds because of my acknowledged opposition to Ahmadinejad's foreign and nuclear policy.[89] He wrote in his indictment that I was guilty of jeopardizing national security by opposing the president's policies.

On the last day of the Iranian calendar (March 20, 2008), I was informed by an official from the Tehran prosecutor that the office had arranged a trial for me during the New Year holidays. He also told me that the office had already decided that I would be sentenced to a two-year suspended sentence and a five-year ban on holding any diplomatic post. I responded to the official by pointing out that that a two-year suspended jail sentence meant that I would not be able to criticize Ahmadinejad's nuclear and foreign policy, and moreover that I would have to keep quiet about the story of my arrest for one year before and one year after the presidential elections of 2009, lest I be forced to serve the sentence in jail. Concerning the five-year ban on holding a diplomatic post, I told him that it implied that Ahmadinejad was supposed to be president for another term, from 2009 to 2013. He told me, "You are very clever."

The same day, I recounted the story of the prosecutor's office to prominent politicians, including Rafsanjani, Nategh-Nouri, Khatami, and Karroubi. Five days before the trial, I met the judge and asked him for a public trial open to the media, but he rejected my request. I asked him to let me study the file to be able to defend myself, but he refused. I then asked why a trial was even necessary if the outcome had already been determined. He acted shocked and denied that this was the case. But four days after my court appearance on March 30, 2008, he issued the same sentence that I had been informed of by the prosecutor's office before the trial.

COMPARING THE LEGAL STATUS OF THE NUCLEAR CASE IN THE ROUHANI AND LARIJANI PERIODS

During the first (Rouhani) period of Iran's nuclear diplomacy and as a result of Tehran's political approach, the IAEA Board of Governors recognized the non-diversion of nuclear materials from Iran's declared facilities and accepted corrective measures taken to address major outstanding issues. The Board of Governors even removed Iran's nuclear case from its provisional agenda in the fall of 2004.

However, the case was taken up again by the Board of Governors in September 2005, which led to its being officially labeled by the UN Security Council as a threat to international peace and security. In late 2005, the Board of Governors approved a resolution accusing Iran of noncompliance with International Atomic Energy Agency regulations under Article XII, Paragraph C of the IAEA Statute and accordingly called for the case to be reported to the UN Security Council.

The resolution did not, however, mention any set date for reporting. It was only after Iran restarted its enrichment program in January 2006 that the Board of Governors passed a new resolution requiring the director general to prepare a report. The Security Council subsequently put Iran's nuclear case on its agenda, resulting ultimately in UN Security Council Resolutions 1696, 1737, and 1747.

In the first period of Iran's nuclear diplomacy, after release of the November 2004 resolution, the Board of Governors returned to the framework of the Safeguards Agreement and the Additional Protocol in dealing with Iran, giving up its earlier calls for inspections and access beyond the Additional Protocol. Just months into the new government's tenure, the September 2005 resolution reversed this accomplishment and called for access to sites and individuals that went far beyond the contents of the Safeguards Agreement and the Additional Protocol.

In the early days of the crisis and after the adoption of the September 2003 IAEA resolution, Iran was required to suspend enrichment activities. Tehran managed to change that "obligatory suspension" to a "voluntary" and "non-legally binding" confidence-building measure whose duration was limited to the period of negotiations. In the nuclear diplomacy of the Ahmadinejad government, UN Security Council resolutions made suspension obligatory for Iran.

In the second period of the nuclear diplomacy, Iran's nuclear program became a "threat to international peace and security" in Resolutions 1696, 1737, and 1747 under Chapter VII of the UN Charter. Articles 39 and 40 (through Resolution 1696) and Article 41 (through Resolutions 1373 and 1747) of Chapter VII were applied to Iran. Tehran had successfully prevented American attempts to achieve this during the first round of its nuclear diplomacy.

Reports and resolutions issued in 2005 and 2006 also presented Iran's missile capabilities as an aspect of the threat to international peace and security posed by Iran, and this perception was accepted in further resolutions adopted by the UN Security Council in 2006.

In the Rouhani period, Iran's nuclear program was a legal-political issue. It was turned into a security-political-legal issue with the IAEA's referral of the Iran case to the Security Council and into a totally security matter during the Ahmadinejad period.

Finally, in the first period of the nuclear diplomacy, a majority of technical problems between Iran and the IAEA were resolved and the nuclear case was viewed by the agency from a largely technical viewpoint. Although there were other outstanding issues that had not been resolved by the Rouhani team and there was no agreement on the duration of suspension and the definition of objective guarantees, there certainly had been major progress. The IAEA had officially announced in the fall of 2004 that ambiguities surrounding the matters of highly enriched uranium contamination and P-2 centrifuges had also been removed. After the restart of operations at the Isfahan uranium conversion facility and of research and development activities in Natanz in 2005–2006, however, the IAEA's director general prepared his reports in such a way that technical ambiguities were highlighted.

CHAPTER EIGHT

IRAN ALONE

THE JALILI PERIOD

IRAN-IAEA RELATIONS IN 2007

Other developments occurred in Iran's nuclear case in 2007 beyond Larijani's resignation. One of the most important achievements was an agreement between Iran and the IAEA known as the "modality agreement," or "work plan." Put forth as a "Plan of Action" in summer 2007, it was developed by Larijani's team and the IAEA to resolve all of the IAEA's remaining ambiguities, including the "alleged weaponization studies." The director general and Larijani devised the modality/work plan focusing on plutonium, P-1 and P-2 centrifuges, the source of uranium contamination in the University of Tehran's Faculty of Technology, metal hemispheres, plutonium-210, and the Gchine mine as the basis for the negotiations.

Iran's cooperation with the IAEA under the work plan led to ElBaradei's February 2008 report, in which the director general mentioned that the two sides had reached an agreement over the six outstanding technical issues cited by the IAEA and that the "alleged studies" on the possibility of military applications in the past were the sole issue that remained unresolved. Iran maintained that this issue had been of marginal importance in the modality agreement and that the director general's emphasis on it was simply the product of pressure from Western countries.

Another major development was a report known as the National Intelligence Estimate that was issued by the sixteen intelligence agencies of the United States. To the great surprise of international observers, the National Intelligence Estimate announced that Iran had halted military nuclear activities in 2003.[1] The report was considered by Tehran to be a rebuke to the West's accusations. In reaction to the report and that of ElBaradei, Tehran renewed its call for the nuclear case to be taken off the Security Council's agenda and returned to the IAEA.[2]

In late December 2007, Moscow made the first of eight fuel deliveries containing a total of 83 tons of low-enriched uranium to the Bushehr nuclear plant.[3] In late January 2008, IAEA Director General Mohamed ElBaradei visited Tehran to meet with Iran's president, foreign minister, the head of Iran's Atomic Energy Organization, and the supreme leader. The IAEA secretariat issued a press release announcing that ElBaradei intended to discuss further cooperation with Iran in order to remove ambiguities surrounding the country's past and present nuclear activities.[4] Agence France-Presse, meanwhile, quoted unnamed European diplomats as saying that cooperation between the IAEA and Iran had reached a crucial juncture and that ElBaradei aimed to persuade Tehran to be more transparent and allow more extensive inspections of its nuclear facilities.[5] European sources were also quoted as saying that ElBaradei should investigate and verify the National Intelligence Estimate finding that Iran had been running a military nuclear program until 2003, at which point it had been discontinued.[6]

ElBaradei's meeting with Supreme Leader Ayatollah Khamenei, the details of which were only recently disclosed in ElBaradei's memoir, were of particular significance. Prior to the meeting, ElBaradei asked U.S. Secretary of State Condoleezza Rice about America's bottom line in terms of conditions for negotiations. In his account, Rice responded by saying "suspension remained a redline she could not cross."[7]

When the issue of suspension was raised in the meeting, Khamenei told ElBaradei that Iran would "never be brought to its knees"—meaning, ElBaradei wrote, "that no amount of sanctions would get Iran to suspend enrichment or end what they recognized as their legitimate right."

ElBaradei recounts Khamenei's position in the meeting:

The IAEA should be Iran's only interlocutor; it had been a mistake to discuss Iran's nuclear program with others. Once the Security Council returned the Iranian file to the Agency, he added, Iran would be ready to implement the Additional Protocol. . . . [Enrichment suspension], he said, was merely a distraction invented by the Americans. The real issue was U.S. anger over Iran's emerging role in the region. Khamenei was ready to engage with the West on all issues of regional security and trade, but he saw no reason for Iran to show flexibility about enrichment. Iran, he insisted, had never had a nuclear weapons program; to do so, he told me, would be against Islam.[8]

As ElBaradei reveals, this was the highest-level overture to the United States and Europe that Iran made for engagement "on all issues of regional security and trade." ElBaradei informed the Americans and Europeans of Khamenei's position immediately after returning to Vienna, but the United States once again passed up the opportunity to engage with Iran.

ElBaradei's sixth trip to Tehran convinced political circles that a new page had been turned in Tehran's cooperation with the IAEA.[9] Iran agreed to continue to cooperate with the IAEA more actively in the framework of this "plan of action,"[10] though some American media outlets still claimed that it was not sufficient. It is important to note that despite Ahmadinejad's rhetoric, cooperation with the IAEA was consistently, if quietly, pursued by the ninth government. Although Ahmadinejad attacked Khatami for accepting inspections beyond the Additional Protocol and thus providing an opportunity for Western spies to access sensitive information, the Additional Protocol occasionally was in reality implemented (unofficially, but in practice) under both Larijani and Jalili as secretaries of the Supreme National Security Council.

After ElBaradei left Tehran, the secretariat of the IAEA issued a statement officially announcing that Iran had agreed to solve outstanding issues in the space of four weeks.[11] The statement also noted that at ElBaradei's meeting with Ayatollah Khamenei, the two sides had agreed to implement the "modality" plan in those four weeks. The Islamic Republic of Iran was also supposed to provide ElBaradei with information on the manufacture of an advanced centrifuge that could speed up the enrichment process.

The Iranian Foreign Ministry responded that Tehran expected the director general to announce an end to disputes over legal and technical aspects of Iran's nuclear case in his March 2008 report.[12] Iranian nuclear officials maintained that the agreement on the "Modality Plan of Action" paved the way for more extensive cooperation between Tehran and the IAEA that would get the nuclear case back on the normal track.[13]

Despite Iran's optimism, the modality plan itself drew criticism from Western and Israeli officials and media outlets. ElBaradei recounts in his memoir,

> The plan made [the Americans] nervous: an uptick in Iran's cooperation with the IAEA weakened the chance of prodding China and Russia into imposing any further sanctions. Plus, if Tehran [succeeded] in resolving the outstanding issues about its past and present nuclear program, the Security Council's demand for Iran to suspend uranium enrichment would lose any logical basis.[14]

A September 5, 2007, editorial in the *Washington Post* entitled "Rogue Regulator" criticized ElBaradei harshly over the modality plan, and the *Jerusalem Post* labeled him a "man of dubious integrity."[15] The *New York Times* quoted his harshest detractors as calling him "drunk with the power of [the] Nobel."[16] Brushing aside such criticism, ElBaradei reported to the Board of Governors that "due to the work plan: a number of nuclear verification issues had been resolved, because Iran had provided long-sought information."[17]

The opposition to ElBaradei's attempts to clarify the nature of Iran's program hardened the Iranian judgment that the Americans and Europeans were not interested in ensuring the peaceful nature of Iran's nuclear activities. In ElBaradei's words,

> The truth was that the Americans wanted only to portray Iran as a noncooperative pariah state, in violation of its international obligations and therefore deserving continued punishment. . . . Despite Larijani's efforts to get back to "prenegotiations," Solana was blocked by the Americans from continuing.[18]

Even as progress was made through the modality/work plan, secret talks were going on in Western capitals about a new sanctions resolution against Iran. Surprising remarks of the American and French presidents and their warnings to Iran in late January 2008 also suggested that a new wave of confrontation was imminent.

THE WEST PREPARES TO ADOPT
A NEW UN SANCTIONS RESOLUTION

Facing staunch opposition from China and Russia to a new sanctions resolution, on top of Iran's agreement to expand cooperation with the IAEA, Washington launched intensive diplomatic maneuvering in order to gain the support of the permanent members of the Security Council for the new resolution. State Department spokesman Sean McCormack emphasized that the United States still pursued adoption of another anti-Iranian resolution in the Security Council.[19] He added that P5+1 member states were not in accord regarding the resolution, and he could not deny that China and Russia were not willing to support another anti-Iranian resolution. The most telling of his remarks, however, was the reaction to Iran's agreement with ElBaradei. McCormack said that ElBaradei and the IAEA could not decide about political matters, and as Dr. Rice had already noted, the IAEA's demands were different from the Security Council's, and it was the Security Council that would make the final decision on Iran.

In reality, publication of the National Intelligence Estimate and Tehran's agreement with the IAEA presented U.S. President George W. Bush with a dilemma. The announcement by Tehran that it would shortly resolve outstanding issues was an impediment to U.S. efforts aimed at putting more pressure on Iran. While China and Russia opposed a new resolution, the EU3 (France, Germany, and Britain) were also more willing to look toward a peaceful solution of the nuclear standoff. Iranian officials, as well, indicated their satisfaction with the new trend in the nuclear case.[20] Everything appeared to be in place to move the nuclear case back to a plane that was less highly charged. An agreement by the P5+1 over a new sanctions resolution in late January 2008, however, did away with all optimism.

In spring 2008, a draft of the third sanctions resolution was submitted to the UN Security Council. The body would not easily let go of Iran's nuclear case. We had frequently warned officials on our side that it is easy for a matter to be taken into the Security Council, but very difficult to get it out. American officials and some of their European counterparts had already noted that the IAEA's demands were different from those of the UN Security Council and that "political" decisions on the nuclear case would be made in New York. Thus, Iran's cooperation with the IAEA could be effective only when combined with political maneuvering. This approach had been followed by Khatami's team and later in the second half of Ali Larijani's term as lead nuclear strategist. The agreement among the P5+1 further refuted the "looking to the East" policy that was the main strategy of Ahmadinejad's foreign policy.

Russia's dual game was evident when its foreign minister, Sergei Lavrov, announced that the new resolution was not punitive. His American counterpart moved fast to say that it was both punitive and very serious.[21] Some analysts close to Ahmadinejad's government claimed that the P5+1 agreement was, in fact, a political tactic to put more pressure on Iran and get the country to fulfill its promise to resolve outstanding issues in four weeks or even sooner.

Interestingly, the P5+1 agreement came one day after some state officials in Iran noted that the nuclear case had been practically closed[22] and President Ahmadinejad even spoke of the UN Security Council resolutions as nothing but "worthless scraps of paper." Public opinion largely ignored the inaccuracy of Ahmadinejad's viewpoints. Sporadic information leaked on the content of the new sanctions resolution indicated that the United States and United Kingdom were bent on expanding the range of Iran sanctions by extending them to commodities with dual uses. They also meant to intensify international supervision over Iran's exports and to include possible sanctions against Melli Bank as the country's most important state-run bank.[23]

Meanwhile, new missile tests by Iran and the launch in early February of the country's first space satellite by the carrier rocket Safir (meaning "messenger" or "ambassador" in Persian)[24] led to a spate of new international criticism of Iran. The satellite launch demonstrated sophistication in multistage separation and propulsion systems. Even the Russian deputy foreign minister warned Tehran that such measures would increase concerns about possible diversion in Iran's nuclear program toward military purposes.[25] Western media also quoted an anonymous source as saying that Iran was testing a new and more advanced centrifuge that would greatly increase the pace of uranium enrichment in the country.[26]

ELBARADEI'S FEBRUARY 2008 REPORT

ElBaradei's February 22, 2008, report on Iran[27] elicited contradictory reactions outside of and inside the country. Foreign media interpreted it as paving the way for a third UN Security Council sanctions resolution, while state-run media in Tehran described it as a "complete victory" for Iran.

Mahmoud Ahmadinejad even wrote an official letter to the supreme leader describing the report as a great victory for Iran.[28] The government's Islamic Propagation Organization issued a statement calling for "thanks-giving ceremonies" to be held nationwide.[29] A few minutes after the report was released, Saeed Jalili, the secretary of the Supreme National Security Council, appeared with a wide smile on his face in a news conference attended by domestic and foreign media and congratulated the Iranian nation at least three times for ElBaradei's report, calling it an "achievement and triumph for the Iranian nation and a result of its steadfastness."[30]

ElBaradei had indeed emphasized the success of cooperation between Tehran and the IAEA, in that most of the questions that the IAEA had posed about Iran's pre-2003 nuclear activities had been answered. He also mentioned, however, that the IAEA's most important question—about possible military dimensions of the nuclear program—remained unresolved. He also complained about a lack of cooperation from Tehran with regard to certain issues—particularly Tehran's rejection of the Additional Protocol. Finally, he stated clearly that Iran had failed to meet the UN Security Council's demand to suspend enrichment.

The report stated that six outstanding issues had been resolved: the source of the contamination of highly enriched uranium at the University of Tehran Faculty of Technology, Iran's production of polonium-210, the use of the uranium from Iran's Gchine mine, Iran's test separations of plutonium from irradiated uranium, its P-1 and P-2 centrifuges, and the document from the A. Q. Khan network on the production of uranium hemispheres. Also, the IAEA had found no evidence to prove diversion of declared materials toward a military program.

As ElBaradei notes in his recent memoir,

We had made significant strides: the last of our questions about the low- and high-enriched uranium particles we had detected at various locations in Iran had finally been answered. The Iranians had explained their polonium experiments, their activities at the Gchine mine, and the procurement activities of the former head of the Physics Research Center. The last of the discrepancies about Iran's past procurement of P-1 and P-2 centrifuges had been addressed in my November 2007 report. While there had been a few minor delays, the Iranians had held steadily to their commitment to the work plan. It was the most consistent and committed cooperation we had experienced in years. Only one issue remained: the alleged weaponization studies that had come to us from U.S. intelligence.[31]

This allusion to weaponization studies, which implied that Iran had been doing research on building a nuclear bomb, was an important point censored by Iran's state-run media.[32] This reference to weaponization studies was, of course, taken as sufficient basis for the adoption of a third anti-Iran sanctions resolution by the UN Security Council.

It should be noted that even on the eve of a new punitive resolution's passage, ElBaradei was working behind the scenes with P5+1 members for a new offer for Iran. In early 2008, ElBaradei proposed to French President Nicolas Sarkozy a new freeze plan: no further expansion of Iran's enrichment activities and Iran's agreement to allow the IAEA to conduct a robust inspection program in exchange for an end to seeking new sanctions and a commitment by the West to provide Iran with French reactors. He told Sarkozy that the complete suspension of enrichment would "no longer be a meaningful request." Sarkozy agreed to support the proposal. ElBaradei left the meeting and called Aghazadeh to meet him in Vienna immediately. However, less than a day later, the French ambassador to the IAEA told ElBaradei not to convey the proposal to Iran until the French had provided "clarifications." Three days later, ElBaradei received a verbal message that the French would engage with Iran directly, not through his mediation. "Obviously, people around Sarkozy had convinced him that the Americans would react negatively to his agreeing to my proposal."[33] One American analyst advised me that Sarkozy's advisers were "at least as hard line as the Americans" and that they would not have let ElBaradei mediate a deal with Iran regardless of the American reaction.

Also in early 2008, the French foreign minister suggested that ElBaradei go public with his new proposal for "double suspension," with Iran suspending enrichment and the Security Council suspending efforts to seek new sanctions. ElBaradei preferred to call it a "pause" to avoid the word "suspension." The Russians, Chinese, and Europeans welcomed the proposal, and Larijani called ElBaradei requesting further clarification, but the Americans respectfully rejected the proposal by saying that the previous resolution was clear on what Iran needed to do.[34]

ElBaradei then whittled his four-principle plan of August 2006 down to just three stipulations:

- Explicit acknowledgement of Iran's nuclear rights including enrichment with the "time-out" recognized as simply a temporary measure to create time for an agreement.
- An Iranian commitment to cooperate with the IAEA in full transparency.
- A commitment by both sides to work toward the full normalization of relations between Iran and the West, including in the political, security, and economic fields.[35]

Iran gave positive signals toward the proposal, but John Sawers stepped in, calling ElBaradei to tell him that the United Kingdom would issue a statement based on his three principles and the idea of a double time-out but that it "intended to pursue a dual-track strategy and push for *another* [emphasis added] Security Council resolution, with additional 'limited' sanctions." ElBaradei informed Larijani, who was dismayed. Rice, meanwhile, made it clear in a conversation with ElBaradei that she was "not keen on the word *normalization*, nor on explicitly spelling out Iran's right to enrichment."[36]

Once more, ElBaradei's initiative for a peaceful resolution was scuttled by the Washington-London axis, with its rejection of the goal of normalization and Iran's enrichment rights and its intention to go forward with another sanctions resolution.

In March 2008, before an IAEA Board of Governors' meeting, the Swiss prepared a paper along the same lines as ElBaradei's proposal, but Washington strongly disapproved of the Swiss initiative to work with Iran toward a solution.[37] Instead, according to the Arms Control Association, even as the P5+1 spearheaded the adoption of a new sanctions resolution, the group "agreed to 'repackage' the June 2006 proposal in order to specify some of the benefits that they would offer Iran as part of a long-term agreement on its nuclear program and to better demonstrate the nature of those benefits to the Iranian public."[38]

SECURITY COUNCIL RESOLUTION 1803: FOURTEEN AYES AND ONE ABSTENTION

Resolution 1803, the third sanctions resolution, was adopted by the Security Council on March 3, 2008.[39] It passed by a vote of fourteen ayes, no nays, and one abstention. Although the pro-state media in Iran had expressed the hope that Libya, Indonesia, South Africa, and Vietnam would vote negatively on the new resolution, none of them did, and only Indonesia abstained.

Resolution 1803, adopted again within the framework of Chapter VII of the UN Charter, welcomed Iran's recent cooperation with the IAEA and resolution of some "outstanding issues" and noted that the P5+1 was ready to give more room to diplomatic efforts aimed at solving the crisis at hand. It stressed, however, the need for Tehran to suspend uranium enrichment. It also warned that it would continue its efforts until Iran complied with Resolutions 1696, 1737, and 1747, which required Tehran to suspend uranium enrichment and implement the Additional Protocol.

The most important part of Resolution 1803 was the introduction of land, air, and maritime sanctions similar to sanctions imposed on Iraq during the 1990s. For the first time, member states were authorized to inspect cargo bound for or arriving from Iran at their seaports and airports and to search Iran-bound ships and planes suspected of carrying forbidden materials.[40] The Security Council also called on member states to withhold from Iran all material, goods, equipment, and technology with dual uses that could be utilized in Iran's nuclear or missile programs.[41]

Resolution 1803 intensified sanctions by calling on all countries to exercise vigilance in entering into new commitments for publicly provided financial support for trade with Iran.[42] The Security Council also called on all countries "to exercise vigilance over the activities of financial institutions in their territories with all banks domiciled in Iran, in particular with Bank Melli and Bank Saderat." The Security Council requested "within 90 days a further report from the Director General of the IAEA on whether Iran has established full and sustained suspension of all activities mentioned" in Resolutions 1737, 1747, and 1803.

Since adoption of Resolution 1747 on March 24, 2007, the United States tried to bring about the consensus necessary for adoption of tougher sanctions against Iran, though it seemed that Washington was able neither to achieve that consensus nor to get the next resolution rapidly adopted. Iran's success in reaching an agreement with the IAEA on the "modality" option and resolution of outstanding issues had caused the UN Security Council members to oppose another resolution before ElBaradei offered his new report. They argued that further sanctions would be unnecessary while Iran was negotiating outstanding issues with the IAEA.

They were also concerned that further sanctions would dampen Iran's willingness to work with the IAEA: ElBaradei had noted that austerity imposed by the UN Security Council would interrupt Iran's cooperation with the IAEA. At the same time, the report produced by the United States intelligence community on the absence of a military nuclear program in Iran was a further surprise to White House officials and a boost to opponents of sanctions. The United States had focused sharply on the implementation of the UN Security Council resolutions when it was trying to encourage other countries to agree to more sanctions on the grounds of a nuclear weapon program in Iran and lack of transparency in Iran's nuclear activities.

The 2007 National Intelligence Estimate said that "we assess with high confidence until fall 2003 Iranian military entities were working under government direction to develop nuclear weapons," and "we assess with moderate confidence Tehran had not restarted its nuclear weapon program as of mid-2007." Nuclear policy during Khatami's presidency played an essential role in convincing the U.S. intelligence organizations that, at least after 2003, Iran's nuclear program and intention were for peaceful purposes and not nuclear weaponry. This was an important achievement of Khatami's nuclear policy. Ahmadinejad's nuclear team failed to take appropriate advantage of the achievement to convince the international community about the peacefulness of Iran's nuclear program.

The United States had started consultations with other members of the P5+1 on the adoption of a new resolution a few months after passage of the previous resolution in March 2007. Washington primarily aimed to get the agreement of the P5+1 on new sanctions and then press non-permanent members of the UN Security Council to vote for the next resolution. Libya, South Africa, Vietnam, and Indonesia were the four non-permanent members of the UN Security Council that had indicated their opposition to hasty measures on the part of the Security Council. South Africa announced that it would wait for ElBaradei's report before discussing a new resolution. Therefore, the resolution was postponed for a month.

After ElBaradei submitted his new report, the United States, which had prepared a draft resolution months earlier, asked non-permanent members to give their viewpoints. Reservations considered by Libya, South Africa, Vietnam, and Indonesia increased Washington's pressure on them. The French president, meanwhile, did his best to get the South African government aligned. Finally, Indonesia was the sole country to abstain.

The Eastern bloc and Non-Aligned Movement were expected from the very beginning to avoid opposing the United States and its allies either by being absent on the voting day, or by abstention. Most of those countries were Iran's friends, but because of mounting international pressure they decided to agree to the resolution. The United States reckoned on a positive vote from all members to prove that they were unanimous on Iran's nuclear program. Adoption of Resolution 1803 both rebutted the "looking to the East" policy and proved that Iran's strategic friends such as China, Russia, and the Non-Aligned Movement were not willing to pay a high price for supporting Tehran. It also showed that technical cooperation with the IAEA alone was not enough to prevent political decisions being made by the P5+1 on the nuclear case. Some believe that the example of Libya shows that full and proactive cooperation with the IAEA is the way to avoid negative political consequences. But Libya decided to have no nuclear program, relinquished its nuclear facility, and paved the way for NATO's invasion in 2011.

Nevertheless, resolution of six outstanding issues further weakened the U.S. position. ElBaradei was thus under tremendous pressure to keep the case on outstanding issues open, and in his February 2008 report called for more transparency on Iran's military nuclear studies (referred to as "alleged studies" by the Iranian media) as the sole key outstanding issue that remained unresolved.

Iran responded by rejecting the new resolution as "unjust." Foreign minister Mottaki charged several members of the UN Security Council with trying to politicize the nuclear case.[43] He also argued that, given Iran's inalienable right to peaceful use of nuclear energy, and the fact that all the IAEA reports found a lack of diversion from Iran's nuclear program,* "it is clearer than at any time before that reporting the case to the UN Security Council was a purely political measure and the Council's measure in adopting resolutions against Iran is illegitimate and in stark contrast to the UN Charter and established principles of international law."

This view was shared by ElBaradei, who resented the Security Council for passing such a resolution with little regard to his agency's findings or the ongoing Iranian cooperation:

> Iran agreed to address the weaponization issue under the work plan and our discussions began. . . . Then, two days before the Board was scheduled to review the report, the Security Council adopted their resolution [1803], with more sanctions on Iran. To put it another way, the council issued the verdict before the deliberation. I had in fact seen a draft resolution that did not even refer to my report. Not only was this a procedural fault, it gave the impression—perhaps accurately—that the council was taking action based on predetermined policy objectives rather than on facts.[44]

Mottaki and ElBaradei were right in concluding that the Iranian nuclear program was a political issue rather than just a legal one. Indeed, this was one of the major disputes between the Rouhani and Larijani nuclear teams: We (the Rouhani team) were emphasizing that Iran's nuclear file is more a political issue, while Larijani's team saw it from the beginning as merely a legal case needing to be resolved between Iran and the IAEA, without the involvement of countries from the EU3, Russia, and China. Mottaki's statement showed that finally they understood the case to be more political than legal.

Mahmoud Ahmadinejad,[45] for his part, announced on April 9, 2008, that Iran would increase the speed of uranium enrichment by a factor of

---

* Editor's note: Mottaki characteristically omitted the IAEA reports and resolutions that stated that the Agency was still unable to verify that Iran's nuclear program was exclusively peaceful.

five by introducing new centrifuges to its nuclear industries. Ahmadinejad also announced that Iran had installed 6,000 centrifuges and was bent on increasing their number to 50,000.[46] The West responded with skepticism to his remarks, with U.S. Secretary of State Condoleezza Rice noting that Ahmadinejad's remarks were not believable.[47] Ahmadinejad officially announced five days later that Iran was ready to share its nuclear technology with all countries.[48] Ahmadinejad's remarks, which were made in a meeting with the Philippine foreign minister, Alberto Gatmaitan Rómulo, revealed the flip side of the policy pursued as "invasive and non-passive" by the ninth government's supporters but considered "provocative" by its critics.

Olli Heinonen, IAEA deputy director for safeguards, who was termed a "spy" and "CIA agent" by the mainline press in Iran, arrived in Tehran on April 22, 2008.[49] Following Heinonen's negotiations in Tehran, the secretariat of the IAEA issued a statement announcing new agreements with Iran. Western media reported that Heinonen and Iran had reached agreement on major points referred to in ElBaradei's February report as to the relationship of Iran's nuclear program with its missile program, and military tests on highly explosive materials. Heinonen had reached similar agreements with the Iranian officials a year earlier, which led to the IAEA announcement that a number of outstanding issues had been resolved. ElBaradei later raised other issues that the IAEA considered outstanding.

In the meantime, Iran offered a new package to UN Secretary General Ban Ki-moon and foreign ministers of the P5+1 aimed at achieving a "lasting and comprehensive" agreement with the West, including on the nuclear issue.[50] The package contained no new proposal. Mottaki, however, wrote a letter to the P5+1 stating that Iran had prepared a package of political, security, economic, and nuclear proposals after extensive studies, to be offered to the P5+1. The Iranian minister added that the package was based on justice and mutual respect and could form a basis for overarching negotiations. He described the package as an exceptional opportunity for cooperation and emphasized that Iran's approach to the package was a strategic one.

The package stated: "The Islamic Republic of Iran is ready to start serious and targeted negotiations to produce a tangible result. The negotiations can be evaluated after a specific period of time (a maximum of 6 months) to decide about its continuation." The content of the package, however, was vague. The first paragraph, for example, suggested that Iran and the P5+1 talk about protecting "the right and dignity of human beings and respect for the cultures of other nations."

As for the nuclear case, Tehran announced that it was ready "in a comprehensive manner and as an active and influential member of the NPT and the IAEA" to consider the following issues:

- Acquisition of further assurance about the non-diversion of the nuclear activities of different countries.
- Establishment of enrichment and nuclear fuel production consortia in different parts of the world, including Iran.
- Cooperation to provide access and utilize peaceful nuclear technology and facilitate its use by all states.
- Nuclear disarmament and establishment of a follow-up committee for all states.
- Improved supervision by the IAEA over the nuclear activity of different states.
- Cooperation on nuclear safety and physical protection for all states.
- Efforts to promote export control of nuclear materials and equipment for all states.

ELBARADEI'S REPORT: BACK TO SEPTEMBER 2003

The general reaction of the West, especially the United States, to Iran's proposed package was cold. The atmosphere grew more hostile still with a new report issued by the IAEA director general on May 26, 2008, in which ElBaradei noted that since the previous report, Iran had continued to operate the original 3,000 centrifuges and that installation work had continued on four other sets of cascades as well.

Unsurprisingly, after its cooperation on the work plan had done nothing to prevent UN Security Council Resolution 1803, Iran reduced its cooperation on the weaponization issue to a minimum. This had only encouraged further suspicions. A special section of the report was dedicated to "Possible Military Dimensions" of Iran's nuclear program, in which ElBaradei detailed military studies that could possibly be used in the development of nuclear weaponry:

One aspect of the alleged studies refers to the conversion of uranium dioxide to UF_4, also known as green salt. A second aspect concerns the development and testing of high voltage detonator firing equipment and exploding bridgewire (EBW) detonators including, inter alia, the simultaneous firing of multiple EBW detonators; an underground testing arrangement; and the testing of at least one full scale hemispherical, converging, explosively driven shock system that could be applicable to an implosion-type nuclear device. A third aspect of the studies concerns development work alleged to have been performed to redesign the inner cone of the Shahab-3 missile re-entry vehicle to accommodate a nuclear warhead.[51]

ElBaradei added, however, "It should be noted that the Agency currently has no information—apart from the uranium metal document—on the actual design or manufacture by Iran of nuclear material components of a nuclear weapon or of certain other key components, such as initiators, or on related nuclear physics studies." He said that the IAEA had found no evidence to prove the use of nuclear materials in the alleged studies. Even so, he pressed for clarification of the roles of certain military institutes in Iran's nuclear program and emphasized that the IAEA could not verify non-diversion to the production of nuclear material from possible undeclared activities in Iran's nuclear program.

Following the publication of ElBaradei's report, in which he made frequent use of such phrases as "military nuclear studies of Iran" and "nuclear weapon," Iran's representative to the IAEA, Ali Asghar Soltanieh, declared that documents provided to the IAEA by the United States on purported Iranian military nuclear activities were forged. In an interview in Vienna, Soltanieh said that the contents of those documents were fabricated by the CIA and that "they should have done a better job."[52]

Olli Heinonen, the deputy director general of the IAEA, then took part in a closed-door session to present an unprecedented report in which he stated that documents delivered to the IAEA on Iran's military nuclear studies had been provided by ten countries. The new information compiled by the IAEA triggered renewed hostility and suspicions among Western countries about Iran's interest in nuclear weapons. Gregory Schulte, the U.S. representative to the IAEA, said that as the director general reports, these various activities are "relevant to nuclear weapon research and development."[53]

A few days after ElBaradei's report referring to military nuclear studies in Iran, the American media claimed for the first time that Iran might have acquired blueprints for a nuclear bomb on the black market. David Albright, head of the Institute for Science and International Security, said the A. Q. Khan network might have supplied Tehran or Pyongyang with the more advanced and much more useful bomb blueprints that had just surfaced. "They both faced struggles in building a nuclear warhead small enough to fit atop their ballistic missiles, and these designs were for a warhead that would fit. These would have been ideal for two of Khan's other major customers, Iran and North Korea."[54] Albright's article followed allegations by the *Guardian* a week earlier to the effect that nuclear bomb blueprints and manuals on how to manufacture weapons-grade uranium for warheads may have been sold or circulated on the international black market by a Swiss expert.[55]

The revelations led to renewed speculation about a possible military attack on Iran, with threats to this effect from Israel, the United States, and even EU members such as France and Italy. ElBaradei responded to these rumors by threatening to resign his post in the event of such an attack.[56]

IRAN'S EIGHTH MAJLES: A NEW START FOR THE NUCLEAR CASE?

The inauguration of the eighth Parliament since the Islamic Revolution in May 2008 with Ali Larijani as its Speaker raised expectations that Ahmadinejad's control over nuclear policy would be counterbalanced and that pragmatic forces would once more take the initiative. Given Larijani's diplomatic background, some analysts maintained that the focus of Iran's Majles would gradually shift away from domestic policy toward international affairs. In his first address as Majles Speaker, Larijani criticized the "mysterious diplomatic passing of Iran's nuclear case between the IAEA and 5+1" and officially announced that the Iranian Parliament would not "tolerate that approach and will determine new limits for cooperation with IAEA."[57] Clearly, Larijani intended for Parliament to take a more activist role in the issue.

This was significant because all action taken by the preceding (2004–2008) Majles on the nuclear issue followed the lead of the executive and was largely limited to emotional reactions to international censure of Iran. An example was a vote in November 2005 that called for the termination of voluntary suspension of uranium enrichment if the case should be referred to the UN Security Council.

After the election of the eighth Parliament, more moderate figures close to Ayatollah Hashemi Rafsanjani expressed their unhappiness about the current nuclear policy more openly. Ali Akbar Velayati, a former foreign minister and pragmatic adviser to the supreme leader, made conciliatory remarks. Rafsanjani drew the ire of the pro-Ahmadinejad media by emphasizing the need to negotiate with the West and to avoid adventurism. The hard-line newspaper *Kayhan*'s reaction to Velayati's remarks was that,

> News agencies and some American and European officials have distorted Dr. Velayati's remarks about his criticism of radical figures and . . . have taken his criticism to be targeted at President Ahmadinejad. They have tried to imply that his stance, as senior adviser to the Supreme Leader for international affairs, is different from the ongoing nuclear policies and have reached the erroneous conclusion that Ahmadinejad is to be removed from the nuclear case! Despite their illusion, Dr. Velayati has noted in his article, which has been sent to three western newspapers, and also in an interview with *Jomhouri Eslami* newspaper, that it is impossible for Iran to suspend uranium enrichment and that the issue is not open to negotiation.[58]

The supreme leader finally intervened in July 2008. He issued a clear statement that the sole authority handling the nuclear case was the Supreme National Security Council and its president, that is, Mahmoud Ahmadinejad, and that the National Security Council's policies were based on the unanimous conclusions reached by all branches of the government.[59]

The behind-the-scenes dispute between pragmatic and radical politicians took place at a time when Tehran and the West were exchanging diplomatic package proposals. In early 2008, Mahmoud Ahmadinejad rejected in advance a new incentive package being prepared by the P5+1, saying during an interview with a Japanese news agency that Tehran would negotiate only with the IAEA.[60] His remarks did not dissuade the P5+1 from presenting its package anyway; Javier Solana conveyed it to Mottaki on July 15, 2008, and it was simultaneously made available to the media.

The following letter to Iran introduced the new P5+1 proposal:

We, the Foreign Ministers of China, France, Germany, Russia, the United Kingdom and the United States of America, joined in this endeavor by the European Union High Representative for the Common Foreign and Security Policy, are convinced that it is possible to change the present state of affairs. We hope that Iran's leaders share the same ambition. In June 2006, we set out an ambitious proposal for a broad-based negotiation. We offered to work with Iran on a modern nuclear energy program, with a guaranteed fuel supply. We were also prepared to discuss political and economic issues, as well as issues regarding regional security. These proposals were carefully considered and designed to address Iran's essential interests and those of the international community. Today, bearing in mind the provisions of UN Security Council resolution 1803, we restate our offer to address constructively these important concerns and interests. Our proposals are attached to this letter. Iran is of course free to suggest its own proposals. Formal negotiations can start as soon as Iran's enrichment-related and reprocessing activities are suspended. We want to be clear that we recognize Iran's rights under the international treaties to which it is a signatory. We fully understand the importance of a guaranteed fuel supply for a civil nuclear program. We have supported the Bushehr facility. But with rights come responsibilities, in particular to restore the confidence of the international community in Iran's program. We are ready to work with Iran in order to find a way to address Iran's needs and the international community's concerns, and reiterate that once the confidence of the international community in the exclusively peaceful nature of your nuclear program is restored, it will be treated in the same manner as that of any Non-Nuclear Weapon State party to the Non Proliferation Treaty. We ask you to consider this letter and our proposals carefully and hope for an early response. The proposals we have made offer substantial opportunities for political, security and economic benefits to Iran and the region. There is a sovereign choice for Iran to make. We hope that you will respond positively; this will increase stability and enhance prosperity for all our people.

The P5+1 offered to cooperate with Iran in numerous fields if the country fulfilled its commitment to suspend enrichment and to comply with resolutions adopted by the IAEA Board of Governors and the UN Security

Council. Incentives offered included reaffirmation of Iran's peaceful nuclear rights, assistance in nuclear technology and infrastructure development, fuel supply and disposal guarantees, support for Iran's greater integration into the global economy, cooperation with Iran's aviation sector, and the promotion of further dialogue to improve political relations with Iran, as well as peace and stability in the Middle East.

Although the new package lacked fundamental changes, it included both positive and negative points from an Iranian perspective. The package did not mention the alleged studies into nuclear weaponry cited by ElBaradei's previous report, suggesting that they were of little consequence to political negotiations.* It was in fact similar to the packages offered in August 2005 and July 2006. It seemed that the P5+1 had addressed the new package to the Iranian people. Publication of the complete text of the package by Solana in a news conference with Manouchehr Mottaki proved that the West was appealing to Iranian public opinion.

There was a difference between the letter written to the Iranian foreign minister by the P5+1 and the package that was offered. The letter read, "Formal negotiations can start as soon as Iran's enrichment-related and reprocessing activities are suspended." In the package, however, the suspension was mentioned as a legally binding request from the Security Council (in line with Resolution 1803), which from an Iranian point of view is inconsistent.

The new package lacked major changes, but it opened up the possibility for further talks by putting more emphasis on common ground between the two sides. Mechanisms proposed through the package could have made it possible for Tehran to ask for concessions from the P5+1.

The package was quickly overtaken by other events, however, and forgotten. Just one week after presentation of the package, the EU ratified new sanctions against Iran, which included a freeze on Melli Bank's assets in Europe. In response, Majles Speaker Ali Larijani warned the West, "The end of this game will unravel soon."[61] Concurrent with Larijani's warning, Iran's hard-line media launched a propaganda drive calling for the discontinuation of negotiations with the European Union and urged the government to withdraw from the NPT.[62] They argued that Iran had

---

* Editor's note: The letter from Solana referred importantly to the need to restore confidence in the exclusively peaceful nature of Iran's nuclear program. This, of course, included the alleged weaponization studies, even if the letter did not specifically mention them.

shown goodwill in its negotiations with Solana but that the European side was still pressuring Iran by all means available and was adopting a stance closer to that of the United States.

In another development, a statement signed by 70 percent of the members of Parliament warned the P5+1 that further sanctions would just make Iran more resolute in defending its rights. Their statement read,

> We, representatives of the eighth term of the Islamic Consultative Assembly, voice our all-out support for national determination and the policies adopted by the Supreme National Security Council and we think that negotiations with 5+1 are a good opportunity for its member states to solve the existing problems. They should know that adopting new resolutions will get them nowhere, but will make us determined to defend the rights of our nation and consider other measures like halting the implementation of the Additional Protocol.[63]

GENEVA TALKS AND THE LOSS OF ALL HOPE

Saeed Jalili, Tehran's chief nuclear negotiator, and the P5+1 resumed negotiations in mid-summer 2008. The talks were noteworthy due to the presence of U.S. Undersecretary of State William J. Burns even as they raised new hopes, which were unfortunately lost before long.[64] Burns was the first American official to take part in nuclear negotiations with Iran, though according to well-informed French and American experts, Jalili downplayed the significance of this development. According to an American expert, Burns was introduced at the meeting and stated that the United States welcomed a full dialogue with Iran on a range of issues, only for Jalili to respond that Iran had always assumed the Americans were at the table and to dismiss the idea that the shift in U.S. policy presented significant new opportunities.

With the unprecedented participation by the United States in talks seemingly yielding few results, Jalili presented a non-paper in which he proposed a new modality for comprehensive talks between Iran and the P5+1 to be composed of the following three stages:[65]

Stage 1: Preliminary Talks

In this phase, negotiations would continue for a maximum of three rounds between Jalili and Solana, with Solana representing the P5+1. The parties would reach an agreement on modality and the next phase of negotiations, including its timetable and draft agenda. Meanwhile, committees would be established with clear agendas.

Stage 2: Initiation of Negotiations

After the completion of the first phase, negotiations would begin at the ministerial level. In this stage, the seven participating countries would meet the following conditions:

- The P5+1 would avoid any unilateral or multilateral measures or enforcement of new sanctions against Iran, either independently or through the UN Security Council. The group would even nullify certain unilateral measures that had already been taken by member countries against Iran.
- Iran would continue to cooperate with the IAEA.
- At least four sessions of negotiations would be held and attended by Solana; the foreign ministers of P5+1; Jalili, Iran's foreign minister; and the head of the Atomic Energy Organization of Iran.
- The following principles would govern negotiations:
- Participants would avoid raising any point that would prevent progress in negotiations.
- Discussions would focus on common grounds.
- All parties would agree on the schedule, agenda, and priorities of the negotiations.
- Negotiations would end with the release of a joint statement explaining agreements achieved by parties to the negotiations.
- Following the statement, three specialized committees would finalize those agreements.

Stage 3: Negotiations

After the completion of the second stage of negotiations, the P5+1 would reverse existing Security Council sanctions and resolutions. At the beginning of the third stage, all seven countries would prepare and sign a comprehensive agreement for cooperation in economic, political, regional, international, nuclear, energy, security, and defense fields. After achieving a comprehensive agreement, Iran's nuclear issue would be taken out of the Security Council's agenda and returned to the IAEA to be addressed on an ordinary basis.

Iran's non-paper stressed that the negotiations would be "based on the commonalities of the two packages" that Iran had presented in May and that the P5+1 had presented in June. Western governments, however, did not take Saeed Jalili's written message seriously, and the international media treated it as something of a joke.[66] Numerous typographical errors in Jalili's message preoccupied some Western media outlets to the extent that they completely forgot about the prospect it raised for negotiations.[67] One American analyst told me that the reason that the proposal was ridiculed was not just its typographical errors, but also its one-sidedness, which was viewed as absurd by the other diplomats at the meeting.

Iran's nuclear dossier had come a long way since 2003. Iran's stepped-up cooperation with the IAEA, long negotiations with the Europeans, the American National Intelligence Estimate of November 2007, and the 2007 modality agreement all served to lay the groundwork for new agreements. The presence of William J. Burns at the P5+1 talks also provided an exceptional opportunity. The Americans pursued three goals through Burns's attendance:

- To show agreement with the other members of the P5+1.
- To prove that they supported diplomatic means.
- To convince the other P5+1 countries that if negotiations failed, there would be no alternative to more sanctions.

The ninth Iranian government maintained that the presence of Burns in Geneva was a sign that the United States was withdrawing from its past positions. Critics warned that U.S. involvement could either pave the way for an agreement or lay the grounds for further measures by the UN Security Council. In a speech in Mashhad, however, Ahmadinejad rejected any moves to even slow down the expansion of Iran's enrichment capacity: "Those who claimed Iran should negotiate for at least 10 years to get

20 enrichment cascades running have now given up after Iran launched hundreds and thousands of centrifuges and are now calling on us not to go beyond the current point in our nuclear activities."[68]

The Western media depicted Ahmadinejad's speech in Mashhad as an announcement that Iran had commissioned thousands of centrifuges in recent months. Global press reports along these lines, and a lack of denial on the part of Iran, initiated a new wave of international disapproval. The reports raised the possibility that Iran's claim was exaggerated as an act of defiance to the great powers and speculated that the Iranian president's statement might cause the Geneva talks to fail, irking European countries and the United States. Meanwhile, Agence France-Presse quoted the Iranian radio and the AP quoted the Fars News Agency as saying that once in Mashhad, Ahmadinejad had announced the launch of 5,000 to 6,000 centrifuges.[69] The website of USA Today emphasized that the Iranian president's remarks about commissioning 6,000 centrifuges shattered hopes and would raise tension in the region. ABC News also opined that there was no alternative but to increase sanctions against Tehran.[70] Fox News claimed that launching 6,000 centrifuges would mean that Iran would produce nuclear weapons sooner than predicted by Israeli and American intelligence services.[71] Such an atmosphere prompted Rafsanjani, the chairman of the Expediency Council, to call for more caution on the part of the Iranian nuclear officials.[72]

U.S. participation in negotiations with Iran raised hopes about both nuclear negotiations and Iran-U.S. bilateral relations. Oil prices in international markets fell from $140 per barrel to $120, but Javier Solana expressed his concern in an interview about the lack of any response from Iran's top nuclear negotiator to the P5+1 package proposed in July. He added that the Europeans expected an outright yes or no to the package.

Saeed Jalili was circumspect. He said that weaving an Iranian carpet took a long time because human taste is mingled with art and beautiful designs and that the end result is both appealing to customers' tastes and durable. Jalili was sending a message to Western countries, which were anxious about lengthy negotiations, that although negotiations might take a long time, the end result would be rewarding and lasting. Some Western circles maintained that Iran was just buying time. Some were fine with that because long negotiations were in the interests of both sides.

In 2003, Iran wanted tight time limits on talks about suspension of enrichment while it was eager for protracted talks for broader cooperation. But this time there were two other reasons that Iran wanted protracted talks. First, given the technical and legal complexities of the case, Iran was not able to respond on short notice to all ambiguities surrounding a program that had been started long before the Islamic Revolution. Some of the past activities cited by the IAEA occurred so far in the past that current Atomic Energy Organization officials did not know about them or have records detailing them readily available. Files on these activities were in many cases not well organized, meaning that researching them took a long time.

Second, Iran and the United States both had an interest in protracted negotiations. Iran needed to buy time to increase the credibility of its claims while enriching uranium, as well as time to undermine the credibility of claims by the United States and Israel about a military dimension to Iran's nuclear program. And as a top European diplomat involved in Iran's nuclear issue told me,

> I believe that P5+1 handling of the nuclear issue has been bedeviled by U.S. reluctance to give sufficient weight to accumulating evidence that since 2003 Iran has decided to respect its NPT obligation to refrain from manufacturing or otherwise acquiring nuclear weapons. This misjudgment freezes the P5+1 into positions which preclude any movement towards the areas of mutual interest with Iran that, I am convinced, exist.

One may ask how, if Iran's nuclear negotiators were not fully informed about their country's nuclear activities, they could reject American and Israeli claims as not credible. Despite the fact that we were not informed about detailed technical aspects of Iran's past and present nuclear activities, we were confident that none of the previous Iranian administrations since the revolution had pursued military nuclear activities. We trusted that the supreme leader's *fatwa* banning the use or production of nuclear weapons as ensuring this, and hence we could confidently reject foreign claims that Iran was secretly pursuing nuclear weapons.[73]

Some Western scholars question whether this *fatwa* has ever been published, while in the supreme leader's official message to the International Conference on Nuclear Disarmament, he said:

We believe that besides nuclear weapons, other types of weapons of mass destruction such as chemical and biological weapons also pose a serious threat to humanity. The Iranian nation which is itself a victim of chemical weapons [in the war with Iraq] feels more than any other nation the danger that is caused by the production and stockpiling of such weapons and is prepared to make use of all its facilities to counter such threats. We consider the use of such weapons as *haram* [unlawful, forbidden] and believe that it is everyone's duty to make efforts to secure humanity against this great disaster.[74]

Iran's permanent envoy to the United Nations, Mohammad Khazaee, registered that the text of the Ayatollah Khamenei's message as an official UN document.[75]

Indeed, although in 2003, Washington had claimed that Iran was only three to five years away from having a nuclear bomb, the 2007 American National Intelligence Estimate indicated that Iran was a long way from building a nuclear bomb and that there had been little evidence, at least since 2003, to suggest that Iran was involved in a military nuclear program.[76] Some intelligence entities, and especially Israel, did not agree with the National Intelligence Estimate, however, and suggested that the nuclear program was just a cover for a military program. On the other side, China, Russia, and Non-Aligned Movement countries rejected alarmist claims and called for the continuation of negotiations until a peaceful solution was found.

In summary, Iran consistently insisted on the peacefulness of its nuclear program and was prepared to give guarantees to this effect. In his first month in office, Ahmadinejad even made positive gestures in a speech to the UN General Assembly toward a proposal for the establishment of a nuclear fuel consortium with the United States and Europe to build confidence in Iran's uranium enrichment activities. The United States and Israel were unpersuaded of Iran's intent and continued trying to convince the world that Iran presented an imminent nuclear threat.

In this context, and given the redline that had previously existed for Iran's elected leadership against negotiating directly with the United States, the Ahmadinejad government stunned the world by indicating its readiness to engage in official negotiations with the United States on the nuclear issue, preferably out of the framework of the P5+1. Although the Americans had previously announced through a high-ranking official that suspension of uranium enrichment was a precondition for any form of negotiation with Iran, this demand was gradually forgotten and the United States had sent William J. Burns, a high-ranking State Department official, to attend Larijani-Solana negotiations in Geneva.

There were many reasons behind Washington's withdrawal from its formal position, some of which have already been discussed. An important point is the role played by the Democratic Party and Barack Obama's stand on the wars in Iraq and Afghanistan, as well as his introduction of an "engagement" policy with Iran during the 2008 presidential campaign. This may have spurred George Bush to send Burns to attend the negotiations. Also, a plan to open an American interests section in the Swiss Embassy in Tehran was leaked to the media.[77] Tehran's immediate positive reaction further tempted the White House to take tentative steps toward engagement.

In the summer of 2008, Iranian analysts were suggesting that Europe had changed its position toward the nuclear case after seeing Washington's newfound conciliatory stance on Iran. They believed that Solana expected Iran to take two important steps: first, to avoid increasing the number of operational centrifuges and, second, not to enrich uranium above 4.8 percent. This raised new hope about direct talks between Tehran and Washington.

Under President Khatami and through negotiations by the former nuclear team, Iran had managed to divide Europe's positions from those of Washington and this had enraged the United States. Ahmadinejad's policy, which was supported by the supreme leader, could have done the same if carried out in the correct way, steering away from radical rhetoric and propaganda. However, the lack of a realistic proposal from the Iranian side and the unreadiness of the P5+1 to recognize Iran's inalienable nuclear rights, including to enrichment, and enter into a comprehensive package on the nuclear issue led to the ultimate convergence between the U.S. and European positions. Some experts maintain that the Security Council has acknowledged that once confidence is restored that Iran's nuclear activities are exclusively peaceful, Iran would be allowed to resume enrichment with negotiated guarantees of its peaceful purposes. Therefore, the decisive issue remains whether Iran and others could agree on what would be objective guarantees that Iran's ongoing enrichment would not lead to a military application of nuclear energy. But the fact is that the Security Council resolution is not transparent on the enrichment issue and that neither the EU3 nor the P5+1 has ever negotiated with Iranians in such a transparent way. Since 2003, they always have declined to clarify the rights for enrichment during nuclear negotiations.

ELBARADEI'S SEPTEMBER 2008 REPORT

ElBaradei circulated a new report on September 15, 2008. His previous report, issued in May 2008, had paved the way for the adoption of a new sanctions resolution, and the new report followed the same lines.

The report was shorter than its predecessors and contained almost no new points. It rehashed concerns about military studies and requested further information from Iran:

> There remain a number of outstanding issues, identified in the Director General's last report to the Board, which give rise to concerns about possible military dimensions to Iran's nuclear program. As indicated in the Director General's report, for the Agency to be able to address these concerns and provide assurances regarding the absence of undeclared nuclear material and activities in Iran, it is essential that Iran, inter alia, provide the information and access necessary to resolve questions related to the alleged studies. . . .[78]

One month later, in October 2008, the secretariat of the Supreme National Security Council published the complete text of Saeed Jalili's letter to the P5+1, which included Tehran's complaints against its negotiating partners. The two-page letter accused the P5+1 of bullying instead of rationally addressing ambiguities and called on the West not to pass up further opportunities to find common ground.[79] The salient point about the letter was the use of "could have" instead of "can" when Jalili wrote, "Undoubtedly, welcoming this proposal, taking advantage of time and opportunities, and avoiding of illogical behavior *could have* [emphasis added] provided good grounds for constructive cooperation." The use of the past tense suggested to international observers that Jalili's letter was in fact meant to declare the Geneva negotiations a failure.

The EU and the U.S. State Department downplayed the letter's significance. EU foreign policy chief Javier Solana emphasized that the EU's policy, which focused on the continuation of negotiations, would not change. He added that Jalili's letter was "just a letter."[80]

FAILURE TO GAIN SECURITY COUNCIL MEMBERSHIP: MESSAGES AND CONSEQUENCES

Concurrent with Jalili's letter, President Ahmadinejad launched a new project for Iran to become a non-permanent member of the UN Security Council during 2009–2010. It had been fifty-three years since Iran held a seat on the Security Council.

With Indonesia leaving its non-permanent seat, Tehran entered into a competition with Tokyo to take Jakarta's place. This came at a time when the last sanction resolution, which Iran considered an illegal measure, had just been adopted by the UN Security Council. The Security Council had also issued a statement in December 2005 about Mahmoud Ahmadinejad's remarks on the elimination of Israel and questioning the reality of the Holocaust.[81] The attempt, then, to gain membership in an international body whose resolutions were called "worthless scraps of paper" by the Iranian president and was called a place for "the world's arrogant and bullying powers"[82] was very ambitious, to put it mildly.

In a meeting with the ambassadors of 57 Muslim countries at the United Nations in June 2008, Manouchehr Mottaki asked for support for Iran's accession to the Security Council as the sole Muslim candidate from Asia. He also addressed the closing ceremony of the fifteenth meeting of foreign ministers of Non-Aligned Movement by saying, "Iran is a candidate [for] membership at the Security Council; please support it."[83]

Despite these diplomatic and public relations efforts, only 32 countries voted for Iran's membership. Japan, with 158 votes, won the Security Council seat for the tenth time. Ahmadinejad had predicted that Muslim and Non-Aligned Movement countries would vote for Iran, but few of those countries ultimately supported Iran. Support by only 32 of 192 countries highlighted Iran's international isolation.[84]

Why did Iran insist on seeking UN Security Council membership in the face of a competitor as prominent as Japan, thus demonstrating to its enemies its international isolation? Despite frequent instances of anti-Iran consensus in the IAEA and the UN Security Council, Ahmadinejad did not believe that Iran was truly isolated internationally and argued that only Israel and a few Western countries were against Iran's nuclear program. Many analysts maintain that Ahmadinejad really believed his own claims that 150 countries supported Iran's nuclear program and that his rhetoric was not just propaganda. He believed that member states of the Organization of the Islamic Conference and Non-Aligned Movement, along with the Group of 77,[85] supported Iran's nuclear program. The result, therefore, was quite shocking to him.

The vote raised the question of whether Ahmadinejad would review his foreign policy approach and correct his perception of the international system. Later developments showed, however, that instead of coming to grips with reality, he chose to slam the UN structure by calling it "unjust." In other words, Ahmadinejad and his aides believed that Iran's failure to be elected to the UN Security Council was simply proof of the unjust nature of the international system, rather than of Iran's unpopularity. And he repeated his denigration of UN Security Council resolutions as nothing but "worthless scraps of paper."[86]

AHMADINEJAD ADDRESSES THE GENERAL ASSEMBLY, PAVING THE WAY FOR RESOLUTION 1835

When the UN General Assembly convened in 2008, Ahmadinejad insisted that he deliver his fourth address there. In his address, Ahmadinejad showed no sign of flexibility but appeared as a religious preacher who called on all countries to worship God and return to the right path of God and his prophets in order to realize justice.[87] He continued to describe the Israelis as "criminal and occupationist Zionists." He said:

[In] Palestine, 60 years of carnage and invasion is still ongoing at the hands of some criminal and occupying Zionists. They have forged a regime through collecting people from various parts of the world and bringing them to other people's land by displacing, detaining, and killing the true owners of that land. With advance notice, they invade, assassinate, and maintain food and medicine blockades, while some hegemonic and bullying powers support them. The Security Council cannot do anything and sometimes, under pressure from a few bullying powers, even paves the way for supporting these Zionist murderers. It is natural that some UN resolutions that have addressed the plight of the Palestinian people have been relegated to the archives unnoticed.[88]

He bitterly attacked the United States and European powers, emphasizing that Israel was close to final collapse and that there was no way to save it from the quagmire it had created with its patrons. He stressed his past positions on the nuclear case and, while downplaying the importance of the UN Security Council resolutions, took the Security Council to task.

Ahmadinejad's harshly worded speech paved the way for the adoption of another sanctions resolution and helped once again to unify the P5+1. On September 28, 2008, five days after Ahmadinejad's address to the General Assembly, the UN Security Council adopted a fourth sanctions resolution. All fifteen members of the UN Security Council voted for the resolution without serious opposition or even abstention. Even Indonesia, which had abstained from voting for Resolution 1805, supported Resolution 1835.[89]

Zalmay Khalilzad, then U.S. ambassador to the United Nations, welcomed adoption of the resolution. He said it proved international unity over Iran's nuclear issue and showed that Iran should work with the international community.[90] Vitaly Churkin, the Russian ambassador to the United Nations, also stated that the new resolution proved that the world was willing to find a diplomatic solution to the nuclear case, saying that in practical terms it obviated the need for a military option against Iran.[91] U.S. Secretary of State Condoleezza Rice also said that the resolution proved the unity of P5+1 member states following differences with Russia over Georgia.[92] The German foreign minister, Frank-Walter Steinmeier, lauded the resolution by saying that if such a resolution had not been adopted, "the Iranian government would have been more than happy."

Resolution 1835 can be analyzed from other points of view as well. By avoiding the introduction of new sanctions, the UN Security Council showed that it hoped to reach a negotiated solution through interaction with Iran. This line had already been followed by such countries as Russia, China, and even Germany. The Iranian delegation, however, announced that the resolution was unjust and not constructive, adding that Iran was determined to pursue its inalienable right to peaceful use of nuclear technology.[93] The secretary of the Supreme National Security Council described the new resolution as more of a statement than a resolution.[94]

Iran's government also issued a statement describing its nuclear program as peaceful, and characterizing the UN Security Council's involvement as unjust and politically motivated. Tehran had no plans to withdraw from its positions.[95]

RESOLUTION 1835: NEW DOUBTS ABOUT THE NINTH GOVERNMENT'S FOREIGN POLICY

Although Resolution 1835 cast new doubts on the basis of the ninth government's aggressive foreign policy, every address by Ahmadinejad brought the situation back to the starting point. With his speeches having provoked three anti-Iranian resolutions, some Iranian analysts wondered whether he was helping the national interests of Iran.

Among other questions, Resolutions 1803 and 1835 raised questions about the benefits of reliance on Russia. In the past one hundred and fifty years, Russia had been the only country to try to annex large parts of Iran. After World War II, Russia kept some of its forces in Iran's Azerbaijan province and even appointed a governor for them. This drew a strong re-action from the United States and the United Kingdom, forcing Russia to withdraw its troops. Moscow had tried throughout the nuclear crisis to pose as a friend to Iran, but at the same time it had supported all UN Security Council resolutions and charged Iran dearly for the contracts, cooperation, and activities under way for the completion of the Bushehr nuclear power plant and the air defense systems it had agreed to provide. It therefore was natural for critics to slam Ahmadinejad for his overreliance on Russia. The Russian foreign minister, however, denied that his country had reached a deal with the West over Iran.[96]

Past stances taken by Russia on Iran suggested that the Russians might ask for more concessions from Tehran in return for blocking the adoption of more punishing resolutions. This possibility certainly occurred to some high-ranking Iranian officials. It was not clear, however, how seriously the ninth government's foreign policymakers took such warnings. In fact, there is ample evidence to show that the ninth government did *not* take the experts' views seriously and—despite changes in its nuclear negotiating team—continued to follow its previous policies.

CHAPTER NINE

U.S. ENGAGEMENT

AHMADINEJAD, OBAMA, AND THE IRANIAN NUCLEAR FILE

From September 27, 2008, when the Security Council voted to issue Resolution 1835 against the Islamic Republic, until approximately twenty months later, that is, June 9, 2010, when Resolution 1929 was issued, the file on Iran's nuclear activities for a variety of reasons fell into a kind of diplomatic, political, and even security slump.

Before Resolution 1835, the UN Security Council and the P5+1 group had issued a statement and four resolutions (1696, 1737, 1747, 1803) against Iran and had adopted sanctions against it. With this in mind, some predicted, based on comparative models, especially North Korea, that the pace of resolutions against Iran after Resolution 1835 would accelerate and even herald sanctions on Iran's sales of crude oil. Other observers and veteran diplomats, with an eye to upcoming presidential elections in both the United States and Iran, argued that Resolution 1835 would be the starting point of a new and relatively lengthy era. In fact, Resolution 1835 was followed by a period of paralysis, confusion of the Western world, diplomatic and political stagnation, and a kind of passivity in the Europe-America bloc.

This period of paralysis was full of, among other things, rhetoric, unproductive negotiations, changing tactics, meaningless plans and contingencies, and agreements that failed from the start. Despite this, however, there were also important developments, including the overhaul by the newly elected Obama administration of extreme approaches toward Iran, rapprochement between Moscow and Washington, greater cohesion in the European Union, some nuclear and military advances by the Islamic Republic, and new political maneuvers by Tehran. The outcome, whether intended or unintended, was that the Obama administration by March 2010 found itself in the same position vis-à-vis Iran in which George W. Bush had been in March 2008. Some Obama administration officials, of course, reject this judgment.

The most important message of UN Security Council Resolution 1835 was its reaffirmation of Resolutions 1696 (July 31, 2006), 1737 (December 23, 2006), 1747 (March 24, 2007), and 1803 (March 3, 2008). Its unwelcome message for Tehran was that the Western world had still not found a strategy to deal with Iran other than "diplomacy together with resolutions."

Resolution 1835 can be called a kind of joint international message to Iran after the development of a new state of affairs in the Iranian nuclear file. It was a state of affairs in which factors such as America's invasion of Iraq and Afghanistan, the presidential election of the United States and the emergence of the Barack Obama phenomenon, Israel's attack on Gaza, the dramatic and unprecedented rise in the price of oil, the spreading of the pervasive economic crisis on the international level, and of course other factors major and minor allowed Tehran to face the international community from a position of far greater strength and with more room to maneuver. Iran's internal political dynamics, however, did not foster confidence that the government could take advantage of the convergence of these events.

The failure of the Western bloc, especially the United States, to expand new sanctions against Iran encouraged some in Tehran to believe that Tehran could, without worrying about an effective and serious response from the international community, develop its nuclear activities and every now and then, in the form of military maneuvers, show off a new generation of mid-range or even ballistic missiles and other domestic military achievements to the world.

It is interesting to note that concurrently with the passage of Resolution 1835, the U.S. House of Representatives approved by a vote of 298–117 a nuclear agreement between the United States and India. This also sent a message to Tehran, the subcontinent, and the countries along the Persian Gulf. India had refused to sign onto the NPT as a non–nuclear-weapon state. Despite this, on March 2, 2006, during a trip to New Delhi, U.S. President George W. Bush signed an agreement with Indian Prime Minister Manmohan Singh that committed America to provide India with peaceful nuclear technology. In this agreement Washington also persuaded India to reduce its reliance on Iran for energy supplies and garnered the support of India in the international campaign against Iran's nuclear activities. Both of these provisions were explicitly stressed by Condoleezza Rice while testifying at the U.S. Senate and House of Representatives committee hearings.[1]

In the meantime, Iran took its first practical action after the passage of Resolution 1835 by trying to gain membership on the IAEA's Board of Governors. The annual meeting of the 152 member countries of the IAEA began on October 3, 2008. Pakistan's period of representation in the Board of Governors was ending, and Iran was competing with Syria, Afghanistan, and Kazakhstan for this key seat. The United States supported Afghanistan and Kazakhstan. Tehran initially strove for membership and then supported Damascus but was defeated by the maneuvers of the Western bloc in the Board of Governors. In August 2007, Israel had bombed a nuclear reactor, claiming that Syria was secretly building it with assistance from North Korea, in violation of IAEA Safeguards Agreements.

Contradictory signals from Tehran continued during this period. On October 3, Ali Asghar Soltanieh, Iran's representative to the IAEA, stated after a conference in Brussels, "As long as legally binding international guarantees for the provision of nuclear fuel do not exist, Iran will continue with uranium enrichment."[2] This statement was immediately interpreted in some Western media outlets as a new stance for Tehran, and some analysts imagined that Iran had announced that, if it obtained necessary international guarantees for the provision of nuclear fuel, it would give up enrichment. However, two days later Soltanieh himself said in an interview with the newspaper *Asharq Alawsat* that his statements had been distort-ed. He said that uranium enrichment would continue in Iran for at least thirty years and that Iran would not trust any country for the provision of nuclear fuel to its (future) power plants. Soltanieh in this same interview offered his appreciation to the Russian government for the delivery of fuel sufficient for one year to the Bushehr power plant. That same day, Foreign Minister Manouchehr Mottaki, in a joint news conference with Nicolás Maduro, his Venezuelan counterpart, said explicitly, "Even if many coun-tries give guarantees for the provision of nuclear fuel to Iran, we will con-tinue operations relating to uranium enrichment."[3]

On October 6, Saeed Jalili, secretary of Iran's Supreme National Secu-rity Council, in a two-page letter to Javier Solana that fiercely criticized the P5+1 group, implicitly signaled Iran's preparedness to engage in a new round of talks. In his response to the letter, Solana signaled the continu-ation of P5+1 policy of incentives and threats toward Iran and reaffirmed that the policies of the European Union would not change.[4] About two weeks later, in continuation of its response to the Security Council resolu-tion, the Ahmadinejad administration announced the beginning of the detailed design phase for a 360-megawatt power plant in Darkhovin, in Iran's southwest, and said that some Western countries that it did not iden-tify had expressed readiness to engage in the design and construction of the power plant.[5] The Atomic Energy Organization of Iran also publicly announced that it would support, financially and organizationally, all the research of graduate and doctoral students in the nuclear field, and espe-cially that related to the fuel cycle, the development of human resources in the nuclear industry, and the management of nuclear waste. This call was sent out to all of Iran's scientific research centers and universities. On November 13, 2008, representatives of the P5+1 countries once again met in Paris to look into recent developments in Iran's nuclear program; the meeting came to an end without reaching any special result.

THE AMERICAN PRESIDENTIAL ELECTION AND THE BARACK OBAMA PHENOMENON

America's presidential election and the rise of Barack Obama had im-portant effects on Iran's nuclear file for at least some months.

The crux of Obama's argument during the presidential campaign was that a self-confident and effective American superpower must not be afraid to sit at the negotiating table with its enemy. The argument had gained currency among Democrats who believed that Washington, especially in the field of foreign policy, must behave differently than in the past in order to decrease the level of public disapproval of America in the Middle East and increase its own "smart power" and its impact in the international arena.

Even Obama's opponent, John McCain, in his election campaign statements, tried to present his own position on Iran as different from that of Bush and, like Obama, defended the policy of diplomatic negotiations with Tehran. This approach by both McCain and Obama at least showed the convergence of an important segment of the political community in Washington on a policy that been advocated for twenty years by pragmatic and technocratic forces in Iran and America.

During the past two decades, especially during the sixteen-year period of Hashemi Rafsanjani and Khatami, the refusal of the White House to understand the political realities of Iran and the lack of understanding of American domestic political realities on the part of the Iranians caused the strengthening of radical factions and political thought in both capitals. Inflexible policies on the part of the United States reinforced the belief in Iran's military-security sector that such strategies as confidence building and interaction with the West, pursued by the Rafsanjani and Khatami administrations, had yielded few results and that Tehran should have presented America with the dilemma of choosing between a war with tremendous costs or accepting the existence of the Islamic Republic and the reality of Iran's Islamic Revolution. As someone who has for twenty years endeavored through Iran's foreign policy to eliminate problems between Iran and the West, I believe that the Western world, under American leadership, by pursuing incorrect and narrow-minded policies for the duration of the sixteen-year period of the Rafsanjani and Khatami administrations, lost important opportunities for the improvement of relations between Iran and the West.

At any rate, with Obama's rise to power, an important segment of the moderate American media was in favor of talks between the United States and Iran without preconditions. There was a belief that direct talks with Tehran could facilitate solutions to three major problems for the United

States: nonproliferation, Iraq, and Afghanistan. The clear thrust of this line of thinking was toward an agreement with Tehran on halting enrichment and agreements on the internationalization of Iranian enrichment and other mechanisms for transparency such as the implementation of the Additional Protocol, which would clear the path for serious and direct negotiations with Iran about other issues of critical importance. Some even supported commencing negotiations before the 2009 Iranian presidential elections and expanding talks after Iran's election (with whomever was elected president). There was opposition in the United States, of course. Extremists such as John Bolton, the former U.S. ambassador to the United Nations in the Bush administration, claimed that America had been the true loser of the nuclear negotiations with Iran. Bolton and others in the United States encouraged Obama to keep open the option of attacking Iran's enrichment facilities.

In contrast, experts such as Flynt Leverett and Hillary Mann Leverett, formerly of the U.S. National Security Council, spoke of a "grand bargain" with Tehran and stressed that in exchange for the necessary reassurance from Tehran, America should commit to refrain from pursuing regime change in Iran and accept Iran's role in the maintenance of order in the Persian Gulf region. According to these experts, the Obama administration ought to follow an approach comparable to that of Nixon and Kissinger in their establishment of amicable relations with China in the 1970s.

The subject of Iran has been one of America's major political problems since 1979. Strategist Kenneth Pollack explained in his 2004 book, *The Persian Puzzle*, that from the time of the victory of the Islamic Revolution in February 1979, all six U.S. presidents defined reining in Iran as one of their most important foreign policy priorities, and all six failed.

I believe that despite very deep differences that exist between the foreign policies of the Democrats and the Republicans and their substantive and formal disagreements about Iran, the strategies of Democratic and conservative Republican U.S. presidents toward Iran have not differed greatly over the past three decades. All of their approaches have followed the same shared strategy. The ultimate goal of all American presidents has been, first, to remove the threat posed to Israel by Iran, and second, to create a strategic ally out of Iran. For America, strategic relations with no country in the region are more important or desirable that those with Iran. The goal of a variety of strategies has been the restoration of Tehran-Washington relations, that is, turning back the clock on relations to the prerevolutionary period, in which Iran was a pliable U.S. ally. Despite this goal, none of America's presidents has been able to come up with a reasonable and comprehensive strategy that would serve the shared vital interests of both Iran and America.

However, Obama, for the first time in thirty years, put forward a U.S. "engagement" policy with Iran and announced his readiness for direct negotiation with Iran without preconditions. In 2005, the supreme leader of the Islamic Republic for the first time in the twenty-one years of his leadership, had removed the redline on negotiations with America. The unprecedented letters from President Mahmoud Ahmadinejad to President Bush and then President Obama on the issue of relations with Iraq as well as the nuclear issue, and Ahmadinejad's suggestion for "debate" or direct negotiations with Obama, were special privileges allowed to Ahmadinejad, privileges that had been denied to previous administrations by the hardheaded opposition of Ayatollah Khamenei.

With little progress made in Obama's engagement policy, it seems that the United States has increasingly tried to get the international community to accept that Iran is a real and full-scale threat to global security. To this end Obama's diplomatic team has endeavored to convince the international community that Iran has no intention of cooperating and that no path other than a serious confrontation with Tehran remains for the international community. This confrontation has begun with crippling sanctions and could even culminate in a military strike. The difference between the Bush and Obama administrations is that the Obama administration is pursuing this hard approach through greater international consensus and the mechanisms of international bodies such as the International Atomic Energy Agency, the UN Security Council, and the P5+1.

The Obama administration has pursued efforts to transform Western public opinion from a trend toward Islamophobia to presenting Iran as a country which, with the propagation of radical Shi'i Islam, attempts to interfere in the affairs of the Middle East through the support of extremist organizations such as Hamas and the Lebanese Hizbollah, incite anti-Western sentiment, and spread militant fundamentalism. Since the Arab Spring of 2011, the situation has changed. Analysts in the West believe that Iran is supporting repression in Syria, exacerbating the crisis in Lebanon, and is very undemocratic internally despite the wave of democratization struggles across the region. The West interprets the democratic movements in the Middle East as spontaneous uprisings against unjust, repressive regimes, not unlike the Green Movement, which arose in Iran as a series of demonstrations against alleged electoral fraud in Ahmadinejad's 2009 reelection. From the perspective of the government of Iran, however, the developments in the Middle East are a clear signal that pro-American dictators are collapsing, in a sense echoing the 1979 revolution in Iran. Iran blames the United States for supporting dictatorships in the region and praises the popular democratic movements as opposing American political domination.

CHANGE IN EUROPEAN POLICIES

After Barack Obama's electoral victory, a sort of switching of roles between America and Europe became evident. Throughout the Bush administration, Britain, Germany, and France—the European members of the P5+1—generally emphasized the use of a combination of diplomacy and pressure as a counterpoint to the constant American threats of sanctions, pressures, and even military strikes. However, after Obama became president and Vice President Joseph Biden announced at a security conference in Munich America's readiness for talks with Iran,[6] President Sarkozy of France advocated (at the same conference) an increase in sanctions as the only way to make Iran give up its nuclear program. Chancellor Merkel of Germany made similar statements, as did some British officials. Even Russia did not object to the request for more sanctions.[7]

Although this change of roles can be viewed as following "good cop/bad cop" tactics, I believe that the true reason for this change of roles was the foreign policy of Tehran since Ahmadinejad's election in 2005.

In the October 21, 2003, agreement between Iran and the foreign ministers of the EU3, one of the important objectives of Iran's former nuclear negotiating team was to finalize a Trade and Cooperation Agreement with Europe and memoranda of understanding on political, security, and nuclear issues. This would have provided a basis for comprehensive cooperation between Iran and Europe, with Iran becoming Europe's main energy partner so that most of the security, political, and economic threats against the Islamic Republic in the previous three decades would be minimized.

The Ahmadinejad administration, without understanding the role that the European Union could play in balancing America and Israel to the Islamic Republic's benefit, followed a path that replaced confidence building with divergence from—and sometimes conflict with—Europe.

Ahmadinejad, who started his first year in the presidency by denying the Holocaust[8] and creating a great wave of Iranophobia in the world, launched into strange and unprecedented rhetoric that imposed heavy and unwarranted costs on Tehran. Such rhetoric, which included the claim in 2010 that the U.S. government was involved in the September 11 terrorist attacks,[9] was heard time and time again from Ahmadinejad and his friends. It served no purpose except to enrage Europe and America and even some countries such as Russia that are ordinarily sympathetic to Iran.

Ahmadinejad stated, "President Obama is under the pressure of capitalists and the Zionists" and, like former President George W. Bush, is a "cowboy."[10] Addressing his rhetoric directly to the president,[11] Ahmadinejad said: "Mr. Obama, you've just come from the outside; wait a while for your sweat to dry, gain some experience, observe things for a while, you don't need to read every paper they put in front of you. Know that bigger and greater ones than you couldn't succeed. And your station is lower than theirs!"[12] About then French Foreign Minister Bernard Kouchner, he said, "What does Mr. Kouchner say? Because he talks a lot; the French themselves say to us that he doesn't have an ounce of sense in his speech and doesn't know what he's saying. He doesn't really understand the implications of what he's saying but he talks anyway."[13]

The radicals in Iran were of the belief that Europe had from the beginning not been the appropriate partner for Iran in nuclear negotiations because Europe did not have sufficient power or status in the negotiations. The radical faction believed that the European Union hadn't given any concessions to Iran to reciprocate for the sixteen years of confidence building and engagement policies of the Rafsanjani and Khatami administrations and that the continuation of such policies would result in the continuous advance of the West at the expense of Iran's security and national interests. It was from that point of view that the "looking to the East" doctrine was developed. Despite this, Ali Larijani, one of the founders of this theory, but also one of the more pragmatic and moderate of the Principlists, before his resignation (or dismissal by Ahmadinejad) changed his focus from the Eastern bloc to the EU and Javier Solana.

At any rate, from Ahmadinejad's election until UN Security Council Resolution 1929 in the summer of 2010, Iran's political relations with Europe grew consistently colder. Seven years after the signing of the Sa'dabad Agreement, Iran had not only lost its place as a top trading partner of Europe in the region, but had also emerged in the form of a serious security threat as Europe's biggest political dilemma. This continued until, after the election of Obama, the European Union surpassed the United States in taking a hard line on Iran on some matters.

ISRAEL'S APPROACH TO OBAMA'S NEW TACTICS

The Obama administration's policy of engagement with Iran met with considerable concern in Tel Aviv. Before America's November 2008 presidential election, Israeli officials made both secret and public statements and analyses that concluded that the only remaining path to stop Iran's nuclear program was to attack the country's atomic facilities. Reports about an Israeli plan to attack Iran with or without America's help were published in the foreign media. Rumors of pressure on the United States to give the green light to Tel Aviv or to conduct the attack itself in the last months of the Bush administration continued to emerge for several weeks. In the end, the Bush administration declared that America would, for the present, not adopt this approach, and Israeli officials went along with that.

Approximately one month before the U.S. presidential election, the Israeli press—and particularly the newspapers *Haaretz, Yedioth Ahronoth*, and the *Jerusalem Post*—published lengthy news and analysis pieces that could be seen as intended to dissuade the incoming American administration from direct, high-level negotiations with Iran without preconditions.

However, cables disclosed by WikiLeaks have suggested that the Israeli government wanted the United States to negotiate with Iran, though again, only *with* preconditions. After Obama's electoral victory, Israeli sources adjusted to the idea that the United States would seek direct negotiations without preconditions. Within the Israeli debate, a mix of tactical approaches was considered. In an interview with *Le Figaro*, Israeli

President Shimon Peres called on the world to form a united front against Iran.[14] Israeli officials continuously stressed that Iran was a real threat and that America must not forget this reality. Direct negotiations without preconditions or any other kind of negotiations with Iran would be fruitless, in this view. Nevertheless, the Obama administration wanted to at least try negotiations. And if negotiations failed, the United States would then be able to attract global support to the path of confrontation with Iran.[15]

In order for confrontation to work, countries like Russia must support it. Therefore, according to Israel and U.S. foreign policy "hawks," the United States ought to pursue close cooperation with Moscow and even cancel missile shield plans to provide for the close and serious cooperation of Russia in the campaign of resistance to Tehran's nuclear activities. Israel's worry about the delivery of a Russian S-300 antiaircraft missile system to Iran was one of the issues that Tel Aviv brought to the attention of the Obama administration.[16] Israeli officials wanted to create a firm timetable for the implementation of Obama's policies, so that if negotiations with Iran did not produce results by then, the West would take effective action against Iran.[17]

One of the first actions of Obama's secretary of state, Hillary Clinton, after taking office was to telephone Israeli Foreign Minister Tzipporah "Tzipi" Livni to talk about the nuclear challenge of Iran. According to the international media, they reached an agreement on increasing pressure on Tehran.[18] Despite this, Obama administration officials expressed concern over the possibility of an Israeli surprise attack on Iran's nuclear facilities or the increase of pressure from Tel Aviv on Washington for the execution of a military plan against Iran. On the eve of Benjamin Netanyahu's first visit to Washington as prime minister on May 18, 2009, Obama warned Netanyahu in a secret message not to surprise the White House with plans for a military attack on Iran during his trip.[19]

IAEA Director General Mohamed ElBaradei's report on Iran's nuclear program for the December 2008 meeting of the Board of Governors was released on November 19, 2008. In the report, ElBaradei estimated the total quantity of UF_6 produced at the Isfahan uranium conversion facility from March 2004 until November 3, 2008, to be 348 tons. He also emphasized that the agency's concerns about possible military dimensions of Iran's atomic program had increased.

ElBaradei requested that Iran provide information and documentation necessary to resolve questions related to alleged military studies, provide more information about Iran's uranium ore, and elucidate material procurement activities and research and development by military-affiliated institutions and companies related to nuclear matters. ElBaradei also asked Iran to clarify questions concerning the production of nuclear equipment and parts by companies connected to defense industries. The report stated that the IAEA had unfortunately not been able to advance very far on the question of Iran's alleged military studies and other important remaining issues and that Tehran had been asked to accept the Additional Protocol of the NPT and provide the agency with access to individuals, information, and locations as necessary for inspectors.

The report was published after the Atomic Energy Organization of Iran had answered some of the IAEA's questions in a 117-page report and once again requested that ElBaradei provide the original documents about Iran's military studies that had been the basis of accusations by Western, and especially American, intelligence services. One week after the publication of this report, Gholamreza Aghazadeh, Iran's Atomic Energy Organization chief, announced that Iran planned to install 50,000 centrifuges over the course of five years in order to be able to produce thirty tons of low-enriched nuclear fuel yearly. He stated that Iran had 5,000 operational centrifuges. This point was stressed by ElBaradei in Paris several days later and in his March report to the Board of Governors, in which he also indicated that despite its aggressive and controversial stand, Iran had slowed the pace of its centrifuge installation. ElBaradei welcomed the fact that Iran had not installed any new centrifuges over the previous months.

I believe that the halt in adding centrifuges was a political decision rather than the result of technical problems. The Ahmadinejad administration had put itself in a position in which it could not openly accept any provision for enrichment suspension, and so instead it stopped installing new centrifuges as a political gesture to test the West's reaction and see if political negotiations could be facilitated. ElBaradei's disclosure showed that behind all the aggressive and controversial public statements of the Ahmadinejad government, a sort of tacit negotiation was taking place that had secured a kind of unofficial suspension of the installation of centrifuges. Similar pauses had occurred during the administration of

Mohammad Khatami as well, with the difference that at that time, the domestic and global publics were aware of the agreements between Iran and the P5+1. Because of the populist nature and political maneuvers of the Ahmadinejad government and because of the radical slogans it had used regarding the nuclear case, the government was forced to conduct any international agreements out of sight of the media and the public and to present any development in the nuclear case as a "great victory" of its official policies.

Of course, political circles and media in this period also discussed whether Iran's technical pause was the result of sabotage operations against Iran's nuclear program, the assassination of Iranian nuclear scientists, or the conduct of cyber warfare by the intelligence apparatuses of America and Israel using viruses and worms to damage computer and guidance systems at the Bushehr power plant and the Natanz enrichment facility. In late 2008, *Haaretz* quoted Meir Dagan, then head of Mossad, as saying that he had promised that he would seek to disrupt Iranian nuclear activities by any means possible. On November 18, 2008, Iran, citing these reports, executed Iranian businessman Ali Ashtari after his conviction on charges of spying for Israel.[20] The *New York Times* also cited cyber operations by Israel's intelligence service against Iranian nuclear facilities[21] and capabilities as the likely reason for the 23 percent reduction of the number of centrifuges operating in Natanz. (According to the 2010 report, the total number of Iranian centrifuges in May 2009 was 4,920; by August 2010, the figure was 3,772.)

In November 2008, Mark Fitzpatrick, director of the International Institute for Strategic Studies program on nonproliferation and disarmament, in a 100-page paper entitled "The Iranian Nuclear Crisis: Avoiding Worst-Case Outcomes," argued that the Western world should recognize the difference between weapons capability and weapons production and that production could be prevented through deterrence and containment strategies. He also wrote that he considered enrichment in Iran to be a fact of life, supported diplomacy and sanctions to halt Iran's nuclear program, and opposed military action against the Islamic Republic. He cautioned that an attack on Iran would lead to the country's withdrawing from the NPT and becoming more determined than ever to advance its nuclear program and even build nuclear weaponry.

Other U.S. nonproliferation experts such as Matthew Bunn made arguments along the same lines.

Bunn, an associate professor of public policy at Harvard University's John F. Kennedy School of Government, argued:

> Zero centrifuges in Iran would be the best outcome for the United States and international security. But there is virtually no chance that Iran will agree to zero enrichment in response to any set of sanctions and inducements the United States can plausibly put together. Insisting on zero will mean no agreement, leaving the world with the risks of acquiescence or military strikes. It is time to begin thinking about what the least bad options might look like. Allowing some enrichment on Iranian soil may offer the lowest risks to U.S. security of the many bad options now available.[22]

On January 24, 2009, the *Sunday Times* of London cited Western diplomats as saying that Iran's reserves of yellowcake were close to exhausted and would be used up within a few months.[23] Tehran was therefore trying to obtain yellowcake from producer countries to provide for its needs, but some Western countries, including the United States, United Kingdom, France, and Germany, had undertaken extensive diplomatic efforts to prevent its transfer to Iran. Ali Asghar Soltanieh, Iran's representative to the IAEA, claimed that Iran could obtain the uranium it needed from mines within the country. An American nuclear expert told me that this statement is threatening because Iran does not have sufficient production capacity in its mines to refuel Bushehr or another power plant but has enough to produce material for nuclear weapons if it decides to do so.

In his report for the March 2009 meeting of the Board of Governors, ElBaradei announced that the pace of development of Iran's nuclear program—especially with regard to enrichment and centrifuge installation—had slowed, and that the total amount of UF_6 produced at Isfahan since his previous report was approximately nine tons. This showed that, whether for technical or political reasons or due to reduced supplies of yellowcake, the speed of work at Iran's enrichment facilities had slowed considerably. I believe that this reduction of the pace of work at the enrichment facilities was indeed based on a political decision to send a message to the West and to facilitate progress in negotiations without publicly compromising.

In ElBaradei's report, possible military studies by Iran were discussed in much stronger and more explicit language. The director general cited a lack of any progress in determining if there was truth to allegations of military dimensions because of lack of cooperation on the part of Iran.

Shortly after this report was issued and in the context of White House demands for the "immediate investigation" of Iran's nuclear program by the international community, Gholamreza Aghazadeh, head of Iran's Atomic Energy Organization, denied that the pace of construction and installation of centrifuges in Iran had declined, saying that there had been no political decision to this effect. With this statement, he was trying to reject rumors on undeclared suspension. He also reiterated that a new generation of centrifuge machines, superior in technology and speed to the previous generation, would be installed at nuclear facilities.

At that juncture, some Western and Russian media outlets reported for the first time President Obama's letter to Dmitri Medvedev, his Russian counterpart, laying the basis for a tacit agreement on Iran, in which the United States would adapt its plans for a missile shield in Europe in exchange for Moscow's help in achieving America's goals on the Iranian nuclear issue.[24] In January 2007, America had made an offer to Poland and the Czech Republic, both former Soviet satellites and now members of the EU and NATO, to host a missile defense system comprising ten interceptor missiles in Poland and a radar system in the Czech Republic.

According to the United States, the program was meant to counter the threat of nuclear missiles from countries like Iran and North Korea, but Russia opposed the establishment of this system, fearing that it was in fact aimed at eventually countering Russia's missile deterrent. The offer to exchange Russia's help with Iran for changes in the missile shield program had been proposed earlier by some American politicians. A few days later, Medvedev denied news of this bargain on the sidelines of a G20 meeting in London, saying that there was no quid pro quo concerning Iran and the missile shield.[25] One week later, Barack Obama said during a speech at a meeting of the leaders of Europe in Prague that Iran's nuclear program was still a threat and that a missile defense shield in Eastern Europe should be pursued as long as that threat remained.

After meeting on the sidelines of the London G20 summit, Obama and Medvedev stressed in a joint statement the use of negotiations and diplomacy in resolving the Iran nuclear issue. The developments of the ensuing months showed that political maneuvers were taking place behind the scenes.

The first practical action taken by the Obama administration was a meeting of the P5+1 to reassess the "suspension for suspension" proposal. ElBaradei had proposed this idea to Ali Larijani some time before, but it had failed because of opposition from Ahmadinejad. The April 8, 2009, meeting of the P5+1 concluded with a compromise announcement that, like previous statements of the P5+1, G8, and EU3, officially recognized Tehran's right to peaceful nuclear energy and stressed the use of direct diplomacy with Iran in the context of incentive and punishment policies but set aside "stick and carrot" rhetoric.

Media outlets close to the hard-line neoconservatives allied with Ahmadinejad called the announcement a victory for Iran and an indication of the success of his aggressive policy. One day later, Ahmadinejad, at a conference organized for Iran's "Nuclear Technology Day" (20 Farvardin/ April 9), announced with the air of a victor two new conditions in Tehran's negotiations with the P5+1. He said that Iran, given new circumstances, was adding two new points to its previously offered package: Tehran's participation in the management of global disarmament and in economic crisis management.[26]

That same day, the U.S. State Department officially confirmed that an American representative would attend the upcoming P5+1 negotiation with Iran and stated that America's participation would be in accordance with the Obama administration's desire for direct negotiations with Iran based on mutual interest and respect.

The truth is that the dispatch of an individual at the level of U.S. undersecretary of state for direct negotiations with Tehran was an unusually promising development since the time of Tehran-Washington negotiations about Iraq and Afghanistan. William J. Burns, who was the number three official of the U.S. State Department during the latter period of the Bush administration, joined the P5+1 negotiations with Tehran during that period in an observer capacity, due largely to heavy pressure from critics of the administration.[27] But his presence now in P5+1 negotiations with Tehran, in the maneuvering space that emerged from the victory of Barack Obama, had the potential to open new doors, especially because

Obama, unlike his predecessor, was willing to move forward with negotiations without preconditions or threats.

A high-level American official intimated that the goals of the United States in dispatching Burns to P5+1 negotiations with Iran were to try to diplomatically resolve existing problems in relations with Iran, gauge Iran's aims, and assess the honesty of Iran's claim that it was pursuing only peaceful energy.

Although minor changes in American behavior toward Iran had begun to take place since the end of the Bush period, talk of a new approach by Washington toward Iran became more serious with the coming into office of Barack Obama. This change caused a number of policy activists inside Iran to imagine that the era of hostility in Iran-U.S. relations had come to an end. Just before the Persian New Year, these activists, who favored the immediate agreement of Tehran to direct negotiations with America, met with a warning from Ayatollah Khamenei. He stressed that America had first to prove in practice its goodwill toward Iran.

At that juncture, some American sources alluded to a reassessment of policy and the possibility of the United States altering its previous basic stance toward Iran. According to these sources, the United States and its allies were in the process of a policy review that would lift demands relating to the shutting down and sealing off of Iran's nuclear facilities and permit Iran to continue enrichment for the duration of negotiations.[28] One informed European analyst told me that during Obama's visit to Europe, the possibility that Iran might not agree to immediately shut down its nuclear facilities, as requested by the Bush administration, had been discussed. This was, however, denied by the U.S. secretary of state, Hillary Clinton, who also emphasized that the United States would not be lifting its conditions requesting that Iran halt its enrichment program before negotiations could begin.

NUCLEAR CELEBRATION

With approximately three months remaining before Iran's presidential election, the ninth government organized a large event for its newly designated "Nuclear Technology Day." In early April it announced two new achievements of Iran: the inauguration of a factory producing fuel rods and a nuclear fuel production complex in Isfahan, as well as the construction of new types of centrifuges. The head of Iran's Atomic Energy Organization declared that with the installation of these centrifuges, the enrichment capacity at Natanz would increase 2.5 times. He also said that the number of active centrifuges at Natanz was 7,000.[29] The announcement of news about the Iran's nuclear advances met with skepticism in Washington.

In Ahmadinejad's fiery speech on Nuclear Technology Day, which also marked the official start of the presidential election campaign, he responded to America's offer for direct negotiations. He trumpeted the victory of his administration on the nuclear issue in several parts of the speech and claimed that if he hadn't been elected in 2005 and hadn't given up suspension, the Western world would have sought to shut down high school experimental and mathematics programs and some university engineering departments in Iran. He once again stressed in this speech that "all have accepted that Iran is a global power."

BARACK OBAMA'S LETTER TO AYATOLLAH KHAMENEI

In early May 2009, President Obama wrote a letter to Ayatollah Khamenei. Though the contents of the letter have not been made public, it was the second practical step of the new American administration on the path to resolving the Iranian nuclear issue. I was told that in his letter, President Obama sent a clear signal for rapprochement between Tehran and Washington. Great differences in opinion about the timing of the letter existed within the U.S. administration and among Iran experts, pivoting on whether to wait until after the June elections in Iran. The letter discussed Iran's nuclear program and the commencement of bilateral talks. The letter was delivered to officials of Iran's Foreign Ministry through the Swiss Embassy in Tehran, which represents American interests in Iran.[30]

Approximately two weeks later, Ayatollah Khamenei responded. The contents of this letter also remained secret. Later, however, the *New York Times* wrote that according to American officials, Ayatollah Khamenei's letter had caused disappointment and frustration among high-ranking U.S. officials. After receiving Ayatollah Khamenei's letter, Obama sent a second letter of his own. In a brave initiative, Obama announced preparedness for discussion of all issues of interest to the two sides and put forth the names of U.S. representatives for direct Tehran-Washington talks: William J. Burns, then-under secretary of state, and Puneet Talwar, senior director for the Gulf States, Iran, and Iraq on the National Security Council. Obama's second letter was sent a few days before the election, and Ayatollah Khamenei did not respond. The lack of a response from the Iranian leadership naturally was cause for surprise and resentment at the White House, but two points must be made clear. First, it was natural that Iran's supreme leader waited until after the election to reply to the second letter, because choosing the officials who would serve as Iran's representatives for official negotiations would be subject to the composition of the new administration, and, second, Iran's political conditions transformed in a radical and unexpected way after the election. Following the disputed presidential election of June 2009, the United States sided with the Green Movement in Iran. I believe this was the main reason the supreme leader did not respond to Obama's second letter—he had lost confidence in Obama's engagement policy with Iran.

There were two major interpretations of the sending of Obama's second letter. An important portion of Iranian observers believed that the sending of this letter before Iran's presidential election showed a soft line and in fact that any kind of softness toward Tehran before the election could affect the election's outcome and even improve the chances of Ahmadinejad, against whom three candidates were fiercely competing. A second handful of observers stressed that waiting until after the election would be more dangerous and that the choice of correspondence with Ayatollah Khamenei, given his status, was important because it meant that engagement would be carried on irrespective of who won the election. This group opined that if Ahmadinejad won the presidency for a second time, Obama's letter would be viewed as indicative of America's weakness and complaisance with Iran's existing situation.

I believe that the writing of this letter, with the type of language that it used, and in its timing, was a mistake that was indicative of the lack of understanding of the actual power relations in Iran and the particularities of Ayatollah Khamenei's character. Although Ayatollah Khamenei is regarded as the ultimate decisionmaker in foreign and domestic policies and has sweeping authority in practically all of the branches of administration of the country, the complexities of power in Iran's internal politics mean that for initiatives (such as Barack Obama's letter) to be effective, there is a need for extensive preparation and follow-ups. Otherwise, it is clear that such a letter will meet with a critical and admonishing response from Iran's supreme leader. In my opinion, Obama should have responded to Ahmadinejad's letters respectfully in order to avoid humiliating and discouraging Ahmadinejad from pursuing further engagement. After that or simultaneously, he could have sent a letter to the supreme leader, thus engaging with both figures.

DEVELOPMENTS OF THE JUNE 12, 2009, ELECTION

The Iranian presidential election had a broad impact on Tehran's domestic, foreign, security, and even military policies. Although neoconservatives in America favoring war were not interested in the victory of reformist and technocratic forces in Iran's elections, I believe that at least the Obama administration was hopeful that after the election it would be able to deal with a more moderate and pragmatic government that could produce results in the engagement policy, pursue confidence building with the international community, and reduce the volume of conflict in the region.

Mir Hossein Mousavi's breathtaking challenge of Mahmoud Ahmadinejad in the end turned into an all-out political confrontation. Mousavi had been prime minister for eight years during the Iran-Iraq war, and had enjoyed Imam Khomeini's support. Ahmadinejad, meanwhile, benefited from all the advantages of incumbency and government resources. The day after the election, the supreme leader announced that Ahmadinejad had received 24 million votes (with about 14 million votes for Mousavi) and vouched for the validity of the election's results. A few days later, the Council of Guardians, the organ that constitutionally supervises national elections, confirmed the validity of the election results. Despite this, Mir Hossein Mousavi insisted that extensive fraud had taken place in the election. He branded the election a magic act, and emphasized that he would never surrender to this game and would refuse to recognize the government's legitimacy.

Mehdi Karroubi, another of Imam Khomeini's close friends who was the Speaker of Majles for eight years (1996–2004) and who was another reformist opponent of Ahmadinejad's, alleged that there had been widespread electoral fraud and called the results ridiculous. Hashemi Rafsanjani, the head of the Assembly of Experts and Expediency Council and former president, Majles speaker, and war commander of the Khomeini era, was not prepared to recognize the election's validity either. Widespread protests had broken out over the results of the election, and Rafsanjani's first Friday prayer sermon, which was given with the intention of providing advice on how to get through the crisis, showed his own objections to the election results and to the confrontation with the people and with protesters.

The opposition accused the government of a military coup d'état, and the government in turn accused the opposition of being linked to hirelings and spies of the United States, the United Kingdom, and Israel, which aimed to overthrow the system through a velvet revolution. It reached the point where the minister of intelligence claimed that over the course of the election, America and the West paid $17 million to instigate the overthrow of the Islamic Republic. Ayatollah Ahmad Jannati, chairman of the Council of Guardians and one of Ahmadinejad's most important supporters, claimed that the United States, acting through Saudi Arabia, had given a billion dollars to the protest leaders and promised to pay up to fifty million dollars more if regime change were successful.[31]

In the postelection confrontation, millions of protesters and supporters took to the streets. These clashes led to the closing of many media outlets, the arrest and prosecution of hundreds of journalists and opposition political and social activists, the dissolution or closing of the offices of three major reformist political parties (Mosharekat Party, the Mojahedin of the Islamic Revolution Organization, and the National Trust Party), and the arrest and prosecution of thousands of citizens across Iran. Although no precise or reliable figure for the number slain or arrested during these postelection events has been published, Brigadier General Ali Fazli, a senior Revolutionary Guard Corps commander who had an important role in managing the response to the protests, said that ten thousand people had been arrested in the unrest.[32]

These protests were unprecedented and reverberated across the world. Ayatollah Khamenei for the first time in two decades acknowledged that "the reputation of the system among the nations of the world was ruined" and officially recognized that during the clash with protesters, especially in the incidents of prisoner mistreatment and killings at Kahrizak detention center and the attack on the University of Tehran student dormitories, "crimes" had taken place.[33] These enormous and unprecedented incidents undoubtedly had a deep impact on Iran's foreign relations and especially on its nuclear file.

Given that according to the constitution, Iran's general policies must be endorsed by the supreme leader, as well as the reality that Iran's general nuclear policies during the Khatami and Ahmadinejad administrations were determined by Ayatollah Khamenei, an overnight transformation of foreign and nuclear policies should not have been expected with the victory of the reformists and pragmatist forces. But the complex structure of power in Iran provided the opportunity for governments and specialized agencies, in cooperation with the Office of the Supreme Leader, to adjust policies and adopt new policies.

Something like that also occurred in the time of the previous nuclear team. For me, as one who had seen up close the domestic political issues related to the nuclear case, it was completely clear that the supreme leader did not personally support the implementation of the Additional Protocol or suspension of enrichment activities during the Khatami period, but because such measures were recommended by the Supreme National Security Council and most institutions and officials in the Khatami administration, Ayatollah Khamenei reluctantly and after much debate signed off on them.

After the June 2009 Iranian election, one of the important problems of the West was how to approach the newly reelected president. Western governments were under pressure from individuals and organizations not to officially recognize the Ahmadinejad government. Overlooking the violent repression after the election and talking with the Ahmadinejad administration were no simple task for Western governments, especially the United States.

The legitimacy of Ahmadinejad's presidency came to be questioned both at home and abroad, and the situation and credibility of the Islamic Republic were seriously damaged. This situation completely changed Iran's outlook on future negotiations with the West, as America and Europe were accused of barefaced interference in Iran's internal affairs with the goal of overthrowing the Islamic Republican system.

This could be seen in Ayatollah Khamenei's first Friday sermon following the presidential election. It was then that the supreme leader revealed having received a letter from President Obama a month earlier. American officials had not publicized this letter. Now Khamenei portrayed President Obama's message in an interesting way: "Unfortunately, what happened was exactly what was expected. The American Government and the new establishment and president with their interest in just and appropriate relations—about which they wrote a letter and sent a message and announced over loudspeakers and repeated at private parties—said that we want to normalize our relations with the Islamic Republic. Unfortunately they did the opposite. In the eight months after the elections they adopted the worst possible stance. The American President introduced the street rioters as a civil movement. . . . You cannot talk about friendship but at the same time hatch plots and try to harm the Islamic Republic."[34]

The truth is that although Barack Obama had talked during his election campaign of direct talks with high-level Iranian officials, he had also said that Mahmoud Ahmadinejad might not be the right person for these talks. Dennis Ross, who at the time was one of Obama's advisers, said to the *Wall Street Journal* that Ayatollah Khamenei was the only Iranian official who could issue the order to suspend enrichment activities and for this reason talks should be with him. Barack Obama also on multiple occasions had emphasized that Ayatollah Khamenei was the ultimate decisionmaker in the Islamic Republic.

In the volatile postelection environment, the opposition in Iran envisioned the possibility that the Ahmadinejad administration would make concessions to the Western world with the goal of decreasing foreign pressure and allowing a greater focus on domestic issues. To be sure, Iran's nuclear activities are directly approved and overseen by the supreme leader and from this perspective are transgovernmental affairs. However, because of the developments related to the election, the issue of enrichment became more than a matter of mere face-saving in Iran. After the election, any kind of concessions in negotiations would, from the view of the outside world and domestic opponents of Ahmadinejad, be interpreted as a retreat of the leadership and the administration from its foreign policy and nuclear positions. This in turn would weaken the Ahmadinejad administration both at home and abroad.

Another objective consequence of the June 2009 election was the creation of a kind of political obstinacy among government and opposition supporters. Because of this obstinacy, which of course was not in the national interest of Iran, every action taken by the Ahmadinejad administration (regardless of whether it was correct or a mistake) was met with a wave of critical articles and declarations from the opposition on websites, satellite TV networks, and even on the floor of the Majles.

THE IAEA'S NEW DIRECTOR GENERAL

In 2009, Mohamed ElBaradei was preparing to step down after serving three terms as the IAEA director general. On July 2, in the sixth round of voting, Yukiya Amano was able to garner the support of 23 of 35 IAEA Board of Governors members to succeed El Baradei. Amano's position toward Iran was quite similar to that of America. An October 2009 U.S. State Department cable disclosed by WikiLeaks stated that he was "solidly in the U.S. court on every key strategic decision."[35] In February 2009, Amano had declared that Iran should cooperate with the agency through useful and productive talks and that it should refrain from nuclear activities.

Around the same time, Gholamreza Aghazadeh resigned as chief of Iran's Atomic Energy Organization. He had overseen the organization for twelve years and was the last remaining person in the ninth government from the reformist period. Responsibility for managing the organization immediately passed to Ali Akbar Salehi, a man experienced in Iran's nuclear diplomacy.

There was much speculation about the reason or reasons for Aghazadeh's resignation. Two reasons, however, were certain: first, differences of opinion between Aghazadeh and Ahmadinejad's team; and second, Aghazadeh's support for Mir Hossein Mousavi in the presidential election, which stemmed from the close relationship of the two since the 1980s. Some people close to Aghazadeh also believed that he resigned because he recognized sanctions and the continued nuclear crisis as undesirable and harmful to Iran's national interests and did not want to be remembered in history as playing a key role in them. I personally believe that Aghazadeh's strong support for Mir Hossein Mousavi in the disputed presidential election was the main reason for his resignation.

Although Bernard Kouchner, the French foreign minister, called Aghazadeh's resignation a very important development, the resignation didn't generate any particular criticism or controversy within Iran. One of the reasons for this silence was that he was a serious supporter of Mousavi; furthermore, his replacement, Ali Akbar Salehi, was widely respected for his expertise.

On August 3, 2009, the *Times* of London, in a controversial report that cited Western intelligence services as sources, claimed that Tehran had obtained the technology for nuclear warhead construction and was waiting for a green light from senior Islamic Republic officials to produce them. The newspaper asserted that the reason for Iran's decision to halt its military nuclear program in 2003 (as cited by the U.S. government's National Intelligence Estimate) was that it had reached its goal in obtaining the necessary knowledge for the construction of an atomic bomb. According to the article, if permission were granted by senior Islamic Republic officials for the production of an atomic bomb in Iran, it would take six months to enrich a sufficient quantity of uranium and another six months to build the warhead.

In summer 2009, Tehran penned a proposal to ban attacks on nonmilitary nuclear facilities, which would reaffirm a 1990 UN resolution—also proposed by Iran—entitled "Prohibition of All Armed Attacks Against Nuclear Installations Devoted to Peaceful Purposes Whether Under Construction or in Operation." In an official letter sent to the IAEA, Iran requested that the proposal be voted on in the upcoming September meeting of the agency's 150 member nations. Iranian officials emphasized that this proposal was unrelated to Israel's position of threatening to attack Iran's atomic facilities.

At this juncture, much speculation was published about whether Israel would attack Iran, which of course met with sharp and threatening responses from Iranian military officials. On April 12, 2009, Israeli President Shimon Peres threatened once again that in the absence of an international agreement on Iran's nuclear program, Israel would attack. On April 24, 2009, United Press International, quoting sources in Jerusalem, claimed that Israel had made the decision to attack Iran's air force but Tehran was notified of this decision by Moscow and had transported 140 of its fighters from one air base to a different location. These sources claimed that a military air maneuver had been planned by the Iranian army but was canceled because of the possibility of an Israeli attack.

On May 22, 2009, the Israeli newspaper *Haaretz* published the results of an opinion poll that showed that 85 percent of Israelis were afraid of the danger of Iran, with one in four saying that if Iran obtained nuclear weaponry, they would flee Israel. At the end of July, Israeli Defense Minister Ehud Barak stated during the course of a talk with his American counterpart that Israel would not take "any option" off the table in relation to Iran's nuclear program. On July 16, 2009, the *Times* of London reported on Israeli naval movements with the probable aim of attacking Iran and cited Israel's military movements as a clear indication of the government's inclination to attack Iran.

Needless to say, the presentation of Iran's proposal to the IAEA was a kind of preemptive action to prevent an American or Israeli military attack on Iran's nuclear facilities. This showed that from 2005 on, Ahmadinejad administration officials and leaders of the Islamic Republic, despite some stances made for the sake of publicity, took seriously the possibility of an attack on Iran's nuclear facilities. The Supreme National Security Council, military, and Foreign Ministry regularly make assessments of military threats and prepare according to the seriousness that they ascribe to those threats. Their assessments no doubt had an effect on the way Tehran interacted with the international community and on Iran's nuclear planning.

Of course, similar worries arose in 2003 with America's military invasion of Iraq and the simultaneous opening of the Iranian nuclear file. The potential of military attack on Iran was important in the Khatami team's calculations and nuclear policies, although it was not the key variable in shaping the confidence-building strategy.

Over the course of previous decades, numerous resolutions had been passed on the prohibition of any kind of attack or threat of attack against nuclear installations that were devoted to peaceful aims, and such attacks were recognized as violating the articles of the UN Charter, international law, and the IAEA Statute. Despite this, the instances of Israeli attacks on Iraq's Osirak and Syria's Al Kibar nuclear facilities showed that Israel would not step back from its redline of defending its existence and military supremacy in the region. It is obvious that repeating such an action against Iran could not be ruled out.

Iran's proposal was also considered to be a sort of response to the shared concerns of countries along the Persian Gulf, which believed that the leakage of radioactive materials from Iranian nuclear facilities in the instance of a military or terrorist attack could be a disaster for the entire region. Of course, countries along the Persian Gulf coast in no way supported Iran's cause, but by submitting such proposals, Tehran strove to attract their tactical agreement and support on the path to its own political goals.

In my belief, this proposal sought to weaken the coalition that had come together against Iran's nuclear activities under the global leadership of the West and to open up a new front against Israel with the support of the Arabs and the Non-Aligned Movement.

IRAN'S NEW OFFER: THE SECOND PACKAGE

Ahead of P5+1 meetings and amid talk of bringing more pressure on Iran, Tehran announced the presentation of a new package for the Western world and its readiness for negotiations with the P5+1. The aim was to reverse Russian and Chinese support for the expansion of sanctions and once again open up a rift within the Western world. Although many Western experts were of the belief that Iran made this announcement solely with the aim of reducing the probability of the implementation of new sanctions, China and Russia expressed optimism toward the new package. This came as talk of sanctions on exporting gasoline to Iran, proposed by the U.S. Congress, as well as the implementation of greater trade and financial restrictions on Iranian institutions, were among the most important subjects of P5+1 negotiations, as led by the United States. China, which was in the process of helping Iran build new refineries and had considerable interests in economic cooperation with Tehran, showed little desire for new sanctions against Iran, as did Russia.

Iran at that time was struggling tooth and claw with the domestic crisis over the June 2009 presidential election. Some foreign observers suggested that because of its precarious position on both domestic and foreign political fronts, Tehran would inevitably choose between two options: either it would grant the domestic opposition considerable concessions, or it would make concessions at the negotiating table with the West with the goal of reducing international pressure. This notion gave way to a belief on the part of some countries such as Russia that Iran's viewpoint had become more moderate and, for this reason, the Security Council should wait to see how things played out and let the new Iranian government take action on the nuclear case. During this same juncture, however, Mahmoud Ahmadinejad stressed in numerous speeches that Tehran would not negotiate on its nuclear rights and recommended instead that issues such as the "management of the world" be discussed in negotiations with America.[36]

In any case, Iran's foreign minister transmitted Ahmadinejad's new package offer to representatives of the P5+1 in Tehran on September 9, 2009. At around the same time, Iran's ambassador in Brussels presented the package to Javier Solana. The package was introduced as meetings of the IAEA Board of Governors were under way and representatives of countries such as the United States were arguing in sharp-toned speeches that Iran was very close to obtaining nuclear weaponry and had increased its reserves of enriched uranium. The U.S. ambassador to the IAEA, Glyn Davies, asserted that "Iran is now either very near [to], or in possession already of, sufficient low-enriched uranium to produce one nuclear weapon, if the decision were made to further enrich it to weapons-grade," an indication of "dangerous and destabilizing possible breakout capacity."[37]

The Ahmadinejad administration's five-page package offer contained stipulations similar to those of the administration's previous package. The difference, according to Iranian officials, was that it had been brought up to date to reflect recent circumstances, developments, and crises. As expected, Iran gave absolutely no indication in the package that it would suspend enrichment or comply with the requests of the UN Security Council resolutions. This showed that the Obama administration's strategy of direct negotiations with Iran had not brought about any change in the stances of the Ahmadinejad government or the supreme leader toward America. In its new offer, Tehran declared its readiness for negotiation with the United States and its allies on all international issues from stability in the Balkans to development in Latin America. In truth this package was set according to Ahmadinejad's ambitious and sensational theory for "management of the world." The proposal was written in the style of Ahmadinejad's speeches and letters to world leaders and began with ethical expressions in the style of the holy books.

Upon receiving the proposal package, the White House and EU security chief Javier Solana requested an immediate meeting with Tehran for an inquiry into Iran's exact nuclear goals and the Islamic Republic's intention in providing such a package. Media outlets close to Ahmadinejad said that this approach by the Obama administration indicated an acceptance of Iran's arguments on the nuclear subject despite the lack of any mention of nuclear issues in the proposal package.

It must not be forgotten that America at the time was not prepared to enter into a grand bargain with Iran, but because of Obama's pro-engagement rhetoric did not want to be seen as rejecting an Iranian initiative offhandedly, and so preferred to buy time to eventually reject the proposal in the framework of the P5+1.

Some experts described the immediate declaration of preparedness for negotiations with Iran as a final opportunity for the Obama administration. Particularly given that it was made at a time when Iran was burning with the fervor of street protests and the government had had serious confrontation with its critics, the request for negotiations was not without costs for the Obama administration.

Despite the fact that America initially took this package seriously (or at least appeared to for propaganda purposes), hopes dissolved into disappointment, giving serious impetus to the change of America's strategy from negotiation to sanctions. State Department spokesman P. J. Crowley, as he explicitly rejected the package offer, stressed that the Obama administration intended to decide by the end of the year about its offer to Iran for negotiations, or whether to withdraw the offer and implement further sanctions for the purpose of halting the country's nuclear program.

ElBaradei revealed in his recent memoir that, also in September 2009, "A message had come back from Ahmadinejad saying that he was 'ready to engage in bilateral negotiations, without conditions and on the basis of mutual respect.' There were additional details, related to Iran's willingness to help in Afghanistan and elsewhere."[38] This was a clear attempt by Ahmadinejad to reach Obama for a grand bargain. All evidence indicates that Obama did not respond.

On September 16, 2009, with Iran still embroiled in domestic conflict following the election, a documentary film was aired on the state TV broadcast (Seda-o-Sima) aimed at discrediting the Khatami administration's policies on the nuclear file. Ahmadinejad had transformed the issue from a national matter to one of factional propaganda and rough political competition. The film showed that, when it came to the nuclear file, the Ahmadinejad administration was more than anything concerned with managing the domestic aspect of the crisis. Protecting national interests on the issue was much less important than satisfying some of Ahmadinejad's domestic supporters.

Entitled *The Nuclear File*, the documentary film had striking similarities in structure and narrative to a collection of documentaries that had been broadcast on state television on the subject of plots for a "colored revolution" and "velvet coup d'état." It had no goal except to completely discredit and marginalize reformists, moderate Principlists, and technocratic forces in Iran's political structure. At one point in the film, the narrator tries to present the Sa'dabad negotiations as "degrading," without the slightest mention that the negotiations were conducted under Ayatollah Khamenei's direct counsel and approval.

The film sought to condition public opinion in advance of nuclear negotiations. If the West refused Iran's requests and terms over the course of negotiations and issued the order for greater pressure and put Iran into the vice of enmity, the government could explain it from a national position based on dignity. Or, if concessions were made to the West, it would be presented as more reasonable and acceptable than previous agreements of the reformist government. In tandem with this shaping of public opinion, the effort was to portray the Ahmadinejad administration as the first administration to come to the negotiating table with the upper hand and from a position demanding dignity, while all previous Iranian negotiators had been meek and eager to make concessions.

JALILI-BURNS NEGOTIATIONS AND THE SECRET FORDOW FACILITIES

With only a few days remaining before the new round of P5+1 negotiations with Iran, the shocking news emerged in September 2009 of another enrichment facility called Fordow, located on the outskirts of the religious city of Qom. The existence of this undeclared facility was revealed personally by the president of the United States. It astonished the world and changed the dynamics of the imminent negotiations.

The new round of P5+1 negotiations with Iran had been planned for the first week of October 2009. Before the start of negotiations, Javier

Solana gave a negative response to the question of whether the Europeans would provide new offers to Iran, maintaining his "suspension for suspension" stance. This was to be the first meeting between the P5+1 and Iran in 2009 and the first since Obama's inauguration. The U.S. president had decided that a high-ranking American representative, Undersecretary of State William J. Burns, would join the negotiation. The face-to-face negotiations of Iranian Supreme National Security Council Secretary Saeed Jalili and Burns could have breathed new life to the tired soul of the negotiations and returned the nuclear issue to its 2003 status.

Under these circumstances, it was shocking when, days before the start of talks, on September 25, Obama, in a joint news conference with Gordon Brown and Nicolas Sarkozy, accused Iran of having a secret underground enrichment center. The three asserted that Iran had for a long time kept the construction of this facility in Qom secret and had kept it out of view of IAEA inspectors. The statements of Obama, Brown, and Sarkozy before the inauguration ceremony of a G20 meeting in Pittsburgh certainly led to an increase in tensions between the European countries and Iran. The apparent goals of the revelation were to weaken Iran's position in the negotiations, attract more support and cooperation from China and Russia, and draw global public attention to Iranian nuclear secrecy. An alternative explanation of the timing, given by one American former diplomat, was that Iran had found out that the United States and its allies had discovered the existence of the Fordow facility and was going to declare the facility and claim that it had not been hiding it. The United States, United Kingdom, and France then rushed to make the announcement in order to preempt the Iranians while the facility remained undeclared.

At approximately the same time as the joint news conference, Tehran announced in a letter to the IAEA the start of construction on its second enrichment facility. A few hours after the Obama-Brown-Sarkozy news conference, Atomic Energy Organization head Ali Akbar Salehi announced through a published bulletin that the activities of the Fordow facility, like those of Iran's other nuclear facilities, would be in compliance with IAEA regulations. To defend the public face of the ninth government, he congratulated the supreme leader and people of Iran on the facility's construction.

From that time on, ninth government officials and diplomats continuously stressed that the creation of Fordow was not a secret effort and that they hadn't prevented IAEA inspectors' access to anything. The P5+1 did not accept these claims. In order to reduce tension, Tehran immediately announced its willingness to permit IAEA inspections of the facility. Iranian officials argued that according to the Comprehensive Safeguards Agreement, Tehran was required to notify agency inspectors of the existence of a site 180 days before the introduction of radioactive materials into the facilities, and that the Fordow facility had still been at the stage of physical construction. Countering this argument, Western nuclear experts, including those from the IAEA, asserted that according to Security Council resolutions, Safeguards Agreement, and Subsidiary Arrangements (which Ali Asghar Soltanieh even announced that the Iranian government would implement a portion of following a request of ElBaradei to Ahmadinejad), Iran was obliged to have informed the IAEA when the decision was made to construct the site.

With the disclosure of the secret Qom facility, the rhetoric of the international community toward Iran changed completely and the atmosphere became considerably more tense. Russian President Dmitri Medvedev expressed impatience with Iran's behavior and stressed that if Tehran didn't cooperate in the October 1 meeting, other methods would have to be adopted vis-à-vis the Iranian nuclear file. Shortly before the October talks, U.S. Secretary of Defense Robert Gates rejected the statements of Iran's president and said, "If they wanted it for peaceful nuclear purposes, there's no reason to put it so deep underground, no reason to be deceptive about it, keep it a . . . secret for a protracted period of time."[39] Also in late September, British Prime Minister Gordon Brown said, "The level of deception by the Iranian government . . . will shock and anger the whole international community, and it will harden our resolve," adding that it was time "to draw a line in the sand."[40]

Obama's disclosure of the Qom facility shocked not only the international community, but also many of the Iranian diplomats involved in the nuclear file. I myself heard about the Fordow facility for the first time watching Obama's news conference. It is necessary to note that because of the Iranian security apparatus's lack of trust in many Foreign Ministry diplomats, as far as I know, none of the diplomats on Khatami's nuclear negotiation team was informed about such issues. The name "Fordow" never even came up in our meetings. It seems to me that the facility did not exist until after Ahmadinejad took office. That said, as spokesman for the Khatami team, I more than once heard important news for the first time from IAEA officials or the foreign media and then had to work on reformulating plans to manage the crises that the news gave rise to.

When I was arrested by the Ahmadinejad government in April 2007, I was openly accused of giving intelligence about Iran's nuclear program to the Europeans. After a year of interrogation and examination by three judges, a spokesman for the judiciary announced in April 2008 that all three judges had dismissed the charges as baseless and issued verdicts of acquittal. Neither I nor other members of Khatami's nuclear negotiation team had any insider information about the technical dimensions of Iran's activities that I could have provided to foreigners. In fact, I believe that even Khatami, the president at the time, Rouhani, the secretary of the Supreme National Security Council responsible for the nuclear file, and Kharrazi, the foreign minister, heard about the P-2 centrifuge issue for the first time from the IAEA and the foreign media and had no previous information on the matter.

This thick wall between the technical and political sides of nuclear programs exists in many nuclear countries, and this issue was naturally among the serious problems faced by Khatami's negotiation team. It has puzzled me to this day how Western intelligence services and the IAEA could have more information about Iran's nuclear program than the members of the country's own nuclear negotiating team during the Khatami period, and yet we were accused of engaging in espionage by providing the West with nuclear intelligence.

Shortly after the Fordow disclosure, CIA Director Leon Panetta announced in an interview with *Time* magazine that Western intelligence agencies had first become aware of the Fordow facility in 2006 because of unusual activity in the mountains in the region of Qom. Iran was transferring antiaircraft batteries to the area, indicating that secret activities were under way. Panetta said that he was told about the site in January 2009 in the White House transition period before he assumed leadership of the CIA. Working with English and French intelligence services, the United States had conducted covert operations in that area to ascertain the nature of the construction activity.[41]

Two days after Obama revealed the Fordow facility and the leaders of the international community began discussing how to respond to it, Iran tested three short-range missiles with ranges of 90–125 miles. One day later, on September 28, 2009, Iran announced that the Revolutionary Guard Corps had tested mid-range missiles capable of striking Israel, parts of Europe, and American bases on the Persian Gulf. Reports indicated that the tests of the mid-range, liquid-fuel Shahab-3 and solid-fuel Sejil-2 missiles were conducted successfully.

Against this backdrop, on October 1, 2009, the "Geneva 2" talks between Iran and the P5+1 began with Burns and Jalili among the participants. After the meeting, news was released that the negotiations had achieved satisfactory results. The most important news of the day, however, was that the U.S. undersecretary of state and the secretary of Iran's Supreme National Security Council had met for direct negotiations lasting 45 minutes on the sidelines of the meeting. Given the thirty-year freeze in diplomatic relations between the two countries, this meeting of high-level Iranian and American diplomats in Geneva raised great hopes.

Although Israeli Vice Prime Minister Silvan Shalom dismissed negotiations with Iran as a "waste of time," Javier Solana, at a news conference that same day after the second round of talks,[42] assessed the negotiations as positive and mentioned that the next round of talks had been set for October 18. Solana expressed optimism that the two sides would be able to build on the progress that had been made.

In the talks in Geneva on October 1, Tehran had appeared to agree on a plan to transfer a major portion of its enriched uranium reserves (1,200 of 1,600 kilograms low-enriched uranium) out of the country, in exchange for fuel for the Tehran Research Reactor. Later on this plan generated great controversy, but at this juncture the Western media and even media outlets close to America's neoconservatives saw some promise in the proposed transfer, even if they suspected that Tehran was doing it under duress because of the Fordow revelation. Many among Iran's reformists, moderates, and conservatives, however, opposed this exchange. They argued that the 1,600 kilograms of low-enriched uranium were Iran's most important form of leverage for future bargaining and obtaining concessions. In the view of the exchange's conservative and reformist opponents, if Iran surrendered this leverage, Iran's bargaining power with the international community would undoubtedly decline, and pressure on Iran to give up its enrichment program would increase considerably.

At the time of the direct meeting between Burns and Jalili, some Obama administration officials wanted negotiations to create a breakthrough but were mindful of past false hopes and current challenges. Fordow was a cautionary tale, in the sense that Iran had secretly built the facility even while seeming to negotiate with the P5+1. But there was a possibility that Iran would conclude it needed to compromise to repair the damage to its position. U.S. National Security Adviser James L. Jones, in an interview with CNN, asserted that policies were on the right track and downplayed a *New York Times* article, which stated that Iran had acquired the information necessary to build a "workable" atomic bomb.[43] Jones called Iran's acceptance of inspections of the Fordow facility very important.[44] Other elements in the House and Senate, encouraged by Israeli views, argued that negotiations with Iran would not go anywhere and that sanctions needed to be stepped up. For this reason, Obama administration officials were constantly warning that Tehran had to address international concerns and that if it balked at cooperating with the international community, it would meet with painful punishments. That said, the Geneva agreement had the potential of reducing domestic pressure against Obama's moderate Iran policy.

It is interesting to note that after the Geneva 2 negotiations, a new tagline came into usage among diplomats and media outlets close to the Ahmadinejad administration: "peaceful atomic awakening movement." Its proponents believed that Iran had become the flag bearer of a "peaceful atomic awakening movement" in the region: Its resistance to the West had created a wave of demand and awakening in the region in such a way that many Arab countries in the region began looking to develop this technology themselves.

On a trip that Khatami's nuclear negotiating team made to Arab countries before Iran's June 2005 presidential election, Dr. Rouhani had expressed, with the aim of confidence building, Iran's preparedness for joint investment and nuclear cooperation with Arab and other Islamic countries. To a person, all of the Arab leaders of the region thanked him but showed no interest. One of the Arab leaders, while thanking Rouhani, even replied, "I didn't hear anything from you about this, and you didn't make such an offer to me!"

OCTOBER 19 NEGOTIATIONS

In June 2009, Iran requested that the IAEA provide fuel for the Tehran Research Reactor. The Tehran reactor needed 116 kilograms of uranium enriched to 19.75 percent, and this fuel had been purchased from Argentina around two decades earlier. According to a later *Time* magazine account, after this Iranian request, high-level Obama administration officials attended three secret, multiparty negotiations with Iranian officials, beginning in June 2009. These secret negotiations also included representatives of the IAEA, Russia, and France.[45]

In the course of these negotiations, the American government, in tandem with the IAEA, proposed that 80 percent of Iran's low-enriched uranium be sent to Russia for further enrichment to 20 percent, and then to France for conversion into fuel rods. It was determined that a team of Obama administration officials, together with officials from France and Russia, would conduct negotiations with Iranian diplomats on this enriched uranium transfer. The groundwork for these negotiations was laid October 1 in the meeting of Saeed Jalili with the P5+1, and the second phase of these negotiations was set for October 19.

According to the *Time* account, the White House played a central role in shaping the proposed deal. During President Obama's July 1 trip to Russia, his senior adviser on arms control and proliferation, Gary Samore, gave the Russians a proposal according to which if Iran agreed to export its enriched uranium to Russia, Moscow could enrich the uranium to the level needed for the Tehran Research Reactor and then France would convert the uranium into fuel rods and transfer it back to Iran. The Russians immediately welcomed this proposal. After that, meetings were held among high-level officials from Iran, the IAEA, Russia, the United States, and France to arrange the details of the plan.

In mid-September 2009, shortly before the end of Mohamed ElBaradei's tenure, Obama personally notified the IAEA director general that the United States was interested in looking into this proposal. ElBaradei then raised the subject with Iran's representative to the IAEA. After contacting Iran, Ali Asghar Soltanieh expressed his country's approval of the plan. When in late September Russian President Dmitri Medvedev traveled to New York to participate in a UN General Assembly meeting, Obama pressured him to endorse the proposal for the transfer of enriched uranium from Iran. Obama then had a telephone conversation with ElBaradei in which they discussed the details of the exchange, which were introduced in the October 1 negotiations between Iran and the P5+1 in Geneva and the subject of talks between William Burns and Saeed Jalili.

American officials insisted that if Iran did not commit to this agreement, it would face further sanctions. At that time, Russia and China were expressing opposition to the expansion of sanctions against Iran and were continuously pushing for nuclear negotiations. This matter was cause for disagreement among P5+1 countries. During a trip to Moscow with the goal of persuading Russia on the implementation of sanctions against Iran, Hillary Clinton received stiff opposition, to the point where Russian Foreign Minister Sergei Lavrov, after four hours of meetings with his American counterpart, declared to reporters that "threats, sanctions and threats of pressure" on Iran would be "counterproductive."[46]

Nevertheless, some members of Iran's negotiating team in Vienna hinted for the first time that Iran's delegation might not engage in talks with France's representatives on the provision of fuel to the Tehran reactor. The Iranian officials said that France was not an acceptable partner in this field because of its poor record of nuclear cooperation with Iran, especially related to the Eurodif company.[47] Hours later, media outlets close to the Iranian government announced that because of the Islamic Republic of Iran's opposition based on France's lack of adherence to its previous commitments, Paris would "definitely" not be included in the consortium of countries to provide fuel for the Tehran Research Reactor. Iran's delegation announced, "Talks with these countries offering to provide fuel to the Tehran reactor [are] lacking in the necessary guarantees and France has definitely been removed from the negotiation process." The United States, Russia, and the IAEA were incredulous, as France was the only country other than Argentina possessing the technology to convert the fuel into fuel rods. Tehran's request was soon dropped, and the ninth government abandoned its publicity campaign on the issue.

One of America's goals with this plan was the reduction of regional tension, as this exchange would forestall any possible Israeli plans to attack Iran's nuclear facilities. Given that some unofficial sources were reporting that Iran had achieved the capability to build an atomic bomb in the space of one year, the removal of most of Iran's enriched uranium from the country would create confidence that the path to a nuclear-armed Iran had been extended by at least a year. Therefore, the Obama administration was, on the one hand, trying to buy time to reassure Israel and hard-line American neoconservatives, and on the other, in need of a display of progress in the strategy of engagement with Iran, a policy that for the past year had yielded few achievements that Obama could show off domestically.

The Ahmadinejad administration was equally eager for a victory on the global stage, in light of the domestic crisis it faced. On a September 2009 trip to New York, Ahmadinejad said that he was doing everything possible to resolve issues with America but that the United States had not responded appropriately, with Obama failing even to reply to his letter.

In my opinion, this plan was truly in Iran's national interests. I was from the start and still am opposed to Ahmadinejad's approach to foreign and nuclear policy, and it is for this reason that I was arrested.[48] But this doesn't mean that if Ahmadinejad does something good in the foreign policy arena, I automatically oppose it. The fuel exchange plan, of which Ahmadinejad approved, had six important benefits for Iran:

- This exchange could have been the first step toward the official recognition of enrichment in Iran by the P5+1.
- The plan could have been the first important action intended for confidence building between Iran and the West during the Ahmadinejad period. This was particularly significant given the president's harsh and extremist statements on such subjects as the Holocaust, wiping Israel off the map, and his defiance of UN Security Council and IAEA resolutions. Ahmadinejad had brought unprecedented distrust in relations between Iran and the West, and this plan could be seen as the first move by Ahmadinejad to repair the relations.
- This plan could have reinforced Obama's position against pressures from the Israel lobby and neoconservatives to take a harder line on Iran.
- This plan could have strengthened the positions of Russia, China, and the Non-Aligned Movement in defending Iran.
- If this plan had been carried out, the subsequent UN Security Council Resolution 1929 of June 2010, which expanded sanctions against Iran, would not have been passed.

- This plan could have broken the existing impasse in Iran's negotiations with the United States and opened the way for Iran-U.S. negotiations on bilateral relations, as well as on Afghanistan and Iraq. This would have been a great step forward for advancing peace and stability in the region.

Notwithstanding these potential benefits of the proposed fuel swap, the Iranian government began backing away from it, largely due to domestic political maneuvering.

Before the agreement in Geneva, Ahmadinejad had not coordinated this plan with Iran's supreme leader. According to Iran's constitution, the supreme leader—not the president—is the final decisionmaker on foreign policy matters. According to the Iranian constitution, this plan should have been discussed at and coordinated with the Supreme National Security Council and should have received the supreme leader's approval.

Ahmadinejad earlier had criticized both of Iran's former nuclear negotiation chiefs (Rouhani and Larijani) about their agreements with the IAEA, EU3, and later P5+1, going so far as to accuse them of treason and submissiveness and of surrendering. Now an opportunity was created for Larijani and Rouhani to reciprocate. In the crisis conditions prevailing within the country because of the presidential election, Ahmadinejad's domestic opponents didn't want him to be able to consolidate his position in Iran or internationally by reaching an agreement with America. Leaders such as Mir Hossein Mousavi and Expediency Council Secretary Mohsen Rezaei joined Ali Larijani, now the Speaker of the Majles, in criticizing the proposed exchange. Even some hard-line Principlists argued that this plan was a ploy of the ninth government and the West against Iran's national interest.

Meanwhile, some other critics believed that if Iran were willing now to import fuel for the Tehran Research Reactor, what was the justification for the costly effort in the preceding years to enrich uranium in Iran and incur rounds of UN sanctions? About two decades earlier, at the climax of the war with Iraq, Iran's government had secured uranium needed for the Tehran Research Reactor from Argentina. For this reason, critics believed that Iran could have avoided the extravagant (political) cost of enrichment and Security Council sanctions and instead quietly negotiated to obtain fuel as it had in the 1980s.[49]

The expansive propaganda of the Western media in painting the transfer of most of Iran's enriched uranium reserves out of the country as a great victory for the Western world was also a factor in Iran's ultimate rejection of the deal.

In addition to critics of the government and some reformist forces, a great wave of opposition on this issue came from Principlists in the Majles. This was in part rooted in political competition, and in part due to the fact that Iranians were worried about being tricked by the West. The plan called for transferring out of the country, and for an extended period of time, most of the uranium that Iran had enriched in the previous years, but what guarantees were there that the West would then follow through on its part of the bargain?

In Washington, congressional worries about pursuing Barack Obama's approach on the matter of the enriched uranium exchange were no less than those of Iran. Some in Washington were afraid that in planning such a proposal, the U.S. government would fall into its own trap—meaning that the Iranian government, by responding to this initiative, would suck Washington into endless negotiations. There was a serious concern among some U.S. officials that time was being wasted and that Iran would be able to buy time through the tactic of unproductive negotiations on this issue.

It is interesting to note that despite radical rhetoric, Ahmadinejad tried his utmost to open direct, bilateral dialogue with the United States. On the October 2009 Geneva deal, as ElBaradei remembers, "We were at an impasse. I called on Salehi, who, to my surprise, said they would deliver the entire twelve hundred kilograms if the United States were their counterpart in the agreement, instead of Russia or France." Iran, in other words, wanted to use this as an opportunity to engage in talks directly with the United States. According to ElBaradei, "This is what Ahmadinejad told me they wanted all along." But unfortunately, this last attempt by Iran to engage comprehensively with the United States failed, as the United States officially informed ElBaradei that it "would not be a partner in the agreement."[50]

Although I believe that Obama was prepared for engagement, due to domestic political constraints—specifically, the Israel issue—he was not able to go for the grand bargain that Iran was looking for. It was only after this negative reaction from Washington that ElBaradei was informed that uranium would be transferred out of Iran only in batches of four hundred kilograms, and only after Iran received the promised fuel.[51]

After the third round of talks on October 19, 2009, ElBaradei announced that a draft agreement about the enrichment of Iranian uranium in Russia for use in the Tehran reactor had been circulated and emphasized that this plan had been tacitly approved by Iran and Russia. The IAEA gave the negotiating sides two days to give a definite answer on the plan. That same day, the head of the Islamic Republic's negotiating delegation in Vienna said that the other sides must reply to Iran after obtaining instructions from their capitals.

Hours after ElBaradei's statement, France, the United States, and shortly thereafter Russia announced their approval of the draft agreement circulated by the IAEA and expressed hope that Iran would indicate its response to ElBaradei's request within two days. Despite this, Soltanieh announced that Tehran would give its official response one week later. The Western press reported that Iran had refused to accept the IAEA's draft agreement for the sale of nuclear fuel.

One week later, Iran's representative in Vienna announced that Tehran would continue its negotiations with the IAEA about the transfer of fuel and that Iran's economic and technical concerns about the provision of fuel for the Tehran Research Reactor had to be taken into consideration in the text of any agreement or contract emanating from the negotiations. ElBaradei confirmed that the agency had received Tehran's reply verbally, while reiterating that the agreement did not need to be changed.

At the end of a two-day meeting in Brussels, the 27 member countries of the European Union requested that Iran accept the IAEA's proposal for the provision of fuel to the research reactor. At a meeting with Israeli officials in Jerusalem, Hillary Clinton also said that Tehran had a limited window of time to respond to the IAEA draft agreement on uranium enrichment.

At the peak of pressure on Iran to accept the plan, it became clear that Iran now wanted different terms than those that had been discussed in the October negotiation in Vienna. Iran now proposed that it not send its enriched uranium abroad before the fuel in question arrived at the Tehran reactor. First fuel rods would be transferred to Iran and only after that would a portion of Iran's uranium reserves be sent abroad. The exchange would take place on Iranian soil. Iran also wanted to transfer its uranium out of the country in installments, not all at once, after the receipt of fuel for the Tehran reactor. This counterproposal came as the U.S. secretary of state said repeatedly that the Vienna Group's offer to Iran and the text of the nuclear fuel agreement would not be changed.

The director general of the IAEA, in a new and tactical approach that ran counter to the Vienna negotiation process, announced that to overcome Iran's objections to the transfer of uranium to Russia, Iran's uranium could be transferred to Turkey instead.

In my opinion, none of the conditions proposed by Iran were serious. In the later trilateral Iran-Turkey-Brazil agreement of May 2010, Tehran didn't secure any of these demands. I believe that internal opposition to the Geneva plan caused Iran to choose the tactic of proposing these conditions without rejecting the basics of the P5+1 plan in order to buy time to increase its uranium reserves to 2.5 tons. This would mean that even after the transfer of 1,200 kilograms out of the country, it would retain more than 1,000 kilograms in low-enriched uranium reserves, which would reduce the risk to Iran of the exchange.

At any rate, based on decision of Ayatollah Khamenei, Tehran in effect rejected the fuel exchange agreement. Soltanieh accordingly announced in an interview with *Der Spiegel* that if the Western world did not sell Iran fuel, the country would produce fuel enriched to 20 percent on its own.

Under these conditions, the IAEA Board of Governors met on November 26, 2009, in Vienna and for the first time since February 2006 issued a resolution against Iran. It also requested the immediate suspension of construction of the Fordow facility. Of the 35 members of the Board of Governors, 25 countries voted in favor and three (Venezuela, Cuba, and Malaysia) voted against the resolution. Afghanistan, Brazil, Egypt, Pakistan, South Africa, and Turkey abstained from voting, and the representative from Azerbaijan left the meeting before the vote was conducted.

In his speech commencing the meeting, ElBaradei described Iran's positions, especially on the fuel exchange deal, as discouraging. In responding to the new resolution, Iran's representative to the IAEA stated that Tehran would not implement a single word of the resolution's requests. He said that Iran would reduce the level of its cooperation with the IAEA to a minimum and stop voluntarily allowing inspectors access to its nuclear facilities beyond the Comprehensive Safeguards Agreement.

Two days later, Ahmadinejad's cabinet ordered the Atomic Energy Organization to implement plans for the creation of ten enrichment sites on the scale of Natanz. The agency's head, Ali Akbar Salehi, likewise said, "The Cabinet's decision for the building of 10 new enrichment sites and investigation into 20% enrichment is a powerful answer to the unacceptable action of the 5+1 in the recent Board of Governors meeting."

Following Tehran's decision to build ten new enrichment sites, Turkish Prime Minister Recep Tayyip Erdogan publicly discussed for the first time in a meeting with Barack Obama Ankara's efforts and readiness to mediate between Iran and the P5+1 on the nuclear issue. American officials welcomed this offer.

Ahmadinejad's order to Iran's Atomic Energy Organization to construct ten enrichment centers drew two foreign reactions: It was called a political "threat" and a technical "bluff." International political officials tried to take advantage of this issue and once again accuse Iran of violating Security Council resolutions and to threaten Iran with further sanctions. International analysts questioned whether Iran really had the necessary technical capability to build ten new enrichment centers. The answer to this question was not easy. After about fifteen years of continuous work on the Natanz facility, Iran had been able to install at most 9,000 centrifuges at the facility. The IAEA report indicated that Iran had, as of 2011, fewer than 5,000 centrifuges in operation. For the facility to be complete and for the development of an industrial-level fuel cycle, 50,000 centrifuges must be installed. By this count, ten new enrichment centers on the scale of Natanz would require 500,000 centrifuges, which would take a very long time to build. And even if Iran could produce so many centrifuges, where would it get the uranium necessary to feed them?

Some American and European circles wondered whether Iran announced plans to build ten new facilities in anticipation of the possibility that other previously undeclared enrichment plants would be discovered. Iran could reply that it had officially announced its intention to build ten new enrichment complexes and that it didn't see any need, under the Safeguards Agreement, to provide information to the IAEA about the location of these construction sites.

Iran had only one nuclear power plant, at Bushehr, and by contract its fuel would be provided by Russia for a decade. Building new power plants would take one to two decades, provided that Iran was not under strict sanction and that some countries were prepared for nuclear cooperation with Iran. Given this reality, what was the purpose of accelerating the announcement of building new enrichment facilities?

Considering the great cost of the Natanz facilities and the serious economic problems that Iran faced domestically, would Iran really be able to embark upon such expensive projects? If Iran could secure raw uranium and yellowcake and had the technical capability to outfit two new enrichment sites, Western analysts asked, why was the Natanz facility after five years using only 10 percent of what its operational capacity was supposed to be (50,000 centrifuges)?

Some commentators even speculated that Iran was trying to provoke Israel or America to attack Iran. According to Mark Fitzpatrick of the International Institute for Strategic Studies, the plan to build ten enrichment centers was mere boasting on Iran's part, though it unfortunately made an attack on Iran more probable and the expansion of sanctions easier.[52]

Finally, at this juncture, the Iranophobia strategy, which had also been used in previous periods, was pursued with greater vigor in some Western (especially American, British, and Israeli) media outlets. The *Times* of London reported that Iran was in the final stages of testing for an atomic bomb and claimed that a document had come to light on a four-year program by Tehran to test "neutron initiators" (a neutron initiator is the part of a nuclear bomb that triggers the fission chain reaction).[53] The newspaper went on to quote an unnamed "Asian intelligence source" as claiming that an Asian country had supplied Iran with neutron initiators. According to the newspaper, Tehran was working on the nuclear initiator project a recently as 2007. The *Guardian* also reported that Tehran may have experimented with designs for advanced nuclear warheads. According to the report: "The very existence of the technology, known as a 'two-point implosion' device, is officially secret in both the United States and Britain, but according to previously unpublished documentation in a dossier compiled by the International Atomic Energy Agency, Iranian scientists may have tested high-explosive components of the design."[54] The *Times* of London published news about some Russian nuclear scientists helping Iran in constructing a nuclear bomb. According to the newspaper's report, denied by the Russian Foreign Ministry, Israeli leaders on a trip to Moscow had provided the Kremlin with a list of the names of these scientists.[55]

THE DECISION TO ENRICH TO 20 PERCENT

In early January 2010, Tehran indicated that it would give the West until the end of the month to make a decision on the provision of fuel to the Tehran Research Reactor and threatened that if the West did not reach an agreement with Iran on reactor fuel by then, Iran would move forward with the production of nuclear fuel for the reactor on its own. It seems that at this point the countdown to the expansion of Iran sanctions had started in earnest, though this countdown at first ticked away very slowly due to clear opposition from countries like China and a lack of enthusiasm from countries like Russia.

Although some high-level European officials threatened that new sanctions could be put in place as soon as February 2010, later developments including China's lack of high-level participation in P5+1 meetings in New York in spring 2010 and the statements of Russian officials showed that reaching a consensus in the UN Security Council on the expansion of Iran sanctions would take more than one month.

In early February 2010, Mahmoud Ahmadinejad defended the fuel exchange plan in an interview on Iranian state television, while his domestic opponents criticized the plan. Ahmadinejad's statements were welcomed by Moscow and by some media outlets as indicating Tehran's assent to the fuel swap based on the IAEA's proposal. Later statements, however, by Manouchehr Mottaki, the foreign minister, that the exchange would have to be done on Iranian soil and that Tehran would have to receive the 20 percent enriched fuel before transferring its low-enriched uranium to Russia forced many to come to the conclusion that the position taken by Ahmadinejad on television was mostly just propaganda in response to domestic criticism.

Despite this, in my view, Ahmadinejad's numerous statements defending a fuel exchange and his attacks on domestic critics over the issue showed that the Ahmadinejad administration sought a deal of some kind with the West, and specifically with the United States, to reduce the acrimony of the nuclear confrontation. Vigorous domestic opposition from reformist and Principlist critics of the administration and ultimately the opposition of the supreme leader defeated the fuel exchange deal.

In a speech during a meeting in Munich in February 2010, Mottaki asserted that timing, location, and quantity were important matters for Tehran on the uranium exchange issue and emphasized that as long as Iran had not received the needed guarantees, the proposal would not be implemented. He did, however, speak of the future of the agreement in optimistic tones.[56]

On February 7, 2010, under the direct order of Ahmadinejad, the production of 20 percent-enriched uranium officially commenced. Two days later, with Ali Akbar Salehi in attendance, 3.5 percent-enriched uranium was introduced into centrifuges at Natanz to be enriched up to 20 percent.

The decision to enrich to 20 percent, of which Iran officially notified the IAEA on February 8, drew an immediate and harsh response from the Western world. Following a meeting with U.S. Defense Secretary Robert Gates, Italian Prime Minister Franco Frattini demanded that Iran stop stalling and said that the international community should not allow Iran to continuously change its positions on enrichment within Iran and the transfer of uranium abroad. For his part, Gates, in a meeting with French President Sarkozy, advocated increased pressure on Iran. Russia similarly indicated that the expansion of sanctions on Iran was likely, with Konstantin Kosachev, head of the Foreign Affairs Committee of Russia's Duma, stating that Tehran's decision was "a step back" and "this opened the way for supporters of sanctions against Iran."[57] The new IAEA director general, Yukiya Amano, likewise expressed his concern over Iran's move to begin enrichment to 20 percent.

Amid such condemnation, Washington made a new offer to Iran: America and other countries would provide Iran with the isotopes it needed for medical purposes and, in exchange, Iran would forgo enrichment up to 20 percent. Soon thereafter, the United States, Russia, and France sent a joint letter to the IAEA sharply criticizing Iran's actions in increasing the level of uranium enrichment and proposing that if Iran were not inclined to accept the IAEA's offer, it could procure medical radioisotopes from the global market "as a reasonable, timely and cost effective alternative to the IAEA's proposal."[58] On February 2011, Salehi, the head of Iran's Atomic Energy Organization, officially declared: "If they are ready to supply the fuel rods for TRR [the Tehran Research Reactor], we would stop the entire process of 20% enrichment."[59]

Finally on February 11, Mahmoud Ahmadinejad gave news of the production of the first consignment of 20 percent-enriched uranium.[60] On this matter, White House spokesman Robert Gibbs, expressing doubts about Iran's abilities to produce nuclear fuel domestically, said, "We do not believe they have the capability to enrich to the degree to which they now say they are enriching," adding that Iran's claims were "based on politics, not on physics."[61] Iran's achievement, however, was confirmed by the International Atomic Energy Agency,[62] and it was a hefty achievement indeed.

THE ASSASSINATION OF IRANIAN NUCLEAR SCIENTISTS

In January 2010, unexpected news of the assassination of Massoud Ali-Mohammadi, a prominent physicist at the University of Tehran, came out, making headlines across the world. Several major interpretations of this news were published.

News outlets close to the postelection opposition movement said that Ali-Mohammadi was one of 420 professors who had published a statement explicitly supporting Mir Hossein Mousavi in the 2009 presidential election. There is no doubt that Ali-Mohammadi was among the critics of postelection conditions in Iran. Therefore, media outlets close to the Green Movement pointed an accusatory finger at the government and hard-line domestic elements and rogue groups, and turned his funeral, at which there was a heavy presence of security forces, into a political rally. The nature of the assassination operation also showed that it had been organized in a complex and professional manner.

Ahmadinejad administration officials immediately called the assassination the work of Israeli and/or American intelligence services aimed at disrupting Iran's nuclear program. Shortly thereafter, government sources and associated media outlets claimed that an obscure monarchist group called Tondar, which they said was related to the Iran Royal Association, had taken responsibility for the killing and that the United States had a hand in the plot.[63] The American government, of course, called this accusation "absurd." The Iran Royal Association, for its part, said that its supposed announcement claiming responsibility was the work of the cyber unit of Iran's Revolutionary Guard Corps and denied any role in the killing.[64]

Some observers believed that the nuclear physicist's assassination was a serious warning to individuals who might cooperate with Iran's nuclear program. At that time, the Ministry of Intelligence and Revolutionary Guard had stepped up considerably their security and intelligence probes of scientists and other involved with Iran's nuclear program. Others posited that the assassination had been carried out by the armed opposition to the regime with the goal of creating unrest and insecurity in the country's political sphere.

In 2007, another Iranian nuclear expert, Ardeshir Hosseinpour, who was employed at the Isfahan uranium conversion facility, had died under mysterious circumstances, with some reports alleging involvement by Israel's Mossad.[65] That same year, Alireza Asghari, a former deputy minister of defense and Revolutionary Guard commander, went missing during a trip to Turkey, and some Western and regional media reported that he had sought political asylum in the United States.[66] These events around the same time as the highly controversial affair involving Shahram Amiri showed that behind the scenes and despite Iran-West diplomatic negotiations, a war of intelligence services was going on.

The Amiri affair opened up a new conflict between Iran and America, and specifically between the two countries' intelligence apparatuses. The story began in spring 2009, when Shahram Amiri, a nuclear scientist, left Iran for Saudi Arabia and then disappeared after three days. In October, Foreign Minister Mottaki met with UN Secretary-General Ban Ki-moon on the sidelines of General Assembly meetings to complain about the disappearance of four Iranians—including Amiri and Asghari—in which Tehran believed the United States had a hand.[67] Mottaki went on to publicly accuse the United States of kidnapping Amiri, saying, "We've obtained documents about the U.S. involvement in Shahram Amiri's disappearance,"[68] and saying that it was mere speculation on the part of the Western media that Amiri was involved with Iran's Atomic Energy Organization.

After that, the affair took on a new form. Some Western media outlets reported that Shahram Amiri had sought political asylum in the United States and that he was the main source of new intelligence about the Fordow site. On two occasions, Iran summoned the Swiss ambassador in

Tehran, who often serves as an intermediary between Iran and the United States, and requested Amiri's return to the country from the United States. The American media portrayed him as a spy for the CIA in Iran who had for a long time provided the United States with important information about the dimensions of Iran's secret nuclear program. Iranian officials denied that he had worked in any way with the country's Atomic Energy Organization.

The release of two contradictory videos from Amiri in June 2010 turned the affair into an even greater international spectacle. The first video of Amiri was broadcast on Iranian state television on June 7 and had apparently been recorded on April 5 in Tucson, Arizona. In the low-quality webcam video, Amiri said that he had been kidnapped by U.S. and Saudi intelligence services and then flown to the United States, where he was tortured and forced to say that he defected with evidence of Iranian nuclear secrets. Within a day, a second video was released on YouTube in which Amiri, well-dressed under studio lighting and apparently reading from a script, said that he was happy and free in the United States and wanted to stay in the country to continue his education. He added that he had no involvement in any Iranian weapons research.[69] Then, on June 29, Iranian state television broadcast a third video of Amiri, in which he said that he had escaped from U.S. agents in Virginia and dismissed the second video as a "complete fabrication."[70] ABC News later reported, citing informed American sources, that Iran's Intelligence Ministry had threatened that if Amiri did not release an Internet video stating that he had been kidnapped by the U.S. government, his son would be harmed.[71]

On July 13, 2010, Amiri unexpectedly appeared at the Iranian interest section of the Pakistani Embassy in Washington requesting assistance to return to Iran. The next day, he boarded a flight out of the United States. While Iranian officials reiterated the allegation that he had been abducted by the CIA, according to a U.S. State Department spokesman, Amiri's departure showed that he had not been coerced into coming to or staying in the United States: "He has been in the United States of his own free will and obviously he is free to go."[72]

Amiri received a hero's welcome in Tehran and said in a subsequent interview that he had rejected an offer of $50 million by the United States to cooperate and to claim to have a laptop containing evidence of an Iranian nuclear weapons program. About the same time as his return to Iran, Foreign Minister Mottaki responded to a reporter's question about whether Amiri should be recognized as a hero by saying that Iran first had to verify his claim of being abducted and find out what had happened during his stay in the United States.

After returning to Iran, Shahram Amiri disappeared from view, and no news was published about him or his family. There was speculation that he was under investigation by the Ministry of Intelligence. Immediately after Amiri's return to Iran, it was reported that he had received more than $5 million from the CIA to provide intelligence on Iran's nuclear program. According to the article, Amiri had been paid but now that he had returned to Iran would be unable to access the money because of UN sanctions.[73]

Many believe that the Shahram Amiri affair resembles that of KGB officer Vitaly Yurchenko. In 1985, Yurchenko defected to the United States during an assignment in Rome and began to cooperate with the CIA. Just months later, however, Yurchenko fled to the Soviet Embassy in Washington, from where he gave a news conference claiming that he had been drugged and kidnapped by CIA agents. Upon returning to the Soviet Union, Yurchenko was awarded the Order of the Red Star but nonetheless was subject to a secret investigation by the KGB.[74]

In my opinion, Amiri was from the start not an important player. He was not a nuclear scientist, nor did he hold an important position, such that he would possess valuable information. Thus, all the controversy was baseless. He might have just been playing a spy game of some sort.

CHAPTER TEN

THE CRISIS WORSENS

AMANO'S FIRST REPORT ON IRAN

On February 18, 2010, Yukiya Amano's first report on Iran to the IAEA Board of Governors was published. It consisted of ten pages and 51 paragraphs and followed up on the Western world's sharp criticism of Tehran. Some of its requests were similar to those in Mohamed ElBaradei's reports, though Yukiya Amano's requests were considered more explicit and forceful. The new director general showed that unlike his predecessor, he had no intention of issuing equivocal reports. Amano showed more determination to obtain answers to questions about the goals and nature of Iran's nuclear program.

In my view, this report was the harshest of its kind in the six-plus years of the Iran nuclear crisis. The most important part of the report was the connection it established between Iran's nuclear activities and its weapons and missile production. In much more explicit terms than preceding reports, the February 18 report referenced the possible military dimensions of Iran's nuclear program and expressed concern about the possible existence of past and present undeclared activities related to nuclear warhead development by military entities connected to the regime.

Among questions and ambiguities related to possible military dimension explicitly mentioned in this report were the following:

> Whether Iran was engaged in undeclared activities for the production of UF$_4$ [uranium tetrafluoride, also known as green salt] involving the Kimia Maadan company; whether Iran's exploding bridgewire detonator activities were solely for civil or conventional military purposes; whether Iran developed a spherical implosion system, possibly with the assistance of a foreign expert knowledgeable in explosives technology; whether the engineering design and computer modeling studies aimed at producing a new design for the payload chamber of a missile were for a nuclear payload; and the relationship between various attempts by senior Iranian officials with links to military organizations in Iran to obtain nuclear related technology and equipment.[1]

Paragraph 43 of the report went on,

> The Agency would also like to discuss with Iran: the project and management structure of alleged activities related to nuclear explosives; nuclear related safety arrangements for a number of the alleged projects; details relating to the manufacture of components for high explosives initiation systems; and experiments concerning the generation and detection of neutrons.

The report stressed that from August 2008 on, while stating that claims related to possible military dimensions of its nuclear program were baseless and any information the agency had obtained pointing to such dimensions was falsified, Tehran had refused to take part in any talks with the IAEA about these issues or to grant more access or information.

In short, this report accused Iran, directly or indirectly, of pursuing a military nuclear and missile program, an unprecedented move for IAEA director general reports.

The new IAEA director general also criticized Iran's construction of the Fordow plant without informing the agency as contravening the country's commitments and stressed that Iran had not granted inspectors access to design documents or to companies involved in the enrichment facility's design. This report emphasized in more explicit terms than ElBaradei's previous reports that it could not verify that Iran was not enriching uranium at sites other than the country's two declared enrichment facilities.

The report stressed that Iran had not carried out the requests of any UN Security Council resolution, nor had it cooperated with the IAEA on matters such as the sampling of heavy water tanks, alleged military studies, and the implementation of the Additional Protocol. Amano repeated ElBaradei's earlier statements that Iran's March 2007 decision to suspend the implementation of Code 3.1 of the Subsidiary Arrangements, which Iran had agreed to implement in 2003, with the approval of the Supreme National Security Council and the country's leadership, was illegal under Article 39 of Iran's Safeguards Agreement and that the article's implementation was legally mandated. The report emphasized that Iran had not informed the agency in a timely fashion of the decision to build either the Darkhovin or Fordow facilities, as was required under Code 3.1.

Amano's report sharply criticized the declared increase in the level of enrichment of uranium-235 from 5 percent to 20 percent and Iran's failure to promptly announce this increase to the agency, which it called a clear violation of the Safeguards Agreement. Amano stressed that because of Iran's late notification, IAEA inspectors did not have the necessary opportunity to monitor adherence to the Safeguards Agreement in the enrichment process. The lack of implementation of Code 3.1, Amano noted, had decreased the agency's confidence in the absence of undeclared nuclear sites in Iran.

In response to this harsh report, Iran's representative to the IAEA declared in a February 24 letter that the director general's report was not fair or truthful. Iran decried the omission of the fact that all of the declared nuclear materials in the country were under the supervision of the agency and accounted for. The letter pointed out that the report failed to mention past reports' judgment that there was not clear evidence of a nuclear-weapons program in Iran. Also, the United States and other countries did not allow the IAEA to provide Tehran with documents related to claims of military-nuclear studies, a point that the director general did not acknowledge. The letter concluded, after an account of instances of Tehran's cooperation with the agency, by calling Amano's report unprofessional, politicized, and biased, all for the purpose of increasing pressure on Iran.

On March 20, 2010, Barack Obama stated in a Persian New Year message to the Iranian people that "we are working with the international community to hold the Iranian government accountable because they refuse to live up to their international obligations. But our offer of comprehensive diplomatic contacts and dialogue stands." Obama also spoke of the pursuit of expanded sanctions against Iran to prevent Tehran from obtaining nuclear technology.[2]

A meeting of G8 foreign ministers began on March 29 under the shadow of new reports from the international media about secret efforts by Iran to build two new sites like the Fordow facility. The meeting, which was organized for the discussion of global security, was hosted by Canada and treated Iran's nuclear activities as military in nature and Iran as a danger to international peace and security.[3]

Several days later, Obama expressed one of his hardest-line stances on Iran to date. In an interview with CBS, the president suggested that new sanctions would be the only thing to deter Iran from developing nuclear weapons: "All the evidence indicates that the Iranians are trying to develop the capacity to develop nuclear weapons. They might decide that, once they have that capacity that they'd hold off right at the edge—in order not to incur more sanctions."[4]

On April 9, 2010, and during the celebration of Iran's Nuclear Technology Day, which had always been a stage for propaganda for the ninth government and for Mahmoud Ahmadinejad personally, the third generation of Iranian centrifuges was unveiled. This new model, Ahmadinejad said, had six times the enrichment capability of the centrifuges in use at the time. He claimed that Iran was the only country that had mastery over the entire enrichment process from start to finish. Addressing countries that possessed nuclear warheads, he said, "When a tool is in your hands you use it to threaten other nations, and thus encourage those countries to obtain weapons themselves."[5]

Iran's Atomic Energy Organization head, Ali Akbar Salehi, emphasized that the construction of the Fordow site would continue. He said further that "the government has decided to create other similar sites across the country with suitable natural defenses, and has already begun preliminary location scouting and the first stages of evaluating new locations."

On April 12, the United States hosted an unprecedented nuclear security summit in Washington, D.C., which was attended by the leaders of more than forty countries. The summit was arranged before the latest director general's report on Iran and neither Iran nor North Korea was invited. In a news conference with South African President Jacob Zuma the day before the summit began, Obama stressed the necessity of preventing terrorists from obtaining nuclear weapons. Secretary of State Hillary Clinton added in an interview with ABC's This Week, "We want to get the world's attention focused where we think it needs to be, with these continuing efforts by al-Qaeda and others to get just enough nuclear material to cause terrible havoc, destruction, and loss of life somewhere in the world."[6] Immediately after Chinese President Hu Jintao's trip to Washington to participate in the conference, the Chinese government issued a statement indicating its possible support for a new round of sanctions against Iran.[7]

The two-day nuclear security summit followed by one week the publication of the Obama administration's fifty-page Nuclear Posture Review outlining America's new nuclear strategy. The strategy was a change from previous U.S. nuclear policy and bore the clear imprint of Obama's stance on nuclear arms reduction. Several elements of the review are relevant to the Iran nuclear issue.

The Nuclear Posture Review declared that non–nuclear-weapon states that are signatories of the NPT and in compliance with their nonproliferation obligations are safe from American nuclear retaliation, even if such countries attack America by cyber or biological means. However, two countries—Iran and North Korea—could be excluded from this guarantee: North Korea because it possesses nuclear weapons, and, potentially Iran, insofar as it is not in compliance with its nonproliferation obligations. The clear message of the strategy to Tehran and Pyongyang was: If you do not follow the rules and if you are recognized as a violator of the Non-Proliferation Treaty, then all options for countering you—even a preemptive nuclear strike—will be on the table.

Although the Nuclear Posture Review sought to reduce the role of nuclear weapons and emphasize the goal of nuclear disarmament, the implied threat to Iran and North Korea of the use of nuclear weapons was directly connected to the Cold War era concept of "deterrence" and showed that

America still reserved the option to use nuclear weapons as deterrents. Obama's nuclear policy implicitly placed a special emphasis on the nuclear deterrence option, that is, the option for America to attack any country that is likely building or possesses nuclear arms. The Obama administration did not want to relinquish the weapon of fear.

The threat of nuclear attack not only runs contrary to the tenets of the Non-Proliferation Treaty, but also could provide a good excuse for Iran to build nuclear weapons. When a great nuclear power such as the United States in its official Nuclear Posture Review openly threatens a country under the pretext of deterrence (and even disarmament) with nuclear attack, doesn't that encourage that country to go nuclear itself to guarantee its own security? One may argue that if proliferation is a threat to international peace and security, and if a state violates the NPT and acquires nuclear weapons and commits aggression, it could be valid under the International Court of Justice opinion to threaten to use nuclear weapons to prevent or respond to a threat to the existence of one's state (or ally). This argument may be valid but does not apply to Iran, as it is a member of the NPT, is cooperating with the IAEA, and does not possess nuclear weapons.* A nuclear-weapon state should not individually threaten a non–nuclear-armed state with nuclear attack.

Iran was named along with North Korea as proliferation challenges even though the two cases were completely different from one another. North Korea had withdrawn from the NPT and tested nuclear weapons, while Iran was committed to the NPT and possessed no nuclear arms. In addition, the process of global powers' negotiations with Pyongyang was always completely different from the process of negotiating with Iran, and the structure of power within Iran was completely different from North Korea's system.

In my view, pairing Iran and North Korea together facilitated some of the propaganda goals of the United States and its Western allies, but it was a mistake that would exacerbate the Iran nuclear crisis considerably. It signaled to Iran that the United States wanted to make Iran pay the price like North Korea for possessing nuclear weapons, even though Iran, unlike

---

* Editor's note: The IAEA has declared that Iran is not in compliance with its safeguards obligations and is not cooperating fully in answering outstanding questions or in implementing IAEA resolutions.

North Korea, did not possess such weapons. This begged the question that if Iran was already paying the price, why not actually go for the bomb and get the benefits of nuclear deterrence?

One very important point in the Nuclear Posture Review was its emphasis on nuclear terrorism. From Obama's perspective, the greatest short-term, medium-term, and long-term threat to America's national security was the prospect of militant, non-state actors obtaining nuclear weapons. Given the accusations of supporting terrorism directed at Tehran, the focus on nuclear terrorism was another way in which the Nuclear Posture Review zeroed in on countries like Iran.

In revising its nuclear policy, the United States greatly restricted the conditions under which it would possibly use nuclear weapons. Also, according to the revised U.S. strategy, the country would not produce new nuclear warheads, a decision that commendably fulfilled Obama's campaign promises. Despite this, a relatively long and difficult path remained to ending the era of hypocritical policies that gave the necessary pretext to states interested in possessing nuclear weapons.

Key figures in Iran responded defiantly to the new U.S. nuclear strategy.[8] Supreme Leader Ali Khamenei: "The international community should not let Obama get away with nuclear threats. . . . We will not allow America to renew its hellish dominance over Iran by using such threats."[9] Khamenei initially called President Obama's statements on the Nuclear Posture Review "disgraceful" and an indication that "the U.S. government is wicked and unreliable."[10] President Mahmoud Ahmadinejad's response: "World summits being organized these days are intended to humiliate human beings. . . . These foolish people who are in charge are like stupid, retarded people who brandish their swords whenever they face shortcomings, without realizing that the time for this type of thing is over."[11] Iran's armed forces chief of staff Hassan Firouzabadi: "If the U.S. seriously threatens Iran and takes an action against Iran, none of the American soldiers in the region would return to the United States alive."[12] Ahmad Vahidi, Iran's defense minister and former chief of the Revolutionary Guard Corps Quds Force, said, "We, too, announce that we will use all options to defend ourselves."[13]

Parliament Speaker Ali Larijani said that "the U.S. President is taking the same previous arrogant and hegemonic approach through demagogic gestures."[14] Three-quarters of the Majles also signed a petition calling on the Foreign Ministry to lodge a formal complaint with the United Nations on the grounds that the United States represents a "threat against international peace."[15] Iran's ambassador to the United Nations, Mohammad Khazaee, wrote a letter to the United Nations describing the statements by President Obama and Secretary Gates as "nuclear blackmail" against Iran, "a serious violation" of the UN charter, and "a real threat to international peace and security."[16]

Nevertheless, on April 17, 2010, less than one week after the Washington nuclear security conference, Tehran organized an "International Nuclear Disarmament Conference" of its own that was attended by ten foreign ministers and fourteen deputy foreign ministers as well as nuclear experts from 60 countries.[17] This conference, which had in truth been organized with the intention of refocusing international criticism from Tehran to Tel Aviv, had on its official agenda the consideration of issues like the revision of the NPT, means of preventing double standards, mechanisms for the just oversight and control of nuclear activities across the world, and disarmament in the Middle East.

Iranian officials made every effort to score publicity points and exploit the conference, which commenced with a message from Supreme Leader Khamenei and a speech by Mahmoud Ahmadinejad. In his message, Ayatollah Khamenei called America "the only perpetrator of atomic crime in the world" and stressed his religious *fatwa* against weapons of mass destruction in saying, "We recognize the use of these weapons as forbidden [*haram*] and the protection of mankind from this great disaster as the duty of all." He also told the conference that "the world's only atomic criminal lies and presents itself as being against nuclear weapons proliferation, while it has not taken any serious measures in this regard."[18]

In the opening ceremony of the conference, Ahmadinejad laid out five propositions for global disarmament, saying that Iran was prepared to help in the "management of global disarmament" and share with other countries its knowledge and experience in the nuclear field.[19] Ahmadinejad's five proposals were as follows:

1. The establishment by the UN General Assembly of an independent international working group on nuclear disarmament and non-proliferation.

2. The suspension from the IAEA and its Board of Governors of any countries possessing, using, or supplying nuclear weapons.

3. A revision of the NPT by independent and non–nuclear-armed countries.

4. A collective effort to reform the structure of the UN Security Council, including either abolishing veto rights or extending such rights to countries from South America, Africa, Europe, and Asia.

5. The establishment of a working group from those attending the Tehran International Nuclear Disarmament Conference in order to pursue the decisions reached in the conference.

The Iranian event had a less impressive guest list than the conference in Washington, with no major foreign heads of state in attendance. Iranian officials attributed the paltry and low-level turnout by foreign officials to American pressure and obstructionism. The title chosen for the conference, "Nuclear Energy for All—Nuclear Weapons for No One," showed that Tehran was attempting a sort of competition with the United States and P5+1 for leadership of the management of nuclear issues. Iran's foreign minister held private talks with American attendees (former officials and diplomats) behind closed doors to discuss U.S.-Iran relations.[20]

On April 24, 2010, the Western media reported on some new agreements between Iran and the IAEA that had the potential of reducing tension between Tehran and Washington. The reports, quoting unnamed diplomats, claimed that Iran had promised the agency greater cooperation and agreed to allow increased IAEA monitoring of the Natanz site that had for the previous two months been enriching uranium to a high level.

In early May, the eighth NPT review conference began in an atmosphere very different from that of previous conferences. The new president of the United States had pushed for a change in approach and was serious about placing nuclear disarmament on the agenda. After the expiration of the START I treaty between the United States and countries of the former Soviet Union, which provided for the reduction of nuclear arsenals, Obama signed a follow-up New START Treaty with Russia, which bound both countries to reduce the number of their deployed nuclear warheads and nuclear missile launchers. The New START Treaty, along with the release of the new U.S. Nuclear Posture Review, and the convening of the Washington nuclear security summit with dozens of heads of state, had set the stage for Washington's leadership of the NPT Review Conference.

THE JOINT TEHRAN DECLARATION

On May 17, 2010, the leaders of Turkey, Brazil, and Iran met in Tehran to find a way to revive the October 2009 nuclear fuel exchange deal. This occurred as the P5+1 was preparing to adopt new sanctions through the UN Security Council. Iran was frustrated and so sought to bring new actors into the diplomatic process who would be more sensitive to its perspectives and interests. Turkey, as a regional power, and Brazil, as an international power defending enrichment rights, were excellent candidates to fill this role, as Tehran enjoyed good relations with both countries. Including Turkey and Brazil, Iran hoped, would break the hold of the West on nuclear diplomacy and create a more balanced atmosphere.

Diplomatic activism by Turkey and Brazil on the Iran nuclear crisis had been under way for months before this meeting. Turkish Prime Minister Recep Tayyip Erdogan, who had shortly before gone on a tour of European countries (where Iran was an important topic of discussion), had expressed support for a solution to disputes related to Iran's nuclear program through diplomatic means instead of the implementation of economic sanctions. Together with Brazilian President Luiz Inácio (Lula) da Silva, Erdogan had stressed the need for cooperation and renewed efforts to find a new means to a peaceful resolution of the Iran nuclear issue at the Washington conference on nuclear security, and he reiterated his opposition to the imposition of further sanctions on Iran.

Because Brazil and Turkey were at this time both rotating members of the UN Security Council, these efforts raised hopes for a practical way out of the nuclear crisis. On April 28, 2010, Lula had emphasized in a news conference that he intended to convince the permanent members of the Security Council that sanctions against Iran would solve nothing. A few days after that, he reminded the world during a meeting with Venezuelan President Hugo Chávez that Brazil had not made any offer to Iran for the export of uranium—as had been alleged—and emphasized that Tehran had not yet showed that its nuclear program was intended exclusively for peaceful aims but that he was hopeful that talks with Iran could provide the necessary reassurance and prevent further sanctions.

According to an official 2008 International Monetary Fund report, the volume of Iran's commercial exchanges with Latin American countries had increased threefold since 2006 to reach $9.2 billion, of which $2 billion was with Brazil. It is natural that advancing Brazil's economic interests was among Lula's goals with his trip to Tehran. Brazil, which has experienced impressive economic growth and is considered to be an important emerging power, also sought with its diplomatic activism on the Iran nuclear issue to carve out its place on the global political stage.[21] Turkey has similar interests. By mediating the Iran nuclear issue, Turkey could promote its status as an important regional power.

After the U.S. president urged Turkey and Brazil "to impress upon Iran the opportunity presented by this offer to 'escrow' its uranium in Turkey while the nuclear fuel is being produced,"[22] a trilateral meeting of Iran, Turkey, and Brazil was held on May 17 on the sidelines of a conference of the G15, a group of major powers among developing countries, in Tehran. After the meeting, the three countries issued a ten-paragraph declaration focused on the exchange of nuclear fuel that was later called the Tehran Declaration and turned into one of the main propaganda maneuvers of the Ahmadinejad administration. Its highlights:

1. The declaration, like all the resolutions of the IAEA Board of Governors and UN Security Council, emphasized Iran's commitment to the NPT and the rights of the Islamic Republic to the peaceful use of nuclear energy (including fuel-cycle activities) without discrimination.

2. The Tehran Declaration described the fuel exchange deal as "a starting point to begin cooperation and a positive constructive move forward among nations" and called for the avoidance of "all kinds of confrontation through refraining from measures, action and rhetorical statements that would jeopardize Iran's rights and obligations under the NPT."

3. The most important part of the joint declaration was its fifth paragraph, which stated, "The Islamic Republic of Iran agrees to deposit 1200 kg LEU [low-enriched uranium] in Turkey. While in Turkey

this LEU will continue to be the property of Iran. Iran and the IAEA may station observers to monitor the safekeeping of the LEU in Turkey."

4. After that the declaration emphasized that upon the receipt of a positive response from the Vienna Group (the United States, Russia, France, and the IAEA), further details of the fuel exchange and relevant arrangements between Iran and the Vienna Group, which had explicitly agreed to transfer to Iran 120 kilograms of fuel needed for the Tehran Research Reactor, would be provided in a written agreement.

One Western analyst told me that one major problem with the deal was that it depended on no sanctions being agreed upon in the UN Security Council, while requiring nothing of Iran to address outstanding IAEA and Security Council demands for transparency. The declaration did not commit Iran to cease enriching uranium to 20 percent, since Obama's letter said nothing about a U.S. requirement that Iran halt its enrichment program, or even stop enriching uranium at near-20 percent levels.[23] Nevertheless, the agreement faced opposition from Iranian officials until the morning Erdogan arrived in Tehran. Erdogan recounted that Foreign Minister Ahmet Davutoglu informed him that morning that negotiations had proceeded successfully, and he decided to travel immediately to Iran to seal the deal before proceeding with a scheduled trip to Azerbaijan.

Although the trilateral fuel exchange agreement had the potential to create difficulties for the Obama adminstration in its pursuit of expanded sanctions against Iran, White House press secretary Robert Gibbs said in a news conference that the Tehran Declaration would not change America's policy toward Iran or its effort to impose further sanctions against the country. Secretary of State Hillary Clinton, following a meeting with Congress, announced that the permanent members of the UN Security Council had reached an agreement on a draft resolution against Iran.[24] This declaration met with criticism from Brazil's president, and Turkey's Erdogan.[25] Erdogan wrote to the leaders of 26 countries expressing frustration that the trilateral agreement among Iran, Turkey, and Brazil had been spurned, as he considered it an important step for the peaceful resolution of the Iranian nuclear issue.[26]

Shortly thereafter, in response to the American criticism, Brazil provided to the *New York Times* a secret letter from Barack Obama writen on April 20, 2010, in which he asked that Brazilian President Lula work to secure an agreement with Iran.[27] Obama said he welcomed an initiative by Lula and the prime minister of Turkey to facilitate Iran's agreement for a fuel swap.[28]

In his letter, Obama noted that the Tehran Research Reactor "is an opportunity to pave the way for a broader dialogue dealing with the more fundamental concerns of the international community regarding Iran's overall nuclear program." Specifically, Obama stated that "for us, Iran's agreement to transfer 1,200 kg of Iran's low-enriched uranium (LEU) out of the country would build confidence and reduce regional tensions by substantially reducing Iran's LEU stockpile." The Brazil-Turkey nuclear deal stipulated that Iran will transfer 1,200 kilograms of low-enriched uranium out of the country. On the issue of timing for a fuel swap and third-country custody of the Iranian uranium, Obama wrote: "We understand from you, Turkey, and others that Iran continues to propose that Iran would retain its LEU on its territory until there is a simultaneous exchange of its LEU for nuclear fuel. . . . I would urge Brazil to impress upon Iran the opportunity presented by this offer to 'escrow' its uranium in Turkey while the nuclear fuel is being produced." As part of the Brazil-Turkey deal, Iran agreed to take the "opportunity" presented to "escrow" its uranium in Turkey, for one year, pending the delivery of new fuel for the Tehran Research Reactor.[29]

The trilateral Iran-Brazil-Turkey declaration was noteworthy in several ways. The Ahmadinejad government had for a long time sought to include new players in nuclear negotiations and harshly criticized the former nuclear negotiating team under Dr. Rouhani's leadership for allowing negotiations with the international community to be limited to the P5+1. These criticisms indicated to me a lack of understanding of the international balance of power and the political structure of organizations such as the European Union, IAEA Board of Governors, and UN Security Council. The Tehran Declaration showed that the entrance of other countries onto the stage of serious negotiations would serve Tehran only as a "political maneuver" and make little actual difference.

The Tehran Declaration, of course, created an incomparable opportunity for a political maneuver benefiting Iran just before a new round of UN Security Council sanctions. This was achieved to the extent that the international media paid a good deal of attention to the statements of Turkey's prime minister, Brazil's president, and high-level Ahmadinejad administration officials that the agreement left no room for new sanctions.

Yet, the agreement was too late and too minor to derail the Security Council's movement toward more sanctions. The positions taken by the United States, EU, Britain, France, and Germany after the signing of the Tehran Declaration showed that the countries emphasized that, first, their stances were based principally on the previous agreement of Tehran and the Vienna Group, and second, Tehran had opportunistically signed the agreement to create a rift within the Western world.

The argument that Iran signed the declaration as a tactical measure to weaken efforts to implement new sanctions should be taken seriously. The agreement stated that if Western countries agreed to it, the October 2009 negotiations between Iran and the Vienna Group would begin again practically from scratch. The declaration stated that Tehran would, within a month of receiving the approval of the Vienna Group and a "written agreement and proper arrangement," confirm its readiness to entrust 1,200 kilograms of its low-enriched uranium stocks to Turkey. The qualification that a "written agreement and proper arrangement" was necessary meant from a legal standpoint that Tehran could request negotiations to begin before any fuel exchange in order to secure the written agreement referenced by the Tehran Declaration.

These negotiations bore an interesting resemblance to the quadrilateral talks between Iran and the EU3 in October 2003 that led to the Sa'dabad Agreement. Like the suspension agreed to at Sa'dabad, the swap deal promised to minimize the amount of low-enriched uranium in Tehran's possession. The difference between the two was that the Sa'dabad Agreement, which was signed by the foreign ministers of Germany, Britain, and France, was accepted by the entire world, and it immediately and drastically reduced the severity of the Iran nuclear crisis. By contrast, immediately after the Iran-Brazil-Turkey fuel exchange agreement, the great powers secured the passage of UN Security Council Resolution 1929—the worst resolution ever for the Ahmadinejad administration.

The political and economic dimensions of an agreement among Iran, Brazil, and Turkey would have ushered in a new era in international relations, because although confidence in such an agreement would have been very premature, it would have showed that countries could in the future effectively address many global issues by forming temporary blocs with narrowly defined goals. This was, of course, the dream of Mahmoud Ahmadinejad from the start, and he based his relations with Latin America on this goal. However, Ahmadinejad's crude diplomacy, lack of understanding of the realities of international relations, and provocative and unnecessary statements caused this dream to go unfulfilled.

Naturally, Brazil and Turkey thought more than anything of their national interests, and their efforts can thus be understood as pragmatic. Brazil tried on the one hand to enhance its international image while it forged a deal where the P5+1 had been unable, yet on the other hand to avoid antagonizing the great powers by agreeing to go along with the sanctions resolution that eventually proceeded.

Nevertheless, the Tehran Declaration enabled Iran to inflict damage on Washington's relations with Brazil and Turkey and created credibility problems for the United States, as the two countries had entered into the agreement after receiving the green light from Washington. And, according to the agreement, Iran would have transferred only 1,200 out of 2,500 kilograms of low-enriched uranium reserves out of the country. (If Iran had agreed to such a deal in October 2009, when it was first negotiated, and exported 1,200 kilograms of low-enriched uranium, it could have then enriched more than one thousand kilograms of additional uranium by April 2010.)

UN SECURITY COUNCIL RESOLUTION 1929 AND NEW SANCTIONS

From Iranian policymakers' points of view, although Mohamed ElBaradei had put tremendous pressure on Iran from 2003 to 2009 and despite the belief among some factions in Iran that he was a puppet of the West, a majority of Iran's decisionmakers acknowledged that ElBaradei had done his best to maintain a balanced and independent position between Iran and the P5+1. That ElBaradei was an Arab had two implications: On the one hand, the Arab world was by and large very concerned about the prospect of a nuclear Iran, and ElBaradei might have shared this concern; on the other hand, he shared the region's perspective and sensitivities about double standards of the United States vis-à-vis Muslim countries and Israel.[30] His successor, Yukiya Amano, however, was firmly in the Western camp. In the Iranian point of view, he had no independence and simply followed the instructions of the United States and Europe.[31]

On May 31, the new IAEA director general in his second report about Iran's nuclear activities[32] announced the installation of a new cascade of 164 centrifuges that would allow enrichment up to 20 percent. The report named Iran as the non–nuclear-weapon state enriching to such a high level.[33] Amano explicitly referenced these ambiguities, as well as the now-familiar topic of "alleged studies" as pointing to "possible military dimensions."[34] The report also provided other reasons for suspicion toward Tehran, such as information about ten new enrichment sites, including the new fuel enrichment plant at Fordow, which was not declared to the agency in a timely manner.

The UN Security Council went ahead on June 9, 2010, and adopted the sixth round of sanctions on Iran in Resolution 1929.[35] All the permanent Security Council members voted in favor. Only Brazil and Turkey voted against the resolution, with Lebanon abstaining. Resolution 1929 greatly increased the cost of Iran's nuclear activities. It included "smart sanctions" carefully designed to target influential figures and organizations in Iran's nuclear program—especially the Islamic Revolutionary Guard Corps. The new sanctions also targeted Iran's banking system and economy more broadly.

Excerpts of the most important new sanctions provisions:[36]

- All states shall prevent the sale, transfer, provision, manufacture, maintenance, or use of arms and related materiel.
- Iran shall not undertake any activity related to ballistic missiles capable of delivering nuclear weapons.
- Iran is further restricted from acquiring various technical items related to nuclear and missile development.
- All states are to inspect all cargo to and from Iran in their territory.

- All states are to seize and dispose of items whose supply, sale, transfer, or export is prohibited by the resolution.
- All states shall prohibit the provision of fuel or supplies, or other servicing of vessels, to Iranian-owned or -contracted vessels, including chartered vessels, if they have information that provides reasonable grounds to believe they are carrying items prohibited by the resolution.
- All member states are to communicate to the Sanctions Committee any information available on transfers or activity by Iran Air's cargo division or vessels owned or operated by the Islamic Republic of Iran Shipping Lines to other companies that may have been undertaken in order to evade the sanctions and requests of the committee to make that information widely available.
- All states are to prevent the provision of financial services (including insurance or reinsurance) or the transfer to entities organized under their laws (including branches abroad) of any financial or other assets or resources.
- All states shall exercise vigilance when doing business with entities incorporated in Iran, including those of the Islamic Revolutionary Guard Corps and Islamic Republic of Iran Shipping Lines, if they have information that such business could contribute to Iran's proliferation-sensitive nuclear activities or the development of nuclear weapon delivery systems or to violations of past resolutions or this resolution.
- States are to prohibit in their territories the opening of new branches or representative offices of Iranian banks, and also prohibit Iranian banks from establishing new joint ventures, if they have information that these activities could contribute to Iran's proliferation-sensitive nuclear activities or the development of nuclear weapon delivery systems.
- All states are prohibited from doing business with the Islamic Revolutionary Guard Corps and companies associated with it.
- The assets of 40 Iranian companies are frozen and one person is blocked; 35 individuals previously under lighter travel restrictions have been placed under a travel ban.

- A "panel of experts" will be appointed to oversee the implementation of UN sanctions, report violations, and provide recommendations for continuous improvement in the implementation of sanctions.
- The Security Council shall review Iran's actions in light of the report, to be submitted within ninety days.[37]

Several months later, Dennis Ross, special assistant to President Obama, gave an overview of the impact of new sanctions against Iran:[38]

- Across multiple sectors, an increasing number of international companies and foreign subsidiaries of American companies have cut ties with Iran. These include: Toyota, Kia, Daimler, Siemens, Lukoil, Allianz, GE, Honeywell, Caterpillar, and many others.
- Iran access to financial services from reputable banks has been severely restricted, and the country is facing major obstacles to conduct major transactions in dollars or euros. Several international financial institutions have also halted or drastically reduced their business in Iran, including BNP Paribas, Korea Exchange Bank, Lloyds, and Société Générale.
- Major fuel suppliers, such as Total and Tüpras, have reduced their fuel shipments to Iran, forcing Iran to divert its own fuel production capabilities to cover domestic needs. Additionally several European jet fuel suppliers have canceled fuel delivery contracts with Iran Air.
- Iran's inability to pay loans and maintain insurance coverage led to the recent seizure of three Iranian ships in Singapore.
- Investors in Iran's energy sector from around the world are pulling out of projects, making it far more difficult for Iran to modernize its aging energy infrastructure or develop new oil and gas fields despite significant reserves. These include Royal Dutch Shell, the Spanish firm Repsol, the Japanese energy firm Inpex, and the Italian multinational ENI. Tens of billions of dollars in oil and gas development deals have been put on hold or discontinued in the last few years.
- In late September, the Iranian rial experienced a sudden drop in value by 10–20 percent in street trading, and the Central Bank was

forced to intervene to stabilize the currency. Iran is struggling to sell its currency abroad and access hard currency from its traditional suppliers. The dip in the rial was also influenced by public anxiety over access to hard currency. The Iranian people are concerned that their government cannot manage the economy.

- The Iranian government is struggling to implement its long-awaited subsidy reform plan, which will force it to significantly raise prices on heavily subsidized gasoline and other items. However, the government keeps delaying price hikes over fears of public unrest. With high unemployment and inflation, Iran has little margin for error.

Resolution 1929 once again brought attention to the concerns of the international community over Iran's nuclear program and stressed the need for negotiations, while outlining the necessary steps for Iran to restore confidence in the peacefulness of its nuclear program, which would lead to a possible suspension or termination of the sanctions. In the days that followed, Brazil's foreign minister announced the end of Brazil's mediation on the Iran nuclear issue and stated that he didn't think that Brazil or Turkey were really in a position to serve as mediators. Brazil later announced in an official statement that it would implement the stipulations of Resolution 1929 against Tehran.

UNILATERAL SANCTIONS AGAINST IRAN BEYOND THE REQUIREMENTS OF RESOLUTION 1929

Sanctions strengthened from 2005 on had already put Tehran under immense pressure. Hundreds of foreign banks had cut off their dealings with Iran.[39] Summer 2010, however, marked a new low for Iran, with a huge wave of sanctions that went beyond Security Council resolutions against Iran. These sanctions were sure to inflict considerable and irreparable damage to the Iranian economy and industry in the long run, despite the Ahmadinejad administration's rhetoric.

A few days after Resolution 1929 was adopted, Senator Chris Dodd, the chairman of the Senate Banking Committee, and Representative Howard Berman, ranking member of the House Foreign Affairs Committee, presented to the U.S. Congress a draft unilateral sanctions bill to update and expand the Iran Refined Petroleum Sanctions Act of 2009. On June 24, the House bill for unilateral sanctions against Iran's energy sector and economy was passed with 408 votes in favor and eight opposed.[40] The same day, the Senate approved the bill with a 99–0 vote. This bill encouraged foreign governments to direct state-owned and private entities to cease all investment in, and support of, Iran's energy sector and all exports of refined petroleum products to Iran. It also imposed sanctions on the Central Bank of Iran and any other Iranian financial institution engaged in proliferation activities or support of terrorist groups and called for the U.S. government to work with allies to protect the international financial system from deceptive and illicit practices by Iranian financial institutions involved in proliferation activities or support of terrorist groups.[41]

On June 16, 2010, the U.S. Treasury Department announced a set of measures, including sanctions and asset freezes and seizures, to curtail Iran's nuclear and missile programs through restricting Iran's ability to use international financial and transportation infrastructure.[42] The following is a brief summary of entities targeted by the U.S. sanctions on Iran:[43]

- Five companies affiliated with Islamic Republic of Iran Shipping Lines.
- Twenty-seven vessels connected to the shipping lines, as well as 71 renamed vessels that had already been identified for sanctions.
- Post Bank of Iran, on the grounds that it was acting on behalf of the sanctioned Bank Sepah.
- The Iranian Revolutionary Guard Corps Air Force and Missile Command, as well as the two firms affiliated with the Revolutionary Guard Corps, Rah Sahel and Sepanir Oil & Gas Engineering Company, and two commanders from the Revolutionary Guard leadership.
- Two individuals linked to Iran's weapons of mass destruction programs, and the Naval Defense Missile Industry Group.
- Twenty-two entities in insurance, petroleum, and petrochemical industries linked to the government of Iran.

Sanctions against Iran adopted through the U.S. Congress, as well as other unilateral American sanctions, have enabled the U.S. government to pressure both American and foreign companies to cut economic ties with Iran. The U.S. government has also placed a comprehensive sanction on the sale of refined petroleum products, including gasoline, diesel, and jet fuel, to Iran.[44] It has warned that foreign companies violating these unilateral sanctions will be barred from their U.S. operations. This led the Swiss company Glencore International, one of the largest suppliers of gasoline to Iran, to cease its operations there,[45] as did the United Kingdom's BP.[46]

Prominent members of the international community followed the U.S. lead and implemented their own unilateral sanctions above and beyond the requirements of Resolution 1929. In June 2010, 27 European Union countries adopted wide-ranging unilateral sanctions against Iran, including a ban on investment in the Iranian oil and gas sector and restrictions on the trade, industry, insurance, banking, shipping, and transportation sectors. Restrictions were placed on currency exchange and on Iranian banks and financial institutions opening new branches, expanding their operations, or going into partnership with European banks. Additionally, a number of Islamic Revolutionary Guard Corps commanders and Revolutionary Guard-affiliated companies, and economic and military entities were sanctioned.[47]

On September 8, 2010, South Korea's government passed sanctions against Iran, suspending the activities of Iranian banks and blacklisting 102 companies and institutions and 24 individuals.[48] That same month, Japan's cabinet announced the implementation of unilateral sanctions that blocked the assets of individuals and organizations associated with Iran's nuclear program and restricted economic transactions with the country. Restrictions on Japanese investment in oil and gas projects in Iran were also adopted.[49] Canada and Australia imposed economic and financial sanctions against Iran, primarily in the energy sector. Australia introduced additional sanctions based on the European Union's measures.[50]

These unilateral sanctions, coupled with the UN Security Council sanctions, have inflicted a major blow to Iran's financial transactions worldwide. The main hub for Iran's international financial activities was the United Arab Emirates, which came under tremendous pressure to limit Iran's economic activity, particularly in Dubai. These measures succeeded and have created a great deal of difficulty for Iranian financial and commercial companies, including a vast community of small businesses operating out of the UAE. In addition, the UAE froze the accounts and assets of companies and individuals suspected of involvement in the production or dissemination of weapons and dozens of companies involved in money laundering and transportation of sensitive items to Iran.[51]

Unilateral sanctions by the United States and European Union have shaken Iran's relationship with some of its closest trading partners, with far more detrimental effects than previously expected. An increasing number of multinational companies have also ceased their economic activity with Iran under pressure from the United States (or out of fear of losing the American market). This has led to a reduction in oil exports from Iran destined for Japan by 11 percent and almost 40 percent for China since the beginning of 2010.

These sanctions have caused a great deal of strain on the Iranian oil and gas industries, the main source of government revenue, and will continue to do so. Iran holds the world's second-largest proven oil reserves, after Saudi Arabia, with 130 billion barrels.[52] However, due to Western and especially American sanctions on investments in upstream oil fields and infrastructure, Iran's oil and gas industry suffers from a lack of up-to-date infrastructure and investment to tap into this vast resource, thus leading to a decrease in production levels and exports.

According to Iranian parliamentary officials, maintaining Iran's production of approximately 5.1 million barrels of crude oil per day requires drilling new wells and investing hundreds of billions of dollars, particularly in the use of new technologies and gas reinjection.[53] The Research Center of Iran's Parliament estimates that Iran's oil and gas industries need $500 billion over the next fifteen years in new investments in order to achieve Iran's twenty-year development plan. Unfortunately, international sanctions and a shortage of domestic resources have proved to be severe obstacles to the current administration in making adequate investments in this area or attracting needed foreign investment in recent years.

Iran's Mehr News Agency reported that the statistics for 2010 released by the Organization of Petroleum Exporting Countries showed that while Iran's oil refining capacity in the period increased by 18 percent, the highest within OPEC, the country lost its decade-long position as second exporter within the organization to Nigeria. Nigeria increased its exports by 300,000 barrels per day an average, reaching 2.464 million barrels per day; Iran's crude export was 2.248 million barrels per day, the report said.[54]

While America and the European Union adopted unilateral sanctions against Iran, Russia criticized the measures and even deemed them illegal.[55] In response to Russia's criticism, U.S. officials have stated that the unilateral sanctions against Iran are complementary to the efforts of the UN Security Council, which have targeted institutions and persons associated with Iran's nuclear program. However, Russian Foreign Minister Sergei Lavrov reiterated in a May 2010 interview that Russia would continue to oppose any unilateral sanctions against Iran.[56]

AHMADINEJAD'S REACTION TO INTERNATIONAL SANCTIONS AND CRITICISM

On June 28, 2010, Mahmoud Ahmadinejad responded to Resolution 1929 at a news conference with local and foreign journalists by announcing the postponement of Iranian nuclear negotiations as a penalty to "teach [the P5+1] a lesson on how to have debate and a discussion with nations." He went on to state that further negotiations with the P5+1 would be based on four preconditions:[57]

1. Countries that wanted to negotiate with Iran had to make their position clear in regard to Israel's nuclear arsenal and announce if they accept it or not.
2. The P5+1 countries had to declare whether they are for or against strengthening the NPT through a review conference, which in practice meant pushing countries such as Israel to join the NPT to end double standards.
3. The P5+1 countries had to clarify their objective in the negotiations with Iran, that is, whether they wanted animosity or friendship, and whether or not they wanted to be rational in negotiations with Iran.
4. The countries involved in the negotiations had to be expanded. It was Iran's intention to include Brazil and Turkey in the negotiations following the Tehran Declaration.

Many foreign observers assume that the statements made by Ahmadinejad about major global issues and his derogatory remarks about Israel and the characters of Western leaders arise from the foreign policy of the government. Ahmadinejad's approach to diplomacy is directed at domestic consumption and garnering popularity in the streets of many Muslim countries. However, I strongly believe that most of these statements reflect Ahmadinejad's illusions about and limited comprehension of complex foreign policy issues. We should be mindful of the fact that Mahmoud Ahmadinejad had no experience in diplomacy and foreign policy when he took office in 2005.

The fact is that within Iran and even among conservatives, including influential figures such as Ayatollah Sadegh Larijani,[58] the head of the judiciary and Ali Larijani's brother, discontent is growing with the bizarre language Ahmadinejad uses when representing Iran in the international arena. Hence he has been both privately and publicly cautioned about the way he conducts himself on the international scene and about the tone of his rhetoric and insults. Apart from a few individuals within Ahmadinejad's inner circle, no prominent politician in Iran, whether reformist, conservative, or technocrat, defends his offensive rhetoric, which has brought criticism from the international community and has been detrimental to the interests of Iran.

Nonetheless, Ahmadinejad enjoys the international spotlight for his inflammatory comments. He has repeatedly taken international trips and attended functions that under normal diplomatic protocol would be attended by officials of a level no higher than ambassador or deputy minister. For example, in March 2010, Ahmadinejad attended the NPT Review Conference in New York, raising eyebrows because of the nearly 180 countries present at the conference, he was the only head of state.[59]

Ahmadinejad's populist and propagandist discourse regarding sanctions, and his disparaging remarks about Western officials, the Security Council, and even the International Atomic Energy Agency, have been intended to shore up his domestic political support. However, in my opinion they have been gross mistakes that have enabled Western authorities and media outlets to label the Iranian government as "extremist" and "undermining of international security" and to push for unprecedented sanctions and pressures on Iran. In the thirty-two years of its existence, the Islamic Republic had never faced the level of sanctions imposed on it by international institutions and nations as it has under Ahmadinejad's watch.

The approach that Ahmadinejad's government has taken toward the UN Security Council and IAEA Board of Governors can be best understood through the following four episodes or behaviors, which have themselves been contradictory at times.

On most of the occasions when the Security Council met to draw up new resolutions, the president or his close advisers and supporters in Parliament would reassure the public that no resolutions would be passed against Iran as there were internal disagreements in the Security Council.[60]

Immediately after the issuance of each resolution, representatives of Iran in Vienna or New York or the Foreign Ministry spokesman issued an immediate rebuttal, stressing that Tehran would not adhere to the resolution.

Soon after these resolutions, Ahmadinejad has personally denounced the resolutions as "torn paper,"[61] "worthless," "garbage," and "cowboy logic,"[62] while simultaneously telling the Iranian people that the resolutions were a "divine favor" from God.[63]

Ahmadinejad has also adopted the policy of retaliating tit for tat with each new resolution. For example:

- Five days before the deadline given by Security Council Resolution 1696 for Iran to halt its nuclear activities, President Ahmadinejad inaugurated the heavy-water production site at Arak,[64] the project that came into operation during the Khatami period.

- After passage of Resolution 1737, the Ahmadinejad government limited the entry of IAEA inspectors and announced the installment of 3,000 centrifuges at the Natanz facility.[65]

- Approximately two weeks after the passing of Resolution 1747 in spring 2007, Ahmadinejad claimed that Iran had reached an industrial level of enrichment and had entered the club of nuclear countries. Ahmadinejad's government also announced that the day would henceforth be named the "National Day of Nuclear Technology."[66] Ahmadinejad's declaration that Iran had joined the "nuclear club" was particularly controversial because the term is generally reserved for nuclear-weapon states, while the Iranian government has always maintained that its nuclear program is for peaceful purposes and advocated for the nonproliferation of nuclear weapons. The statement was also a great exaggeration: Reaching an industrial level of nuclear activity to generate reactor fuel requires an average of 50,000 to 60,000 operating centrifuges; Iran has not reached those levels and was estimated to have approximately 10,000 centrifuges as of 2011.

- Approximately a month after Resolution 1803 was adopted in March 2008, Mahmoud Ahmadinejad announced the installment of an additional 6,000 centrifuges at the Natanz enrichment facility during the celebrations of Iran's second National Day of Nuclear Technology.[67]
- Following the passage of Resolution 1835, the Ahmadinejad government announced the commencement of the design stage for a 360-megawatt nuclear reactor at Darkhovin.[68]
- Soon after the disclosure by President Obama of the existence of the Fordow enrichment facility, Tehran announced that it had successfully tested the Shahab-3, a medium-range missile with liquid fuel, and Sejil-2, a solid fuel missile with a range of 2,000 kilometers modeled on the previous Ashura missile.[69]
- Following the IAEA resolution issued after the disclosure of the Fordow facility and the breakdown of negotiations between Tehran and the P5+1 on a fuel exchange, Ahmadinejad ordered the construction of ten new enrichment facilities. He also announced that Iran would enrich uranium at 20 percent.
- After the passage of Resolution 1929, Ahmadinejad announced the postponement of further negotiations and provided four preconditions for the resumption of talks.
- Some days before the passage of Resolution 1929, Ahmadinejad officially threatened that in case of another UN Security Council resolution, Iran would stop nuclear negotiations with the P5+1 countries.[70]

Nevertheless, Tehran has continued to have dialogue and cooperation with the IAEA and to engage with the P5+1 on different levels, though since Jalili has taken charge of the nuclear file, there have been no genuine and productive negotiations with the P5+1 as of the end of 2011. Only one serious negotiation took place, in October 2009 in Geneva regarding fuel exchange, and it failed miserably. The passage of Resolution 1929 signaled an increasing shift by Russia and China away from sympathy for Iran's position and toward greater frustration with the Islamic Republic.

HAS RUSSIA DISTANCED ITSELF FROM IRAN?

When Mahmoud Ahmadinejad attended the Shanghai summit in Moscow a few weeks after the disputed presidential elections in June 2009, he was warmly welcomed by Russian President Medvedev. Subsequent developments, however, have led Russia to distance itself from Tehran; relations have hit such a low note that Ahmadinejad has derogatorily commented that "Vladimir Putin is playing into the American game."[71]

The most important factor influencing Russia's realignment toward the West regarding Iran has been the efforts of Barack Obama in reengaging Moscow and Russia's own national interest, which have culminated in strategic agreement on major issues ranging from cancellation of the installation of a U.S. missile defense system in Eastern Europe to policies regarding Central Asia and the Caucasus.[72] This suggests that Russia had been using Iran as a bargaining chip to reduce the presence of NATO around Russia's borders.

Russia was deeply disturbed by the revelation of the secret construction of an enrichment facility at Fordow near Qom.[73] When President Obama relayed the information regarding the discovery of the secret project to his Russian counterpart Medvedev, the revelation destroyed Russia's trust in the sincerity of the Iranians with regard to their nuclear activities.

Iran's change of heart regarding the exchange of 1,200 kilograms of Iran's low-enriched uranium for fuel for the Tehran Research Reactor also fostered Moscow's resentment. Russia and France were supposed to be the major players in the exchange and provide the necessary enriched uranium at 20 percent for the Tehran reactor. Despite Iran's initial agreement to this deal in October 2009, the conditions it later added ultimately killed the deal.

A few months later, Ahmadinejad ordered the production of 20 percent enriched uranium to begin in Iran, and during trilateral negotiations in Tehran with Brazil and Turkey, insisted that Iran's uranium be deposited in Turkey instead of Russia. Tehran did not trust Russia any more than it did the West.

From the beginning of the Iranian nuclear case, Russia has tried to maintain a political balance in which it would use its "Iranian card" to get concessions from the West and at the same time prevent Iran from creating friction between Washington and Moscow. I recall a meeting with Russian

President Vladimir Putin at the Kremlin in 2004; he told us that Tehran should not expect Moscow to be on a boat in which Iran is the only passenger when the whole international community is on another boat. In May 2010, Russian Foreign Minister Sergei Lavrov stated that the new sanctions were inevitable, adding, "To our great regret, during years—not months—Iran's response to these efforts has been unsatisfactory, mildly speaking."[74]

At the same time, Moscow has wanted to show more loyalty to Tehran than the Europeans have in order to retain business opportunities in Iran. A few weeks after my arrest in April 2007, news media outlets published the story that I had been arrested because of reports submitted by Russia's intelligence agency to its Iranian counterpart, claiming my close interaction and cooperation with the Europeans against Ahmadinejad's nuclear policy.[75] These reports were not denied by officials in Tehran and Moscow or by the pro-Ahmadinejad media in Iran.[76]

Another factor in the strained relations between Moscow and Tehran can be attributed to developments after the presidential election. The Kremlin initially congratulated Ahmadinejad for his victory in the elections[77] but was later embarrassed when protesters showed their dissatisfaction with Moscow's support for Ahmadinejad by burning the Russian flag and chanting "Death to Russia." This became one of the key slogans of the protesters.[78] More embarrassment occurred at the Disarmament Conference held April 17–18, 2010, in Tehran. In the final statement of the conference, with the Russian deputy foreign minister present, Iran severely criticized the five nuclear powers including Russia. The critical remarks were swiftly denounced by Russia's foreign ministry spokesman, Andrei Nesterenko.[79]

Pressure exerted on Moscow by Israel and some Arab countries should not be ignored. In the past several years various media outlets have reported that some regional Arab states, particularly Saudi Arabia, have promised Moscow that they will reward the Kremlin handsomely through lucrative arms deals if Russia ceased its support for Tehran.[80] In an attempt to persuade Moscow to sever its ties with Tehran, Israeli leaders have portrayed Iran as the primary destabilizing force to peace and security in the region and a threat to Russia's national interests. During a visit of Ehud Olmert to Moscow in October 2007, Russian Foreign Minister Sergei Lavrov promised that the Kremlin would take strong measures to stop Tehran from militarizing its nuclear program.[81]

Another issue between Russia and Iran centers on Russia's delays in supplying armaments, as symbolized by the S-300 antiaircraft missile system. Iran's interest in acquiring the S-300 ground-to-air missile system from Russia was initially discussed during two visits to Moscow by Hassan Rouhani in 2003 and 2004. I was present at these talks. The negotiations were extremely hard, and I felt that it was a difficult decision for Moscow to agree to the deal. During that time, our cooperation with the IAEA, including adherence to the Additional Protocol, created trust between Moscow and Tehran, which culminated in Russia's agreement to sell the S-300 to Iran. The sale of the S-300 and other missile technologies was later suspended by the Russian president after Resolution 1929 was passed.[82]

In August 2011, Iran's ambassador to Moscow, Mahmoud Reza Sajjadi, announced that Tehran had filed a complaint against Russia with an international court of arbitration over the cancellation of an S-300 missile contract. Moscow was surprised by Iran's move, insisting that it had had no choice but to cancel the long-agreed delivery because of UN sanctions.[83]

It is very strange to me that the Iranian military did not move urgently to implement the agreement despite the Supreme National Security Council's insistence that it do so. If Iran's agreement with Moscow had been implemented on schedule and foreign policy had not shifted so suddenly, the S-300 missile system would have been delivered to Iran in 2007–2008, long before the UN sanctions prohibiting delivery went into effect. Such a deal would have been a great measure to secure Iran's nuclear facility.

A final sticking point in the relations between Moscow and Tehran was suspicion surrounding the involvement of Russian operatives in the Stuxnet computer worm attack on the Bushehr nuclear plant.[84] It has emerged that even well before the Stuxnet affair, Russia may have taken part in efforts to slow progress in Iran's nuclear program through sabotage. In May 2010, the Israeli daily *Yedioth Ahronoth* reported, based on documents provided by WikiLeaks, that Russian President Vladimir Putin had personally ordered the "sabotage" of Iran's Bushehr nuclear plant four years earlier. The document details February 2006 talks between the U.S. ambassador to Israel and the head of Israel's Atomic Energy Commission, the latter of whom describes talks with high-level Russian officials in which he was told that

Putin had ordered the deliberate delay of progress at the Bushehr plant. The Russians would delay providing fuel rods to the reactor and had "made changes to the hardware that they were supposed to send to the Bushehr reactor so as to slow down the Iranian nuclear program even further."[85]

REASONS BEHIND CHINA'S SUPPORT FOR SANCTIONS AGAINST IRAN

Beijing's insistence on resolving the Iranian nuclear issue through negotiations has been a key protection against severe sanctions. However, during Ahmadinejad's tenure, Beijing has shifted its support toward the American position. China and the United States reached an agreement that if any sanctions are imposed against Tehran by America and its European allies, Beijing's considerable interests in Iran's energy, trade, and financial sector would be protected.[86] According to some reports, Beijing secured guarantees from Washington that Chinese companies would be protected and exempt from unilateral U.S. sanctions on Iran.[87]

It is critical to note that since Ahmadinejad's shift in foreign policy toward the East, China has benefited from lucrative contracts to help develop Iran's upstream oil industry. China's share of oil and gas contracts in Iran has increased sharply, with approximately $50 billion in contracts concluded or closed since 2005. There are also separate contracts between Chinese companies[88] and various Iranian oil companies to build ten offshore and onshore devices and floating cranes.[89]

China was apparently able to convince the authorities in Tehran that by voting for Resolution 1929, Beijing was able to make the resolution less damaging to Iran than it would have been otherwise. The deputy of Iran's National Security and Foreign Policy Commission of the Majles, after meeting with commission officials, reiterated that China and Russia had voted positively to prevent a tougher version of Resolution 1929 from being adopted.[90] However, this depiction of their votes is unlikely, as Ahmadinejad took the unprecedented step of sending a derogatory and aggressive message to the Russians for having voted positively on the resolution and gave warning to Beijing.

The reorientation of policies toward the East during the presidency of Ahmadinejad—if it had been conducted in a correct and calculated manner—could have yielded valuable economic partnerships and also increased Iran's international status as an active and influential member of the Shanghai Pact and the wider international community. China's foreign policy is based on development advancement, while Ahmadinejad's foreign policy is based on ideological advancement. Ideological advancement became Iran's foreign policy after the 1979 revolution. Hashemi Rafsanjani and Mohammad Khatami during their respective presidencies between 1989 and 2005 tried to meld ideological advancement and development-centered policies, and for that reason came under attack from both extreme left- and right-wing factions within the government. Ahmadinejad's government brought ideological advancement back to the forefront of Iran's foreign policy approach. The consequences have been plain to see, including in relations with China.

TALKS IN GENEVA

In late October 2010, with the proposal for the low-enriched uranium for research reactor fuel exchange having remained unresolved for more than a year, there were reports in the international media that the United States and European Union had introduced a modified package that would require Iran to put more low-enriched uranium on the table. This proposal was justified by the fact that Iran had continued to enrich uranium for more than a year and therefore had a larger stockpile. Low-enriched uranium is of concern to the West as possible feed for further enrichment to rapidly produce weapons-grade uranium.[91] The P5+1 therefore increased the amount of UF_6 requested from Iran in exchange for nuclear fuel from 1,200 kilograms in the 2009 proposal to 1,995 kilograms. The new proposal was released in the expectation that Tehran and the P5+1 would resume negotiations after the U.S. congressional elections in November.

Saeed Jalili and EU foreign affairs chief Catherine Ashton opened the talks between Iran and the P5+1 in Geneva in December 2010. The two sides agreed to hold the next round of talks in the Turkish city of Istanbul in late January 2011. Jalili said Tehran would not agree to suspend uranium enrichment during the January meeting. Ashton characterized the talks in Geneva as "detailed, substantive" and said the talks in January would "discuss practical ideas and ways of cooperating towards a resolution of our core concerns about the nuclear issue."[92]

Iran's top negotiator in the Geneva talks stressed that Iran had agreed only to hold more talks with the P5+1 within the framework of "cooperation based on common points." He dismissed Ashton's statement that the upcoming talks in Istanbul would focus on Iran's nuclear program and fuel provision.[93]

Meanwhile, on December 13, 2010, Ahmadinejad abruptly dismissed his foreign minister[94] while Mottaki was abroad in Senegal on official business. Ahmadinejad named Ali Akbar Salehi to become the caretaker foreign minister while retaining his role as head of Iran's atomic energy agency.[95] Dr. Salehi received his Ph.D. in nuclear engineering from MIT in 1975. Many believed that dismissal of Mottaki would facilitate international negotiations with Iran over Iran's nuclear program.[96]

Salehi announced in January 2011 that Iran is one of the few countries capable of producing fuel rods and plates to be used for peaceful purposes and credited the West's sanctions and lack of cooperation for Iran's progress. "Actually the West's attitude made us reach this point," he said.[97]

Just days ahead of the talks between Iran and the 5+1 group in Istanbul, Ahmadinejad made it clear that Iran would not negotiate over its nuclear rights. "We are pushing ahead with our nuclear program, and they (the hegemonic powers) are issuing resolutions, let them issue thousands of resolutions. That is not important. What is important is that Iran has become a nuclear state. Let them say that Iran is seeking to build an atomic bomb. That is not important."[98]

TALKS IN ISTANBUL

The P5+1 and Iran met on January 21, 2011, in Istanbul. Iran's delegation was led by Saeed Jalili, secretary of the Supreme National Security Council, and included Supreme National Security Council Deputy Ali Bagheri, Atomic Energy Organization and Ministry of Foreign Affairs Adviser Hamidreza Asgari, Ministry of Foreign Affairs European Deputy Ali Ahani, and Supreme National Security Council Press Deputy Abolfazl Zohrevand. Washington's delegation was led by the then undersecretary of state for political affairs William J. Burns and included State Department nonproliferation advisers Robert Einhorn and James Timbie, National Security Council Senior Director for the Persian Gulf Puneet Talwar, National Security Council Director on Nonproliferation Rexon Ryu, and National Security Council Spokesman Mike Hammer.[99]

Separately, Saeed Jalili and the EU's Catherine Ashton met for ninety minutes. Zohrevand reported that the meeting was held in a "positive" climate. But Western officials reported little progress. A Western diplomat who requested anonymity remarked, "They talked a lot but the positions remain the same. . . . It would be fair to say that the bilateral [meeting] was inconclusive."[100]

Hammer told journalists in Istanbul: "The P5+1 is united and committed to credible engagement, the onus is on Iran to take concrete and convincing steps. We are not engaging in talk for talk's sake, but rather to develop a process by which Iran can address the international community's long-standing concerns on the nuclear program."[101]

Ashton reported that Iran had insisted as preconditions to the negotiations that the UN Security Council lift its sanctions and that the P5+1 recognize Iran's right to enrich. Ashton also said no new talks had been scheduled but the "door remains open."[102] As already noted, the P5+1 increased by two-thirds the amount of low-enriched uranium required from Iran in exchange for fuel for the Tehran Research Reactor under a tentative deal struck in Vienna more than year earlier. The U.S. goal was to reduce the amount of 3.5 percent low-enriched uranium that Iran had on hand to less than the amount required to make one bomb, if enriched further to weapon grade. The P5+1 countries also asked Iran to halt all enrichment to 20 percent, the enrichment level of the research reactor fuel. This request was rejected by Iran.[103]

WANDERING TOWARD THE BRINK

Prior to the meetings, I was questioned by academics at Princeton University, where I am an associate research scholar, and other universities on the possibility of these talks being successful. I predicted that the talks would not result in any substantial outcome or agreement. The reasons were clear. The P5+1 countries were insisting on a piecemeal approach on the nuclear issue, asking Iran to take steps for confidence building such as the proposed fuel swap, suspension of enrichment activities, and implementation of the Additional Protocol. They were concentrating on the nuclear issue and not a grand bargain. The Iranians, however, were looking for a comprehensive package to resolve major issues including nuclear, regional, and international disputes. For the Iranians, the nuclear issue is a bargaining chip to reach a global compromise with the P5+1, specifically the United States. This mismatch was reflected in the statements by negotiating partners after the meetings. The Iranians emphasized the broader aspect of the negotiations, while the Europeans focused on issues related to the nuclear dispute.

Reports emerged that the Obama administration was prepared to accept some enrichment activities in Iran as long as the enrichment was not to weapons grade. The goal would be to get Iran to not store stockpiles of enriched uranium and to operate a limited number of centrifuges under strict monitoring.[104] I was told more specifically by well-informed analysts and academics that the Obama administration was prepared to accept enrichment activities in Iran at the then-current level of about 4,000–5,000 centrifuges on the condition that Iran not stockpile enriched uranium and that it allow intrusive surveillance and commit to full transparency measures. This proposal was, however, reportedly rejected by Britain and France.[105]

This was very interesting to me because, in the spring of 2005, I had proposed to the EU3 a three-phased plan to start with a pilot plant at Natanz, consisting of a minimum of 3,000 centrifuges and to export all the production of low-enriched uranium from Natanz and excess UF_6 from Isfahan. These measures were aimed to permit the negotiations to continue for a maximum of one year, in order to reach agreement on measures to guarantee that Iran's nuclear activities would be exclusively peaceful. At that time, Berlin and Paris were flexible, while the UK negotiating partner told me that the United States would not accept even "one centrifuge" in Iran. It is ironic that after five years, the Americans are closer to my 2005 proposal, while the Europeans have backtracked from their position.

As part of Iran's annual revolution celebrations in February 2011, President Mahmoud Ahmadinejad unveiled prototypes of four locally made satellites—Rasad (Observation), Fajr (Dawn), Zafar (Victory), and Amir Kabir-1—while a senior commander showed off the engines of a Safir-B1

(Ambassador-B1) rocket. Iran also warned its adversaries that it had "complete domination" of the entrance to the Persian Gulf.[106]

In April 2011, Fereydoun Abbasi Davani, who succeeded Ali Akbar Salehi as the head of the Atomic Energy Organization of Iran, announced that following the successful production and testing of second and third generations of Iranian-brand centrifuges, "We will boost the enrichment level of uranium up to 20 percent, based on the country's requirements, and in doing so, we will not seek anyone's permission." He cited plans to build several nuclear research reactors as justification for increased production of 20 percent enriched uranium.[107]

The IAEA confirmed that Iran had informed the agency in January of its intention to install two 164-machine cascades of its newly developed centrifuges, called the IR-2m and the IR-4, at its pilot enrichment plant for testing. Iran had previously tested these improved models, but only in cascades of up to 20 machines. In this regard, the former IAEA safeguards chief Olli Heinonen indicated in a March 2 presentation that the IR-2m has about three times the potential capacity of the P-1.[108]

Nevertheless and despite all these developments, Gary Samore, President Obama's top nonproliferation adviser, said in April 2011 that "the good news though is that Iran's technical capacity really has slowed down. I mean, they really have experienced enough technical difficulties, and secret projects have been exposed, so all of that I think has given—in my view—the world some number of years to work on this problem before Iran is in a position where it could make a political decision to build nuclear weapons."[109]

In his June 2011 report on Iran's compliance with its NPT obligations and the UN Security Council resolutions, IAEA Director General Yukiya Amano stated that the IAEA had received new evidence of possible military dimensions to Iran's nuclear activities, a claim that was dismissed by the Islamic Republic.[110] A month later, Amano identified Iran, along with North Korea and Syria, as a virtual nuclear rogue nation for its continued refusal to comply with international obligations under the NPT. During the twenty-third UN Conference on Disarmament Issues in Japan, Amano said that Iran was not cooperating with IAEA officials in providing credible assurance about the absence of undeclared nuclear material and activities.[111]

In response, Fereydoun Abbasi Davani announced that under the supervision of the IAEA, Iran will increase by threefold its production of 20 percent enriched uranium. Abbasi also said that the country will shift its urani-um enrichment activities from the central Iranian city of Natanz to Fordow in Qom province south of the capital, Tehran, adding that Iran would not stop 20 percent enrichment at Natanz until production at Fordow was up to speed. At the same time, President Ahmadinejad told reporters that con-struction of a new generation of indigenous centrifuges was under way.[112]

Later, on August 22, 2011, Abbasi said that some centrifuges had been transferred to the Fordow facility under the monitoring of the IAEA.[113] Just before this announcement, the IAEA's safeguards chief, Herman Nackaerts, concluded a five-day trip to Iran's main atomic sites, including the uranium enrichment sites in Natanz and Qom and the heavy-water reactor in Arak.[114]

A nuclear scientist at Princeton University, who requested anonymity, wrote me the following: "Iran already has enough 20-percent-enriched en-riched uranium for a full replacement core for the Teheran Research Reac-tor and is making annually about twice as much as required to keep it in fuel thereafter. A large stockpile of 20 percent enriched uranium would make an Iranian breakout about four times quicker."

Another nuclear scientist at Harvard University, who also requested anonymity, wrote me the following:

Iran has currently 4400 kgs of LEU hexafluoride [UF_6].[115] The tripling of the current production of 20 percent enriched uranium means that practically all new LEU produced will go as a feed to 20 percent en-riched uranium production. Taking all this, one year from now, Iran will have 200 kgs of 20 percent uranium hexafluoride and, at least, 4400 kgs 3.5 percent LEU hexafluoride. This will increase during months to come. This will not be sufficient for a realistic break-out? Likely not. . . . However, we see that Iran is clearly "hedging" under the civilian umbrella and is on the path to beome a nuclear weapons capable state. I do not think that Iran will [now] back off from this path. What I see is that there is technically maximum one year to settle this issue unless we can live with another nuclear capable state in the Middle East with its implications.

The dead end in the negotiations resulted in the P5+1's expanding the sanctions, while the Iranians reacted by, as promised, accelerating their rate of production of 20 percent enriched uranium threefold, both of which led to heightened tensions among all parties involved. Iran was moving forward in nuclear activities that others found alarming and that violated IAEA and UN Security Council resolutions. Various attempts to negotiate confidence-building measures had failed. The Security Council was continuing to add sanctions. All sides in the ongoing crisis appeared to be moving toward a precipice whose exact location was unknown.

BACK TO THE BEGINNING: MAJOR SHIFT TOWARD KHATAMI'S TENURE

During August and September 2011, Iran made a major shift toward President Khatami's nuclear diplomacy by offering substantive confidence-building and transparency measures.

1. The New Russian "Step-by-Step" Proposal

In an attempt to cool the situation, Sergei Lavrov, the Russian foreign minister, visited Washington on July 13, 2011, and suggested a "step-by-step" or "phased" plan. After meeting with President Obama and Secretary of State Hillary Clinton, he said: "We propose, on each requirement of the IAEA, to create some kind of a road map, starting from the easiest questions and in the end there will be the most difficult ones that would require time . . . the response to each specific step of Iran would be followed by some reciprocal step, like freezing some sanctions and shortening the volume of sanctions."[116]

In an unprecedented statement by a P5+1 member, Russian Deputy Prime Minister Igor Ivanov said: "We believe that neither further sanctions, nor intimidation and application of force could be regarded an efficient tool to solve these issues. . . . I don't believe in this horror story that Iran will obtain nuclear weapons next year or in 2013."[117] I was told by a Princeton nuclear scientist that the Russians first proposed this plan in October 2010 and have made some modifications since. The proposed plan was based on gradual steps to be taken by both parties as follows:[118]

Iran	P5+1
Step 1	**Step 1**
Would not add new centrifuges	Would suspend some of the Resolution 1929 sanctions, including financial sanctions and inspection of ships. This step would be done in two phases:
Limit enrichment to the existing site at Natanz	Phase 1. After IAEA report on implementation of Iranian Step 1a
Stop production of a new generation of centrifuges	Phase 2. After IAEA report on implementation of Iranian Steps 1b and 1c
Step 2	**Step 2**
Allow IAEA surveillance of centrifuge production	Suspend all P5+1 sanctions, except those related to the Nuclear Suppliers Group (this would be done in two phases)
Implement Subsidiary Arrangement Code 3.1	Begin gradual lifting (i.e., make suspension permanent) of unilateral sanctions by the P5+1
Limit production of enriched uranium to a maximum of 5%	Take confidence-building measures in the Persian Gulf
Step 3	**Step 3**
Implement Additional Protocol	Suspend all UN Security Council sanctions (this would also be done in two phases)
Step 4	**Step 4**
Suspend all enrichment and related activities mentioned by the UN Security Council for 3 months	Begin final lifting of all sanctions after the first IAEA director general report to the IAEA board and UN Security Council.
	Remove Iran's file from IAEA Board of Governors agenda after second report
	Begin implementation of incentives mentioned in P5+1 packages on cooperation in different fields

Every step taken by Iran would be verified by the IAEA.

At the end of July 2011, Washington decided to send Robert Einhorn from the State Department to Moscow to discuss the plan. Following that meeting on August 15, the Russian government sent the secretary of its Security Council, Nikolai Patrushev, to Tehran to confer with Iranian officials on the proposal.[119] The next day, Patrushev returned to Moscow along with Iran's foreign minister, Ali Akbar Salehi, to discuss the Russian plan.[120]

On August 16, 2011, Ahmadinejad accepted the approach laid out in the Russian proposal. The president's website quoted Ahmadinejad as telling Patrushev that Iran agreed with Russia's "step-by-step proposal and is ready to make suggestions to cooperate and interact in this regard."[121] While in Tehran, Patrushev also met with his counterpart, Saeed Jalili, who confirmed that the Russian proposal could be a basis for initiating a dialogue on regional and international cooperation in the field of peaceful nuclear activities."[122] That same day, in a news conference with his Russian counterpart Sergei Lavrov in Moscow, Ali Akbar Salehi reiterated that Iran was ready to resume negotiations on its nuclear program and that the Russian proposal will aid the process.[123]

Iran's ambassador to the IAEA, Ali Asghar Soltanieh, even said that Iran had started the step-by-step plan. In October 2011, he told *Arms Control Today* that "as my foreign minister said after the meeting with his Russian counterpart, we have welcomed the initiative . . . what has happened recently in the context of the IAEA is the visit of the deputy director-general, Mr. [Herman] Nackaerts . . . which in fact [was] the biggest step toward transparency and cooperation. Therefore, we have in fact started this process of taking a step in a proactive approach, and therefore we are waiting to see what the steps are from the other side."[124] Iran welcomed the initiative despite the fact that it included, among other things, suspension for three months of all enrichment and related activities mentioned by the UN Security Council, implementation of the Additional Protocol, implementation of the Subsidiary Arrangements, and limitation of enrichment to 5 percent.

A day before these visits, I wrote in the U.S. Institute of Peace's "Iran Primer" that the plan could be successful if it defines an endgame entailing Iran's full rights to enrichment, lifting of sanctions, and removal of Iran's nuclear dossier from the UN Security Council and the IAEA Board of Governors.[125]

The Russian plan is the most realistic package put forward by a member of P5+1 since 2003 that could lead toward final resolution of the crisis over Iran's nuclear program. Unfortunately, German and French officials told Princeton University graduate students visiting Berlin and Paris during October 30 to November 5, 2011, the EU and the United States had rejected the Russian plan.

Meanwhile, on August 27, 2011, Iran announced that it had launched production of carbon fiber, a material with potential use in a strategic material employed in uranium centrifuges as well as high-tech civilian and military products such as the casings of missiles. Defense Minister Ahmad Vahidi said Iran decided to manufacture the strategic material domestically because the UN embargo had blocked its access to carbon fiber on foreign markets. "That had caused a bottleneck in Iran's production of advanced and smart defence systems," Vahidi said. He claimed that Iran has mastered the entire process of carbon fiber production. Iran uses carbon fiber for more advanced centrifuges, which spin uranium gas to produce enriched uranium.[126] Vahidi also declared that the Iranian Defense Ministry started mass production of 73-millimeter anti-tank rockets capable of piercing and destroying armored vehicles from a distance of 1,300 meters.[127]

2. Five-Year Blank Check to the IAEA on Transparency Measures

At the end of August 2011, the IAEA delegation headed by Herman Nackaerts, the safeguards chief, visited Tehran. During a five-day tour of Iran's nuclear facilities, he visited the new Fordow enrichment site, the Isfahan fuel production factory, the IR40 Arak Reactor and the heavy-water factory in its vicinity, and the Bushehr Nuclear Reactor.

Ali Asghar Soltanieh described the tour in an interview published by *Arms Control Today*. He said:

> We had decided to make sure that the [IAEA] and the Department of Safeguards and Mr. Nackaerts would have a sort of blank check and he can go wherever he wants, and in fact it happened . . . he requested to see the production of the heavy-water plant . . . he was able to visit that plant . . . he requested that we grant access to see the R&D, research and development, on the advanced centrifuges . . . and he was able to see all the advances in research and development on different generations of centrifuges. He also had the opportunity to see the workshop as well as the simulation activities. I declared that nobody in the whole world has shown these centrifuges and R&D to the inspectors of the IAEA. Even in EURATOM [the European Atomic Energy Community], they are not showing [such facilities to] the inspectors. . . . Therefore, we have done something unprecedented in the history of IAEA; and I hope that, with this biggest step, which is 100 percent transparency, we have given

a strong message to all involved, particularly those who have been negotiating with us, the P5+1. Also [I hope] that they receive this message,
that if there is no language of threat, sanctions, or this sort of obsolete
policy of carrot and stick, that if the approach is of a logical, civilized
request in a very friendly, cooperative environment, then the answer is
yes . . . hopefully, all countries and the IAEA [will] show maximum vigilance to protect this new trend of cooperation transparency, and we will
not be faced with disappointing words or actions that will disappoint us
for continuing such cooperation and transparent measures even beyond
our legal obligation as we did during his last visit.[128]

A reliable source told me that during this visit, the director of Iran's
Atomic Energy Organization, Fereydoun Abbasi Davani, offered Nackaerts a "real deal":

> . . . to remove all ambiguities and technical issues including the alleged
> weaponization studies, Iran would cooperate with the IAEA beyond its
> legal obligations for five years by offering a maximum level of transpar-
> ency, including implementation of the Additional Protocol and the Sub-
> sidiary Arrangement Code 3.1, and dealing with the possible military
> dimension, and in exchange, Iran's nuclear file would be normalized in
> the IAEA and the UN Security Council's sanctions removed.[129]

This source also told me that Amano discussed Iran's new far-reaching
overture with the P5+1, but unfortunately Washington, Berlin, Paris, and
London rejected it.

3. Suspension of Building Ten New Enrichment Sites

In early August 2011, during his meeting with Amano, Fereydoun Abbasi Davani told the IAEA chief that Iran does not have plans to build
new enrichment facilities over the next two years, even though Iran had
previously announced plans to build ten new enrichment facilities. Ali
Soltanieh confirmed the decision officially. He said: "This is the updated
decision because we had been exploring the possibilities; all the decisions
will be a function of the political environment of the whole world and also
the technical requirements. Therefore, based on these things, the decision
is really clear: we have decided for 20 percent [enrichment] in Fordow and
the rest of the activities up to 5 percent are going to be at Natanz."[130]

4. Limiting Enrichment to 5 Percent

In the third week of September 2011, during his visit to New York to attend the UN General Assembly, Iranian President Mahmoud Ahmadinejad announced Iran's readiness for another great move toward a confidence-building measure with the P5+1. He said that Tehran would stop producing 20 percent enriched uranium if it is guaranteed fuel for a medical research reactor.[131]

Ahmadinejad repeated the offer often enough, and with confirmation from his foreign minister, that it must have had the backing of Iran's supreme leader, Ayatollah Khamenei. While the 20 percent enriched uranium is to make fuel for the Tehran Research Reactor, which produces radioisotopes for medical uses, it could be enriched quickly to weapons-grade uranium (90 percent enriched). Ahmadinejad's offer therefore could certainly lower concerns that Iran will make a dash toward developing atomic bombs in the near future.[132]

5. Releasing the American Hikers

The fifth goodwill gesture also came during Ahmadinejad's visit to New York. He announced that two American hikers, imprisoned for more than two years since crossing over the border into Iran, would soon be released as a humanitarian gesture (a third hiker had been released a year earlier).[133] A day after Ahmadinejad's announcement, Joshua Fattal and Shane Bauer bounded down the steps of the aircraft that took them from Iran to Oman, rushing into the arms of the loved ones who had sought their freedom.[134]

Meanwhile Iran's foreign minister, Ali Akbar Salehi, announced that Tehran will inaugurate a new unit in the next three months to produce plate fuel for the Tehran Research Reactor. He said that a first plate, made of uranium enriched to 20 percent, would be tested in the reactor, which was running on low-enriched nuclear fuel imported from Argentina in 1993. Salehi also revealed that Majid Shahriari, a nuclear scientist killed in a bomb attack last year, had been the driving force behind the fuel production project at a facility in Isfahan. "When Shahriari was martyred, I was concerned that he was the only one who knew how to do the job. But, after visiting Isfahan, I saw that he had tutored around 20 youths in a workshop. Today we have thousands of nuclear scientists. There is almost nothing beyond our reach in the nuclear field if we aim for it," Salehi said.[135]

THE U.S.-EU RESPONSE TO IRAN'S GOODWILL

The West responded to Iran's five pillars of goodwill with its own six pillars.

1. Rejecting the 20 Percent Offer

The United States immediately dismissed Iran's offer to suspend 20 percent enrichment of uranium as not credible because Ahmadinejad "makes a lot of empty promises," a State Department spokeswoman said.[136]

2. Rejecting the Russian Step-by-Step Proposal

After meeting with the political directors of the P5+1 foreign ministries, Catherine Ashton, the EU foreign affairs chief, said:

> We discussed the recent developments of the Iranian nuclear program as reflected in the latest IAEA report. We remain determined and united in our efforts to work towards a comprehensive, negotiated, long-term solution—involving the full implementation by Iran of [the UN Security Council] and IAEA Board of Governors Resolutions . . . we reaffirmed the need for Iran to co-operate fully with the IAEA and to satisfactorily address all its concerns, including those on possible military dimensions to its nuclear program, as reflected in IAEA reports. . . . We reaffirm our offer of June 2008 and the proposals we made to Iran in Istanbul in January. . . . We reaffirm our unity of purpose and collective determination through joint diplomatic efforts based on these principles and in the context of our double-track strategy to resolve our shared concerns about Iran's nuclear program. . . . In this context, if Iran is prepared to engage more seriously in concrete discussions aimed at resolving international concerns about its nuclear program, we would be willing to agree on a next meeting with the Iranian side at an early and mutually convenient date and venue.[137]

By insisting both on the full implementation of the Security Council resolutions and the P5+1 June 2008 offer, this statement in effect undercut both Russia's step-by-step plan and Ahmadinejad's offer to suspend 20 percent enrichment.

3. Adopting a Resolution on Terrorism in the United Nations

The United States claimed on October 11, 2011, that it had uncovered a plot by two men with links to Iran's Quds Force, the international arm of Iran's Revolutionary Guard Corps, to assassinate the Saudi ambassador to the United States, Adel al-Jubeir, by planting a bomb in a Washington restaurant.[138]

President Obama said he wanted to see the "toughest sanctions" aimed at the Iranian regime. Nevertheless, just three days after the new accusations, both the White House and the State Department had to counter skepticism and disbelief. Many experts in the United States and the world, myself included, believed it was "too amateurish, too far-fetched."[139] Iran denied that it was in any way involved in such a plot and called the allegation a "baseless political and media show." The State Department confirmed it has been in direct contact with Iran, a rarity considering the two countries have no official diplomatic relationship.[140]

Reuters reported on October 13 that Saudi Arabia had also accused Iran of fomenting instability but pledged a "measured response" over the alleged plot. Saudi Foreign Minister Prince Saud al-Faisal said that the evidence showed "Iran is responsible" for the alleged plot and said Tehran had tried to "meddle" in the affairs of Arab states before. The United Kingdom imposed new sanctions on five Iranian individuals accused of plotting the assassination of the ambassador, and the United States continued lobbying allies to apply more pressure on Iran.[141]

On October 18, UN Secretary-General Ban Ki-moon confirmed that he had received documents on the matter from the United States, Iran, and Saudi Arabia and had referred the case to the UN Security Council. Susan Rice, the American ambassador to the United Nations, said she had met with fifteen Security Council members to discuss a course of action against Iran.

In connection with the case, the United States arrested Mansour Arbabsiar, an Iranian-American, and named Gholam Shakouri as another suspect. While the United States alleged that Shakouri is a member of the Quds Force, Iran stated that he is a "key" member of the People's Mojahedin Organization who travels under two other names: Gholam-Hossein Shakouri and Ali Shakouri. The People's Mojahedin Organization of Iran is an exiled Iranian dissident group listed by the United States as a terrorist group and which the Islamic Republic also considers an archenemy.[142]

Iran's leadership reiterated that the allegation had been engineered to further isolate Tehran. Iran's supreme leader, Ayatollah Ali Khamenei, said the alleged plot was a "meaningless and nonsensical accusation.[143] At another occasion, he said:

> Iran has 100 undeniable documents proving the United States has been behind terrorist acts in the Islamic state and elsewhere in the Middle East. By presenting those 100 documents, we will disgrace America in the world. America tried to exert pressure on Iran and rescue itself from the Wall Street movement and its problems by the absurd terrorist scenario. The course of events has changed in the world and, by the grace of God, the fight of virtue, with the pioneering Iran has started against the pharaoh of hegemony will continue to its final collapse.[144]

On November 16, 2011, a draft resolution was circulated by the United States and Saudi Arabia to the UN Secretariat accusing Iran of involvement in a plot aimed at assassinating the Saudi envoy to Washington. Iran's ambassador to the United Nations, Mohammad Khazaee, warned the body against pursuing the issue, calling the resolution unprecedented and a dangerous move and saying that it violates the dignity of the organization. He stressed, "The U.S. aims to practice its narrow-minded policies through the UN General Assembly by offering the resolution which is based on false allegations." He called the action a "threat for regional and international security."[145]

Despite Iran's warning, the UN General Assembly adopted the resolution on November 18 by a vote of 106–9, with 40 abstentions, condemning terrorism in all its forms and specifically deploring the alleged plot. The legally nonbinding resolution called upon Iran to comply with all of its obligations under international law, particularly in regard to efforts to bring those involved in the plot to justice.[146]

The fact that so many countries supported the United States and Saudi Arabia rather than Iran despite so much skepticism about the accusation was a repudiation of Ahmadinejad's diplomacy.

4. The New IAEA Report on Possible Military Dimensions

On November 8, 2011, the IAEA issued a report, mainly based on U.S. intelligence, on research, experiments, and other activities in Iran geared to possible military applications of Iran's nuclear program. Here are some of the highlights of its findings:

- Iran has started moving nuclear material to the underground Fordow nuclear site and installed two cascades of 174 centrifuges. They were not yet connected and were the first-generation IR-1 model that Iran has installed at its main Natanz enrichment plant. Iran has installed 8,000 centrifuge machines at Natanz; of those, around 6,200 are in operation. It has produced 4,922 kilograms of low-enriched uranium since 2007, or enough for a handful of nuclear weapons if enriched to weapons grade.

- The information indicates that, prior to the end of 2003, these activities took place under a structured program. There are also indications that some activities relevant to the development of a nuclear explosive device continued after 2003, and that some may still be ongoing.

- While some of the activities identified in the report's appendix have civilian as well as military applications, others are specific to nuclear weapons.

- The IAEA has "serious concerns" regarding possible military dimensions to Iran's nuclear program. After carefully and critically assessing the available extensive information, "the Agency finds the information to be, overall, credible."

- Iran has sought to procure equipment, materials, and services that would be useful in the development of a nuclear explosive device and has been provided with nuclear explosive design information. Iran has also sought information on how to convert highly enriched uranium into a metal, a step needed to make a nuclear core for a weapon. Iran has developed "exploding bridgewire" detonators.

- Iran has conducted large-scale explosive experiments in the region of Marivan and manufactured simulated nuclear explosive components using high-density materials such as tungsten. In 2000, Iran also built a large explosion containment vessel at Parchin.

- Iran carried out nuclear device modeling studies in 2008 and 2009, worked to manufacture small capsules suitable for carrying components filled with nuclear material, and planned and carried out preliminary experiments that would be useful for the testing of a nuclear bomb.

- Iran has studied how to fit nuclear payloads into the reentry vehicle of the Shahab-3 missile and examined how they would function in theory during launch and flight. The activities may be relevant to a non-nuclear payload but would be highly relevant to a nuclear-weapon program. Iran also has worked on developing a prototype triggering system that would allow a reentry vehicle payload to explode in the air above a target, or upon hitting the ground.[147]

Following the new IAEA report, a new U.S.- and European-led push to censure Iran in an IAEA Board of Governors resolution faced resistance from Russia, China, and a bloc of developing countries. This raised the possibility of a breakdown of the P5 consensus against Iran that has prevailed since the beginning of Ahmadinejad's tenure.

The United States said it was alarmed by the IAEA report, adding that it would unilaterally and multilaterally pursue further economic sanctions against the Islamic Republic and would consider "a range of possibilities."[148] European Union foreign ministers also spoke out in favor of tougher sanctions against Iran. "The EU Council will continue to examine possible new and reinforced measures and revert to this issue at its next meeting, taking into account Iran's action," it said in a statement.[149]

In October 2011, China[150] and Russia had warned the IAEA against publishing the report, saying it would block any chance of serious talks with Iran.[151] Following the release of the report, Moscow said it will not support new and harsher sanctions against Iran, arguing that "the international community will view all additional sanctions against Iran as an instrument of regime change in Tehran." Deputy Foreign Minister Gennady Gatilov told reporters that "we cannot accept this approach; Russia will not consider such proposals." He added that the imposition of further sanctions against Iran will not help strengthen the nuclear nonproliferation regime.[152] Russia also said that the IAEA report contained no new evidence. Moscow's position confronted the P5+1 with a choice between a tough stance that alienates Russia and China or a gentler, more inclusive approach that the United States, France, and the United Kingdom believe does not reflect the seriousness of the IAEA report.[153]

Meanwhile, Israel tested a missile capable of carrying a nuclear warhead and striking Iran, fanning a public debate over whether the country's leaders are agitating for a military attack on Tehran's atomic facilities. While Israeli leaders have long warned that a military strike was an option, the most intensive round of public discourse on the subject was ignited by a report in the Israeli newspaper *Yedioth Ahronoth* that said the prime minister, Benjamin Netanyahu, and the defense minister, Ehud Barak, favored an attack.[154]

Distancing themselves from IAEA Director General Yukiya Amano's report on Iran, members of the Non-Aligned Movement issued a statement criticizing the language used in the IAEA chief's report: "NAM notes with concern the possible implications of the continued departure from standard verification language in the summary of the report of the Director General," said the statement, which was read during the IAEA Board of Governors meeting on behalf of 120 NAM member states, including India. The statement sharply criticized Amano for accepting at face value Western intelligence information on Iran's nuclear activities. New Delhi maintained that Tehran has an "inalienable right" to use atomic energy for peaceful purposes but needs to abide by "international rules and obligations."[155]

As a permanent member of the UN Security Council, China opposed plans by U.S.-led Western states to impose tougher UN sanctions against Iran and called for further dialogue to resolve concerns about the Islamic Republic's nuclear program. "We always believe that dialogue and cooperation is the right way to solve the Iranian nuclear issue and that sanctions cannot fundamentally resolve the case. We hope the IAEA will be fair and objective, and actively committed to clarifying the salient issues through cooperation with Iran," Chinese Foreign Ministry spokesman Hong Lei said.[156]

Iran's Foreign Minister, Ali Akbar Salehi, said the director general of the IAEA must be held accountable for his report on Iran's nuclear program. In an interview with *Der Spiegel*, Salehi said, "Recent charges leveled against Iran in Yukiya Amano's report were unfair and unjustified. Iran has met all IAEA requirements to prove the peaceful nature of its nuclear program. No other country in the world has cooperated as much as Iran with the IAEA. The nuclear issue is just a pretext to weaken Iran by all available means."[157]

Iran's ambassador to the IAEA, Ali Asghar Soltanieh, calling the report a historic mistake, unbalanced, unprofessional, and politically motivated, said it repeats "obsolete and repetitive" charges that the Islamic Republic proved were fabricated in a comprehensive 117-page response four years earlier.[158]

Credible international experts also criticized the report. Robert Kelley, an American nuclear engineer and former IAEA inspector who was among the first to review the original data in 2005 and whose experience includes inspections ranging from Iraq and Libya, to South Africa in 1993, described the report as a "real mish-mash" that includes some "amateurish analysis":

> It's very thin, I thought there would be a lot more there, it's certainly old news . . . it's really quite stunning how little new information is in there. . . . The first is the issue of forgeries. There is nothing to tell that those documents are real. . . . My sense when I went through the documents years ago was that there was possibly a lot of stuff in there that was genuine, [though] it was kind of junk.[159]

The IAEA exposed in its report that a Russian scientist worked in Iran for five years during the 1990s in the weaponization group that was responsible for the final stage in the assembly of a nuclear bomb. The *Washington Post* revealed the name of the Russian scientist as Vyacheslav Danilenko. He immediately denied the reports by the IAEA and the newspaper.[160]

The Speaker of Parliament, Ali Larijani, said on November 13 that the IAEA report suggested that the agency was increasingly a political tool of the United States.[161] The Parliament urged the government to reduce its cooperation with the IAEA, and a day later, the Parliament's National Security and Foreign Policy Commission decided to discuss options for doing exactly that. The head of the committee, Alaeddin Boroujerdi, said that "we believe that [Iran's] cooperation with the IAEA needs reconsideration."[162] A member of the Iranian Parliament, Sirous Borna Baldaji, said: "The Islamic Consultative Assembly [Parliament] is expected to exert serious pressure on the government in the next few weeks to study Iran's withdrawal from the NPT."[163]

I told the *Bulletin of the Atomic Scientists* that the IAEA had, unfortunately, broken the rules of the game. The issues between the agency and member states should remain confidential. When the content of the IAEA reports on Iran are leaked to the media ahead of their distribution among the agency's member states, this is highly unprofessional, against the statute of the agency, and damaging to the credibility of the IAEA as an impartial international body. It also suggests that the allegations are dictated to the agency from somewhere else in order to make the case for ratcheting up pressure on Iran. The publication of these allegations was, I believe, a significant step backward.[164]

Following the IAEA report, the IAEA Board of Governors passed a resolution on November 18, 2011, expressing "deep and increasing concern" over Iran's nuclear activities. The resolution stressed the importance of establishing dialogue between the atomic agency and Iran and called on Tehran to "comply fully and without delay with its obligations under relevant resolutions of the UN Security Council."[165] Diplomats described the great-powers' draft as a compromise text between the Western states, which would have preferred tougher language, and Russia and China, which resisted. It stopped short of actions with teeth such as reporting Iran once again to the Security Council.[166]

Ali Asghar Soltanieh, Iran's ambassador to the IAEA, said the resolution would only strengthen Tehran's resolve. "The only immediate effect is further strengthening the determination of the Iranian nation to continue its nuclear activities for peaceful purposes without any compromise," he said.[167]

The Swiss government took the lead in toughening sanctions against Iran, adding 116 names, including that of the Iranian foreign minister and four current and former members of the Atomic Energy Organization of Iran, to the list of people subject to Swiss sanctions.[168]

On November 18, 2011, for the first time, Iran rejected an IAEA invitation to attend a meeting for Middle Eastern countries to discuss a Middle East nuclear-weapon–free zone. Soltanieh said of the IAEA director general,

Amano had not even talked about Israeli nuclear capabilities[;] how can we positively respond to the invitation of Mr Amano? . . . As long as Israel is not joining the NPT . . . and [does not] denounce and destroy all nuclear weapons capabilities, we will not be able to realize this expectation of the international community for a nuclear weapons-free zone. . . . While we are a strong proponent of a nuclear weapons-free zone we don't think that the meeting . . . will be fruitful and successful.[169]

Starting in the middle of 2011, Britain and France pressed Amano to report to the board that Iran's nuclear program included activities in support of the development of nuclear weapons, to provide support for the passage of a resolution that could lead to further sanctions against Iran. But China and Russia were opposed.[170] The Western states had to accept a weak resolution that everyone would agree to rather than take the risk that a tougher text would be opposed by China and Russia. Nevertheless, in effect, the West has been pushing Iran to close the door on nuclear diplomacy out of fear that it is part of a strategy to achieve regime change. I believe this path will, regrettably, lead to confrontation.[171]

5. Adopting a New Resolution on Human Rights

On October 10, 2011, the European Union sanctioned 29 Iranian officials accused of human rights violations in Iran.[172] A few days later, on October 19, the UN special rapporteur for human rights in Iran, Ahmed Shaheed, presented a report on the situation of human rights in Iran to the General Assembly's third committee, which deals with social, humanitarian, and cultural affairs. He alleged that Iran has displayed a pattern of systemic violations of fundamental human rights.[173] He voiced concern over alleged violations in the country's judicial system, citing practices such as torture, cruel or degrading treatment of detainees, and the imposition of the death penalty without proper safeguards. The report highlighted the house arrest and forced isolation of opposition leaders Mir Hossein Mousavi and Mehdi Karroubi and their wives, with all forms of communications cut to the places where they were detained. Mark Toner, U.S. State Department deputy spokesman, called upon the international community to use this occasion to redouble its condemnation of Iran.[174] Iran, for its part, denied the allegations and criticized the report as being poorly sourced, unfair, and simply untrue.[175]

Nevertheless, on November 21, 2011, the UN General Assembly passed a resolution condemning human rights abuses in Iran with a record number of votes in support. The 193-member assembly passed the resolution condemning "torture and cruel, inhuman or degrading treatment" by Iranian authorities with 86 votes in favor, six more than the previous year, 32 against, down eight from 2010, and 59 abstentions. In a speech to the General Assembly's Human Rights Council, the Iranian government representative, Mohammad Javad Larijani, an adviser to the country's supreme leader, called the resolution "substantially unfounded and intentionally malicious."[176]

Why are so many countries turning against Iran? In my critique of Ahmadinejad's policy, I have said it is because of miscalculations and the bluster of his administration, his foreign policy in particular. That doesn't mean, of course, that U.S. policy has been correct. But the fact remains that in the past few years, many countries, including some counted as allies, seem to have lost patience with Iran.

6. Sanctioning the Central Bank of Iran and Recognizing the Human Suffering in Iran

On November 21, 2011, just days after the IAEA report and on the same day that the UN Assembly passed the resolution on human rights, the United States took steps targeting Iran's Central Bank and its energy sector. The Obama administration named the Bank of Iran (Bank Markazi) a "primary money laundering concern" amid mounting international pressure against Iran. Britain, Canada, and France cut all ties with Iranian banks, including the Central Bank. French President Sarkozy sent a letter to Western leaders recommending an immediate freeze on Bank Markazi's assets. Although the U.S. action did not formally sanction the bank, the "money laundering" designation is expected to result in serious consequences for its operations. The United States also announced sanctions on a list of companies it says are involved in supporting Iran's nuclear program, as well as new measures targeting Iran's production and sales of petrochemicals and oil exports. Secretary of State Hillary Clinton called the measures "a significant ratcheting up of pressure on Iran."[177]

Days before, the U.S. Senate began considering its own harsh sanctions against the Central Bank of Iran aiming to "collapse the Iranian economy." Senator Mark Kirk said the intent is to cause so much suffering among ordinary Iranians that they will be forced to rise up against the regime, "and, if that doesn't work, we will go to war with Iran."[178] This is the same approach taken against Iraq that helped kill half a million Iraqis with a decade of crippling sanctions. It failed to topple Iraq's brutal dictatorship and ultimately ended in devastating war that cost the lives of thousands of

Americans and tens of thousands of Iraqis, and also cost the U.S. economy hundreds of billions of dollars.

But now, Congress and the administration seem eager to punish the Iranian nation and even Iranian-Americans for the actions of the Iranian government. In early November 2011, the House Foreign Affairs Committee passed a bill that would make it illegal for U.S. diplomats to engage their Iranian counterparts, strip the president's authority to license upgrades of Iran's aging civilian aircraft, and impose indiscriminate sanctions that would hurt individual Iranians.[179] One of the bill's top supporters, Representative Brad Sherman, said, "Critics [of the sanctions] argued that these measures will hurt the Iranian people. Quite frankly, we need to do just that."[180] It should be pointed out that blocking overdue upgrades of Iran's civilian aircraft doesn't just endanger innocent Iranians; it also puts at risk the lives of the nearly one million Iranian-Americans who travel to Iran.

On November 23, Ahmadinejad denounced European countries that are tightening sanctions on Iran as puppets of a U.S. master and said he was surprised at their moves to isolate Tehran's Central Bank. "We have had no relations with America for the past 32 years . . . but we are surprised by these European puppets, who immediately repeat whatever their master says like impotent servants. . . . They have said 'we should cut relations with the central bank and block the money of the Iranian people' . . . any expropriation of the Iranian people's foreign exchange reserves is considered major theft, and the Iranian people will treat those who do this as thieves," he told a large crowd gathered at an outdoor venue near Tehran.[181]

On November 28, Iran's Parliament singled out Britain after it became the first state to impose direct sanctions on Iran's Central Bank. The Majles erupted in a fresh frenzy of animosity toward its old imperial foe as members of Parliament, chanting "death to England," voted to expel Britain's ambassador to Tehran.[182]

Anger over the West's negative responses to Iran's multiple goodwill gestures caused more damage to Iran-West relations. A day after Parliament's decision to expel the British ambassador, Iranian protesters stormed the British Embassy in Tehran, tossing firebombs and burning documents and taking hostage six embassy staff members. Police reacted immediately and secured their release, but hundreds of protesters continued gathering in front of the British Embassy chanting, "God is the Greatest," "Down with the UK," "Down with the U.S.," and "Down with Israel."[183]

The United States and European Union condemned the assault, and representatives at the UN Security Council immediately drafted a statement calling on the Iranian authorities "to protect diplomatic and consular property and personnel."[184] Britain's foreign secretary, William Hague, said Britain held Iran's government responsible and promised "other, further, and serious consequences."[185]

In a statement, Iran's Foreign Ministry expressed regret over the incident and called it the unacceptable actions of a few protesters that occurred despite the efforts of Iranian security forces to stop them. The statement stressed Iran's respect for international law and the government's commitment to protect diplomatic missions. It also said an immediate investigation had been ordered.[186]

As the year ended, tensions between Iran and the West were escalating. In December, President Obama described as a success his "engagement policy," which had systematically imposed the toughest sanctions ever on Iran even while proclaiming that all options were on the table. "When we came into office, the world was divided, Iran was unified and moving aggressively on its own agenda. Today, Iran is isolated, and the world is unified in applying the toughest sanctions that Iran has ever experienced," he said.[187] Obama had come under heavy criticism from Republican candidates for president who said he was not being tough enough. Earlier, U.S. Ambassador to Israel Dan Shapiro said that Washington has been fully cooperating with Israel when it comes to Iran. "There is no issue that we coordinate more closely than on Iran," Shapiro told reporters at a briefing in Tel Aviv.[188]

In early January 2012, Iran managed to successfully test the country's first nuclear fuel rod for the Tehran Research Reactor[189] and began 20 percent enrichment of uranium at Fardow. Iran had already informed the IAEA that centrifuges installed in the underground facility at Fardow were ready to start spinning and enrich uranium to 20 percent purity. A U.S. State Department spokeswoman, Victoria Nuland, said the enrichment constitutes a "further escalation" of Iran's violation of its international obligations.[190]

Later in the month, Iran's foreign minister, Ali Akbar Salehi, said Iran will install its first 20 percent nuclear fuel plates at the Tehran Research Reactor within a month. "After our opposite parties refused to carry out their obligations in providing fuel for the Tehran Research Reactor, we moved towards 20 percent enrichment in line with our rights," Salehi said on the sidelines of the 18th African Union Summit in Addis Ababa.[191]

On January 11, another Iranian scientist was assassinated. Mostafa Ahmadi Roshan, a director at the Natanz uranium enrichment facility and a professor at Tehran's technical university, was killed while driving to work. The method of terror attack was similar to previous attacks on Iranian nuclear scientists.[192] He was at least the fifth scientist with nuclear connections to be killed since 2008.

The latest assassination brought forth a stream of reactions. UN Secretary General Ban Ki-moon issued a vague condemnation of the killing, saying attacks on "any people, whether scientist or civilian," are not acceptable.[193]

Iran's Foreign Ministry sent protest notes to London and Washington pointing out that the assassination of Iranian nuclear scientists began immediately after John Sawers, the head of MI6, discussed the launch of covert operations against Iran.[194]

U.S. officials denied any role in Roshan's death. "I want to categorically deny any United States involvement in any kind of act of violence inside Iran," Secretary of State Hillary Clinton said. Tommy Vietor, a National Security Council spokesman, added: "The United States had absolutely nothing to do with this. We strongly condemn all acts of violence, including acts of violence like this."[195]

A confidential source who is a former Israeli cabinet minister and senior Israeli Defense Force officer said that Roshan's killing was the work of the Mossad and the MEK, a violent anti-regime group in Iran that has been designated by U.S. State Department as a terrorist organization.[196]

Not everyone expressed outrage over the attack. One of the Republican presidential candidates who has taken a hard line on Iran's nuclear program welcomed the news of the scientist's assassination. "On occasion scientists working on the nuclear program in Iran turn up dead. I think that's a wonderful thing . . . I think we should send a very clear message that if you are a scientist from Russia, North Korea, or from Iran, and you are going to work on a nuclear program to develop a bomb for Iran, you are not safe," former senator Rick Santorum said at a campaign stop in Greenville, South Carolina.[197]

Patrick Clawson, director of the Iran Security Initiative at the Washington Institute for Near East Policy, said a covert campaign was far preferable to overt airstrikes by Israel or the United States on suspected Iranian nuclear sites. "Sabotage and assassination is the way to go, if you can do it," he said. "I think the cocktail of diplomacy, of sanctions, of covert activity might bring us something. . . . I think it's the right policy while we still have time."[198]

Meanwhile, in December 2011, amid tougher sanctions and talk of a military strike, Iran threatened to close the strategic Strait of Hormuz, the route for about one-sixth of the global flow of oil. Obama warned Tehran against any action that would impede the flow of oil from the Persian Gulf. In a letter to Iran's supreme leader, Obama said that closing the Strait of Hormuz is a redline for Washington.[199] An informed source told me that the letter had been delivered to Iran through three channels: Oman, Iraq, and Iran's ambassador to the United Nations. Ali Akbar Salehi said in an interview with *Le Monde* that Iran would close the strait only if it is attacked.[200]

Pressure on Iran continued to mount when, for the first time since the 1979 Islamic Revolution, the European Union approved a ban on oil imports from Iran starting July 1, 2012. (Saudi Arabia promptly assured the international community that it would pump more oil to keep prices from rising.[201]) As part of the effort to target Iran's source of financing, the EU also decided to freeze assets of the Iranian Central Bank in Europe as well as of eight other entities and to ban the trade in gold, precious metals, diamonds, and petrochemical products from Iran.[202] French President Nicolas Sarkozy played a key role in pushing the EU action.[203]

Obama praised the EU sanctions and vowed that the United States also "will continue to impose new sanctions to increase pressure on Iran."[204] In early February 2012, he issued an Executive Order placing new sanctions on Iran including its Central Bank, as an amendment to the wide-ranging defense bill he signed into law at the end of 2011. In a letter to Congress, he said the tougher sanctions are warranted "particularly in light of the deceptive practices of the Central Bank of Iran and other Iranian banks."[205]

The Russian foreign minister, Sergei Lavrov, however, said such sanctions have nothing to do with a desire to strengthen nuclear nonproliferation, but instead are "aimed at stifling the Iranian economy and the population in an apparent hope to provoke discontent."[206]

In an unprecedented statement, Yukiya Amano said that the IAEA has "credible information that Iran is engaged in activities relevant to the development of nuclear explosives." While making it very clear that Iran does not have nuclear weapons, Amano told *Gulf News* after a session on Iran at the World Economic Forum in Davos, Switzerland, that Iran was engaged in the design of weapons, computer modeling, neutron initiators, high explosives, and detonators.[207] I believe with such an odd and surprising statement, Amano reinforced Iranian officials' contention that he is doing the bidding of the United States, Israel, and the EU.

Israel, as the only Middle East country possessing a nuclear arsenal, continued to issue thinly veiled threats on the use of military force against Iran. "If sanctions don't achieve the desired goal of stopping [Iran's] military nuclear program, there will be a need to consider taking action," Defense Minister Ehud Barak said.[208]

On February 2, *Washington Post* columnist David Ignatius reported that U.S. Secretary of Defense Leon Panetta believes that "there is a strong likelihood that Israel will strike Iran in April, May or June—before Iran enters what Israelis described as a 'zone of immunity' to commence building a nuclear bomb. Very soon, the Israelis fear, the Iranians will have stored enough enriched uranium in deep underground facilities to make a weapon—and only the United States could then stop them militarily."[209]

Russian officials took pains to warn against a military strike by the United States or Israel. An attack would destabilize the world, Sergei Lavrov said. "The consequences will be extremely grave. It's not going to be an easy walk. It will trigger a chain reaction and I don't know where it will stop."[210] The Russian ambassador to NATO, Dmitry Rogozin, told reporters in Brussels that "if Iran is involved in any military action, it's a direct threat to our security."[211]

Nikolai Patrushev, the Russian Security Council secretary, said military escalation is likely, with a U.S. strike being a "real danger." He said:

> Israel is pushing the Americans toward it. . . . They are trying to turn Tehran from an enemy into a supportive partner, and to achieve this, to change the current regime by whatever means. . . . They use both economic embargo and massive help to the opposition forces . . . for years we have been hearing that the Iranians are going to create an atomic

bomb, [but] still nobody has proved the existence of a military component of Iran's nuclear program.[212]

Barbara Slavin, a senior fellow at the Atlantic Council, confirmed Russia's
position. She wrote: "The Barack Obama administration is increasingly giving the impression that it supports a policy of regime change against Iran—a
policy that could backfire and convince Iran to build nuclear weapons. . . .
Senior U.S. officials have suggested recently that mounting economic sanctions are meant to 'tighten the noose" around the Iranian government." She
quoted Paul Pillar, a CIA veteran and former Middle East chief on the U.S.
National Intelligence Council, as saying that "the Iranians are convinced
that [regime collapse] is our goal."[213]

In a defiant speech at a Friday prayer ceremony in January in Tehran,
Ayatollah Khamenei responded to the latest economic pressures and military
threats made by the United States, Israel, and the EU, saying,

> Threatening Iran and attacking Iran will harm America. . . . Sanctions
> will not have any impact on our determination to continue our nuclear
> course. . . . In response to threats of oil embargo and war, we have our
> own threats to impose at the right time. . . . I have no fear of saying that
> we will back and help any nation or group that wants to confront and
> fight against the Zionist regime [Israel]. . . . Americans say all options
> are on the table, even the option of [a] military strike [against Iran] . . .
> Any military strike is ten times more harmful for America. Such threats
> show that they have no sufficient discourse against Iran's logic and discourse
> . . . no way but using force and bloodshed to achieve [their] goals, which
> further harms America's rulers' international and domestic credibility. . . .
> Such sanctions will benefit us. They will make us more self-reliant. . . .
> We would not achieve military progress if sanctions were not imposed
> on Iran's military sector. . . . More imposed pressures mean more self-
> reliance for Iran. . . . Sanctions are beneficial also because it makes us
> more determined not to change our nuclear course. . . . Iran will not
> change its nuclear course because of sanctions.[214]

Despite such tough rhetoric, I do believe that in this period Iran turned
to the nuclear policy of Khatami's tenure and opened some opportunities
for negotiation. Iran's response to Russia's step-by-step proposal does not appear to be complete acceptance but rather a willingness to talk about it and

to accept the major issues. Fereydoun Abbasi Davani's transparency offer was indeed dramatic, because it included the implementation of the Additional Protocol, Subsidiary Arrangement Code 3.1, and the alleged studies on a "possible military dimension." The suspension of the threat to build ten more enrichment sites and the willingness to limit enrichment to 5 percent in exchange for Tehran Research Reactor fuel are also very meaningful ideas and should be regarded as substantive overtures. Releasing the hikers was a good thing; they never should have been tried as spies in the first place.

Overall, Iran's initiative came late, at a time when the West was in no mood for further negotiation. Nevertheless, the West should have welcomed the opportunity to forge a more comprehensive agreement on the nuclear issue.

CONCLUSION

COMPARING THE NUCLEAR POLICIES
OF KHATAMI AND AHMADINEJAD

Achievements of the Khatami Government's Nuclear Diplomacy[1]

This section analyzes the challenges, approaches, and achievements of Mohammad Khatami's nuclear negotiation team, as well as those of its successors under the Ahmadinejad administration. In short, Khatami's interactive diplomacy, which was a continuation of Hashemi Rafsanjani's "détente" policy, was highly successful in achieving its goals, given the circumstances facing Iran after the August 2002 revelations that Iran was building an underground uranium enrichment facility at Natanz.

The Khatami administration was successful in its primary goal of preventing economic or political sanctions and indeed the referral of the Iranian nuclear file to the UN Security Council as a threat to international peace and security. Furthermore, in November 2004, Iran succeeded in getting the file returned to the ordinary agenda of the International Atomic Energy Agency (IAEA) Board of Governors.

Iran managed to avoid war or international isolation even as it continued to develop its civilian nuclear program. Among the U.S. State Department documents disclosed by WikiLeaks was a secret telegram, sent in 2005, in which American diplomats said that their conversations with Israeli officials indicated that there was no longer any likelihood of a military strike against Iran.[2] This is a credible document showing that Iran's nuclear policies under Khatami removed the threat of military attack from Israel or the United States.

The diplomatic process in fact created the time for Iran to work out numerous technical issues in hardware and software design. Isfahan's uranium conversion plant was finished and made operational. The number of centrifuges was increased from 150 to 1,274 in the Natanz enrichment plant. This showed the world that Iran had mastered the nuclear fuel-cycle technology.

The management of the nuclear crisis had positive ramifications domestically. Fears of imminent war and instability were quieted, and investors gained confidence in Iran's economy. Offers of economic cooperation gleaned in negotiations with the European Union also seemed to promise greater access for Iran to the global economy. Obstacles to Iran's membership in the World Trade Organization were removed, and early negotiations set in motion Iran's accession to a Trade and Cooperation Agreement with the EU.

In terms of soft power, Iran also made gains during Khatami's tenure. Iran's negotiators managed to frame the dispute with Iran as a matter of preserving rights to peaceful nuclear cooperation, which many developing countries subsequently echoed.[3] With the Paris Agreement in 2004, Europe even pledged to enforce Iran's nuclear rights. Many countries, particularly in the developing world, became convinced during this period that Iran posed no military threat to the region and came to sympathize with its protestations in defense of its rights to a peaceful program and fuel-cycle development under the NPT.

Washington's unilateralism was undermined, at least as far as Iran's nuclear case was involved, and progress made it clear that Europe's multilateral negotiations were a much better approach to solving international problems. U.S. efforts to use the IAEA as a tool to serve its own anti-Iran agenda and secure international condemnation of Iran as noncompliant with international treaty obligations were effectively thwarted.

The United States failed to orchestrate international consensus against Iran because the EU, Russia, China, and Non-Aligned Movement countries rejected the U.S. demand for referral of Iran's nuclear file to the UN Security Council for imposing sanctions.

Iran cooperated extensively with the IAEA during this period and clarified many of the technical ambiguities reported by the agency, although some ambiguities remained and the IAEA asked for further cooperation. Tehran also earned a seat on the IAEA's multilateral nuclear approaches committee. Iran's improved relationship with the IAEA showed that the agency was not simply under the thumb of Western powers set on confrontation with Iran.

Iran's nuclear negotiators succeeded in transforming suspension of uranium enrichment and implementation of IAEA's Additional Protocol to a "voluntary" short-term measure aimed at confidence building.

More broadly, diplomacy surrounding the nuclear crisis showed that engagement with Europe was a viable strategy and that Iran could strengthen its position vis-à-vis Russia, on whom it had been dependent for nuclear fuel and to an extent political support, by increasing cooperation with the EU. Stepped-up cooperation with Europe also helped neutralize the threat of damaging U.S. sanctions on Iran and at the high-water mark of the Khatami team's efforts raised hopes for the transfer of nuclear technology for medical, agricultural, and power plant projects, a reversal of decades of sanctions-enforced technological isolation.

Steps toward Iran-Europe security cooperation also created an opportunity for Iran to take a new and prominent role in the region. The agreement for cooperation to establish a WMD-free zone in the Middle East raised the prospect of increased international pressure on Israel to disarm.

The Ahmadinejad Administration's Nuclear Diplomacy

Beginning with parliamentary elections in 2004 and culminating in Ahmadinejad's 2005 election, moderate and reformist figures were marginalized as the hard-line radical Principlists and conservative factions rose to predominant power in Iran's executive, judiciary, and legislative branches as well as its military and security structure.

Moderates and reformers had sought to resolve conflicts with the West under Presidents Rafsanjani and Khatami. During their administrations (1989–2005), Iran made far-reaching overtures and showed goodwill and flexibility on a number of issues:

- Iran played a key role in securing the release of Western hostages in Lebanon in the late 1980s. The United States promised Iran "goodwill for goodwill" but did not, in fact, reciprocate when Iran followed through with its end of the bargain.

- Iran responded positively to a European proposal for talks on critical issues in the early 1990s. During my visit to Dublin in summer 1990 as director general of the Foreign Ministry, I established a structure for an Iran-EU dialogue and we agreed to begin serious negotiations on such issues as the peace process in the Middle East, terrorism, weapons of mass destruction, and human rights. Iran remained neutral during Iraq's 1990 invasion of Kuwait, accepting about one million Iraqi and Kuwaiti war refugees.

- Iran announced during the Rafsanjani and Khatami period a policy of noninterference in the Israeli-Palestinian peace process and neutrality on any solution accepted by the Palestinian people. Iran expressed a readiness to work with Europe in fighting terrorism and in nonproliferation of weapons of mass destruction. During my time as ambassador to Germany (1990–1997), I proposed that Iran and the EU establish joint committees to combat terrorism and WMD bilaterally, regionally, and internationally. Unfortunately, my German interlocutor told me that Bonn could not persuade Washington to approve such a high level of cooperation.

- Iran accepted the Chemical Weapons Convention and the Biological Weapons Convention, hoping to enjoy the ordinary rights to peaceful chemical and biological technologies. Although Iran has complied fully with both conventions, Western countries never lifted their restrictions against Iran. Iran also accepted the Comprehensive Nuclear Test Ban Treaty. Although world powers were extremely concerned that Iran would object to the extension of the Non-Proliferation Treaty after twenty-five years, Iran voted for the extension of the treaty at the 1995 NPT Review Conference.

- Iran cooperated with the UN General Assembly's Human Rights Council in the 1990s by admitting the UN special human rights rapporteurs. Iran played a key role in the biggest prisoner exchange deal in the Middle East in 1996, which led to the release of Palestinian prisoners in Israel in return for the bodies of two Israeli soldiers. Also, a number of Antoine Lahad's forces were released.[4] Germany played a mediatory role, and I coordinated the deal between the German authorities and Hassan Nasrallah, the chairman of Hizbollah of Lebanon.[5] Iran announced in the 1990s that it would not send assassins to kill Salman Rushdie, would not interfere in other countries' internal affairs, and would show respect for international law.[6]

- Iran was among the first countries to condemn the 9/11 terror attacks. After 9/11, Iran cooperated with the Afghan opposition and the United States to rout the Taliban, supported the new government in Afghanistan, and fought al-Qaeda. Iran arrested and tried numerous al-Qaeda members and extradited approximately 500 to their respective countries.[7]

- Iran also cooperated with the United Nations to repatriate about two million Afghan refugees residing on its soil and—working with United States, Russia, and India—provided support to the Northern Alliance.

- After the downfall of Saddam, Iran cooperated extensively with Iraq's new government and spared no effort in helping to reestablish security in Iraq. Prior to the U.S. invasion of Iraq, Saddam Hussein sent a high-ranking envoy to Tehran proposing strategic cooperation between Baghdad and Tehran. Saddam even offered to pay reparations for Iraq's invasion of Iran if Tehran cooperated strategically against the United States, but Iran rejected the offer.

- Khatami promoted a "dialogue of civilizations" in order to achieve détente with the West and bolster international peace and security. Iran actively pursued membership in the World Trade Organization and worked to open the country's markets to foreign investors.

The Principlists opposed this moderate diplomacy, maintaining that during the sixteen years of Rafsanjani and Khatami, the country had made numerous concessions to the West with little to show for it. They argued that it was wrong to trust Europe or the West because they had shown no reciprocal goodwill toward Iran.

Indeed, the United States did ratchet up sanctions on Iran despite the overtures of the Rafsanjani and Khatami administrations. Even as Iran was cooperating with the United States in Afghanistan, Washington sought to isolate Iran in its region. In his 2002 State of the Union address, President George W. Bush labeled Iran as a member of an "axis of evil" with Iraq and North Korea.

The Principlists suggested that the accusations by the United States and its allies of terrorism, WMD development, and human rights abuses had not abated but in fact increased as a result of the flexibility and compromises of the reformists and moderates. According to their argument, Europe would simply follow America's lead on Iran and could not be relied on because EU and other Western countries are not interested in making useful economic and industrial investments in Iran and are looking only to export their own products to the country.

The Principlists considered Iran's democracy and stability to be incomparable to any other Middle Eastern country. The unremitting pressure on Iran by the United States and its allies, even as they supported autocracies across the region, proved to Iran's radicals that the West was interested not in democracy, human rights, or regional stability, but in dominating client states and their oil resources.

The Principlists likewise viewed the West's policies toward nuclear weapons and other WMD as deeply hypocritical and argued that conciliatory policies would not ease Western pressure on Iran. In part this stemmed from the West's history of supporting Saddam Hussein as he used chemical weapons against Iran but then actively working to prevent Iran from acquiring peaceful nuclear, chemical, and biological technologies after it accepted the relevant international conventions. By contrast, Israel, which has not acceded to any of those conventions and possesses the largest WMD arsenal in the Middle East, receives unconditional support from the United States and is allowed to import WMD technology from Western countries.

Pakistan and India did not sign the NPT, resisted pressure from the West including sanctions, and eventually tested nuclear bombs. Yet the West did not stop seeking close relations with both countries, and indeed increased cooperation with both, including, in the case of India, nuclear cooperation. Similarly, despite the fact that Iran cooperated with the IAEA for twenty consecutive months (from 2003 to 2005) and even opened some military facilities to IAEA inspections, and although the agency frequently announced the lack of evidence of any military diversion in Iran's nuclear program, European countries on August 5, 2005, called on the country once more to suspend all enrichment activities, a repetition of their summer 2003 demand. The Principlists therefore deemed that all cooperation with the IAEA had been in vain.

Radicals used such arguments to attack and marginalize moderates and reformists, emerging as the dominant political force in Iran after the June 2005 presidential elections with a new foreign policy agenda. They decided to ignore demands by the West, including the G8, EU, and even UN Security Council, deeming them illegitimate. This defiance, they believed, would force their international opponents to back down and eventually accept Iran's enrichment plan.

They gave priority to relations with the Muslim world, the developing countries, and Eastern powers such as China, India, and Russia over cooperation with the West. The radicals believed that their position was supported by Muslim world public opinion fed up with the double standards applied by the United States and the West. This public support would eventually force the West to rethink its stance on Iran.

I heard some of these arguments directly from Mahmoud Ahmadinejad some days after the 2005 presidential election, when he invited me to a meeting as one of his candidates for foreign minister. As recounted earlier, I rejected the offer because of his approach to foreign policy. I have been involved in Iran's foreign policy for more than two decades, including critical issues such as the Salman Rushdie affair, Western hostages in Lebanon, the nuclear issue, and Afghanistan and Iraq. I agree that the treatment of Iran by the West has not been fair during the past century and that American and British officials have clearly owned up to some of their big mistakes toward Iran, including organizing the military coup that brought down the popular government of Mohammad Mossadegh in 1953; supporting the past dictatorial rule of the Shah; and encouraging Saddam to attack Iran and supporting him throughout his eight-year war against Iran.[8]

I, however, believe that although cooperation between Iran and the West has not produced optimal outcomes, it has yielded a number of considerable successes:

- Iran's moderate foreign policy on Iraq facilitated the downfall of Saddam Hussein in 2003—up to then the number one threat to Iran's integrity, national security, and interests. In invading Iran in 1980, touching off the Iran-Iraq war, Saddam caused 300,000 deaths and $600 billion in damage. U.S.-Iran cooperation was the key to getting rid of Saddam and to creating the new era in Iraq after decades of dictatorship.

- Iran's major nuclear capabilities were achieved during the Rafsanjani and Khatami administrations. In early 2003, Mohamed El-Baradei, the director general of the IAEA, announced that Iran had acquired enrichment technology. This announcement came two and a half years before the Ahmadinejad presidency. More than 1,200 centrifuges were built in Natanz; the Arak facility produced heavy water; and the Isfahan uranium conversion facility produced UF_6 before Ahmadinejad was elected in June 2005.

- Iran was on the threshold of war with the Taliban government and al-Qaeda in Afghanistan in late 1990s. There is no doubt that the Taliban and al-Qaeda were the second most important threat to Iran's national interest and security, a threat that was removed through cooperation between the United States and the moderate government in Iran.[9]

- The United Nations supported an initiative by Iranian moderates by declaring the year 2001 as the "United Nations Year of Dialogue among Civilizations," reaffirming the purposes and principles of developing friendly relations among nations to strengthen universal peace and to achieve international cooperation in solving international problems of an economic, social, cultural, or humanitarian character.[10]

- Europe and Japan were the major creditors of the reconstruction of Iran after the eight-year war with Iraq. From 1990 to 1993, Iran was, after Brazil, the main credit recipient from the German state insurance company Hermes.[11] Tens of billions of dollars were obtained to promote economic, industrial, and technological development in Iran and to repair damage totaling hundreds of billions of dollars caused by Iraq's invasion. As mentioned before, moderates had major achievements on the nuclear issue.

Disadvantages of Nuclear Diplomacy
during the Khatami Presidency

The first negotiating team's diplomatic efforts sought to show Iran to be a rational actor and to build confidence with the international community. The attitude of many of the great powers that the Islamic Republic was inherently irrational and radically ideological in its policymaking was, after all, a major obstacle for Iran. Rather than consistently showing flexibility, the wisest course of action for Iran may have been to mix reasonableness with shows of more stubborn brinkmanship and unpredictability. Our flexibility led the Europeans to believe that there was less need for them to compromise.

If, however, Iran had pretended that it could turn to either moderation or radicalism, depending on the international reaction to its nuclear activities, it would in fact have facilitated progress in negotiations toward a mutually acceptable agreement. If, for example, Iran had temporarily behaved radically in the lead-up to the signing of the Paris Agreement, perhaps Europe would have taken a different and more palatable (for Iran) approach to the matter of "objective guarantees," which ended up being one of the main impediments to a lasting resolution. Instead, the EU3 was under the unrealistic impression that it could pressure Iran into long-term suspension of uranium enrichment.

Khatami's nuclear team was precluded by guidance from the supreme leader, Ayatollah Khamenei, from entering into direct interaction with the world's most powerful country, the United States. Thus, the Iranian team could only negotiate with the EU, Russia, China, and the Non-Aligned Movement. Although the U.S. bloc, including the United States, UK, Canada, and Australia, constituted a minority at the IAEA Board of Governors, they were a powerful minority that was quite effective in getting the board to pass strongly worded resolutions on Iran. The supreme leader's ban on direct negotiation with the United States effectively limited the potential for Iranian crisis management diplomacy. The United States also refused to negotiate directly without preconditions.

Although the supreme leader approved all of the Khatami administration's nuclear policies,[12] his later statements show that he did so only grudgingly.[13] Ayatollah Khamenei preferred and praised the Ahmadinejad administration's "psychology of the offensive" in nuclear policy and blamed Khatami's "defensive policy" for setbacks.[14]

Our disagreements with the radical conservatives in Iran's policymaking apparatus and media constituted a major impediment to our activities. We could never get them to trust and go along with our strategy as the best option under existing conditions. We were under particularly heavy pressure in the last stages of negotiations leading up to the Paris Agreement. For their part, our European counterparts were not in a position to endorse important agreements and measures because they were obliged to attune their position to the United States, which in many cases was not on board.

Roberto Toscano, Italy's ambassador to Iran from 2003 to 2008, explained to me how the absence of the United States frustrated EU3 negotiations with the Khatami team:

> I believe that the so-called EU3 did not achieve any significant result in their attempt at finding a solution for the Iranian nuclear question for two basic reasons. First, the Iranians have always seen the U.S. as the real adversary/interlocutor, and the Europeans as partners that could be interesting for bilateral relations, but doubting that they could be truly relevant in matters of security and strategy. . . . However, the real issue was not their view of the EU, but rather the concrete problem, which they often lamented, that any agreement with the Three was actually *ad referendum*, since the real decider was not sitting at the table.

Technical crises that arose during this period were mostly the result of lack of coordination between Iran's diplomats and its Atomic Energy Organization. While Iran was trying to build maximum confidence with its negotiating partners by announcing that it had reported all aspects of Iran's nuclear activities to the IAEA, new allegations surfaced as to blueprints for P-2 centrifuges, testing with plutonium, highly enriched uranium contamination found in certain nuclear equipment and facilities in the spring of 2003, missing UF_6 gas, and conflicts between Tehran's statements and the results of plutonium test samples. These caused serious problems for the Sa'dabad and Brussels agreements and practically obliterated any possibility of direct involvement of the United States in a diplomatic approach to the nuclear case. As previously mentioned, none of Iran's diplomats involved in negotiation had any information about the technical details of the country's nuclear activities, nor were we qualified to understand technicalities.

The partial suspension of enrichment irked Iran's leaders across the board and fueled the criticisms of the hard-liners. We tried our best to convince our European interlocutors about this reality, and the pressure that we were under as a result, but the EU3 did not believe us and thought that we were bluffing while they were trying to satisfy the United States through prolongation of suspension. So there needed to be a better plan beyond suspension to close the case.

Advantages of the Ninth Government's Diplomacy

From the start, the Ahmadinejad government stressed the importance of protecting Iran's nuclear achievements by opposing suspension of enrichment and implementation of the Additional Protocol. This policy, pursued regardless of its political costs, led to increasing the number of active centrifuges in Natanz from 1,274 in November 2004 to about 9,000 as of the end of 2011.

Iran established a new enrichment facility in Qom and began moving centrifuges from the Natanz enrichment plant for installation at the fortified Fordow facility near Qom. Iran mastered the capability of 20 percent enrichment and decided to triple its production of this material. The IAEA confirmed Iran's achievement on newly developed centrifuges, called the IR-2m and the IR-4; the IR-2m has about three times the potential capacity of the P-1. Iran also mastered technology to build fuel rods for the Tehran Research Reactor.

Ahmadinejad's nuclear policies were in line with those of Ayatollah Khamenei, as the supreme leader told the nation in a Friday prayer sermon several weeks after the June 2009 presidential election.[15] He also officially stated that his political and economic views were at odds with Rafsanjani's and close to those of Ahmadinejad.[16]

Thanks to Ayatollah Khameni's unprecedented and powerful support for Ahmadinejad and his nuclear policy, the ninth government has enjoyed the full support of the state-run media, as well as important players loyal to the supreme leader in all branches of the Iranian state. This is a significant advantage to the Ahmadinejad administration for aligning domestic public support with its nuclear strategy, which the Khatami government lacked.

While the Rafsanjani and Khatami administrations were barred from direct negotiation with the United States, Ayatollah Khamenei gave Ahmadinejad permission for such talks because of his confidence that Ahmadinejad's policies would align with his own stance. Hence, Ahmadinejad wrote letters to George W. Bush in May 2006[17] and Barack Obama in November 2008[18] and again in March 2010,[19] and the Supreme National Security Council announced that Iran was prepared to negotiate with any country except Israel. The exchange of letters between Ayatollah Khamenei and President Obama in 2009[20] was a particularly bold measure, showing Iran's readiness to reconcile with the United States for an agreement on the nuclear issue. And as revealed by Mohamed ElBaradei in his memoirs, in September 2009 Ahmadinejad had the IAEA chief transmit the message to Obama that Iran was "ready to engage in bilateral negotiations, without conditions and on the basis of mutual respect."[21]

Movement to direct negotiations with the United States—necessary to resolve the crisis—was impeded, however, by Ahmadinejad's rhetoric on the Holocaust, Israel, and the 9/11 terrorist attacks, which raised enormously the political costs to U.S. Democrats of softening their stance on Iran. Nonetheless, the taboo on direct U.S.-Iran talks had been broken, and the American presence in the diplomatic process around the nuclear issue during the Ahmadinejad period means that if engagement is truly embraced, the two capitals will be able to pursue a comprehensive and mutually acceptable deal through direct channels.

The Ahmadinejad administration managed to increase Iran's uranium enrichment abilities and present the world with a nuclear program that had reached the point of no return. Although this was a success, the question is "at what cost?"

Disadvantages of the Ninth Government's Diplomacy and the Missed Opportunities

The ninth government's first nuclear team was chosen from officials with security perspectives. Ahmadinejad has marginalized the Foreign Ministry during his tenure. Ahmadinejad's ambassador to China described the Foreign Ministry as "the lowest organization in foreign policy making and just a personnel office for the presidency,"[22] and Khatami's ambassador to Paris characterized the Foreign Ministry under Ahmadinejad as "a ministry just for protocol and propaganda."[23]

As has been explained, the ninth government's "looking to the East" policy exaggerated the cohesion, abilities, and willingness of the "Eastern bloc" to confront the West and as a result made little headway. Indeed, in some instances, it even consolidated Eastern and Western countries against Iran. Support for UN Security Council resolutions from China, India, and Russia, as well as the lack of support for Iran evinced by the Non-Aligned Movement and other Eastern countries when the nuclear case was reported to the Security Council, attest to this fact. Even Javad Mansouri, Iran's ambassador to China under Ahmadinejad (2005–2010), described the "looking to the East" policy as one of the mistakes of the ninth government,[24] and its failure was a blow to the credibility of Iran's foreign policy.

Some days after he was appointed as secretary of the Supreme National Security Council and top strategist on Iran's nuclear file in August 2005, Dr. Larijani proposed to me that I become either Iran's ambassador to China or the head of nuclear affairs in the Foreign Ministry. I rejected both offers. I declined the Beijing posting because I knew the Ahmadinejad administration would expect me to persuade China to resist U.S. and EU efforts to refer Iran's nuclear file to the UN Security Council, and I was convinced that this was a futile mission. Ambassador Mansouri, who took on the task, acknowledged after half a decade of efforts in Beijing that this was the case. I rejected Larijani and Mottaki's offer to become the head of nuclear affairs at the Foreign Ministry because I knew that the new government's nuclear policy would cause the Iranian nuclear file to be referred to the UN Security Council. I did not want to be responsible for the ignominy of the referral and sanctions. This was one of the major negative consequences of Ahmadinejad's nuclear policy, and it was harmful to Iran's national security and interests.

Ahmadinejad's diplomacy also enabled the great powers to redefine enrichment suspension from being voluntary as recognized by the P5+1 during Khatami's tenure, to now being completely obligatory under UN Security Council resolutions. The UN resolutions also called on Iran to allow inspections beyond the Additional Protocol, as opposed to the IAEA resolution in November 2004, which had stated that the IAEA would limit inspections to the framework of the Additional Protocol.

Ahmadinejad's policies handed the United States and its allies unprecedented international support for pressing Iran as a Chapter VII "threat to international peace and security." The UN Security Council, for the first time, linked Iran's nuclear and missile programs. Iran's nuclear dossier, which had been removed from the emergency docket of the IAEA Board of Governors in November 2004, was from summer 2005 onward the subject of new IAEA director general reports and board resolutions every three months.

The international community slapped Iran with devastating economic sanctions and expanded sanctions to include the Arak heavy-water reactor. Resolution 1737 took the further step of prohibiting construction operations related to the nuclear program. The great powers made it clear that sanctions could be lifted only on the conditions that: first, all issues considered outstanding by the IAEA were resolved; second, the IAEA could verify for certain that there was no undeclared nuclear material in Iran; and third, the world gained more trust in the peaceful nature of Iran's nuclear program and Iran was in a better position to deal with the West.

Furthermore, Ahmadinejad's foreign and nuclear policy enabled the United States and the West to pass UN Security Council Resolution 1929 and impose crippling unilateral sanctions on financial transactions and oil imports, making Iran the most sanctioned country in the world and perhaps in history.

In practice, this meant a call for unlimited suspension because of the ambiguity of the conditions and difficulty in certifying when they had been met. Under Ahmadinejad's watch, the number of outstanding technical issues on the IAEA's Iran dossier began to rise again, specifically the IAEA's claims on the weaponry dimension of Iran's nuclear program.

The unnecessary controversies that Ahmadinejad created also raised the domestic political costs in Washington of talking to Iran. This contributed to the failure of Obama's engagement policy, despite direct and high-level Iran-U.S. talks. Tension with the United States did not decrease and actually has dramatically increased.

Additionally, with progress on nuclear negotiations at a deadlock, the United States, Israel, and some European allies attempted to sabotage and conduct covert actions against Iran's nuclear facilities and Iranian nuclear scientists. This marked the beginning of a cyber war against Iran.

Ahmadinejad's foreign policy enabled the United States and Israel to win over the EU, Russia, China, India, Japan, and other countries on the referral of Iran's dossier to the Security Council and to orchestrate unprecedented sanctions resolutions against Iran at the United Nations. Furthermore, the United States was able to persuade many countries, including Japan, South Korea, EU member states, Canada, and Australia to impose unilateral sanctions beyond the realm of the UN resolutions.

Last but not least, the MEK was removed from the EU's list of terrorist organizations, where it had been placed due to tremendous diplomatic efforts during the Rafsanjani and Khatami periods. This change was due in part to frustration over Iran's nuclear program.

Meanwhile the U.S. Navy went so far as to order all units under its command to re-label the Persian Gulf as "the Arabian Gulf."[25] International criticism of Iran on the grounds of human rights violations and terrorism increased considerably. On March 24, 2011, the UN Human Rights Council decided by a vote of 22–7 to reestablish a UN special mechanism on human rights in Iran.[26] The mechanism had been removed during the Khatami period. The renewed focus on human rights contributed to the general air of suspicion and hostility toward Iran in the international community that did little to advance the country's defense of its nuclear rights. Global public opinion has turned sharply against Iran, a trend that facilitated the passage of new resolutions on human rights and terrorism in November 2011 in the United Nations, raising the possibility of a military strike.

Iran still has had opportunities to improve its international position. The seeming triumph of American hard military power during the George W. Bush administration transformed into costly quagmires in Iraq and Afghanistan. With U.S. military capacities stretched and little appetite for further adventurism in the Middle East, geopolitics shifted to a focus on soft power and the balance of influence, where Iran enjoys unique advantages. The fall of authoritarian U.S.-allied governments in the Arab Spring of 2011 has created further opportunities for Iran to expand its influence and manage relations with the United States through a multifaceted regional strategy.

On the economic front, too, spiking oil prices, which have averaged about $120 a barrel during the Ahmadinejad presidency compared with $15 during the Rafsanjani period and $30–40 during the Khatami periods, have cushioned the blow of economic sanctions and brought unprecedented revenue to the government.

This boon to the budget has, however, raised new questions and criticism about Iran's high unemployment rate and other economic problems. According to Majles MP Ghodratollah Alikhani in a March 2011 speech, "Current government revenue [$600 billion] is equivalent to the entire income from oil of the country of the previous 100 years; with this income, unemployment should have been uprooted and industry should not have been faced with adversity, but according to economic experts only 30 percent of the country's industry is in operation."

Iranian economic experts have contested the official unemployment rate of 10 percent cited by the Ahmadinejad administration and rosy figures of job creation since 2010 provided by the Ministry of Labor and Social Affairs. According to Ali Mousavi, a member of the Majles Social Affairs Commission, the unemployment rate as of April 2011 was close to 20 percent.[27] In Tehran, Ahmad Tavakkoli, a prominent Principlist member of the Majles, said Iran's dependence on imports has risen from 35 percent to 75 percent during Ahmadinejad's presidency (2005–2011). He cited an increase of more than 600 percent in imports of wheat over the period.[28] Furthermore, the value of the Iranian currency dropped an unprecedented 60 percent as of January 2012.[29]

That's why I believe that through a more reasonable policy that would have prevented the referral of Iran's nuclear file to the UNSC and the subsequent sanctions, Iran could have had unprecedented achievements at a much lower cost.

THE MISTAKES AND MISSED OPPORTUNITIES OF THE WEST

A solution that is acceptable to both sides requires an understanding of the concerns of both the international community—especially Western countries—and the Iranian nation. Because the international media focus is almost entirely on the West's interests, Western public opinion is largely unaware of Iranian concerns. Therefore, I want to focus on this issue, and in the process note some strategic mistakes on the part of the West, in the hope that doing so may help achieve a fair and peaceful settlement of this important international crisis.

After the Revolution

Article IV of the NPT notes that all parties to the treaty undertake to facilitate the exchange of equipment, materials, scientific and technological information, and cooperation for the peaceful uses of nuclear energy with other members. Iran signed the NPT in 1968, and the Iranian Parliament ratified the treaty in 1970.

Following the Islamic Revolution in 1979, Iran remained committed to the NPT. From the Iranian point of view, the West, intent upon fomenting regime change in Iran, ignored all commitments it had accepted through mutual contracts with Iran and within the framework of the NPT. Now, Western countries are urging Iran to respect international treaties while forgetting that, according to the same treaties, they should have implemented contracts for which Iran had paid them billions of dollars. However, they have never respected their obligations under the NPT, and most have not even refunded the money that had been given by Iran for the implementation of the contracts.[30] This was the *first mistake* by the West that made Iran seek self-sufficiency in nuclear energy.

Support for the Iraqi dictator in his eight-year war against Iran was the second strategic mistake made by the West in relation to Iran and the entire Middle East. Every day, Iranian citizens were pounded by missiles that massacred women and children. Thousands of Iranians lost their lives or were critically injured in chemical attacks by Saddam's army; twenty years after the war, victims of chemical weapons are still dying of their injuries. This has had a great impact on the Iranian nation and policymakers. Ignoring Iraq's depradation was the *second mistake* by the West.

Thus, Iran's measures to become self-reliant in peaceful nuclear technology, missile, and other military industries started after 1985 in the later years of the war. Under the circumstances, Iran had no choice but to become self-sufficient in order to gain deterrence and defensive power. Iran's current nuclear and missile capabilities grew out of this important historical background; faced with similar conditions, no advanced nation would have done otherwise. Additionally, Iranians came to view Western governments' stances on WMD nonproliferation as selective and hypocritical. In discussing *deterrence*, I do not mean the possession of nuclear weapons, but obtaining the capability of enrichment in accordance with the NPT, which would practically enable a country to develop nuclear weapons if it decided to do so, though it is the firm policy of Iran not to go after the nuclear bomb.

The Rafsanjani Period

After the war and the election of President Hashemi Rafsanjani, a period of reconstruction and détente began. The issue of Western hostages in Lebanon provided an opportunity for the reduction of tensions in Iran's relations with the West. At that juncture (1987–1988), I served as director general for Western Europe at the Iranian Ministry of Foreign Affairs.

Western leaders, especially the U.S. president and secretary of state, sent many messages to their Iranian counterparts calling for Iran's humanitarian intervention to secure the release of Western hostages in Lebanon. The proposed U.S. formula was "goodwill for goodwill" in frequent messages to Rafsanjani. In one of these messages, Washington noted that Iran's show of goodwill by helping with the release of the American hostages would be answered with unexpected and surprising goodwill on the part of the United States. Mahmoud Vaezi, who was deputy foreign minister for Europe and the Americas, and I were tasked by Rafsanjani and then-minister of foreign affairs Ali Akbar Velayati to follow the case in order to free the Western hostages.

Within a few months, Iran's humanitarian efforts led to the release of all Western hostages in Lebanon. In return, however, the United States intensified economic sanctions against Iran and increased its hostile policies.[31] That response was shocking, to say the least. The unprecedented economic sanctions visited upon Iran after the war and resolution of the hostage-taking situation were aimed at preventing reconstruction of the country after eight years of war—a war that had claimed the lives of about 300,000 Iranians and cost Iran at least $600 billion.

This was the West's *third mistake*, which nipped in the bud any chance of détente with Iran and further motivated Iran to become self-sufficient in military and peaceful nuclear technology.

In 1994–1995, while I was Iran's ambassador to Germany, the West tried to persuade Iran to sign the Chemical Weapons Convention. Germany had the best relations with Iran among Western countries. One day, I was called to the Chancellery, where I was given a sealed letter from the German chancellor directed to the Iranian president. In the letter, the chancellor asked for ratification of the convention and promised in return to remove all limitations on the provision of advanced chemical technologies and equipment to Iran. The chancellor reiterated that this convention would open the doors to the export of advanced chemical technology to Iran. Iran ratified the convention, but neither Germany nor other Western countries removed their limitations on chemical technology exports to Iran, even though they were obliged by the convention to do so. This was the *fourth mistake* made by the West.

Thus, the Iranian nation and its leaders were taught the following lessons regarding the West's strategy:

- From the point of view of the West, Iran should remain committed to WMD conventions despite all of their limitations, controls, and inspections, while at the same time being deprived of peaceful technologies as laid out and promised by the WMD conventions.
- Despite the fact that all NPT member states are committed to cooperate with each other on peaceful nuclear activities, the West would not comply with its contractual commitments. As a result, Iranian projects with billions of dollars of investment would remain unfinished.
- The West would support the use of weapons of mass destruction against Iran if and when that became necessary.
- Self-sufficiency would be the only choice for Iran to save billions of dollars of investments, to enjoy the legitimate rights outlined in the NPT, and to have deterrence capability[32] against foreign aggression.
- The strategy of the West is to keep Iran weak and vulnerable. The West would do anything to impede Iran's self-sufficiency and capability in defense and sophisticated technology. Therefore, some secrecy is unavoidable to realize Iran's objectives.

The Khatami Presidency and Post–9/11 Era

Mistakes continued to be made by the West after Rafsanjani's presidency. According to Dr. Bruno Pellaud, the former deputy director general of the International Atomic Energy Agency, "In May 2003, the Swiss ambassador to Iran, Tim Guldimann, handed over to U.S. officials a road map for comprehensive talks that had been approved by Iran's supreme religious leader, Ayatollah Ali Khamenei. In May as well, the Iranian ambassador to the UN, Javad Zarif, did likewise through his own American channels to the State Department."[33] If the United States had responded appropriately, the existing atmosphere surrounding Iran's nuclear issue could have been completely different.

Ambassador James Dobbins, the Bush administration's special envoy for Afghanistan, Kosovo, Bosnia, Haiti, and Somalia, confirmed the proposal. By 2003, he said,

> The Khatami government had made substantial overtures of coopera-tion to Washington twice, first after the U.S. victory in Afghanistan, and again after the U.S. invasion of Iraq. . . . This approach was more formal and far-reaching, encompassing offers of cooperation on nuclear tech-nology, Iraq, terrorism, and Middle East peace as well as Afghanistan. The Iranian offer was conveyed though the Swiss government, which was responsible for representing U.S. interests in Tehran. This proposal, like its predecessor, was never seriously considered in Washington and once again the Iranians never received a response. . . . U.S. officials have never explained in any detail why they ignored the Iranian overtures of 2002 and 2003.[34]

This missed opportunity in the earliest phase of the crisis was the *fifth mistake* made by the West.

Mohamed ElBaradei, director general of the IAEA, visited the Natanz facility in early 2003 and announced that Iran was among the countries—others included Brazil, Argentina, Germany, and Japan—that had nuclear fuel-cycle technology. The announcement echoed far and wide. Prior to nuclear negotiations with Iran, which started in October 2003, the Eu-ropean Union called for the cessation of Iran's nuclear program.[35] The re-quest was in striking contrast to the NPT, which recognized "the inalien-able right of all the Parties to the Treaty to develop research, production and use of nuclear energy for peaceful purposes without discrimination and in conformity with Articles I and II of this Treaty."

The request, therefore, increased Iran's suspicions and led to more seri-ous questioning. All parties to the nonproliferation and disarmament treaties are obligated to certain limitations. They must conduct nuclear, chemical, and biological activities within the framework of the relevant treaty and under the supervision of appropriate international bodies such as the IAEA. This would entitle them to peaceful technology and to the cooperation of all countries for the development of their peaceful technology. Iran has acceded to all conventions and treaties, including the NPT and the Chemical Weapons Convention, and no international authority has been able to prove any form of deviation in Iran's program toward production of nuclear, chemical, or biological weapons. While the IAEA still has questions about possible military aspects of the program—questions that Iran has yet to answer—these questions are related to past and not present activities.

Lack of trust in Iran's intentions was the reason given by the EU for requiring Iran to bring its nuclear activities to a full stop. Iran concluded that if this trend continued, the West would subsequently ask Tehran to give up all nuclear, chemical, and biological activities, and Iran, as a member of the treaties, to give in to all restrictions and relinquish its rights. Although EU, U.S., and Security Council resolutions provide for a resumption of enrichment in Iran if and when the country has restored international confidence and resolved remaining issues with the IAEA, Iran's concern is that such "confidence" would not be restored for decades (as it believes is precisely the West's intention) and that enrichment would be held hostage to all outstanding matters of dispute with the West, including human rights, the Middle East peace process, weapons of mass destruction, terrorism, and missile capability.

Therefore, Iran decided to remain a party to the disarmament treaties and, at the same time, continue all peaceful activities under the supervision of international bodies, not accepting cessation of those activities under any conditions. The West could have asked for more "transparency" in Iran's activities and full supervision of the IAEA over Iran's nuclear program rather than calling for "cessation" or "suspension" of the program. The request for cessation (as distinct from transparency), was the *sixth mistake* committed by the West because it led to more distrust toward the West in Iran and disillusionment with disarmament treaties. Indefinite cessation, after all, meant depriving Iran of its legitimate international right.

From the beginning of the Iran nuclear crisis in 2003 to the present time, the West has pushed the IAEA and the UN Security Council to compel Iran to allow inspections and access to facilities beyond the requirements of the Comprehensive Safeguards Agreement and its Additional Protocol. Such a demand for inspections *beyond* the Safeguards Agreement and the Additional Protocol limitlessly raises the ceiling on what could be requested by the IAEA or Security Council. The Safeguards Agreement and the Additional Protocol should provide the sole legal framework for interactions among all members—any request that steps beyond that framework should not have been raised. This was the *seventh mistake* of the West and the P5+1.

From the start, the West should have made it clear that Iran's nuclear enrichment rights would be respected by allowing a pilot program, which would have provided more time and a more amicable atmosphere for Iran to continue confidence-building measures, enabling both parties to resolve the issue. In October 2003 and after much resistance from Iran, foreign ministers of the EU3 agreed to give up on their "cessation" request, and both sides accepted temporary suspension of part of Iran's nuclear activities for inspection by the IAEA, though just as a confidence-building measure that was not legally binding. More than one year after the beginning of suspension and following frequent inspections of Iran's nuclear facilities by the IAEA, the agency announced that no sign of diversion of declared material toward a nuclear-weapon program had been found in Iran. Obviously, Iran could not continue with suspension of nuclear activities for an unlimited period. In the spring of 2005 during a visit to EU3 countries, I, as spokesman for Iran's nuclear negotiating team, proposed the following package to the EU3:

- Isfahan's uranium conversion facility would start to work and export its entire product to South Africa in return for an equivalent amount of yellowcake.
- The Natanz facility would work at the level of a pilot plant.
- Negotiations would continue for a maximum of one year, during which the two sides could achieve, respectively, "objective guarantees" about diversion toward a weapons program in Iran's nuclear program and "firm guarantees" of nuclear, technological, and economic cooperation between Iran and the EU.

I reiterated that, regardless of the outcome of its forthcoming presidential election, Iran would never compromise on its legitimate right to have an enrichment program and would, in the absence of negotiations, restart its enrichment activities. Germany and France were positive overall toward the proposed package in private talks, but a UK official told me that they were concerned about the position of the United States and would be ready to negotiate on this package only after the presidential elections.[36] The EU3 made a strategic mistake in postponing negotiations. The United States was not on board in this period, and the EU was not able to deliver alone. This was the *eighth mistake* made by the West. Had the package been accepted, there would have been no need to send Iran's case to the Security Council or to impose sanctions on the country.

In general, the EU and United States missed a great opportunity during the Rouhani period and Khatami presidency when Iran displayed maximum goodwill, transparency, and overtures of confidence building. During this period (2003–2005), Iran did suspend its enrichment activities and, in addition, voluntarily allowed implementation of the Additional Protocol, which gave the IAEA access to Iran's centrifuge production activities. The IAEA confirmed that there was no evidence of diversion of Iran's declared material; the EU and IAEA recognized Iran's right to have a civilian nuclear program; and in November 2004 Iran's nuclear file was taken off the agenda of periodic IAEA board meetings. This was the right time to finalize a mutually acceptable package, but it didn't happen because of the misguided ambitions of the West. In an interview concerning his 2011 memoir about his time as IAEA director general, Mohamed ElBaradei lamented the West's refusal to compromise and therefore its missed chance to strike a deal with Iran during this period, before the rise of the more obstinate Ahmadinejad administration:

> The Iranians were willing in 2003, but the administration of then U.S. President George W. Bush was not. Then, in 2010, when President Barack Obama extended his hand, the Iranians couldn't take it, because of domestic political power struggles. . . . I adhere strictly to the facts, and part of that is that the Americans and the Europeans withheld important documents and information from us. They weren't interested in a compromise with the government in Tehran, but regime change—by any means necessary.[37]

Indeed, the West's position on the nuclear issue played a large role in the change of Iran's elected government from reformist and moderate under Khatami to one dominated by hard-line radicals under Ahmadinejad. As early as June 2004, a year before EU3-Iran talks broke down, ElBaradei told EU3 and U.S. ambassadors,

> Iran's hard-liners were gaining power because of the meager results from cooperation with the IAEA. A policy of pressure alone . . . would not work, "particularly since no one in the West has clear evidence of an Iranian nuclear weapon program." With no incentives, the Iranians might take any number of actions: they could restart their enrichment program, back away from their Additional Protocol, or even withdraw from the NPT.[38]

The Ahmadinejad Period

Strategic mistakes and missed opportunities on the part of the West continued during Ahmadinejad's presidency. In 2009, Iran had communicated to IAEA Director General ElBaradei that replacement fuel was needed for the Tehran Research Reactor.[39] ElBaradei then worked behind the scenes with the United States, Russia, and France to devise a proposal whereby Iran would receive fuel for the reactor in return for transferring from Iran the existing stockpile of low-enriched uranium that Iran had produced.[40] Such a deal would satisfy Iran's interest in keeping the reactor running to produce medical isotopes, while building international confidence that Iran would not convert its LEU into highly-enriched uranium which could be used in nuclear weapons. Iran communicated a strong interest in such a deal, and negotiations were held in Geneva in October 2009 to hammer out the details. Importantly, the United States was represented in the Geneva meetings by Undersecretary of State William J. Burns, who met bilaterally with Saeed Jalili, the secretary of Iran's Supreme National Security Council. This was the highest-level bilateral meeting between the two states in thirty years. In Geneva, the negotiators of the United States, Russia, France, and Iran principally agreed.[41]

Opponents of President Ahmadinejad, who had supported the deal, mobilized to accuse the president and his negotiator of making a bad bargain. Among the leaders of the critics was Majles Speaker Ali Larijani, whom Ahmadinejad had vilified when he was the chief nuclear negotiator early in Ahmadinejad's first presidential term.[42]

Following domestic disputes, Iran proposed some conditions to modify the deal that had been negotiated in Geneva. Whereas the October plan called for Iran to send its low-enriched uranium to a third country before fuel for the Tehran Research Reactor could be fabricated and delivered to Iran, Iran now demanded that the LEU should be exchanged at the same time as fuel was delivered, and that the exchange take place on Iranian soil.[43] Meanwhile, Iran would keep producing more LEU. The P5+1 rejected this counterproposal. Iran then announced that it would make fuel for the Tehran Research Reactor itself, and therefore began enriching uranium to 20 percent, which is much closer to weapon-grade uranium than the 3.5 percent enriched uranium it had been producing before.[44]

A short time after the October meeting in Geneva, the Iranian government told El Baradei that Tehran would be willing to make the deal directly with the United States. Washington rejected the offer. Then, as I was told by a reliable source, Mohammad Khazaee, the Iranian Ambassador to the UN, informed his U.S. counterpart that Iran would be ready for the deal as agreed in Geneva with no precondition. But surprisingly Susan Rice, the U.S. Permanent Representative to the United Nations raised suspension of enrichment as a precondition while suspension was not a prerequisite to Geneva deal.

The collapse of the October deal, and the subsequent move by Iran to enrich to 20 percent, increased tensions between Iran and the P5+1, and intensified the international sense of crisis. In early 2010, following the April Nuclear Security Summit in Washington, the leaders of Brazil and Turkey stepped forward to try to revive diplomacy. They traveled to Tehran and negotiated with Iranian leaders a new plan to swap fuel for the Tehran Research Reactor for LEU from Iran. The new plan was announced on May 17. It called for Iran to transfer to Turkey 1,200 kilograms of LEU in exchange for receipt of new fuel for the Tehran Research Reactor within one year. While the amount of LEU that Iran would transfer was the same that Tehran had agreed to in October 2009, Iran had in the meantime increased its stockpile of the material. Western critics of the May package highlighted this, though the October proposal would not have required Iran to stop additional production of LEU in any case. Critics also noted that the May deal was contingent on states, including the P-5, refraining "from measures, actions, and rhetorical statements that would jeopardize Iran's rights and obligations under the NPT." Because the deal was announced just days before a scheduled UN Security Council meeting to consider further sanctions on Iran, this provision suggested that Iran's primary objective was to preclude further sanctions, and that Iran could choose to cite any subsequent statements or actions by other states as a justification for reneging on the deal. For these and other reasons, the West, led by the United States, rejected the proposal and cast aspersions not only on Iran but also on Prime Minister Erdogan and President Lula.

The May 17 declaration was not a solution for the impasse over Iran's nuclear program, but it could have been a positive step forward and a start for a broader negotiation that unfortunately was missed. This was the *ninth mistake* made by the West. As Iran saw Western suppliers shrug off their responsibility—as provided in the Non-Proliferation Treaty and the International Atomic Energy Agency Statute—it started domestic plans to enrich uranium to 20 percent. Some six months after the rejection of Tehran's offer by the West, Iran had produced 40 kilograms of 20 percent enriched uranium and hoped to soon witness the injection of the first batch of Iranian-made fuel into the Tehran Research Reactor, thus gaining the capability of producing fuel rods and plates to be used for peaceful purposes.[45]

Salehi, who was then the head of the Atomic Energy Organization of Iran and acting foreign minister, said: "Iran's progress in this area was a result of the West's lack of cooperation and sanctions, and the more they delay in holding a new round of negotiations with us, the more progress we make in fuel production and after a while the issue of [a] fuel swap will become meaningless."[46] This was a great achievement for Iran, though simultaneously it further complicated the nuclear negotiations.

On August 16, 2011, President Ahmadinejad's website announced that he had agreed with Russia's step-by-step proposal.[47] It was a far-reaching overture by Iran because the Russian plan included not adding new centrifuges, limiting enrichment to the existing site at Natanz, stopping production of a new generation of centrifuges, allowing IAEA surveillance of centrifuge production, implementing the Additional Protocol and Subsidiary Arrangement Code 3.1, limiting production of enriched uranium to a maximum of 5 percent, and even suspending all enrichment and related activities mentioned by the UN Security Council for three months. The West's failure to negotiate the step-by-step proposal was its *tenth mistake.*

In summer 2011, the IAEA team, led by deputy Director General Herman Nackaerts, visited Tehran. Iran offered him a blank check for any inspection he wanted. The team visited the Research and Development (R&D) sections of heavy-water facilities and new generation of centrifuges. This initiative was in line with the Additional Protocol. By this step, Iran registered itself at the IAEA as the first country ever to permit the agency to visit R&D centrifuge facilities. At the end of the visit, the head of Iran's Atomic Energy Organization, Abbasi-Davani, offered "full IAEA supervision," including implementation of the Additional Protocol for five years, provided that sanctions against Iran are lifted. Again the offer was rejected by the United States and the EU.[48] The West's failure to welcome Iran's offer on "IAEA's full supervision" was its *eleventh mistake,* because Ahmadinejad had clearly shifted toward the nuclear policy that had been pursued during Khatami's tenure.

It is important to note that all of this has played out while Israel, India, and Pakistan—which have not been forced by the West to join the NPT—hold large stocks of weapons of mass destruction while enjoying the full support of the West.[49] Not only the Iranian nation, but all Muslim countries, believe that the West is pursuing a double-dealing strategy of unconditional support for Israel on the issue of weapons of mass destruction in order to dominate the Middle East region, while preventing Muslim countries from developing peaceful nuclear, chemical, and biological technologies. This is the *twelfth mistake* made by the West in the Middle East. It has made Iran more determined to insist on its inalienable right to peaceful nuclear technology. The West should put an end to its discriminatory behavior, encourage all countries to accede to disarmament treaties, and give up the use of nuclear weapons as a means of threat.

The twelve broad mistakes made by the West have made Iran all the more resolute in safeguarding its rights. As of the end of 2011, Iran has about 10,000 active centrifuges and more than four tons of low-enriched uranium. If the P5+1 does not drop its demand of suspension of enrichment and find a face-saving, nondiscriminatory, and lasting solution acceptable for both sides, Iran will continue to expand its nuclear activities. But the Obama administration has not clarified that it recognizes what must be done in order to reach a mutually acceptable diplomatic solution to the nuclear crisis.

On September 23, 2010, President Obama stated in an address to the UN General Assembly,

> The United States and the international community seek a resolution to our differences with Iran, and the door remains open to diplomacy should Iran choose to walk through it. But the Iranian government must demonstrate a clear and credible commitment and confirm to the world the peaceful intent of its nuclear program.[50]

In an interview with BBC Persian the next day, Obama added that if Iran chose to act responsibly, "They would then be able to have their rights for a peaceful nuclear program under the Nuclear Non-Proliferation Treaty. And that would remove the sanctions and would allow them to fully enter the international community in a way that would tremendously benefit the Iranian people."[51]

In December 2010, Hillary Clinton made explicit for the first time in an interview with the BBC that the United States, as well as the international community, could accept a verifiably peaceful enrichment program in Iran if international concerns about the country's nuclear program were allayed.[52]

However, it is questionable to what degree this truly signaled a new approach to Iranian uranium enrichment. In April 2011, top Obama adviser Gary Samore[53] explained the continuity in policy between the Bush and Obama administrations:

> The Bush administration said that once Iran satisfied concerns about its nuclear program, then Iran could have a peaceful nuclear program like any other NPT party. The Obama administration has said the same thing, but Secretary Clinton has gone a little bit further, and she's been explicit that once Iran has complied with the Security Council resolutions, and satisfies concern and restores confidence in its nuclear activities, then it has the same rights as any NPT party. And in the NPT there are no restrictions on the development of enrichment capability for peaceful purposes. So she has said explicitly what the Bush administration implied, but didn't say explicitly. *But both the Bush administration and the Obama administration have emphasized that the first step is*

for Iran to comply with the UN Security Council resolutions and restore confidence in its nuclear program (emphasis added).[54]

It seems from this statement that the Obama team has continued to demand that Iran comply with UN Security Council resolutions (which as discussed have included demands that Iran halt enrichment indefinitely and allow unlimited inspections beyond its international legal obligations by the IAEA for an indefinite period) *before*—and in practical terms perhaps years before—the United States and the international community reciprocate with any recognition of Iran's nuclear rights, by agreeing to let Iran continue fuel-cycle activities, or by lifting sanctions. If that is the case, there is no difference between Obama's approach and that of his predecessor, and the current policy is in practice a continuation of discriminatory restrictions on peaceful nuclear activities beyond international treaty requirements that Iran has been protesting for the past nine years.

It is also possible, however, that Obama envisions that a deal through which Iran would provide all the transparency, access, and guarantees necessary to assure the IAEA and international community that its nuclear capabilities are not, and will not be, diverted for military applications, and in exchange have sanctions lifted and recognition of the legitimacy of its nuclear program granted. If this is the case, then Obama's approach may bring real progress.

A WAY OUT

The UN Security Council, international community, and successive U.S. administrations have wrestled with the Iranian nuclear issue for the past nine years. The West's policies have fluctuated between persuasion and coercion in an unsuccessful attempt to resolve the issue. Linked as the nuclear issue is with the destiny of President Obama's engagement policy with the Muslim world, Israel and its own security policies, and the future of Iran-U.S. relations, a resolution of the crisis is imperative. Yet neither the United States nor the international community has thus far been able to find a solution for this problem.

As the above narrative of the continuity in basic Iranian aims during the Khatami and Ahmadinejad administrations demonstrates, regardless of who rules Iran, the principles of Iran's nuclear policy will remain the same. The full rights of Iran to peaceful nuclear technology, including uranium enrichment, will remain a non-negotiable issue. I will never forget what Dr. Rouhani told me about the supreme leader's position on enrichment. Ayatollah Khamenei told him in 2004, "I would never abandon the rights of the country as long as I am alive. I would resign if for any reason Iran is deprived of its rights to enrichment; otherwise this may happen after my death."

Of course, nuclear negotiating tactics would be different depending on whether the leadership is moderate, reformist, or conservative, as we have seen from the comparisons of nuclear diplomacy during Khatami's and Ahmadinejad's times in office. But no Iranian politician—neither the ruling political figures nor leaders of the opposition—can risk surrendering uranium enrichment.

Nevertheless the current deadlock on the nuclear issue is the result of two miscalculations. The first was by the United States and its European allies. In 2003–2005, we told the EU3 frequently that the right to enrich is a redline for Iran. They would not be able to deprive Iran of this right by prolonging the negotiations and Iran's unilateral suspension. Iran would restart enrichment at any cost. They did not believe us. The second miscalculation relates to a powerful school of thought in Tehran. We told the members of this school that restarting enrichment unilaterally would result in Iran's being referred to the UN Security Council, the invocation of Chapter 7 of the UN Charter citing Iran's nuclear program as a threat to international peace and security, and the imposition of sanctions and more on Iran. But we were told that this was all a Western bluff and would not happen.

By now both parties have learned their lessons. The West should have learned that Iran will not forgo its legitimate rights and Tehran has learned that the threats of referral and sanctions were not a bluff. Now it is time for diplomacy.

A Negotiable Framework to Resolve Iran's Nuclear Dilemma

A negotiable framework is needed to resolve the Iran-U.S. nuclear deadlock. After many years of mutual hostility, no one should expect this to be an easy task with a quick result. And the domestic political situations following the disputed Iranian presidential election of June 2009 and the Republican victories in the U.S. congressional elections in November 2010 will make it even more difficult. Nevertheless, diplomacy, even under the present circumstances, has a much greater chance of success than sanctions if both sides could be realistic and flexible in putting together a negotiable package that would be face-saving in terms of their respective domestic political situations.

The reality is that it is now too late to keep Iran from learning how to enrich uranium. However, enriching uranium and building a weapon are two different things. In his February 16, 2011, Worldwide Threat Assessment to the U.S. Senate Select Committee on Intelligence, retired Lieutenant General James Clapper, director of national intelligence, concluded that Iran was "keeping open the option to develop nuclear weapons, in part by developing various nuclear capabilities that better position it to produce such weapons, should it choose to do so. We do not know, however, if Iran will eventually decide to build nuclear weapons." A month later, speaking with Senator Carl Levin at another Senate committee, Clapper confirmed that the U.S. intelligence community had concluded with a high level of confidence that Iran had not restarted nuclear weapons work halted in 2003.[55]

I hold to the assessment that Iran has not made a decision to acquire a nuclear weapon—as distinguished from a nuclear-weapon option.[56]

Also, I believe that, in parallel to nuclear negotiations, Tehran and Washington have made tremendous efforts for rapprochement during the Obama and Ahmadinejad presidencies. Despite some of his counterproductive statements and policies, Ahmadinejad has made efforts to improve relations with the United States that are unprecedented since the 1979 revolution.

Ahmadinejad is the first president since the victory of the Islamic Revolution to be allowed to announce that his government was ready to take part in direct and unconditional negotiations with the United States.[57] He is the sole postrevolutionary president to have written a direct official letter to a U.S. president (President George W. Bush) and to have congratulated another (Barack Obama) on the occasion of his election.[58] Negotiations on Iraq between Iran and the U.S. ambassador in Baghdad in 2007, and, as stated previously, the meeting between Saeed Jalili, the secretary of the

Iranian Supreme National Security Council, and Undersecretary of State William J. Burns in Geneva in early October 2009, were unprecedented instances of direct high-level contacts between Tehran and Washington since the Islamic Revolution in 1979.[59]

The efforts have not been limited to official channels. Track 2 (non-governmental) and Track 1.5 (talks between Iranian government officials and former U.S. officials) diplomacy has also been extremely active during Ahmadinejad's presidency. Ahmadinejad's special adviser, Mojtaba Hashemi Samareh, participated in talks organized by the Pugwash organization in Austria in 2008, in which former secretary of defense William Perry and two U.S. congressmen also participated. During the period 2005 to 2011, former U.S. officials have met frequently with Iran's foreign minister, deputy foreign minister, its ambassador to the United Nations, and other Iranian ambassadors to discuss the possibility for rapprochement.[60]

Such meetings are unprecedented in the past thirty years and are no longer taboo. That the supreme leader lifted for Mahmoud Ahmadinejad the redline on direct negotiations and relations with the United States has been a very positive and important development.[61] Despite some differences, most of these contacts should have been coordinated with the supreme leader, who, according to the Iranian constitution, is the ultimate decisionmaker on all matters of Iran's foreign policy.

Public statements indicate that the supreme leader is skeptical concerning the sincerity of U.S. statements regarding engagement, stating that, "From the very beginning, Iran has intended not to prejudge and observe practical steps taken in line with the 'change' motto. What we have seen in practice during this period has been against their oral remarks . . . . Our nation would not be deceived by their tactical smiles."[62] I believe that Ayatollah Khamenei has not yet, however, reached a final conclusion on the possibilities of rapprochement with the United States.

Attempts by the two capitals to put into practice the present engagement policy have not been successful because neither Washington nor Tehran has a grand strategy—or even a road map. While in general terms the United States wants to normalize relations with Tehran, the present engagement policy lacks a well-defined strategy for dealing either with the Iranian nuclear issue or with U.S.-Iran relations more generally.

What is needed is what I call a negotiable framework, which contains a comprehensive solution package for these two different dimensions of the U.S.-Iran problem. And here, I believe that the best way to ensure that Iran's nuclear capabilities do not become a threat to the interests of the United States, Europe, or other countries is to move toward a fully engaged, normal, and cooperative relationship with Iran. This requires two things:

1. Contextualizing the nuclear and other issues within a bilateral, regional, and international framework; and
2. Understanding that there will be no final resolution to the issue of Iran's nuclear program as long as the bilateral relationship between Tehran and Washington continues to be dominated by hostilities, threats, and mistrust.[63]

It is critical in this context to understand that Iran's insistence on enriching uranium on its soil reflects its centuries-old determination to protect its independence. It is not just survival of the Islamic system; it is seen as a matter of national survival. Iran's priority is to defend its legitimate right to a peaceful nuclear program, including enrichment. This was, is, and will remain a redline for Iran. The United States must understand that Iranians of all political stripes view outside pressure, sanctions, intimidation, and threats of military strikes as foreign aggression to be resisted. The Americans need to understand Iran's deep-rooted concern regarding foreign intervention. Tehran and Washington should change their focus from confrontation to cooperation in supporting proposals for regional security in the Persian Gulf and the elimination of weapons of mass destruction from the entire Middle East.[64]

Iran has a range of options, from enriching uranium for peaceful use, to using its nuclear-weapons potential as a bargaining chip, to actually developing nuclear weapons. There is no acceptable way for the West to eliminate these options. Its central goal therefore must be to ensure that Iran does not make the fateful decision to develop a nuclear weapon or to produce highly enriched uranium or plutonium that could be used to make nuclear weapons.[65]

In recent years, Iran has exchanged many proposals with the EU3 (2003–2005) and the P5+1 (2006–2009), but unfortunately none of them has worked. Any viable solution needs to meet the bottom lines of all sides. For Iran, this means reliable civilian nuclear energy, a guarantee of its rights under the NPT to enjoy peaceful nuclear technology including enrichment, maintenance of its pride and achievements in the nuclear technology area, and removal of security threats. For the United States and Europe, the bottom line is "no nuclear weapons" and no "short-notice nuclear weapon breakout capability."[66]

A face-saving solution acceptable to both parties is critical not only for Iran-West relations but also for the Middle East and global peace and security. We need diplomacy within a negotiable framework—a solution that addresses the concerns of both parties. As a career diplomat who has worked for more than two decades on improving relations between Iran and the West, I believe the framework that will be described below could provide a way out for both the confrontation over Iran's nuclear program and Iran-U.S. relations.

PHASED GRAND AGENDA

The P5+1 have proposed small steps to build confidence and provide a temporary compromise, to be followed with an enduring solution to the controversy over Iran's nuclear position. In contrast, Iran wants to be sure of the entire game plan and endpoint, that is, a road map toward an eventual grand bargain, before committing itself to anything. A mutually acceptable solution to the nuclear issue must go far beyond the nuclear issue itself and address related issues that are vital to peace and stability in the Middle East.

There is still time for the P5+1, Iran, the IAEA, and other interested parties to resolve the nuclear dispute through diplomacy. Rapprochement between Iran and the United States is a key element in resolving the present impasse on the nuclear issue and heading forward to more comprehensive cooperation between Iran and the West on regional and international issues. I believe the foundation for a final agreement already exists in:

- The NPT and Iran's Safeguards Agreement with the IAEA.
- The *fatwa* by Iran's supreme leader that prohibits the production, storage, or use of nuclear weapons. Iran regards utilizing nuclear weapons as forbidden by the Islamic faith and believes it is incumbent on everyone to safeguard humanity from such weapons. The supreme leader stated as much in his messages.[67] In February 2011 he said: "We are not seeking nuclear weapons because the Islamic Republic of Iran considers possession of nuclear weapons a sin... and believes that holding such weapons is useless, costly, harmful and dangerous."[68] From Iran's point of view, the *fatwa* is clear evidence of Iran's opposition to the proliferation of nuclear weapons and the highest credible assurance that Iran is sincere in its drive to use nuclear energy only for peaceful purposes.[69]
- President Obama's statement that, after Iran "confirm[s] to the world the peaceful intent of its nuclear program," the United States will accept "their rights for a peaceful nuclear program under the Nuclear Non-proliferation Treaty. And that would remove the sanctions and would allow them to fully enter the international community. . . . We respect Iran's right, like all countries, to access peaceful nuclear energy. That is a right embedded in the NPT. We recognize Iran's rights. *But with those rights come responsibilities.* I would like nothing more than to reach the day when the Iranian government fulfills its international obligations—a day when these sanctions are lifted, previous sanctions are lifted, and the Iranian people can finally fulfill the greatness of the Iranian nation."[70]

Secretary of State Hillary Clinton recently stated more specifically that Iran "can enrich uranium at some future date once they have demonstrated . . . [themselves to be] in accordance with international obligations."

Nevertheless, the following is my attempt to outline a reasonable diplomatic solution. It is important that any conditions linked to implementation of the elements of the package be avoided.

A. Nuclear Package

The P5+1 should assure Iran that, in the event of an agreement, it will:

- Remove Iran's nuclear dossier from the agendas of the IAEA Board of Governors and the UN Security Council.
- Recognize Iran's right to nuclear technology, including enrichment.
- Lift the sanctions.
- As required by the NPT, cooperate with Iran in the development of peaceful nuclear technology to the same extent as they do with other non-weapon states.

In response and to reassure the P5+1 on non-diversion to military purposes, Iran would take the following steps:

- Operationalize the supreme leader's *fatwa* banning the acquisition of nuclear weapons by passing legislation to that effect in the Iranian Parliament: declaring Iran a non–nuclear-weapon state, strengthening legal export control mechanisms for nuclear material and technology, and guaranteeing a permanent ban on the development, stockpiling, and use of nuclear weapons; and requiring the highest standards of physical security at all Iranian nuclear facilities where nuclear materials are present, especially enrichment facilities, and criminalizing the possession of such material outside such facilities other than during authorized transit between facilities.
- Iran would establish a consortium with other countries to manage fuel-cycle activities within Iran, based on the official proposal made by Ahmadinejad during his September 2005 speech at the UN General Assembly meeting. This would enhance the transparency of Iran's nuclear program and thereby reduce regional and international concerns.
- With the Parliament's approval, Iran would resume provisional implementation of the Additional Protocol and the Subsidiary Arrangements to its Safeguards Agreement. In addition, Iran would offer to ratify and bring the Additional Protocol into force as soon as the package is realized.
- Iran would commit to cooperate with the IAEA on the removal of all remaining questions about its past nuclear-related activities, including the IAEA's Possible Military Dimension (PMD) issues. A new work plan between Iran and the IAEA, similar to what was

signed in summer 2007, should be worked out for resolving the remaining questions.[71]

- Iran would make its centrifuge production fully transparent to the IAEA.
- During a period of confidence building, Iran would promise not to reprocess spent fuel from power or research reactors.
- If provided with modern light-water research reactors, and for a period of confidence building, Iran would make a commitment to refrain from constructing further heavy-water-moderated research reactors once Arak is completed.

B. Iran-U.S. Package

In parallel to the deal on the nuclear issue, a separate comprehensive package, including major bilateral, regional, and international issues, should be negotiated on U.S.-Iran relations. While Iran's nuclear issue could be negotiated in the framework of the P5+1 talks, the separate comprehensive package should be negotiated directly between Tehran and the United States.

Tehran and Washington need a broader way to think about each other in the context of their security objectives. U.S. security objectives in the Middle East continue to grow and become more complex and dangerous because of the unpredictable and volatile events in the Arab world and the mounting tensions with Iran. Iran's interests and activities in the region are involved in virtually each of these American security objectives.

A new strategy is essential to avoid conflict and address threats to security objectives in the region. The United States should seek a broad relationship with Iran based on mutual respect, noninterference, equality, justice, and common interests. No significant progress can be made toward achieving the U.S. security objectives without first convincing Iran that the United States is prepared to discuss all agenda items in U.S.-Iranian relations.

Iran and the United States should have a realistic assessment of potential areas where they could have common interests, such as Afghanistan, stopping the drug trade, opposing al-Qaeda, and limiting the role of the Taliban. Unfortunately, pursuit of these wider ranges of potential common interests has so far been held hostage both to preoccupation with the nuclear file and the domestic political emotional climate in both capitals.

C. A Middle East WMD-Free Zone

The UN Security Council, in cooperation with regional powers, should proactively pursue a WMD-free zone in the Middle East. Iran was the first country in the Middle East to propose such a zone in a UN General Assembly resolution. In the four decades since, there has been zero progress toward this goal because Israel has repeatedly obstructed it. Israel's nuclear policy and its refusal to join the NPT could fuel nuclear-weapons proliferation in the region in the next decade. That is why there is an urgent need for a serious initiative to establish a WMD-free zone in the Middle East, which could potentially facilitate a regional security arrangement, increase the prospects for finding a just solution to the Arab-Israeli conflict, and prevent regional proliferation.

D. An End to Double Standards

The fact that the P5+1 countries maintain strategic and aid relations with Israel, India, and Pakistan, which have nuclear weapons and are not parties to the NPT, while at the same time they pressure Iran, which has not acquired nuclear weapons, sends a message to other countries that once they get the bomb they are immune. The P5 countries must also move more quickly to fulfill their own NPT commitments to nuclear disarmament. In the absence of such actions, the NPT will lose its legitimacy.

To be realistic, Steps C and D cannot be preconditions to Steps A and B, but whatever conditions are applied to Iran's enrichment program should be applied to other countries that have enrichment capabilities and the associated nuclear-weapon option. Iran will not be willing to accept special conditions indefinitely. This is an opportunity to create a new protocol—call it Additional Protocol 2—for all countries that have dual-use nuclear cycle capabilities.

I presented the outline of my proposal for the first time at the Carnegie International Nuclear Policy Conference in Washington on March 29, 2011. Some days later, a European diplomat who was present at my talk and is well informed about the details of Iran's nuclear dossier wrote me the following:

> I am in almost entire agreement with the contents of the paragraphs leading up to your description of a possible package basis for a U.S./

Iran deal. I believe that P5+1 handling of the nuclear issue has been bedeviled by U.S. reluctance to give sufficient weight to accumulating evidence that since 2003 Iran has decided to respect its NPT obligation to refrain from manufacturing or otherwise acquiring nuclear weapons. This misjudgment freezes the P5+1 into positions which preclude any movement towards the areas of mutual interest with Iran that, I am convinced, exist. I do not see, though, grounds to hope that any U.S. administration will abandon these positions any time soon, least of all for the kind of comprehensive negotiation (bilateral plus nuclear) that you advocate. The positions are too comfortable politically for abandonment to be likely. They please or at least avoid displeasing AIPAC [the American Israel Public Affairs Committee], evangelical Christians, neocon ideologues, the military-industrial complex, and all those Americans who have not forgotten the hostage crisis and/or fear/hate Muslims.

The key question is whether the United States and its allies are interested in ensuring that Iran's activities are peaceful or whether they are using Iran's nuclear program as a rationale to advance an ultimate agenda of destabilization and regime change in the Islamic Republic. If there is no genuine and sincere will for a compromise and peaceful resolution of the nuclear issue, then no realistic scenario can work. And if that is the case, we can expect a real confrontation with disastrous consequences for all parties.

NOTES

INTRODUCTION

1. The Non-Aligned Movement is an international organization with a general platform opposing imperialism and great power hegemony. The movement's membership includes, as of 2011, 118 countries from across the developing world. In a UNISCI discussion paper on the role of the movement in the nuclear issue, Iran's ambassador to the IAEA, Ali Asghar Soltanieh, wrote, "Since the nuclear issue of Iran was raised in 2003 the NAM chapter started its activities in Vienna. It has always taken positions based on the very principles which the movement's foundation was based on. The emphasis [is] on the multilateralism and challenge against the nuclear disarmament and non-proliferation, on one hand, and non-compromising position on inalienable and non-discriminatory right for peaceful uses of nuclear energy." See Ali A. Soltanieh, "Iran Going Nuclear?" UNISCI Discussion Paper 10, January 2006.

2. "Evaluation of Iran's Nuclear Policy after a decade," kaleme.com, www.kaleme. com/1390/08/19/klm-79696.

3. U.S. Embassy, Cairo, "Scenesetter for Requested Egyptian FM Aboul Gheit Meeting with the Secretary," WikiLeaks, February 9, 2009, www.wikileaks.ch/cable/2009/02/09CAIRO231.html.

4. U.S. Embassy, Doha, "Senator Kerry's Meeting with Qatar's Amir," WikiLeaks, August 30, 2011, www.wikileaks.ch/cable/2010/02/10DOHA70.html#.

5. U.S. Embassy, Riyadh, "Saudi King Abdullah and Senior Princes on Saudi Policy Toward Iraq," WikiLeaks, April 20, 2008, www.wikileaks.ch/cable/2008/04/08RIYADH649.html.

6. U.S. Embassy, Paris, Secretary of Defense Gates' Meeting with French Foreign Minister Kouchner, February 9, 2010, WikiLeaks, February 10, 2010, www.wikileaks.ch/cable/2010/02/10PARIS174.html.

7. U.S. Embassy, Amman, "Wary of U.S.-Iran Engagement, Jordan Offers Words of Caution," WikiLeaks, April 2, 20009, www.wikileaks.ch/cable/2009/04/09AMMAN813.html.

8. Ibid.

9. Ibid.

10. U.S. Embassy, Manama, "General Petraeus with King Hamad: Iraq, Afghanistan, Iran, NATO Awacs, Energy," WikiLeaks, November 4, 2009, www.wikileaks.ch/cable/2009/11/09MANAMA642.html#.

11. U.S. Embassy, Abu Dhabi, "Crown Prince Sounds Alarm on Iran," WikiLeaks, July 20, 2009, www.wikileaks.ch/cable/2009/07/09ABUDHABI736.html.

12. Ibid.

13. U.S. Embassy, Abu Dhabi, "Abu Dhabi Crown Prince Talks Iran Concerns with General Moseley," WikiLeaks, February 7, 2007, www.wikileaks.ch/cable/2007/02/07ABUDHABI187.html.

14. Ibid.

15. U.S. Embassy, Abu Dhabi, "MBZ on Iraq, Iran, Pakistan," WikiLeaks, May 16, 2005, www.wikileaks.ch/cable/2005/05/05ABUDHABI2178.html.

16. U.S. Embassy, Tel Aviv, "PM A/S Shapiro's July 22-23 Visit to Israel," WikiLeaks, July 30, 2009, www.wikileaks.ch/cable/2009/07/09TELAVIV1688.html.

17. U.S. Embassy, Tel Aviv, "APHSCT Townsend Takes Stock of BMENA Region with Mossad Director Dagan," WikiLeaks, July 26, 2007, www.wikileaks.ch/cable/2007/07/07TELAVIV2280.html.

18. U.S. Embassy, Stockholm, "GAERC JULY 26-7 Agenda: Sweden's Preliminary Items," WikiLeaks, July 14, 2009, www.wikileaks.ch/cable/2009/07/09STOCKHOLM428.html.

19. U.S. Embassy, Kabul, "Afghanistan's Outlook on Iran: A Karzai Insider's View," WikiLeaks, February 3, 2010, www.wikileaks.ch/cable/2010/02/10KABUL436.html.

20. U.S. Embassy, Cairo, "Senator Lieberman's February 17 Meeting with Gamal Mubarak," WikiLeaks, February 23, 2009, www.wikileaks.ch/cable/2009/02/09CAIRO326.html#.

21. U.S. Embassy, Tel Aviv, "Israeli Intentions Regarding the Iranian Nuclear Program," WikiLeaks, March 17, 2005, www.wikileaks.ch/cable/2005/03/05TELAVIV1593.html#.

22. U.S. Embassy, Tel Aviv, "Codel Cardin Discusses Iran, Syria, Palestinians, and Israeli Election with Benjamin Netanyahu," WikiLeaks, February 26, 2009, www.wikileaks.ch/cable/2009/02/09TELAVIV457.html.

23. U.S. Embassy, Tel Aviv, "Assistant Secretary of Defense Vershbow Meets with Senior Israeli Defense Officials," WikiLeaks, November 16, 2009, http://wikileaks.ch/cable/2009/11/09TELAVIV2482.html#.

24. Ibid.

25. Ian Black, Harriet Sherwood, and Saeed Kamali, "Wikileaks Claims Are 'Psychological Warfare,' Says Ahmadinejad," Guardian, November 29, 2010, www.guardian.co.uk/world/2010/nov/29/wikileaks-claims-psychological-warfare-ahmadinejad.

26. "Public Opinion favors military action against Iran," Radio Farda, July 13, 2010, www.radiofarda.com/content/f2_Iran_nuclear_limited_options_military_attack_sanctions_US_Israel/2098394.html.

27. "Overwhelming Majority of Muslims in Favor of Iran's Nuclear Program," *Kayhan*, September 28, 2010, http://kayhannews.ir/890706/2.htm#other201.

28. Matthew Kroenig, "Time to Attack Iran: Why a Strike Is the Least Bad Option," *Foreign Affairs*, January/February 2012, www.foreignaffairs.com/articles/136917/matthew-kroenig/time-to-attack-iran.

29. Alan J. Kuperman, "There's Only One Way to Stop Iran," *New York Times*, December 23, 2009.

30. James M. Lindsay and Ray Takeyh, "The Force Needed to Contain Iran," *Washington Post*, February 21, 2010.

31. Setareh Tabatabaie, "Military Attack on Iran: A Combination of Ignorance and Naiveté," National Iranian American Council (NIAC) Insight, September 29, 2010, www.niacinsight.com/tag/joe-lieberman.

32. Jamal Abdi, "Lieberman to Push for Iran War Resolution?" Wednesday, November 17, 2010, NIAC Council, www.niacouncil.org/site/News2?page=NewsArticle&id=6850&security=1&news_iv_ctrl=-1.

33. Joseph I. Lieberman, "Back to a Bipartisan Foreign Policy," *Wall Street Journal*, November 16, 2010, available at http://lieberman.senate.gov/index.cfm/news-events/speeches-op-eds/2010/11/wsj-oped-back-to-a-bipartisan-foreign-policy.

34. Michael Comte, "US senator sees 'confrontation' with China, war with Iran," Agence France-Presse, November 6, 2010.

35. Sarah Oliai, "Senator Graham Calls for Military Strikes on Iran if Sanctions Fail," NIAC, April 6, 2011, www.niacouncil.org/site/News2?page=NewsArticle&id=7261&security=1&news_iv_ctrl=-1.

36. Jim Lobe, "Stirrings of a New Push for Military Option on Iran," Inter Press Service, July 9, 2010, http://ipsnorthamerica.net/print.php?idnews=3188.

37. Ibid.

38. CNN, Piers Morgan Tonight, "One-on-One with Prime Minister Benjamin Netanyahu," March 17, 2011, transcript, http://transcripts.cnn.com/TRANSCRIPTS/1103/17/pmt.01.html. See also Natasha Mozgovaya, "Netanyahu: Only fear of possible strike could stop Iran's nuclear progress," *Haaretz*, March 18, 2011, www.haaretz.com/news/diplomacy-defense/netanyahu-only-fear-of-possible-strike-could-stop-iran-s-nuclear-progress-1.349942.

39. "Netanyahu rejects nuclear power, advocates action against Iran," M&C News, March 18, 2011, http://news.monstersandcritics.com/middleeast/news/article_1627018.php/Netanyahu-rejects-nuclear-power-advocates-action-against-Iran.

40. Robert E. Hunter, "Rethinking Iran," *Survival* 52-5, September 29, 2010.

41. Israeli TV Channel Two, July 8, 2010.

42. "Ross talks Iran, Israel with AIPAC," *Politico*, October 25, 2010, www.politico.com/blogs/laurarozen/1010/Ross_talks_Iran_Israel_with_AIPAC.html#.

43. Howard Schneider, "Israel Backs Obama's Push for Sanctions on Iran," *Washington Post*, January 1, 2010, A08, www.washingtonpost.com/wp-dyn/content/article/2009/12/31/AR2009123101934.html.

44. Ibid.

45. Barak Ravid, Amos Harel, Zvi Zrahiya, and Jonathan Lis, "Netanyahu trying to persuade cabinet to support attack on Iran," November 2, 2011, www.haaretz.com/print-edition/news/netanyahu-trying-to-persuade-cabinet-to-support-attack-on-iran-1.393214.

46. American Foreign Policy Project, "Gateway to Iran," available at www.americanforeignpolicy.org.

47. Mohamed ElBaradei, *The Age of Deception* (New York: Metropolitan Books, 2011), 135.

48. Ibid., 252, 255.

49. John Limbert, "The Obama Administration," Iran Primer, United States Institute of Peace, http://iranprimer.usip.org/resource/obama-administration.

50. Dalia Dassa Kaye, "A WikiLeaks disconnect," *Los Angeles Times*, December 6, 2010, www.latimes.com/news/opinion/commentary/la-oe-kaye-wiki-mideast-20101206,0,1756847.story.

51. Steven Simon, "An Israeli Strike on Iran," Council on Foreign Relations, November 2009.

52. Timothy J. Geraghty, "Iran Expands Its List," *Wall Street Journal*, January 3, 2010.

53. "The Iranian Nuclear File Is Completely Closed," Asr Iran, November 2011, www.asriran.com/fa/news/144647.

54. Marc Lynch, "Keep the Iran war talk quiet," Foreign Policy.com, Middle East blog, October 28, 2010, http://lynch.foreignpolicy.com/posts/2010/10/28/keep_the_iran_war_talk_quiet.

55. Matthew Bunn, "Beyond Zero Enrichment," Policy Brief, Belfer Center, John F. Kennedy School, Harvard University.

56. "The Impact of Sanctions on Iran's Nuclear Program," Arms Control Association briefing, March 9, 2011, www.armscontrol.org/print/4708.

57. David Albright and Jacqueline Shire, "Iran's Growing Weapons Capability and Its Impact on Negotiations," *Arms Control Today*, December 2009.

58. Robert Kagan, "How Obama Can Reverse Iran's Dangerous Course," *Washington Post*, January 27, 2010.

59. Richard Haass, "Enough is Enough," *Newsweek*, January 22, 2010.

60. See Race for Iran blog, www.raceforiran.com/the-iraqization-of-americas-iran-debate-mohammad-javad-larijani-and-the-mainstream-media.

61. Rachel Slajda, "Giuliani, Tom Ridge Go To Paris To Support Iranian Marxist Terrorist Group," TPMMuckraker, December 23, 2010, http://tpmmuckraker.talking pointsmemo.com/2010/12/giuliani_tom_ridge_speak_out_to_support_iranian_ ma.php.

62. Scott Peterson, "Iranian group's big-money push to get off US terrorist list," *Christian Science Monitor*, August 8, 2011, www.csmonitor.com/World/Middle-East/2011/0808/ Iranian-group-s-big-money-push-to-get-off-US-terrorist-list.

63. "The NCRI - MKO - MEK - PMOI facts," Iran Affairs, November 13, 2009, www. iranaffairs.com/iran_affairs/2009/11/the-mko-mek-pmoi-facts.html.

64. Ali Fatemi and Karim Pakravan, "War With Iran? US Neocons Aim to Repeat Chalabi-Style Swindle," Truthout News Analysis, July 15, 2011, www.truth-out.org/war-iran-us-neocons-aim-repeat-chalabi-style-swindle/1310659549.

65. Anna Fifield, "Iranian exiles pay US figures as advocate," *Financial Times*, July 29, 2011.

66. Ben Katcher, "Obama Going Down the Sanctions Path," Race for Iran, December 29, 2009.

67. "Ross talks Iran, Israel with AIPAC," Laura Rozen on Foreign Policy, Politico.com, www.politico.com/blogs/laurarozen/1010/Ross_talks_Iran_Israel_with_AIPAC.html#.

68. Press Releases: Briefing With Secretary of the Treasury Timothy Geithner, September 29, 2010.

69. "Strategic Implications of the Iranian Nuclear Program," Aspen European Strategy Forum Berlin, September 22–24, 2010.

70. David Elliott, "In New Iran Sanctions Bill, Congressman Targets Iranian Passenger Planes," NIAC, September 29, 2010, www.niacouncil.org/site/News2?page=NewsArti cle&id=6719&security=1&news_iv_ctrl=-1.

71. "Strike Continues in Gold Market and Foreign Currencies' Value Increases," rahesabz. net, www.rahesabz.net/story/24465.

72. "Iran's currency rate keeps depreciating," Xinhuanet.com, January 19, 2012, http:// news.xinhuanet.com/english/world/2012-01/19/c_122603760.htm.

73. "Government asks Iranians to stop buying dollars," Reuters, November 19, 2011.

74. Ahmadinejad: "Hundreds More Sanctions Would Not Change Our Path," rahesabz.net, www.rahesabz.net/story/30070.

75. "Thank God that out country is under sanctions; we pray for more sanctions," Khabar Online, www.khabaronline.ir/news-110810.aspx.

76. "Iran's Rafsanjani Chides Ahmadinejad over Sanctions," Reuters, September 14, 2010, www.reuters.com/article/2010/09/14/us-iran-sanctions-rafsanjani-idUSTRE68 D1UN20100914.

77. Robert Zeliger, "Divisions Emerge Among Iran's Conservatives," PBS *Newshour*, September 16, 2010, www.pbs.org/newshour/updates/middle_east/july-dec10/ iran_09-16.html.

78. "Iran Sanctions, Options, Opportunities and Consequences," Hearing of the National Security and Foreign Affairs Subcommittee of the House Oversight and Government Reform Committee, December 15, 2009.

79. Suzanne Maloney and Ray Takeyh, "The Self-Limiting Success of Iran Sanctions," *International Affairs*, November 2011, available at www.brookings.edu/articles/2011/11_iran_sanctions_maloney_takeyh.aspx.

80. James Dobbins is former assistant secretary of state for Europe, and former special assistant to the president. He is the director of the International Security and Defense Policy Center at the Rand Corporation. Testimony at the Hearing Before the Subcommittee on National Security and Foreign Affairs of the Committee on Oversight and Government Reform, U.S. House of Representatives, December 15, 2009, Serial No. 111-43, www.gpo.gov/fdsys/pkg/CHRG-111hhrg55100/html/CHRG-111hhrg55100.htm.

81. Dobbins testimony, December 15, 2009.

82. ElBaradei, *The Age of Deception*, 113.

83. Dobbins testimony, December 15, 2009.

84. ElBaradei, *The Age of Deception*, 203.

85. Ibid., 215–20.

86. Jay Solomon, "Iranian Diplomat in U.S. Opens Window on Tehran," *Wall Street Journal*, June 29, 2010, http://online.wsj.com/article/SB10001424052748704846004575332754213432126.html.

87. Dov S. Zakheim, "The Military Option," Iran Primer, United States Institute of Peace, http://iranprimer.usip.org/resource/military-option.

88. Rob Grace, "Abandoning Sabotage in Iran," Foreign Policy in Focus, October 22, 2010, www.fpif.org/articles/abandoning_sabotage_in_iran.

89. Tim Weiner, "U.S. Plan to Change Iran Leaders Is an Open Secret Before It Begins," *New York Times*, January 26, 1996, www.nytimes.com/1996/01/26/world/us-plan-to-change-iran-leaders-is-an-open-secret-before-it-begins.html.

90. Barbara Slavin, "U.S. aims to spend money in Iran," *USA Today*, April 10, 2005, www.usatoday.com/news/washington/2005-04-10-us-iran_x.htm.

91. Rob Grace, "Covert ops sabotage US-Iran ties," *Asia Times*, October 27, 2010, http://atimes.com/atimes/Middle_East/LJ27Ak02.html.

92. Ibid.

93. Anne Penketh, "Bush tried to sabotage Iran's nuclear plans," *Independent*, January 12, 2009, www.independent.co.uk/news/world/americas/bush-tried-to-sabotage-irans-nuclear- plans-1301576.html.

94. "U.S. Tries Sabotage Against Iran's Nuclear Program," Nuclear Threat Initiative, Global Security Newswire, May 24, 2007, www.nti.org/gsn/article/us-tries-sabotage-against-irans-nuclear-program.

95. John Markoff and David E. Sanger, "In a Computer Worm, a Possible Biblical Clue," *New York Times*, September 29, 2010, www.nytimes.com/2010/09/30/world/middleeast/30worm.html?pagewanted=2&_r=1&ref=world.

96. Elinor Mills, "Expert: Stuxnet was built to sabotage Iran nuclear plant," CNET, September 21, 2010, http://news.cnet.com/8301-27080_3-20017201-245.html.

97. William J. Broad, John Markoff, and David E. Sanger, "Israeli Test on Worm Called Crucial in Iran Nuclear Delay," *New York Times*, January 15, 2011, http://www.nytimes.com/2011/01/16/world/middleeast/16stuxnet.html.

98. "Clinton dismisses outgoing Mossad chief's assessment about Iran nuclear program," *Haaretz*, January 10, 2011, www.haaretz.com/news/diplomacy-defense/clinton-dismisses-outgoing-mossad-chief-s-assessment-about-iran-nuclear-program-1.336173.

99. David E. Sanger, "Iran Fights Malware Attacking Computers," *New York Times*, September 25, 2010, www.nytimes.com/2010/09/26/world/middleeast/26iran.html.

100. David Albright and Andrea Stricker, "Iran's Nuclear Setbacks: A Key for U.S. Diplomacy," Iran Primer, United States Institute of Peace, January 18, 2011, http://iranprimer.usip.org/blog/2011/jan/18/iran%E2%80%99s-nuclear-setbacks-key-us-diplomacy.

101. "Obama Adviser Gary Samore: 'The Ball Is Very Much in Tehran's Court,'" Radio Free Europe/Radio Liberty, January 18, 2012, www.rferl.org/content/interview_samore_russia_iran_us_policy/3557326.html.

102. Markoff and Sanger, "In a Computer Worm, a Possible Biblical Clue"; Tyler Durden, Nuclear Sabotage in Iran? Zero Hedge, July 22, 2010, www.zerohedge.com/article/nuclear-sabotage-iran.

103. IAEA Board of Governors, "Implementation of the NPT Safeguards Agreement and relevant provisions of Security Council resolutions in the Islamic Republic of Iran," Report by the Director General, September 2, 2011, http://isis-online.org/uploads/isis-reports/documents/IAEA_Iran_2Sept2011.pdf.

104. Arash Aramesh, "Iran Says Computers Cleansed of Virus," Progressive Realist, October 4, 2010, http://progressiverealist.org/blogpost/iran-says-computers-cleansed-virus.

105. "Five spies to stand trial: Prosecutor," Tabnak, October 13, 2010, www.tabnak.ir/en/pages/?cid=1719.

106. David Ignatius, "Buying time with Iran," *Washington Post*, January 9, 2011, www.washingtonpost.com/wp-dyn/content/article/2011/01/07/AR2011010706247.html.

107. Ali Akbar Dareini, "Iran says it has uncovered second cyber attack," Associated Press, April 25, 2011.

108. Rob Grace, "Abandoning Sabotage in Iran."

109. Simon Henderson, "Diplomacy, Sanctions, and Sabotage: Putting Pressure on Iran," Real Clear World, January 20, 2011.

110. "Iran's Intelligence Ministry: Murderer of Nuclear Scientist Alimohammadi Arrested," http://mardomak.us/story/59427.

111. Ibid.

112. "Iran arrests elements of recent terrorist attacks against nuclear scientists: minister," Xinhuanet, December 3, 2010, http://news.xinhuanet.com/english2010/world/2010-12/03/c_13632645.htm.

113. "Mossad, CIA, and MI6 Behind the Assassination of Nuclear Scientists," Raja News, http://rajanews.com/detail.asp?id=72425 (Farsi).

114. "Ahmadinejad: I swear to God, if they attempt to assassinate another nuclear scientist, I will bring every member of UNSC to trial," rahesabz.net, www.rahesabz.net/ story/28269.

115. Jeffrey Goldberg, "Another Iranian Nuclear Scientist Shot Dead," *Atlantic*, July 29, 2011, www.theatlantic.com/international/archive/2011/07/another-iranian-nuclear-scientist-shot-dead/242747.

116. "Mossad killed Iranian scientist, Der Spiegel reports," JTA, August 2, 2011, www.jta. org/news/article/2011/08/02/3088812/mossad-killed-iranian-scientist-der-spiegel-reports.

117. Ghormeh Sabzi, "Shot Scientist not Involved in Nuclear Program," Iranian.com, July 25, 2011, www.iranian.com/main/2011/jul/shot-scientist-not-involved-nuclear-program.

118. Alan Cowell and Rick Gladstone, "Iran Reports Killing of Nuclear Scientist in 'Terrorist' Blast," *New York Times*, January 11, 2012, www.nytimes.com/2012/01/12/world/ middleeast/iran-reports-killing-of-nuclear-scientist.html?pagewanted=all.

119. "Iranian supreme leader blames U.S., Israel for scientist's death," CNN, January 13, 2012, http://articles.cnn.com/2012-01-13/middleeast/world_meast_iran-scientist-killed_ 1_iranian-nuclear-scientist-iranian-supreme-leader-leader-ayatollah-ali-khamenei?_ s=PM:MIDDLEEAST.

120. Simon Henderson, "Diplomacy, Sanctions, and Sabotage: Putting Pressure on Iran," PolicyWatch 1743, January 19, 2011.

121. Ignatius, "Buying time with Iran."

122. Ibid.

123. "Clinton dismisses outgoing Mossad chief's assessment about Iran nuclear program," Reuters, January 10, 2011.

124. See Michael Brendan Dougherty, "Rick Santorum: Dead Foreign Scientists Are A 'Wonderful Thing'" (video), October 27, 2011, Business Insider Politics, www. businessinsider.com/rick-santorum-dead-north-korean-scientists-are-a-wonderful-thing-2011-10.

125. Ali Vaez and Charles Ferguson, "Killing Iranian Nuclear Scientists Is Counterproductive and Wrong," *Atlantic*, January 13, 2012, www.theatlantic.com/international/archive/ 2012/01/killing-iranian-nuclear-scientists-is-counterproductive-and-wrong/251340.

126. "MI6 chief says spying crucial to stop Iran nuclear drive," Agence France-Presse, October 29, 2010, available at www.iranian.com/main/2010/oct/uks-top-spy-watching-iran.

127. "Iran blasts US, UK for N-assassination," Press TV, January 13, 2012, www.presstv.ir/ detail/220809.html.

128. "Iran sends rare letter to U.S. over killed scientist," Reuters, January 14, 2012, www. reuters.com/article/2012/01/14/us-iran-idUSTRE80D0NI20120114.

129. "Instructions to Establish Iran's Cyber Army Issued," aftabnews, http://aftabnews.ir/vdcb8wb8grhbf8p.uiur.html.

130. "Iran says it has evidence CIA behind assassination of nuclear scientist," *Washington Post*, January 13, 2012, www.washingtonpost.com/world/middle-east/mourners-for-slain-iran-nuclear-expert-chant-against-us-israel-amid-calls-for-retaliation/2012/01/13/gIQA62kjwP_story.html.

131. "Iran says ready for nuclear talks with world powers: FM," Xinhuanet.com, January 18, 2012, http://news.xinhuanet.com/english/world/2012-01/18/c_131367440.htm.

132. William O. Beeman, "Stuxnet Worm Attack Against Iran—An Exercise in Overkill," New American Media, January 18, 2011, http://newamericamedia.org/2011/01/the-stuxnet-worm-attack-against-iranan-exercise-in-overkill.php.

133. "Operation Earnest Will," Wikipedia, http://en.wikipedia.org/wiki/Operation_Earnest_Will.

134. IAEA Board of Governors, "Implementation of the NPT Safeguards Agreement and relevant provisions of Security Council resolutions in the Islamic Republic of Iran, Report by the Director General," November 8, 2011, http://isis-online.org/uploads/isis-reports/documents/IAEA_Iran_8Nov2011.pdf.

135. "Report: Iran's nuclear capacity unharmed, contrary to U.S. assessment," *Haaretz*, January 22, 2011, www.haaretz.com/news/international/report-iran-s-nuclear-capacity-unharmed-contrary-to-u-s-assessment-1.338522.

136. Peter Crail, "Iran Prepares Improved Centrifuges," *Arms Control Today*, April 2011, www.armscontrol.org/act/2011_04/Iran.

137. "Iran: Sanctions, Options, Opportunities, and Consequences," Hearing Before the Subcommittee on National Security and Foreign Affairs, U.S. House of Representatives, December 15, 2009, www.gpo.gov/fdsys/pkg/CHRG-111hhrg55100/html/CHRG-111hhrg55100.htm.

138. Ibid.

139. Ibid.

140. Seymour Hersh, "Iran and the Bomb," *New Yorker*, June 6, 2011.

141. "'Iran could produce a nuclear weapon within two months' it is claimed as UN atomic watchdog reveals concerns," *Daily Mail*, www.dailymail.co.uk/news/article-1394901/Iran-produce-nuclear-weapon-months-claimed-U-N-atomic-watchdog-reveals-concerns.html.

142. "Nuclear Trident renewal underway," AhlulBayt Islamic Mission, March 14, 2007, www.aimislam.com/nuclear-trident-renewal-underway.

143. PRC/Iran: Premier Wen Pushes Rahimi on Dialogue: China Urges Cooperation with IAEA, P5-Plus-1, WikiLeaks, October 22, 2009, www.wikileaks.ch/cable/2009/10/09BEIJING2932.html#.

144. "Israeli Foreign Minister Lieberman in Moscow," WikiLeaks, June 5, 2009, www.wikileaks.ch/cable/2009/06/09MOSCOW1488.html.

145. "How Hashemi Rafsanjani courted King Abdullah," Ayandehnews, July 11, 2011, www.ayandenews.com/news/32460.

146. "They talk about friendship with Israel while being hostile to Saudi Arabia," interview with Rafsanjani, Diplomacy Iran, www.entekhab.ir/fa/news/31732.

147. "Saudi King Abdullah and Senior Princes on Saudi Policy Toward Iraq."

148. "Iran minister: Former nuclear official a spy," Press TV, August 25, 2010, http://previous.presstv.ir/detail.aspx?id=140046&sectionid=351020101.

CHAPTER ONE

1. Abbas Milani, "The Shah's Atomic Dreams," Foreign Policy, December 29, 2010.

2. Athan Theoharis, Richard Immerman, Loch Johnson, Kathryn Olmsted, and John Prados, The Central Intelligence Agency, Security Under Security (Westport, Conn.: Greenwood Press, 2006).

3. U.S. Department of State, "Atoms for Peace Agreement With Iran," U.S. Department of State, Bulletin 36, April 15, 1957, 629.

4. Arshad Sharif, "Western Help to Iran's Nuclear Programme," Dawn, January 30, 2004.

5. A protected enclosure used to work with and test radioactive material.

6. "Iran's Nuclear Activities before the Revolution and Attitude of Western Media," Mehr News Agency, June 10, 2004.

7. The crude oil price soared from 1.5 dollars per barrel in January 1971 to 11.65 dollars per barrel in January 1974.

8. Mark Fitzpatrick, "Motivations behind Iran's enrichment program," paper prepared for NTI/CSIS workshop on New Approaches to the Nuclear Fuel Cycle, July 26–27, 2011, Washington, D.C.

9. Farah Stockman, "Iran's Nuclear Vision First Glimpsed at MIT," Boston Globe, March 12, 2007.

10. Stockman, "Iran's Nuclear Vision First Glimpsed at MIT."

11. Milani, "The Shah's Atomic Dreams."

12. Quihillat, one of the most prominent foreign scientists, had served as head of Argentina's Energy Commission for years and after quitting his post, was introduced to the Iranian government by IAEA. He brought ten top scientists, who were of great help in developing Iran's nuclear program.

13. Yousaf Butt, "Spinning Iran's centrifuges," Asia Times, August 16, 2011.

14. "The Carter administration, which took office in January 1977, went even further in terms of restricting nuclear cooperation with Iran. Although Washington assured Tehran that it would not 'discriminate' against Iran's wishes to reprocess U.S.-origin fuel, it decided to reverse the Ford administration's willingness to offer reprocessing and enrichment assistance to Iran and required Iran to accept comprehensive IAEA safeguards as a condition for any Iranian nuclear exports." See "Iran's Strategic Weapons

Programmes—A Net Assessment," edited by Gary Samore, International Institute for Strategic Studies, Strategic Dossier, 2005, 11; Mark Fitzpatrick, "Iran's Nuclear, Chemical and Biological Capabilities—A Net Assessment," International Institute for Strategic Studies, Strategic Dossier, 2011, 9.

15. Butt, "Spinning Iran's centrifuges."

16. Dafna Linzer, "Past Arguments Don't Square With Current Iran Policy," *Washington Post*, March 27, 2005, www.washingtonpost.com/wp-dyn/articles/A3983-2005Mar26. html.

17. Akbar Etemad, former head of IAEO, interview on Iran's nuclear energy program, 1997.

18. National Security Decision Memorandum (NSDM) 292, April 22, 1975.

19. Sydney Sober, address to the symposium on "The US and Iran, An Increasing Partnership," held in October 1977.

20. Etemad interview, 1997.

21. Muhammad Sahimi, "Iran's Nuclear Program," six-part series by published in *Payvand*, www.comw.org/pda/fulltext/03sahimi.html.

22. The initial capital invested in Sofidif was 100,000 francs. Forty percent of the money had been supplied by IAEO and 60 percent by a subsidiary of the French Atomic Energy Commission.

23. Iran Atomic Energy Organization, "Iran's Nuclear Activities and Interactions with other Countries before Islamic Revolution," May 16, 2004.

24. Milani, "The Shah's Atomic Dreams."

25. Maziar Bahari, "The Shah's Plan Was to Build Bombs," *New Statesman*, September 11, 2008.

26. "Special National Intelligence Estimate: Prospects for Further Proliferation of Nuclear Weapons," SNIE 4-1-74, Central Intelligence Agency, 38, available at www.gwu. edu/~nsarchiv/NSAEBB/NSAEBB240/snie.pdf.

27. Milani, "The Shah's Atomic Dreams." Interestingly, at the time, Richard Cheney was the White House Chief of Staff and Donald Rumsfeld the Secretary of Defense.

28. Linzer, "Past Arguments Don't Square With Current Iran Policy."

29. Haleh Vaziri, "Iran's Nuclear Quest: Motivations and Consequences," translated by Heidar Ali Baluchi, *National Security Quarterly*, no. 2, winter 2000.

30. Etemad interview, 1997.

31. Declassified American government documents and hearing transcripts show that the United States knew of Iraq's frequent use of chemical weapons from 1983, despite which it officially resumed diplomatic ties with Iraq in 1984 and continued to export "chemical, biological, nuclear, and missile-system equipment . . . that was converted to military use in Iraq's chemical, biological, and nuclear weapons program." See Arshin Adib-Moghaddam, *Iran in World Politics: The Question of the Islamic Republic* (New York: Columbia University Press, 2008), 106–109.

32. "Timelines: July 3, 1988, the U.S. Navy accidentally shot down a passenger plane from which country?" *Epoch Times*, www.theepochtimes.com/n2/world/timelines-

on-july-3-1988-the-us-navy-accidentally-shot-down-a-passenger-plane-from-which-country-58577.html.

33. Mark Fitzpatrick, "Motivations behind Iran's enrichment program."

34. Dagoberto Bellucci, "Nuclear Energy in Iran," http://dagobertobellucci.wordpress.com/2011/12/31/nuclear-energy-in-iran.

35. Ibid.

36. Coredif was an Iranian-French company established concurrently with Sofidif by IAEO, the French Atomic Energy Commission, and Eurodif.

37. R. K. Ramazani, "Making a U.S.-Iranian Nuclear Deal," Agence Global, November 9, 2009, www.agenceglobal.com/Article.asp?Id=2187.

38. "Iran's Nuclear Program," ABC News, April 16, 2006, http://abcnews.go.com/International/story?id=1834763&page=1.

39. David Albright and Andrea Stricker, "Iran's Nuclear Program," Iran Primer, United States Institute of Peace, http://iranprimer.usip.org/resource/irans-nuclear-program.

40. Maseh Zarif, "Technology Sources for Iran's Nuclear Program," AEI Iran Tracker, July 24, 2009, www.irantracker.org/nuclear-program/technology-sources-irans-nuclear-program; and "Iran Country Profiles, Nuclear," Nuclear Threat Initiative, www.nti.org/country-profiles/iran/nuclear.

41. Although in Iran's Islamic republican system the *Rahbar*, or supreme leader, is the highest-ranking authority on all policy matters, nuclear activities were largely left in the hands of the elected presidential administrations of Rafsanjani and his successor, Mohammad Khatami, up until the emergence of the current nuclear crisis. A more detailed description of Iran's nuclear decisionmaking process is provided in Chapter 2.

42. Mohammad Sahimi, "Iran's Nuclear Program. Part I: Its History," Payvand News, October 2, 2003, www.payvand.com/news/03/oct/1015.html; and Mark D. Skootsky, "U.S. Nuclear Policy Toward Iran," June 1, 1995, http://people.csail.mit.edu/boris/iran-nuke.text.

43. "Iran Country Profiles, Nuclear."

44. Ibid.

45. Paul Kerr, "IAEA Says Iran Failed to Disclose Key Nuclear Activities," *Arms Control Today*, March 2004, www.armscontrol.org/act/2004_03/Iran.

46. Ibid.

47. IAEA (United Nations), "Amendment to Agreement between the International Atomic Energy Agency and the Government of Iran for assistance by the Agency to Iran in establishing a Research Reactor Project," December 9, 1988, http://treaties.un.org/doc/Publication/UNTS/Volume%201562/volume-1562-I-8865-English.pdf.

48. "Foreign Suppliers to Iran's Nuclear Development," James Martin Center for Nonproliferation Studies, http://cns.miis.edu/wmdme/flow/iran/reactor.htm.

49. Gareth Porter, "Argentina's Iranian nuke connection," *Asia Times*, November 15, 2008, www.atimes.com/atimes/Middle_East/HK15Ak03.html.

50. "Iran's Bushehr nuclear plant begins operation," BBC News, May 10, 2011, www.bbc.co.uk/news/world-middle-east-13351134.

51. Semira Nikou, "Iran Primer: Timeline of Iran's Nuclear Activities," November 2, 2010, www.pbs.org/wgbh/pages/frontline/tehranbureau/2010/11/iran-primer-timeline-of-irans-nuclear-activities.html.

52. "Iran Nuclear Timeline," Iran Nuclear Watch, August 1, 2006 http://irannuclearwatch.blogspot.com/2006/08/iran-nuclear-timeline.html; and "North Korea Provided Nuclear Aid to Iran: Intelligence Reports," *Daily Times*, July 7, 2005, www.dailytimes.com.pk/default.asp?page=story_7-7-2005_pg7_4.

53. Nikou, "Iran Primer: Timeline of Iran's Nuclear Activities."

54. "Iran Nuclear Timeline."

CHAPTER TWO

1. These policies were not without controversy, and the so-called radical school, suspicious of any rapprochement or flexibility with the West on grounds that it would reduce Iran once again to a position of dependency, remained influential, if temporarily sidelined, during the 1990s.

2. "Iran and Afghanistan," American Foreign Policy Project, November 9, 2009, http://americanforeignpolicy.org/iran-afghanistan/iran-and-afghanistan.

3. The PMOI, also known by the initials MEK and MKO, was created as an anti-Shah Islamic-Leftist group in the 1960s involved in numerous militant activities, including the assassination of figures in the Shah's regime and American officials in Iran (before the 1979 revolution, Ayatollah Khomeini rejected a PMOI request for a *fatwa* permitting such assassinations). After the revolution, the organization came to oppose the Islamic Republic and assassinated hundreds of officials and religious figures, including the president, head of the judiciary, prime minister, ministers, and more than twenty members of parliament. PMOI members joined forces with Saddam Hussein in the Iran-Iraq war and mounted numerous assassination and terrorist attacks. Though it continues to advocate regime change in Iran and remains on the U.S. government's list of terrorist groups, the group claims to have renounced violence.

4. "Interview with Mohamed ElBaradei, director general of International Atomic Energy Agency," CNN, December 13, 2002.

5. "The 1997 IAEA Additional Protocol at a Glance," Arms Control Association, www.armscontrol.org/factsheets/IAEAProtoco.

6. The name reflects the drafting of the protocol in 1993 with the intention of implementing it in two years.

7. Iran went on to accept the Additional Protocol and subsidiary arrangements in October 2003, as will be subsequently discussed.

8. John S. Wolfe, "Statement to the 2004 NPT PrepCom," April 30, 2004.

9. Zarif started his career in the Foreign Ministry as an expert in Iran's UN mission and later served as the deputy foreign minister for international affairs.

THE IRANIAN NUCLEAR CRISIS

10. Also a career diplomat, Khoshrou had previously served as the ambassador to Australia. He was close to President Khatami and the reformist camp.

11. Zamaninia spent most of his career at Iran's UN mission. After two decades in New York, he returned to Iran to serve as the Foreign Ministry's Director General for International Affairs. In 2005, he went on to be posted as ambassador to Malaysia, but was one of three ambassadors (along with the ambassadors to France and Germany) recalled from their posts and fired in the early months of the Ahmadinejad presidency.

12. In its statement on May 5, 2003, the European Union affirmed the right of all NPT State Parties to development, research, production, and application of nuclear energy for peaceful purposes and compliance with the NPT without discrimination. However, they emphasized that any abuse of nuclear programs for production of nuclear weapons was not covered by that right and constituted a breach of the NPT. The statement was released during the first session of the Preparatory Committee for the NPT Review Conference.

13. Hence, I will in subsequent chapters, in my exploration of Iran's policies and positions, devote considerable emphasis to the diversion issue.

14. "We will not ignore the proliferation implications of Iran's advanced nuclear program. We stress the importance of Iran's full compliance with its obligation under the NPT. We urge Iran to sign and implement an IAEA Additional Protocol without delay or conditions. We offer our strongest support to comprehensive IAEA examination of this country's nuclear program," G8 declaration, Evian, France; May 23, 2003.

15. "Talking to Tehran," Conflicts Forum, http://conflictsforum.org/2007/talking-to-tehran.

16. Resolution 1373, adopted in the wake of the September 11 attacks, calls on nations to freeze assets of terrorists and share intelligence on terrorism.

17. See "Spring Iran Proposal," Arms Control Association, www.armscontrol.org/pdf/2003_Spring_Iran_Proposal.pdf.

18. Tim Guldimann is the Swiss ambassador to Germany.

19. The Molybdenum, Iodine, and Xenon Radioisotope Production Facility, located at the Tehran Nuclear Research Center.

20. Mohamed ElBaradei, *The Age of Deception* (New York: Metropolitan Books, 2011), 119.

21. The British representative argued that as long as the Safeguards Agreement had not been implemented, problems had not been solved and concerns had not been addressed, and so no nuclear material should enter the half-built plant in Natanz. The Canadian representative called on Iran to hold off on introducing nuclear material into the Natanz plant until the IAEA produced its report on Iran's nuclear activities and their true nature. The representative of Australia likewise asked Iran to avoid introducing nuclear material to the Natanz plant until the true nature of its nuclear activities had been clarified.

22. The *Los Angeles Times* reported on June 17, 2003, that American officials have not been able to report Iran's case to the United Nations Security Council. It quoted an expert on weapons of mass destruction as saying that the reconciliatory tone of the International Atomic Energy Agency's Board of Governors had amazed him and perhaps the Board thought that a reconciliatory approach would encourage Iran to cooperate more with IAEA. Douglas Frantz, "U.N. Nuclear Chief Nudges Iran," *Los Angeles Times*, June 17, 2003, http://articles.latimes.com/2003/jun/17/world/fg-irannuke17.

23. International Atomic Energy Agency, "Transcript of the Director General's Press Statement," IAEA Headquarters, Vienna, delivered on June 19, 2003, www.iaea.org/newscenter/transcripts/2003/transcr19062003.html.

24. "The war in Iraq has already driven a wedge through the European Union. But the real test case for the EU's foreign policy credibility will be Iran." See "Iran Will Be the Test for European Foreign Policy," *Financial Times*, June 1, 2003; the article argued that the Europeans ought to adopt tough policies toward Iran in order to reduce the existing gap between the EU and the United States.

25. "Interview with the Director General of the IAEA," *Al-Hayat*, November 12, 2003.

26. Velayati was Iran's foreign minister for sixteen years, starting in the early 1980s (following Iraq's invasion of Iran) and continuing during the Rafsanjani period (1989–1997).

27. Rouhani was a member of parliament for almost twenty years in the 1980s and 1990s. Throughout most of this period, he was the deputy speaker of parliament and the head of the parliament's foreign policy committee. During the Iran-Iraq war, he was the top aide to Rafsanjani while the latter commanded the war effort.

28. "Interview with John Bolton," Associated Press, August 13, 2003.

29. Text of ElBaradei's address to the 47th meeting of IAEA, September 15, 2003, available at www.acronym.org.uk/docs/0309/doc26.htm#iaea.

30. "Iran Warns Deadline on Nukes May Backfire," Associated Press, September 13, 2003, available at www.foxnews.com/story/0,2933,97252,00.html.

31. "Press conference of Foreign Ministry spokesman," ISNA News Agency, September 14, 2003.

32. "Interview with Iran's representative to the IAEA," BBC News, September 19, 2003.

33. Mehrzad Boroujerdi, "Iran's New Foreign Minister: Ali Akbar Salehi," January 31, 2011, Iran Primer, U.S. Institute of Peace, http://iranprimer.usip.org/blog/2011/jan/31/iran's-new-foreign-minister-ali-akbar-salehi.

34. ElBaradei, *The Age of Deception*, 4.

35. The Board of Governors "requests Iran to work with the Secretariat to promptly and unconditionally sign, ratify and fully implement the additional protocol, and, as a confidence-building measure, henceforth to act in accordance with the additional protocol," Board of Governors' Resolution, September 2003.

36. "The Agency environmental sampling at Natanz has revealed the presence of two types of highly enriched uranium, which requires additional work to enable the Agency to arrive at a conclusion," Board of Governors' Resolution, September 2003.

37. "IAEA inspectors found considerable modifications had been made to the premises at the Kalaye Electric Company prior to inspections that may impact on the accuracy of the environmental sampling," Board of Governors' Resolution, September 2003.

38. "Reports that were given to us at the Supreme National Security Council did not reflect such critical conditions. In August 2002, when Iran's underground enrichment facilities were revealed by foreign news agencies, officials emphasized that the Islamic Republic of Iran's activities were quite legal and that there was no reason for concern. In June 2003, when the Agency presented its first report, related officials believed that the dossier

contained nothing to concern Iran and said the row would end in that meeting," Dr. Hassan Rouhani, former secretary of the Supreme National Security Council, interview with *Daily Iran*, special issue on the nuclear crisis, March 2005, 9.

39. The Principlists constitute the main right-wing/conservative political movement in Iran. They are more religiously oriented and more closely affiliated with the Qom-based clerical establishment than their moderate and reformist rivals, believing that the whole system of governance should be run on the principles of Islam. Two religious institutes, *Jame-e Modaressin* (a group of about 50 prominent clerical scholars based in Qom) and *Jame-e Rohaniat-e Mobaraz* (a group founded by Ayatollahs Rafsanjani and Khamenei of 30–40 prominent clerics in Tehran) provided the ideological foundations for the Principlists and played key roles in the country's religious organization.

40. Robert F. Worth, "A Struggle for the Legacy of the Iranian Revolution," *New York Times*, June 20, 2009, www.nytimes.com/2009/06/21/weekinreview/21worth.html?_ r=1&ref=world&pagewanted=print.

41. Jeffrey M. Jones, "In U.S., 6 in 10 View Iran as Critical Threat to U.S. Interests: International terrorism viewed as top threat to U.S.," Gallup Politics, February 16, 2010, www.gallup.com/poll/125996/view-iran-critical-threat-interests.aspx.

42. Hossein Baqerzadeh, "Countdown to Collapse of the Iranian Government Has Started," Akhbar Rooz, September 26, 2003.

43. Fox News, the U.S. media outlet closest to the neoconservatives, interviewed Senator Sam Brownback on June 22, 2003. In that interview, Brownback was asked about the U.S. president's remarks that the United States could not tolerate Iran's nuclear program advancing any further. The interviewer then asked him what options were available to the United States. Brownback said the options were quite clear. The first step, he said, would be to support the Iranian expatriate opposition and democracy-seeking movements inside the country. The second step, according to Brownback, would be to pressure Iran in coordination with the international community. He then stated that when these two policies had succeeded in isolating Iran, the last step would be military operations against the country. Transcript available at www.votesmart.org/public-statement/11703/fox-news-sunday-transcript-interview-with-sam-brownback.

44. Ayatollah Rafsanjani, serving as an interim Friday Prayer leader, emphasized that there was no dispute among political groups over signing or rejecting the Additional Protocol and called rumors to that effect psychological warfare by enemies of Iran; "Tehran Friday Prayer sermons by Ayatollah Hashemi Rafsanjani," ISNA, September 12, 2003.

45. See "What Can International Actors Do to Promote Democratic Change in Iran?" Council on Foreign Relations, transcript, October 15, 2003.

46. See "Does participation in the NPT have a benefit?" Teribon, April 23, 2010, www. teribon.ir/archives/5347.

47. Ibid.

48. See "Alami's letter to Kofi Annan," www.akbaralami.com/Public/ContentBody.aspx? ContentID=10.

49. "Rafsanjani: We can have a relationship with the US based on mutual respect," Khabar Online, www.khabaronline.ir/news-162146.aspx.

50. "Rafsanjani blames Khamenehi [*sic*] for years of sour relations with America," *Iran Times*, July 19, 2011, http://iran-times.com/english/index.php?option=com_content&view=article&id=2259:-rafsanjani-blames-khamenehi-for-years-of-sour-relations-with-america&catid=98:whats-left&Itemid=425.

51. Ibid.

52. Ibid.

53. Muhammad Sahimi, "The Neoconservatives' Strategy for Regime Change in Iran: Propaganda, Ethnic Unrest, Godwin's Law, and Finding Iranian Curveball, Ahmad Chalabi, and Iyad Allawi," Payvand News, September 7, 2006, www.payvand.com/news/06/sep/1074.html.

54. The *Financial Times* wrote on June 1, 2003, that Europe needed to prove that conditional talks with Iran could be an effective means of addressing the nonproliferation of nuclear weapons and other weapons of mass destruction. The daily added that European countries ought to convince Tehran that Europe and Iran have common interests and thus show Washington and the whole world that more inspections would be useful. The article concluded that if the European Union failed to do so, it would be a catastrophic failure for the foreign policy of the Union. See Steven Everts, "Iran Will Be the Test for European Foreign Policy," *Financial Times*, June 1, 2003.

55. Rouhani's and my meeting with Putin in Moscow in October 2003 after Tehran's Agreement.

56. The membership of the SNSC, which was created in 1989 and whose purpose is detailed in Article 176 of Iran's constitution, includes the president, heads of the parliament and judiciary, various ministers and commanders of the armed forces.

57. "The Islamic Republic firmly declared months ago that it was willing to seriously negotiate the adoption of the Additional Protocol, remove ambiguities, and if expedient, accept the Protocol. They know that this decision has been made at the highest level and will be implemented. We follow this policy despite their unkindness and impoliteness. Our reservations are similar to those that were considered by the United States at the International Atomic Energy Agency," part of Ayatollah Hashemi Rafsanjani's remarks in Tehran Friday Prayer sermons, Mehr News Agency, October 4, 2003.

58. "Address by Dr. Hassan Rouhani to members of the High Council of Cultural Revolution," *Rahbord Quarterly*, no. 37, 11.

59. Then an adviser to the Supreme Leader and a former prime minister.

60. Then the secretary of the Expediency Council and former head of the Revolutionary Guards.

61. "Address by Dr. Hassan Rouhani to members of the High Council of Cultural Revolution."

CHAPTER THREE

1. The negotiating team comprised Javad Zarif, the permanent representative to the UN; Reza Alborzi, the ambassador to the UN in Geneva; Ambassador Cyrus Nasseri, adviser to the Foreign Minister; Mohammad Saeedi, Deputy of the Iran Atomic Energy Organization; and me as the official spokesman and Head of the Foreign Relations Committee of the National Security Council.

2. International media outlets point out that the concerns stirred by the United States at an international level about Iran were threateningly similar to those that had led to the invasion of Iraq. See Webster Griffin Tarpley, "Bush-Cheney Heading for Nuclear Rendevous at Desert One," www.rense.com/general67/heading.htm.

3. As will be subsequently discussed, this redline was to shift after Ahmadinejad's election as president.

4. "All issues on which we reached agreement with the three European ministers had been determined beforehand by the Islamic regime. Even if we had not reached an agreement with said ministers, we would have announced unilaterally that we would sign the Additional Protocol and present a full picture of Iran's nuclear activities to the IAEA, and we would have declared that Iran would partially suspend the fuel cycle. I mean that it had been approved [in the meeting of high-ranking officials] that even if we did not reach an agreement with the three European countries, we would take the above measures unilaterally," "Address by Dr. Hassan Rouhani, former secretary of the Supreme National Security Council, to members of the High Council of Cultural Revolution," *Rahbord Quarterly*, no. 37, 10.

5. Mohamed ElBaradei, *The Age of Deception* (New York: Metropolitan Books, 2011), 140.

6. In his report to the Board of Governors on November 10, 2003, Mohamed ElBaradei described his meeting with Iran's chief nuclear negotiators: "On 16 October 2003, at the invitation of the Iranian Government, the Director General met in Tehran with H.E. Dr. H. Rouhani, Secretary of the Supreme National Security Council of Iran, to discuss the open issues requiring urgent resolution. These issues related to the use of nuclear material in the testing of centrifuges (including the presence of LEU and HEU particles at the Kalaye Electric Company and at Natanz); the testing of conversion processes; the purpose of uranium metal production; the existence of laser isotope enrichment; and details of Iran's heavy water reactor program. At this meeting, Dr. Rouhani stated that a decision had been taken to provide the Agency, in the course of the following week, with a full disclosure of Iran's past and present nuclear activities. He also expressed Iran's readiness to conclude an Additional Protocol and, pending its entry into force, to act in accordance with the Protocol and with a policy of full transparency."

7. ElBaradei, *The Age of Deception*, 131.

8. "Report by Head of Mossad Foreign Intelligence to Members of Knesset," *Haaretz*, November 17, 2003.

9. Conal Urquhart, "Israel warns Iran on N-weapons," *Guardian*, December 21, 2003, www.guardian.co.uk/world/2003/dec/22/israel.iran.

10. The *New York Times* reported on October 19, 2003, that the Iranian president had stipulated that Tehran was probably going to suspend its uranium enrichment program.

Asked whether Iran was willing to stop uranium enrichment in line with requests from the United States and EU, Khatami said that Iran would take all necessary steps to solve the problem while expecting its nuclear rights to be respected. It was the first time that a high-ranking Iranian official talked about possible suspension of Iran's nuclear enrichment program.

11. ElBaradei, *The Age of Deception*, 140.

12. "Address by Ayatollah Khamenei to Iranian officials," IRNA, November 3, 2003.

13. The Supreme Leader said allegations that the recent measure was an act of submission were not compatible with realities and emphasized that the measure was a political and diplomatic move and carried no sign of submission. See "Address by Khamenei," IRNA, November 3, 2003.

14. "While the Iranian government is authorized to develop peaceful nuclear energy, it has voluntarily decided to suspend all uranium enrichment and reprocessing activities as defined by IAEA," ISNA news agency, Tehran, October 21, 2003.

15. "What the Agency currently knows does not differ much compared to the past. We had hidden some of our activities and thought that nobody knew anything about them. However, that information had already been published through master's degree and doctoral theses and scientific papers. A portion of that information had already been relayed to IAEA by China and Russia," "Address by Dr. Hassan Rouhani to members of the Supreme Council of Cultural Revolution."

16. Behind closed doors in talks with the IAEA, Iranians justified their *previous* secrecy—during the 1980s and 1990s—as being their only option at the time. Because Iran was left with billions of dollars of unfinished projects after the 1979 revolution and was unable to openly obtain needed technology and materials due to sanctions by the United States and its allies, the country was left with no choice but to buy them secretly for inflated prices. Iran's policymakers were of the opinion that the country needed to master the fuel cycle to avoid complete dependence on the Russians, whom they regarded as unreliable and who charged them excessive prices.

17. "Resolving questions regarding the conclusion of Agency experts that process testing on gas centrifuges must have been conducted in order for Iran to develop its enrichment technology to its current extent," part of resolution adopted by Board of Governors of International Atomic Energy Agency, September 2003.

18. "On 16 September 2003, the IAEA met with representatives of Iran to discuss the results of the analysis of the environmental samples taken at the Kalaye Electric Company in August 2003, which had revealed the presence of highly enriched uranium (HEU) particles and low-enriched uranium (LEU) particles which were not consistent with the nuclear material in the declared inventory of Iran. Also discussed were the results of the environmental sampling taken at PFEP [pilot fuel enrichment plant], which had revealed the presence of other types of HEU particles, as well as LEU and other particles, not of a type on Iran's inventory," part of director general's report to Board of Governors, November 2003.

19. "In its letter of 21 October 2003, Iran acknowledged that 'a limited number of tests, using small amounts of UF_6, [had been] conducted in 1999 and 2002' at the Kalaye Electric Company. In a meeting with enrichment technology experts held during the

27 October–1 November 2003 visit, Iranian authorities explained that the experiments that had been carried out at the Kalaye Electric Company had involved the 1.9 kg of imported UF_6, the absence of which the State authorities had earlier attempted to conceal by attributing the loss to evaporation due to leaking valves on the cylinders containing the gas," part of director general's report to Board of Governors, November 2003.

20. "In a meeting on 1 November 2003, the Iranian authorities stated that all nuclear material in Iran had been declared to the Agency, that Iran had not enriched uranium beyond 1.2% U-235 using centrifuges and that, therefore, the contamination could not have arisen as a result of indigenous activities. The Agency has now obtained information about the origin of the centrifuge components and equipment which Iran claims to be the source of HEU contamination. The Agency will continue its investigation of the source of HEU and LEU contamination, including through follow-up with other relevant parties," part of director general's report to Board of Governors, November 2003.

21. ". . . based on the information currently available to the Agency, the results of the environmental sample analysis tend, on balance, to support Iran's statement about the foreign origin of most of the observed HEU contamination. It is still not possible at this time, however, to establish a definitive conclusion with respect to all of the contamination, particularly the LEU contamination," part of director general's report to Board of Governors, February 2006.

22. "In a letter dated August 19, 2003, Iran acknowledged that it had carried out UO_2 to UF_4 experiments on a laboratory scale during the 1990s at the Radiochemistry Laboratories of the Tehran Nuclear Research Center using some of the imported depleted UO_2 referred to in the previous paragraph. Until August 2003, Iran had claimed that it had carried out no UF_4 production experiments. This activity was acknowledged by Iran only after the July 2003 waste analysis results of samples taken to verify experiments using nuclear material imported in 1991 indicated the presence of depleted UF_4 mixed with natural UF_4," part of Director General's report to Board of Governors, November 2003.

23. Director general's report to IAEA's Board of Governors, June 2004.

24. Agence France-Presse reported on October 28, 2003, that Iran's case would be referred to the United Nations Security Council due to clear breaches of the Non-Proliferation Treaty. See "Iran soon to inform IAEA of agreement to snap nuclear inspections," Agence France-Presse, October 28, 2003.

25. ITAR-TASS reported that Russian President Vladimir Putin had emphasized in a meeting with the secretary of Iran's Supreme National Security Council that Russia considered access to peaceful nuclear technology to be Iran's undeniable right and opposed the U.S. position. Putin stressed that voluntary suspension of the fuel cycle by Iran would build confidence with the international community about nature of Tehran's nuclear program. See "Iran suspends uranium enrichment programme," November 10, 2003, ITAR-TASS, November 10, 2003.

26. "Nuclear program of Iran," Wikipedia, http://en.wikipedia.org/wiki/Nuclear_program_of_Iran#2002.E2.80.932006; "Bolton Confident Proliferation Security Initiative Is Legitimate. Says PSI will be 'extremely efficient' effort against WMD," U.S. Department of State, November 13, 2003.

27. See "U.N. and U.S. in Dispute over Iran's Nuclear Plans," *Reuters*, November 13, 2003.

28. The word "refer" in the sense of sending a case to the Security Council is not used in the Statute of the International Atomic Energy Agency or the Non-Proliferation Treaty. Article 12, Clause C of the International Atomic Energy Agency Statute mentions "reporting" in the sense of reporting a case to the Security Council, and the word "notify" is used in Article 3 of the Statute. According to Article 3, Paragraph 4, Clause B of the statute, "if in connection with the activities of the Agency there should arise questions that are within the competence of the Security Council, the Agency shall notify the Security Council." According to this paragraph, the IAEA shall notify the Security Council of activities within the purview of the Security Council "as the organ bearing the main responsibility for the maintenance of international peace and security." IAEA is even entitled to take measures to suspend the rights and privileges resulting from membership for a country that had not complied with its obligations.

29. "The Rise of Nuclear Iran: An Interview with Ambassador Dore Gold," *inFocus Quarterly*, Winter 2009, www.jewishpolicycenter.org/1525/rise-of-nuclear-iran.

30. The Board "welcomes Iran's decision voluntarily to suspend all enrichment-related and reprocessing activities and requests Iran to adhere to it, in a complete and verifiable manner"; from "Implementation of the NPT Safeguards Agreement in the Islamic Republic of Iran," resolution adopted by the International Atomic Energy Agency's Board of Governors on November 26, 2003.

31. William J. Broad, "Sleuths Patrol Nations for Nuclear Mischief," *New York Times*, December 30, 2003.

32. I should mention that neither I nor other diplomats on the negotiation team had any inside information about the exact scope or technicalities of Iran's nuclear activities.

33. "In response to an Agency question as to why the P-2 design, and related work on it, had not been included in Iran's 21 October 2003 declaration, the Iranian authorities stated that they had, due to time pressure in preparing the declaration on the centrifuge research and development program, neglected to include it. . . . In further discussions on this issue in February 2004, the Iranian authorities provided additional explanations for the non-inclusion in the October 2003 declaration of information related to the P-2 design and related work . . . . (they said) the declaration only included information intended to correct the failures of Iran in reporting under its Safeguards Agreement and the information was not required to be reported under its Safeguards Agreement, but only under the Additional Protocol," part of the report by the Director General of the International Atomic Energy Agency to the Board of Governors; February 24, 2004.

34. Douglas Frantz and Josh Meyer, "For Sale: Nuclear Expertise," *Los Angeles Times*, February 22, 2004.

35. "Malaysian police report implicates Dr A.Q. Khan," *Dawn*, February 21, 2004, http://archives.dawn.com/2004/02/21/top3.htm.

36. Many articles appeared in the international media about these discoveries, asserting that international inspectors had found out that Iran had hidden drawings related to a powerful centrifuge used for uranium enrichment in violation of its obligation to reveal all aspects of its atomic activities. These articles claimed the new revelation added to

uncertainty as to whether Iran had bought plans for building an atomic bomb on the black market, e.g., www.command-post.org/nk/2_archives/cat_iran.html.

37. "As reported in November 2004, Iran asserted that no work was carried out on the P-2 design (or any centrifuge design other than the P-1) prior to 2002. Iran said that priority had been placed at that time on resolving difficulties being encountered by Iran in connection with the P-1 centrifuge," part of the Director General's report to the IAEA Board of Governors, September 2, 2005.

38. The *Washington Post* reported on February 24, 2004, that IAEA inspectors had found out about Iran's experiments with polonium. The report called the revelation the latest instance of undeclared Iranian nuclear activities. The paper also noted that information about Iran receiving parts and drawings of P-2 centrifuges to enrich uranium had previously been disclosed. "Neither polonium, nor centrifuges were mentioned in Iran's detailed report and IAEA officials say that discovery of P-2 centrifuge parts and drawings is a hard blow to the Agency's trust in Iran." The paper also quoted an analyst as saying that the Iranians describe the omission as a simple oversight, but IAEA officials thought otherwise. See Karl Vick, "Another Nuclear Program Found in Iran," *Washington Post*, February 24, 2004.

39. "Text of Iran's protest to Mohamed ElBaradei's report," Mehr News Agency, March 8, 2004.

40. "Analysis of samples taken from domestically manufactured centrifuge components show predominantly LEU contamination, while analysis of samples from imported components show both LEU and HEU contamination. It is not clear why the components would have different types of contamination if, as Iran states, the presence of uranium on domestically manufactured components is due solely to contamination originating from imported components," part of the IAEA Director General's report to Board of Governors, February 2004.

41. The *New York Times* ran a story by William J. Broad on February 28, 2004, saying that European diplomats and American specialists have noted that according to inspectors' findings, part of the highly enriched uranium contamination which was detected on Iran's nuclear installations had been carried over from Russia. The report also quoted European diplomats as saying that scientists at the IAEA's specialized laboratories in Austria had found similarities between the atomic properties of Russian uranium and the samples collected by IAEA inspectors from Iranian centrifuges. William J. Broad, "Uranium Traveled to Iran via Russia, Inspectors Find," *New York Times*, February 28, 2004, A4.

42. "As previously reported to the Board of Governors . . . the Iranian authorities have stated that none of the imported UF_6 had been processed, and, specifically, that it had not been used in any centrifuge tests. It was observed during Agency verification in March 2003, however, that some of the UF_6 (1.9 kg) was missing from the two small cylinders. The Iranian authorities have stated that this might be due to leakage from the cylinders resulting from mechanical failure of the valves and possible evaporation due to their storage in a place where temperatures reach 55 degrees centigrade during the summer," part of the Director General's report to the IAEA Board of Governors, August 26, 2003.

43. "Iran has estimated that the original amount of plutonium in the solution was approximately 200 μg. Until sample results are available, the Agency cannot verify

the accuracy of that estimate. However, based on Agency calculations, the amount of plutonium produced in 3 kg of depleted uranium targets under the declared irradiation conditions should have been substantially higher. The reason for this apparent discrepancy is not yet clear. The matter remains under discussion with Iran," part of the Director General's report to the IAEA Board of Governors, February 24, 2004.

44. Hassan Rouhani, "National Security and Nuclear Diplomacy," Center for Strategic Research, 2012, 205, 231.

45. A "non-paper" is a piece of unofficial diplomatic correspondence.

46. ElBaradei, *The Age of Deception*, 140.

47. Ibid., 132–33.

48. "The Americans put tremendous pressure on [the EU3] and they finally gave up their commitments. We were first informed about U.S. pressure through political channels before it was revealed by the European press that Bush had contacted Blair and criticized the agreement signed by the three countries with Iran," "Dr. Hassan Rouhani's address to members of the High Council of Cultural Revolution."

49. "Europe Rejects US Proposed Paragraphs in Draft Resolution," Mehr News Agency, March 7, 2004.

50. "The Non-Aligned Movement is satisfied with increasing cooperation between Iran and IAEA and hopes that cooperation will continue until a complete solution to the issue is achieved in the shortest possible time. . . . We appreciate [the] role of the European members of [the] Non-Aligned Movement and other countries for bolstering that cooperation and ask other members to support their move and join them," part of NAM statement in Board of Governors' meeting, March 10, 2004.

51. The *Financial Times* quoted U.S. Undersecretary of State Nicholas Burns as warning his European counterparts to be tough on Iran during negotiations and reject any proposal that would allow a partial resumption of Iran's nuclear program. He added that the United States would only support negotiations on the basis of a complete halt to all nuclear activities of Iran; see "US Warns EU3," *Financial Times*, May 25, 2005.

52. There were reports that enrichment activities had taken place in Shiyan, east of Tehran, after which the Iranian government had destroyed all buildings and converted it into a park in order to cover up evidence. The IAEA sent a team to investigate the rumors, and it found no evidence of contamination.

53. "The Europeans gradually reached the conclusion that we had not accepted suspension in those fields where we were facing technical problems and had only agreed to suspend those activities in which we had no technical problems. They have mentioned this in their recent talks. They say Isfahan UCF and the facility that converts UF_4 to UF_6 were completed at that time. When we were negotiating with the Europeans in Tehran, we were still installing equipment in some sections of Isfahan UCF and there was a long way to go before the project was complete," address by Dr. Hassan Rouhani to members of the High Council of Cultural Revolution.

54. The U.S. Congress asked the European Union to avoid resuming trade talks with Iran until the country had stopped all activities that could be used for the production of nuclear weapons forever and had dismantled all centers for uranium enrichment and

reprocessing. The congressional resolution also called on the EU to take measures such as imposing sanctions on Iran to convince the country to fulfill its obligations toward the IAEA.

55. The eight industrial states announced in their statement on June 11, 2004, that they were determined to face the consequences of Iran's advanced nuclear program.

56. "Seyed Mohammad Khatami's press conference," ISNA, June 17, 2004.

57. "In fact, today we are under no obligation with regard to enrichment and we are sure to make decisions and announce them along with the measures that we are going to take in the upcoming days," statement by Dr. Hassan Rouhani at a press conference, Mehr News Agency, June 20, 2004.

58. Member states of the Non-Aligned Movement noted in their statement on June 18, 2004, that they believed the binding Paragraphs 7 and 8 of the resolution reflected on subjects that lay outside the IAEA's jurisdiction. The Non-Aligned Movement also opined that the two binding paragraphs deprived countries of their undeniable right to produce and use peaceful nuclear energy. . . ." They additionally noted that said paragraphs would undermine the importance and role of safeguards and the reasons for prescribing them.

59. The London-based International Institute for Strategic Studies (IISS) released a book titled *Iran's Strategic Weapons Programme* on September 13, 2005, supervised by Gary Samore. The book had alleged that Iran had done a major test aimed at converting 27 tons of U_3O_8 to UF_6 in August 2004, though the test faced serious technical problems. It added that difficulties in pre-commissioning Isfahan's UCF indicated that the facility has been rushed to production phase before being completely ready for it. According to the book, the announced plan for UF_6 production at the facility had a capacity of about 30 tons of U_3O_8 per month even though Iran had in the past only been able to produce 27 tons of it over six months.

60. The *Washington Post* reported on May 25, 2005, that diplomats attending Iran-EU3 negotiations in Brussels over Iran's nuclear program had claimed that the Bush administration was open to the possibility of allowing Iran to launch preliminary uranium enrichment activities in the near future. The report said the measure would be part of a final agreement and for which Iran would be required to continue suspension until the end of nuclear negotiations. The paper also quoted an unnamed U.S. official as saying that the United States was not willing to reach an agreement and that the White House expected the European countries to call for the complete cessation of Iran's nuclear enrichment program, especially at the Isfahan facility. "Europeans Open Talks With Iran on Nuclear Program," *Washington Post*, May 25, 2005, www.washingtonpost.com/wp-dyn/content/article/2005/05/24/AR2005052401365.html.

61. Jean du Preez and María Lorenzo Sobrado, "IAEA Board Gives Iran Yet Another Chance," James Martin Center for Nonproliferation Studies, September 27, 2004, http://cns.miis.edu/stories/040927.htm.

62. The legal evidence for this point will be discussed in subsequent sections.

63. The Board of Governors "deeply regrets that the implementation of Iranian voluntary decisions to suspend enrichment-related and reprocessing activities, notified to the Agency on 29 December 2003 and 24 February 2004, fell significantly short of the

Agency's understanding of the scope of those commitments and also that Iran has since reversed some of those decisions; stresses that such suspension would provide the Board with additional confidence in Iran's future activities; and considers it necessary, to promote confidence, that Iran immediately suspend all enrichment-related activities, including the manufacture or import of centrifuge components, the assembly and testing of centrifuges, and the production of feed material, including through tests or production at the UCF," part of the Board of Governors' resolution, September 18, 2004.

64. "Also concerned that, at its Uranium Conversion Facility, Iran is planning to introduce 37 tonnes of yellowcake, as this would run counter to the request made of Iran by the Board in resolution GOV/2004/49," part of the Board of Governors' resolution, September 18, 2004.

65. "Requests the Director General to submit in advance of the November Board meeting:

- a report on the implementation of this resolution;

- a recapitulation of the Agency's findings on the Iranian nuclear programme since September 2002, as well as a full account of past and present Iranian cooperation with the Agency, including the timing of declarations, and a record of the development of all aspects of the programme, as well as a detailed analysis of the implications of those findings in relation to Iran's implementation of its Safeguards Agreement," part of the IAEA Board of Governors' resolution, September 2004.

66. "Interview with Hossein Nejabat," Mehr News Agency, September 29, 2004.

67. Safa Haeri, "Iran Asks the World to Nuclear Party," *Asia Times*, September 24, 2004, www.atimes.com/atimes/Middle_East/FI24Ak02.html.

68. From 1999–2009, Solana served as the European Union's High Representative for Common Foreign and Security Policy, Secretary General of the Council of the European Union, and Secretary-General of the Western European Union.

69. See the report by the Associated Press on the failure of expert talks between Europe and the U.S. on Iran's nuclear activities, October 16, 2004.

70. "About 3–4 months ago, we had presented a plan to the Europeans and the new plan offered by Europe on Thursday was, in fact, a response to our plan," Dr. Hossein Mousavian, spokesman of Iran's negotiating team, interview with Islamic Republic of Iran News Network, October 27, 2004.

71. The Persian section of Cologne Radio announced on October 29, 2004, that as the November meeting of the IAEA's Board of Governors approached, the EU3 was looking for a way to tone down Iran's debate and had, thus, increased diplomatic contacts with Washington and Iran. The report said it seemed that one year of talks between Iran and Europe had failed, while achieving an agreement could boost the EU's credibility in solving international disputes in a non-American fashion.

72. "Contrary to the general understanding, the Paris Agreement is not the end of the process, but only a beginning for real negotiations to achieve understanding. Since Iran had already completed its structural facilities related to the fuel cycle at that time, it was possible to suspend enrichment for a couple of months without damaging the fuel production program. The European side, on the other hand, agreed to get the situation back to normal during those months to pave the way for broad-based negotiations in

a calm atmosphere," part of a report by the former Secretary of the Supreme National Security Council to President Mohammad Khatami, July, 30, 2005.

73. "The E3/EU recognize that this suspension is a voluntary confidence building measure and not a legal obligation," Paris Agreement, Paragraph 6.

74. "The E3/EU recognize Iran's rights under the NPT exercised in conformity with its obligations under the Treaty, without discrimination," Paris Agreement, Paragraph 3.

75. *Newsday* opined on November 17, 2004, that, like it or not, President George W. Bush would have to remove Iran from the so-called "axis of evil" list and accept the agreement between Iran and the EU. It said that it was time for Bush to get in line with the European agreement, which did not include U.S. demands for permanent suspension of Iran's nuclear enrichment and was a far cry from the threats of harsh economic sanctions that the United States pushed for.

76. In the June 26, 2004, joint U.S.-EU statement on nonproliferation of weapons of mass destruction, it was explicitly stated that countries that the IAEA was inspecting for non-technical breaches of the NPT and the Safeguards Agreement should not take part in decisionmaking in the proposed council or special committee.

77. "Multilateral Approaches to the Nuclear Fuel Cycle, Expert Group Report submitted to the Director General of the International Atomic Energy Agency," February 22, 2005.

CHAPTER FOUR

1. "Noting specifically the Director General's assessment that Iranian practices up to October 2003 resulted in many breaches of Iran's obligations to comply with its Safeguards Agreement, but that good progress has been made since that time in Iran's correction of those breaches and in the Agency's ability to confirm certain aspects of Iran's current declarations," part of Board of Governors' resolution, November 29, 2004.

2. "Also noting specifically the Director General's assessment that all the declared nuclear material in Iran has been accounted for, and that such material is not diverted to prohibited activities, but that the Agency is not yet in a position to conclude that there are no undeclared nuclear materials or activities in Iran," part of the Board of Governors' resolution, November 29, 2004.

3. "Welcomes Iran's continuing voluntary commitment to act in accordance with the provisions of the Additional Protocol, as a confidence building measure that facilitates the resolution of the questions that have arisen, and calls on Iran once again to ratify its Protocol soon," part of the Board of Governors' resolution, November 29, 2004

4. Interview with Javier Solana, EU foreign policy chief, *Euronews*, December 1, 2004.

5. See Proposal by Iran, Presented to Political and Security Working Group, Geneva, January 17, 2005, available at www.armscontrol.org/pdf/20050117_Iran_Proposal_PSWG.pdf.

6. Nasseri was a career diplomat, and previously served as Iran's Ambassador to the UN mission in Geneva and the Foreign Ministry's Director General for International Affairs.

7. Interview with George W. Bush, NBC News, January 18, 2005.

8. Aghazadeh began his political career after the revolution working under then–editor-in-chief Mir Hossein Mousavi at the *Jomhuri-e Islami* newspaper. He was Iran's oil minister during the Rafsanjani presidency and then became head of the AEOI under President Khatami.

9. Mohamed ElBaradei, *The Age of Deception* (New York: Metropolitan Books, 2011), 143.

10. The steering committee refers to the meetings of the EU3 ministers with the Iranian negotiators (me, Zarif, Nasseri, Alborzi, and Saeedi), the results of which were discussed at the ministerial level. The meetings included the Brussels meeting in February 2004 and the meeting in Paris (Paris Agreement) in November 2004.

11. *Iran's Strategic Weapons Programmes: A Net Assessment* (London: IISS, 2005).

12. Arms Control Association, *History of Official Proposals on the Iranian Nuclear Issue*. www.armscontrol.org/factsheets/Iran_Nuclear_Proposals.

13. The *Washington Post* reported on May 25, 2005, that diplomats attending Iran-EU3 negotiations in Brussels over Iran's nuclear program claimed that the Bush administration would allow Iran to launch preliminary uranium enrichment stages in the near future. However, this would only be part of a final agreement and Iran was expected to continue suspension until the end of the nuclear negotiations. The paper also quoted an unnamed U.S. official as saying that the United States was not interested in such an agreement and the White House expected the Europeans to call for the complete cessation of Iran's nuclear enrichment program, especially at the Isfahan UCF. See Dafna Linzer, "Europeans Open Talks With Iran on Nuclear Program," *Washington Post*, May 25, 2005, A21.

14. "George Bush Agrees to Limited Enrichment in Iran," Reuters, June 1, 2005.

15. ElBaradei, *The Age of Deception*, 201–202.

16. Arms Control Association, *History of Official Proposals*.

17. *Iran's Strategic Weapons Programmes*.

18. *Iran's Strategic Weapons Programmes*.

19. Mike Shuster and Melissa Block, "NIE Report on Iran Contradicts Bush Claims," NPR, December 3, 2007, www.npr.org/templates/story/story.php?storyId=16846056.

CHAPTER FIVE

1. The *Washington Post* reported that diplomats present at Iran-EU negotiations in Brussels had noted that European officials, unlike their American counterparts, were willing to accept the start of preliminary uranium enrichment by Iran in the future. However, this was to be part of a final agreement and they expected Iran to suspend its nuclear activities until that time. The paper also quoted an American official who spoke on the condition of anonymity as saying that the Bush administration was not interested in such an agreement and stressing that the White House expected Europe to help make Iran stop its enrichment program, including at the Isfahan facilities. See Dafna Linzer, "Europeans Open Talks With Iran on Nuclear Program," May 25, 2005, www.washingtonpost.com/wp-dyn/content/article/2005/05/24/AR2005052401365.html.

2. The Ahmadinejad administration was commonly referred to as the "ninth government," meaning the ninth presidential administration since the 1979 Revolution.

3. "During negotiations with the three European countries, they agreed that the operations should continue; that is, that enrichment on a small-scale or laboratory scale may be carried out. They should not change their position. We maintain that all concerns should be addressed and they should also respect our demands. The best solution is to establish a link between these two issues," Dr. Manouchehr Mottaki's interview with Japan's NHK television, available at ISNA News Agency, March 6, 2006.

4. "Although Europeans are formulating their final plan, there is evidence that Europeans have conceded on some issues, which they rejected before Iran's achievement of nuclear technology," report by Dr. Hassan Rouhani to former president Mohammad Khatami, July 31, 2005.

5. Dr. Ali Larijani, new secretary of the Supreme National Security Council, quoted in Baztab, June 5, 2005.

6. "Nuclear Dossier: Numerous Concessions Given by Tehran in Return for Nothing," Baztab, April 27, 2005. Javad Va'idi, a powerful figure in the secretariat of the Supreme National Security Council under Ali Larijani, published special issues on foreign policy and the nuclear case in the Persian daily *Hamshahri* before political developments in the summer of 2005. Those issues provide further evidence of the outlook of critics of the first two years of negotiations.

7. "Interview with Mohsen Rezaei," Baztab, September 27, 2005.

8. "Answering the West's Questions by Revealing Secrets of the Islamic System," Baztab, February 19, 2005.

9. "Rereading the Most Controversial Iranian Case of the Century," Baztab, November 22, 2005.

10. "Rereading the Most Controversial Iranian Case of the Century."

11. "We should not negotiate our rights," *Kayhan*, September 11, 2005.

12. "Stripping suspension of its legal nature and turning it into a political game was not an achievement, but the result of a mistake because as Mohamed ElBaradei has announced, the IAEA did not have any problem with Iran in this regard, but since we have politicized it, we have to give concessions to Europeans to break the deadlock." See "Mr. Rouhani and Unfair Judgment," Baztab, August 9, 2005.

13. An elected body of high-level clerics whose main purpose is to appoint Iran's Supreme Leader and assess his qualifications.

14. "Negotiating from a Weak Position," Baztab, December 5, 2004.

15. Dr. Mahmoud Ahmadinejad's proclaimed plan during presidential elections; article 8-2-5.

16. Ibid., article 8-2-9 and article 4-2-8.

17. Mottaki was a Parliamentarian who was in the Foreign Ministry as deputy minister and ambassador to Turkey and Japan.

18. "US Military Strike on Iran Likely, Ex-CIA Chief Says," Huffington Post, September 3, 2010.

19. This position is taken in remarks made by various Iranian officials including Ayatollah Hashemi Rafsanjani, chairman of the Expediency Council; Mahmoud Ahmadinejad, the current president of Iran; Mohammad Khatami, the former Iranian president; and many other military and security authorities.

20. "Dr. Mohammad Javad Larijani's remarks," Entekhab News Agency, December 5, 2006.

21. "Address by Dr. Mahmoud Ahmadinejad," Fars News Agency, January 5, 2006; Kayhan Barzegar, "Balance of Power in the Persian Gulf: An Iranian View," Belfer Center for Science and International Affairs at Harvard University, http://belfercenter.ksg.harvard.edu/files/Barzegar-Balance-of-Power-in-the-Persian-Gulf.pdf.

22. "Condoleezza Rice Proposes U-Turn on Iran," Aftab, February 24, 2007.

23. The internal U.S. government study group report headed by former secretary of state James Baker, a Republican, and former representative Lee Hamilton, a Democrat, primarily addressed U.S. policy in Iraq, but recommended that the United States immediately engage in negotiations with Iran to help stabilize the former country. Iran's foreign minister welcomed the proposal even as the Bush administration dismissed it. Scott MacLeod, "Iran Reacts Favorably to the Baker-Hamilton Plan," Time, www.time.com/time/world/article/0,8599,1568431,00.html.

24. "Ahmadinejad's Letter to Bush," Washington Post, May 9, 2006.

25. "Ahmadinejad: Iranian Nuclear Train Will Not Stop," Radio Zamaneh, January 26, 2006.

26. "The innovative and preemptory positions taken by the president in the international arena, like proposing establishment of a human rights investigation group in Iran and Western countries, proposing live televised debate with the U.S. president, rejecting the Holocaust, posing fundamental questions and causing diplomatic problems for the Western countries. . . have led to the emergence of a proactive or aggressive diplomacy for the Islamic Republic of Iran," Meisam Shirvani, website of the Islamic Revolution Documents Center, Points Concerning the Assessment of the 9th Government's Foreign Policy, August 2, 2007.

27. Ben Birnbaum, "Majority of Arab World views Nuclear Iran," Washington Times, August 6, 2010.

28. "Fundamental Policies Remain Unchanged," ISNA, June 24, 2005.

29. "Iranian Press Menu on 3 July 2005," BBC Monitoring Middle East, July 3, 2005, 11.

30. "Iran tells U.N. it will resume some uranium processes," Associated Press, August 1, 2005.

31. "Britain, at EU helm, 'deeply concerned' at Iran nuclear move," Agence France-Presse, August 8, 2005.

32. "France calls Iran's resumption of nuclear activities a 'serious' unilateral step," AP Worldstream, August 8, 2005.

33. "Germany warns of 'disastrous consequences' if Iran gets nuclear arms," Agence France-Presse, August 8, 2005.

34. Ibid.

35. "Iran Offers to Talk on Nuclear Plans; Bush Calls Aim 'Positive,'" Bloomberg, August 9, 2005.

36. Director General Statement, IAEA website, August 2, 2005.

37. "Two Urgency Plans for Full Suspension and Ratification of the Additional Protocol to be Discussed in the Majles," ISNA, September 9, 2005.

38. The *Los Angeles Times* reported that Iran had delivered an unsigned statement to ambassadors of Germany, France, and Britain in Tehran in rejecting the European proposal. The statement, which was served by the Iranian Foreign Ministry's director general for political affairs, Pirouz Hosseini, maintained that the requests made on Iran were too much while proposing too little in return. This was taken as an indication that the European countries had no plan to act in a balanced way; the proposal was called an insult to the Iranian nation for which Iran sought apologies from the three European countries. See Sonni Efron, "Iran's Nuclear Program Goes Back Online; Tehran bluntly rejects European offer, begins processing uranium. The West is likely to try more diplomacy before seeking U.N. sanctions," *Los Angeles Times*, August 9, 2005.

39. Part of the August 2005 plan noted that if Iran required a guaranteed fuel supply for the coming years, it would be able to get the needed fuel by guaranteeing that it would stop its own fuel-cycle program. The request did not include manufacture and application of light-water research reactors as well as light-water electricity reactors.

40. According to the August 2005 plan, the European Union/three European countries expected Iran to stop building a heavy-water research reactor in Arak, which had given rise to some concerns about proliferation of nuclear weapons.

41. Taken from the European Union's August 2005 proposed plan to Iran.

42. Mohamed ElBaradei, *The Age of Deception* (New York: Metropolitan Books, 2011), 144.

43. "Full text of Iran's response to the proposal of three European countries," ISNA, August 10, 2005.

44. Some western analysts argue that the obligation to facilitate nuclear access is only for states that are complying with their NPT and IAEA obligations. Iran was in breach. But from the Iranian point of view, Iran had not violated the NPT in any major way, and if the country were to be deprived of access to peaceful nuclear energy, then there was no reason to remain a member of the NPT.

45. "South Africa's initiative on Nuclear," Mehr News Agency, August 14, 2005.

46. In his last trip to South Africa, Hassan Rouhani met with Thabo Mbeki, the South African president, and discussed the framework of a new plan with him, which was welcomed by Mbeki. He immediately wrote a letter to top officials of the EU3 and the U.S. president to outline his plan, which was accepted by leaders of those countries to be put on the agenda of negotiations. However, the plan was lost during the political developments that followed the presidential elections of 2005.

47. "Urges Iran to re-establish full suspension of all enrichment related activities including the production of feed material, including through tests or production at the Uranium Conversion Facility, on the same voluntary, non-legally binding basis as requested in previous Board resolutions, and to permit the Director General to re-instate the seals

that have been removed at that facility"; Para. 3, Board of Governors' resolution, August 11, 2005.

48. "Expresses serious concern at the 1 August 2005 notification to the IAEA that Iran had decided to resume the uranium conversion activities at the Uranium Conversion Facility in Isfahan," Para. 1, Board of Governors' resolution, August 11, 2005.

49. "New security chief says Tehran not to restrict talks to EU," BBC Monitoring Middle East, August 25, 2005.

50. "Head of Iranian nuclear file comments on his visit to India," BBC Monitoring Middle East, September 3, 2005.

51. "Iran's top nuclear negotiator arrives in Pakistan," BBC Monitoring Middle East, September 7, 2005.

52. "Interview with a French diplomat," *Al-Sharq al-Awsat*, September 10, 2005.

53. Reacting to the report of the IAEA director general concerning Iran's nuclear activities, Iran submitted a text titled "Supplementary Information about the Director General's Report" (Gov/2005/67) on September 13, 2005. Part of the document, which focuses on the extraordinary meeting of the Board of Governors in August 2005, noted that according to the Paris Agreement, Iran decided to suspend uranium enrichment as a confidence-building measure and not as a binding, legal measure as long as a lasting agreement had not been achieved. Long before resumption of activities at Isfahan's UCF, Iran had warned in various meetings including a ministerial session in Geneva that any proposal by the EU3 which denied Iran its inalienable right to the fuel cycle would be against the Paris Agreement and make negotiations more difficult. In view of the above developments, Iran had no other choice but to resume enrichment activities at the Isfahan UCF. However, European countries reacted hurriedly to Iran's measures and called for a special meeting of the Board of Governors for a trivial matter related to a bilateral agreement. This unwise measure by three European countries has undermined the process of confidence building and dialogue to a great extent.

54. "Larijani: Iran's New Initiative can Break the Deadlock," Mehr News Agency, August 26, 2005.

55. Larijani told reporters that since the president had come up with a suitable initiative to solve the nuclear problem, they had to wait until the new cabinet was established because the president hoped that some ministers who had experience with the nuclear case would start cooperating with the Supreme National Security Council. He stipulated that the IAEA director general had welcomed the Iranian president's proposal and expressed hope that the proposal would prove useful in future negotiations. "Ali Larijani's press conference after his return from Vienna," ISNA, August 27, 2005.

56. "Iran to come up with new proposals over nuclear talks with Europe," Agence France-Presse, August 26, 2005.

57. Responding to Larijani's remarks about the presence of other countries in negotiations over Iran's nuclear case, Department of State spokesman Sean McCormack claimed that this was only a tactic to change the subject and that even the European countries had not been impressed by Larijani's proposal. See Nasser Karimi, "Iran calls for nuclear negotiations to include countries outside Europe," Associated Press, August 25, 2005.

58. Oliver Meier, "Interview with Ambassador Ali Asghar Soltanieh, Iran's Permanent Representative to the International Atomic Energy Agency," Arms Control Association, January 23, 2006, www.armscontrol.org/interviews/20060123_Soltanieh.

59. "The Secretary of the Supreme National Security Council warned European countries and the United States that in the event that they resorted to force against Iran, the country would resume enrichment immediately, stop implementation of the Additional Protocol and consider withdrawal from the NPT," ISNA News Agency, September 20, 2005.

60. The draft resolution prepared by the EU3 was based on a proposal to report Iran to the Security Council according to article 12C of the IAEA Statute. They had also argued that according to Article III of the Statute the Security Council, as the organ bearing the main responsibility for the maintenance of international peace and security, should put Iran's nuclear case on its agenda.

61. Supporters of the resolution included Argentina, Australia, Belgium, Canada, Ecuador, France, Germany, Ghana, Hungary, India, Italy, Japan, Korea, the Netherlands, Peru, Poland, Portugal, Singapore, Slovakia, Sweden, UK, and the United States. Yemen, Algeria, Brazil, China, Mexico, Nigeria, Pakistan, Russia, South Africa, Sri Lanka, Tunisia, and Vietnam abstained to vote for the resolution and the sole negative vote came from Venezuela. Website of the International Atomic Energy Agency, September 24, 2005.

62. Article XII, Paragraph C, Statute of the IAEA, www.iaea.org/About/statute_text.html#A1.18.

63. ElBaradei, *The Age of Deception*, 146.

64. "Requests the Director General to continue his efforts to implement this and previous Resolutions and to report again, including any further developments on the issues raised in his report of 2 September 2005 (GOV/2005/67) to the Board. The Board will address the timing and content of the report required under Article XII.C and the notification required under Article III.B.4;" Paragraph 3, Board of Governors' September 2005 resolution on Iran

65. "[The Board of Governors] urges Iran: To implement transparency measures, as requested by the Director General in his report, which extend beyond the formal requirements of the Safeguards Agreement and Additional Protocol, and include access to individuals, documentation relating to procurement, dual use equipment, certain military owned workshops and research and development locations…," part of Paragraph 4 of the Board of Governors' resolution, September 2005.

66. According to international procedure, the Security Council can require Iran to implement the request of the Board of Governors for the ratification of the Additional Protocol. As historical evidence, the Security Council ratified its resolution 687 on April 3, 1991, and forced the Iraqi government to ratify the convention on prohibition of microbial weapons.

67. "Iran's Official Response to Board of Governors Resolution," ISNA, September 26, 2005.

68. "Iran rules out pre-conditions in nuclear talks," Mehr News Agency, July 23, 2005, available at www.payvand.com/news/05/dec/1169.html.

69. The managing editor of *Kayhan*, Hossein Shariatmadari, maintained that Iran ought to clearly announce that if its nuclear case were referred to the Security Council, it would leave the NPT. Shariatmadari criticized Iran's statement in reaction to the Board of Governors' resolution, opining, "I believe that Iran's statement was passive and we expected more from a revolutionary and principlist government. While the illegal resolution says that Iran's case should be illegally referred to the Security Council, announcing the country's readiness to continue negotiations with Europe is unacceptable," "Iran should withdraw from the NPT," ISNA, September 25, 2005.

70. In the speech, given at a conference on "The World without Zionism," Ahmadinejad said, "I hope the Palestinian nation will remain aware and alert as they have been during the past 10 years of struggles. This is a short juncture and when passed, God willing, annihilation of the Zionist regime would be quite easy."

71. "Iran: Thursday, October 27," CNN.com, October 27, 2005.

72. Jill Lawless, "World expresses dismay over Iranian president's remarks on Israel," Associated Press, October 27, 2005.

73. Lawless, "World expresses dismay over Iranian president's remarks on Israel."

74. "Chirac blasts Iranian leader's 'senseless' Israel comments," Agence France-Presse, October 27, 2005.

75. "Moscow criticizes Ahmadinejad's statement on Israel," RIA Novosti, August 28, 2005.

76. "Dublin condemns Ahmadinejad's statement on Israel," *Dublin Post*, October 27, 2005.

77. "Europeans consider Ahmadinejad's remark unacceptable," ISNA, October 28, 2005.

78. Ibid.

79. Ibid.

80. "Israel urges UN to exclude Iran," BBC News, October 27, 2005, http://news.bbc.co.uk/2/hi/middle_east/4382594.stm.

81. "World reaction to Iranian President's words," QuandO blog, October 28, 2005, www.qando.net/details.aspx?Entry=2824.

82. "Iran's Final Solution Plan," StudentNewsDaily.com, November 3, 2005, www.studentnewsdaily.com/commentary/irans_final_solution_plan.

83. Parchin is an industrial complex east of Tehran and is affiliated with the Defense Ministry. It produces weaponry and civilian products.

84. "Iran's readiness to resume negotiations," Mehr News Agency, November 6, 2005.

85. The Non-Aligned Movement (NAM) troika refers to the three countries chairing the organization in the previous, present, and next term.

86. Additional points of interest in the report were as follows:

    • ElBaradei admitted that Tehran had permitted access to individuals who were previously unreachable by the Agency.

    • The report noted that information provided by Iran on P-2 centrifuges was incomplete and that Iran had not presented any additional information to prove that it had not used second generation P-2 centrifuges between 1995 and 2002.

- The reported admitted that no progress or new developments had taken place with regard to uranium mining or activities related to plutonium or beryllium.

- ElBaradei noted that after meeting with Larijani on November 1, access was given to Agency inspectors to visit military sites in Parchin, with no unusual activity observed.

- He announced that there had been no new developments with regard to questions and access related to the Shiyan site.

87. "Iran to stop suspension in case of referral to UNSC," IRNA, November 20, 2005.

88. "IAEA failed to pass resolution against Iran," IRNA, November 24, 2005.

89. "Iran would not budge on enrichment," Mehr News Agency, December 5, 2005.

90. "Iran-EU to continue talks," IRNA, January 5, 2005.

91. "Russia Presented its proposal to Iran," IRNA, January 5, 2005.

92. The statement noted that El-Baradei had reminded Iran of the importance of suspension of all enrichment activities by Iran as stipulated by the IAEA. The director general stressed the right of all countries, including Iran, to peaceful use of nuclear technology while asking Iran to take the steps required by the IAEA for a resolution of outstanding issues related to the true nature of Iran's nuclear program. El-Baradei also asked Iran to adopt all voluntary measures for confidence building and to resume talks with all concerned parties; statement by IAEA secretariat, www.iaea.org/Publications/Documents/Board/2006/gov2006-15.pdf.

93. The Iranian embassy in Moscow issued a press release on January 12, 2006, which was published by Novosti news agency. The statement noted that the Islamic Republic of Iran had adopted voluntary and non-legally binding suspension of enrichment activities to build confidence over its nuclear program. However, the suspension had inflicted heavy losses on the country and had brought activities of nuclear researchers, scientists and technicians to a standstill, causing serious concern for researchers as well as the Iran Atomic Energy Organization.

94. "Iran calls for renewed EU3 nuclear talks in letter," Reuters, January 17, 2006.

95. "The west calls for suspension," Mehr News Agency, January 21, 2006.

96. "R&D activities under supervision of the IAEA are legal," Mehr News Agency, January 18, 2006.

97. The Iranian foreign minister told parliamentary reporters that, in view of all conditions, the possibility of reporting Iran's nuclear case to the Security Council was remote. See "The possibility of reporting Iran's nuclear case to the Security Council is unlikely," ISNA, January 18, 2006.

98. ISNA reported the deputy head of the Iran Atomic Energy Organization as saying that Iran had told the IAEA that it would simply resume R&D activities. Saeedi also noted that Iran differentiated between research activities related to nuclear fuel and its production and would continue with suspension of nuclear fuel production, "Iran would resume R&D activities in Natanz," ISNA, January 10, 2006.

99. Ali Asghar Soltanieh, Iran's representative to the IAEA, threatened that if Iran's case were referred to the Security Council, Iran would cease its voluntary cooperation with IAEA inspectors; BBC, January 19, 2006.

100. Norman Lamont, "Talking to Iran is a better idea than more sanctions," *Financial Times*, January 23, 2006, www.ft.com/cms/s/0/e93c3a9c-8bb4-11da-91a1-0000779e2340. html.

101. "Iran threatens to carry out enrichment on industrial scale: Larijani," Agence France-Presse, January 23, 2006.

102. "Iran would stop voluntary cooperation with the IAEA," ISNA, January 19, 2006.

103. "Iranian Foreign Minister Says Uranium Plan Still on Agenda for Moscow Meeting," Space War, November 12, 2006, www.spacewar.com/reports/Iranian_Foreign_Minister_Says_Uranium_Plan_Still_On_Agenda_For_Moscow_Meeting_999.html.

104. "Iran says Russian nuclear proposal a basis for compromise," Agence France-Presse, January 25, 2006.

CHAPTER SIX

1. "Bush seen resisting calls to toughen Iran policy," Reuters, January 31, 2006.

2. "Europe lacked the capacity to solve the nuclear issue," ISNA, January 31, 2006.

3. "Parliament: No bargain on inalienable Rights of Iran," ISNA, February 1, 2006.

4. "Implementation of the NPT Safeguards Agreement and relevant provisions of Security Ccouncil resolutions in the Islamic Republic of Iran," report by the Director General, November 8, 2011, iNFCIRC/214.

5. Eric Brill, "The Iran Nuclear Dispute—A New Approach," October 2010, http://brillwebsite.com/writings/Irannuclear.html.

6. Brill, "The Iran Nuclear Dispute," 20.

7. Ibid.

8. "Nuclear proliferation: Engaging Iran," *Los Angeles Times*, June 9, 2011, http://articles.latimes.com/2011/jun/09/opinion/la-oe-ambassadors-iran-20110609.

9. Peter Crail, "Iran's Nuclear Program: An Interview with Iranian Ambassador to the IAEA Ali Asghar Soltanieh," *Arms Control Today*, October 2011, www.armscontrol.org/act/2011_10/Iran-Nuclear-Program-Interview-Iranian-Ambassador-Ali-Asghar-Soltanieh.

10. "Iran would end voluntary cooperation with IAEA," ISNA, February 4, 2006.

11. Ibid.

12. "Iran Reported to Security Council," BBC News, February 4, 2006, http://news.bbc.co.uk/2/hi/middle_east/4680294.stm.

13. Paragraph M of February 2006 resolution of Board of Governors.

14. ". . . to report on the implementation of this and previous resolutions to the next regular session of the Board, for its consideration, and immediately thereafter to convey, together

with any Resolution from the March Board, that report to the Security Council," part of the February 2006 resolution of the Board of Governors.

15. Additionally, Paragraph 1 of the executive part of the resolution called on Iran to go beyond the formal requirements of the Safeguards Agreement and Additional Protocol and to provide information about dual use equipment, certain military-owned workshops as well as documentation relating to procurement. In Paragraph 3, the Board of Governors implied that Iran's reports to the IAEA were not "correct" and "complete." The resolution referred to the document concerning casting uranium metal into hemispheric forms.

16. "We cannot withstand all threats with a simple strategy. To resist enemies, we need a multifaceted strategy as well as dynamic and increasing strategic power. Our enemies intend to corner us, but we must be active in the region and the world. We cannot achieve our goals by just crying out. Those who know the world will not err. We must be more alert. Our people expect us, the statesmen, to do this at the lowest cost; and God willing this will be the case. We need complex strategies in the world; therefore, we must expand the circle of our advisers and take advantage of anything to prevent them from cornering us," part of an address by Dr. Hassan Rouhani at Imam Khomeini Holy Shrine, ISNA News Agency, February 11, 2006.

"I believe that in the process of getting the world to recognize Iran's right to this technology, Iran should go for understanding and building confidence with parties that are concerned about Iran building a nuclear bomb to solve this problem. I have frequently told my friends and Europeans that such pressures and excuses against Iran benefit neither Iran, nor Europeans and Americans. I hope this problem will be solved through negotiation, understanding and the IAEA. I hope my friends in Iran will endeavor to prevent further difficulties with the nuclear case," part of an interview with former Iranian president Mohammad Khatami by Al Jazeera TV, ISNA News Agency, February 26, 2006.

17. "No progress in EU talks with Iran," breakingnews.ie, February 21, 2006, www.breakingnews.ie/world/no-progress-in-eu-talks-with-iran-245620.html.

18. Paul Kerr, "Russia, Iran Sign Deal to Fuel Bushehr Reactor," *Arms Control Today*, November 2006, www.armscontrol.org/print/2398.

19. Ibid.

20. "Larijani arrives in Moscow for nuclear talks," *Turkish Weekly*, March 1, 2006, www.turkishweekly.net/news/26860/larijani-arrives-in-moscow-for-nuclear-talks.html.

21. The Russian president announced that the proposal for establishment of uranium enrichment sites to produce nuclear fuel would pave the way for finding political solutions to pressing problems, Novosti News Agency, February 3, 2006.

22. The Russian foreign ministry announced in a statement that its embassy in Tehran had delivered an official note containing the proposal to the Iranian officials. According to the note, Russia still stuck to its previous proposal for the establishment of a joint venture company by Iran and Russia to enrich uranium. See Nasser Karimi, "Tehran Vows to Defy the U.N.," Associated Press, December 24, 2006.

23. The foreign ministry spokesman today announced that Iran has received no well-defined plan from Russia. He added, "Any plan or proposal recognizing Iran's right to enrich

uranium on its own soil will be taken positively and Iran will be ready to discuss it," weekly briefing by the foreign ministry spokesman, ISNA News Agency, December 25, 2006.

24. "Iran sees many problems with Russia's idea, but there is no reason for us not to welcome new ideas. Considering the Russian proposal will depend on its framework," Ali Larijani in an interview with Islamic Republic of Iran Broadcasting, January 2, 2006.

25. Mottaki said, "We think that the Russian plan includes components, such as various locations for enrichment, or diversity of company members, which can provide a good ground for a mutual agreement," joint press conference of Iranian and Indonesian foreign ministers in Tehran, ISNA News Agency, January 25, 2006.

26. Discussing the Russian plan, Javad Va'idi, undersecretary of the Supreme National Security Council for security affairs, noted that since Iran had already started enrichment on its soil, there was no reason for joint enrichment with Russia, ISNA News Agency, February 4, 2006.

27. The Students' Basij Organization emphasized Iran's inalienable right to independence and protection of its national dignity while announcing that Russia's proposal for transfer of enrichment facilities to its soil was unacceptable. It warned officials against falling in the West's new trap, analytical statement of Students' Basij Organization about uranium enrichment on Russian soil. See ISNA News Agency, January 4, 2006.

28. Sergei Kislyak, the Russian deputy foreign minister, announced that uranium enrichment by Iran in Russia would be possible only if Iran suspended its nuclear activities. He added that the proposal would depend on Iran's further compliance with resolutions adopted by the IAEA Board of Governors. See "Russia ready for N-venture if Iran resumes U-freeze," 12ozprophet.com forum, www.12ozprophet.com/forum/archive/index.php/t-105082.html.

29. "Talks with EU, Progress with Russians," Mehr News Agency, March 2, 2006.

30. Ibid.

31. George Jahn, "Diplomats say Iran cleaned nuke work," Associated Press, March 7, 2006.

32. "Nuclear dilemma is over, marginal issues left," IRNA, March 17, 2006

33. Mohamed ElBaradei, *The Age of Deception* (New York, Metropolitan Books, 2011), 192.

34. "Europe welcomes Iran-US direct talks," *Aftabeyazd*, March 20, 2006.

35. United Nations Security Council, Security Council Calls on Iran to Take Steps Required by IAEA Board of Governors; Requests Report from IAEA Director General in 30 Days," www.un.org/News/Press/docs/2006/sc8679.doc.htm.

36. "Iran rejects UNSC demand on suspension," ISNA, April 3, 2006.

37. "Wolf Blitzer Interview With Vicente Fox; Interview With Hoshyar Zebari," CNN.com, April 2, 2006, http://transcripts.cnn.com/TRANSCRIPTS/0604/02/le.01.html. Retrieved 2006-05-04 .

38. "EU calls for diplomatic solution," IRNA, April 13, 2006.

39. Ibid.

40. Ibid.

41. "Condoleezza Rice calls for sanctions or even force against Iran," *Pravda*, April 14, 2006, http://english.pravda.ru/world/asia/14-04-2006/79206-iran-0.

42. The Complementary Access can take place with 24 hours' notification to any declared site. However, in connection at a site, two hours' notification would be sufficient.

43. "Interview with Seyed Hossein Mousavian, spokesman of the Iranian nuclear negotiating team," Mehr News Agency, June 26, 2005.

44. This is considered low-enriched uranium.

45. Also considered low-enriched uranium.

46. Elaine Sciolino, "U.S., Britain and France Draft U.N. Resolution on Iran's Nuclear Ambitions," *New York Times*, May 3, 2006, www.nytimes.com/2006/05/03/world/middleeast/03iran.html.

47. Christine Hauser, "Iranian President Writes Letter to Bush," *New York Times*, May 8, 2006, www.nytimes.com/2006/05/08/world/middleeast/08cnd-iran.html.

48. Bernard Gwertzman, "Drozdiak: German Chancellor Likely to Press Bush for Direct Talks with Iran," (interview) May 2, 2006, www.cfr.org/germany/drozdiak-german-chancellor-likely-press-bush-direct-talks-iran/p10575.

49. "Interview with U.S. Secretary of State Condoleezza Rice," Associated Press, May 13, 2006.

50. Mark N. Katz, "Policy Watch: Putin and Ahmadinejad," UPI.com, August 13, 2006, http://digilib.gmu.edu:8080/jspui/bitstream/1920/5907/1/PutinAhmadinejad.pdf.

51. The Secretary of the Supreme National Security Council warned that sanctions against Iran would lead to suspension of the country's cooperation with IAEA. However, he promised that if Iran's nuclear case were returned to the IAEA Board of Governors, Iran would voluntarily implement the Additional Protocol and take other relevant steps. "Interview with Ali Larijani," ISNA, April 25, 2006.

52. The Iranian foreign minister stressed that Iran would never consider suspension of nuclear activities. "Interview with Manouchehr Mottaki," *Kayhan*, May 2, 2006. Subsequent developments proved that pressures exerted by the United States and Israel as well as miscalculations on the part of Iran rendered this "carrot and stick" policy totally useless from the outset.

53. Germany, France, and the United Kingdom offered incentives to Iran, including nuclear power plants and guarantees on nuclear fuel, if Iran gave up uranium enrichment. They also promised to help with the construction of light-water reactors in Iran and guarantee a regular supply of nuclear fuel for five years. They also asked Iran to accept the deal to transfer its enrichment facilities to Russia. American diplomats noted that the EU had asked the United States to consider sales of new planes to Iran. In return, Iran was supposed to suspend all aspects of its enrichment program, along with construction of the heavy water reactor in Arak, to reassure the world that it was not trying to build nuclear weapons. See "History of Official Proposals on the Iranian Nuclear Issue," Fact Sheet, Arms Control Association, www.armscontrol.org/factsheets/Iran_Nuclear_Proposals.

54. United Nations, "Iran: Historical Chronology," Security Council Report, www.securitycouncilreport.org/site/?c=glKWLeMTIsG&b=2733227.

55. "EU's Javier Solana: Brokering Deal With Iran on 6/6/6? Solana pushes Iran for nuclear deal," Godlike Productions Message Board, June 6, 2006, www.godlikeproductions. com/forum1/message245437/pg1; "The challenge of a nuclear Iran," Bitter Lemons International, September 7, 2006, www.bitterlemons-international.org/previous.php? opt=1&id=148.

56. "Iran's Nuclear Program: Basic Facts," Foreign Ministry of Iran, 2008.

57. "World powers may soon make progress on Iran," *Taipei Times*, May 26, 2006, www. taipeitimes.com/News/world/archives/2006/05/26/2003310173.

58. ElBaradei, *The Age of Deception*, 194.

59. Ibid., 199.

60. "Text of P5+1 nuclear package of incentives offered to Iran," Iran Focus, July 18, 2006, www.iranfocus.com/en/?option=com_content&task=view&id=7947.

61. "Iran's steadfastness resulted in western retreat," Raja News, May 26, 2006.

62. "U.S. Proposes Talks with Iran on Nuclear Weapons," PBS, May 31, 2006, www.pbs. org/newshour/bb/middle_east/jan-june06/rice_05-31.html.

63. This referred to the five permanent members of the UN Security Council plus Germany. In Europe the group was often called the E3+3, meaning the EU3 plus the U.S., China, and Russia.

64. U.S. Department of State, "Press Conference on Iran," May 31, 2006, http://2001-2009.state.gov/secretary/rm/2006/67103.htm.

65. Guy Dinmore and Roula Khalaf, "Bush bows to pressure and offers Iran talks," *Financial Times*, June 1, 2006.

66. Bill Samii, "Iran: Tehran Responds To U.S. Offer Of Direct Talks," Radio Free Europe/ Radio Liberty, June 2, 2006, www.rferl.org/content/article/1068853.html.

67. "US ready to flexibility," Baztab website, June 5, 2005.

68. "Larijani-Solana talks positive," Mehr News Agency, June 6, 2006.

69. Karl Vick and Dafna Linzer, "Proposal Would Let Iran Enrich Uranium; Tehran Must Meet U.N. Guidelines," *Washington Post*, June 7, 2006.

70. "Elements of a proposal to Iran as approved on 1 June 2006 at the meeting in Vienna of China, France, Germany, the Russian Federation, the United Kingdom, the United States of America and the European Union," High Representative for CFSP, June 1, 2006, www.consilium.europa.eu/ueDocs/cms_Data/docs/pressdata/en/reports/90569.pdf.

71. Gary Samore, ed., *Iran's Strategic Weapons Program: A Net Assessment* (London: IISS, 2005).

72. "U.S. Willing to Delay Sanctions on Iran," NewsMax.com, September 27, 2006, http:// archive.newsmax.com/archives/articles/2006/9/27/141413.shtml.

73. "Iran is ready for talks if there is no precondition," ISNA, June 13, 2006.

74. After Mahmoud Ahmadinejad's remarks, U.S. Secretary of State Condoleezza Rice said Iran's early response to the P5+1 package had been positive and called for an official

response from Tehran. See "The US considers Iran's early response positive," Mehr News Agency, June 17, 2006.

75. "Iran will respond P5+1 within 10 days," IRNA, June 15, 2006.

76. "Official: Iran Will Never Stop Nuclear Program," NewsMax.com, June 23, 2006, http://archive.newsmax.com/archives/articles/2006/6/23/90941.shtml.

77. Gareth Smyth, "Khamenei appoints body to oversee Iran's foreign policy," *Financial Times*, June 27, 2006, www.ft.com/intl/cms/s/0/c78dba8a-062d-11db-9dde-0000779 e2340.html#axzz1ncMVaSI7.

78. The President announced that Iran will declare its stance on Europe's proposals in late August. See "Mahmoud Ahmadinejad's address to people in Hamedan," ISNA, June 21, 2006.

79. "Iran," Country Profiles, Nuclear Threat Initiative, March 2012, www.nti.org/country-profiles/iran/nuclear; United Nations, "Iran: Historical Chronology."

80. "G8 Foreign Ministers Forecast Key Issues Relating to International Security," stevencwelsh.com, July 15, 2006, www.stevencwelsh.com/cdi-archive/g8-071506.php.

81. "Iran warns the P5+1," IRNA, July 20, 2006.

82. "The United States has once again failed in forging consensus in the Security Council on Iran sanctions. Experts maintain that it will take at least three more months before the Security Council would be able to overcome differences, and no more sanctions will be considered until then. "The US failed to secure consensus against Iran," Raja News, July 30, 2006.

83. Text of Security Council Resolution 1696 against Iran's nuclear program.

84. Ibid.

85. ElBaradei, *The Age of Deception*, 199–200.

86. Chapter VII of the UN Charter is about "action with respect to threats to the peace, breaches of the peace, and acts of aggression." According to Article 39 of Chapter VII, "The Security Council shall determine the existence of any threat to the peace, breach of the peace, or act of aggression and shall make recommendations, or decide what measures shall be taken in accordance with Articles 41 and 42, to maintain or restore international peace and security." Based on Article 40, "the Security Council may . . . call upon the parties concerned to comply with such provisional measures as it deems necessary or desirable." According to Article 41, "The Security Council may decide what measures not involving the use of armed force are to be employed. These may include complete or partial interruption of economic relations and of rail, sea, air, postal, telegraphic, radio, and other means of communication, and the severance of diplomatic relations." According to Article 42, "Should the Security Council consider that measures provided for in Article 41 would be inadequate or have proved to be inadequate, it may take such action by air, sea, or land forces as may be necessary to maintain or restore international peace and security."

87. ElBaradei, *The Age of Deception*, 201.

88. Ibid., 203.

89. *Iran's Nuclear Program: Basic Facts* (Tehran: Foreign Ministry of Iran, 2008), 190.

90. The measure taken by Iran concurrent with the Zolfaqar military exercises was met with a wary reaction by the West and concerned Israel. Knesset deputies claimed that inauguration of the Arak heavy-water facility would aid Iran's access to nuclear weaponry and called on the Israeli government to prepare to attack Iran. Again, Tehran's analysis had been based on the premise that obtaining superior nuclear technology, which would make Iran independent of the West, would be a big bargaining chip in international negotiations and would force the United States to accept realities concerning Iran.

91. The report included two major points that paved the way for more pressure on Iran:

    "Iran has not addressed the long outstanding verification issues or provided the necessary transparency to remove uncertainties associated with some of its activities. Iran has not suspended its enrichment related activities; nor has Iran acted in accordance with the provisions of the Additional Protocol."

    "The Agency will continue to pursue its investigation of all remaining outstanding issues relevant to Iran's nuclear activities. However, the Agency remains unable to make further progress in its efforts to verify the correctness and completeness of Iran's declarations with a view to confirming the peaceful nature of Iran's nuclear programme."

92. ElBaradei, *The Age of Deception*, 206.

93. Ibid., 204.

94. Ibid., 204–205.

95. "Iran said to offer 2-month atomic enrichment halt," Reuters, September 10, 2006.

96. David Ignatius, "Signals from Tehran," *Washington Post*, February 23, 2007, www.washingtonpost.com/wp-dyn/content/article/2007/02/22/AR2007022201454.html?nav=emailpage.

97. Ignatius, "Signals From Tehran." The important point here is that some of the most outspoken critics of Khatami's nuclear policies and "suspension" of enrichment took a U-turn and asked Tehran to accept the two-month suspension as a confidence-building measure toward the West under certain conditions. The Baztab website, which had taken the sharpest critical positions on the nuclear strategy of the previous nuclear team, wrote: "In view of new emphasis put by Mr. Solana on the continuation of negotiations with Iran, the Islamic Republic of Iran can suspend enrichment for a period of two months after all members of the P5+1 sign paragraph 11 of the Solana-Larijani agreement as the last chance for the continuation of negotiations between Iran and the P5+1." Later, some Iranian media noted that Larijani's agreement with Solana was never realized due to strong opposition from the president. See "Signs of compromise on nuclear issue," Baztab, November 14, 2006; "The president rejects suspension," Raja News, November 20, 2006.

98. "Iran must suspend enrichment before talks–Chirac," Reuters, September 20, 2006. The French foreign minister, Philippe Douste-Blazy, told reporters that Europe was awaiting a rapid answer from Iran. France had proposed a bilateral suspension in which the West would suspend its efforts to enforce new sanctions against Iran through the UN Security Council, if Iran suspended its enrichment program. However, U.S. Secretary of State Condoleezza Rice noted that Iran should suspend enrichment before any negotiation could be resumed.

99. International Atomic Energy Agency, "Statement to the Sixty-First Regular Session of the United Nations General Assembly by IAEA Director General Dr. Mohamed ElBaradei," October 30, 2006, www.iaea.org/newscenter/statements/2006/ebsp2006n020.html#dprk.

100. Larijani, on a trip to Moscow, said, "If the UN Security Council approved the resolution proposed by Europeans without considering Russia's corrective proposal, we would review our relations with the IAEA." Again, Tehran continued its aggressive policy of threatening to leave the NPT as a way of deterring enactment of the resolution. "Moscow May Dump Iran for WTO Membership," *Kommersant*, November 11, 2006, www.kommersant.com/p720813/r_500/Russia_Iran_WTO_US.

101. IAEA, "Implementation of the NPT Safeguards Agreement in the Islamic Republic of Iran, Report by the Director General," November 23, 2006, http://iaea.org/Publications/Documents/Board/2006/gov2006-64.pdf.

102. He added, "We announced that the Iranian parliament was ready to approve a bill and if the nuclear case is referred to the UN Security Council, the government will be obliged to halt voluntary implementation of the Additional Protocol, and those who have not paid attention to that warning will be responsible for the consequences." Following Iran's new approach, which aimed to divide supporters of Iran sanctions by threatening to leave the NPT, Soltanieh said that the above conditions already existed in the country and a draft bill had been drawn up. "If the UN Security Council approved any resolution on the basis of Article 41 of the UN Charter, Iran would revise cooperation with the IAEA," he said. "Iran would halt implementation of Additional Protocol if the nuclear file is referred to UNSC," Mehr News Agency, November 23, 2006.

103. Richard Weitz, "Iran Again Fails to Secure Shanghai Treaty Organization Membership," *World Politics Review*, August 28, 2007, www.worldpoliticsreview.com/articles/1070/iran-again-fails-to-secure-shanghai-cooperation-organization-membership.

104. It is clear that at this juncture Iran was just used as a tactic by Russia and not a part of a greater strategy. The Russians liked Iran to cause trouble for western countries, but did not want and do not want Iran's policies to interfere with their own conservative and double standards. At the same time, Russia was Iran's rival in another field. Russia was very willing at that moment to play the role of interlocutor between Arabs and Israelis and this factor could have overshadowed bilateral relations between Tehran and Moscow, creating distance between them.

105. Sergei Lavrov emphasized that Russia was ready to support the UN decision banning the export of nuclear materials and sensitive technologies to Iran. He added that negotiations with the P5+1 on a resolution against Iran would be held the following week. "FM: Russia Ready to Back Sanctions Against Iran," albawaba.com, December 1, 2006, www.albawaba.com/news/fm-russia-ready-back-sanctions-against-iran.

106. Under these conditions, it seemed that Russia was entering a new phase in which it cast the Iran nuclear standoff as wholly a security matter, which was the main goal pursued by the United States and Israel. The remarkable position taken by a Russian foreign ministry official on the new draft resolution against Iran is notable. He maintained that the draft resolution would virtually isolate Iran, but would not be a firm guarantee that it would not pursue its nuclear ambitions. That approach was later manifested with regard to completion of the nuclear power plant in Bushehr. Nuclear cooperation

between Iran and Russia had officially started in 1992. Subsequent to the disintegration of the former Soviet Union, relations between Moscow and Tehran have always been a matter of dispute between Russian and American leaders, with pragmatic politicians of the Kremlin using it as a valuable bargaining chip. It seems that the Russian government has considered Iran a very important country in moderating relations with the West and Russia's position in the international system: it was interacting both with Tehran and the West in order to secure its own national interests.

CHAPTER SEVEN

1. "Technical and legal review and analysis of Security Council resolution 1737," Mehr News Agency, January 4, 2007, www.mehrnews.com/fa/NewsDetail.aspx?NewsID=430273.

2. "President's address to the Cabinet," Fars News Agency, December 25, 2006.

3. Also, Seyed Mohammad Ali Hosseini, spokesman of Iran's foreign ministry, called Resolution 1737 unfair, and noted that it would not affect the nation's resolve to continue peaceful nuclear activities.

4. "Britain expects Iran sanctions passed Saturday," Reuters, December 23, 2006.

5. "US wants more sanctions on Iran," Agence France-Presse, December 23, 2006.

6. "Assessing the Leader's nuclear diplomacy after a decade," kaleme.com, November 10, 2011, www.kaleme.com/1390/08/19/klm-79696.

7. "Iran: Guardian Council confirms Majlis nuclear ratification," Payvand News, December 27, 2006, www.payvand.com/news/06/dec/1292.html.

8. "Target Iran—Countdown Timeline," globalsecurity.org, www.globalsecurity.org/military/ops/iran-timeline-bush.htm.

9. "Larijani warns the West," *Resalat*, January 6, 2007.

10. The White House spokesman immediately reacted by saying that if Iran did not cooperate more with the IAEA, its image in the international arena would diminish further and the IAEA would be prompted to issue more reports on non-cooperation and noncompliance of Iran with its obligations as per the Safeguards Agreement and UN Security Council resolutions. The spokesman expressed hope that Iran's government would give up threats and comply with UN Security Council demands, "White House asks Iran to comply on nuclear prog," Reuters, December 28, 2006.

11. Paragraph 18 of the resolution called for the establishment of a committee to follow up on the Iran nuclear issue. The most important tasks of the committee were as follows:

    • Seeking information from all countries about their economic exchanges with Iran;

    • Reviewing cooperation between Iran and the IAEA;

    • Creating a list of individuals, companies, and institutions to be inspected or subject to sanctions;

    • Reporting at least every 90 days to the Security Council.

The committee was similar to the "sanctions committee" set up to deal with Iraq crisis, though the case of Iran was different from Iraq. Although Resolution 1737 only addressed sanctions targeted toward Iran's nuclear and missile programs, the resolution also paved the way for further restrictions on the country's interactions in political and economic arenas. This was particularly serious because the UNSC resolutions under Chapter VII are legally binding for all member states of the UN, and Paragraph 19 of Resolution 1737 explicitly required all UN member states to report to the Committee within 60 days of the adoption of the resolution on the steps they had taken to implement the resolution's mandates. This had the effect of raising tensions with Iran's neighbors and other international partners.

The resolution's second paragraph emphasized the need for Iran to suspend uranium enrichment and implied that suspension was a precondition for the resumption of negotiations, which in the face of continued Iranian rejection brought all efforts to reach an understanding to a practical standstill.

12. Jack Boureston and Jennifer Lacey, "Nuclear Technical Cooperation: A Right or a Privilege?" Arms Control Association, September 2007, www.armscontrol.org/print/2702.

13. "Iran bars entry for 38 nuclear inspectors," Reuters, January 22, 2007, available at www.msnbc.msn.com/id/11682871/ns/world_news-mideast_n_africa/t/iran-bars-entry-nuclear-inspectors.

14. Guy Jackson, "Iranian Ready to Resume Talks but Set to Announce New Technologies," *Space War*, February 11, 2007, www.spacewar.com/reports/Iranian_Ready_To_Resume_Talks_But_Set_To_Announce_New_Technologies_999.html.

15. In a meeting with Ali Akbar Velayati, Russian President Vladimir Putin said he was very happy about continuing working dialogue between the two countries, while expressing hope that diplomatic consultations would lead to suitable solutions to existing problems. "Ali Akbar Velayati's meeting with Putin," RIA Novosti, February 9, 2007.

16. The Director General of the IAEA, Mohamed ElBaradei, argued that it was possible for both sides of the nuclear problem to come to a face-saving agreement. He urged Iran to suspend uranium enrichment in return for a waiver of international sanctions against Tehran as a prelude to the resumption of diplomatic negotiations, "ElBaradei's press conference on the sidelines of Davos Economic Forum," Agence France-Presse, January 27, 2007.

17. Alejandro Wolff, the acting U.S. Ambassador to the United Nations, rejected ElBaradei's request to waive sanctions in return for suspension of enrichment activities by Iran and noted that the resolution was quite clear. Wolfe added that based on the resolution adopted on September 23, sanctions could be lifted only when Iran totally stopped all uranium enrichment activities and plutonium tests. See Bill Varner, "ElBaradei's Idea for 'Timeout' With Iran Is Rejected by U.S.," Bloomberg, January 29, 2007, www.bloomberg.com/apps/news?pid=newsarchive&sid=aIY6psePXtfA&refer=home.

18. "As reported by BBC and AFP, some European countries have also rejected ElBaradei's initiative for lifting sanctions in return for a total freeze of Iran's nuclear activities. German and British diplomats have said that the initiative could not be implemented right now and the Security Council Resolution should be enforced," "EU rejects ElBaradei's initiative,"Aftab, January 1, 2007.

19. The Iranian Foreign Ministry spokesman announced that the proposed "time-out" was an outdated idea which would not help to solve the nuclear problem and would not be considered by Iran, "Spokesman's weekly briefing," IRNA, July 8, 2007.

20. "Larijani's deputy announced that a time-out was a flawed idea in line with past proposals for suspension of enrichment activities. He added that the initiative would not break the existing deadlock." "Larijani: ElBaradei's initiative would not break the existing deadlock," Mehr News Agency, July 4, 2007.

21. Referring to centrifuge operation without the introduction of gas.

22. Following his meeting with Putin, Velayati told reporters that Iran welcomed the Russian president's initiative as a logical step that considered Iran's concerns. "Tehran welcomes Moscow's initiative," IRNA, February 8, 2007.

23. "Iran ready to consider all possibilities during negotiations," *Ebtekar*, February 1, 2007.

24. Barbod Fadaie-Far, "Uranium Dispute a Gordian Knot for Both Sides," Mianeh. net, March 5, 2007, http://mianeh.net/article/uranium-dispute-gordian-knot-both-sideshttp://mianeh.net/article/uranium-dispute-gordian-knot-both-sides.

25. The same line was followed by most print media outlets supporting the new government's diplomatic approach, including Raja News and *Kayhan*.

26. As a result of that agreement, Iran managed to exclude the Arak heavy-water reactor and Isfahan's UCF from suspension and continue its research and development as well as the manufacture of needed parts in Natanz.

27. Gareth Porter, "German Official Urges Compromise on Iran Enrichment," Anti-War. com, July 4, 2006, www.antiwar.com/orig/porter.php?articleid=9238.

28. Enriched uranium is a kind of uranium in which the percent composition of uranium-235 has been increased through the process of isotope separation. *Low-enriched uranium* (LEU) has a lower than 20 percent concentration of ^{235}U. For use in commercial light-water reactors (LWR), the most prevalent power reactors in the world, uranium is enriched to 3 to 5 percent ^{235}U. Highly enriched uranium (HEU) has a greater than 20 percent concentration of ^{235}U or ^{233}U. The fissile uranium in nuclear weapons usually contains 85 percent or more of ^{235}U (known as weapon(s)-grade), though for a crude, inefficient weapon 20 percent is sufficient (called weapon(s)-usable); some argue that even less is sufficient, but then the critical mass for unmoderated fast neutrons rapidly increases, approaching infinity at 6 percent ^{235}U. For critical experiments, enrichment of uranium to over 97 percent has been accomplished.

29. "Iran stopped enrichment," Associated Press, March 5, 2007.

30. "IAEA Pushes Iran to Accept Cameras at Key Atom Site," Sudan Vision, March 31, 2007, www.sudanvisiondaily.com/modules.php?name=News&file=print&sid=19686.

31. "The Threat from Iran" (updated March 2012), Jewish Virtual Library, www. jewishvirtuallibrary.org/jsource/talking/23_Iran.html.

32. "Iran would be cooperative if P5+1 returned the nuclear file to IAEA," *Resalat*, March 18, 2007.

33. "Letter from Iran's representative in IAEA, Ali Asghar Soltanieh, to Mohamed ElBaradei," Mehr News Agency, March 12, 2007.

34. "P5+1 agree on new sanctions," *Jahanesanat*, March 15, 2007.

35. Resolution 1747 called "upon all States and international financial institutions not to enter into new commitments for grants, financial assistance, and concessional loans, to the Government of Iran, except for humanitarian and developmental purposes." It also called "upon all States also to exercise vigilance and restraint regarding the entry into or transit through their territories of individuals who are engaged in, directly associated with or providing support for Iran's proliferation of sensitive nuclear activities or for the development of nuclear weapon delivery systems." The names of companies and institutions subject to UN Security Council sanctions were as follows: Ammunition and Metallurgy Industries Group (AMIG); Isfahan Nuclear Fuel Research and Production Centre (NFRPC) and Esfahan Nuclear Technology Centre (ENTC) (Parts of the Atomic Energy Organization of Iran's [AEOI] Nuclear Fuel Production and Procurement Company, which is involved in enrichment-related activities); Kavoshyar Company (subsidiary company of Iran Atomic Energy Organization); Parchin Chemical Industries (Branch of DIO, which produces ammunition, explosives, as well as solid propellants for rockets and missiles); Karaj Nuclear Research Centre (Part of AEOI's research division); Novin Energy Company (aka Pars Novin) (Operates within AEOI and has transferred funds on behalf of AEOI to entities associated with Iran's nuclear program); Cruise Missile Industry Group (aka Naval Defense Missile Industry Group) (Production and development of cruise missiles. Responsible for naval missiles including cruise missiles); Bank Sepah and Bank Sepah International (Bank Sepah provides support for the Aerospace Industries Organization [AIO]); Sanam Industrial Group (subordinate to AIO, which has purchased equipment on AIO's behalf for the missile program); Ya Mahdi Industries Group (subordinate to AIO, which is involved in international purchases of missile equipment); Qods Aeronautics Industries (Produces unmanned aerial vehicles [UAVs], parachutes, para-gliders, para-motors, etc.); Pars Aviation Services Company (Maintains various aircraft including MI-171, used by IRGC Air Force); Sho'a' Aviation.

36. Nazila Fathi, "Iran Claims Progress in Enriching Uranium," *New York Times*, April 9, 2007.

37. The Anglo-Iranian Oil Company was an antecedent of today's BP.

38. "Ahmadinejad: Iran is member of nuclear club," IRNA, April 9, 2007. Ahmadinejad used the phrase "nuclear club" to mean countries that had mastered enrichment, seemingly oblivious to the eyebrows raised over the fact that the term is generally used with reference to nuclear-*armed* countries.

39. "Iran completed the nuclear fuel cycle," ISNA, April 11, 2007.

40. "Israel at Sixty: Tests of Endurance," Herzliya Conference, January 20–23, 2008, www.herzliyaconference.org/_Uploads/2814ShmuelBarIranianAhmadinejad.pdf.

41. See "Israel-Iran," website, http://israeliran.net.

42. "Iran has technical problems to start uranium enrichment on an industrial scale," *Ebtekar*, April 13, 2007.

43. David Albright and Jacqueline Shire, "A Witches' Brew? Evaluating Iran's Uranium-Enrichment Progress," Arms Control Association, November 2007, www.armscontrol.org/act/2007_11/Albright.

44. "Implementation of the NPT Safeguards Agreement and Relevant Provisions of Security Council Resolution 1737 (2006) in the Islamic Republic of Iran, Report by the Director General," March 7, 2007, www.iaea.org/Publications/Documents/Board/2007/gov2007-08.pdf.

45. "Iran's Larijani terms his nuclear talks with Solana as 'very good,'" Payvand News, April 26, 2007, www.payvand.com/news/07/apr/1310.html.

46. Jason Webb, "No breakthrough seen for Iran-EU nuclear talks," Reuters, May 30, 2007, available at www.iiss.org/whats-new/iiss-in-the-press/press-coverage-2007/may-2007/no-breakthrough-seen-for-iran-eu-nuclear-talk.

47. "G8 nations warn Iran over nuclear enrichment," International Reporter, June 1, 2007, www.internationalreporter.com/News-2165/g8-nations-warn-iran-over-nuclear-enrichment.html.

48. "Larijani-Solana talks," Aftab, May 31, 2007. It should be noted that some in the international community had begun to question whether the call for suspension was still practical, given the expansion of Iran's enrichment activities and capabilities. ElBaradei told the *New York Times* that Iran had already mastered enrichment and the purpose of the demand for suspension had been "overtaken by events." The United States was extremely angry with the statement and Condoleezza Rice went so far as to threaten ElBaradei that the United States would cut the IAEA's budget. ElBaradei, *The Age of Deception*, 252–53.

49. "Larijani: Iran-EU Nuclear Talks Near Unity View," china.org.cn, April 27, 2007, www.china.org.cn/english/International-Iran/209206.htm.

50. "Iran's Larijani Does Not Rule Out Suspension of Uranium Enrichment," *WNC: Focus*, August 6, 2007, available at http://dlib.eastview.com/browse/doc/12419426.

51. "G8 urges Iran to suspend," Aftab, June 20, 2007.

52. Time-out plan was first brought up by ElBaradei, the former director general of IAEA, in a press conference. It was another version of the "suspension for suspension" initiative and called on Tehran and the P5+1 to both suspend enrichment activities for a short period of time, and punishments considered by the Security Council, the United States, and Europe. This was meant to pave the way for resumption of negotiations, but the plan was snubbed by both sides.

53. "Iran would allow IAEA to visit Arak Heavy Water," Aftab, July 14, 2007.

54. "Limited suspension is possible," Mehr News Agency, July 23, 2007.

55. Ibid.

56. "Larijani resigned," Fars News Agency, October 20, 2007.

57. "It seems that Iran has succeeded in its aggressive approach to the nuclear case and we must expect more of the radical politicians while moderate ones are marginalized," RFE/RL, October 22, 2007. "Larijani's resignation was mostly due to differences in methods, performance and tactics regarding not only the nuclear case, but also other security and strategic matters," *Al Jazeera*, October 2007.

58. "Larijani resigned due to differences with President Ahmadinejad," *Ebtekar*, October 23, 2007.

59. "Safavi criticized Ahmadinejad's policies," Norouz News, October 24, 2007.

60. "Surprising resignation," BBC Radio, October 23, 2007.

61. BBC radio pointed to the appointment of Saeed Jalili as the new secretary of the Supreme National Security Council and concluded that since Jalili was close to the president, the appointment was a sign of the rising power of radical politicians.

62. Dariush Qanbari, a member of the Majles National Security and Foreign Policy Commission, explained the possibility that Mottaki would resign by saying that there were profound differences between the foreign minister and the president and since Mottaki was close to Larijani, his dismissal was quite possible. Qanbari said the resignation would have adverse effects on foreign negotiators and the country's national interests. See "Mottaki at a juncture, to stay or leave," Aftab News, October 24, 2007.

63. "Mottaki at a juncture, to stay or leave."

64. "Ahmadinejad denies rumors on Larijani's resignation," IRNA, October 21, 2007.

65. "Velayati on Larijani's resignation," Mehr News Agency, October 22, 2007.

66. "Government says Larijani's resignation was based on personal motives," ISNA, September 24, 2007.

67. The Expediency Council is a high-level government body whose members are nominated by the Supreme Leader and whose main function is to adjudicate disputes between the legislature and the Guardian Council. It also considers general economic, social, cultural, political, and foreign policies and proposes them to the Supreme Leader. The Center for Strategic Research works on policy issues for the Expediency Council and is one of the country's most prominent think tanks.

68. "The West needs to change its policy and Iranian officials need to be more cautious," *Etemad*, November 21, 2007.

69. "Iran arrests ex-nuclear official: Former nuclear negotiator reportedly arrested in Tehran 'for security reasons,'" *Al Jazeera*, May 2, 2007, www.aljazeera.com/news/middleeast/2007/05/2008525122041998100.html.

70. I was accused, among other things, of sharing classified information and collaborating with European intelligence services.

71. Christiane Amanpour, "Hossein Mousavian Is Arrested," CNN, May 3, 2007.

72. Kimia Sanati, "Iran: Espionage Allegations Weaken Ahmadinejad's Coalition," Goliath Business News, December 5, 2007, http://goliath.ecnext.com/coms2/gi_0199-7261805/IRAN-ESPIONAGE-ALLEGATIONS-WEAKEN-AHMADINEJAD.html; Amir Taheri, "Iran Playing a Clever Game," Arab News, October 28, 2006, http://archive.arabnews.com/?page=7&section=0&article=77057&d=28&m=10&y=2006.

73. In its new year special edition on April 16, 2007, *Kargozaran* newspaper introduced Mousavian as its "Man of the Year," writing that a great event like discovering a "spy" in the former nuclear team would be a bounty to those who charged the government's critics with affiliation to the United States and claimed that they are traitors and spies. "It will also prove that all critics of Ahmadinejad's nuclear diplomacy are affiliated with the west and the ninth government's foreign policy approach is the best existing approach for Iran."

74. *Kargozaran* pointed in its March 18, 2008, issue to my appointment during the Hashemi Rafsanjani presidency as the first post-revolution ambassador to Germany, as well as my role, alongside one of Rafsanjani's sons, in a special diplomatic mission to Saudi Arabia. *Kargozaran* was the official newspaper of the Kargozaran political party. The party was known as being pro-Rafsanjani, and its central committee included numerous ministers from Rafsanjani's cabinet.

75. Rooz Online news website wrote on May 6, 2007, that I was known as the spokesman of Rafsanjani's policies outside Iran and was responsible for explaining viewpoints of one of the most important political currents of Iran.

76. Jon Wolfsthal, nonproliferation expert at the Center for Strategic and International Studies (CSIS) in Washington, told AP that my arrest may have shown that there was a group in Iran that tried to prevent empowerment of pragmatic figures led by Hashemi Rafsanjani. See Nasser Karimi, "Iran arrests former nuclear negotiator," Associated Press, May 3, 2007.

77. *Kargozaran* wrote on March 18, 2008, that even if my sharp criticism of Ahmadinejad's diplomacy were ignored, my key post at the Expediency Council's Center for Strategic Research was enough to enrage conservatives. "It seems that being a trustee to Hashemi Rafsanjani, vice president of the Center for Strategic Research, and critic of nuclear policies is considered an unforgivable crime."

78. An Australian periodical, *Diplomatic Noise*, described me as one of three international Iranian diplomats among the 25 most famous diplomats of the Middle East. This was probably why my arrest soon grabbed the headlines in the international media. *Kargozaran*, March 18, 2008.

79. Mohammad Atrianfar was quoted by the *Financial Times* on May 2, 2007, as saying that my arrest was a sign of new pressure and that my friends expected Hassan Rouhani and Ayatollah Hashemi Rafsanjani to step in on my behalf if I were not released soon.

80. Cyrus Nasseri was accused of financial corruption. This allegation was also a part of the smear campaign against the former nuclear negotiation team. He was cleared of the charges after a year.

81. "Ahmadinejad: former nuclear negotiation team urged the West to impose sanction resolutions," Mehr News Agency, December 10, 2010.

82. "Tavakkoli asks Mousavian for forgiveness/13 of Mousavian's charges were baseless," Mehr News Agency, September 15, 2008, www.mehrnews.com/fa/NewsDetail. aspx?NewsID=749825.

83. "Office of the President: Mr. Tavakkoli! You asked forgiveness once again," *Donya-e-Eqtesad*, September 15, 2008, www.donya-e-eqtesad.com/Default_view.asp?@=122366.

84. "I am certain Your Excellency has now realized the secret of this side's silence," Mehr News Agency, September 16, 2008, www.mehrnews.com/fa/NewsDetail. aspx?NewsID=750791.

85. "Director of the Ansar News site was sentenced in the Mousavian case," Mehr News Agency, March 17, 2009, www.mehrnews.com/fa/NewsDetail.aspx?NewsID=850556.

86. "Warrant for the site director of 'Edalatkhaneh' was issued," Mehr News Agency, November 17, 2008, www.mehrnews.com/fa/NewsDetail.aspx?NewsID=784388.

87. "The aim of my complaint was the revival of the moral values of the Revolution," Mehr News Agency, November 18, 2008, www.mehrnews.com/fa/NewsDetail.aspx?NewsID=784847.

88. "Mousavian is not guilty/Espionage charges and providing documentation to foreigners is not an issue," Mehr News Agency, November 27, 2007, www.mehrnews.com/fa/NewsDetail.aspx?NewsID=594144; "The details of Mousavian's sentence/Two-year suspension and acquitted of espionage charges again," Mehr News Agency, April 8, 2008, www.mehrnews.com/fa/NewsDetail.aspx?NewsID=661995.

89. In Evin prison and during the interrogations, I wrote dozens of pages describing why I disagreed with Ahmadinejad's foreign and nuclear policy.

CHAPTER EIGHT

1. National Intelligence Estimate, November 2007; see Chapter Four, Appendices; complete text of NIE.

2. "Iran's nuclear file should be taken out of the UNSC," IRNA, December 24, 2008.

3. "Russia, Iran may set up JV to operate Bushehr NPP in 3 months," Belarus Export, www.belarus-export.com/news/363/index75.html.

4. "Saudi cannot be launchpad for Iran attack: report," Agence France-Presse, January 12, 2008.

5. Ibid.

6. "U.N. Chief Seeks Answers on Iranian Nuclear Issues," Reuters, January 11, 2008.

7. Mohamed ElBaradei, *The Age of Deception* (New York, Metropolitan Books, 2011), 267.

8. Ibid., 273–74.

9. "New page in Tehran—the IAEA's cooperation," *Jomhouri-Eslami*, January 13, 2008.

10. Also known as a "work plan" or "modality agreement"; the purpose of the plan was to resolve all technical ambiguities.

11. "IAEA Announces New Nuclear Accord With Iran," Reuters, January 14, 2008, available at http://archive.arabnews.com/?page=4&section=0&article=105644&d=14&m=1&y=2008.

12. "Interview with spokesman of the Ministry of Foreign Affairs," Mehr News Agency, January 13, 2008.

13. "Interview with Foreign Minister Manouchehr Mottaki," IRNA, January 14, 2008.

14. ElBaradei, *The Age of Deception*, 258.

15. Caroline Glick, "ElBaradei's Nuclear Policy," *Jerusalem Post*, August 27, 2007.

16. Elaine Sciolino and William J. Broad, "An Indispensable Irritant to Iran and Its Foes," *New York Times*, September 17, 2007.

17. ElBaradei, *The Age of Deception*, 259.

18. Ibid., 259.

19. Matthew Lee, "US to pursue new Iran sanctions," *USA Today*, January 16, 2008, www.usatoday.com/news/washington/2008-01-16-3591335936_x.htm.

20. "Tehran is sure about a speedy solution to its nuclear crisis. We think that the situation is good and we are getting ready to solve this problem once and for all," Ali Baqeri, deputy minister of foreign affairs in an interview with reporters in Madrid, Spain, on the occasion of a conference on dialogue among civilizations. See George Jahn, "Iran Hopes for Solution in Nuke Dispute," Associated Press, January 16, 2008, available at www.accessnorthga.com/detail-pf.php?n=205868.

21. "The U.S. says resolution is punitive and very serious," *Etemad*, January 18, 2008.

22. "News conference of government spokesman, Dr. Elham," Fars News Agency, January 4, 2008.

23. "Iran's Melli Bank: the target of sanctions," *Space War*, June 24, 2008, www.spacewar.com/reports/Irans_Melli_Bank_the_target_of_sanctions_999.html.

24. "Iran provides space launch info," Press TV, January 4, 2008.

25. "Moscow warns Tehran on satellite launch," *Resalat*, February 6, 2008.

26. Jason Ditz, "Reports: Iran 'Struggling' to Get New Centrifuges Up and Running, IAEA Says Iran to Install More Centrifuges Using Old Design," Antiwar.com, February 27, 2012, http://news.antiwar.com/2012/02/27/reports-iran-struggling-to-get-new-centrifuges-up-and-running.

27. International Atomic Energy Agency, "Implementation of the NPT Safeguards Agreement and relevant provisions of Security Council resolutions 1737 (2006) and 1747 (2007) in the Islamic Republic of Iran, Report by the Director General," February 22, 2008, www.iaea.org/Publications/Documents/Board/2008/gov2008-4.pdf.

28. The complete text of Ahmadinejad's letter to the Supreme Leader is as follows: "I congratulate Imam Zaman (AS), Your Excellency, and the revolutionary and courageous nation on the historical triumph of the noble Iranian nation in its confrontation with hegemonic powers over the nuclear case. As you know, this triumph is owed to empathy and steadfastness of the faithful . . . Iranian nation under your lead and special favors of Imam Zaman (AS). I thank you for your support and guidance, incessant efforts of scientists and specialists, endeavors of our diplomats, as well as intelligence and self-confidence of the great Iranian nation and assure you that the nation and your revolutionary children in the government will continue to defend the lofty cause of the Islamic Revolution until realization of all its goals. . . ." "President congratulated the Leader on nuclear achievements," IRNA, February 23, 2008.

29. "The latest report of the director general of the IAEA on Iran's nuclear activities is more golden evidence of the peaceful nature of our country's nuclear activities. The director general has been under tremendous pressure during the past few weeks to present his report by ignoring facts and in such a way as to harm Iran in accordance with the will of the United States and the Zionist regime," part of the statement released by the Islamic Propagation Organization in reference to El-Baradei's report on February 22, Fars News Agency, February 23, 2008. "IPO calls for thanksgiving ceremonies," Fars News Agency, February 23, 2008.

30. "Jalili congratulated the Iranian nation," ISNA, Fars, Mehr, and IRNA, February 22, 2008.

31. ElBaradei, *The Age of Deception*, 279.

32. "The one major remaining issue relevant to the nature of Iran's nuclear program is the alleged studies on the green salt project, high explosives testing and the missile re-entry vehicle. This is a matter of serious concern and critical to an assessment of a possible military dimension to Iran's nuclear program. The Agency was able to show some relevant documentation to Iran on 3–5 February 2008 and is still examining the allegations made and the statements provided by Iran in response. Iran has maintained that these allegations are baseless and that the data have been fabricated. The Agency's overall assessment requires, inter alia, an understanding of the role of the uranium metal document, and clarifications concerning the procurement activities of some military related institutions still not provided by Iran. The Agency only received authorization to show some further material to Iran on 15 February 2008. Iran has not yet responded to the Agency's request of that same date for Iran to view this additional documentation on the alleged studies. In light of the above, the Agency is not yet in a position to determine the full nature of Iran's nuclear program. However, it should be noted that the Agency has not detected the use of nuclear material in connection with the alleged studies, nor does it have credible information in this regard. The Director General has urged Iran to engage actively with the Agency in a more detailed examination of the documents available about the alleged studies which the Agency has been authorized to show to Iran," Paragraph 54, Director General's report, February 22, 2008.

33. ElBaradei, *The Age of Deception*, 278–79.

34. Ibid., 243–45.

35. Ibid., 245–46.

36. Ibid., 246–47.

37. Mathieu van Rohr, "US Irked By Over-Eager Swiss Diplomats," Spiegel Online International, December 14, 2010.

38. Arms Control Association, "History of Official Proposals on the Iranian Nuclear Issue," www.armscontrol.org/factsheets/Iran_Nuclear_Proposals.

39. See United Nations, "Security Council Tightens Restrictions on Iran's Proliferation-Sensitive Nuclear Activities, Increases Vigilance over Iranian Banks, Has States Inspect Cargo," press release, March 3, 2008, www.un.org/News/Press/docs/2008/sc9268.doc.htm.

40. "Calls upon all States, in accordance with their national legal authorities and legislation and consistent with international law, in particular the law of the sea and relevant international civil aviation agreements, to inspect the cargoes to and from Iran, of aircraft and vessels, at their airports and seaports, owned or operated by Iran Air Cargo and Islamic Republic of Iran Shipping Line, provided there are reasonable grounds to believe that the aircraft or vessel is transporting goods prohibited under this resolution or resolution 1737 (2006) or resolution 1747 (2007)." Security Council Resolution 1803.

41. The resolution also extended sanctions already imposed on companies and persons connected with Iran's nuclear activities, and in three appendices produced a list of 13 Iranian companies and 13 top managers of Iran's nuclear programs in addition to those already mentioned in prior resolutions. It called on all countries to freeze the assets of the aforesaid companies and persons and "to exercise vigilance and restraint regarding the entry into or transit through their territories of individuals who are engaged in, directly associated with or providing support for Iran's proliferation sensitive nuclear activities or for the development of nuclear weapon delivery systems." That prohibition was also extended to five new Iranians involved in Iran's nuclear activities and others whose names had been mentioned in Resolution 1803 and its predecessors.

   Names of the following persons were mentioned in Resolution 1803: 1. Amir Moayyed Alai (involved in managing the assembly and engineering of centrifuges); 2. Mohammad Fedai Ashiani (involved in the production of ammonium uranyl carbonate and management of the Natanz enrichment complex); 3. Abbas Rezaee Ashtiani (a senior official at the AEOI Office of Exploration and Mining Affairs); 4. Haleh Bakhtiar (involved in the production of magnesium at a concentration of 99.9 percent); 5. Morteza Behzad (involved in making centrifuge components); 6. Dr. Mohammad Eslami (Head of Defense Industries Training and Research Institute); 7. Seyyed Hussein Hosseini (AEOI official involved in the heavy-water research reactor project at Arak); 8. M. Javad Karimi Sabet (Head of Novin Energy Company, which is designated under resolution 1747 [2007]); 9. Hamid-Reza Mohajerani (involved in production management at the Uranium Conversion Facility (UCF) at Isfahan); 10. Brigadier-General Mohammad Reza Naqdi (former Deputy Chief of Armed Forces General Staff for Logistics and Industrial Research/Head of State Anti-Smuggling Headquarters, engaged in efforts to bypass the sanctions imposed by resolutions 1737 [2006] and 1747 [2007]); 11. Houshang Nobari (involved in the management of the Natanz enrichment complex); 12. Abbas Rashidi (involved in enrichment work at Natanz); 13. Ghasem Soleymani (Director of Uranium Mining Operations at the Saghand Uranium Mine).

42. "Calls upon all States to exercise vigilance in entering into new commitments for publicly provided financial support for trade with Iran, including the granting of export credits, guarantees or insurance, to their nationals or entities involved in such trade, in order to avoid such financial support contributing to the proliferation of sensitive nuclear activities, or to the development of nuclear weapon delivery systems, as referred to in resolution 1737 (2006)," Para. 9, Resolution 1803.

43. "Mottaki: world powers trying to politicize the nuclear case," Mehr News Agency, March 27, 2008.

44. ElBaradei, *The Age of Deception*, 280–81.

45. In reaction to Security Council Resolution 1803, Ahmadinejad called it "a gift from the Security Council to the Iranian people" (*Etemad*, March 6, 2008). However, he had already promised that no new resolution would be adopted against Iran. He told reporters that Resolution 1803 "proved Iran's weight as a big international power and . . . proved that the Iranian nation outweighed all the world powers" (*Etemad*, March 6, 2008). Ahmadinejad also announced that Iran would thenceforth work with no other country or institution, save for the IAEA.

46. "Ahmadinejad: Iran to increase number to 50,000," IRNA News Agency, April 9, 2008.

47. "Condoleezza Rice: Ahmadinejad's remarks were not believable," *Etemad*, April 10, 2008.

48. "Iran ready to share its peaceful nuclear technology," Fars News Agency, April 15, 2008.

49. "CIA agent in the IAEA," *Kayhan*, April 24, 2008.

50. "The Islamic Republic of Iran believes that sustainable peace and security in the region and the world, economic relations, free trade, energy security, the war on terror, fighting drugs and the use of the nuclear energy for peaceful purposes are very good common grounds for long-term cooperation. In view of the existing conditions at regional and international levels, the Islamic Republic of Iran believes that a new and overarching plan is needed to realize sustainable cooperation and constructive interaction," part of Manouchehr Mottaki's letter to the P5+1 and Ban Ki-Moon; May 22, 2008.

51. International Atomic Energy Agency, "Implementation of the NPT Safeguards Agreement and Relevant Provisions of Security Council Resolutions 1737 (2006), 1747 (2007) and 1803 (2008) in the Islamic Republic of Iran, Director General's Report," May 26, 2008.

52. "Interview with Ali Asghar Soltanieh," Reuters, June 2, 2008.

53. Kenneth R. Timmerman, "New Documents Show Iran Still Working on Nukes," NewsMax, March 8, 2008, www.newsmax.com/KENTIMMERMAN/IRANIAN-NUCLEAR-PROGRAM/2008/03/06/ID/337418.

54. Ian Traynor, "Blueprint for nuclear warhead found on smugglers' computers," *Guardian*, June 16, 2008, http://m.guardian.co.uk/world/2008/jun/16/nuclear.pakistan?cat=world&type=article.

55. The article identified the Swiss expert as Urs Tinner, an engineer who has ties to the A. Q. Khan network. He was detained in prison for more than four years before being released in late 2008. See Ian Traynor, "Nuclear bomb blueprints for sale on world black market, experts fear," *Guardian*, May 31, 2008, http://m.guardian.co.uk/world/2008/may/31/nuclear.internationalcrime?cat=world&type=article.

56. "IAEA's ElBaradei Threatens to Quit if Iran Is Attacked," democracynow.org, June 23, 2008, www.democracynow.org/2008/6/23/headlines.

57. "Parliament will determine new limits for cooperation with the IAEA," *Kargozaran*, June 12, 2008.

58. "Velayati: suspension is impossible," *Kayhan*, July 7, 2008.

59. "The Leader: NSC is the sole authority handling the nuclear case," Fars News Agency, July 17, 2008.

60. "Ahmadinejad rejects a new incentive package," *Resalat*, April 5, 2008.

61. "Larijani warns the west," Fars News Agency, June 27, 2008.

62. "Iran should withdraw from the NPT," *Kayhan*, June 30, 2008.

63. "Parliamentarians determined to defend the rights of the nation," IRNA, July 2, 2008.

64. "Iran and P5+1 resume nuclear talks," Mehr News Agency, August 15, 2008.

65. "Iran's New Package of Proposals to 5+1: A Fateful Test of the Honesty of Western Countries," IRNA, July 22, 2008.

66. "Iran's New Package of Proposals to 5+1."

67. The *New York Times*, for example, highlighted spelling errors in the two-page document, including a missing "p" from "comprehensive" and the misspelling of "non-paper" as "none-paper." The *New York Times* article went on to say that the errors had made Russian Foreign Minister Sergei Kislyak burst out laughing. Other American and European press also focused on this issue to marginalize nuclear negotiations between Iran and six countries. They also opined that dictation errors were a sign of the inefficiency of the Iranian nuclear diplomats. The *New York Times* piece commented that the content of the message was as disappointing as its diction. Elaine Sciolino, "Iran Offers 2 Pages and No Ground in Nuclear Talks," *New York Times*, July 22, 2008. "Many western news agencies, especially BBC, AP, Deutsche Welle, and AFP focused on the *New York Times*'s report and tried to marginalize the original negotiations which [were] attended for the first time by a U.S. representative." "U.S. participation has been marginalized," Shahab News, July 23, 2008.

68. "Ahmadinejad rejects moves to slow down Iran's enrichment capacity," Fars News Agency, July 27, 2008.

69. "Report: Ahmadinejad says Iran now possesses 6,000 centrifuges," YnetNews.com, July 26, 2008, www.ynetnews.com/articles/0,7340,L-3573312,00.html.

70. "Nuclear program no threat: Iranian ambassador," ABC News, February 26, 2008, www.abc.net.au/news/stories/2008/02/26/2173441.htm.

71. Ibid.

72. "Rafsanjani invites officials to be more cautious," Mehr News Agency, July 26, 2008.

73. Bill Weinberg, "Iran issues anti-nuke fatwa," World War 4 Report, August 12, 2005, www.ww4report.com/node/929.

74. "Supreme Leader's Message to International Conference on Nuclear Disarmament," Khamenei website, April 17, 2010, http://english.khamenei.ir/index.php?option=com_content&task=view&id=1287&Itemid=16.http://english.khamenei.ir/index.php?option=com_content&task=view&id=1287&Itemid=16

75. "Imam Khamenei's fatwa on banning WMDs registered as UN document," Comfort Zones blog, April 26, 2010, http://perwi21.blogspot.com/2010/04/imam-khameneis-fatwa-on-banning-wmds.html.

76. In late 2007, ElBaradei had an intelligence briefing at the American mission to the UN, in which they described their concerns that Iran had, at least in the past, conducted activities indicating an intention to develop nuclear weapons, but acknowledged that they had no evidence that Iran had undeclared nuclear material. ElBaradei, *The Age of Deception*, 262.

77. Since the victory of the Islamic Revolution, the U.S. interests section has been located at the Swiss embassy in Tehran. Democrat diplomats and senators proposed that Washington should be represented in Iran by something like the interest section it already ran in Cuba, where American diplomats would be working to provide certain services like issuing visas.

78. International Atomic Energy Agency, *IAEA Director General's Report*, September 15, 2008.

79. "The international community may find it amusing that when a logical question is put forth, the other party to negotiation resorts to pressure instead of giving a clear response. This illogical behavior attests to the absence of convincing answers to the Islamic Republic of Iran's questions and raises doubts that some powers only see negotiations as a temporary tactic. The international community cannot ignore the lack of willingness on the part of bullying powers to engage in logical negotiations," excerpt of Saeed Jalili's letter to the P5+1, October 8, 2008.

80. "Iran points finger at nuclear accusers," Reuters, August 8, 2008, available at www.stuff. co.nz/world/664226/Iran-points-finger-at-nuclear-accusers.

81. United Nations, "Security Council Press Statement on Remarks by Iran's President," September 12, 2005, www.un.org/News/Press/docs/2005/sc8576.doc.htm.

82. "Mahmoud Ahmadinejad's remarks," Fars News Agency, March 15, 2008.

83. Bill Varner, "Iran launches bid for Security Council seat," Gstaad Project blog, http:// gstaadblog.wordpress.com/2008/07/04/IRAN-LAUNCHES-BID-FOR-SECURITY-COUNCIL-SEAT.

84. Neil MacFarquhar, "3 Nations Win Security Council Seats," *New York Times*, October 17, 2008, www.nytimes.com/2008/10/18/world/18nations.html.

85. The Group of 77 (G-77) was established on June 15, 1964, by seventy-seven developing countries signatories of the "Joint Declaration of the Seventy-Seven Countries" issued at the end of the first session of the United Nations Conference on Trade and Development (UNCTAD) in Geneva. The Group of 77 is the largest intergovernmental organization of developing countries in the United Nations, which provides the means for the countries of the South to articulate and promote their collective economic interests and enhance their joint negotiating capacity on all major international economic issues within the United Nations system, and promote South-South cooperation for development. See The Group of 77 at the United Nations, www.g77.org/doc.

86. "President Ahmadinejad's speech," IRNA; September 19, 2008.

87. "Ahmadinejad Address Before the UN General Assembly," IRNA, September 25, 2008.

88. "Iranian President Ahmadinejad's 2008 UN Address," FinalCall.com News, September 24, 2008, www.finalcall.com/artman/publish/article_5253.shtml.

89. Resolution 1835 did not contain new economic sanctions against Iran, but it asked Tehran to implement the content of previous resolutions without delay, especially suspension of uranium enrichment. The short, ten-paragraph resolution emphasized the UN Security Council's "commitment within this framework to an early negotiated solution to the Iranian nuclear issue" while supporting the policy of "sanctions and encouragement." It also called upon Iran to comply "fully" and "without delay" with its obligations. Resolution 1835 was an international message to Iran in line with new conditions in the nuclear case following the occupation of Afghanistan and Iraq by the United States, the U.S. presidential election, the rise of Barack Obama, Israel's invasion of Gaza, the unprecedented rise in oil prices, early signs of a pervasive global economic crisis, and many other factors which allowed Tehran more maneuvering room

in its confrontation with the international community. Permanent members of the UN Security Council, including the United States, UK, France, and Russia, noted that the new resolution was a sign of the "international community's convergence on preventing Iran from building the nuclear weapon."

90. "UN passes Iran nuclear resolution," *National*, September 28, 2008, www.thenational. ae/news/world/middle-east/un-passes-iran-nuclear-resolution.

91. "UN passes Iran nuclear resolution."

92. Louis Charbonneau, "Russia Says U.S. Blocking Nuclear Arms Reduction Talks," Reuters, September 29, 2008.

93. "UN resolution against Iran was absolutely abusive and unjust" IRNA, September 29, 2008.

94. Ibid.

95. From September 29 to October 4.

96. "Russia denied deal on Iran," *Jomhouri Eslami*, October 3, 2008. Some analysts maintained that Russia's support for Resolution 1835 was a tactical measure which should be assessed in the context of Moscow's Caucasian diplomacy. The analysts argued that Russia's role was a "two-edged sword" affecting Iran, on one side, and the P5+1, on the other. Russia's role was instrumental in organizing the P5+1 to reach a consensus over the new resolution. If this analysis is true, it follows that one edge of that sword constantly targeted Iran. Although Moscow managed to appease the P5+1 by pioneering presentation of the new draft resolution, they created the general impression that they may try to gain more influence on Tehran in return for preventing adoption of stricter resolutions. The Iranian diplomatic apparatus should be prepared to handle this possible situation.

CHAPTER NINE

1. See C. Christine Fair, Indo-Iranian Ties: Thicker Than Oil," *Middle East Review of International Affairs*, vol. 11, no. 1, March 2007, http://meria.idc.ac.il/journal/2007/issue1/jv11no1a9.html#_edn1; Henry D. Sokolski, *Gauging U.S.-Indian Strategic Cooperation*, March 5, 2007, Senate Committee on Foreign Relations, Hearing on U.S.-India Civilian Nuclear Agreement, April 5, 2006, www.foreign.senate.gov/hearings/2006/hrg060405a.html; Prakash Karat, "The Indo-US Nuclear Deal: Struggle to Defend National Sovereignty," *Marxist*, vol. XXIII, no. 3, July to September, 2007, www.cpim.org/marxist/200703_marxist-nuclear%20deal-prakash.pdf; Ninan Koshy (edited by John Gershman), "India and the Iran Vote in the IAEA," *Foreign Policy in Focus*, October 27, 2005, www.fpif.org/articles/india_and_the_iran_vote_in_the_iaea; Harsh V. Pant, "India's Relations with Iran: Much Ado about Nothing," *Washington Quarterly*, 34:1, Winter 2011, www.twq.com/11winter/docs/11winter_Pant.pdf.

2. "Iran hints at nuclear rethink if gets guarantees," *USA Today*, October 2, 2008, www. usatoday.com/news/world/2008-10-02-3591335936_x.htm.

3. "FM: Iran not to halt uranium enrichment for foreign nuclear fuel supply," Xinhua, October 5, 2008, http://news.xinhuanet.com/english/2008-10/05/content_10152169. htm.

4. "Iran says Solana asks for continuation of nuclear talks," Xinhua, November 8, 2008, http://news.xinhuanet.com/english/2008-11/08/content_10324746.htm.

5. Nuclear Threat Initiative, "Iran Nuclear Chronology, 2008," www.nti.org/media/pdfs/ iran_nuclear.pdf?_=1316542527.

6. "Biden Addresses Munich Conference," *Washington Post*, February 7, 2009, http:// voices.washingtonpost.com/44/2009/02/07/biden_addresses_munich_confere.html.

7. Oliver Rolofs, "45th Munich Security Conference Ushers in Political Spring," www. securityconference.de/MSC.307.0.html?&L=1.

8. Nasser Karimi, "Ahmadinejad Denies Holocaust Yet Again," Huffington Post, September 19, 2009, www.huffingtonpost.com/2009/09/18/ahmadinejad-denies-holoca_n_291056.html.

9. Ed Pilkington, "Ahmadinejad accuses US of 'orchestrating' 9/11 attacks to aid Israel," *Guardian*, September 23, 2010, www.guardian.co.uk/world/2010/sep/23/iran-unitednations.

10. Michael C. Moynihan, "Mahmoud Ahmadinejad: Obama a 'Cowboy' Just Like Bush," Opposing Views, April 7, 2010, www.opposingviews.com/i/mahmoud-ahmadinejad-obama-a-cowboy-just-like-bush.

11. Ahmadinejad was reportedly insulted that Obama did not respond to his congratulations for the latter's electoral victory, even complaining of this to ElBaradei. Mohamed ElBaradei, *The Age of Deception* (New York: Metropolitan Books, 2011), 303.

12. Ali Akbar Dareini, "Ahmadinejad Mocks Obama: Iran President Blasts Nuclear Strategy, Calls Obama 'Cowboy,'" Huffington Post, April 7, 2010, www.huffingtonpost. com/2010/04/07/ahmadinejad-mocks-obama-i_n_528110.html.

13. See video at www.metacafe.com/watch/3819884.

14. "Israeli president calls on world to unite against Iran," Breitbart, July 23, 2005, www. breitbart.com/article.php?id=070723221255.bhwlxs2o&show_article=1.

15. Amos Harel and Avi Issacharoff, "Does Israel stand alone against Iran?" *Haaretz*, April 28, 2010, www.haaretz.com/blogs/2.244/does-israel-stand-alone-against-iran-1.285167.

16. Spencer Ackerman, "Nyet! Russia Now Won't Sell Badass Missile to Iran," Wired.com, September 22, 2010, www.wired.com/dangerroom/2010/09/nyet-russia-now-wont-sell-badass-missile-to-iran.

17. Harel and Issacharoff, "Does Israel stand alone against Iran?"

18. "U.S., Israel to Work Closely on Iran," Global Security Newswire, January 23, 2009, http://gsn.nti.org/gsn/nw_20090123_6842.php.

19. "Obama warns Netanyahu: Don't surprise me with Iran strike," *Haaretz*, May 14, 2009, www.haaretz.com/print-edition/news/obama-warns-netanyahu-don-t-surprise-me-with-iran-strike-1.275993.

20. "Iran Executes Alleged Israeli Spy," Sky News, November 22, 2008, http://news.sky.com/skynews/Home/World-News/Iran-Executes-Ali-Ashtari-Businessman-Accused-Of-Spying-For-Israels-Mossad-Security-Service/Article/200811415159108.

21. William J. Broad, John Markoff, and David E. Sanger, "Israeli Test on Worm Called Crucial in Iran Nuclear Delay," New York Times, January 15, 2011, www.nytimes.com/2011/01/16/world/middleeast/16stuxnet.html?pagewanted=all.

22. Matthew Bunn, "Beyond Zero Enrichment: Suggestions for an Iranian Nuclear Deal," Policy Brief, Belfer Center for Science and International Affairs, Harvard Kennedy School, November 2009, http://belfercenter.ksg.harvard.edu/publication/19695/beyond_zero_enrichment.html.

23. Robin Pagnamenta, Michael Evans, and Tony Halpin, "Iran in scramble for fresh uranium supplies," Times Online, January 24, 2009, www.timesonline.co.uk/tol/news/world/middle_east/article5576589.ece.

24. "President Obama letter to Russia's Dmitry Medvedev offered deal on Iran," New York Daily News, March 3, 2009, www.nydailynews.com/news/national/2009/03/02/2009-03-02_president_obama_letter_to_russias_dmitry.html.

25. "Moscow rebuffs Obama's secret Iran-missile shield deal," France 24, April 3, 2009, www.france24.com/en/20090304-moscow-rebuffs-obamas-secret-iran-missile-shield-deal-.

26. Meir Javedanfar, "Obama factor reaches Iran," Guardian, April 7, 2009, www.guardian.co.uk/commentisfree/2009/apr/06/iran-nuclear-power.

27. Julian Borger, "Nuclear talks lead to rare meeting between US and Iran," Guardian, October 1, 2009, www.guardian.co.uk/world/2009/oct/01/iran-nuclear-geneva-talks.

28. Ebrahim Mottaqi, "Will Enrichment Continue in Iran's Nuclear Policy?" Iran Review, December 13, 2010, www.iranreview.org/content/Documents/Will_Enrichment_Continue_in_Iran%E2%80%99s_Nuclear_Policy_.htm.

29. Najmeh Bozorgmehr and Daniel Dombey, "Iran Hails Nuclear Progress," Financial Times, April 9, 2009, www.ft.com/cms/s/0/151adb18-2523-11de-8a66-00144feabdc0.html#axzz1TXXsWLNO.

30. "Obama sent second letter to Khamenei," Washington Times, September 3, 2009, www.washingtontimes.com/news/2009/sep/03/obama-sent-second-letter-to-irans-khamenei.

31. "Karroubi's reaction to Ayatollah Jannati's remarks: 'I will take you to court," Khabar Online, July 29, 2010, www.khabaronline.ir/news-79407.aspx.

32. "Corps commander admitted to the arrest of ten thousand people last year," Kalmeh Mirror blog, September 7, 2010, http://klm.blogsky.com/1389/06/17/post-70.

33. "Leadership views about the crimes in the university dormitory and Kahrizak," Fararu, August 26, 2009, www.fararu.com/vdciywap.t1au52bcct.html.

34. Juan Cole, "Khamenei Blames Obama for post-election Disturbances Demands non-intervention as prerequisite to improved ties," Informed Comment, March 22, 2010, www.juancole.com/2010/03/khamenei-blames-obama-for-post-election.html.

35. Julian Borger, "Nuclear WikiLeaks: Cables show cosy US relationship with IAEA chief," Guardian Global Security Blog, November 30, 2010, www.guardian.co.uk/world/julian-borger-global-security-blog/2010/nov/30/iaea-wikileaks.

36. "Ahmadinejad slams world unilateralism," Press TV, September 22, 2010, www.presstv.ir/detail/143479.html.

37. Catherine Philp, "Iran may have enough enriched uranium to build a bomb, US warns," Times, September 10, 2009, www.timesonline.co.uk/tol/news/world/middle_east/article6828300.ece

38. ElBaradei, The Age of Deception, 295.

39. "US to Iran: Prove Your Nuclear Program Is Peaceful," CNN, September 27, 2009, http://articles.cnn.com/2009-09-27/politics/us.iran_1_iranian-atomic-energy-agency-qom-site-nuclear-program?_s=PM:POLITICS.

40. PBS Newshour, "Leaders Warn Iran Over Secret Enrichment Site," September 25, 2009, www.pbs.org/newshour/updates/international/july-dec09/iran_09-25.html.

41. Bobby Ghosh, "CIA Knew About Iran's Secret Nuclear Plant Long Before Disclosure," Time, October 7, 2009, www.time.com/time/world/article/0,8599,1929088,00.html. The importance of intelligence-security approaches in confronting the Iranian nuclear issue was pointed to about one year later by Sir John Sawers, head of Britain's MI6. As Sawers told the Society of Editors in London in the first public address by a chief of the UK's intelligence agency, "The revelations around Iran's secret enrichment site at Qom were an intelligence success. They led to diplomatic pressure on Iran intensifying, with tougher UN and EU sanctions, which are beginning to bite. . . . Stopping nuclear proliferation cannot be addressed purely by conventional diplomacy. . . . We need intelligence-led operations to make it more difficult for countries like Iran to develop nuclear weapons."

42. "Israel Views Iran Talks as 'Waste of Time,'" October 3, 2009, DiwanLebnan.org, http://diwanlebnan.org/en/zionist-entity/40.html.

43. William J. Broad and David E. Sanger, "Report Says Iran Has Data to Make a Nuclear Bomb," New York Times, October 3, 2009, www.nytimes.com/2009/10/04/world/middleeast/04nuke.html?scp=7&sq=iran+nuclear&st=nyt.

44. "State of the Union with John King, Interview with General Jim Jones; Interview with Senators John Kyl and Barbara Boxer; Governor Jennifer Granholm Gets the Last Word; A Company Born on the Prairie," CNN, October 4, 2009, http://transcripts.cnn.com/TRANSCRIPTS/09/10/04/sotu.05.html.

45. Massimo Calabresi, "Obama's Secret Iran Talks: Setting the Stage for a Deal?" Time, October 19, 2009, www.time.com/time/magazine/article/0,9171,1931722,00.html.

46. Mary Beth Sheridan, "Russia Not Budging on Iran Sanctions," Washington Post, October 14, 2009, www.washingtonpost.com/wp-dyn/content/article/2009/10/13/AR2009101300221.html.

47. "Soltanieh: Iran has not and will not implement Security Council resolutions," Aftab, January 25, 2011, www.aftabnews.ir/vdcjyyevouqe8vz.fsfu.html.

48. The second judge who examined my case in March 2008, while clearing me of espionage charges, issued a guilty verdict that explicitly stated that the reason for my sentencing

was my opposition to Ahmadinejad's nuclear and foreign policies. It was true that I opposed these policies, as I officially acknowledged during interrogations and my legal defense, and for this reason by the court's final judgment in April 2008 I was banned from holding any diplomatic post for five years.

49. Neither of the only two producers of the fuel—France and Argentina—were at all inclined to sell it. France had adopted the most hard-line position toward Iran, and Argentina had a political issue with Iran, over its alleged role in the 1984 bombing of a Jewish center in Buenos Aires that resulted in 85 deaths.

50. ElBaradei, *The Age of Deception*, 307–308.

51. Ibid., 311.

52. "Sanctions would only encourage enrichment - Iranian expert Interview with Mark Fitzpatrick," IISS, August 10, 2010, www.iiss.org/whats-new/iiss-in-the-press/press-coverage-2010/august-2010/sanctions-would-only-encourage-enrichment-iranian-expert.

53. "U.S. intelligence officials later concluded that the document was forged," Inter Press Service, January 2, 2010, http://ipsnews.net/news.asp?idnews=49833.

54. Julian Borger, "Iran Tested Advanced Nuclear Warhead Design—Secret Report," *Guardian*, November 5, 2009, www.guardian.co.uk/world/2009/nov/05/iran-tested-nuclear-warhead-design.

55. "Israel names Russians helping Iran build nuclear bomb," Times Online, October 3, 2009, www.timesonline.co.uk/tol/news/world/middle_east/article6860161.ece.

56. Ulrich Rippert, "Munich Security Conference steps up threats against Iran," Global Realm, February 12, 2010, http://theglobalrealm.com/2010/02/12/munich-security-conference-steps-up-threats-against-iran.

57. "Global community condemns Iran's decision," Voice of Russia, February 8, 2010, http://english.ruvr.ru/2010/02/08/4252555.html.

58. "Spokesman Reiterates Iran's Readiness to Buy N. Fuel," Fars News Agency, February 17, 2010. http://english.farsnews.com/newstext.php?nn=8811281417.

59. "Ali Akbar Salehi: The head of Iran's Atomic Energy Agency talks to Al Jazeera's Nazanine Moshiri," *Al Jazeera*, February 13, 2010, http://english.aljazeera.net/programmes/talktojazeera/2010/02/2010212174415727175.html.

60. Ivan Oelrich and Ivanka Barzashka, "Deconstructing the meaning of Iran's 20 percent uranium enrichment," *Bulletin of the Atomic Scientists*, May 19, 2010, www.thebulletin.org/web-edition/features/deconstructing-the-meaning-of-irans-20-percent-uranium-enrichment.

61. "Iran nuclear program based on politics not physics," *Dawn*, February 12, 2010, http://archives.dawn.com/archives/93821.

62. "Implementation of the NPT Safeguards Agreement and relevant provisions of Security Council resolutions 1737 (2006), 1747 (2007), 1803 (2008) and 1835 (2008) in the Islamic Republic of Iran," Report by the Director General, February 18, 2010, www.iaea.org/Publications/Documents/Board/2010/gov2010-10.pdf.

63. "Monarchists Take Responsibility for Iran Assassination," Press TV, January 12, 2010. http://edition.presstv.ir/detail/115962.html.

64. "Iranian media: Iran suspects Israel, U.S. behind scientist's killing," CNN, January 12, 2010, http://articles.cnn.com/2010-01-12/world/iran.professor_1_massoud-ali-mohammadi-iranian-media-islamic-revolution?_s=PM:WORLD.

65. Yossi Melman, "US Website: Mossad Killed Iranian Nuclear Physicist," *Haaretz*, February 4, 2007, www.haaretz.com/news/u-s-website-mossad-killed-iranian-nuclear-physicist-1.211920.

66. See for example, "Iran to UN: Israel kidnapped former gov't official," *Jerusalem Post*, January 1, 2011, www.jpost.com/Headlines/Article.aspx?id=201728.

67. Manal Lutfi, "Iran Blames US for Missing Scientist," *al-Sharq al-Awsat*, October 8, 2009, www.asharq-e.com/news.asp?section=1&id=18397.

68. Julian Borger, "Iran: US Behind Missing Scientist," *Guardian*, October 7, 2009, www.guardian.co.uk/world/2009/oct/07/iran-usa.

69. "Videos Deepen Mystery Over Iranian Nuclear Scientist Amiri," BBC News, June 8, 2010, www.bbc.co.uk/news/10264193.

70. "Missing Iranian scientist appears at embassy in US," BBC News, July 13, 2010, www.bbc.co.uk/news/10609461.

71. Matthew Cole, "US: Iran Threatens Family of Nuclear Defector Shahram Amiri," ABC News, June 28, 2010, http://abcnews.go.com/Blotter/iran-threatens-family-nuclear-defector/story?id=11034885.

72. "Iran scientist Shahram Amiri free to leave, US insists," BBC News, July 13, 2010, www.bbc.co.uk/news/10617656.

73. Matthew Cole, "Iran Nuke Defector Left Behind $5 Million in CIA Cash," ABC News, July 15, 2010, http://abcnews.go.com/Blotter/shahram-amiri-iran-nuke-defector-left-million-cia/story?id=11171171.

74. James Kelly, "The Spy Who Returned to the Cold," *Time*, April 18, 2005, www.time.com/time/magazine/article/0,9171,1050566,00.html.

CHAPTER TEN

1. "Implementation of the NPT Safeguards Agreement and relevant provisions of Security Council resolutions 1737 (2006), 1747 (2007), 1803 (2008) and 1835 (2008) in the Islamic Republic of Iran, Report of the Director General," International Atomic Energy Agency, February 18, 2010, www.iaea.org/Publications/Documents/Board/2010/gov2010-10.pdf.

2. "Remarks of President Obama Marking Nowruz," White House, March 20, 2010, www.whitehouse.gov/the-press-office/remarks-president-obama-marking-nowruz.

3. "Iran dominates G8 foreign ministers meeting," CBC News, March 30, 2010, www.cbc.ca/news/canada/story/2010/03/30/g8-ministers-meeting.html.

4.	"Obama: 'Ratchet Up' Pressure on Iran," CBS News, April 2, 2010, www.cbsnews.com/stories/2010/04/02/earlyshow/main6356438.shtml.

5.	"Iran unveils 'faster' uranium centrifuges," BBC News, April 9, 2010, http://news.bbc.co.uk/2/hi/8611864.stm.

6.	"Obama hosts two-day summit on nuclear security," CNN, April 11, 2010, http://articles.cnn.com/2010-04-11/politics/nuclear.security.summit_1_nuclear-weapons-terrorists-and-rogue-states-weapons-and-technology?_s=PM:POLITICS.

7.	"China to work with US on Iran sanctions," *Guardian*, April 13, 2010, www.guardian.co.uk/world/2010/apr/13/china-us-iran-sanctions.

8.	Maseh Zarif, "Defiance & Distraction: Iranian Regime Responds to Nuclear Posture Review," AEI Iran Tracker, April 27, 2010, www.irantracker.org/news-highlight/defiance-distraction-iranian-regime-responds-nuclear-posture-review.

9.	Parisa Hafezi, "Iran Denounces U.S. 'Nuclear Threats,' to Hold Drill," Reuters, April 21, 2010, www.reuters.com/article/2010/04/21/us-iran-wargames-gulf-idUSTRE63K17320100421.

10.	"Iran's Khamenei condemns Obama's 'nuclear threat.'" Agence France-Presse, April 11, 2010.

11.	"Iran's Ahmadinejad says nuclear summit 'humiliating,'" Reuters, April 12, 2010, www.reuters.com/article/idUSTRE63B30H20100412.

12.	"Iran's DM Stresses Popularity of Islamic Establishment in Iran," Fars News Agency, April 12, 2010, http://english.farsnews.com/newstext.php?nn=8901231449.

13.	Ibid.

14.	"Larijani: the US nuclear policy bellicose," ISNA, April 11, 2010, www.isna.ir/ISNA/NewsView.aspx?ID=News-1516883&Lang=E.

15.	Nazila Fathi, "Iranian Anger Rises over Obama's Revised Nuclear Policy," *New York Times*, April 11, 2010, www.nytimes.com/2010/04/12/world/middleeast/12iran.html.

16.	"Iran: US using 'nuclear blackmail,'" *Tehran Times*, April 15, 2010, www.tehrantimes.com/index_View.asp?code=217530.

17.	"Nuclear disarmament conference opens in Tehran," *Siasat Daily*, April 17, 2010, www.siasat.com/english/news/nuclear-disarmament-conference-opens-tehran.

18.	"Iran leader Khamenei brands US 'nuclear criminal,'" BBC News, April 17, 2010, http://news.bbc.co.uk/2/hi/8627143.stm.

19.	"Iran leader Khamenei brands US 'nuclear criminal.'"

20.	Author conversation with American participants in the discussion with Mottaki.

21.	Brazil's own nuclear activities were not irrelevant to this diplomatic action, either.

22.	"Obama's Letter to Lula Regarding Brazil-Iran-Turkey Nuclear Negotiations," May 27, 2010, Política Externa Brasileira, www.politicaexterna.com/11023/brazil-iran-turkey-nuclear-negotiations-obamas-letter-to-lula.

23. "President Obama Should Be Honest about the Iran-Turkey-Brazil Nuclear Deal," Race for Iran, May 27, 2010, www.raceforiran.com/president-obama-should-be-honest-about-the-iran-turkey-brazil-nuclear-deal.

24. "Major powers agree on Iran resolution—Clinton," Reuters, May 18, 2010, www.reuters.com/article/idUSWBT01391920100518.

25. "Lula: 'Nuclear weapons make the world more dangerous, not agreements with Iran," *Buenos Aires Herald*, June 9, 2010, http://axisoflogic.com/artman/publish/printer_60273.shtml.

26. "Erdogan: Support nuclear deal," *Jerusalem Post*, May 22, 2010, www.jpost.com/IranianThreat/News/Article.aspx?id=176121.

27. "Obama's Letter to Lula Regarding Brazil-Iran-Turkey Nuclear Negotiations."

28. "Brazil reveals Obama letter in spat over Iran nuclear deal," *Today's Zaman*, May 29, 2010, www.todayszaman.com/news-211443-brazil-reveals-obama-letter-in-spat-over-iran-nuclear-deal.html.

29. "President Obama Should Be Honest about the Iran-Turkey-Brazil Nuclear Deal."

30. In his recent book, *The Age of Deception*, ElBaradei explains at length and in detail this pressure exerted by the United States, and also expresses his critical views of the West's double standards.

31. Both Ahmadinejad and Soltanieh have harshly and publicly criticized Amano. In reaction to Amano's June 2011 report on Iran, Ahmadinejad stated, "We think the IAEA director moves in a direction that harms the agency's credibility. Politically-motivated stances don't suit the IAEA chief." Soltanieh likewise accused Amano of bias, saying, "He is not doing his job. Instead, with his reports, he is paving the way for more confrontation." Sylvia Westall and Fredrik Dahl, "Six Powers Push Defiant Iran to Address Nuclear Fears," Reuters, June 10, 2011; Nasser Karimi and Ali Akbar Dareini, "Ahmadinejad Criticized IAEA Chief," Associated Press, June 7, 2011.

32. "Implementation of the NPT Safeguards Agreement and relevant provisions of Security Council resolutions 1737 (2006), 1747 (2007), 1803 (2008) and 1835 (2008) in the Islamic Republic of Iran."

33. The report added that while the agency continued to verify the non-diversion of *declared* nuclear material in Iran, Iran had not provided the necessary cooperation to permit the IAEA to confirm that all nuclear material in Iran was intended for peaceful usage. More specifically, Iran was not implementing the requirements contained in the relevant resolutions of the Board of Governors and the UN Security Council, including the implementation of the Additional Protocol.

34. "Campaign Against Sanctions and Military Intervention in Iran," June 2, 2010, www.campaigniran.org/casmii/index.php?q=node/10249.

35. Prior to the passing of resolutions 1929, resolutions 1696, 1737, 1747, 1803, 1835, and 1887 had been implemented by UNSC, which makes Resolution 1929 the seventh such action taken against Iran. However it should be noted that Resolution 1887 (September 24, 2009) which was issued by Barack Obama, aimed at nuclear disarmament in the world. Even though reference to Security Council Resolution 1929 and Resolution

1887 have no direct relevance to Iran, it meant that the Iranian issue would be treated as a security threat to international peace within the Security Council.

36. United Nations Security Council, "Resolutions," June 9, 2010, www.un.org/Docs/sc/unsc_resolutions10.htm.

37. United Nations Security Council, "Resolutions," June 10, 2010.

38. "Remarks by Dennis Ross, Special Assistant to the President and Senior Director for the Central Region AIPAC National Summit," White House Press Office, October 25, 2010, www.whitehouse.gov/the-press-office/2010/10/25/remarks-dennis-ross-special-assistant-president-and-senior-director-cent.

39. "Sanctions on Iran: Reaction and Impact," AEI Iran Tracker, www.irantracker.org/us-policy/sanctions-iran-reactions-and-impact.

40. Teymoor Nabili, "Drip, drip, drip," Al Jazeera blog, December 30, 2009, http://blogs.aljazeera.net/category/country/islamic-republic-iran?page=4.

41. "Bill Summary & Status 111th Congress (2009–2010), H.R.2194," Congressional Research Service Summary, April 30, 2009, http://thomas.loc.gov/cgi-bin/bdquery/z?d111:HR02194:@@@D&summ2=0&.

42. "America imposes sanctions on 37 companies associated with Iran Shipping Lines," Radio Farda, October 28, 2010, www.radiofarda.com/content/F11_Iran_nuclear_issu_new_US_sanctions_iranian_front_companies/2203262.html.

43. Fact Sheet: U.S. Treasury Department Targets Iran's Nuclear and Missile Programs, Treasury Announces New Sanctions on Iran, Including First Set of Actions in Response to President Obama's Call for Vigorous Enforcement of United Nations Security Council Resolution 1929, Iran Watch, June 16, 2010, www.iranwatch.org/government/US/Treasury/us-treasury-1929implementation-061610.htm.

44. Steven Stanek, "U.S. Senate approves tough new sanctions on Iran," *National*, January 30, 2010, www.thenational.ae/news/worldwide/middle-east/us-senate-approves-tough-new-sanctions-on-iran.

45. Spencer Swartz, "Swiss Firm Halts Its Sales of Gas to Iran," Wall Street Journal Online, January 9, 2010, http://online.wsj.com/article/SB126300336665822669.html.

46. "Halt of gas exports of 10 oil giants to Iran," Khabar Online, June 28, 2010, www.khabaronline.ir/news-71592.aspx.

47. "Details of EU sanctions on Iran were released," BBC News, January 27, 2010, www.bbc.co.uk/persian/iran/2010/07/100727_l38_eu_sanctions_details.shtml.

48. "South Korean bank imposes sanctions," Deutsche Welle, October 7, 2010, www.dw-world.de/dw/article/0,,6087895,00.html.

49. "Iranian traders in Dubai feel the heat of unilateral sanctions," Voice of America, September 24, 2010, www.voanews.com/persian/news/iran-uae-trade-sanctions-us-eu-09-24-10-103717059.html.

50. "Australia: Will implement unilateral sanctions on Iran," Aftab News Network, July 29, 2010, www.aftabnews.ir/vdcbsab85rhbg5p.uiur.html.

51. "Iranian traders in Dubai feel the heat of unilateral sanctions."

52. "Oil production and price drop," Radio Zamaaneh, July 12, 2010, http://zamaaneh. com/analysis/2010/07/post_1533.html.

53. "Interview with Emad Hosseini, spokesman of Islamic Consultative Assembly Energy Committee," Mehr News Agency, July 2, 2010.

54. "OPEC: Iran no more second exporter within organization," Iran Independent News Service, July 19, 2011, www.iranwpd.com/index.php?option=com_k2&view= item&id=1940:opec-iran-no-more-second-exporter-within-organization& Itemid=66.

55. "Russia's Medvedev criticizes Iran sanctions: report," Reuters, June 17, 2010, www.reuters.com/article/2010/06/18/us-nuclear-iran-medvedev-idUSTRE65H 0M720100618http://www.fararu.com/prta06nm.49nwa15kk4.html.

56. "Russia warns U.S. against unilateral Iran sanctions," Reuters, May 13, 2010, www. reuters.com/article/2010/05/13/us-russia-iran-us-idUSTRE64C1SU20100513.

57. "Iran's terms for negotiations—Five major conditions," Mehr News Agency, June 28, 2010, www.mehrnews.com/fa/NewsDetail.aspx?pr=s&query=احمدی‌نژاد&NewsID=110 8482.

58. Michael Theodoulou, "Ahmadinejad resorts to gutter language," National, www. thenational.ae/news/world/middle-east/ahmadinejad-resorts-to-gutter-language#full.

59. "Ahmadinejad as Iran's Deputy Foreign Minister," Radio Farda, March 22, 2011, http:// www.radiofarda.com/content/f3_ahmadinejad_newyork_nuclearsummit/2031332. html?page=2&x=1.

60. "Ahmadinejad defiant ahead of UN nuclear sanctions vote," BBC News, June 8, 2010, www.bbc.co.uk/news/10262088.

61. Ahmadinejad's speech to the gathering of people March 15, 2007; his speech on April 10, 2008 in Mashhad; his speech at a press conference on August 7, 2010; and his speech in New York on his September 18, 2010 visit, Mehr News Agency.

62. "Before we proceed down the nuclear path/Our foreign policy is a determinant in the international arena/Control of inflation is a matter of honor," Mehr News Agency, January 21, 2007, www.mehrnews.com/fa/NewsDetail.aspx?pr=s&query=%D9%82% D8%B7%D8%A7%D8%B1%20%D9%87%D8%B3%D8%AA%D9%87%E2%80 %8C%D8%A7%DB%8C&NewsID=437580.

63. Official Iranian Government website, July 19, 2010, www.dolat.ir/NSite/FullStory/ ?id=191050.

64. "The President inaugurates the Arak heavy water production facility," Mehr News Agency, August 26, 2006, www.mehrnews.com/fa/NewsDetail.aspx?pr=s&query=احمدی‌نژاد News ID=371388.

65. "Details of Iran's conditions for talks/5 important conditions for Iran," Mehr News Agency, June 28, 2010, www.mehrnews.com/fa/NewsDetail.aspx?NewsID=438558.

66. "Iran was among the countries producing nuclear fuel," Mehr News Agency, April 9, 2007, www.mehrnews.com/fa/NewsDetail.aspx?pr=s&query=احمدی‌نژاد&NewsID=467 938.

67. "Beginning of the installation stage of 6 thousand centrifuges/New to be announced tonight," Mehr News Agency, April 8, 2008, http://www.mehrnews.com/fa/NewsDetail.

aspx?pr=s&query=%D8%A7%D8%AD%D9%85%D8%AD%DB%8C%E2%80%8
C%D9%86%DA%98%D8%A7%D8%AF&NewsID=661723.

68. "Beginning of the detailed planning stage of Darkhovin Nuclear Power Plant," Mehr News Agency, October 19, 2008, www.mehrnews.com/fa/NewsDetail. aspx?pr=s&query=احمدنیژاد&NewsID=767801.

69. "Long-range Shahab-3 and Sajil missiles were fired," Fars News Agency, September 28, 2009, www.farsnews.net/newstext.php?nn=8807060418.

70. "Camp of lies," *Kayhan*, http://kayhannews.ir/890319/2.htm#other206-Kayhan-6/ 11/2010.

71. "Ahmadinejad: US directs 'propaganda drama' against Iran with Russia," ISNA News Agency, July 24, 2010, http://isna.ir/Isna/NewsView.aspx?ID=News-1579781&Lang=E.

72. "Relations between Moscow and Tehran get colder by the day," Deutsche Welle, September 28, 2010, www.dw-world.de/dw/article/0,,6052729,00.html.

73. Randi Talbot, "Obama hypes news of Iranian nuclear facility near Qom at G20," United for Peace of Pierce County, September 25, 2009, http://ufppc.org/us-a-world-news-mainmenu-35/9024-news-obama-hypes-news-of-iranian-nuclear-facility-near-qom-at-g20.html.

74. "World Leaders on Sanctions to Halt Iran's Nuclear Weapons Program," Realité EU, June 4, 2010, www.realite-eu.org/site/apps/nlnet/content3.aspx?c=9dJBLLNkGiF&b= 2315291&ct=8023335.

75. "The relations between Nourizadeh and Fatemeh Rajabi," Aftab News, May 7, 2007, www.aftabnews.ir/vdcfyvdv.w6dxmagiiw.html.

76. "The relations between Nourizadeh and Fatemeh Rajabi."

77. "Russia, China congratulate Ahmadinejad on vote win," Reuters, June 16, 2009, www. reuters.com/article/2009/06/16/us-iran-president-sb-idUSTRE55F0YA20090616.

78. "Russia is the enemy of Iran," RIA Novosti, July 20, 2009, http://pe.rian.ru/articles/ digest/20090720/122395850.html.

79. "Russia will not support the final declaration of the Conference on Disarmament in Tehran," Trend News Agency, April 24, 2010, http://fa.trend.az/news/nuclearp/1675743. html.

80. "Weapons purchase from Moscow through Bin Sultan port, if Russia decreases its support for Iran," Mehr News Agency, July 15, 2008, www.mehrnews.com/fa/ NewsDetail.aspx?NewsID=717092.

81. "Russian FM: Committed to preventing military nuclearization in Iran," Doc's Talk blog, October 7, 2008, http://docstalk.blogspot.com/2008/10/russian-fm-committed-to-preventing.html.

82. "Medvedev announced the list of sanctions against Iran," Jamejam Online, September 23, 2010, www.jamejamonline.ir/newstext.aspx?newsnum=100886522751.

83. "Russia 'surprised' by Iran's legal complaint over S-300," *Daily Star*, August 25, 2011, www.dailystar.com.lb/News/Middle-East/2011/Aug-25/Russia-surprised-by-Irans-legal-complaint-over-S-300.ashx#axzz1W3hZ4Trf.

84. "Russian experts flee Iran's dragnet for cyber worm smugglers," Debka File, October 3, 2010.

85. "Russia Sabotaged Iran Nuclear Programme: Report," Agence France-Presse, May 19, 2011.

86. "Will Russia or China be considered as the historical enemy?" Khabar Online, May 31, 2010, www.khabaronline.ir/news-65658.aspx.

87. Michael D. Swaine, "Beijing's Tightrope Walk on Iran," *China Leadership Monitor*, no. 33, June 28, 2010, available at http://carnegieendowment.org/files/CLM33MS.pdf.

88. The most important Chinese contracts in areas of the upstream oil industry are:

    • Yadavaran oil field development project contract worth more than $2 billion with Sinopec China,

    • North Pars gas field development project worth approximately $16 billion with China Sinopec,

    • Phase 11 of the South Pars development project worth $5 billion with China International Oil Company (CNPCI),

    • North Azadegan field development project worth 1.6 billion dollars with China's CNPC,

    • Exploration and development blocks with Garmsar and Chinese Sinopec,

    • Building the second phase of Iran LNG plant with HEFC China,

    • Exploration Project of Golshan and Ferdowsi fields with China,

    • Oil field development project with Kassel Oil Company and China,

    • Offshore Oil Field Development Project with Masjed Soleiman Oil Co. and China (CNPCI).

89. "$50 billion deal with China," *World Economics*, January 28, 2010, www.donya-e-eqtesad.com/Default_view.asp?@=194069.

90. "Russia and China vote in support of the sanctions resolution was based on 'sympathy,'" BBC News, June 14, 2010, www.bbc.co.uk/persian/iran/2010/06/100614_l03_russia_sanctions.shtml.

91. David E. Sanger, "Obama Set to Offer Stricter Nuclear Deal to Iran," *New York Times*, October 27, 2010, www.nytimes.com/2010/10/28/world/middleeast/28iran.html?_r=4&ref=nuclear_program.

92. Glenn Kessler, "Iran talks end with little sign of progress," *Washington Post*, December 8, 2010, www.washingtonpost.com/wp-dyn/content/article/2010/12/07/AR2010120701362.html.

93. "Talks with Iran, intl. opportunity," December 7, 2010, Press TV, www.presstv.ir/detail/154369.html.

94. "Manouchehr Mottaki fired from Iran foreign minister job," BBC News, December 13, 2010, www.bbc.co.uk/news/world-middle-east-11984931.

95. "Iran Replaces Foreign Minister," Fars News Agency, December 13, 2010, http://english.farsnews.com/newstext.php?nn=8909221576.

96. Laura Rozen, "Iran Kremlinology as Ahmadinejad sacks foreign minister," Politico. com blog, December 13, 2010, www.politico.com/blogs/laurarozen/1210/Iran_ Kremlinology_as_Ahmadinejad_sacks_foreign_minister.html.

97. "Iran's 20% Enriched N. Fuel Stockpile Stands at 40kg," Fars News Agency, January 8, 2011, http://english.farsnews.com/newstext.php?nn=8910181207.

98. "Resolutions cannot hinder Iran's progress: Ahmadinejad," Tabnak News, January 18, 2011, www.tabnak.ir/en/news/4485/resolutions-cannot-hinder-iran's-progress-ahmadinejad.

99. Ibid.

100. Nicolas Cheviron and Farhad Pouladi, "Defiant Iran insists on enrichment, talks 'inconclusive,'" Agence France-Presse, January 22, 2011, http://sg.news.yahoo.com/iran-nuclear-wrangling-world-powers-20110120-230821-001.html.

101. Laura Rozen, "International Iran nuclear talks resume in Turkey, as U.S. hand appears strengthened," Politico.com blog, www.politico.com/blogs/laurarozen/0111/International_Iran_nuclear_talks_get_underway_in_Turkey.html.

102. "Iran nuclear talks end in stalemate," *Guardian*, January 22, 2011, www.guardian.co.uk/world/2011/jan/22/iran-nuclear-talks-end-stalemate.

103. Sanger, "Obama Set to Offer Stricter Nuclear Deal to Iran."

104. Shlomo Shamir, "EU offering to okay Iran nuclear program in return for UN supervision," *Haaretz*, www.haaretz.com/news/diplomacy-defense/eu-offering-to-okay-iran-nuclear-program-in-return-for-un-supervision-1.329547.

105. "New details of America's plan for accepting Iranian enrichment and the disputes of the 5+1," Raja News, December 12, 2010, http://rajanews.com/detail.asp?lang_id=&id=72447.

106. "Iran proclaims 'complete domination' over entrance to Persian Gulf," *Haaretz*, February 7, 2011, www.haaretz.com/news/international/iran-proclaims-complete-domination-over-entrance-to-persian-gulf-1.341839.

107. "Iran plans to build several nuclear research reactors: nuclear chief," Xinhua News, April 12, 2011, http://news.xinhuanet.com/english2010/world/2011-04/12/c_13825552.htm.

108. Peter Crail, "Iran Prepares Improved Centrifuges," *Arms Control Today*, April 2011, www.armscontrol.org/act/2011_04/Iran.

109. "Obama Adviser Gary Samore: 'The Ball Is Very Much in Tehran's Court,'" Radio Free Europe/Radio Liberty, April 14, 2011, www.rferl.org/content/interview_samore_russia_iran_us_policy/3557326.html.

110. "Iran to triple enriched uranium output," Press TV, June 9, 2011, www.presstv.ir/detail/183886.html.

111. "IAEA head chides Iran, N. Korea, Syria," United Press International, July 27, 2011, www.upi.com/Top_News/World-News/2011/07/27/IAEA-head-chides-Iran-N-Korea-Syria/UPI-72331311787311.

112. "Iran to triple enriched uranium output."

113. Fredrik Dahl, "Iran shows U.N. official all nuclear sites: envoy," Reuters, Aug 23, 2011, www.reuters.com/article/2011/08/23/us-iran-nuclear-idUSTRE77M6ZW20110823.

114. "Top IAEA Inspector Tours Iranian Atomic Facilities," Global Security Newswire, August 23, 2011, http://gsn.nti.org/gsn/nw_20110823_9080.php.

115. 1.5 kg of UF_6 contains 1 kg of uranium.

116. "Russia Proposes 'Phased' Resolution of Iran Nuclear Standoff," Global Security Newswire, July 14, 2011, http://gsnweb.nationaljournal.com/gsn/nw_20110714_9546.php.

117. "Russia Seeks New Strategy for Iran Talks," Global Security Newswire, February 7, 2011, http://gsnweb.nationaljournal.com/gsn/nw_20110207_4968.php.

118. The plan was discussed in a graduate course at Woodrow Wilson School of Princeton University.

119. "Secretary of Russia's Security Council Due in Tehran mid August," Fars News Agency, August 2, 2011, http://english.farsnews.com/newstext.php?nn=9005110193.

120. "Salehi says will discuss Russia 'step-by-step' plan in Moscow," Mehr News Agency, July 29, 2011, www.mehrnews.com/en/newsdetail.aspx?NewsID=1370328.

121. "Ahmadinejad Welcomes Russia's Nuclear Proposal," Radio Free Europe/Radio Liberty, August 16, 2011, www.rferl.org/content/ahmadinejad_welcomes_russia_nuclear_proposal/24298968.html.

122. "Ahmadinejad accepts a Russian proposal on Iran's nuclear program," All Voices, August 16, 2011, www.allvoices.com/contributed-news/9996835-ahmadinejad-accepts-a-russian-proposal-on-irans-nuclear-program.

123. "Iranian FM: Tehran ready to resume nuclear talks," Associated Press, August 16, 2011.

124. Peter Crail, "Iran's Nuclear Program: An Interview with Iranian Ambassador to the IAEA Ali Asghar Soltanieh," Arms Control Today, October 2011.

125. Semira N. Nikou, "Hossein Mousavian: Iran is Ready to Negotiate—If, Interview with Seyed Hossein Mousavian," Iran Primer, United States Institute of Peace, August 15, 2011, http://iranprimer.usip.org/blog/2011/aug/15/hossein-mousavian-iran-ready-negotiate-if.

126. "Iran launches production of banned carbon fiber," August 27, 2011, www.iranfocus.com/en/index.php?option=com_content&view=article&id=23643:iran-launches-production-of-banned-carbon-fiber&catid=8:nuclear&Itemid=45.

127. "Iran Starts Mass-Production of Home-Made Anti-Armor Rockets," Fars News Agency, August 29, 2011, http://english.farsnews.com/newstext.php?nn=9006070052.

128. Crail, "Iran's Nuclear Program."

129. David E. Sanger, "Easing Stance, Iran Offers Inspectors 'Supervision' of Nuclear Program," New York Times, September 5, 2011, www.nytimes.com/2011/09/06/world/middleeast/06iran.html.

130. Peter Crail, "Iran's Nuclear Program."

131. Louis Charbonneau, "Iran's Ahmadinejad revives nuclear fuel swap offer," Reuters, September 22, 2011, www.reuters.com/article/2011/09/22/us-nuclear-iran-ahmadinejad-idUSTRE78L6F620110922.

132. Ali Vaez amd Charles D. Ferguson, "An Iranian Offer Worth Considering," *New York Times*, September 29, 2011, www.nytimes.com/2011/09/30/opinion/30iht-edvaez30.html.

133. George Stephanopoulos, "Iranian President Ahmadinejad Guarantees Hikers' Release: 'When We Said We Will Release Them, We Will Release Them,'" ABC News, September 20, 2011, http://abcnews.go.com/blogs/politics/2011/09/iranian-president-ahmadinejad-guarantees-hikers-release-when-we-said-we-will-release-them-we-will-release-them.

134. "Freed American hikers arrive in Oman," CNN, September 21, 2011, http://articles.cnn.com/2011-09-21/middleeast/world_meast_iran-hikers_1_sarah-shourd-fattal-and-bauer-cindy-hickey?_s=PM:MIDDLEEAST.

135. "Iran to Start N. Fuel Plate Production in Months," Fars News Agency, October 28, 2011, http://english.farsnews.com/newstext.php?nn=9007270902.

136. "US dismisses Iran's nuclear offer as 'empty promises,'" Agence France-Presse, September 30, 2011, www.google.com/hostednews/afp/article/ALeqM5id8BKfZAlF7E9UJG3uZjl_u6avig?docId=CNG.ef9852b3bf30a3a9a6e5f826fa351e18.481.

137. "Statement on Iran by EU High Representative Catherine Ashton on behalf of the E3/EU+3," September 21, 2011, www.consilium.europa.eu/uedocs/cms_Data/docs/pressdata/EN/foraff/124694.pdf.

138. "Alleged Iran plot referred to UN," *Irish Times*, October 17, 2011, www.irishtimes.com/newspaper/breaking/2011/1017/breaking22.html.

139. Philip Crowther, "Obama urges more Iran sanctions over alleged Saudi murder plot," Reuters, October 14, 2011, www.english.rfi.fr/americas/20111014-obama-urges-more-iran-sanctions-over-alleged-saudi-murder-plot.

140. Ibid.

141. "U.K. imposes sanctions on Iranians," *USA Today*, October 18, 2011.

142. "Allegations of Iran Assassination Plot Referred to UN Security Council," *Eurasia Review*, October 18, 2011, www.eurasiareview.com/18102011-allegations-of-iran-assassination-plot-referred-to-un-security-council.

143. "UN chief Ban sends Iran plot case to Security Council," Reuters, October 17, 2011, http://af.reuters.com/article/worldNews/idAFTRE79G1VF20111017.

144. "Khamenei: Iran 'to unveil 100 US plot documents,'" World Bulletin, November 2, 2011, http://www.worldbulletin.net/?aType=haber&ArticleID=81139.

145. "Iran UN envoy warns of new resolution's aftermaths," Payvand News Service, November 16, 2011, www.payvand.com/news/11/nov/1166.html.

146. "UN Members Condemn Alleged Iranian Plot on Saudi Official," VOA News, November 18, 2011, www.voanews.com/english/news/-UN-Members-Condemn-Alleged-Iranian-Plot-on-Saudi-Official-134162448.html.

147. Fredrik Dahl and Sylvia Westall, "Iran worked on nuclear bomb design: U.N. watchdog," Reuters, November 8, 2011, www.reuters.com/article/2011/11/08/us-nuclear-iran-iaea-idUSTRE7A75N420111108.

148. Natasha Mozgovaya, "U.S. calls UN report on Iran nuclear program 'alarming,' vows further sanctions," *Haaretz*, September 11, 2011, www.haaretz.com/news/diplomacy-defense/u-s-calls-un-report-on-iran-nuclear-program-alarming-vows-further-sanctions-1.394651.

149. Sebastian Moffett and Justyna Pawlak, "EU ministers postpone decision on new Iran sanctions," Reuters, November 14, 2011, www.reuters.com/article/2011/11/14/us-eu-iran-idUSTRE7AD2AE20111114.

150. "U.S. Miscalculates on IAEA Report: Russia Repudiates New Sanctions as 'Instrument of Regime Change,'" Tikun Olam, www.richardsilverstein.com/tikun_olam/2011/11/10/u-s-miscalculates-on-iaea-report-russia-repudiates-new-sanctions-as-instrument-of-regime-change.

151. "REFILE-Russia says UN Iran report to strain nuclear talks," Alert.net, October 25, 2011, http://www.trust.org/alertnet/news/refile-russia-says-un-iran-report-to-strain-nuclear-talks.

152. "New Iran sanctions a 'regime change tool'—Russia," RT Online, November 9, 2011, http://rt.com/politics/iran-sanctions-russia-un-921.

153. Fredrik Dahl and Sylvia Westall, "Big power unity on Iran at stake at UN nuclear meet," Reuters, November 15, 2011, www.reuters.com/article/2011/11/15/us-nuclear-iran-iaea-idUSTRE7AE27620111115.

154. "Israeli army test-fires missile capable of reaching Iran," *Guardian*, November 2, 2011, http://www.guardian.co.uk/world/2011/nov/02/israeli-army-test-fires-missile?intcmp=239.

155. Shubhajit Roy, "India with NAM in slamming IAEA report on Iran," *Indian Express*, September 17, 2010, www.indianexpress.com/news/india-with-nam-in-slamming-iaea-report-on-ir/ 682728.

156. "China rejects new anti-Iran sanctions," Press TV, November 10, 2011, www.presstv.ir/ detail/209333.html.

157. "Amano must answer for Iran report," Press TV, November 13, 2011, http://presstv. com/detail/209942.html.

158. "IAEA report a historic mistake, Iran says," Press TV, November 9, 2011, http://edition. presstv.ir/detail/209099.html.

159. Scott Peterson, "Iran nuclear report: Why it may not be a game-changer after all," *Christian Science Monitor*, November 9, 2011, www.csmonitor.com/World/Middle-East/2011/1109/Iran-nuclear-report-Why-it-may-not-be-a-game-changer-after-all.

160. "Russian scientist denies being 'father' of Iran's nuclear weapons program," Hydrablog, October 10, 2011, http://hydrablog.csusm.edu/2011/11/russian_scientist_denies_being. html.

161. Jason Ditz, "Iranian Parliament Tells Govt to Reduce IAEA Cooperation," AntiWar. com, November 13, 2011, http://news.antiwar.com/2011/11/13/iranian-parliament-tells-govt-to-reduce-iaea-cooperation.

162. "Iran's parliament to discuss means of cooperation with IAEA: lawmaker," Vietnam. net, November 14, 2011, http://english.vietnamnet.vn/en/world-news/15297/iran-s-parliament-to-discuss-means-of-cooperation-with-iaea--lawmaker.html.

163. "Iranian Parliament likely to press gov't to withdraw from NPT," Trend, November 16, 2011, http://pda.trend.az/en/1957724.html.

164. Ali Vaez, "Seyed Hossein Mousavian: The West is pushing Iran in the wrong direction," *Bulletin of the Atomic Scientists*, November 18, 2011, http://thebulletin.org/web-edition/features/seyed-hossein-mousavian-the-west-pushing-iran-the-wrong-direction.

165. Kyle Kim, "UN atomic watchdog passes resolution, Iran says nuclear program won't be stopped," *Global Post*, November 18, 2011, www.globalpost.com/dispatch/news/politics/111118/un-atomic-watchdog-passes-iran-nuclear-program-resolution.

166. Fredrik Dahl and Sylvia Westall, "Powers pressure Iran, IAEA chief 'alerts world,'" Reuters, November 17, 2011, www.reuters.com/article/2011/11/17/us-nuclear-iran-iaea-idUSTRE7AG0RP20111117.

167. "IAEA resolution strengthens our resolve: Iran," *Khaleej Times*, November 18, 2011, http://www.khaleejtimes.com/DisplayArticle09.asp?xfile=data/middleeast/2011/November/middleeast_November454.xml&section=middleeast.

168. "Swiss toughen sanctions against Iran," Swissinfo.ch, November 18, 2011, www.swissinfo.ch/eng/politics/Swiss_toughen_sanctions_against_Iran.html?cid=31590594.

169. Fredrik Dahl and Sylvia Westall, "Iran to boycott Middle East nuclear talks," Reuters, November 18, 2011, www.reuters.com/article/2011/11/18/us-nuclear-iran-zone-idUSTRE7AH27C20111118.

170. Mark Hibbs, "Waiting for Russia's Next Move on Iran," Q&A, Carnegie Endowment for International Peace, November 22, 2011, http://carnegieendowment.org/2011/11/22/waiting-for-russia-s-next-move-on-iran/7nzn.

171. Vaez, "Seyed Hossein Mousavian: The West is pushing Iran in the wrong direction."

172. "New EU sanctions to hit Syria commercial bank, 29 Iranians," Agence France-Presse, October 6, 2011, www.google.com/hostednews/afp/article/ALeqM5iOMVz_eC6l3v9Kc-hvoUWdfzzZ2w?docId=CNG.c05571d1da8b533f5fbbc6407b4da20d.5d1.

173. "Iran: UN human rights expert concerned over judicial abuses," UN News Centre, October 19, 2011, www.un.org/apps/news/story.asp?NewsID=40112.

174. "Human Rights Rapporteur on Iran," VOA News, October 28, 2011, www.voanews.com/policy/editorials/Human-Rights-Rapporteur-On-Iran-132799138.html.

175. "Iran rejects UN report on 'rights abuses,'" *Al Jazeera*, October 20, 2011, www.aljazeera.com/news/middleeast/2011/10/201110205193213355.html; "Iran denies UN report on increasing human rights violations," One Million Voices for Iran, www.speak4iran.org/wordpress/?p=762.

176. "UN resolution on Iran rights gets record votes," Agence France-Presse, November 21, 2011, www.google.com/hostednews/afp/article/ALeqM5h3le83ePfM65U89CCwHkNtGDI3pw?docId=CNG.156c7bd071cf4eb15b665238e235daca.381.

177. Howard LaFranchi, "US targets Iran's central bank as world takes aim at Iran's nuclear program," *Christian Science Monitor*, November 21, 2011, www.csmonitor.com/USA/Foreign-Policy/2011/1121/US-targets-Iran-s-central-bank-as-world-takes-aim-at-Iran-s-nuclear-program.

178. "No to Indiscriminate Sanctions, No to War with Iran," National Iranian American Council, https://secure3.convio.net/niac/site/Advocacy?cmd=display&page=UserActio n&id=189&autologin=true&JServSessionIdr004=kafbpppuw1.app333b.

179. "House Committee Adopts Indiscriminate Sanctions, Anti-Diplomacy Bill," National Iranian American Council, November 2, 2011, www.niacouncil.org/site/News2?page= NewsArticle&id=7687&security=1&news_iv_ctrl=-1.

180. John Glaser, "Senator Proposes New Sanctions on Iran's Central Bank," AntiWar.com, November 17, 2011, http://news.antiwar.com/2011/11/17/senator-proposes-new-sanctions-on-irans-central-bank.

181. "Iran's Ahmadinejad slams European 'puppets' of U.S.," Reuters, November 23, 2011, www.reuters.com/article/2011/11/23/us-iran-sanctions-ahmadinejad-idUSTRE7 AM0ZI20111123.

182. Adrian Blomfield, "Tehran votes to expel Britain's ambassador," *Telegraph*, November 27, 2011, www.telegraph.co.uk/news/worldnews/middleeast/iran/8918875/Tehran-votes-to-expel-Britains-ambassador.html.

183. Douglas Stanglin, "Iranian students storm British Embassy in Tehran," *USA Today*, November 29, 2011, http://content.usatoday.com/communities/ondeadline/post/2011/11/-iranian-students-break-into-british-embassy-in-tehran/1?csp=34news.

184. Flavia Krause-Jackson, "UN Security Council Condemns Attacks on U.K. Embassy in Tehran," Bloomberg/*Business Week*, November 29, 2011, www.businessweek.com/news/2011-11-29/un-security-council-condemns-attacks-on-u-k-embassy-in-tehran. html.

185. Alan Cowell and Rick Gladstone, "Protesters storm British embassy in Tehran," GoUpstate.com, November 29, 2011, www.goupstate.com/article/20111129/ZNYT03/111293006/1051/news01?Title=Protesters-storm-British-embassy-in-Tehran.

186. "Iranian Foreign Ministry expresses regret over British embassy storming," Xinhua, November 30, 2011, http://news.xinhuanet.com/english2010/world/2011-11/30/c_131277828.htm.

187. Natasha Mozgovaya "Obama: Iran won't be allowed to develop nuclear weapons," *Haaretz*, August 12, 2011, www.haaretz.com/news/middle-east/obama-iran-won-t-be-allowed-to-develop-nuclear-weapons-1.400406.

188. Ibid.

189. According to the public relations office of Iran's Atomic Energy Organization (IAEO), the rod has undergone various physical and dimensional tests and has been inserted into the core of Tehran's Research Reactor. The fuel rod has been exposed to radiation of about 1,500 megawatt hours and passed neutron-related tests in terms of radioactivity level and non-leakage of the radioactive materials during initial phases at diverse power levels, the report added. See "Iran produces first nuclear fuel rod," Press TV, January 1, 2012, www.presstv.ir/detail/218778.html.

190. "Underground Iran nuclear enrichment makes diplomatic path suddenly rockier (+video)," *Christian Science Monitor*, January 9, 2012, www.csmonitor.com/USA/Foreign-Policy/2012/0109/Underground-Iran-nuclear-enrichment-makes-diplomatic-path-suddenly-rockier-video.

191. "Iran to install 20% N-plates in 30 days," Press TV, January 29, 2012, www.presstv.ir/detail/223804.html.

192. Ladane Nasseri and Nicole Gaouette, "Iran Says Scientist's Murder Reveals Global Terror Campaign," Bloomberg/*Business Week*, January 17, 2012, www.businessweek.com/news/2012-01-11/iran-nuclear-scientist-killed-in-blast-in-tehran-fars-says.html

193. "Mourners for slain Iran nuclear expert chant against US, Israel amid calls for retaliation," *Washington Post*, January 13, 2012.

194. "Iran blasts US, UK for N-assassination," Press TV, January 11, 2012, www.presstv.ir/detail/220809.html.

195. "US condemns Iranian nuclear scientist killing," *Al Jazeera*, January 12, 2012, www.aljazeera.com/news/americas/2012/01/201211244648837585.html.

196. "Israeli Source: Assassination of Iranian Nuclear Scientist Joint Mossad-MEK Operation," Tikun Olam, January 11, 2012, www.richardsilverstein.com/tikun_olam/2012/01/10/iran-blames-israel-for-assassinating-another-iranian-nuclear-scientist.

197. Michael Brendan Dougherty, "Rick Santorum: Dead Foreign Scientists Are A 'Wonderful Thing,'" (Video), October 27, 2011, www.businessinsider.com/rick-santorum-dead-north-korean-scientists-are-a-wonderful-thing-2011-10#ixzz1mfkDIaFV.

198. Scott Shane, "Adversaries of Iran Said to Be Stepping Up Covert Actions," *New York Times*, January 11, 2012, www.nytimes.com/2012/01/12/world/middleeast/iran-adversaries-said-to-step-up-covert-actions.html?pagewanted=2&_r=2.

199. Ali Akbar Dareini, "Iranian lawmaker: Obama proposed talks; US denies," Associated Press, January 19, 2012.

200. "Le nucléaire est devenu la clé de voûte du nationalisme iranien," *Le Monde*, February 4, 2012.

201. Ibid.

202. Ewa Krukowska and Gregory Viscusi, "EU Agrees to Ban Iran Oil Imports to Target Nuclear Program," Bloomberg, January 23, 2012, www.bloomberg.com/news/2012-01-22/european-union-likely-to-agree-on-iranian-oil-ban.html.

203. Barbara Slavin, "New Sanctions Aimed at Averting Wider Conflict," Inter Press Service, January 25, 2012, http://ipsnews.net/news.asp?idnews=106549.

204. Abdel Fattah Hussein, "U.S. President Barack Obama praised new sanctions announced by the European Union on Monday on Iran," AllVoices.com, January 24, 2012, www.allvoices.com/contributed-news/11368099-us-president-barack-obama-praised-new-sanctions-announced-by-the-european-union-on-monday-on-iran.

205. Julie Pace, "Obama Signs Executive Order Imposing New Sanctions On Iranian Government, Central Bank," Huffington Post, February 6, 2012, www.huffingtonpost.com/2012/02/06/obama-iran-executive-order_n_1257186.html.

206. Vladimir Isachenkov, "Russia: New Sanctions Against Iran Too Stifling," Associated Press, January 18, 2012, available at http://cnsnews.com/news/article/russia-new-sanctions-against-iran-too-stifling.

207. Francis Matthew, "IAEA has proof of Iran's nuclear-related activities," Gulfnews.com, January 27, 2012, http://gulfnews.com/news/region/iran/iaea-has-proof-of-iran-s-nuclear-related-activities-1.972177.

208. "Ayatollah Ali Khamenei gives fiery speech promising retaliation against U.S. for Iran sanctions," *National Post*, February 3, 2012, http://news.nationalpost.com/2012/02/03/ayatollah-ali-khamenei-gives-fiery-speech-promising-retaliation-against-u-s-for-iran-sanctions.

209. David Ignatius, "Is Israel preparing to attack Iran?" *Washington Post*, February 2, 2012, www.washingtonpost.com/opinions/is-israel-preparing-to-attack-iran/2012/02/02/gIQANjfTkQ_story.html.

210. Isachenkov, "Russia: New Sanctions Against Iran Too Stifling."

211. "Russia says would be threatened by Iran military action," Reuters, January 13, 2012, www.reuters.com/article/2012/01/13/us-iran-russia-nato-idUSTRE80C1BI20120113.

212. "Real danger of US strike on Iran: Russia," Daily Nation, January 12, 2012, www.nation.co.ke/News/world/Real+danger+of++US+strike+on++Iran++Russia+/-/1068/1304528/-/vslfs6z/-/index.html.

213. Barbara Slavin, "Obama Administration Edges Toward Iran Regime Change," Inter Press Service, January 11, 2012, http://ipsnews.net/news.asp?idnews=106416.

214. "Ayatollah Ali Khamenei gives fiery speech promising retaliation against U.S. for Iran sanctions."

CONCLUSION

1. Since this book represents an analytical study, it is not right to compare nuclear diplomacies of Ahmadinejad and Khatami because that comparison has been done in various parts of the text. However, since it is not logical to repeat all that material here, this chapter is dedicated to comparison of the two diplomacies from various aspects, and it would be more useful if considered in the general framework of the book's discussion.

2. Jeffrey Goldberg "Did Israel Rule Out a Strike on Iran? (updated)," *Atlantic*, April 10, 2011, www.theatlantic.com/international/archive/2011/04/did-israel-rule-out-a-strike-on-iran-updated/237063.

3. "Majority in U.S. Support Military Action Against Iran," NewsMax.com, June 25, 2003, http://archive.newsmax.com/archives/articles/2003/6/24/221018.shtml; "Poll: Iran not a nuclear threat," CNN World, March 30, 2005, http://articles.cnn.com/2005-03-30/world/iran.poll_1_nuclear-program-nuclear-threat-iran-and-syria?_s=PM:WORLD.

4. Seyyed Hossein Mousavian, *Iran-Europe Relations: Challenges and Opportunities* (New York: Routledge, 2008), 41.

5. Gary C. Gambill and Ziad K. Abdelnour, "Hezbollah: Between Tehran and Damascus," *Middle East Intelligence Bulletin*, vol. 4, no. 2, February 2002, www.meforum.org/meib/articles/0202_ll.htm.

6. Daniel Pipes, "Is Salman Rushdie a Free Man?" Policywatch, October 2, 1998, www.danielpipes.org/5746/is-salman-rushdie-a-free-man.

7. "Report: Iran arrests al Qaeda, Taliban suspects," CNN World, February 14, 2002, http://articles.cnn.com/2002-02-14/world/ret.iran.arrests_1_hamid-reza-asefi-afghanistan-qaeda?_s=PM:WORLD.

8. Lionel Beehner, "Timeline: U.S.-Iran Contacts," Council on Foreign Relations Backgrounder, March 9, 2007, www.cfr.org/iran/timeline-us-iran-contacts/p12806.

"A U.S. Apology: Secretary of State Madeleine Albright delivered a speech on March 17 apologizing for America's role in the 1953 overthrow of Mohammad Mossadegh (a democratically elected prime minister who threatened to nationalize Iran's oil fields) and acknowledged the coup, which installed the shah, "was clearly a setback for Iran's political development." The Clinton administration partially lifted sanctions on Persian rugs, pistachios, and caviar (but not oil and gas). Because Albright's speech ended with a hectoring of Iran's domestic and foreign policies, the theocratic regime in Tehran responded with a denunciation of the goodwill gesture."

9. The Northern Alliance in Afghanistan cooperated with the United States to fight the Taliban and al-Qaeda and were the most important asset inside Afghanistan for the American military operation. Iran had been a chief supporter of the groups making up the Northern Alliance for the previous two decades, from the time of the Soviet occupation of Afghanistan. The Taliban and al-Qaeda, on the other hand, were backed by a Saudi Arabia-Pakistan-US triangle; but after 9/11 American policy changed completely, and the United States was left fighting against its erstwhile proxies with virtually no assets on the ground in Afghanistan. Only after the Northern Alliance had taken Kabul and much of the country from the Taliban was the U.S. military able to establish a successful presence in the country, and only with Iran's cooperation at the early 2002 Bonn Conference was the Karzai administration established as a successor to the Taliban.

10. United Nations General Assembly, "United Nations Year of Dialogue among Civilizations, Report of the Secretary-General," October 16, 2000, www.un.org/documents/ga/docs/55/a55492.pdf.

11. Mousavian, *Iran-Europe Relations*, 209,

12. "Leader has supported a revolution in nuclear management," Farda News, September 22, 2009, www.fardanews.com/fa/news/91630.

13. "Denial of government benefits and continued gossip, destruction not criticism," Fars News, August 23, 2008, www.farsnews.com/newstext.php?nn=8706021267.

14. "Ayatollah Khamenei, Ahmadinejad, and news that was erased," Click (blog), September 3, 2008, www.click20.blogsky.com/1387/06/13/post-259; "Denial of government benefits and continued gossip, destruction not criticism," www.farsnews.com/newstext.php?nn=8706021267.

15. See Abbas Milani, "Iran Primer: The Green Movement," PBS, October 27, 2010, http://www.pbs.org/wgbh/pages/frontline/tehranbureau/2010/10/iran-primer-the-green-movement.html.

16. "Supreme leader: End of the showdown in the streets," Asr Iran, June 19, 2009, www.asriran.com/fa/pages/?cid=75581.

17. "Ahmadinejad's Letter to Bush," *Washington Post*, May 9, 2006, www.washington-post.com/wp-dyn/content/article/2006/05/09/AR2006050900878.html.

18. "Translation of Ahmadinejad's Letter," November 6, 2008, *Washington Post*, www.washingtonpost.com/wp-dyn/content/article/2008/11/06/AR2008110603030.html.

19. Laura Rozen, "White House: Obama received letter from Ahmadinejad," *Politico*, April 17, 2010, www.politico.com/blogs/laurarozen/0410/White_House_Obama_received_letter_from_Ahmadinejad_.html.

20. "Obama sent second letter to Khamenei," *Washington Times*, September 3, 2009, www.washingtontimes.com/news/2009/sep/03/obama-sent-second-letter-to-irans-khamenei.

21. Louis Charbonneau, "Ahmadinejad Wanted Direct Talks with US: ElBaradei," Reuters, February 15, 2011, http://us.mobile.reuters.com/article/topNews/idUSTRE71E5JG20110215?feedType=RSS&feedName=topNews.

22. "Former ambassador denounces Ahmadinejad about the appointment of ambassadors,"Aftab News, December 31, 2010, http://aftabnews.ir/vdciuyaz5t1azv2.cbct.html.

23. "Deputy Minister of Foreign Affairs of the Reformist Government: The sleep that has invaded the diplomatic apparatus today is the biggest pain in the country's diplomatic apparatus/the UAE and some of the Arab countries of the region are the first threat to Iran's national security/the Ministry of Foreign Affairs is lacking a strategic vision of global developments and has been transformed into a Ministry of Advertisement and Propaganda/the apparatus must become the trustee of translation and analysis of all WikiLeaks documents," Parleman News, December 30, 2010, http://parlemannews.com/?n=13948.

24. "Former ambassador denounces Ahmadinejad about the appointment of ambassadors," Aftab News, December 31, 2010, http://aftabnews.ir/vdciuyaz5t1azv2.cbct.html.

25. "U.S. Navy orders use of 'Arab Gulf,'" Press TV, November 27, 2010, http://presstv.com/detail/152838.html. "Actually, "The Arabian Gulf" was used by the U.S. Navy ships when working with Arab host nations. To clarify the issue and later in a press release, it was made clear that the U.S. State Department, the U.S. Navy and the Defense Department continue to use "Persian Gulf" in accordance with the DoD Captioning Style Guide.

26. "Human Rights Council Votes 22 to 7 to Establish Special Rapporteur," International Campaign for Human Rights in Iran, March 24, 2011, www.iranhumanrights.org/2011/03/hrc-rapporteur-res-passed.

27. "Conflicting Reports on Iran's Unemployment Rate," Payvand News, April 7, 2011, www.payvand.com/news/11/apr/1062.html; "Representative of Qazvin: Only 30 percent of the industries are working/The job creation figures of Ahmadinejad are

very far from the reality," Peyke Iran, March 15, 2011, www.peykeiran.com/Content.aspx?ID=30144.

28. "The ratio of Iran's dependence on imports went from 35 percent to 75 percent in 5 years," Mehr News Agency, July 27, 2011, www.mehrnews.com/fa/newsdetail.aspx?NewsID=1368875.

29. Parisa Hafezi and Mitra Amiri, "Iran's rial falls to record low on U.S. sanctions," Reuters, December 31, 2011, www.reuters.com/article/2012/01/03/iran-currency-dollar-idUSL6E8C30JN20120103.

30. "Weapons of Mass Destruction, Bushehr – Background," Global Security, www.globalsecurity.org/wmd/world/iran/bushehr-intro.htm.

31. Mousavian, *Iran-Europe Relations*.

32. Again, by deterrence capability, I mean that Iran would not possess nuclear weapons, but have the option of rapidly building them if faced with an existential threat.

33. "Iran Nuclear Issue, Missed Opportunities," Lecture at Princeton-LISD Seminar, November 13, 2010,

34. James Dobbins, "Negotiating with Iran: Reflections from Personal Experience," *Washington Quarterly*, 33:1, January 2012, www.twq.com/10january/docs/10jan_Dobbins.pdf.

35. "678 Days of Nuclear Crisis management (2003–2005)," Center for Strategic Research of Iran, 2006.

36. Ibid.

37. Dieter Bednarz and Volkhard Windfuhr, "'Egypt's Military Leadership Is Reacting Too Slowly,' SPIEGEL Interview with Mohamed ElBaradei," Spiegel Online, April 19, 2011, www.spiegel.de/international/world/0,1518,757786,00.html.

38. Mohamed ElBaradei, *The Age of Deception* (New York, Metropolitan Books, 2011), 136.

39. Yukiya Amano, "Introductory Statement to the Board of Governors," March 1, 2010, www.iaea.org/newscenter/statements/2010/amsp2010n001.html.

40. Peter Crail, "Iranian Response to LEU Fuel Deal Unclear," *Arms Control Today,* November 2009, www.armscontrol.org/act/2009_11/Iran.

41. Steven Erlanger and Mark Landler, "Iran Agrees to Send Enriched Uranium to Russia," *New York Times,* October 1, 2009, www.nytimes.com/2009/10/02/world/middleeast/02nuke.html.

42. Michael Slackman, "Iran's Politics Stand in the Way of a Nuclear Deal," *New York Times,* November 2, 2009, http://www.nytimes.com/2009/11/03/world/middleeast/03iran.html.

43. "Iran Demands Uranium Exchange Within Borders," *Global Security Newswire,* November 24, 2009, www.nti.org/gsn/article/iran-demands-uranium-exchange-within-borders.

44. "Iran 'starts enriching nuclear fuel to 20%' at Natanz," BBC News, February 9, 2010, http://news.bbc.co.uk/2/hi/8505426.stm.

45. "Iran has produced 40 kg of 20% enriched uranium: local media," Xinhua.net, January 8, 2011, http://news.xinhuanet.com/english2010/world/2011-01/08/c_13682042.htm.

46. "Iran's 20% Enriched N. Fuel Stockpile Stands at 40kg," Fars News Agency, January 8, 2011, http://english.farsnews.com/newstext.php?nn=8910181207.

47. "Ahmadinejad Welcomes Russia's Nuclear Proposal," Radio Free Europe/Radio Liberty, August 16, 2011, www.rferl.org/content/ahmadinejad_welcomes_russia_nuclear_proposal/24298968.html.

48. Hossein Mousavian, "How to Engage Iran: What Went Wrong Last Time—And How to Fix It," *Foreign Affairs*, February 9, 2012, www.foreignaffairs.com/articles/137095/hossein-mousavian/how-to-engage-iran?page=2.

49. Hossein Mousavian, Statement at SOAS University Conference on WMD in the Middle East, 2006.

50. David Jackson, "Obama will be interviewed for audience in Iran," *USA Today*, September 30, 2010, http://content.usatoday.com/communities/theoval/post/2010/09/obama-will-be-interviewed-for-audience-in-iran/1.

51. "Obama interviewed by BBC Persian (as released by the White House)," *Washington Post*, September 24, 2010, http://projects.washingtonpost.com/obama-speeches/speech/418.

52. "Clinton Testifies on Iran Sanctions, Nuclear Enrichment, and the MEK," National Iranian American Council, March 3, 2011, www.niacouncil.org/site/News2?page=NewsArticle&id=7111&security=1&news_iv_ctrl=-1.

53. Samore is special assistant to the president and White House coordinator for arms control and weapons of mass destruction, proliferation, and terrorism.

54. "Obama adviser Gary Samore, 'The Ball is Very Much in Tehran's Court,'" RFE/RL, April 14, 2011, www.rferl.org/content/interview_samore_russia_iran_us_policy/3557326.html.

55. Seymour Hersh, "Iran and the Bomb," *New Yorker*, June 6, 2011.

56. "Nuclear program of Iran," Wikipedia, http://en.wikipedia.org/wiki/Nuclear_program_of_Iran.

57. Mahmoud Ahmadinejad, "The Iranian Nation Is Ready to Negotiate with the United States but Under Equitable Conditions and Mutual Respect," BBC News, February 10, 2009, www.bbc.co.uk/persian/iran/2009/02/090210_he_iran_rev.shtml.

58. "Mahmoud Ahmadinejad congratulated Obama for winning majority vote of the American people and asked him to answer the calls for serious changes in US domestic and foreign policies," *Jam-e Jam*, November 6, 2008, www.jamejamonline.ir/newstext.aspx?newsnum=100953717049.

59. "For the first time following the victory of the Islamic Revolution, representatives of Iran and the United States talked directly on the sidelines of Geneva negotiations. The meeting was held between secretary of the Supreme National Security Council Saeed Jalili and U.S. Undersecretary of State William Burns," Aftab News, www.aftabnews.ir/vdciyqa3.t1arw2bcct.html .

60. Laura Rozen, "Revealed: Recent U.S.-Iran nuclear talks involved key officials (UP-DATED)," Cable, ForeignPolicy.com, January 30, 2009, http://thecable.foreignpolicy.com/posts/2009/01/29/americas_secret_back_channel_diplomacy_with_iran.

61. "Will the Taboo of Direct Talks with U.S. Shatter?" Tabnak, September 30, 2008, http://tabnak.ir/fa/pages/?cid=19797.

62. "Revolutionary leader: If officials are smart, they will not swallow America's tricks."

63. Ben Katcher, "Don't Let Israel Set an Artificial Clock on Negotiations," Race for Iran, December 28, 2009.

64. R. K. Ramazani, "Iran's Independence and the Nuclear Dispute," *Daily Progress*, December 20, 2009.

65. "Overview," American Foreign Policy Project, How to Deal with Iran, Fall 2009.

66. Abbas Maleki, "Iran's Nuclear File: Recommendations for the Future," *Daedalus*, issue 1, volume 139, Winter 2010.

67. "Nuclear Trident renewal underway," Ahlul Bayt Islamic Mission, March 14, 2007, www.islamicdigest.net/v8core/?p=385.

68. Office of the Supreme Leader Sayyid Ali Khamenei, "Iran to break authority of powers that rely on nukes," February 22, 2012, www.leader.ir/langs/en/index.php?p=contentShow&id=9183.

69. The full text of the leader's *fatwa* is available at http://mrzine.monthlyreview.org/2010/khamenei180410.html.

70. "Remarks by the President on United Nations Security Council Resolution on Iran Sanctions," White House, June 9, 2010, www.whitehouse.gov/the-press-office/remarks-president-united-nations-security-council-resolution-iran-sanctions.

71. "IAEA says Iran nuclear accord 'significant step,'" ChannelNewsAsia.com, August 31, 2010, www.channelnewsasia.com/stories/afp_world/view/297067/1/.html.

INDEX

A. Q. Khan's enrichment equipment
    smuggling network, 53, 238, 305
Abbasi Davani, Fereydoun, 26, 28, 405–
    406, 411, 429, 457, 467
Abdullah, Amir, 35–36
Abdullah, King, 248
access
    granting unrestricted, 73
    required beyond NPT, 72
accusations, against Mousavian, 283–284
Additional Protocol
    accepting with reservations, 94
    under both Larijani and Jalili, 291
    equated with 1828 Treaty of
        Turkmenchai, 69
    European approach to the issue of, 109
    high-level Western diplomats urging
        acceptance, 60
    Iran was required to comply with, 251
    no room for negotiations about, 74
    presented as an international obligation,
        75
    resuming provisional implementation
        of, 466

signing considered to be humiliating,
    80
Additional Protocol 2, 469
Afghan refugees, Iran repatriating, 435
aggressive diplomacy, 221, 256
aggressiveness, of the ninth government,
    199–201
Aghazadeh, Gholam Reza, 95, 101, 163,
    207, 233, 237, 253, 332, 335, 344,
    497n8
Ahani, Ali, 402
Ahmadinejad, Mahmoud
    accepting approach laid out in the
        Russian proposal, 409
    accusing former negotiators of "treason"
        and "cowardice," 280
    aggressive policy boosting Iran's
        international standing, 267
    announcing
        final victory in the nuclear case
            (2006), 234–235
        increased speed of uranium
            enrichment, 301–302
        Iran's heavy water facility at Arak

put into operation, 253
production of nuclear fuel on an
industrial scale, 273
response to the P5+1 proposal, 247
willingness to stop producing 20
percent enriched uranium, 412
appointments of, 191
approach idealistic and aggressive, 277
approach to diplomacy directed at
domestic consumption, 394
arguments directly from after 2005
presidential election, 437
assailed Khatami's nuclear policies, 280
on assassinations, 26
attending NPT Review Conference in
New York as only head of state, 394
attending Shanghai summit in Moscow
warmly welcomed by Medvedev, 397
benefits of fuel exchange plan, 358–359
criticisms of past approach, 188–190
defending fuel exchange plan in, 365
differences with Mottaki, 278
diplomacy enabling great powers to
redefine enrichment suspension from
being voluntary to being completely
obligatory, 443
discussion with Mousavian without a
single point of agreement, 187
dismissed his foreign minister on
December 13, 2010, 402
dismissing WikiLeaks as a staged and
worthless psychological warfare
campaign, 8
efforts to improve relations with the
United States unprecedented, 461
elected president, 175
emphasis on promoting a "regional-
based" foreign policy, 191
enjoying international spotlight for his
inflammatory comments, 394
faced with mounting domestic criticism
in winter of 2007, 281
first foreign trip to New York, 207
five propositions for global
disarmament, 378–379

foreign policy, 401, 445
forming temporary blocs with narrowly
defined goals, 385
good news propaganda campaign,
236–237
illusions about and limited
comprehension of complex foreign
policy issues, 394
Iran would not negotiate over its
nuclear rights, 402
isolation of Iran, not believing, 317–318
launching a new project for Iran to
become a non-permanent member of
UN Security Council, 317
letters
to American officials, 83
to supreme leader describing report
as a great victory for Iran, 295
to U.S. presidents, 203, 240, 442
new centrifuge model, 374
news of production of first consignment
of 20 percent-enriched uranium on
February 11th 2010, 367
nuclear policies in line with those of
Ayatollah Khamenei, 441
numerous statements defending a fuel
exchange, 365
Obama, not right person for talks with,
343
opponents mobilized, 454
opposition to suspension for suspension
proposal, 336
ordering production of 20 percent
enriched uranium, 397
policies handing the U.S. and its allies
unprecedented international support,
444
populist and propagandist discourse,
394
positive gestures in a speech to UN
General Assembly, 314
presenting himself as champion of
nationalization of Iran's nuclear
industry, 274

proposal for consortium to manage
Iran's enrichment program, 207–210
reaction to international sanctions and
criticism, 393–396
receiving strong domestic support for
his initiative proposal, 209
rejecting
in advance a new incentive package
prepared by P5+1 in 2008, 306
any moves to even slow down
expansion of enrichment capacity,
311
the Holocaust and creating a great
wave of Iranophobia in the world,
329
relations between Persian Gulf and Iran
at a low point, 36
reorientation of policies toward the East
during presidency of, 400–401
response to new U.S. nuclear strategy,
377
retaliating with each new UN
resolution, 395–396
sanctions no effect on Iran's economy,
20
saying incentives package was a step
forward, 247
scathing rhetoric against Mousavian,
280
speeches
in October 2005 expressing hope
for annihilation of Israel's Zionist
regime, 214–215
addressing General Assembly,
318–320
before Assembly of Experts, 190
on Nuclear Technology Day, 338
provoking three anti-Iranian
resolutions, 320
stressing nuclear rights and
negotiations with America, 347
spoke of UN Security Council
resolutions as "worthless scraps of
paper," 294
statement on Amano, 534n31

stating defiantly that sanctions lost
their efficacy, 261
suggestion for debate or direct
negotiations with Obama, 327
summit meeting of the Shanghai
Cooperation Organization in Beijing,
248
Tehran had thrown away the brakes
and reverse gear of the nuclear train,
265
telling reporters that construction
of a new generation of indigenous
centrifuges was under way, 406
tried utmost to open direct, bilateral
dialogue with United States, 360
unnecessary controversies raised
domestic political costs, 444
unveiling prototypes of four locally
made satellites, 404
on uranium enrichment activities, 270
victory of considered by Europeans as
a symbol of Islamic fundamentalism,
191
Vladimir Putin is playing the American
game, 397
welcoming sanctions by the
international community, 187
Ahmadinejad administration
arresting Mousavian, 36
equally eager for a victory, 358
main propaganda maneuver, 381
making agreement with enrichment
suspension costly and even
impossible, 267
making statements against European
Union, 214
managed to increase Iran's uranium
enrichment abilities, 442
new diplomatic activism by, 263–264
nuclear diplomacy, 433–438
opposing suspension of enrichment
and implementation of Additional
Protocol, 441
ordering creation of ten enrichment
sites on scale of Natanz, 363

package offer, 348
replacing confidence building with
    divergence from Europe, 329
taking seriously possibility of an attack
    on Iran's nuclear facilities, 346
Ahmadinejad period, 185, 454–459
Ahmadinejad's presidency, legitimacy came
    to be questioned, 342
aid programs, suspension of to Iran, 272
air strikes, who should launch, 11
Akhondzadeh, Mehdi, 69
Alami, Akbar, 81
Alborzi, Reza, 488n1
Albright, David, 24
Albright, Madeleine, 547n8
al-Faisal, Saud, 248
Algiers Accord (1981), 23
Alikhani, Ghodratollah, 446
Alimohammadi, Massoud, 25, 367
al-Jubeir, Adel, 414
all options, remaining on the table, 11
alleged studies, on possibility of military
    applications, 289–290
al-Maliki, Nouri, 199
al-Qaeda, 435, 547n9
Alstom Atlantic, 47
Amano, Yukiya
    apologized for mistakes in the past, 29
    attending important meetings of high
        committee, 371–380
    Britain and France pressing to
        report Iran's activities in support of
        development of nuclear weapons, 421
    "credible information that Iran
        engaged in activities relevant to the
        development of nuclear explosives,"
        427
    criticized by Ahmadinejad and
        Soltanieh, 534n31
    criticized for accepting at face value
        Western intelligence information, 418
    emphasizing activities raising serious
        questions, 31
    expressed concern over enrichment to
        20 percent, 366

first report on Iran (2010), 371–373
    identifying Iran along with North
        Korea and Syria as a virtual nuclear
        rogue nation, 405
    meeting with Fereydoun Abbasi
        Davani, 411
    position toward Iran, 344
    report on Iran, 418
    reporting new evidence of possible
        military dimensions to Iran's nuclear
        activities, 405
    second report announcing new cascade
        of centrifuges allowing enrichment up
        to 20 percent, 386
    Soltanieh's comments on, 420
ambassador to Germany (1990–1997),
    Mousavian's time as, 434
American Atoms for Peace initiative, 41
American bloc, turned into a powerful
    minority at IAEA meeting, 68
American government, in tandem with
    IAEA proposing that 80 percent of
    Iran's low-enriched uranium be sent to
    Russia, 356
American hikers, releasing, 412
American influence, over Iran, 40
American Israel Public Affairs Committee
    (AIPAC), 60, 469
American political maneuvering,
    circumventing, 153
American presidential election, 324–328
American superpower, not be afraid to sit
    at negotiating table, 325
Americans
    closer to Mousavian's 2005 proposal,
        404
    portraying Iran as a non-cooperative
        pariah state, 292
Amir Abdullah, negotiations with, 34–35
Amir Kabir-1 satellite, 404
Amiri, Shahram, 368–370
Anglo-Iranian Oil Company, 516n37
Annan, Kofi, 81, 202, 215, 252
anti-tank rockets, production of, 410

Arab allies, pressing U.S. to prevent Iran from acquiring nuclear-weapons capabilities, 68

Arab countries, pressures exerted on Moscow, 398

Arab League Beirut declaration, acceptance of, 64

Arab Spring of 2011, situation changed since, 327–328

Arak Heavy Water Research Reactor, 130

Arak project, regarded as a potential plutonium production reactor, 256

Arbabsiar, Mansour, 414

Ardebili, Hossein Kazempour, 82

Areva, 204

Argentina, nuclear cooperation with Iran, 54

armaments, Russia's delays in supplying to Iran, 399

arrest, of Mousavian on April 30, 2007 on espionage charges, 280

Arvena, France's government-owned nuclear technology group, 255

Asefi, Hamid Reza, 72, 233

Asgari, Hamidreza, 402

Asgarkhani, Abu Muhammad, 81

Ashtari, Ali, 333

Ashton, Catherine, 26, 401, 403, 413

assassination
    of Iranian nuclear scientists, 25, 367–370, 425
    preferable to airstrikes, 426

Atomic Energy Organization of Iran. *See* Iran Atomic Energy Organization (IAEO)

Atoms for Peace, following logic of, 43–44

August 2005 plan, Tehran objections to, 204–205

Australia, 391

axis of evil, 57–58, 63, 65, 436, 496n75

ayatollahs, revulsion toward WMD, 32

Bagheri, Ali, 402

Baidatz, Yossi, 8

Baker, James, 499n23

Baker-Hamilton report, 199

Baldaji, Sirous Borna, 419

Bank of Iran (Bank Markazi), 422

Barak, Ehud, 345, 418, 427

Bauer, Shane, 412

Baztab conservative news website, 189

Beckett, Margaret, 173

behavior change through sanctions option, 16–23

behind-the-scenes dispute, between pragmatic and radical politicians, 306

Beijing. *See* China

Beijing posting, declined by Mousavian, 443

Berman, Howard, 389

Biden, Joseph, 11, 328

bilateral strategic cooperation, promoting, 140

bin Abdul-Aziz, Abdullah, 34

bin Abdul-Aziz, Fahd, King, 35

bin Abdul-Aziz, Nayef, Amir, 35

bin Isa al-Khalifa, Hamad, King of Bahrain, 6

bin Zayed al Nahyan, Abdullah, 7

bin Zayed al Nahyan, Muhammad, Abu Dhabi Crown Prince, 6–7

Biological Weapons Convention, accepted by Iran, 434

bismuth irradiation project, 122

Blair, Tony, 138, 173, 178, 215

Board of Governors' provisional agenda, Iran's case removed from in 2004, 159

Bolton, John, 10, 60, 116–117, 326

Boroujerdi, Alaeddin, 419

BP, ceasing operations in Iran, 391

Brazil
    end of mediation on the Iran nuclear issue, 389
    as an international power defending enrichment rights, 380
    provided to the *New York Times* a secret letter from Barack Obama, 383
    stepped forward to try to revive diplomacy, 455

trying to enhance its international image, 385
Brazil-Turkey nuclear deal, 383
breakout scenario, in the style of North Korea, 254
bridgewire (EBW) detonators, 304
Brill, Eric A., 227
Britain, first state to impose direct sanctions on Iran's Central Bank, 423
Brown, Gordon, 351, 352
Brownback, Sam, 79, 486n43
Brussels Agreement, 126, 127, 128, 131
Buchris, Pinchas, 7
Bunn, Matthew, 334
Burns, Undersecretary of State, 262
Burns, R. Nicholas, 239, 493n51
Burns, William J., 309, 311, 315, 336–337, 339, 351, 402, 454, 462
Bush, George W.
    Axis of Evil list, 496n75
    committed to a diplomatic solution, 244
    labeling Iran a member of axis of evil, 57–58, 436
    letters to, 83
    remarks in an NBC interview, 163
    signed an agreement with Indian Prime Minister, 323
    signing a "non-lethal presidential finding," 23
    vetoed legislation by Democratic lawmakers requesting a schedule for withdrawal of U.S. troops from Iraq, 199
    visit to Europe in 2005, 178
Bush administration
    costly quagmires in Iraq and Afghanistan, 445
    covert program, 23
    decided to increase pressure on Iran in 2003, 60
    not rejecting possibility of a military attack on Iran, 199
    not willing in 2003, 453

under tremendous pressures domestically to pave way for negotiations with Tehran, 199
Bushehr plant, 53, 172, 192
Bushehr reactor, 54, 55

Canada, imposing economic and financial sanctions against Iran, 391
capital, flight of from the country in 2003, 79
carbon fiber, production of, 410
carrot and stick policy, Iran's, 240
Carter administration, 44, 480–481n14
cases, reported to UN Security Council for noncompliance with Safeguards Agreements, 211–212
Ceausescu, Nicolae, 212
Center for Strategic Research, 279, 282, 518n67
Central Bank, sanctioning, 422
Central Intelligence Agency (CIA), 23
Central Treaty Organization (CENTO), 40
centrifuge crisis, 120–121
centrifuge enrichment, restart of at Natanz pilot plant, 220–223
centrifuge installation, Iran slowed pace of, 332
centrifuge production, making fully transparent to IAEA, 467
centrifuge testing, with uranium hexafluoride, 112–113
centrifuges
    advanced (IR-2m and IR-4), 30, 405, 441
    assembly, 134, 138
    avoiding introduction of gas into, 101
    decision to resume assembling immediately, 137
    halt in adding as a political decision, 332
    Iran testing a new cascade of 162, 255
    maximum output of, 275

P-2, 120–121
planning to install 50,000, 332
putting 3,000 more into operation in
    reaction to UN Security Council
    resolution, 263
required at Natanz, 363
secondhand imported, 112
third generation of, 374
cessation, requesting, 451, 452
Chávez, Hugo, 380
chemical attacks, by Saddam's army, 447
chemical technologies and equipment,
    promise to remove all limitations on
    provision of advanced to Iran, 449
chemical weapons, Iraq's use of, 481n31
Chemical Weapons Convention, 434, 448
China
    American politicians realizing power
        of, 196
    companies protected and exempt from
        unilateral U.S. sanctions, 400
    contracts
    in areas of upstream oil industry,
        538n88
    to help develop Iran's oil industry, 400
        with Iran for oil and natural gas, 13
    foreign policy based on development
        advancement, 401
    interest in expanding relations with
        United States, 93–94
    not likely to back a military option
        against Tehran, 197
    not tolerating an Iranian nuclear bomb,
        32–33
    opposed plans by U.S.-led Western
        states to impose tougher UN
        sanctions against Iran, 418
    opposition
        in 2009 to expansion of sanctions
            against Iran, 357
        to a new sanctions resolution, 293
    optimism toward a new package in
        2009, 347
    on periphery of negotiations, 182

    relatively mild stance on Tehran, 67
    showing little desire for new sanctions
        against Iran, 347
    support for sanctions against Iran,
        400–401
    ten-year nuclear cooperation agreement
        in early 1990, 54
    urging United States to talk with Iran,
        33
    warned IAEA against publishing 2011
        report, 417
    withdrew offer to sell Iran a nuclear
        reactor in 1991, 54
Chirac, Jacques, 138, 163, 164, 178, 215,
    253
Churkin, Vitaly, 319
civil nuclear program, EU support for
    development of Iran's, 204
civilian aircraft, blocking overdue upgrades
    of Iran's, 423
clandestine action, against Iran's nuclear
    facilities, 23, 28
clandestine negotiations, Ahmadinejad
    bitterly criticizing, 277
clandestine programs, rumors flying about
    Iran's, 133
Clapper, James, 461
Clash of Civilizations discourse, following
    9/11, 78
Clawson, Patrick, 426
Clinton, Bill, 55
Clinton, Hillary, 11, 19, 24, 27, 331, 357,
    361, 382, 407, 422, 425, 458
CNN documentary, including satellite
    images of three nuclear sites, 58
Cold War, similarity with current standoff,
    194
Cold War alliance system, of the U.S., 40
Committee on Multilateral Approaches to
    the Nuclear Fuel Cycle, 155
competition, with other regional power, 50
comprehensive deal, as possible and
    essential, 37

Comprehensive Nuclear Test Ban Treaty,
Iran accepted, 434
Comprehensive Safeguards Agreement
Articles 18 and 19 of, 211
failure to observe provisions of, 65
with IAEA, 58
required Tehran to notify agency
inspectors of existence of a site, 352
compromise, chance for, 164–165
computer sabotage program, covert, 24
concessions, given by Iran to Europe, 160
conciliatory approach, to the September
2003 resolution, 84
confidence-building process, 135, 451
confrontational approach, to the
September 2003 resolution, 80–81
connection, between nuclear activities and
weapons production, 371
conservative factions, rose to power in
Iran, 433
consortium
establishing to manage fuel-cycle
activities within Iran, 466
proposed with other countries on Iran's
enrichment activities, 208
contamination crisis, 122
continuity in policy, between Bush and
Obama administrations, 458–459
conversion process, 113–114
cooperative partnership, with Iran, 33
Coredif Company, dissolution of, 53
Council of Guardians, 340
countries, losing patience with Iran, 422
covert actions, conducted against Iran's
nuclear facilities and scientists, 444
crisis, strategies in response to, 80–86
crisis management, Tehran successful in,
159
crisis resolution strategy, formulating,
98–99
criticism, high-water mark of, 190
Crowley, P. J., 349
crude oil prices, 1971-1974, 480n7
currency (rial), experiencing drop in value,
19

cyber warfare, 24, 28, 333, 444

Dagan, Meir, 7, 27, 333
Dalton, Richard, 228
Danilenko, Vyacheslav, 419
Darkhoein oil field, 46
Darkhovin
360-megawatt power plant in, 324
design stage for a 360-megawatt nuclear
reactor at, 396
Daudzai, Muhammad Omar, 7
Dauth, John, 60
Davani, Fereydoun Abbasi, 26, 28, 405–
406, 411, 429, 467
Davies, Glyn, 348
Davutoglu, Ahmet, 382
de Rynck, Stefaan, 201
deadlock on nuclear issue, result of
miscalculations, 460
"Death to Russia," 398
decision, to enrich to 20 percent, 365–367
demand, for Iran to suspend initiation of
uranium enrichment at Natanz facility,
68
détente policy, of Hashemi Rafsanjani, 431
deterrence, 375, 447
development program, focused on next-
generation technology (IR-2m), 32
dialogue
of civilizations, 57
in mutual respect, 63
policy of, 57
diplomacy, failures of, 4
diplomatic activism
by Ahmadinejad team, 263–264
by Turkey and Brazil under way for
months, 380
diplomatic activity, flurry of (2007), 264
diplomatic approach, of former nuclear
team, 267
diplomatic blitz, against Iran, 272
diplomatic consultations, in regard to P5+1
plan in 2006, 248
diplomatic efforts, in early 2005, 163
diplomatic negotiations, with Tehran, 325

diplomatic process, created time for Iran, 432

diplomatic solution option, 32–33

diplomats, criticized by the new government, 209

direct talks, with Tehran to facilitate solutions to three major problems, 325

disarmament, proposed working group, 65

Disarmament Conference, held April 17-18, 2010, in Tehran, 398

disarmament treaties, remaining a party to, 451

discontent, with bizarre language Ahmadinejad uses when representing Iran, 394

Dobbins, James, 21, 31, 450, 476n80

Dodd, Chris, 389

domestic and foreign situation, of Iran in September 2003, 75–79

domestic political disputes, virulent at time of crisis, 77

domestic power generation, nuclear technology for, 42

domestic sparring, impacting Iran's ability to conduct coherent foreign policy, 169

double standards, ending, 468–469

double suspension, ElBaradei's new proposal for, 296–297

double-dealing strategy, of unconditional support for Israel, 457

Douste-Blazy, Philippe, 202, 215, 261, 511n98

dry enrichment, plan for, 265

Dunn, Michael, 7

E3+3, defined, 509n63

Eastern bloc
approach to the September 2003 resolution, 83–84
broad-based negotiations with parallel to diplomacy with the West, 115
concept left over from Cold War diplomacy, 86
decided to agree to Resolution 1803, 300

negotiations with, 86–87
profiteer powers without strong strategic bonds, 87

economic cooperation, proposed working group, 65

economic recession, put to an end in Iran in 2005, 181

Eerkens, Jeffrey, 45, 50

Egypt, failed to disclose past nuclear activities, 22

eighth mistake, made by the West, 453

Einhorn, Robert, 403, 408

ElBaradei, Mohamed
on 2006 negotiations, 253–254
February 2008 report, 289, 295–298
announcing a draft agreement about enrichment of Iranian uranium, 361
announcing that Iran had acquired enrichment technology in 2003, 438
attack on Iran as "an act of madness," 12
calling for a five-year suspension in 2005, 177
calling for suspension of Iran's fuel-cycle activities, 101
criticized by U.S. and Israeli press, 292
demanding information from Iran on polonium experiments, 121
describing Iran's positions as discouraging, 362
devising a proposal in 2009 whereby Iran would receive fuel for the Tehran Research Reactor, 454
distinction between purely technical definitions and political demands, 106
emphasized nuclear standoff could still be resolved, 261
emphasized success of cooperation between Tehran and IAEA, 295
freeze-for-freeze initiative in mind, 255
under heavy pressure from the United States and EU on suspension, 124
informing Americans and Europeans of Khamenei's position, 291

initiative for a peaceful resolution
scuttled by Washington-London axis
in 2008, 297

instructed to report on Iran's
compliance with UN's March 28
request, 238–239

Iran already mastered enrichment,
517n48

Iran wanting to engage in talks directly
with United States, 360

lamented West's refusal to compromise,
453

Larijani meeting with, 276

legality of Resolution 1696, 251

limited definition of suspension in
October 2003, 149–150

maintained a balanced and independent
position, 385–386

major legal and technical issues largely
resolved, 180

meetings
with Ayatollah Khamenei, 290–291
with Iran's chief nuclear negotiator,
488n6

mentioning issues related to origins of
contamination, 135

message directly to President Bush in
March 2004, 125

message from Ahmadinejad as ready to
engage in bilateral negotiations, 349

multilateral nuclear approaches
committee, 155

national pride stimulated by policy of
isolation and sanctions, 21

needed to assess nature of Iranian
program, 141

no evidence that Iran is weaponizing,
31

opposition to attempts to clarify nature
of Iran's program, 292

opposition to report to extraordinary
meeting as a legal trap for Iran, 222

on positions and styles of Straw and
Sawers, 173

preparing to step down after serving
three terms as IAEA director general,
344

proposing Iran suspend its enrichment
program (January 2007), 263–264

questioning legality of referral of
Iran's nuclear dossier to UN Security
Council, 230

reaction to Iran's agreement with, 293

recognizing Iran's commitment to
resolving nuclear issue, 164

referral to Security Council based on
search of United State and its allies
for a legal argument, 212

reports
on March 13, 2007, 275
on May 26, 2008, 303–305
September 2008, 316–317
for the March 2009 meeting of the
Board of Governors, 334
to Board of Governors on August 9,
2005, 205
to IAEA Board November meeting
(2005), 218–220
on implementation of Safeguards
Agreement in Iran, 65, 116
Iran's new government shown
flexibility in talks with IAEA, 241
on Iran's nuclear program for
December 2008 meeting of Board
of Governors, 331
on latest developments in the
implementation of nuclear
safeguards in Iran, 271–272
reopening of Isfahan facility, 179
to UN Security Council, 253

requesting Iran resolve questions related
to alleged military studies, 332

resented Security Council passing
Resolution 1803, 301

Salehi meeting with, 71

Salehi's close and friendly relation with,
72

seeing Resolution 1696 as misguided,
252

suspension for suspension proposal, 336

in Tehran on October 16, 2003, 100

telephone conversation with Obama, 356

United States refusing to allow Areva deal with Iran, 204

visits
> to Iran delayed, 59
> Natanz facility in early 2003, 450
> Tehran again in 2003, 68

welcomed Tehran's cooperation with IAEA in 2003, 59

working behind scenes with P5+1 members for a new offer for Iran, 296

working with Russians on a new compromise rejected by Americans, 235

eleventh mistake, made by the West, 457

Elham, Gholamhossein, 277

empowerment, of Iran as a major regional player, 266

engagement policy, Obama's, 327

enriched uranium
> described, 515n28
> exporting, 467
> reserves, 354
> transfer of, 356

enrichment
> asking Iran to suspend as breach of Article IV of Non-Proliferation Treaty, 249
> Board of Governors calling on Iran to suspend, 73
> in Iran as a redline for the United States, 165
> Iran mastered capability of 20 percent, 441
> limiting during a period of confidence building, 467
> limiting to 5 percent, 412
> as more than a matter of mere face-saving in Iran, 343
> no international law forbidding, 228

no Iranian politician can risk surrendering, 460

partial suspension irked Iran's leaders across the board, 441

participation of foreign private and state-run bodies in, 270

passing point of no return on, 237

program
> Iran determined to have a domestic, 220
> proposed plan to transfer to Russia, 233

reported in Shiyan, east of Tehran, 492n52

restarting unilaterally resulting in Iran's refferal to UN Security Council, 460

rights to inalienable under the NPT, 162

shifting from central Iranian city of Natanz to Fordow in Qom, 406

sites
> Iran's secret at Qom, 530n41
> suspension of building ten new, 411–412

suspending based on ElBaradei's definition, 102

suspension
> Tehran's reneging on, 137
> as voluntary, 158–159
> as a voluntary and temporary confidence-building measure, 151
> as a voluntary measure, 119
> of uranium, 228
> without agreement of international community, 268

enrichment of uranium-235, increased from 5 percent to 20 percent, 373

enrichment-related activity, calling on Iran to suspend all, 213

Entezami, Hossein, 221, 222

Erdogan, Recep Tayyip, 363, 380, 382

Erekat, Saeb, 216

espionage and covert action option, 23–30

Etemad, Akbar, 45, 50, 51

EU (European Union)

in 2003 dominated by two separate axes: London-Washington and Paris-Berlin, 90

adopting wide-ranging unilateral sanctions, 391

approved a ban on oil imports from Iran starting July 1, 2012, 426

breaching obligations of the Brussels Agreement, 134

confidence-building process with, 268

contradictory inclinations, 89–91

engagement with, 86

freezing assets of Iranian Central Bank in Europe, 426

increasing cooperation with, 433

interaction with potentially deepening transatlantic divide, 87

leaders condemning Ahmadinejad's remarks, 215

letter to ElBaradei on decision to resume activities at Isfahan facility, 201

missed a great opportunity during Rouhani period and Khatami presidency, 453

missing many opportunities for face-saving solution during nuclear talks, 178

not willing to accept Iran's right to peaceful nuclear technology, 109

proposing new incentive package to Iran, 240–250

ratified new sanctions against Iran, 308

reaction to President Bush's remarks in an NBC interview, 163

reasons for unwillingness to close Iran's nuclear case, 132–134

rejected Russian plan, 409

rift inside, 102–103

sanctioning 29 Iranian officials accused of human rights violations, 421

threatening punitive sanctions, 243–244

timing and acceptability of proposals (2005), 171

urging Iran to cease nuclear activities, 103

wanting to mend "Germany-France-Britain" triangle, 100

war in Iraq driving a wedge through, 485n24

welcoming Russia's proposal, 217

EU3

absence of the U.S. frustrating negotiations with Khatami team, 440

agreeing for first time to include Iran's representatives in consultations, 158

ambassadors presenting comprehensive package of incentives on August 5, 2005, 175

asking Iran on May 10, 2005, to continue suspension, 170

calling for indefinite suspension and to totally desist from building a heavy-water research reactor (August 2005), 203

complicated and difficult negotiations with, 126–127

continued determination to bring case back to normalcy, 129

deciding to end negotiations with Iran after restart of activities at Isfahan uranium conversion facility, 214

failure to abide by Brussels Agreement because of pressure from the United States, 132

general directors negotiations on draft agreement, 102

goal of dissuading Tehran from continuing fuel-cycle activities, 238

ministers decided to end the negotiation, 102

ministries, 100

more willing to look toward a peaceful solution, 293

not accepting 20 centrifuges to function for lab experiments in Paris Agreement, 149

plan (October 2004), 145–147
pressured by Americans, 492n48
proposed elements of a nuclear deal in
    2005, 165–166
public relations situation of, 117
reasons for Iran's rejection of their
    proposal, 147
replaced by P5+1, 185
replying to letter on resumption of
    negotiations between Iran and
    Europe, 219
seven points to agree on, 148
sources of friction between Iran and,
    105
strategic mistake in postponing
    negotiations, 453
transition from to P5+1, 244
treating harshly during negotiations,
    128
unrealistic impression that it could
    pressure Iran into long-term
    suspension of uranium enrichment,
    439
EURATOM (European Atomic Energy
    Community), not showing centrifuges,
    410
Eurodif, provision of enrichment services,
    47
Europe
    dawdling in cooperating with
        Khatami's government, 186
    disillusioned by Iran's obstinacy, 247
    frustrated with Washington's
        unilateralism, 99
    as main political partner, 191
    major creditor of reconstruction of
        Iran, 438
    not opposed to peaceful nuclear
        program for Iran, 241
    seeking a way to pursue nuclear
        negotiations (2004), 145
    on the verge of accepting Tehran's
        enrichment activities in 2005, 169
European bloc
    in 2003 IAEA meeting, 67

negotiations with, 86–87
    reasons for focusing diplomacy more
        on, 86–87
European countries, turning into top
    economic partners, 191
European draft resolution, against the
    Brussels Agreement, 135
European opposition, to reporting Iran to
    UN Security Council, 152
European package, proposed in 2005,
    175–179
European plan (2006), 242–243
European policies, change in, 328–330
European strategy, rhetorical emphasis on,
    99
Europeans
    believing Iran discovered to be
        noncompliant in 2003, 210
    not opposing enrichment on a
        laboratory scale, 186
    salvaging diplomacy with, 139
expansion of capacities approach, 191
Expediency Council, 518n67
exploding bridgewire (EBW) detonators,
    304, 372, 416

Fajr (Dawn) satellite, 404
Fattal, Joshua, 412
fatwa
    against all weapons of mass destruction,
        32, 378
    banning use or production of nuclear
        weapons, 313
    Khomeini rejected PMOI request for a
        fatwa, 483n3
    prohibiting production, storage, or use
        of nuclear weapons, 465
    of supreme leader on nuclear weapons,
        466
Fazli, Ali, 341
fear and hostility, toward Iran, 7
fifth and the last package, proposed by
    Mousavian, 172
fifth mistake, made by the West, 450

financial transactions worldwide, unilateral sanctions inflicting major blow to Iran's, 391
firm guarantees, 161–162, 164, 168, 177
Firouzabadi, Hassan, 377
first mistake, by the West, 447
Fischer, Joschka, 103, 163, 202
fissile uranium, in nuclear weapons, 515n28
Fitzpatrick, Mark, 23–24, 333, 364
Fleming, Melissa, 117
Focus (German magazine), 276
Ford, Gerald R., 44, 45, 51
Fordow facility
    declared to be in compliance with IAEA regulations, 351
    Iran's construction of, 372–373
    near Qom, 441
    news of in September 2009, 350
    suspension of construction of requested, 362
foreign citizens, arrest of, 7
foreign exchange reserves, Iran's high, 19
Foreign Ministry of Iran, 187, 214, 442
foreign policy
    Ahmadinejad's radical strategy, 187
    scene of an exhausting struggle, 78
Foreign Policy Committee, of the Supreme National Security Council, 279
foreign scientists, hired by IAEO as advisers, 43
former nuclear negotiating team
    approach to suspension, 267–271
    negotiations by, 315
    under the oversight of Supreme National Security Council committee, 280
    two redlines, 202
fourth mistake, by the West, 449
fourth plan, offered by Iran's negotiating team on March 23, 2005, 166–168
Fox News, 486n43
Framatom, 46, 47
framework, for a new strategy in dealing with nuclear issue, 97

"Framework for Mutual Guarantees" plan, 268
framework of mutual guarantees, plan for a, 139–140
France, 46, 261, 357
Frattini, Franco, 366
Freedom Watch, neoconservative group, 17
freeze on assets, in Resolution 1757, 260
freeze to freeze initiative, Larijani-Solana negotiation on, 253–256
French, freezing Iranian assets after 1979, 53
French consortium, canceled agreement in June 1979, 47
French Foreign Ministry, diplomatic delegation of the EU3 led by, 102
fuel cycle, issue never negotiable, 162
fuel-cycle committee, 155–156
fuel exchange agreement, rejected by Tehran, 362
fuel exchange plan, benefits for Iran, 358–359
fuel production, Iran's progress in, 456
fuel rods, transferring first to Iran, 361

G8, 62, 145
gas centrifuge program, started in 1985, 53
gas test crisis, 123
Gates, Robert, 6, 352, 366
Gatilov, Gennady, 417
Geithner, Timothy, 6
Geneva, talks in (2010), 401–402
Geneva plan, internal opposition in Iran, 362
geopolitics, focus on soft power and balance of influence, 445
Geraghty, Timothy J., 14–15
Germany, 53
Gibbs, Robert, 367, 382
Giuliani, Rudy, 18
Glencore International, ceasing operations in Iran, 391
global attention, to need for WMD disarmament by Israel, 182

global community, interaction with deemed necessary to build confidence, 85

global public opinion, turned sharply against Iran, 445

Goldschmidt, Pierre, 71

good copy/bad cop routine, from Europe and United States, 163

good news propaganda campaign, making international community more suspicious, 237

goodwill for goodwill, formula proposed by the U.S., 448

Graham, Lindsey, 10

grand agenda, phased, 464–469

grand bargain
approach to September 2003 resolution, 82–83
overtures to United States, 242
with Tehran, 326
with the United States, 125

Green Movement, 17, 328

green salt, 304

Group of 77 (G-77), 526n85

Guldimann, Tim, 63, 65, 450, 484n18

Gulf Cooperation Council, 192

Haass, Richard, 17

Hadley, Stephen, 10

Hague, William, 424

Hakim, Abdul Aziz, 235, 248

Hamilton, Lee, 499n23

Hammer, Mike, 403

hard-line radical Principlists, 433

hard-liners in Iran, 77, 169, 454

Hashemi, Mojtaba Samareh, 277

hawks, in Washington and Tel Aviv, 182

heavy-water production, at Arak, 58

heavy-water research reactor, 146

Heinonen, Olli, 30, 302, 304, 405

Hermes Company, 181, 438

Hersh, Seymour, 31

Herzog, Michael, 10

Hizbollah, rearmed by Iran, 14

high committee, headed by secretary of the Supreme National Security Council, 95

high voltage detonator firing equipment, testing of, 304

highly enriched uranium (HEU), 489n18, 492n41, 515n28

high-quality uranium, in the Saghand region of Yazd province, 53

Hill, Chris, 252

Hizbollah of Lebanon, 435

Hohwü-Christensen, Steen, 228

Holocaust, Ahmadinejad denying, 329

Hong Lei, 418

Hosseini, Pirouz, 500n38

Hosseini, Seyed Mohammad Ali, 263

Hosseinpour, Ardeshir, 25, 368

hostilities, between Iran and the United States, 2

Howard, John, 163

Hu Jintao, 248, 375

human rights, new resolution on, 421–422

human shield, EU3 engagement saving as, 103

humanitarian efforts, by Iran leading to release of all Western hostages in Lebanon, 448

Hussein, Saddam
encouraging to attack Iran, 437
Iran rejecting secret overtures from, 194
Iran's moderate foreign policy facilitating downfall of, 438
proposed cooperation between Baghdad and Tehran, 435
started Iran-Iraq war, 12
support for in his eight-year war against Iran, 447
United States supporting during Iran-Iraq war, 52
West's history of supporting, 436

IAEA. See International Atomic Energy Agency (IAEA)

IAEO. See Iran Atomic Energy Organization (IAEO)

ideological advancement, as Iran's foreign policy after 1979 revolution, 401

Ignatius, David, 427

imports, dependence on, 446

indefinite suspension, wording used for, 246

India

    agreement to supply Iran with a 10-MW research reactor, 54

    not forced by the West to join the NPT, 457

    not signing NPT, 261, 323, 436

    nuclear cooperation with, 436

    nuclear test by, 44

    P5+1 countries maintaining relations with, 468

industrial-scale centrifuges, Iran's plan to commission, 269

inflexible policies, on part of the United States, 325

initiative, by Ahmadinejad, 208

inspections, beyond the Safeguards Agreement and the Additional Protocol, 213, 452

Institute for Science and International Security (ISIS), 24

instructions, regarding machining of uranium metal into hemispheres, 238

interactive diplomacy, of Khatami, 431

International Atomic Energy Agency (IAEA)

    asking Tehran to extend nuclear suspensions in 2004, 124

    aware of major aspects of Iran's nuclear activities, 111

    Board of Governors

        analysis of resolution on Iran (2006), 231–232

        announcing extraordinary meeting February 2, 2005, 220

        calling for an extraordinary meeting of (2005), 205–206

        calling on Iran to undertake and complete all necessary corrective measures, 118

        calling on Iran to undertake and complete the taking of all necessary corrective measures, 136

        demands different from Security Council's, 293

        first Board resolution (September 2003), 71–75

        interval leading up to November 2004 session, 157

        meeting September 2003, 72

        meeting November 2003, 114, 115

        meeting March 2004, 127

        meeting June 14, 2004, 136

        meeting September 13, 2004, 141

        meeting November 26, 2009, 362

        referring Iran's case to UN Security Council, 225–233

        requests acknowledged to be voluntary, 226–227

        resolution (2003), 1, 75

        resolution September 2003, 126

        resolution November 2003, 117–119

        resolution March 2004, 129–131

        resolution September 2004, 141–142

        resolution November 2004, 119, 158, 269–270, 286

        resolution September 2005, 210–214, 286

        resolution November 2011, 420

        statement requesting only that Iran suspend introduction of gas into centrifuges, 106

        three-day extraordinary meeting on Iran's nuclear issue (2006), 226

        unprecedented prolongation of meeting, 128

breaking the rules of the game, 419–420

concerns

    about nature of Iran's nuclear program, 66

    regarding possible military dimensions to Iran's nuclear program, 416 concluding that Iran's explanation about foreign origin of highly enriched uranium contamination likely true, 113

confirmed that there was no evidence of diversion of Iran's declared material, 453

confirming Iran's intention to install two 164-machine cascades of centrifuges, 405

cooperating with on removal of all remaining questions about past nuclear-related activities, 466

cooperation with as tactical, 111

"credible information that Iran engaged in activities relevant to the development of nuclear explosives," 427

director general
   critical report on implementation of NPT Safeguards Agreement in Iran, 127
   persuaded that the term "noncompliance" should not be applied to Tehran's past failures or breaches, 116
   report on the implementation of NPT Safeguards Agreement in Iran issued June 1, 2004, 135

goal to persuade to support Iran's corrective measures and prevent characterization of past activities as noncompliance, 116

informed of limited laboratory activities with plutonium, 114

inspectors
   allowed access into Iran, 229
   allowed access to new locations inside Parchin military site, 216
   barred from traveling to Tehran, 263
   information gathered by used to create computer viruses and facilitate sabotage, 28

reporting noncompliance, 229
   to Romania at request of new government, 212

invitation to Iran to become a member of fuel-cycle group in extended December 2004, 161

Iran's cooperation with under work plan, 289

Iran's remarkable progress in developing nuclear fuel cycle not possible without testing centrifuges or introduction of UF_6, 100

Iran's technical and legal interactions with, 76

new Director General, 344–347

93+2 Additional Protocol, 58

not able to confirm Iran's nuclear activities as totally peaceful, 207

not informed of construction of facilities at Natanz, 58

obtained information about Iran's experiments with polonium, 121

owning 10 percent of Eurodif's stocks, 47

publicizing identities of Iranian nuclear officials, 29

report on Iran (2003), 65

reports
   content leaked to the media, 420
   on possible military dimensions, 416–421

request for cooperation beyond Comprehensive Safeguards Agreement and Additional Protocol, 74

Tehran continuing to have dialogue and cooperation with, 396

international community
   following U.S. lead and implemented own unilateral sanctions, 391
   no authority to force any country to accept a treaty, 74
   slapping Iran with devastating economic sanctions, 444

views on Iran's nuclear activities, 160
international companies and foreign
    subsidiaries of American companies,
    cutting ties with Iran, 388
international concern, over nuclear
    proliferation, 46
International Conference on Drug Abuse
    and Illicit Trafficking in 2003, 62
international consortium for uranium
    enrichment, proposed establishment of,
    270–271
international cooperation, on Iran's nuclear
    program, 49
international criticism, of Iran on grounds
    of human rights violations and
    terrorism, 445
international engagement, policy of, 57
International Institute for Strategic Studies
    (IISS), 333, 494n59
international investments, plans to attract
    stymied in 2003, 79
international isolation, of Iran, 317
international media, misinterpreting
    Ahmadinejad's remarks, 215
international meetings, in 2005, 170
international nuclear cooperation, after
    Islamic revolution, 52–55
"International Nuclear Disarmament
    Conference," Tehran organized on
    April 17, 2010, 378
international peace and security, Iran's
    nuclear activities not constituting threat
    to, 160
international pressures
    on Iran in 2003, 69
    reducing before IAEA Board's meeting
    (2005), 217
international public opinion, stacked
    against Iran, 78
international reaction
    to the September 2005 resolution, 213
    to Ahmadinejad's speech, 215
Iran
    agreeing to talk directly to United
    States, 235

allied with movements throughout the
    Middle East, 12
among first countries to condemn 9/11
    terror attacks, 435
approach to U.S. security objectives, 2
capability to spread conflict, 12
chief supporter of groups comprising
    the Northern Alliance, 547n9
commercial exchanges with Latin
    American countries, 381
commitment to refrain from
    constructing further heavy-water-
    moderated research reactors, 467
condemned terrorist attacks of
    September 11, 2001, 57
conflicting assessments of nuclear
    program and capability, 8
cooperated with Afghan opposition and
    United States to rout the Taliban, 435
cooperating extensively with Iraq's new
    government after fall of Saddam, 435
decided to temporarily halt all talks
    with EU3 (September 2004), 144
decision to cease voluntary
    implementation of provisions of
    Additional Protocol, 239
defense spending a small fraction of
    Israel's, 12
delaying response simply to buy time,
    248
demanding LEU be exchanged at the
    same time as fuel was delivered, 455
diplomats believing that sending Iran's
    case to the UN Security Council was
    a political bluff, 221
exchange of 1,200 kilograms of low-
    enriched uranium for fuel for Tehran
    Research Reactor, 397
hiding progress of nuclear program, 14
as a hostile regional power from U.S.
    point of view, 88
image of in Western public opinion, 78
incorrect assessments of extent and
    severity of the crisis, 77

insistence on enriching uranium on its
own soil, 463
key role in establishing stability and
peace in Iraq and Afghanistan, 197
limited attack on, 197
membership on multilateral approaches
committee, 180
moderates and reformers seeking to
resolve conflicts with the West, 433
new missile tests by, 294
new offer in 2009, 347–350
not accepting any unilateral obligation,
137
not made a single attack against
United States or Israel since the 1979
revolution, 29
not threatening its neighbors, 31
not undertaking non-peaceful nuclear
activities, 112
offered a new package in 2008, 302
only country referred to Security
Council in line with Article III of
IAEA Statute, 212
opting to negotiate with Germany,
France, the United Kingdom, and
Russia, 99
plan to process natural uranium
yellowcake into UF_6 at the Isfahan
conversion facility, 217
political relations with Europe grew
consistently colder, 330
potential of military attack on, 346
refusing to accept IAEA's draft
agreement for sale of nuclear fuel, 361
rejecting an IAEA invitation, 420
remaining neutral during Iraq's 1990
invasion of Kuwait, 434
removing seals installed by IAEA on
uranium suspension sites, 220
requested to halt all activities related to
enrichment and reprocessing, 250
response to P5+1 threats, 5
resuming R&D on peaceful nuclear
energy, 220
security objectives, 3–4

seeking recognition as a regional power,
195
seeking to become self-reliant, 447
slated for referral to Security Council,
213
suspicion of spreading to Russia and
China and Muslim countries, 76
taking a bold step toward a brand
bargain with the United States, 125
threatening Western countries with
retaliation and expanded activities,
222
on the threshold of war with Taliban
government and al-Qaeda in
Afghanistan in late 1990s, 438
transferring nuclear materials and
technologies, 9
trying to gain membership on IAEA's
Board of Governors, 323
ultimate goals no different than any
other countries' goals, 12
undiplomatic treatment of in 2005, 182
wanting different terms, 361
world's second-largest proven oil
reserves, 392
Iran Atomic Energy Organization (IAEO)
contract with British companies in
1975, 49
establishment of, 43
experiments with polonium, 122
negotiations with Jeffrey Eerkens in
1976, 50
not informing nuclear negotiation
team, 123
public relations office of, 544n189
remarks about Iran's decision to launch
Isfahan facility, 170
report delivered to IAEA on October
22, 2003, 111
trying to hide its true intent from the
public, 51
Iran Nonproliferation Act, 55
Iran Nuclear Research and Development
Center, 47

Iran Refined Petroleum Sanctions Act of 2009, 390

Iran Royal Association, 367

Iran-Brazil-Turkey declaration, 383

Iran-EU3 nuclear negotiations, 126

Iran-EU3 Steering Committee, 168, 186

Iran-Europe cooperation, 153, 433

Iran-Europe security partnership, suggested, 182

Iran-France nuclear cooperation, 46–47, 53

Iran-Germany nuclear cooperation, 47–48

Iran-IAEA relations, in 2007, 289–293

Iranian aims, in 2002 proposal, 63

Iranian bomb, learning to live with, 30–31

Iranian currency, value dropping, 446

Iranian governments, all have pushed for Iran's right to peaceful nuclear technology, 37

Iranian nation and its leaders, lessons regarding the West's strategy, 449

Iranian nuclear crisis, options to resolve, 5

"The Iranian Nuclear Crisis: Avoiding Worst-Case Outcomes," 333

Iranian nuclear rights, goal to earn international recognition, 195

Iranian officials, engaged in extensive negotiations in 2003, 71

Iranian opposition, 79

Iranian overtures, of 2002 and 2003 ignored by the U.S., 450

Iranian perspective, on prospect of an American military attack, 194

Iranian politicians
knowing little about technical aspects of disputes between IAEO and IAEA, 75
not viewing U.S. military threat as credible, 15

Iranian presidential election, June 12, 2009, 340–343

Iranian public opinion
as a problem faced by United States, 198–199
West appealing to, 308

Iranian Revolutionary Guard Corps Air Force and Missile Command, 390

Iranian-Argentine agreements, 54

Iranians
large group of American-educated, 40
looking for a comprehensive package, 404
Western governments' stances on WMD nonproliferation as selective and hypocritical, 447

Iran-Iraq war, 12, 52

Iranophobia strategy, 364

Iran's case, on the agenda of all subsequent sessions of IAEA Board of Governors, 213

Iran's nuclear dilemma, negotiable framework to resolve, 460–464

Iran's Strategic Weapons: Programme, 494n59

Iran-U.S. package, in negotiable framework, 467–468

Iraq
American arming for its invasion of Iran (1980–1988), 29
falsity of Washington's claims about, 198
frequent use of chemical weapons, 481n31
missile attacks on Iranian cities, 52
use of chemical weapons against Iran, 52

IR-2m centrifuge, 30, 405, 441

IR-4 centrifuge, 30, 405

Isfahan uranium conversion facility
after restart of operations at, 287
China and, 54
new Iranian government determined to resume activities at, 177
plan calling for speedy inauguration of, 169
production of 110 tons of UF6 at, 239
production of UF_4 and UF_6, 270
reactivating, 179
restart of in 2005, 201–207
suspension of, 270

Islamic faith, utilizing nuclear weapons as forbidden by, 465

Islamic Iran Participation Front, 78

Islamic pole, forming in multi-polar international system of future, 191

Islamic Propagation Organization, 295

Islamic Republic of Iran
misguided U.S. policies toward, 193–194
overtures for cooperation with Washington, 22
on the verge of referral to UN Security Council, 76
viewed as inherently irrational and radically ideological, 439

Islamic Republic of Iran Shipping Lines, 387, 390

Islamic Revolution
international nuclear cooperation after, 52–55
Iran remained committed to NPT, 447

Islamic Revolutionary Guard Corps (IRGC), 15, 387

Israel
approach to Obama's new tactics, 330–337
bolstering Tehran's international standing weakening its own position, 103
bombed nuclear reactor in Syria, 323
continuing to issue thinly veiled threats on use of military force, 427
cyber operations against Iranian nuclear facilities, 333
largest WMD arsenal in the Middle East, 436
military operation in Lebanon as Resolution 1696 discussed in Security Council, 252
not forced by the West to join the NPT, 457
not signed NPT, 261
nuclear policy and refusal to join the NPT, 468

P5+1 countries maintaining strategic and aid relations with, 468
perceiving a nuclear-armed Iran as an existential threat, 33
pressures exerted on Moscow, 398
public statements about a possible limited military attack, 144
pushing Americans toward a strike, 427
tested missile capable of carrying a nuclear warhead and striking Iran, 418
threats to attack Iran, 345
tremendous effort to woo Russia, 257
working to increase tensions between Iran and the international community, 104

Israeli attacks
concern over possibility of, 331
on Iraq's Osirak and Syria's Al Kibar nuclear facilities, 346
possibility of, 138

Israeli government, positions of, 7

Israeli military intelligence officials, stressing necessity of attacking Iran's atomic installations, 103–104

Israeli press, dissuading incoming American administration from direct, high-level negotiations with Iran, 330

Israeli Right, encouraging United States to attack Iran, 10

Israeli strike, 10, 12

Israelis, as criminal and occupationist Zionists, 318

Israel-Palestinian peace process, 14

issues, six resolved, 295

Istanbul, talks in (2011), 402

Ivanov, Igor, 69–70, 91, 116, 217, 234, 407

Jaber Ebne Hayyan pharmaceutical firm, 114

Jalali, Gholamreza, 25

Jalili, Saeed, 277, 295, 309, 312, 316, 324, 351, 401, 402, 403, 409, 454, 461–462, 518n61

Jalili period, 289–320
Jannati, Ayatollah Ahmad, 341
Japan, 13, 391, 438
Japan model, Iran interested in, 33
Jarari, Mohammad Ali, 278
Joint Declaration of the Seventy-Seven
    Countries, 526n85
joint economic cooperation commission,
    Iran and U.S. established, 45
Jones, James L., 355
judges, finding Mousavian innocent of
    espionage, 284

Kalaye Electric Company
    environmental samples taken at in
        August 2003, 489n18
    introducing gas to centrifuges at, 112
    necessity of taking samples at, 66
    tests conducted at, 489n19
    tests on centrifuges installed at using
        Chinese-supplied UF_6, 54
    undeclared tests on centrifuges using
        UF_6, 113
Karroubi, Mehdi, 281, 340, 421
Karzai, Hamid, 7
Kashani, Ayatollah Emami, 281
Kelley, Robert, 419
Kennan, George, 194
Kennedy, John F., 41
Kerry, John, 6
Khalilzad, Zalmay, 319
Khamenei, Ayatollah Ali
    acknowledged crimes had taken place
        during protests, 341
    alleged plot "meaningless and
        nonsensical accusation," 415
    backing of, 412
    blaming CIA and Mossad for killing of
        Iranian nuclear scientist, 26
    calling American only perpetrator of
        atomic crime in the world, 378
    exchange of letters with Obama in
        2009, 442
    gave Ahmadinejad permission for
        negotiation with United States, 442

having final say, 36
    meeting to explain that Iran was
        not committing to open-ended
        suspension, 150
    meeting with ElBaradei, 290–291
    message exchanged with Putin, 264
    nuclear policies determined by, 342
    nuclear policies of, 441
    Obama letter to, 338–340
    only official who could suspend
        enrichment activities, 343
    position on enrichment, 460
    precluding Khatami's nuclear team
        from interaction with the United
        States, 439
    preferred and praised Ahmadinejad
        administration's psychology of the
        offensive, 439–440
    proposed resolution to Palestinian-
        Israeli issue, 216
    rejecting fuel exchange agreement, 362
    responding to latest economic pressures
        and military threats made by United
        States, Israel, and the EU, 428
    road map for comprehensive talks
        approved by, 450
    suspicious of policies of West, 149
    unprecedented and powerful support
        for Ahmadinejad, 441
    vetoing dialogue with Washington, 83
    warning from on American goodwill,
        337
Khamenei, Ali, 377
Kharrazi, Kamal
    ElBaradei meeting with, 68
    meetings in 2004, 132
    negotiated with president and foreign
        minister of China, India, and Japan,
        71
    negotiations with Japanese prime
        minister and with Chinese officials,
        116
    remarks about Iran's decision to launch
        Isfahan facility, 170
Kharrazi, Sadeq, 172

Khatami, Mohammad
  ElBaradei meeting with, 68
  far-reaching overtures and goodwill and
    flexibility, 433
  gesture of cooperation on Afghanistan
    in 2001, 242
  letter implying Iran might end talks
    with European countries, 136
  melding ideological advancement and
    development-centered policies, 401
  phone conversation with Vladimir
    Putin, 132
  policies followed by, 190
  policy of international engagement, 57
  on possible suspension of Iran's nuclear
    enrichment program, 489n10
  promoting a "dialogue of civilizations,"
    435
Khatami, Seyed Muhammad, 279
Khatami administration, successful in
  preventing economic or political
  sanctions, 431
Khatami government, nuclear diplomacy
  achievements, 431–433
Khatami nuclear negotiating team
  "Framework for Mutual Guarantees"
    plan, 268
  Mousavian publicly defending record
    on the nuclear issue, 280
  objectives achieved, 179–182
  precluded by guidance from supreme
    leader from entering into direct
    interaction with United States, 439
Khatami presidency, disadvantages of
  nuclear diplomacy during, 439–441
Khatami's defensive policy, blamed for
  setbacks, 440
Khatami's nuclear diplomacy, major shift
  toward in 2011, 407
Khazaee, Mohammad, 314, 378, 415, 455
Khomeini, Ayatollah, rejected PMOI
  request for a fatwa, 483n3
Khomeini, Imam, opposed weapons of
  mass destruction, 52
Khomeini, Imam Ruhollah, 83

Khoshrou, Gholamali, 61, 70, 114, 484n10
Kimia Maadan company, 372
Ki-moon, Ban, 302, 368, 414, 425
King of Qatar, on Iranian words, 6
Kiriyenko, Sergei, 233, 274–275
Kirk, Mark, 422
Kislyak, Sergei, 216, 257, 507n28, 525n67
Kissinger, Henry, 40, 44, 196
Kosachev, Konstantin, 366
Kouchner, Bernard, 329, 344
Kraftwerk Union, cancelled nuclear power
  projects in 1979, 48

Lahad, Antoine, forces released, 435
Larijani, Ali
  canceled a trip to Europe in 2006, 247
  condemning assassinations, 26
  differences with Ahmadinejad, 275–
    276
  discussions with, 84
  meeting with ElBaradei in September
    2005, 207
  message to Condoleezza Rice, 241
  Mousavian only ex-nuclear negotiation
    team member appointed by, 203
  pragmatic and tuned approach, 277
  presented Iran's official response to
    incentives package, 253
  proposed posts for Mousavian, 443
  resignation from Supreme National
    Security Council, 276, 278
  resignation or dismissal, 277–279
  response to new U.S. nuclear strategy,
    377
  visiting India and Pakistan, 206
Larijani, Ayatollah Sadegh, 394
Larijani, Mohammad Javad, 422
Larijani period, 185–223
laser parts, delivered to Iran, 50
lasers, shipped in October 1978, 45
Lavrov, Sergei, 215, 233, 234, 294, 357,
  393, 398–399, 407, 409, 426, 512n105
Leader. See Supreme Leader (Rabbar)
learning to live with an Iranian bom
  option, 30–31

Lefebvre de Laboulaye, Stanislas, 172–173
Leverett, Flynt, 326
Leverett, Hillary Mann, 326
Levin, Carl, 461
Li Peng, 54
Libya, 133, 212
Lieberman, Joseph, 7, 9
light water reactors (LWR), 515n28
Limbert, John, 16
Livni, Tzipporah "Tzipi," 331
London-Washington axis, guarantor of external links, 90
looking to the East
    continued to have high-level support, 220
    development of, 329
    further refuted, 294
    as a mistake of the ninth government, 443
    proved a failure, 278
    rebutted, 300
    as strategy or tactic, 190–193
    supporters of Iran's, 250
    theory, 206
    total failure of, 256–258
lost UF_4, used in experiments, 114
low-enriched uranium (LEU), 29–30, 401, 489n18, 515n28
Lula, Luiz Inácio da Silva, 380, 383

Maduro, Nicolás, 324
Majles, 305–306, 377–378
Majles deputies, triple urgency plan, 144
major powers, approaches to Iran's nuclear dossier, 88–94
Maltzahn, Paul von, 228
management of the world, Ahmadinejad's theory of, 348
Mansouri, Javad, 443
Mao Zedong, 196
marginalizing the West, not plausible, 192–193
Martin, Paul, 215
Massachusetts Institute of Technology (MIT), 42

Mbeki, Thabo, 174, 178–179, 266, 500n46
McCain, John, 325
McCormack, Sean, 215, 293, 501–502n57
McDonough, Denis, 19
Medvedev, Dmitri
    impatience with Iran's behavior, 352
    trip to New York, 356
    use of negotiations and diplomacy, 335–336
    welcoming Ahmadinejad to Shanghai summit in Moscow, 397
Mehr New Agency, Mousavian interview with, 261
MEK. See also MKO; PMOI
    advocating U.S. support for, 18
    also know as PMOI and MKO, 483n3
    fought alongside Saddam Hussein in the Iran-Iraq war, 18
    removed from EU's list of terrorist organizations, 445
    Roshan's killing speculated to be the work of, 425
    Spokesman's claims, 58
    as a terrorist organization, 18
Melli Bank, 294, 308
Merkel, Angela, 240, 328
Metten, Guillaume, 228
MI6, chief of, 27
militarization, preventing, 3
military aspects, of Iran's nuclear program returned to in Resolution 1696, 251
military dimensions
    IAEA report on, 416–421
    questions and ambiguities related to possible, 372
military institutes, in Iran's nuclear program, 304
military option, keeping on the table, 10
military presence, end to U.S. as a security objective, 3
military strikes
    on Iran as well-night impossible, 197
    as only remaining viable option, 9
    unifying Iranians, 14

military threats, as counterproductive, 15

Minty, Abdul Samad, 175, 178

missile bases, explosion at one of Iran's (2010), 27

missile capabilities, as an aspect of threat to international peace and security, 287

missiles, Iran testing three short-range in 2009, 353

mistakes made by the West, 447, 448, 449, 450, 451, 452, 453, 456, 457

Mitchell, George, 6

MKO, 483n3

modality agreement, 289

Modality Plan of Action, agreement on, 292

moderates, disappointed with the EU3, 138

Mofaz, Shaul, 8, 104

Mojahedin Organization, People's, 414–415

money laundering designation, 422

Morsali, Hojatoleslam, 82

Moscow. *See* Russia

Moscow plan, aiming to increase dependence of Iran's nuclear industry on Russia, 217

Mosely, Michael, 7

Moslehi, Heydar, 25

Mossad, Roshan's killing speculated to be the work of, 425

Mossadegh, Muhammad, 23, 39, 274, 437, 547n8

Mother Agreement, with France, 46

Mottaki, Manouchehr
announcing that Iran would respond to P5+1 proposal, 248
background of, 498n17
dismissed, 402
reaffirming deadline, 249
rejecting U.S. offer, 245
resignation of, 518n62

Mousavi, Ali, on unemployment rate, 446

Mousavi, Mir Hossein, 340, 344, 359, 367, 421, 497n8

Mousavian, Seyed Hossein
arrest a serious warning to Ahmadinejad's other foreign policy critics, 281
arrest of, 279–285
established a structure for Iran-EU dialogue, 434
head of Security Council's Foreign Relations Committee, 95
Iran's ambassador to Germany (1994-1995), 448
meeting with Ahmadinejad July 19, 2005, 186
no insider information about technical dimensions of Iran's activities, 353
only Iranian official to explain the content and consequences of Resolution 1737, 261
past negotiations by, 149
proponent of grand bargain approach, 82
proposed package to EU3 in 2005, 452–453
similar initiative prior to Ahmadinejad, 208
spokesman of Iran's nuclear negotiating team, 144
telling Rouhani that nuclear strategy risked a serious impasse, 124
unofficial visit to EU3 capitals in spring 2005, 171

Mubarak, Gamal, 8

Mubarak, Hosni, 6, 248

Mukasey, Michael, 18

Mullen, Mike, 11

multinational companies, ceasing economic activity with Iran, 392

mutual agreement, procedure for communication of, 64

mutual simultaneous statements, proposed in 2002, 64

Nackaerts, Herman, 406, 409, 410, 411

Najafabadi, Muhammad Ali, 82

Namibia, IAEO prospecting one of world's biggest uranium mines in, 49

Naqdi, Muhammad Reza, 20

Nasr, Vali Reza, 198

Nasrallah, Hassan, 435

Nasseri, Cyrus, accused of financial corruption, 519n80

Nasseri, Sirous, 162, 284, 496n6

Natanz facility
  demand to suspend enrichment at, 68
  drop in number of operating centrifuges, 25
  evidence of highly enriched uranium, 112
  increasing number of operating centrifuges, 267

Natanz pilot plant
  enriching uranium to about 3.6 percent, 239
  restart of centrifuge enrichment, 220–223

Nategh-Nouri, Akbar, 281

National Atomic Energy Commission, Argentina's, 54

National Day of Nuclear Technology, 273, 395, 396

National Intelligence Estimate (2007), 290, 293, 299, 314

national pride, stimulated by policy of isolation and sanctions, 21

negative atmosphere, surrounding nuclear issue in domestic media, 183

negotiable framework
  described, 464–469
  needed, 463
  to resolve Iran-U.S. nuclear deadlock, 460–464

negotiations
  after the beginning of enrichment by the new government, 202
  dramatic changes in, 186
  Iran and United States interest in protracting, 313
  need to restart, 264

official channels cut off between Tehran and the EU3, 139

opposed by several groups inside Iran, 104

partners for, 99

neoconservatives in America, 76, 88

Nesterenko, Andrei, 398

Netanyahu, Benjamin, 8, 10, 331, 418

neutron initiators, program by Tehran to test, 364

neutrons, experiments concerning generation and detection of, 372

New Delhi, maintaining that Tehran has an inalienable right to use atomic energy for peaceful purposes, 418

new Iranian government. See ninth government

New START Treaty, between U.S. and Russia, 379

Ni Ruchi, 33

Nicoullaud, François, 165, 228

Nigeria, increasing export of oil, 392

9/11 terror attacks, international atmosphere subsequent to, 200

93+2 Additional Protocol
  calling for Iran's "unconditional" signing of, 60
  IAEA's activities in Iran carried out within framework of, 159
  Iran's acceptance of as a necessary step, 67
  premature announcement of Iran's willingness to implement, 105
  signed on December 18, 2003, 120
  Tehran deciding to send positive signals on, 71

ninth government
  adhering to aggressive carrot and stick policy, 263
  advantages of diplomacy, 441–442
  aggressiveness of, 199–201
  against any compromise on Iran's nuclear rights, 190
  approach totally different, 186

coming to power at a time of potential
agreement between Iran and EU3,
185
criticisms raised by about the proposed
package, 249
defined, 498n2
diplomatic policy, 232
disadvantages of diplomacy and missed
opportunities, 442–446
expressing support for Russian proposal
without taking steps to implement,
217
first nuclear team chosen from officials
with security perspectives, 442
followed script expected by the
Americans, 247
looking to the East policy, 443
parallel approaches to reduce
diplomatic pressure and prevent
ratification of another resolution, 272
presence of Burns in Geneva, 311
pursued cooperation with IAEA
consistently, 291
reaction by international community to
nuclear policies of, 210
reactions to Resolution 1747, 273–276
trying to deal with demands for
suspension, 270
ninth mistake, made by the West, 456
Nixon, Richard, 40
Non-Aligned Movement
continued talks with, 86
decided to agree to Resolution 1803,
300
described, 471n1
insistence that Iran's continued
cooperation with IAEA be supported,
129
major members voted against Iran, 226
member states conflicted over Iran's
nuclear program, 192
members issued a statement criticizing
language in IAEA chief's report, 418
requirements accepted in November
2004, 160

satisfied with increasing cooperation
between Iran and IAEA (2004),
492n50
statement professing support for Iran,
67
noncompliance
to NPT, 61
with NPT obligations, 211
recognized by inspectors, 229
noninterference, in Israeli-Palestinian
peace process, 434
nonmilitary nuclear facilities, proposal to
ban attacks on, 345
non–nuclear-weapon states
agree to accept Safeguards Agreements
with IAEA, 58
declaring Iran a, 466
non-oil exports, to the European Union,
153–154
non-paper, Jalili presenting, 309–311
nonproliferation, strategically important to
Russia, 92
Non-Proliferation Treaty (NPT), 211
built on three pillars, 58
eighth review conference, 379
failure to observe provisions of, 65
idea of withdrawing from, 81
Iran voted for at the 1995 NPT Review
Conference, 434
recognition of Iran's rights as per, 140
recognizing Iran's basic nuclear rights
under, 151
Safeguards Agreement obligations, 210
signed by Iran in 1968 and ratified by
Iranian Parliament in 1970, 41, 447
North Korea, 30, 196, 376
Northern Alliance in Afghanistan, 547n9
November 25 deadline (2004), 143
nuclear achievements, exaggerating Iran's,
274
nuclear activities
clandestine taken as proof positive on
intent of Iran, 67
clarification of nature of Iran's past,
238

Iran's concealment of history of, 210
release of information about all aspects
of as tactical, 111
nuclear agreement, between Tehran and
Paris on June 27, 1974, 46
nuclear attack, threat of running contrary
to tenets of Non-Proliferation Treaty,
376
nuclear blackmail, by the U.S. against
Iran, 378
nuclear bomb, 32, 305
nuclear capabilities, achieved
during Rafsanjani and Khatami
administrations, 438
nuclear case
allowing Washington to bank on global
sensitivities about nonproliferation,
200
legal status of in Rouhani and Larijani
periods, 285–287
normalization depriving West of most
important leverage, 132
nuclear club, 395, 516n38
nuclear complexes, in 2002, 58
nuclear cooperation agreements, with other
countries, 42
nuclear crisis, management of, 432
nuclear developments, leading to
November 2003 resolution, 114–117
nuclear device modeling studies, in 2008
and 2009, 417
nuclear diplomacy
disadvantages of during Khatami
presidency, 439–441
first period of Iran's, 286
framework of Iran's new, 97–100
second period of, 286–287
nuclear energy
development of as a right, 61
emerged as a symbol of national pride
and modernization, 43
first agreement for nonmilitary use of
(1957), 41
"Nuclear Energy for All—Nuclear
Weapons for No One," 379

nuclear enrichment, 30, 69
nuclear explosives, alleged activities related
to, 372
The Nuclear File (documentary film), 350
nuclear fuel, becoming self-sufficient, 237
nuclear fuel cycle
completed by Iran, 274
deal for a complete, 44
Iran having technology, 450
legitimate right to and interest in
developing, 181
nuclear fuel exchange deal, 380
nuclear fuel producers club, 274
nuclear fuel rod, 424, 544n189
nuclear issue
bargaining chip to reach a global
compromise with P5+1, 404
matter of national consensus and pride
in Iran, 2
as opportunity for U.S. to unite
international community against
Iran, 2
nuclear materials
accounted for in Iran, 158
failure to report imported from China,
58
Iran moving to the underground
Fordow nuclear site, 416
nuclear negotiating team, new team
allowed to negotiate with the United
States, 203
nuclear negotiations, 188, 350
Nuclear Negotiations steering committee,
second session of, 165–169
nuclear package, in negotiable framework,
465–467
nuclear payloads, studying how to fit into
reentry vehicle on Shahab-3 missile,
417
nuclear physicist's assassination, serious
warning to individuals cooperating
with Iran's nuclear program, 368
nuclear policy
public opinion in Iran negative toward,
183

reasons sanctions will not change, 20–21

Nuclear Posture Review
emphasis on nuclear terrorism, 377
listing Iran as a country that could require a U.S. nuclear response, 55
openly threatening a country under the pretext of deterrence, 376
outlining America's new nuclear strategy, 375

nuclear power generation, 43

nuclear power plant, at Bushehr, 363–364

nuclear powers, in Iran's region, 31

nuclear programs
controlled beyond the negotiating team's purview, 183
origin and development of, 39–55
possible military dimensions of, 295
presenting a complete report on, 111
thick wall between technical and political sides of, 353
as a threat to international peace and security, 286

nuclear proliferation
American inconsistency on issues, 252
international crisis about, 44

nuclear rights approach, 81–82

Nuclear Science Institute of CENTO, 41

nuclear scientists
another assassinated on January 11, 2012, 425
Ardeshir Hosseinpour killed in 2008, 25
assassination of Iranian, 367–370

nuclear security summit, in Washington, D.C. in 2010, 375

Nuclear Suppliers Group, China joining, 54

nuclear technology, 42

Nuclear Technology Day, 336, 337–338, 374

nuclear terrorism, emphasis on, 377

nuclear weapons
development of, 303–304

evidence of former regime's efforts to build, 49–51
implied threat to Iran and North Korea of the use of, 375
Iran has not made a decision to acquire, 461
no credible evidence that Iran has made final decision to acquire, 31
possession of providing only a short-term regional advantage, 32
U.S. expanding potential uses of, 55

nuclear working groups, practically stagnant by March of 2005, 165

nuclear-weapon option, 461

Nuland, Victoria, 424

Obama, Barack
accused Iran of having a secret underground enrichment center, 351
in address to the UN General Assembly, 458
clear attempt by Ahmadinejad to reach a grand bargain, 349
describing as a success his engagement policy, 424
efforts to improve relations with Muslim world, 13
in favor of direct talks with high-level Iranian officials, 343
hard-line stances on Iran in March 2010, 374
Israel's approach to new tactics of, 330–337
issued an Executive Order placing new sanctions on Iran including its Central Bank, 426
letters
to Ayatollah Khamenei, 338–340
to Brazilian President Lula, 383
to Dmitri Medvedev, 335
letters to, 83
meeting with Lavrov, 407
not able to go for grand bargain, 360

opportunity presented by offer to
escrow uranium in Turkey, 381
Persian New Year message to the
Iranian people on March 20, 2010,
374
phenomenon of, 324–328
putting forward a U.S. engagement
policy, 327
reassuring Israel, 11
reengaging Moscow, 397
second letter to Khamenei a mistake,
339
signed a bill calling for new sanctions
(2011), 19
stand on wars in Iraq and Afghanistan
as well as introduction of an
engagement policy, 315
stressing necessity of preventing
terrorists from obtaining nuclear
weapons, 375
trip to Russia in 2009, 356
use of negotiations and diplomacy,
335–336
wanting to see toughest sanctions after
Saudi ambassador plot discovered,
414
Obama administration
efforts to transform Western public
opinion, 327
finding itself in the same position as
George W. Bush in March 2008, 322
first practical action taken by, 336
needing to display progress, 358
overhaul of extreme approaches toward
Iran, 322
prepared to accept some enrichment
activities, 404
pursuing hard approach through
greater international consensus, 327
supporting a policy of regime change
against Iran, 428
objective guarantees
critical negotiations on, 162
definition of mechanisms for providing,
165

letting IAEA solve, 164
negotiating, 177
of non-diversion, 168
for non-diversion offered by Iran, 166
on peaceful nature of nuclear program
in Paris Agreement, 151
requested by Europe, 147
required by EU, 161
that nuclear program would not be
diverted, 164
objectives, in final strategy to manage
crisis, 94–96
objectives and achievements, recap of
Iran's, 179–183
obligatory suspension, changed to
voluntary and non-legally binding
confidence-building measure, 286
October deal (2009), collapse of and
subsequent move by Iran to enrich to
20 percent, 455
oil and gas contracts, China's share in Iran,
400
oil and gas industries, 392
oil and Strait of Hormuz, as Achilles' heel
of United States, 198
oil industry, Chinese contracts, 538n88
oil prices, spiking during Ahmadinejad
presidency, 445
Olmert, Ehud, 261, 398
omissions, uncovered since November
2003 resolution, 129–130
opposition leaders, house arrest and forced
isolation of, 421

P-2 centrifuges, 120–121, 491n33, 492n37
P5+1
accused of bullying, 316
agreement one day after "nuclear case
practically closed," 294
asking Iran to halt all enrichment to 20
percent, 403
bringing Washington, Beijing, and
Moscow to the negotiation table, 185
final agreement on new proposal to
Iran, 245

further negotiations based on four preconditions per Ahmadinejad in 2010, 393

insisting on a piecemeal approach on the nuclear issue, 403

Iran continuing to engage, 396

last-ditch effort to reach a comprehensive agreement with, 278

letter to Iran introducing new proposal in 2008, 307

meeting held in Paris on May 2, 2006, 239

meeting to reassess suspension for suspension proposal, 336

member states not in accord regarding the resolution, 293

members of, 4

negotiations with Iran, new round in 2009, 350

new proposal by, 245–246

not buying into Ahmadinejad's initiative, 209

rejected counterproposal, 455

representatives reaching a new agreement on Iran sanctions (March 15, 2007), 273

requiring IAEA to report Iran's case to Security Council (2006), 225

unified by Ahmadinejad's harshly worded speech, 319

united and committed to credible engagement, 403

Pahlavi, Mohammad Reza Shah
Cold War and, 39–40
interest in nuclear weapons, 50
Iran's nuclear activities under, 49
on nuclear weapons, 50
obvious efforts to enrich uranium, 44
policy of accommodating, 51
pushing for plutonium reprocessing and enrichment facilities, 41
supporting past dictatorial rule of, 437

Pahlavi dynasty, dependence on the United States, 44

Pahlavi regime, 40, 50

Pakistan
forced to cooperate with IAEA, 180
not forced by the West to join the NPT, 457
not signing NPT, 261, 436
P5+1 countries maintaining strategic and aid relations with, 468
preventing from building independent nuclear facilities, 45

Palestinian negotiator, not accepting Ahmadinejad's statements on Israel, 216

Panetta, Leon, 353, 427

Paragraph 8, of the November 2003 resolution, 120

Paris Agreement, 149–156
broad-based negotiations to support, 161–164
developments leading to, 143–149
Europe pledged to enforce Iran's nuclear rights, 432
foundation for negotiations on economic relations and resumption of trade talks, 153
long and difficult process after, 157
negotiations leading up to, 440
reassuring international community that Iran would opt for negotiations, 154
short-term suspension of fuel cycle, 269
supporting Iran's accession to the World Trade Organization, 154
suspension both voluntary and for confidence building, 269
Tehran decided to withdraw from, 177

Paris-Berlin axis, 90, 102

Parliament
more activist role in Iran, 305
ratified Nuclear Non-Proliferation Treaty, 41, 447
ultimate authority on implementation of the Additional Protocol, 109

Passive Defense military unit, 25

Patrushev, Nikolai, 408, 409, 427

peaceful activities, continuing under supervision of international bodies, 451

peaceful atomic awakening movement, Iran flag bearer of, 355

peaceful enrichment technology, extremely important for Iran, 14

peaceful nuclear activities, continuation of discriminatory restrictions on, 459

peaceful nuclear capability, protecting through interaction with international community, 179

peaceful nuclear energy, 58, 160

peaceful nuclear program, defending legitimate right to, 463

peaceful nuclear technology, remaining a non-negotiable issue, 460

Pellaud, Bruno, 449

Pelosi, Nancy, 199

People's Mojahedin Organization of Iran, 414–415

Peres, Shimon, 331, 345

period of paralysis, 322

Persian Gulf neighbors, animosity between Iran and its, 34

The Persian Puzzle, 326

Petraeus, David, 6

PFEP (pilot fuel enrichment plant), environmental sampling at, 489n18

phased grand agenda, 464–469

Physikalisch-Technische Bundesanstalt Institute of Germany, 48

Pillar, Paul, 428

pilot centrifuges, number of, 174

Pilot Fuel Enrichment Plant, at Natanz, 271

pilot program, allowing, 452

plan for negotiations and cooperation, offered to U.S. government in 2002, 62–65

Plan of Action, in summer 2007, 289

plate fuel, producing for Tehran Research Reactor, 412

plutonium, 50–51, 114, 123, 239

PMOI, 483n3. See also MEK; MKO

political obstinacy, among government and opposition supporters, 343

political opponents, goal of discrediting Ahmadinejad's, 281–282

political parties, closing of offices of three major reformist, 341

political scene, main factions, 77

political squabbling, over Iran's nuclear activities, 77

Pollack, Kenneth, 326

polonium, 121–122, 492n38

Post Bank of Iran, 390

postelection confrontation, in Iran, 341

Powell, Colin, 60, 120

power plants, 45, 363–364

pragmatic approach, 84–86, 94

pragmatic politicians, concerned about radicalism, 279

preemptive strike, as unrealistic and unfeasible, 11

preemptive strike option, 5–16

Preparatory Commission, for NPT Review Conference, 60

presidential election fever, in Iran, 169–175

president's policies, Mousavian guilty of opposing, 285

Principlist (Conservative) politicians attacking nuclear policy of reformist government of Khatami, 183

deemed that all cooperation with the IAEA had been in vain, 437

insider's access to, 77

Iran's democracy and stability to be incomparable to any other Middle Eastern country, 436

in line with supreme leader's policies, 185

main right-wing/conservative political movement in Iran, 486n39

in the Majles, 360

opposed moderate diplomacy, 435

viewing West's policies toward nuclear weapons and other WMD as deeply hypocritical, 436

pro-American dictators, collapsing, 328

"Prohibition of All Armed Attacks Against
Nuclear Installations Devoted to
Peaceful Purposes Whether Under
Construction or in Operation," 345
propaganda
new government putting too much
emphasis on, 200
orchestrated in right-wing media, 283
policy of the ninth government, 201
protesters, 398, 423
protests, managing response to, 341
psychology of the offensive, 440
public opinion, an issue inside Iran, 78
publics, international indicating approval
of military action against Iran, 9
Putin, Vladimir
access to peaceful nuclear technology as
undeniable right, 490n25
conferring with Ahmadinejad, 248
conveying a special nuclear message to
the Iranian leader, 277
at Kaliningrad, 178
meeting with Velayati, 514n15
message with Ayatollah Khamenei, 264
negotiations with, 163, 164
not on a boat with Iran as only
passenger, 398
ordered "sabotage" of Iran's Bushehr
nuclear plant, 399
phone conversation with Khatami, 132

Qanbari, Dariush, 518n62
Qom facility, disclosure of, 352
Quds Force, 414
Quihillat (scientist), 480n12

R&D activities, 220–221
radical faction in Iran, Europe not an
appropriate partner for Iran, 329
radical school, suspicious of the West,
483n1
Rafsanjani, Hashemi
after election of, 448
briefed by Mousavian, 35

comprehensive bilateral nuclear
agreement with USSR in 1989, 54
endorsing rapprochement, 83
far-reaching overtures and goodwill and
flexibility, 433
melding ideological advancement and
development-centered policies, 401
Mousavian detention a direct message
to, 282
no dispute among political groups
over signing or rejecting Additional
Protocol, 486n44
official comment from in 2003, 94–95
policies followed by, 57, 190
taking sanctions seriously, 20
technocratic government under, 53
Rafsanjani period, 448–449
Rafsanjani presidency, efforts to bring
closer relations with Iran's neighbors,
34
rapprochement, between Tehran and
Washington, 83
Rasad (Observation) satellite, 404
Rauf, Tariq, 71
Ray, Dixy Lee, 42
recipient country, referred to the Security
Council, 229
referral process, legal grounding of the
entire, 226
reformers and pragmatists, improving
relations with international community,
77
reformist Mosharekat Party, 78
regime change
not part of Iran's outlook in the near
future, 22
Obama administration supporting a
policy of, 428
promoting in Tehran, 17
U.S. policies to achieve, 3–4
U.S. strategy seen as a multipronged
approach to bring about, 89
regional consortium, proposed
establishment of, 270

regional countries, little desire to see a
nuclear Iran, 193
religious *fatwa*, against all weapons of mass
destruction, 32, 378
reporting, to the Security Council, 212
resistance, to Brussels agreement inside
Iran,, 132
"Review of Moratorium," mechanism
mentioned in, 246
Revolutionary Guard Corps, 368, 390
Rezaei, Mohsen, 189, 359
Rezayeenejad, Daryoush, 26
Rice, Condoleezza, 60, 125, 137, 196–197,
199, 234, 241, 244–245, 266, 290, 302,
511n98, 517n48
Rice, Susan, 414, 455
Ridge, Tom, 18
Rifai, Zeid, 6
rights, under Article IV of the NPT linked
with fulfillment of Article III, 61
Rio Tinto-Zinc Corporation, Iran
purchased shares of, 49
road map, for comprehensive talks, 450
robust enrichment capability, preference
for, 32
Rogozin, Dmitry, 427
rogue states, list of, 215
role of the military, in Iran's nuclear
programs, 239
Rómulo, Alberto Gatmaitan, 302
Roshan, Mostafa Ahmadi, 26, 425
Ross, Dennis, 343, 388
Rouhani, Hassan
accepted suspension based on
ElBaradei's assurance, 105
address by, 488n4
any proposal excluding enrichment
would be rejected, 171
asking Mousavian to deny his proposal,
208
background of, 485n27
discussion with EU3 ministers, 102
on hiding some activities, 489n15
instructions from supreme leader, 149

meetings
with Ahmadinejad August 9, 2005,
188
with Mbeki, 500n46
with, 488n6
message to EU3 (2005), 174
message to President Bush (2003), 242
Mousavian discussion with, 70
Mousavian report to, 172
Mousavian's offer to resign, 187
not informed about technical problems
by relevant officials of Iranian nuclear
program, 123
potential candidates for 2005
presidential elections, 104
resignation of, 188, 201
statement by, 494n57, 506n16
on supreme leader's position on
enrichment, 460
visits
Algeria, Russia, Tunisia, France,
and Germany, 163
Japan (March 13, 2004), 132
Moscow by, 116
South Africa in late July 2005, 174
Rumsfeld, Donald, 137
Rumyantsev, Alexander, 233
Rushdie, Salman, 435
Russia
committed to deliver nuclear fuel, 55
considering Iran an important
neighbor, 100
criticizing unilateral sanctions against
Iran, 393
delays in completing Bushehr atomic
power plant, 257
deliveries of low-enriched uranium
to the Bushehr nuclear plant in
December 2007, 290
disillusioned by Iran's obstinacy, 247
distancing itself from Iran, 397–400
disturbed by secret construction of
enrichment facility at Fordow near
Qom, 397

dual game evident, 294

enrichment to be transferred to Russian soil, 235

frustrated with Washington's unilateralism, 99

inconsistent and mixed approach to Iran's atomic program, 91

Iran as a bargaining chip, 397

negotiations on Bushehr nuclear power plant, 232–233

not likely to back a military option against Tehran, 197

not tolerating an Iranian nuclear bomb, 32–33

only country to try to annex large parts of Iran, 320

opposing Iranian membership in Shanghai Cooperation Organization, 257

opposition in 2009 to expansion of sanctions against Iran, 357

opposition to a new sanctions resolution, 293

optimism toward a new package in 2009, 347

proposals
    to invest in its enrichment plant, 233–235
    joint stock company to provide Tehran with nuclear fuel, 216
    putting Iran in a difficult situation, 217
    for uranium enrichment on Russian soil, 232–233

putting forward a plan in 2005, 213

rejecting any forceful treatment of Iran, 258

Resolutions 1803 and 1835 raising questions about benefits of reliance on, 320

support for Resolution 1835 as a tactical measure, 527n96

Tehran not trusting, 397

unwilling to allow Iran to pursue enrichment on its soil, 258

urging United States to talk with Iran, 33

wanting to retain business opportunities in Iran, 398

warned IAEA against publishing 2011 report, 417

willing to play a special role in Iran nuclear case, 264

willing to use Iran as leverage, 257

Russian enrichment technology, not to be shared with any country, 257

Russian National Security Council, 217

Russian Nuclear Energy State Corporation (Rosatom), 274

Russian officials, warning against a military strike by United States or Israel, 427

Russian plan
    contradictory positions on, 233
    for joint uranium enrichment in Russia, 257
    most realistic package since 2003, 409
    as a reflection of Russian policies, 256
    as West's new trap, 234

Russian power plant fuel, reprocessing imported, 122

Russian proposal, 219

Russian S-300 antiaircraft missile system, 331

Russian step-by-step proposal, 407–410, 413, 456, 457

Russian view of relations with Iran, 92–93

Russians, on periphery of negotiations, 182

Russo-Persian War, Treaty of, 69

Ryu, Rexon, 403

S-300 antiaircraft missile system, 399

sabotage
    preferable to airstrikes, 426
    United States pursuing, 28

SACE Insurance Company, not cooperating with Iran, 79

Sa'dabad Agreement
    accepted by the entire world, 384

EU3 agreed to pursue negotiations on the basis of short-term suspension, 268
talks leading to, 384
transforming a political and security dispute into a technical and legal dispute, 108
Sa'dabad negotiations, 100–106, 107, 110
Sa'dabad Palace, political protest organized in front of, 111
Saeedi, Mohammad, 255, 488n1
Safavi, Yahya Rahim, 277
Safeguards Agreement
IAEA's, 211
noncompliance of a country with, 227
providing sole legal framework for interactions among all members, 452
responding only on the basis of, 81
safeguards requirements, separate from voluntary confidence-building measures, 180
Safir carrier rocket, 294
Safir-B1 (Ambassador-B1) rocket, 404–405
Sajjadi, Mahmoud Reza, 399
Salehi, Ali Akbar, 24, 42, 71, 72, 120, 344, 351, 360, 363, 366–367, 374, 402, 405, 408, 409, 412, 418–419, 424, 426, 456, 467
Samareh, Mojtaba Hashemi, 186, 187, 462
Samore, Gary, 356, 405, 458, 494n59
sanctions
effect of, 21
entities targeted by U.S., 390
Europeans advocating, 328
as "gift of God to the Iranian nation," 19
Iran's need to go underground to evade, 67
mobilizing the country to resist, 115
not changing Iran's nuclear course, 428
overview of impact of new against Iran, 388–389
as prelude to invasion, 21
reasons to pursue additional, 20
strengthened from 2005 on, 389
ultimately ineffective, 16
sanctions committee, set up to deal with Iraq crisis, 513n11
Santorum, Rick, 27, 425
Sarkozy, Nicolas, 296, 328, 351, 366, 422, 426
satellite
launch, 294
prototypes, 404
Saud al-Faisal, Prince, 414
Saudi Arabia, 6, 55, 414
Saudi security forces, killing Iranian pilgrims in Mecca in 1988, 34
Sawers, John, 27, 173, 241, 297, 425, 530n41
Schaefer, Michael, 171, 172
Schroeder, Gerhard, 164, 178, 202
Schulte, Gregory, 242, 304
second mistake, by the West, 447
secrecy, Iranians justifying previous, 489n16
security atmosphere, as a result of U.S. invasions of Afghanistan and Iraq, 78
Security Council resolution, legitimacy of, 228
security objectives
Iranian, 3–4
of the United States, 2
Sejil-2, solid fuel missiles, 354
self-sufficiency, as only choice for Iran, 449
Semmel, Andrew, 60
September 11 terrorist attacks, Ahmadinejad saying U.S. government involved in, 329
September shock, from IAEA resolution, 78
seventh mistake, of the West and the P5+1, 452
Shah. See Pahlavi, Mohammad Reza Shah
Shahab-3, 354, 396
Shahab-3 missile re-entry vehicle, redesigning inner cone of, 304
Shaheed, Ahmed, 421
Shahriari, Majid, 26, 412
Shakouri, Gholam, 414

Shalom, Silvan, 354
Shapiro, Dan, 424
Shariatmadari, Hossein, 77, 81, 503n69
Sharon, Ariel, 138, 215
Sheikholeslam, Hossein, 82
Sherman, Brad, 423
Shiyan, reports of enrichment activities, 133
short-term extension of suspension, 126
short-term suspension, not complete cessation, 103
siege mentality, worsening Iranians,' 30
Singh, Manmohan, 323
sixth mistake, committed by the West, 451
Slavin, Barbara, 428
smart sanctions, in Resolution 1929, 386–388
SNSC. *See* Supreme National Security Council (SNSC)
Sofidif joint venture company, 47, 481n22
Solana, Javier, 145, 232, 241, 245, 252, 254, 264, 265, 275, 276, 292, 306, 312, 316–317, 324, 348, 350, 354, 495n68
Soltanieh, Ali Asghar, 81–82, 209, 219, 222, 228, 236, 256, 304, 323, 334, 356, 361, 409, 410, 411, 419, 420, 471n1, 505n99, 534n31
South Africa, 54, 174, 205
South Korea, 13, 22, 391
space satellite. *See* satellite
spherical implosion system, 372
spying, crucial to stop Iran's nuclear drive, 27
Stanford Research Institute, 42–43
Stars virus, 25
Steinmeier, Frank-Walter, 253, 319
step-by-step proposal. *See* Russian step-by-step proposal
sticking point, suspension issue, 102
Strait of Hormuz, 12–13, 198, 426
strategic options, after Resolution 1737, 262
Straw, Jack, 103, 145, 173
Students' Basij Organization, 507n27
Stuxnet affair, 399

Stuxnet computer worm, 24, 25, 28, 29
subsidiary arrangements, 58, 59
Subsidiary Arrangements to Safeguards Agreement, 466
successes, of cooperation between Iran and the West, 437–438
Supreme Leader (*Rabbar*)
    acquiesced to Paris Agreement, 150
    announcing election results, 340
    attending important meetings of high committee, 95
    ban on direct negotiation with the United States, 439
    decided to restart uranium conversion facility at Isfahan, 171
    duties of, 482n41
    establishment of diplomatic relations or conducting direct negotiations with U.S. to be redlines, 99
    final decisionmaker on foreign policy matters, 359
    instructing Rouhani to restart UCF activities in Isfahan, 165
    intervened in July 2008, 306
    lifted for Mahmoud Ahmadinejad the redline on direct negotiations and relations with the United States, 462
    operationalizing his *fatwa* on nuclear weapons, 466
    praising nuclear negotiation team, 188
    rejected Paris Agreement, 149
    removed redline in 2005 on negotiations with America, 327
    showing reluctance and reservation, 183
    skeptical concerning sincerity of U.S. statements, 462
    wise alternative to both preserve its nuclear technology and expose its nuclear activities to the world, 107
Supreme National Security Council (SNSC)
    appointed a team of nuclear negotiators (2003), 94
    considering an American military attack a real possibility, 194

Foreign Policy Committee of, 279
holding regular meetings, 70
issuing a statement warning against
approval of anti-Iranian resolution,
250
membership of, 487n56
package of 33 articles on political and
security relations (2005), 161
as sole authority handling nuclear case,
306
special committee to identify and
prepare strategies, 115
suspension
between 2003 and 2005 limited and
temporary, 270
agreeing to in September 2003 with
qualifications, 268
approach of former nuclear team,
267–271
broad definition, 124
compared to transparency, 150
compromising on definition of, 102
considered a redline by the Islamic
Republic, 250
definition of, 101
of enrichment non-legally binding, 230
internal wrangles over, 265–267
linking to some type of security
assurance, 242
making mandatory through a Security
Council resolution, 241
more limited than what September
IAEA resolution called for, 101
not related to transparency, 74
obligatory under Resolution 1696, 251
redefining from "total suspension" to
"introduction of gas into centrifuges,"
268
revised view of, 109
rumors on undeclared, 335
Tehran demonstrating voluntary nature
of, 180
as voluntary, 160
world's understanding of, 180

suspension for suspension proposal, 264,
276, 517n52
suspicion
bolstering hard line of the United
States, 112
surrounding involvement of Russian
operatives in Stuxnet computer worm
attack on the Bushehr nuclear plant,
399
Swiss government, taking the lead in
toughening sanctions against Iran, 420
Swiss initiative, Washington strongly
disapproved of, 297
Switzerland, willing to get involved in
Iran's security case, 264

Tahir, Buhary Syed abu, 121
Taliban, backed by Saudi Arabia-Pakistan-
U.S. triangle, 547n9
Talwar, Puneet, 403
Tavakkoli, Ahmad, 283, 284, 446
technical crises, result of lack of
coordination between Iran's diplomats
and its Atomic Energy Organization,
440
technical issues, resolution of all, 135
Teheran Research Reactor, enough
20-percent-enriched uranium for a full
replacement core, 406
Tehran agreement, mutual victory for Iran
and EU3, 107
Tehran Atomic Research Center, extensive
studies on reprocessing technology, 50
Tehran Declaration
argument that Iran signed it as a
tactical measure, 384
created an incomparable opportunity of
a political maneuver, 384
describing fuel exchange deal as "a
starting point," 381
entrance of other countries onto stage
of serious negotiations, 383
inflicting damage on Washington's
relations with Brazil and Turkey, 385

requiring nothing of Iran, 382
turning into propaganda maneuver, 381
Tehran negotiations, EU's support for
Iran's taking corrective measures with
the IAEA on mutually acceptable
terms, 108
Tehran Nuclear Research Center, 41, 113,
114, 490n22
Tehran Research Reactor
Iran requesting fuel for in June 2009,
355–356
providing fuel for, 425
providing fuel rods for, 467
Tehran statement (October 21, 2003), 106,
107, 109, 110
Tehran-Brussels relations, second crisis in,
138–142
Tehran-IAEA dispute, resolution through
political negotiations, 111–114
Tehran-Washington relations, restoration
of, 327
Tenet, George, 125
tenth mistake, made by the West, 457
terrorism and regional security, proposed
working group, 65
third mistake, of the West, 448
threat and pressure tactics, U.S. success in
subduing Tripoli through, 133
threats
to the peace, 228
turning into opportunities, 99
3+1 group, 99
threshold country, 228
Timbie, James, 403
time-out initiative, Tehran refusing to
accept, 276
time-out plan, 517n52
time-out proposal, 264
Tinner, Urs, 524n55
Tondar monarchist group, 367
Toner, Mark, 421
top secret information, new government
maintaining that former negotiating
team revealed, 189

Toscano, Roberto, 228, 440
Townsend, Frances Fragos, 7, 18
Trade and Cooperation Agreement, 328,
432
traitors, labeling members of the former
negotiating team as, 189
transparency, compared to suspension, 150
transparency measures, 158, 213, 410–411
trial of Mousavian, results of, 285
triangular diplomatic forum, EU3 as, 182
trigger mechanism, 119, 152
trilateral strategy, White House for
containing Iran, 89
triple urgency plan, forcing government
into accepting Additional Protocol, 105
trust, lack of in Iran's intentions, 451
Turkey, 380, 455
twelfth mistake, made by the West, 457
20 percent offer, rejecting, 413

UF$_4$ (uranium tetrafluoride)
also known as green salt, 372
amount lost in process of conversion to
metal, 113–114
converting to UF$_6$, 113
UF$_6$
cylinder, leakage from, 123
gas reserves, 123
introduction into centrifuges in Iran,
100
limited number of tests using small
amounts of, 489n19
UN (United Nations)
adopting resolution on terrorism,
414–415
declaring the year 2001 as the "United
Nations Year of Dialogue among
Civilizations," 438
resolutions calling on Iran to allow
inspections beyond the Additional
Protocol, 443
UN General Assembly
adopting resolution on November 18,
2011, 415

Ahmadinejad address in 2008, 318–320
Ahmadinejad September 2005 speech, 208
UN Human Rights Council, 434, 445
UN Security Council
  Ahmadinejad addressing, 214–217
  America's use of for sanctions as a tool, 22
  Brazil and Turkey rotating members of, 380
  countries referred to, 76
  draft of third sanctions resolution submitted in spring 2008, 293
  emphasis in the Paris Agreement on noninvolvement by, 152
  failure to gain membership, 317–318
  IAEA Board referring Iran's case to, 225–233
  Iran seeking to prevent involvement of, 115
  legality of resolution, 228–230
  new team willing to risk referral of Iran's nuclear dossier to, 203
  nonbinding statement on Iran situation (2006), 235–236
  permanent members of, 4
  possibility of referral to, 115
  reporting Iran's case to considered to be a bluff or empty threat, 85
  Resolution 1373 on MKO, 64, 484n16
  Resolution 1696, 250–252
    as a diplomatic defeat for Iran, 251–252
    rejected immediately by Tehran, 251
    retaliation, 395
  Resolution 1737
    on December 23, 2006, 259–262
    harsher than resolution issued in October 2006 against North Korea, 263
    against Iran, 259–262
    prohibiting construction operations related to nuclear program, 444

    retaliation, 395
    Tehran's strategy following, 262–263
  Resolution 1747, 271–276, 516n35
  Resolution 1803, 298–303
    adoption of, 300
    details of, 523n41
    introduction of land, air, and maritime sanctions, 298
    retaliation, 396
  Resolution 1835, 320
    September 28, 2008, 319
    details of, 526n89
    followed by a period of paralysis, 321
    kind of joint international message to Iran, 322
    as reaffirmation of Resolutions 1696, 1737, 1747, and 1803, 322
    retaliation, 396
  Resolution 1929, 19, 321, 385–389
    adopting sixth round of sanctions, 386
    making Iran the most sanctioned country in the world, 444
    retaliation, 396
    sale of S-300 and other missile technologies suspended by, 399
    shift by Russia and China away from sympathy for Iran's position, 396
    as the worst resolution ever for Ahmadinejad administration, 384
  resolutions on Iraq, 194
  responsible for maintaining international peace and security, 211
  threats
    to refer Iran's case escalating, 219
    to refer Iran's case to as political bluffs, 189
UN special rapporteur, for human rights in Iran, 421
undeclared facility, existence of, 350

underground enrichment facilities, revealed by foreign news agencies, 485–486n38

unemployment rate, economic experts contesting official, 446

unilateral sanctions, 389–393, 444

unilateralism, warmongering U.S. undermined, 179

United Arab Emirates, 6, 391

United Kingdom, 49, 53, 294

UO_2 pellets, produced at Isfahan Nuclear Technology Center, 114

uranium
converting to UF_6, 49
production of 20 percent-enriched, 366
transferring to Turkey instead, 362

uranium 235, enriching, 113

Uranium Conversion Facility at Isfahan, 58, 133, 140

uranium dioxide, conversion to UF_4, 304

uranium enrichment. *See* enrichment

uranium hexafluoride, centrifuge testing with, 112–113

uranium mines, developing Iran's, 49

uranium particles, discovery of highly enriched, 112

U.S. (United States). *See also various America or American entries*
in 2003 IAEA meeting, 67
accommodating Iranian demands for plutonium reprocessing, 44
after hostages in Lebanon released, 448
aims stated in Iran's 2002 proposal, 63–65
alarmed by IAEA report (2011), 417
allowed to use Iran's airspace to launch air strikes in Iraq, 194
announcing Washington's readiness to work on negotiations with Iran (May 31, 2006), 244
being resolute in the face of, 197
bent on expanding range of Iran sanctions, 294
broad relationship with Iran, 468
budget under tremendous pressure, 15

concerned about increasing influence of Iran in Middle East, 195
counting on limitations of, 193–199
covert action in Iran, 23
dismantlement of Iran's enrichment and reprocessing activities, 178
dominating IAEA Board of Governors meeting, 128
double standards vis-à-vis Muslim countries and Israel, 386
economic interests advanced through nuclear cooperation with Iran, 45
exerting tremendous pressures, 182
expressing opposition to construction of Bushehr nuclear power plant, 178
failing to orchestrate international consensus against Iran during Khatami administration, 432
fear-based view of Iran, 5
focus on security issues, 88–89
genuine and sincere will for compromise and peaceful resolution needed, 469
good opportunity to start direct talks with, 82
Iranians interested in direct talks with, 241
keen on nuclear cooperation with Iran for economic reasons, 46
knowledge of Iraq's use of chemical weapons, 481n31
laying foundation for a nuclear Iran, 40–46
looking toward direct talks with Iran, 160
missed a great opportunity during Rouhani period and Khatami presidency, 453
need for Iran's assistance, 196
in negotiations with Iran during 1970s, 44–45
not buying into Ahmadinejad's initiative, 209
nuclear strategy, responses to in Iran, 377

as obstacle on enrichment issue, 162–163

opposing Iran's accession to the WTO, 154

propping up Shah's regime, 40

pursuing close cooperation with Moscow, 331

ready to engage in direct talks with Iran in 2003, 120

realistic assessment of potential areas of common interest with Iran, 468

recognition of Iran's role as a prelude to a grand bargain, 195

refraining from negotiating with China for twenty-five years, 195

rejected Russian plan, 409

rejecting ElBaradei's plan, 254

report produced by intelligence community, 299

reserving option to use nuclear weapons as deterrents, 376

responded to 2002 offer negatively, 65

security objectives of, 2

security of Iran's neighbors hinging on military presence of, 193

stopped all agreements with Iran, 53

strategy regarding Iran, 89, 125

supported Saddam Hussein during Iran-Iraq War in the 1980s, 52

suspected Iran in bombing of Beirut embassy in 1983, 52

suspicious of Iran's nuclear aspirations throughout the 1990s and early 2000s, 55

trying to isolate Tehran through heavy pressures, 194

trying to persuade international and private banks to stop granting loans to Iran, 262

unprecedented change in position, 245

welcoming Russia's proposal, 217

U.S. bloc

insisting that word "noncompliance" be used, 117

powerful minority on the IAEA Board of Governors, 439

U.S. Department of Defense, 55

U.S. House of Representatives, approved a nuclear agreement between United States and India, 323

U.S. Navy, re-labeling the Persian Gulf as "the Arabian Gulf," 445

U.S. Senate, own harsh sanctions against Central Bank of Iran, 422

U.S. State Department, American representative to attend upcoming P5+1 negotiation, 336

U.S. Treasury Department, set of measures including sanctions and asset freezes and seizures, 390

U.S.-allied governments, fall of authoritarian in the Arab Spring of 2011, 445

U.S.-EU response, to Iran's goodwill, 413–429

U.S.-Iran cooperation, key to getting rid of Saddam, 438

U.S.-Iran relations, new low with American hostages, 52

USS Vincennes, 29, 52

Vaezi, Mahmoud, 209, 448

Vahidi, Ahmad, 377, 410

Va'idi, Javad, 81–82, 209, 217, 221, 230, 233, 242, 248, 265, 498n6, 507n26

Velayati, Ali Akbar, 35, 69, 83, 97, 186, 264, 266, 278, 279, 306, 448, 485n26, 514n15

Vietor, Tommy, 425

Villepin, Dominique de, 60

"War of the Cities" in 1958, 52

war-shattered economy, reconstruction of Iran's, 53

Washington's unilateralism, undermined by diplomacy, 432

"way out," rejected by Iran, 147

weapon grade, enriching low-enriched uranium up to, 30

weaponization issue, 303

weaponization studies, 296

weapons of mass destruction (WMD)
diplomacy to promote regional disarmament, 55
elimination from the entire Middle East, 463, 468
full cooperation with IAEA, 63–64
Iran's lack of, 21

West
decision to ignore demands by, 437
encouraging Iranian government's nuclear ambitions, 44
failure of to expand new sanctions against Iran, 322
history of supporting Saddam Hussein, 436
interested in dominating client states and their oil resources, 436
interpreting democratic movements in Middle East as spontaneous uprisings, 328
inviting to agree on a grand bargain, 145
mistakes made by, 447, 448, 449, 450, 451, 452, 453, 456, 457
never respected obligations under NPT, 447
new government opposed to cooperation and interaction and confidence building with, 189
not accepting anything short of suspension of uranium enrichment, 265
playing a large role in change of Iran's elected government to hard-line radicals, 454
preparing to adopt new UN sanctions resolution (2008), 293–294
under pressure not to officially recognize the Ahmadinejad government, 342

rejected proposal and cast aspersions on Prime Minister Erdogan and President Lula, 456

secret talks about new sanctions resolution, 292

sending contradictory signals to, 80

strategy to keep Iran weak and vulnerable, 449

successful in building up regional pressure on Iran to give up uranium enrichment, 266

violated NPT by cutting off al nuclear cooperation with Iran after 1979 Islamic Revolution, 62

West German government, agreements with, 47–48

Western hostages in Lebanon, 434, 448

Western media
depicting Ahmadinejad's speech, 312
propaganda against the new government, 214
propaganda regarding transfer of Iran's enriched uranium reserves out of the country, 360
psychological warfare against Iran, 133

Western partners, not ready to include rights of Iran for enrichment, 247

Western public opinion, largely unaware of Iranian concerns, 446

White House, 325, 356

WikiLeaks, 5, 330

WMD-free zone, in the Middle East, 468

Wolfe, John, 60

Wolff, Alejandro, 514n17

Wolfsthal, Jon, 519n76

work plan, 289

working groups, 65, 182

World Trade Organization (WTO), 181, 432

worthless scraps of paper, UN Security Council resolutions as, 317, 318

Ya'alon, Moshe, 11

Yadavaran oil field in Iran, China developing, 13

yellowcake, 49, 139, 217, 334
Yurchenko, Vitaly, 370

Zafar (Victory) satellite, 404
Zamaninia, Amir, 61, 70, 484n11

Zarif, Javad, 61, 70, 126, 261, 450, 484n9, 488n1
Zohrevand, Abolfazl, 402, 403
zone of immunity, 427
Zuma, Jacob, 375